Foundations in
Europe

Published by
The Directory of Social Change
24 Stephenson Way
London NW1 2DP
tel.: 020 7209 5151, fax: 020 7209 5049
e-mail: info@dsc.org.uk
from whom further copies and a full publications list are available.

The Directory of Social Change is a Registered Charity no. 800517

ISBN 1 900360 86 1

British Library Cataloguing in Publication Data
A catalogue record for this book is available from the British Library

Cover design by Russell Stretten

Edited by Myra Bennett and Rosie Clay

Text designed and typeset by GreenGate Publishing Services, Tonbridge

Printed and bound by Biddles, Guildford

Other Directory of Social Change departments in London:
Courses and Conferences tel.: 020 7209 4949
Charity Centre tel.: 020 7209 1015
Research tel.: 020 7209 4422
Finance and Administration tel.: 020 7209 0902

Directory of Social Change Northern Office:
Federation House, Hope Street, Liverpool L1 9BW
Courses and Conferences tel.: 0151 708 0117
Research tel.: 0151 708 0136

Contents

Section II: Mission, Governance and Organization

Section III: Programme Selection and Management

Section IV: Legal and Fiscal Framework and State

Supervision

Introduction

Trends of the philanthropic sector

Integration, globalization and increasing international communication are growing characteristics of European societies. In the era of the Euro, economic integration is progressing rapidly and political integration ranks high on the agenda of European policy-makers. Global capital market trends affect the more dynamic economies of Europe. Buoyant stock markets, a shift in corporate finance from institutional investment to public flotation on the stock market, and new wealth generated over a long period of boom years have all left their mark on the potential for philanthropic activity. Branches of the new economy are flourishing and new companies as well as new entrepreneurs, shareholders and stakeholders are emerging.

In a number of European countries, these trends have already resulted in a period of sustained growth in philanthropic investment. New foundations are emerging and new forms of philanthropy are being tested. Both owners of personal wealth and corporations are involved in this process, but there is still untapped potential within these groups for more giving. It is therefore timely to revisit the development of philanthropy and provide a basis for research into the philanthropic sectors of European countries, taking a truly comparative approach to assessing their respective potentials.

This is all the more important given the slowly but steadily growing professionalism of philanthropy in Europe. Lagging behind developments in the US, philanthropy in some countries is only just discovering the need to invest in the creation of its own identity, in management capacity building and in public policy advocacy. However, the knowledge base for any such effort has so far been very limited: the European Foundation Centre – a key institution which can contribute to the development of philanthropic investment – is itself only 11 years old. Yet foundations are coming to realize that they share an identity, a potential and an obligation to serve their communities. They cannot ignore the tremendous changes that can result from applying a European-wide economic and political framework to activities supporting the public benefit or the public good. Long before any European institution can move as far ahead as legal steps to create a common framework for philanthropy, we need to create and develop a knowledge base that reflects and evaluates the range of philanthropic reality across different European traditions.

Efforts to this end are being supported by a common shift in the political cultures of many European countries. The age of state interventionism has been followed by the era of the responsible civil society. This change brings about a need to assess what balance can be struck between lean government, civic engagement and self-organization in respect of the services and living conditions to which citizens may have legal or political entitlement. However, both British and continental European politicians have started reflecting on new forms of public-private partnership which put the emphasis on enabling rather than on service-provision or state regulation. The question of the relative responsibilities of the state and the private sector has come under scrutiny owing to the allegedly limited capacity of the state to guarantee reasonable living conditions or to solve social problems.

European traditions of subsidiarity should hold up a model for effective state-civil society relationships, but in fact traditional welfare associations (the churches, the large church-affiliated associations '*Caritas*' and '*Diakonie*' in Germany , unions, even political parties) are losing out to new forms of social capital generated on a more temporary, project driven, passionate and less membership-based level.[1] Philanthropy is being affected by these developments in that it has to adjust to the new value systems of the participatory society and has to legitimize its activities against the background of increased demands for transparency and accountability. The composition of what is described as the third sector is shifting and will bring further changes in future. Those countries which are currently characterized by a high proportion of direct or indirect state funding supporting the third sector (among them Ireland, Belgium and Germany, with more than 60% of third sector funds coming from the public sources)[2] will have to find new strategies for growth in nonprofit activities against a background of tight public budgets. In such countries both the relatively small proportion of philanthropic Euros going into the sector and the sector's capacity to generate income (by providing services and selling them at fees) will have to be developed.

To develop its philanthropic potential, a country increasingly needs to offer competitive national legal and social conditions for applying philanthropy. More and more donors – both private and corporate – have a choice as to the location of their philanthropies. They own wealth and generate corporate business in many different countries and prefer to give back in the country which offers the most favourable legal and social conditions. Global players in the corporate world may consider establishing foundations in countries where the company has subsidiaries. Global investors owning private wealth may actually reason along similar lines, trying to optimize their tax burden and at the same time reflect their portfolio of stock or other assets. We should therefore prepare to address the question of comparative advantage offered to the philanthropist by different legal and social systems, as well as political cultures.

The reference book project

This reference book aims to provide all those interested in such a comparative advantage perspective with information on which to base their judgement. Obviously, literature on international philanthropy has existed before,[3] but this book attempts to set new standards in comparative philanthropic research. The previous German-language Bertelsmann Foundation reference book (*Handbuch Stiftungen*) elaborated on Germany but involved an international group of authors targeting a German audience, providing systematic management know how.[4] The great success of that book encouraged us to plan for this English language volume which, for all the reasons outlined above, had to be conceived as truly European. In 1998 we initiated work on the project and the results of what was termed a major research effort are now presented.

Foundations in Europe is divided into four sections:

- the role of foundations in society
- governance and organization of foundations
- programme management of foundations
- the legal and political framework governing philanthropy.

Whereas the first and last sections of the book are genuinely comparative exercises, the two other sections of the book are more methodological in nature and may not reflect all the wealth of detail on programme management within European Foundations. These sections also honour the increasingly international character of philanthropy by involving authors from the US.

Against the background of the recently completed phase II of the Johns Hopkins international Comparative Nonprofit Sector Project, we were lucky to attract Helmut Anheier to join us to form a team on Section I: The Foundation Sector in Europe. His talent for organizing comparative work and his working relationship with many colleagues allowed us to convene a group of authors of high quality to work on assessing the most characteristic traits of philanthropy in their countries. A number of key decisions were difficult to make and could be arrived at only after extended discussions at authors' meetings.

The guiding definition of a foundation used in all chapters follows the International Classification System of Nonprofit Organizations (ICNPO) criteria for nonprofit organizations. A clear reference was given to a nonprofit-distributing form of philanthropy in a functional sense, regardless of their legal form. A foundation for the purpose of this reference book is defined as:

> an asset with the following characteristics: non-membership based organization; private entity; self-governing structure; nonprofit-distributing entity; serving a public purpose'.[5]

Private purpose foundations, which play an important role in a number of European countries, are therefore only cursorily touched upon rather than analysed at the core of our chapters. To unearth as much appropriate European foundation history as possible, James Allen Smith and Karsten Borgmann were requested to join the team to work separately on an historical overview. James Allen Smith not only brought his admirable scholarly experience to bear but also identified the need for further historical research; it seems that such research promises to provide us with a better understanding of common European traditions and institutional arrangements.

The geographic scope of the book comprises the European Union including its enlargement candidates and countries of the European Economic Area such as Switzerland and Norway; Turkey is included as an example of Muslim traditions of giving in a European country. In Section I of this book the countries of central and eastern Europe are dealt with by Frances Pinter in one separate chapter rather than in individual country chapters. It was assumed that the (re-)emergence of foundations as part of civil society would be a common theme and given the limited availability of empirical evidence could be treated in one chapter comparatively. The author drew both on her substantial practical experience in these countries and specific research done to collect empirical evidence.

The sociological approach to identifying the role of foundations in society had already showed that questions of definition would be very important in trying to organize the comparative research needed in this reference book. For the legal section, which covers almost the same geographic area as Section I, clear preference was given to thematic key issues of the legal framework governing foundations as against a country-by-country description of the empirical situation. Such publications are already available and do not cover the comparative advantage approach to a sufficient degree.[6] We decided therefore to turn Section IV into a research project which would try to view the legal framework in thematic order with regard to five core questions:

- legal forms available for the institutionalization of philanthropy
- procedures when establishing a foundation
- state supervision
- taxation
- cross-border giving of foundations.

Since no individual author could realistically be expected to offer first-hand legal expertise on all the countries involved, we asked the International Institute of Association and Foundation Lawyers, Inc. and its president, Bradley Gallop, at Brussels, to oversee the work on Section IV.

To solve the problem of providing a working basis for the authors of the systematic chapters, Bradley Gallop developed a questionnaire to be used to survey all the jurisdictions involved (all EU member states – with Scotland constituting a separate legal jurisdiction from England and Wales – Switzerland, Liechtenstein, Cyprus, Slovenia, Estonia, Hungary, Czech Republic and Bulgaria), and an outline of the issues to be covered in each chapter. The team of authors then met to discuss the structure of all chapters, and the questionnaire to be used to conduct the survey. The actual survey was done by corresponding members of the International Institute responding and providing empirical information as well as reference to the relevant body of law in their jurisdictions. Bradley Gallop and his staff, with assistance from Abigail Webb, provided the information in an appropriate and edited form to the chapter authors as a basis for their comparative analyses. International Institute members in the survey countries assisted with clarifications and follow-up information.

The information gathered from the research conducted in the 24 jurisdictions involved in this survey was prepared in a visually friendly and comparative format; the resulting summary of the legal and fiscal situation in all the jurisdictions surveyed is contained in Appendix I.

Appendix II contains a non-comprehensive list of legislation and administrative regulations governing charitable foundations in the 24 jurisdictions, and is intended to help readers interested in conducting further research of their own. Legal changes in the UK and Germany in summer 2000 have been included, the cut-off date for any other legal changes was February 2000.

When starting work on the legal section, it became quite evident that in a comparison including both civil and common law countries it would be difficult to establish a common legal definition of its object. The conflict was finally resolved by using a functional definition along the lines of the ICNPO criteria which was also applied in the section on the European foundation sector. This allowed the authors to identify variations in functional equivalents of legal forms or requirements between different jurisdictions. This approach also identified the tremendous difficulties that would arise when trying to establish a foundation under European law; it became clear that any such effort, rather than encouraging philanthropy, could potentially rule out major elements of existing philanthropic reality and diversity. The approach chosen for this reference book therefore provides a starting point which no European philanthropy initiative aiming at the legal systems should ignore.

Sections II and III required less of a research-intensive effort because they had been prepared as part of the work for the German edition of the Bertelsmann Foundation reference book. The chapters were revised by their authors and are now being published for the first time in their original English language versions. Their authors have contributed revised and updated chapters to address the key questions of professional management. A number of authors from both sides of the Atlantic are involved and offer know-how relevant to any foundation volunteer or professional in the English-speaking world.

The contributions in these chapters are based on the observation that the importance of foundations is growing. This implies that issues of strategic focus, legitimacy and management capacity are becoming more important.[7] Foundations need to be concerned with effectiveness to an increasing degree. In order to remain flexible and responsive, foundations need to pay attention to their governance and organizational structures as well as to their human resources. Transparency and accountability are the public equivalents of internal evaluation. Their implementation provides feedback to assure effective, strategic philanthropy which is based on a wide range of professional management tools. Joseph Breiteneicher and Melinda

Marble provide a systematic, in-depth overview of programme management that has helped to professionalize US philanthropy through TPI's groundbreaking work. Thomas K. Reis and Stephanie J. Clohesy provide an overview of the innovative approaches to philanthropy – venture philanthropy and e-philanthropy.

Findings

Work on this book has revealed a surprising wealth and diversity of philanthropic traditions, lines of development, social functions and organizational forms. European foundations are looking back on an uninterrupted history of millennia and have roots in all major cultures, Christian, Muslim and secular. Over the course of centuries, concepts of the public good and public benefits changed and so, correspondingly, did the lists of purposes supported by charitable institutions. From the very beginning, foundations were one of the cornerstones of integration between individuals and the community, both through the services they provided and by the very concept of offering individuals a method for giving back to society.

Foundations were part of the medieval balance between the secular and religious powers, between clergy, nobility and the first city burghers. Foundations were affected by the struggle for the nation state in quite different ways – at the most extreme by Jacobin notions of the strict separation of church and state. More recently, foundations have been shown to be an integral part of democratic development in countries where they have emerged or resurfaced from illegality or expropriation with the general transition to civil society. Needless to say, the challenges of the contemporary world will leave their yet to be identified marks on philanthropy.

The European philanthropic tradition has favoured the establishment of operating, as against grant-making, foundations. This reflects both traditions of subsidiarity and of inter-relatedness with an interventionist state. The scope of services provided by foundations, or organized in a similar legal form, extends to pension schemes provided for the working population. In some countries, foundations emerged as a legal entity, in others they have to be characterized by their purpose being specifically inscribed in legal forms and being guarded under tax law. Whichever legal route was taken, the purpose was to make contributions to some of the key characteristics of a worthwhile society: culture, research and knowledge, education, social welfare and care of those who cannot care for themselves.

Foundations are ties that help to bind societies together. They will continue to develop innovative approaches to this old endeavour in the future. The potential for giving exists in societies of unprecedented wealth. Democratic citizens will continue to invest in the public good – be it loyalty, be it time, be it capital assets.

Loyalties of Europeans are shifting. On the one hand, they are rediscovering the wealth of their regional and local identities; on the other hand, they are bound to live together as Europeans who as yet have to develop a shared notion of the public good. Currently, national jurisdictions are based on the rationale of giving back to national societies. In future, cross-border philanthropy will become increasingly important as a result of an integrated economy, personal mobility, and the development of communities no longer based on geographic proximity alone. Citizens are joining new forms of communities and developing loyalties that will bring about the reality of European civil society. These developments are reflected by the growth of community philanthropy[8] on the local level and of cross-border giving on the global level. The prime responsibility to provide an encouraging framework for these developments still remains with national legislators. The more competitive a jurisdiction, the more is to be gained for the public good.

Acknowledgements

The Bertelsmann Foundation is publishing this book in cooperation with the Charities Aid Foundation and the Directory of Social Change in the UK. The partners will aim to distribute the book to as wide a public as possible, in the philanthropic sector itself and beyond it in the political sphere and among society at large, including the holders of corporate wealth. The concept of this book opposes the notion that its sections address different professions and should therefore be published in separate volumes. It is the clear intention of the editors to produce a source of reference, offering knowledge not merely of a narrowly defined set of professional questions, but of the criteria that need to be kept in mind when trying to identify a European philanthropic sector. Readers from outside the European boundaries will hopefully appreciate the opportunity to acquire an overview on European developments, based on which they can then deepen their knowledge by reading on individual countries.

The team of authors must be applauded for their acceptance of the editorial concept and their enthusiasm in supporting it and working within its boundaries. The editors would also like to express their gratitude for the good cooperation and scholarly team spirit which helped to solve many of the problems which no individual author could have hoped to tackle on her or his own. The editors particularly have to give credit to the unfailing support and inspiration brought to the project by the coordinators of the two large comparative teams, namely Helmut K. Anheier and to Bradley Gallop. Without their assistance the product would have looked different and would have lost a lot of its qualities. The editors wish to thank their colleagues in the Philanthropy Division of the Bertelsmann Foundation, Ilona Ehlert, Dirk Eilinghoff, Runhild Lipke, Alexandra Schmied and Karsten Timmer, for bearing with them and supporting the discussions on both the content and the management of the project. Should any mistakes have failed to come to the attention of the editors, it is their responsibility alone.

Andreas Schlüter, Volker Then and Peter Walkenhorst

Gütersloh, October 2000

Note: Euro equivalents given are as at 1 May 2000

---

1 The Bertelsmann Foundation currently publishes a comparative analysis of social capital development in industrialized societies chaired by Prof. Robert D. Putnam, Harvard University. See Robert D. Putnam, Gesellschaft and Gemeinsinn, Sozialkapital im internationalen Vergleich, Gütersloh 2001 (English edition published by Oxford University Press, forthcoming).

2 See Lester M. Salamon, Helmut K. Anheier, and associates, The Emerging Sector Revisited, A Summary, The Johns Hopkins Comparative Nonprofit Sector Project, Phase II, Baltimore, MD, Appendix Table 3 (deutsch: Der Dritte Sektor, Aktuelle Internationale Trends, The Johns Hopkins Comparative Nonprofit Sector Project, Phase II, Gütersloh 1999.

3 In a comparative perspective Anheier, Helmut K. and Toepler, Stefan (eds.), Private Funds, Public Purpose, Philanthropic Foundations in International Perspective, New York 1999; Salamon, Lester M., Anheier, Helniut K. and others (eds.), Global Civil Society, Dimensions of the Nonprofit Sector, Baltimore, MD 1999; without comparative added value, but interesting in a systematic view Clotfelter, Charles T. and Ehrlich, Thomas (eds.) Philanthropy and the Nonprofit Sector in a Changing America, Bloomington/Indiana 1999; Lagemann, Ellen Condliffe, Philanthropic Foundations, New Scholarship, New Possibilities, Bloomington, Indiana 1999.

4 Bertelsmann Stiftung (ed.), Handbuch Stiftungen, Ziele – Projekte – Management – Rechtliche Gestaltung, Wiesbaden 1998.

5 See Helmut Anheier's chapter in this volume, 2 1. Definitions.

6 E.g. George, Carol Shelbourne (ed.), International Charitable Giving: Laws and Taxation, London, Dordrecht, and Cambridge 1994/1999 as a prime source of reference.

7 Bertelsmann Foundation (ed.), The Future of Foundations in an Open Society, Gütersloh 1999.

8 For community philanthropy, see Bertelsmann Foundation (ed.), Community Foundations in Civil Society, Guetersloh 1999; for German language reference see Bertelsmann Stiftung (ed.), Handbuch Bürgerstiftungen, Ziele – Gründung – Aufbau – Projekte, Gütersloh 2000

Authors

Helmut K. Anheier

Director
Centre for Civil Society
London School of Economics, UK
Professor of Sociology,
Rutgers University, New York, USA

Edith Archambault

Professor of Economics
Director, Laboratoire d'Economie sociale
University of Paris 1 Sorbonne, France

Davut Aydin

Professor of Economics
Faculty of Business Administration
Anadolu University, Eskisehir, Turkey

Werner Bachstein

Lecturer
Social Policy Unit
Vienna University of Economics and
Business Administration
Vienna, Austria

Christoph Badelt

Professor of Economics
Head of Department, Department of
Social Policy, Vienna University of
Economics and Business Administration
Managing Director
Institute for Interdisciplinary Non-profit
Research Vienna, Austria

Gian Paolo Barbetta

Professor of Political Economy
Faculty of Economics
Catholic University of Milan
Milan, Italy

Paul Bater

Senior Research Associate International
Bureau of Fiscal Documentation (IBFD)
Amsterdam, The Netherlands

Joseph C. K. Breiteneicher

President
The Philanthropic Initiative, Inc.
Boston, Massachusetts, USA

Michael Brophy

Chief Executive
Charities Aid Foundation
Kent, UK

Alex Bonn	Attorney at Law Bonn & Schmitt Luxembourg
Karsten Borgmann	Researcher Free University, Berlin, Germany
Ary Burger	Social and Cultural Planning Bureau The Hague, The Netherlands
Stephanie J. Clohesy	Consultant, W. K. Kellogg Foundation Battle Creek, Michigan, USA
Paul Dekker	Social and Cultural Planning Bureau The Hague, The Netherlands
Freda Donoghue	Dr., Director Policy Research Centre, National College of Ireland, Dublin, Ireland
Marco Demarie	Programme Officer Fondazione Giovanni Agnelli Turin, Italy
Ulrich Drobnig	Professor of Law, former Director Max-Planck-Institute for Foreign Private and Private International Law, Hamburg, Germany
Emmanuelle Faure	Deputy Director European Foundation Centre, Brussels, Belgium
Joel L. Fleishman	President The Atlantic Philanthropic Service Company, Inc., New York, USA Prof. of Law and Public Policy, Duke University, USA
Bradley Gallop	Attorney at Law BDG & Associates President, International Institute of Association and Foundation Lawyers Brussels, Belgium
Jorge García-Andrade	Technical Director Confederacion Espanola de Fundaciones Madrid, Spain
Oliver Habighorst	Attorney at Law Partner with White & Case Feddersen LLP, Frankfurt/Main, Germany

Gunilla Hellman	Director of Arts and Culture Foundation for Swedish Culture in Finland Helsinki, Finland
Kjell Herberts	Social Science Research Unit Åbo Akademi University Vasa, Finland
Diana Leat	Professor Voluntary Sector and Not-for-Profit Management, City University Business School, London, UK
Håkon Lorentzen	Research Director Civil Society and Welfare State, Institute for Social Research Oslo; Norway
Craig Kennedy	President The German Marshall Fund of the United States Washington D.C., USA
Melinda G. Marble	Senior Associate The Philanthropic Initiative, Inc. Boston, Massachusetts, USA
Michel Marée	Researcher Université de Liège Centre d'Economie Sociale Liège, Belgium
Carlos Monjardino	Chairman of the Administrative Board Fundação Oriente President Portuguese Foundation Centre Lisbon, Portugal
Sophie Mousny	Researcher Université de Liège Centre d'Economie Sociale Liège, Belgium
Jose Ignacio Ruiz Olabuenaga	Professor of Sociology Department of Sociology, University of Deusto, Bilbao, Spain
Jeppe Parving	Researcher Copenhagen University Copenhagen, Denmark

Frances Pinter	Information Sub-Board Member Open Society Institute Visiting Fellow, Centre for Civil Society, London School of Economics, UK
Cathy Pharoah	Head of Research Charities Aid Foundation, Kent, UK
Kenneth Prewitt	Director U.S. Census Bureau Washington D.C., USA
Thomas K. Reis	Director Venture Philanthropy W. K. Kellogg Foundation Battle Creek, Michigan, USA
John Richardson	Chief Executive Officer European Foundation Centre Brussels, Belgium
Paddy Ross	International Coordinator Charities Aid Foundation Kent, UK
Dirk Rumberg	Head of Corporate Communication Süddeutscher Verlag München, Germany
Andreas Schlüter	Attorney at Law, Brandi Dröge Piltz, Heuer & Gronemeyer, Gütersloh, Germany
James Allen Smith	Advisor to the President J.P. Getty Trust, Los Angeles, USA
Alex Schmitt	Attorney at Law Bonn & Schmitt Luxembourg
Martin Steinert	Researcher Research Institute for Association and Nonprofit Management (VMI) University of Freiburg, Switzerland
Rupert Graf Strachwitz	Director Maecenata Institute for Third Sector Studies Berlin, Germany

Luc Tayart de Borms

Managing Director
King Baudouin Foundation
Chairman, European Foundation
Centre
Brussels, Belgium

Volker Then

Dr. phil, Director
Philanthropy and Foundations,
Bertelsmann Foundation,
Gütersloh, Germany

Sophia P. Tsakraklides

Researcher, Department of Sociology
Yale University
New Haven, USA

Wino J.M. Van Veen

Research and Training Department
Kennedy Van der Laan
Amsterdam, The Netherlands

Vic Veldheer

Social and Cultural Planning Bureau,
The Hague; The Netherlands

Peter Walkenhorst

Director
Philanthropy and Foundations
Bertelsmann Foundation
Gütersloh, Germany

Markus H. Wanger

Dr. iur., Senior Partner
Wanger Law Group
Vaduz, Liechtenstein

Filip Wijkström

Professor of Economics
Stockholm School of Economics
Stockholm, Sweden

▼ Section I ▼
The Foundation Sector in Europe

▼ James Allen Smith and Karsten Borgmann

Foundations in Europe: the Historical Context

1 Introduction

Whether the term is *foundation, endowment, trust, fondacion, fundacao, fonds, Stiftung, stichting, stiftelse or saatio*, words have been employed in every European language to describe private legal entities that possess income-generating assets and devote their resources to public purposes. The connotations of these terms have mutated and evolved over the centuries, just as the multifarious foundations they describe have changed. Ancient and medieval hospitals, monasteries, municipal alms funds, religious confraternities and trade guilds, colleges and universities, mutual benefit associations, banks and cooperatives are among the many types of institutions that have shaped Europe's philanthropic traditions. All have contributed to the development of the modern foundation as well as to the emergence of what we now call the nonprofit, independent or third sector.

At the most fundamental level, foundations are grounded in an initial gift or aggregation of gifts intended to serve a public purpose. Over the centuries the practices for institutionalizing the gift have spurred the development of mechanisms for holding assets, controlling their use from one generation to the next, and monitoring and regulating philanthropic activities. While a number of countries have begun to rediscover foundations in recent decades and to contemplate their roles within the modern state, the aim of this chapter is to tell a much lengthier story about the historical development of European foundations and, thus, to supply a context for understanding contemporary developments.

If the effort to define 'foundation' is fraught with complexity as we try to compare contemporary foundations in some 30 nations, those difficulties are compounded when we explore the past. Throughout most of the historical period surveyed here, legal categories have not distinguished sharply between public and private sectors and there have not been well delineated boundaries between operating charities and foundations. Thus, this chapter must approach the definition of 'foundation' expansively, while trying to keep certain recurring questions in full view.

- How has private gift-giving been institutionalized?
- How have public purposes been conceived from era to era?
- What internal structures have been devized for governing philanthropic institutions?
- How have governmental regimes for supervising charitable and philanthropic activities developed?
- How have the boundaries between governmental and private responsibilities been drawn and redrawn?
- In what ways have attitudes toward wealth and the motivations for private philanthropy changed?

This chapter can provide only a brief, rough sketch of these developments across the continent of Europe. Early on, it is a truly European story that begins in the ancient Mediterranean world and moves west and north in the Middle Ages. In the 17th and 18th centuries, however, it becomes a more fragmented national story as states emerge with their differing political and legal cultures. Foundations experience very different fates as their civil societies assume divergent forms. Nevertheless, this chapter aims to construct a European narrative that spans more than two millennia: the gift-giving that built personal social ties in the ancient world; the almsgiving that strove for personal salvation in the Middle Ages; the charitable reforms that attempted to respond to widespread social and economic crises on the threshold of the modern era; the various efforts to regulate, integrate, or eliminate old charitable institutions as modern nation states were formed; and, finally, the contemporary renewal of concern for civil society as the social welfare state is being reinvented and economies liberalized.

2 *Philanthropia*: foundations in antiquity

Endowments for specific philanthropic purposes existed throughout the ancient Mediterranean world. Plato left funds for the Academy which bore his name. Epicurus, in a precisely detailed will, bequeathed property to sustain his school, which survived for some 600 years after his death. Theophrastus, who presided over Aristotle's Lyceum, made provisions in his will to continue its support. And the Ptolemies founded and sustained the magnificent library in Alexandria. These educational institutions, whose impact has resonated for many centuries, remain perhaps the most famous of ancient philanthropic endowments even if they were not necessarily the most familiar to those who lived in ancient times. Ancient Greeks would have been far more likely to encounter hospices and hospitals. Many donors left gifts at the sites of temples to support hospices (*katagoia*), which served as simple resting places or shelters for those who journeyed to a particular temple. At some prominent pilgrimage sites, these hospices grew into much more elaborate clinics. The hospice in Epidauros at the Temple of Asclepios was one of the most substantial, with some 160 rooms for the visitors who went there seeking cures. In many ancient Greek towns brotherhoods of hospitality were also formed. These associations, perhaps the oldest form of collective philanthropic enterprise in the western world, raised funds to construct and support guest houses (*xenones*).

Donations were used in antiquity for many other public purposes, erecting monuments and public buildings, ransoming captives, providing dowries and other forms of assistance to the poor, and sustaining festivals, banquets, votive offerings and religious sacrifices. However, these gifts were made in a social and political context that did not draw sharp distinctions between private philanthropic acts and public initiatives. In antiquity, private wealth brought with it a host of civic duties and responsibilities. Lacking any institutional mechanisms for collecting regular taxes, the ancient *polis* often relied on public subscriptions for the support of civic projects. Whether in the Greek *polis* or the later Roman republic, generosity was a public virtue, indeed a political virtue, more than an inner moral quality. Winning honour and prestige within one's own social and political network was the paramount motive when gifts were given. 'It is quite clear,' observed Cicero (106–43 BC), 'that most people are generous in their gifts not so much by natural inclination as by reason of the lure of honour – they simply want to be seen as beneficent.'[1]

Roman imperial wealth produced not merely beneficence but grandiosity and magnificence. Indeed, Roman emperors commanded the resources of the state as they embellished their stature with various sorts of foundations. Some of the most substantial imperial

---

[1] Cited in Hands, p. 49.

establishments were for educational purposes, especially to help orphans and poor children; some emperors, notably Antoninus Pius (86–161 AD) and Marcus Aurelius (121–180 AD), also created foundations whose explicit aim was to help poor girls. And even in the most obscure corners of the empire, lesser office holders and private individuals gave donations to help children, to embellish their towns with civic monuments, or to support public games and shows. Pliny the Younger (c. 62–113 AD) left the fullest written record of his benevolence. His gift-giving reveals a sense of fully intermingled public and personal obligations. He remained loyal to his native town of Como, endowing a library and public baths there, donating funds to help poor boys and girls, and promising to meet one-third of the expenses of a new school if the parents of the students would contribute the remainder (an early version of a 2 to 1 matching grant). He also helped those people closest to him, increasing the dowry of a friend's daughter, lending money free of interest to hard-pressed associates, and leaving income producing properties to aid old friends and family retainers. Other Roman citizens also aided their towns, typically by supporting large-scale public works projects: a citizen of Bordeaux built his city's aqueduct; a man named Crinas spent large sums to construct the walls of Marseilles; others left funds for bridges, markets, temples, and perhaps most commonly, public baths, often providing endowment funds so that the baths might be open to all comers, sometimes even including slaves. The philanthropy of Herodes Atticus, Marcus Aurelius' tutor, was similar in kind to the endowments left by other Roman citizens but even grander in scale. Reflecting stunning ambition and scope, his philanthropic projects left their mark throughout Italy and his native Attica. He gave money to restore decaying towns in Greece, to build public baths, aqueducts, race courses, and theatres, including a roofed theatre in Corinth and another in Athens as a memorial to his wife. When he died in 180 AD he bequeathed funds for an endowment that would provide one *mina* each year to every Athenian citizen.

While philanthropic motives and definitions of public purposes differed in fundamental ways from those that propel contemporary donors to establish foundations, ancient benefactors did expect their gifts to endure in perpetuity and their endowments to be well and honestly managed. Yet despite the hope that their gifts would last forever, the Greeks and Romans initially had neither a concept of 'legal personality' nor legal structures capable of protecting a donor's intentions. The donors typically left their bequests in the hands of a trusted individual or a group of friends who would be expected to carry out the donor's desired aims. That group, in turn, would name their heirs and successors, trusting that that set of individuals would continue as the donor intended. As one scholar has characterized it, the Greek foundation was 'from a legal viewpoint no more than a gift with an obligation attached.'[2] With relatively little legal protection, donors obviously put their gifts at risk. There could easily be a break in the chain of responsible possession and the property could be mismanaged or misappropriated after only a few generations.

Early on, then, foundations faced two fundamental and still familiar questions: How can a donor's intentions be protected or lawfully altered? How can a foundation assure itself of responsible governance from one generation to the next? By the second century BC one straightforward solution for Greek donors was to leave the gift to the *polis* or perhaps to a group of magistrates serving within the town's government. Sometimes the donor might also seek to have his intentions embodied in municipal legislation. By the time of the Roman emperor Nerva (96–98 AD) all Roman municipalities were accorded the right to receive gifts and by the time of Hadrian (117–138 AD) the donor's obligations attached to the gift were also legally enforceable. However, because Roman courts were sometimes lax in their enforcement of the donor's wishes, cautious benefactors also sought an imperial edict as further protection for their endowments. The sheer scale of Roman philanthropic activity compelled this legal evolution. As early as the first century BC, Roman law had begun to recognize associations as 'sentient reasonable beings' and 'immutable undying persons'. By the first century AD these primitive juridical forebears of today's charitable corporations, so-called 'fictive legal persons', were allowed to receive bequests. A major step had been taken in the development of foundation law.

Yet despite the fact that a rudimentary legal structure had begun to take shape, it is fair to ask whether this approach to gift-giving is akin to our own conception of philanthropy. The Greek term *philanthropia* connoted both the gods' love for mankind radiating down from Olympus as well as the more earth-bound human sentiments of kindness and affection shared among civilized human beings. Philanthropy also encompassed the gifts made to one's immediate network of friends and political associates as well as donations that manifested a more general concern for the well-being of suffering or needy humankind. The donors' motivations, to the extent that any donor's reasons for giving in any era can ever be fully comprehended,

---

[2] Laum cited in Hands, p. 18.

were inspired by a social world in which honour and reputation were paramount. The Greek and Roman donors sought primarily to be remembered and esteemed for their generosity. Consequently, their endowments often funded festivals, athletic contests, gladiatorial shows and food distributions, and these public displays of generosity were usually designed to draw a crowd to the donor's gravesite or commemorative statue. The community was attracted to these events; the actual needs of the destitute rarely seemed to motivate the ancient donor.

However, the underlying social and psychological dynamic of the gift relationship – that is to say, the reciprocity that sustains the practice of gift-giving in any culture – was well understood by ancient philosophers. 'Giving and returning,' said Aristotle in a succinct insight into the reciprocal nature of the gift, 'is that which binds men together in their living.' In the *Nichomachean Ethics*, Aristotle linked philanthropy to notions of friendship, concerning himself less with grand public acts of generosity than with benevolent and humane attitudes toward those within an immediate circle of friends and acquaintances. With a timeless understanding of the unequal relationship between donor and recipient, Aristotle urged givers to be discriminating in their judgments, giving only to the right people, an appropriate amount, at the right time.[3]

Some 400 years later in his treatise *de Beneficiis*, Seneca (4 BC–65 AD) also explored the nature of the gift and discussed what he termed 'the rules for a practice that constitutes the chief bond of human society.'[4] He complained that people knew neither how to give nor to receive gifts, failing to choose responsible recipients and often generating ingratitude even in the most worthy beneficiaries. 'Many men we find ungrateful,' he observed, 'but many more we make so, because at one time we are harsh in our reproaches and demands, at another, are fickle and repent of our gift as soon as we have made it, at another, are fault-finding and misrepresent the importance of trifles.'[5] Seneca, Cicero and the later Stoic philosophers expanded the scope and meaning of classical philanthropy. They broadened its reach beyond the face-to-face relationships that had characterized the Greek *polis*. Their writings on gifts and generosity reflected the more expansive notions of natural law and citizenship in the Roman commonwealth. The texts of the ancient Greek philosophers, but

---

[3] Cited in Hands, p. 32.

[4] Seneca, p. 19.

[5] Seneca, p. 5.

especially the later Stoic philosophers, informed the writings of the Apostles and the early Christian theologians. Nevertheless, despite the obvious continuities between late classical thinking about *philanthropia* and early Christian teachings on charity, there were also fundamental differences. Underlying motivations, attitudes toward community, and the most fundamental definitions of charitable purposes began to change. While some scholars such as Demetrios Constantelos underscore the basic continuity between ancient philanthropy and early Christian charity, even he acknowledges that motivations were transformed in the early Christian era: '[t]he definite purpose that guided many Byzantine philanthropists was to please God, to receive forgiveness of sins, and to manifest love for their fellow man.'[6] The ancient world provided a scaffolding of laws and institutional forms. After the Emperor Constantine's conversion to Christianity that long-established framework was more fully elaborated. Attitudes toward wealth, poverty, and charitable responsibility were transformed in the wealthy, urban and still relatively secure eastern half of the Roman Empire. In the Middle Ages, that legacy would be inherited and reshaped in the West.

3 *Caritas*: medieval foundations

Christian teachings on charity are the bedrock on which European foundations rest. Over many centuries the elemental Christian duty to give – and the prospects for earning heavenly rewards – was impressed upon the popular mind. The iconic stone images of cathedral tympana and the stained glass of chapel windows are reminders of those centuries-old teachings. Familiar scenes of charity were portrayed: Christ embracing the leper, St Martin ripping his cloak to share it with a beggar, and the many depictions of the seven corporal (and, less often, the seven spiritual) works of mercy. Literary sources are also abundant. The Bible, the commentaries of the Church Fathers, countless sermons and homilies, the teachings of the scholastics as well as the more practical pronouncements embodied in edicts from church councils, papal decrees, monastic rules, and the discourse of canon lawyers have shaped both individual behaviour and institutional practice for much of the past 2000 years. The Gospels of St Paul and St Luke turned philanthropy heavenward, toward service to God, urging a more selfless and universal love for mankind. The Gospel of St Matthew was very specific in enumerating six works of

---

[6] Cited in Constantelos, *Byzantine Philanthropy and Social Welfare*, p. 280.

mercy. Elaborating medieval doctrines of salvation, St Augustine and later religious thinkers added to this list of charitable duties – feeding the hungry, giving drink to the thirsty, clothing the naked, sheltering the homeless, visiting the sick, ransoming captives, and burying the dead. While we might think of these duties as a rudimentary definition of public benefit, we must remember that most medieval charity was shaped by liturgical aims. Although wealthy donors might feel genuine sympathy for the individual beggar, leper or prisoner whenever they gave alms, the social and economic objectives of almsgiving and endowments were decidedly secondary to the aims of prayer and personal salvation.

The doctrinal as well as the institutional framework that shaped European foundations throughout the Middle Ages took its earliest form in the Byzantine east. The writings of the Greek fathers of the church – Clement of Alexandria (c.150–c.215); Basil the Great, Bishop of Caesarea (c.329–79); and John Chrysostom, Patriarch of Constantinople (c.347–407) – provide the earliest and most compelling articulations of Christian charitable duties. For the church fathers of both East and West, the path to God was through philanthropy. John Chrysostom, in perhaps the most radical break with pagan conceptions of philanthropy, believed that Christian charity resided not in the physical act of giving away money or property but rather in the inner spirit of pity and compassion that motivated the donation. Basil considered wealthy persons to be merely administrators of wealth, a view of stewardship that would be echoed centuries later in Thomas Aquinas and John Calvin. Others, most notably Julianus Pomerius, a 6th century bishop in North Africa, built on this argument contending that God was the owner of all property. He maintained that the wealthy individual's claim to ownership was justified only when, after his family's basic material needs had been met, the property was used to benefit others.

The teachings of the Latin church fathers – St Augustine, Bishop of Hippo (354–430); St Ambrose, Bishop of Milan (c.340–97); St Jerome (c. 340–420); and St Gregory the Great (c. 540–604) – also had resonance. Augustine reminded his flock that the rich man's excess was the poor man's necessity. Ambrose preached forcefully, saying in stark words that would be repeated by others, 'To revile the poor is to commit murder.'[7] In his work *Pastoral Care* Gregory also spoke of the duty to give. The historian Michel Mollat summarized these fundamental injunctions: 'Christ is found in the poor; we possess earthly

---

[7] Cited in Mollat, *The Poor in the Middle Ages: An Essay in Social History*, p. 22.

goods only to administer them; all excess belongs to the poor; alms wipe away sin, but God cannot be corrupted by charity; it is the duty of all Christians to give alms.'[8]

The institutional and legal framework that ultimately shaped medieval foundations in the West also took initial form in 4th century Byzantium. In 321 the Emperor Constantine sought to foster charitable activity when he authorized the church to receive legacies. In 325 the seventieth canon of the Council of Nicaea ordered the founding of hospitals in every city, a call heeded in many towns and cities. Many exemplary foundations were established. John Chrysostom founded hospitals in Constantinople, Jerusalem, and Antioch among other places. The Emperor Constantios (337–61) founded a famous leper hospital called the Zoticon that was built, rebuilt, and its endowment replenished by many subsequent emperors. Basil also urged an expansion of charitable practices by calling upon monasteries to engage directly with society rather than serving primarily as places of spiritual exile and retreat. He saw monasteries as institutions capable of offering hospitality to travellers, alms to the needy, and care to the sick. The charters or *typika* of Byzantine monasteries and hospitals were arguably the first explicit statements of charitable purpose often providing exquisitely detailed instructions about numbers of staff members and their particular duties. In 372 Basil himself was responsible for founding a hospital called the Basileias, one of the most renowned foundations of the era. It functioned as a multi-purpose charitable institution. The Basileias sheltered travellers, poor people, the elderly and lepers as well as those afflicted by other diseases. Gregory Nazianzen described the institution as 'a new city, a storehouse of piety, the common treasury of the wealthy [...] where disease is regarded in a religious light [...] and sympathy is put to the test.'[9] He was so impressed with the scope of this famous foundation that he compared it to the Pyramids of Egypt, the gates of Thebes, and the other great wonders of the world.

The Basileias was not unique. There were many other endowed institutions in the eastern parts of the empire established by clerics and laymen alike. And as the endowed institutions of Byzantium grew in number and specialization, they fell into several categories. Patterned on older pagan institutions, the *xenones* or *xenodochia* served as rent-free hostels for travellers and pilgrims and were located in large cities, provincial towns, and at religious sites. Sometimes they also offered

---

[8] Mollat, p. 39.

[9] Cited in Constantelos, pp. 154–5.

medical care. One of the best known and most enduring was the *xenon* established by Sampson, a court physician and priest who lived, in all likelihood, in the 5th century and whose foundation survived until the 15th century. *Gerocomeia*, homes for the aged, and *ptocheia*, homes for the poor and those unable to work, as well as *orphanotropheia*, orphanages, were also established. Often the founders of these institutions simply gave up their own homes and estates, turning them into charitable enterprises.

Policies to encourage and protect foundations were also implemented. The Emperor Justinian (527–65), who founded a number of *xenones* throughout the empire, granted the first recorded tax exemptions and offered additional financial assistance for the construction of new charitable facilities. Perhaps most significantly, he began to voice his concerns about the administrative oversight of charitable institutions. His legal reforms asserted the emperor's responsibility for protecting charitable institutions and making certain that they adhered to their stated purposes. In general, however, responsibility for overseeing charitable institutions fell to lower ranking ecclesiastical authorities. From the time of the Council of Chalcedon in 451, administration of charitable institutions was overseen primarily by the bishops of the diocese; in turn, the bishops might delegate certain responsibilities to deacons, presbyters, or others selected to manage particular institutions. In the late 9th and early 10th century the emperors again clarified their own administrative responsibilities and sought to prevent bishops from diverting philanthropic endowments to non-charitable purposes. In these practices, we begin to glimpse more coherent mechanisms for regular governmental oversight and control of charitable activity.

Throughout the Byzantine world, the diversity of institutions reflected the complexity of poverty and human need in a region still urban at its core, with a population far more mobile than in the West where poverty remained rural and static. Indeed, as the economy deteriorated in the West, with cities dwindling in size and commerce declining, local bishops assumed the basic responsibility for caring for the vulnerable members of their diocese, devoting one-fourth of their income to the needs of the poor and often using their residences as hospices and shelters. Monasteries also began to play an important social and economic function in the countryside, offering hospitality to travellers and charity to the local residents. Whether in town or country, church property was considered to be the 'patrimony' of the poor.

In western Europe during the early Middle Ages, the typical foundations were monasteries. Indeed, they meet many of the modern definitional criteria for foundations. They held assets in the form of land and rental income, pursued public purposes in the form of almsgiving and hospitality, had formal organizational structures shaped typically by either the Benedictine or Augustinian monastic rules, and reflected the pious intentions of individual donors or groups of benefactors. In the early Middle Ages a monastic official, usually known as the porter, controlled one-tenth of the monastic income and oversaw distributions of food or clothing to those who presented themselves at his door. By the late 10th and early 11th centuries, charitable distributions had grown in importance and were overseen by the monastery's almoner. At the larger monasteries the almonry had its own building and was entitled to a fixed portion of the monastic income as well as to leftover food and used garments. Account books from Cluny suggest that about one-third of its income was routinely devoted to charitable purposes, primarily distributions in kind to those in the abbey's immediate vicinity.

In towns during the early Middle Ages bishops sometimes used their own residences to receive the poor, but as early as the 7th century some urban hospitals – serving as places of hospitality rather than as medical institutions – were founded. Hospitals grew in number in the 11th and 12th centuries as populations became more mobile and as urban and commercial life recovered. Hospitals were founded along pilgrimage, crusade and trade routes; they were located, among other places, in the mountain passes of the Pyrenees and Alps and near river crossings or forest pathways. Charitable impulses also led to the creation of foundations that engaged in the building and maintenance of stone bridges, especially along the Rhône. There, religious confraternities and chapters of canons devoted themselves to constructing and maintaining individual bridges. These chapters of canons, governed most often by the Augustinian rule, remained at the centre of the structured life of most urban charitable institutions between the Rhine and the Seine. Their practices, arguably foreshadowing the professionalization of work within the charitable sector, also began to shape internal habits of governance and accountability.

By the middle of the 12th century increasing economic activity yielded even more abundant wealth for charitable purposes. Kings and princes founded institutions as did lesser lords and merchants. Urban culture and the expanding money economy also reshaped thinking about charitable duties. Twelfth century scholars studied the writings of the early church fathers and underscored both the potential abuses of wealth and the obligations of the rich to give, indeed to share their prosperity. As Michel Mollat explains, 'The frequent use of words like *communicare, communicatio, communis, communicandus* in speaking of the obligation to share is characteristic of twelfth-century habits of thought.'[10] A theory of the natural community of property took shape which led to the belief that property owners were merely the administrators of the wealth under their control and that they had an obligation to share their good fortune with others.

An even more profound change in attitudes toward wealth and poverty came with the preaching of St Francis of Assisi (1182–1226) and St Dominic (1170–1221) and the brothers who joined their mendicant orders. In living among the poor and preaching in bustling urban marketplaces, they confronted inequality and suffering head on. The mendicants brought the link between charity and justice to the fore. Finding intrinsic worth in the poor, they no longer viewed them merely as instruments for the wealthy to seek their own salvation through almsgiving. In the 13th and 14th centuries, theologians and canon lawyers also focused on the new money economy, scrutinizing banking and lending practices and decrying the more obvious disparities of wealth in cities and towns. If pride had been the preeminent sin of the early Middle Ages (and humility its virtuous counterpart), avarice took its place at the top of the list of vices in the later Middle Ages (and charity ascended to the pinnacle of virtues). Theologians subjected the practice of almsgiving to more rigorous analysis, asking when, in what manner, and to whom alms should be given. And, even more significantly, they asked precisely how much of one's property should be considered superfluous wealth.

Increased wealth in the 12th century and after brought about new and more diverse types of charitable foundations. Hospitals became more specialized, responding to the varied forms that poverty and suffering could take in an urbanized world. The reawakening of intellectual life in the West led to the founding of new schools and universities. Royal foundations were created as monarchs consolidated their power and prestige, although whether they should be considered public or private institutions is debatable. However, the royal institutions did begin to point the way toward greater governmental oversight and regulation of charitable activity. In France, in about 1190, a royal almonry was established by King Philip Augustus (1165–1223) who also took an interest in founding leper hospitals. The sainted Louis

---

[10] Mollat, p.107.

IX (1214–70) also founded numerous institutions, including the *Hôpital des Quinze-Vingts* for the blind and the *Maison des Filles-Dieu*. In a rudimentary effort at public supervision and centralization, he used the officials of his almonry to oversee the royal hospitals. His almoner appointed hospital administrators, inspected wayward institutions, and audited their account books.

Throughout western Europe in the 11th and 12th century, new foundations began to be established by noble benefactors, wealthy bourgeois donors, and religious confraternities. Leper hospitals were among the most familiar foundations in this period. They reflected both the enduring appeal of the image of a suffering philanthropic Christ and, at the same time, addressed a genuine public health concern. Other types of hospitals were also founded in cities and towns: Paris soon had more than 60 hospitals; Florence more than 30; Ghent nearly 20; and many smaller cities had a dozen or more. A town's general level of prosperity and its population density drove their establishment and determined their size. Hospitals were numerous but more modest in scale in southern France and on the Iberian peninsula. In the towns of England, the Holy Roman Empire, Hungary and Poland, hospitals and other charitable institutions were not founded nearly as early or as rapidly as in northern Italy, France and Flanders.

Charitable giving also began to take new collective forms in the 12th and 13th centuries. Encouraged by the mendicant orders, confraternities of laymen, craft and trade guilds, and urban parishes developed charitable institutions to serve their members. Guilds and religious brotherhoods collected funds to pay for burials, funeral masses, and provide assistance to widows and orphans. Portugal's *Confraria dos Homens-Bons de Beja* was just such an organization, established by royal charter in 1297. Other confraternities, such as Florence's Or San Michele, operated hospitals and alms houses. In parishes another new type of collective institution appeared, operating under different names in different parts of Europe. These parish-based charitable organizations were commonly called Poor Tables or *Heilige Geest Tafels* in the vernacular of Ghent and other Flemish towns; they were known as *tables des pauvres* in French-speaking regions; and elsewhere they were called Pauper's Bowls, as in Barcelona's *Plats dels Pobres*. Wherever they existed, their purposes were similar: to make regular distributions to the needy in kind and in cash (cash and tokens were used increasingly in the 14th century as almsgiving was monetized). Although the distributions followed the church calendar, these institutions did not treat the poor exclusively as participants in a liturgical ritual. Instead, they aspired to provide genuinely useful assistance. Moreover, these organizations are notable because they were often managed by laymen who worked under clerical supervision. And, especially in northern towns, they were accountable to municipal authorities, who not only provided revenues from town coffers but also specified how account books were to be kept, reviewed the records, and investigated abuses. Not only was a process of secularization underway, so was the expansion of local governmental responsibility.

Indeed, charity was sometimes handled by town governments themselves when they created common alms funds. In many respects, these common funds were prototypical community foundations. In Mons, for example, the Common Alms received bequests and donations and served a variety of functions, burying the dead, assisting poor pupils to attend school, making cash and in-kind donations to the poor and, as in many other towns, making low interest loans to workers. In 1318 the three citizens of Mons who were appointed by the town government to oversee the Common Alms also assumed responsibility for monitoring the town's hospitals. During the 14th century municipalities in the Netherlands and northern Italy took on greater responsibility for overseeing hospitals; the practice then spread gradually to Portugal, Castile and England. In some cases, the municipal governments established new institutions (approximately one-quarter of the hospitals established in the Holy Roman Empire were founded by town governments); in other instances, they compelled the merger and consolidation of faltering institutions. Hospitals also became more specialized, focusing on a particular disease or helping the members of a specific trade or occupational group.

In the 14th and 15th centuries, the boundaries between charitable and commercial activity were also quite permeable. Banks offering low interest loans to the poor emerged in different parts of Europe, especially in Italy where the *monti di pieta* functioned as public pawnbroking institutions and made timely loans at low interest. In 1361 Michael of Northbury, the Bishop of London, left a £1000 legacy to establish a fund whose purpose was to provide one-year, interest-free loans to workers. And if the distinctions between charitable and banking institutions were not always clear-cut, neither were the lines between secular and religious aims, spiritual and temporal practices, or public and private control of institutions. Municipal governments or lay donors would often rely on religious orders to provide staff for their hospitals; in turn, bishops or other clerics would retain lay staff members to administer their almonries or poor tables. Municipal authorities could also impose regulations on hospitals or assume legal jurisdiction over disputes concerning hospital inmates and staff. Variations can be found town by town, with conflict in some places, cordial cooperation in others. But the trend by the 14th century was clear: municipal authorities were assuming greater supervisory authority over charitable institutions. They had done so because deteriorating social and economic conditions had placed municipal governments under greater pressure to rationalize charitable resources, protect institutions from the misdeeds of administrators, and maintain social order.

The mismanagement of hospitals, many of them small and under-endowed, was further aggravated after the Black Death as rents and other income declined and as cash payments were made in devalued currencies. These economic problems were alleviated, to a degree, by the growing practice of testamentary bequests. Studies of wills from around 1400 reveal how frequently people of even relatively modest means left bequests to hospitals and other charitable institutions as well as to their parishes or to the mendicant orders and their establishments. They were motivated by the desire to attract a large gathering of poor people to pray for their souls. Indeed, individual charitable donations and bequests were still chiefly motivated by the medieval penitential system. Popular preachers urged members of the bourgeoisie to renounce their wealth and give to the poor. And the merchant classes responded, often devoting as much attention to accounting for their alms as they did to balancing their business ledgers. They saw alms-giving in terms of contracts and exchanges. '[T]he beggar who receives material aid is bound, in exchange, to pray for his benefactor', the historian Bronislaw Geremek explains. 'This view of alms-giving as a contract was not fully formulated until the twelfth century, but it lies at the roots of the psychological motivation for charity.'[11]

But the late Middle Ages also provoked a countervailing suspicion of poor beggars and mendicant preachers. By the 15th and early 16th centuries fears of vagabonds, gypsies, strangers from distant regions, and the criminality of the poor were much more evident. The wretchedness and Christlike suffering of the poor no longer seemed so praiseworthy. Humanist writers even began to deride poverty and to praise the practical benefits of wealth. As concerns for social order

---

[11] Geremek, p. 48.

mounted, charitable institutions started to undergo an even more marked process of secularization and systematic reform. While municipalities were still the locus of reform, central authorities began to take a keener, more disciplined interest in charitable institutions.

4 Reform and renewal in the early modern era

The reforms of charitable institutions in the 16th century marked a new stage in the development of European foundations, accelerating the processes of secularization and of governmental regulation and control. The origins of these reforms have been much debated. They have been interpreted in various lights: as a product of the Reformation and Counter-Reformation, as a consequence of the rise of capitalism, as a result of the secularizing influences of humanists and lawyers, or even as a mere continuation of medieval reform processes long underway. What we know for certain is that in a relatively short period of time charitable reforms were propelled forward in a number of towns: Nuremberg in 1522, Strasbourg in 1523, Mons in 1525, Ypres in 1525, Lille in 1527. The reforms culminated in a much heralded imperial reform edict issued by Charles V in 1531; this edict sanctioned and codified the reforms that had already taken place in many cities of the empire.

Geremek's account of the reforms in Ypres aptly describes what transpired in various towns:

> The social policies introduced in Ypres in 1525 reposed on the by now familiar principles of banning public beggary, organizing aid for the 'genuine poor', combating vagrancy and creating a fund to cover administrative costs. The essential thing, however, was that the city assumed all responsibility for organizing aid to the poor.[12]

During the 16th century many cities centralized assistance to the poor and took control of a hodge-podge of old and inefficient charitable institutions. Non-residents and vagabonds were driven from towns, while able-bodied beggars were put to work. In many towns general alms funds were also created and supported financially with both charitable contributions and newly imposed taxes. In northern Europe, Ypres, Nuremberg, Paris and Lyon supplied the models for the reforms that were undertaken in some 60 or 70 other European cities, Catholic as well as Protestant.

---

[12] Geremek, p. 139.

Throughout Europe these municipal reforms followed at least a decade of sporadically poor harvests and two exceedingly lean harvests in 1521 and 1522, but they were not the first reforms either of parish poor relief systems or of charitable institutions. The secularization of charity in the 1520s merely accelerated a transition that had begun decades earlier. In 1505 Paris' Hotel-Dieu had been placed under the supervision of a commission of laymen, provoking a conflict with the clergy; Grenoble began efforts to aggregate the wealth of its hospitals and religious confraternities in 1513 but did not finally succeed in that consolidation until 1545. In 1520 Francis I (1494–1547) entrusted the reform of hospitals and royal hospices to his Grand Almoner, who was ordered to appoint two overseers in each diocese – one a cleric, the other a layman – charged jointly with supervising reforms. But like the reforms of Charles V, those of Francis I merely signaled the prospects and possibilities of future state intervention. In the 16th century charitable reform was still primarily a matter for local municipal officials.

Charitable reform in Italy also proceeded city by city beginning as early as the late 14th century. Generally speaking, however, there was much easier accommodation and cooperation between municipal and church authorities in Italy. At the end of the 14th century Giangaleazzo Visconti brought Milan's hospitals under secular control and ordered that they be used to house the city's beggars. By the first years of the 15th century both lay and clerical officials were collaborating in an *Officium Pietatis Pauperum* which organized assistance for the poor. In several other Italian cities – Brescia in 1447, Milan in 1448 and Bergamo in 1449 – 'general' hospitals under a central authority were established. Traditional religious brotherhoods often joined with parish and diocesan officials to reform and renew their charitable work. At the same time, new lending institutions such as the aforementioned *monti di pieta* emerged. In Italy the widespread acceptance of the Council of Trent's reform initiatives kept charitable institutions in conformity with church doctrine. Hospitals were brought under the control of bishops, and the secular hospital administrators were made accountable to the diocesan authority; bishops were also made responsible for all legacies left to the poor.

In the first decades of the 16th century charitable reform in England followed the familiar continental pattern. By mid-century, however, the Reformation had set that country on a markedly different course, clearing the path for further municipal and state intervention in all areas of charity, especially in the 1530s after the dissolution of the monasteries. During the 1540s and 1550s, London's authorities created a coherent system of hospitals, assigning to several hospitals the care of the sick and disabled, to another hospital the care of foundlings, and to another the housing of those deemed idle and lazy. In general terms, however, the weakening of monasteries and other medieval foundations led the English to focus on relief at the parish level and to try to enforce more disciplined approaches to almsgiving. Henry VIII (1491–1547) ordered that every town establish a charitable fund to care for the needy. Voluntary alms, not mandatory taxes, were to be given directly to the fund's administrators rather than to individual beggars, unless those seeking alms fell into certain obviously identifiable categories such as the blind or shipwrecked sailors. While the reform of English poor relief is closely linked to the history of charitable foundations and trusts, it is a larger and more complicated story than can be outlined here.

The Statute of Charitable Uses (1601) is the relevant point of departure for understanding English charity after the Reformation and, indeed, for understanding that country's distinctive and substantial charitable sector today. The preamble to the statute offers compelling insights into the changing definitions of public purpose. On the one hand, it echoes the venerable Augustinian works of charity; on the other, it directly addresses contemporary economic and social needs. Its list of charitable purposes included those

> for relief of aged, impotent and poor people [...] for maintenance of sick and maimed soldiers and mariners, schools of learning, free schools, and scholars in universities [...] for repair of bridges, ports, havens, causeways, churches, sea-banks and highways [...] for education and preferment of orphans [...] towards relief, stock, or maintenance for houses of correction [...] for marriages of poor maids [...] for support, aid and help of young tradesmen, handicraftsmen and persons decayed [...] for relief or redemption of prisoners or captives[13]

The aim of the preamble was not to enumerate a complete and comprehensive list of accepted charitable purposes (the list, in fact, has long medieval antecedents) but rather to suggest that some standard of public benefit should be met. More fundamentally, the statute sought to encourage private charitable giving. The statute called for the appointment of *ad hoc* commissioners – the bishop of the diocese and other reliable individuals – who could investigate cases where a

---

[13] Hammack, p. 6.

donor's intentions were not being followed, where properties were badly administered, or funds diverted illegally. The commissioners were given broad powers of investigation, which included the ability to impanel juries and summon witnesses. Their decisions were fully enforceable unless overturned by an appeal to the Chancellor.

Over the course of the 17th century more than 1000 investigations were undertaken and the effect seems to have been to build confidence in the charitable trust as an instrument for pursuing public purposes. Although the historian W. K. Jordan has probably overestimated the monetary value of charitable bequests and other donations in this period, his general conclusion is sound:

> The consequence [of the commissions' work] was that charitable funds were on the whole administered with quite astonishing probity and skill and that a tradition of the highest fidelity in the discharge of duty was quickly established.[14]

An encouraging and protective legal system was not the only cause, but the 17th and 18th centuries were certainly periods of great vitality for the charitable sector in England.

The most innovative change was in the growth of 'associated philanthropy', the pooling of resources to pursue a common purpose, a model similar to one of the era's greatest commercial innovations, namely the joint stock company.[15] Individuals, particularly those of middling income or whose fortunes were of relatively recent vintage, gave to these new philanthropic organizations. They did so without the restrictions implicit in the charitable trust. Indeed, despite the legal protections that trusts had come to enjoy, they were not as often used in the 18th century as they had been in the 17th century and earlier. New charitable associations devoted themselves to different causes. By the early 18th century the favoured institutions were often charity schools, whose mission was to instill Christian faith along with elemental literacy among the working poor. A new cluster of well-supported voluntary hospitals also emerged. Five of them were established in London between 1719 and 1750 and all were genuinely medical institutions pursuing scientific and public health goals. Four of them were created by associations and one by an individual, Thomas Guy. His grand fortune had its origins in book-selling and publishing. He preserved his wealth when he sold his South Seas shares shortly before the investment bubble burst and was able to

---

[14] Jordan, p.117.

[15] Owen, p. 3.

leave over two-thirds of his estate to endow the hospital which still bears his name. The new hospitals operated on a much larger scale than earlier institutions. The Foundling Hospital was, in the judgment of one historian, 'the most imposing single monument erected by 18th century benevolence', ultimately tending to the needs of some 6300 children.[16] The donors' motivations, whether for the Foundling Hospital or the Marine Society, which trained and prepared boys and young men for naval duty, were those of the humanitarians of that era, reflecting mercantilist concerns for a well-trained and flourishing pool of labour.

While most 18th-century English benefactors left legacies to already existing organizations and associations, new endowments were also established. Of the new trusts created in the 18th century, some 50% were for the benefit of the poor; others were for education, paying apprenticeship fees, making loans to tradesmen, paying dowries, and leaving land for public purposes. The historian David Owen concludes:

> The late-century approach was more calculating, more concerned with consequences, and at least certain philanthropists were taking a harder look at the tasks before them [...]. Philanthropists around the turn of the century were a gloomier lot, disillusioned about the easy and inexpensive successes that they had envisioned, and they were, in fact, faced with growing difficulty in financing their own projects.[17]

Gloomy or not, English donors inhabited an environment that would continue to favour charitable enterprises. From the mid-16th century onward a pattern had been set in England that would differ in fundamental ways from developments on the continent. Charitable purposes were outlined in expansive terms beginning with the Statute of Charitable Uses; trusts and endowments were subject to relatively simple registration requirements rather than formal government approval; legal mechanisms, culminating in the Charitable Trust Act 1853 and the creation of the Charity Commission, aimed to protect the intentions of donors and to prevent abuses of trusts; and efforts were continually being made to simplify Chancery Court proceedings so that trusts could redefine their purposes as public needs changed. In sum, a culture of philanthropy had been created – supportive laws, sound governance practices, habits of giving,

---

[16] Owen, p. 53.

[17] Owen, p. 97.

organizational flexibility, mechanisms for oversight and assuring accountability – which left wide scope for privately run institutions to serve public purposes. The institutions of civil society in England enjoyed a degree of autonomy that was virtually unknown on the continent where the consolidation of state power in the 18th and 19th century had a much more severe impact on charitable foundations.

5 Foundations along the divergent paths to nationhood

While sovereign monarchs had taken tentative steps to oversee and to reform charitable practices in the 16th century and had pressed ahead with additional regulatory efforts in the 17th century, the burden of carrying out these reforms lay primarily with municipal governments, parish administrators, and ecclesiastical authorities. Simply put, the nascent nation states did not yet have the administrative capacity or the fiscal resources to take greater responsibility for social welfare and other public benefit activities. Yet over the next two centuries, the processes of state building continued on the continent. Economic changes resulting from industrialization and a more rapid pace of urbanization placed new demands upon governments. Sometimes the state itself assumed greater responsibilities for public welfare; sometimes the bourgeoisie, industrial workers, and emerging professional groups devized new ways of organizing mutual assistance. Across the continent the boundaries between governmental and philanthropic institutions were redefined. Some states integrated their foundations into the growing governmental sector; others offered them encouragement, protection and a high degree of autonomy; still others subdued and dissolved them. The modern European state has taken diverse forms and, as a consequence, has yielded widely differentiated foundation and nonprofit sectors. Thus, as the history of Europe becomes a history of distinct nation states in the 19th and 20th centuries, it is more difficult to make sweeping European-wide generalizations about foundations. It is best for the individual country chapters to carry the various national stories forward. However, we can begin to discern some of the historical forces that have shaped the broad contours of civil societies in different parts of Europe. We can also begin to see some similarities of approach in a few clusters of nations.

In France and several other predominately Catholic countries with strong monarchies, a new conception of the state's role took shape.

Ultimately, these nations would curtail and eliminate foundations, inhibiting the role of both the nonprofit sector and foundations until well into the 20th century. Patterns of statist centralization and control, later reinforced during the revolutionary period by radical Jacobin ideas, emerged early on in France's national experience. Both Louis XIV (1638–1715) and Louis XV (1710–74) had begun to restrict the privileges of old foundations and had forbidden the establishment of new foundations. They saw them as economically inefficient and viewed their escape from taxation as a drain on the royal treasury. Royal letters patent (culminating in a royal declaration of 1698) were issued as the state sought to reform the administration of many of the larger charitable institutions. Royal decrees were used to intervene in basic matters of foundation governance: duties of governing boards were outlined in great detail and boards were restructured with a mix of parish officials, municipal authorities, and representatives of trade and corporate groups serving together. There were also continuing efforts to rationalize haphazard and uncoordinated charitable work by creating general hospitals in various French cities. Though perhaps less zealous, sovereigns in other absolutist countries pursued similar reforms. Indeed, general hospitals could be found in many countries.

A glimpse at the general hospital in Montpellier, founded in 1678, affords a view into the operations, as well as the deficiencies, of this typical late 17th-century foundation. The Montpellier General Hospital was a substantial institution that held some 700 beds, most of them occupied by young children. At its peak, it also distributed assistance to some 4500 people in their homes. In Montpellier as elsewhere, the new general hospitals also had a policing function, seeking out the idle poor, vagabonds, and criminals, subjecting them to trial and punishment, and, in brute reality, incarcerating many of them. Reflecting the economic ideas of the Physiocrats, general hospitals also established programmes to train people for productive work. These hospitals managed to survive not merely on donations and traditional endowments but on a diverse stream of revenues: rights to tolls, diocesan and municipal contributions, fees from parents who left their children in the hospital, and earnings from the sale of cotton, wool and other goods manufactured in the hospital's shops (earned income is not at all a late 20th century innovation for nonprofit institutions). However, these general purpose institutions did not begin to solve the problems of poverty, ill-health, dependency, or unemployment. And ultimately they proved inadequate to the task of effective charitable administration.

Abuses in administering France's charitable institutions, even the relatively new general hospitals and *bureaux de charité*, led to a series of royal inquiries in 1754, 1764, 1770 and 1788. The discovery that regulations were being flouted, that governance was often corrupt, and that book-keeping and audit practices remained inept only served to undermine the credibility of charitable foundations. Like many other general hospitals, Montpellier's hospital was on the verge of bankruptcy in the 1770s. Indeed, after the middle of the 18th century, state officials seemed to lose faith in promoting hospital reform. Communes and towns had proved incapable of carrying out the reforms mandated by the state. Moreover, popular support for charitable institutions, as evidenced in steadily declining bequests and donations, also waned during the 18th century.

In this worsening climate, Enlightenment thinkers articulated a series of arguments against foundations. The Physiocrat and onetime Minister of Finance, A. R. J. Turgot (1727–81), in his famous article on foundations in the *Encyclopedie* expressed his disdain for these vestigial institutions, dismissing them as a 'frivolous vanity'. He argued that:

> Public usefulness is the supreme law and should not be balanced either against a superstitious respect for what one considers the founder's intent [...] or against a fear of harming the presumed rights of a certain group, as if a particular group had any rights *vis à vis* the state.

He feared that in time foundations might absorb all the property of the nation. He believed that the wealth they held was unproductive and severely impeded national economic development.

Measures to curtail foundations and to turn poor relief and other welfare activities over to the state accelerated during the French Revolution. In 1790 the Constituent Assembly established a *Comité de Mendicité* which sharply criticized the charitable institutions of the old regime, contending that charity was undignified and offensive to rational human beings. The *Comité* sought to centralize public welfare and to bring assets held by foundations into more productive use. As Colin Jones argues, 'The Comité de Mendicité had demoted charity from the foremost of all Christian virtues to the rank of adjunct to state finance in the organization of poor relief.'[18]

---

[18] Jones, p. 166.

In the wake of the French Revolution, church and other charitable properties were seized and sold off as *biens nationaux*. Intermediary associations such as guilds and confraternities as well as foundations were banned under the Le Chapelier Act 1791. Parish and small town relief organizations lost many of their revenues. And, for a time, hospitals submitted to dechristianization, their bells silenced, chapels closed, and religious orders expelled. While the most intense revolutionary fervour did not last long (indeed, many of the more extreme strictures were relaxed within a decade), Jacobin attitudes lingered, bolstering the suspicion of endowments and private institutions. The Jacobins and their ideological heirs in France and elsewhere argued that traditional forms of association hindered state activities and usurped the rights of individual citizens. Throughout the 19th century, bequests continued to be tightly regulated and new endowments were discouraged. Indeed, only at the end of the 19th century did a few new foundations begin to appear in France, despite the obstacles; and it was not until 1987 and 1990 that new French laws were implemented to define, govern and encourage foundations.

If the French experience with foundations defines one end of the European spectrum and the English the other extreme, then there are a few countries more closely aligned to the French end. Rooted in a strong absolutist tradition, French statism had analogues and similar consequences for civil societies elsewhere. In Spain, as early as 1798, a decree of Carlos IV ordered the sale of all real-estate belonging to hospitals and other charitable institutions. In Portugal, since the end of the 15th century, monarchs had also sought periodically to reform charitable institutions, consolidating hospitals in Lisbon, encouraging the creation of the *Misericordias* in Lisbon and other towns, and assuming legal jurisdiction over charitable institutions and their properties. With bequests growing ever more numerous and more properties falling into mortmain, further restrictions on legacies for both secular and religious purposes were imposed in 1769.

France's revolutionary, anti-traditional fervour was carried to many parts of Europe by Napoleon's armies and led to the establishment of anti-clerical regimes. In Belgium, for example, the revolutionary climate at the end of the 18th century proved unfavourable to foundations, guilds and similar intermediary organizations. Many religious institutions were suppressed and private individuals were denied the right to set up foundations. The emergence of liberal and secularly oriented governments in Spain, Portugal and Belgium (though often succeeded by strong anti-revolutionary and monarchical counter-movements) caused charitable foundations to suffer further erosion. Premised on the belief that the state rather than the traditional voluntary charitable institutions should have responsibility for the welfare of its citizens, decisive acts were passed in Spain in 1823 and 1836 dissolving the country's medieval foundations and banning new ones. The break with the medieval past was stark. Not until 1978 did the Spanish Constitution explicitly acknowledge the right to create foundations, thus ending nearly two centuries of hostility toward private charitable institutions. In Portugal a series of 19th-century laws repressed the religious orders, secularized the charitable functions of older foundations, and aimed to dissolve still other retrograde charitable institutions. While some new charitable institutions were founded in the 19th century, it was only in the second half of the 20th century that Portugal began to witness the birth of new philanthropic institutions, most notably the Calouste Gulbenkian Foundation established in 1956. While the right to free association was guaranteed in Belgium's Constitution of 1831, it was not until 1921 that nonprofit organizations and foundations were recognized in law. In the final analysis, we must be cautious about gross historical generalizations that smooth out the distinctive course of national histories. But in most of these countries, the legacies of revolution, counter-revolution, and state-building proved unfavourable to the development of the foundation sector. Even today, as subsequent chapters reveal, their foundation sectors remain relatively small and underdeveloped.

Far more robust foundation communities emerged in the Nordic countries. Denmark and Sweden, like England, experienced neither the lingering confessional and ideological cleavages of Reformation and civil war, nor the national struggles for independence against foreign occupation that had shaped the state-building processes in some Catholic countries to the south. Rather than leading to the expropriation of church properties, the Reformation in both Denmark and Sweden allowed links to be forged between church and state. Early on charitable institutions were used in ways that allowed central and municipal governments to expand their welfare functions. As early as 1536 the coronation charter of Denmark's King Christian III declared that the state had obligations to care for the needy and integrated the clergy into local administration. Various Swedish monarchs created their own substantial foundations, establishing hospitals and educational institutions that foreshadowed a widening role for the public sector. After much trial and error, the Danish kings enacted statutes in the mid-17th century that allowed them to regulate and oversee the activities of foundations, although they did not try to gain full control over private charitable assets. In fact, in the early 18th century, the government sought to guarantee and protect the expressed intentions of foundation donors. Later in the century, legal scholars began to ask the perpetual question: How and under what circumstance can the original intentions of a donor be altered? In both Denmark and Sweden, these conditions produced a pluralistic foundation environment, a sector well supported by state, church, and middle-class associations. Indeed, the middle class began to finance activities much more extensive than the traditional *piae causae* defined by canon law. Foundations gained further legitimacy when various 19th-century popular movements, most notably the labour, temperance, and free-church movements, used foundations to advance their causes.

Norway was, by contrast, a poorer and less populous country. It was also a dependent one, subject to Denmark until 1814, then conjoined with Sweden until attaining full independence in 1905. While some Norwegian foundations can trace their origins to medieval gifts from kings or ecclesiastical authorities, others can be dated to the 18th century when relatively small legacies were left to help with the education or support of needy families in an individual donor's town or parish or within his particular trade or occupational group. Magistrates, serving as local representatives of the state, typically administered these legacies. In the early 20th century, administrative responsibility for these local funds passed into the hands of mayors, county judges or other local officials. Finland, first under Swedish dominion and then a part of the Russian empire from 1809 to 1917, saw its oldest foundations shaped by a relatively supportive Swedish monarchy and then circumscribed by less permissive Russian authorities. Until the Finnish Republic became independent in 1917 and then enacted a foundation law in 1930, foundations and private associations could only be established with the approval of the Russian czar.

There are no easy, over-arching generalizations to account for the history of foundations in the territories that now make up modern Germany. Throughout most of Germany's history, power was fragmented among an array of principalities, duchies, baronies, cities and towns. The development of a unified German nation was fitful and, thus, the fate of foundations varied from place to place and era to era. But there were shared historical experiences that have left distinguishing marks upon German foundations and the wider nonprofit sector. The end of the Holy Roman Empire in 1803 wrote a finale to the multitude of more or less autonomous territories that made up this ancient federation. Properties formerly in the hands of ecclesiastical establishments were frequently transferred to the surviving German states, in part as compensation for territories lost to French occupation. Other foundation properties fell under the control of local administrative authorities. In these new circumstances German foundations enjoyed only a very limited autonomy. However, Friederich Carl von Savigny and other legal theorists began to devize and elaborate a theoretical justification for private foundations. They pondered the question of whether foundations could enjoy independent legal status or could merely be attached to associations and corporations. Savigny concluded that they could be independent, although only subject to the tight control and regulation of the state.

In this legally circumscribed form, the idea of the foundation survived German unification. By the end of the 19th century foundations were experiencing a modest revival. Successful industrialists created a number of prominent foundations, research organizations and cultural institutions. German foundations blossomed when wealthy citizens discovered the uses of private philanthropy both as an arena for experimentation with social welfare initiatives and as a mechanism for influencing public policy. Around the turn of the century their wealth also built institutions of higher education in cities such as Leipzig, Frankfurt, Cologne and Mannheim. And recognizably modern foundations also began to appear, most notably the *Carl Zeiss Stiftung* established by Zeiss' business partner, Ernst Abbe. Founded initially to support the University of Jena, it later turned its attention to issues affecting the lives of factory workers.

In the aftermath of World War I foundations did not fare as well. After 1918 many privately organized institutions were incorporated within large confessional and ideologically structured umbrella organizations, the welfare federations (*Wohlfahrtsverbände*). During the 1930s, these national structures were relatively easy to subsume under the corporatist state of the National Socialists. In the same decade, Jewish foundations and workers' organizations were abolished, and most other foundations saw their assets eaten away, if not during the years of hyperinflation and depression, then through the devastation of World War II. The post-war division of Germany took an additional heavy toll on foundations in the East. Only in more recent decades have their numbers and wealth recovered. Of the more than 10,000 foundations in Germany today, half were founded after World War II and nearly one-third after 1985.

There is no single narrative line that can account for the place that foundations hold in Italy. Long-standing regional differences have prevailed. Large towns in the north such as Turin, which was in the embrace of the Dukes (and later Kings) of Savoy, underwent charitable reforms at the hands of both municipal administrators and local princes. These reforms resembled those in France, Spain, and Portugal. And even though the republican city-states of the north had all given way to more autocratic regimes by the 17th century, a habit of civic engagement continued to sustain charitable institutions and individual acts of public patronage well into the 19th century. In contrast, the south remained poor, its wealth based on agrarian estates and seigneurial privileges. Unlike the north, the region did not produce a strong class of urban merchants, craftsmen, and professionals, nor did the south build the sorts of institutions that had played so vital a part in the political and social fabric of the northern city-states. Southern Italy's civil society has remained underdeveloped to the present day.

In the north, French revolutionary ideas spilled over the Alps, propelling liberal governments in that region to abolish many of their medieval guilds and confraternities. However, the *Risorgimento* gave birth to something new in the world of Italian associational activity. Indeed, the 'principle of association' was fundamental to the nationalist movement and inspired not only reform groups and secret revolutionary societies, but also professional, scientific and educational associations. After unification, mutual aid societies and cooperatives sprang up to replace the older self-help arrangements created by medieval trade and craft guilds. The functions of these mutual aid societies were familiar: helping the families of deceased members, offering burial assistance, providing schooling and training through night schools and lending libraries. The cooperative movement spread throughout all segments of society; there were agricultural cooperatives, labour cooperatives, consumer cooperatives and banking cooperatives. In the three decades after unification, mutual aid societies and cooperatives were the principal forms of voluntary activity, but far more characteristic of the north than the south. Although a richly endowed foundation sector did not emerge in the late 19th and early 20th century, a few substantial corporate foundations were founded after World War II. More recently, the banking law reforms of the 1990s have given new impetus to Italy's foundation sector.

While Greece has inherited a venerable philanthropic tradition, it was a tradition in which ecclesiastical foundations were never fully independent from state control. Philanthropy was not understood in ways that drew sharp distinctions either between church and state or between public and private sector. Private resources supported public activities; state funds sustained church functions; and indeed private endowments have often been placed directly in the hands of relevant government ministries. However, some new foundations did emerge during the last century of Ottoman rule when wealthy Greeks residing in western Europe gave substantially to causes in their homeland. They established foundations to preserve their cultural heritage, to foster the war of independence against the Turks, and to meet the welfare needs of their native towns and villages. These benefactors created a framework for town-run albeit privately funded welfare institutions; they also founded private voluntary associations which administered their own programmes. After independence, many bequests were left directly to the Greek state, a practice that continued in the early 20th century. While legislation was passed in the 1920s to protect the intentions of donors, Greece has been slow to develop an autonomous foundation sector in the 20th century.

This *tour d'horizon* suggests that we must focus on the particularities of national experiences if we want to understand how foundations have evolved in Europe over the past 200 years. While general comparative models can give us a respectably crisp snapshot of the present day, it is far more difficult to turn them into moving pictures. The film blurs, the lens is too wide, the cuts are too swift. However, we can delineate some of the factors that have shaped the various environments in which foundations operate. We have seen legal systems that vary in the ease with which foundations can be incorporated, the intentions of donors protected or altered, and the public accountability of foundations overseen. We have observed differing, indeed evolving, conceptions of the division of responsibility between the state and private entities for the provision of social welfare services, education, arts and cultural life and other public benefit activities. We have seen the various ways in which religious traditions have shaped habits of charitable giving and how established churches (or the religious pluralism that is its opposite) have sustained philanthropic institutions. We have witnessed widely varying habits of association and the different sorts of charitable and mutual benefit enterprises that have been formed along lines of economic class and political allegiance. We have seen how relationships with *émigré* groups and with foreign aid organizations and foundations working from abroad (as later chapters will show) can influence the development of civil societies. And finally, we have observed that a country's degree of political stability and its level of economic development – its capacity to generate wealth and its attitudes toward the private accumulation of that wealth – can determine the resources that go into the foundation sector.

6 Conclusions

This history of foundations in Europe is too brief to be more than a suggestive essay. Obviously it points toward topics for more rigourous and detailed research.

- How have ideas of charity, philanthropy, public welfare, mutual benefit, association, and other cognate concepts been articulated in the past?
- How have these ideas been given institutional form and structure in different eras and in diverse locales?
- How have philanthropic institutions interacted with municipal and state governments?
- How have they played a role in national integration?
- How have they been shaped by religious, regional, social and economic cleavages in various countries?
- How have foundations fared under different regimes and in diverse economic conditions?
- And, in the final analysis, what have foundations accomplished?

If this historical essay ends with more questions than it can answer, it does suggest some ways of looking at contemporary foundations. First, we should not see foundations as static legal entities but rather as malleable, adaptable creations capable of functioning in different environments. In order to survive, whatever the time or place, foundations must have a continuing capacity to change. They must do so quite simply because conceptions of public benefit are never static and the boundaries between public and private sectors are constantly shifting. Thus, we should see foundations as flexible instruments for pursuing the public benefit, as tools for both redefining public purposes and reshaping the boundaries of civil society, government and market.

Second, we should pay careful attention to changing philanthropic motives, purposes and strategies. Historically, foundations have been built upon very different motivational schemes: public honour and remembrance, pious fears and salvation, public order and social control, rationality and scientific progress, class consciousness and political advantage and, no doubt, concepts of altruism, magnanimity and generosity toward others. In exploring what has motivated donors, we can begin to understand why foundations are such deeply rooted European institutions and why the idea of the foundation has had an ability to survive and surface anew even when, as in some countries, private philanthropic traditions have been curtailed. In examining its evolving purposes, we can also see what role foundations have played in relationship to the changing functions of the state and market.

Third, foundations should be viewed in a political or, more broadly conceived, a constitutional context. Despite their wealth, foundations are dependent institutions, relying on the framework of law and regulation created by governments and nurtured by the wealth transferred from flourishing economic sectors. Despite their private structures of governance, foundations must be viewed not simply as autonomous institutions but rather in their relationship to the constituent elements of particular societies. The long-term survival of foundations depends on the legitimacy they have earned, whether it is the legitimacy that arises from their role in maintaining a pluralist civil society or their capacity to provide public goods that the government and private business sector do not. As this chapter has shown, foundations have always been vulnerable *vis à vis* governments. They are no less reliant on the continuing willingness of new donors to create foundations and to transfer their wealth to them. Minimally, the legitimacy of foundations depends on sound internal governance practices and high standards of public accountability. Over the long term, however, legitimacy is built on something more, namely a solid record of accomplishment in meeting public needs. But even that legitimacy cannot be secure without a broad public comprehension and acceptance of the unusual status enjoyed by foundations. They are institutions neither shaped by the consumer demands of the marketplace nor controlled by the majoritarian constraints of the ballot box. At the same time, however, they are neither protected by the power of the market nor assured that democratic majorities will continue to tolerate them. To the extent that their role is not well understood, they will always remain vulnerable. The task of this paper has been to add to our understanding of foundations by situating them in the ebb and flow of European history.

Bibliography

Bienvenu, J. -M., 'Pauvreté, misères et charité en Anjou aux XIe et XIIe siècles' in: *Moyen Age*, Vol. LXXII, 1966, pp. 389–424 and Vol. LXXIII, 1967, pp. 5–34, 189–216.

Bulliet, R. W. *The Patricians of Nishapur: A Study in Medieval Islamic Social History*, Cambridge, MA, Harvard University Press, 1972.

Cavallo, S., *Charity and Power in Early Modern Italy: Benefactors and Their Motives in Turin*, 1541–1789, Cambridge, Cambridge University Press, 1995.

Constantelos, D. J., *Byzantine Philanthropy and Social Welfare*, New Rochelle, NY, Aristide Caratzas, 1991.

Constantelos, D. J., *Poverty, Society and Philanthropy in the Late Medieval Greek World*, New Rochelle, NY, Aristide Caratzas, 1992.

Fairchilds, C. C., *Poverty and Charity in Aix-en-Provence, 1640–1789*, Baltimore, Johns Hopkins University Press, 1976.

Davis, N. Z., *Society and Culture in Early Modern France*, Stanford, CA, Stanford University Press, 1965.

Duby, G., *Rural Economy and Country Life in the Medieval West*, Columbia, SC, University of South Carolina Press, 1968.

Geremek, B., *Poverty: A History*, Oxford, Blackwell Publishers, 1994.

Hammack, D. C. ed., *Making the Nonprofit Sector in the United States*, Bloomington and Indianapolis, Indiana University Press, 1998.

Hands, A. R., *Charities and Social Aid in Greece and Rome*, Ithaca, NY, Cornell University Press, 1968.

Henderson, J., *Piety and Charity in Late Medieval Florence*, Oxford, Oxford University Press, 1994.

Himmelfarb, G., *Poverty and Compassion: The Social Ethic of the Late Victorians*, New York, Knopf, 1991.

Ilchman, W. F., Katz, St N. and Queen II, E. L. eds, *Philanthropy in the World's Traditions*, Bloomington and Indianapolis, Indiana University Press, 1998.

Jones, C., *Charity and Bienfaisance, The Treatment of the Poor in the Montpellier Region, 1740–1815*, Cambridge, Cambridge University Press, 1982.

Jordan, W. H., *Philanthropy in England, 1480–1660: A Study of the Changing Pattern of English Social Aspirations*, London, Allen and Unwin, 1959.

Little, L. K., *Religious Poverty and the Profit Economy in Medieval Europe*, Ithaca, NY, Cornell University Press, 1978.

MacMullen, R., *Christianizing the Roman Empire: AD 100–400*, New Haven, CT, Yale University Press, 1984.

Martz, L., *Poverty and Welfare in Habsburg Spain: The Example of Toledo*, Cambridge, Cambridge University Press, 1983.

Mauss, M., *The Gift: The Form and Reason for Exchange in Archaic Societies*, New York, Norton, 1990.

Mollat, M., *The Poor in the Middle Ages: An Essay in Social History*, New Haven, CT, Yale University Press, 1986.

Mollat, M. ed., *Etudes sur l'histoire de la pauvreté au moyen age–XVIe siècle*, 2 vols, Paris, Publications de la Sorbonne, Série 'Etudes', No. 8, 1974.

Norberg, K., *Rich and Poor in Grenoble, 1600–1814*, Berkeley, University of California Press, 1985.

Owen, D., *English Philanthropy, 1660–1960*, Cambridge, MA, Harvard University Press, 1964.

Prochaska, F. K., *Women and Philanthropy in Nineteenth-Century England*, Oxford, Clarendon Press, 1980.

Prochaska, F. K., 'Philanthropy', in *The Cambridge Social History of Britain, 1750–1950*, Vol 3, Cambridge, Cambridge University Press, 1990.

Pullan, Brian, *Rich and Poor in Renaissance Venice: The Social Institutions of a Catholic State to 1620*, Oxford, Oxford University Press, 1971.

Putnam, R., *Making Democracy Work: Civic Traditions in Modern Italy*, Princeton, NJ, Princeton University Press, 1993.

Salamon, L. M. and Anheier, H. K., *The Emerging Nonprofit Sector: An Overview*, Manchester, Manchester University Press, 1996.

Schneewind, J. B. ed., *Giving: Western Ideas of Philanthropy*, Bloomington and Indianapolis, Indiana University Press, 1996.

Seligman, A. B., *The Idea of Civil Society*, Princeton, NJ, Princeton University Press, 1992.

Seneca, *Moral Essays*, Vol. III, Cambridge, MA, Harvard University Press/Loeb Classical Library, 1989.

Slack, P., *From Reformation to Improvement: Public Welfare in Early Modern England*, Oxford, Oxford University Press, 1998.

Tierney, B., *Medieval Poor Law: A Sketch of Canonical Theory and its Application in England*, Berkeley, CA, University of California Press, 1959.

▼ Helmut K. Anheier

Foundations in Europe: a Comparative Perspective

1 Introduction

This volume reveals a type of organization operating across nearly 30 European countries that is neither business nor government and that belongs neither to the two large institutional complexes of market and state nor to the voluntary, nongovernmental associations of the not-for-profit sector. This type of organization is commonly referred to as a foundation or charitable trust holding assets, financial or otherwise, dedicated to serving a public purpose of its choice. Until recently, relatively little was publicly known about such foundations, with the exception of countries like the United Kingdom[1] or Germany,[2] and of course, the United States.[3]

Comparative research on foundations remains rare and usually involves country-specific comparisons,[4] or takes on specific issues such as governance and accountability.[5] Even work that explored the role of nonprofit organizations more generally, most prominently the

---

[1] Leat, *British Foundations*.

[2] Anheier/Romo; Strachwitz.

[3] Renz/Mandler/Tran; Ylvezaker; Odendahl.

[4] See Anheier/Toepler.

[5] Van der Ploeg.

Johns Hopkins Comparative Nonprofit Sector Project,[6] did not focus on foundations explicitly.[7] Although their work is clearly relevant to the task at hand, and will indeed inform our approach and analysis throughout, foundations remain a largely uncharted part of modern societies. Salamon and Anheier treated only grant-making foundations as a separate statistical category, subsuming other forms such as operating foundations alongside nonprofit organizations at large.[8] As a result, we know little about the world of foundations *in toto*, covering different types and forms.

Significantly, it is not because we could expect to add little in terms of substance and relevance to our understanding of modern societies that foundations remain uncharted from a comparative perspective. Rather, the sheer complexity and richness of the phenomenon, historically, legally, politically as well as culturally, seems to preclude any systematic attempt to compare foundations cross-nationally. Indeed, among the first impressions one can gain from a cursory glance across Europe's foundation world is the great variety and diversity not only in terms of type, size, activities and role but also in the prevailing 'philanthropic culture' of particular countries. In this context, and against the backdrop of the various country reports, the purpose of this chapter is to fill some of the most glaring gaps in our comparative understanding of foundations in Europe.

1.1 Private funds, public purpose

In some countries like the United Kingdom, charitable trusts occupy a prominent place in a political economy and national culture that has shown remarkable stability over time. Foundations, typically referred to as charitable trusts, are relatively numerous, and they operate in wide range of activities.[9] Even though relations with government have changed over time, the independence and role of

---

[6] Salamon/Anheier, *The Emerging Nonprofit Sector*; Salamon *et al.*

[7] The same can be said of research that looked into the role of the third sector across different European countries; see Badelt.

[8] The decision to allocate operating foundations, including those with limited grant making functions, to their major area of economic activity (social services, education, health etc.) was correct in the context of the Johns Hopkins Comparative Nonprofit Sector Research Project. The decision, however, underreports the true scale of foundation activity as defined in this chapter. For example, the share of *grant-making* foundations of total full-time equivalent nonprofit sector employment in France is less then 0.01%; if *operating* foundations are included, the share jumps to 3% of total full-time equivalent nonprofit sector employment. Salamon *et al.* focused on, and reported, the former figure, but not the latter.

[9] Vincent/Pharoah.

foundations has never been seriously challenged.[10] In the Nordic countries, too, foundations have long played a role in welfare provision, research funding and in international relations; and they are also a popular, if sometimes controversial vehicle for setting up family trusts and for the preservation of 'dynastic capital' among the elite.[11] Having developed gradually, foundations are numerous and number over 10,000 in Denmark[12] and between 20–30,000 in Sweden.[13] Similarly, the growth and stability of the foundation world in the Netherlands is in large part a result of the development of the Dutch welfare system, of which foundations are an integral part both in terms of service delivery and financing.[14]

In contrast to the 'steady state' of British, Dutch or Scandinavian philanthropy, foundations in other countries like Austria look back to an uneven, perhaps even dramatic, history. At the beginning of the last century, Austria's foundations numbered over 60,000[15] – a high number even by today's standards. One hundred years later, after two World Wars, hyperinflation, Nazism, and a reconstruction period that favoured state actors within a strict corporatist framework, Austrian foundations number fewer than 1000. It seems that foundations in Austria never fully recovered from the political and economic jolts of the 20th century. German foundations share some of the same misfortunes, but managed a remarkable revival after the 1970s in particular. Nearly half of the existing foundations in Germany today were established during the last three decades.[16] Even though some of the country's foundations date back over 1000 years to the high Middle Ages, it is only a slight exaggeration to state that the German foundation sector today is essentially a product of the post-war period.[17]

Next to such 'boom and bust' patterns we find cases like Ireland, where foundations remain few in numbers, never having played a particularly prominent role, either in the country's political and economics development, or in its social welfare system.[18] Similarly,

---

[10] Kendall/Knapp.

[11] Lundstroem/Wijkström.

[12] See chapter by Hellman/Parving.

[13] See chapter by Wijkström.

[14] See chapter by Burger/Dekker/Veldheer.

[15] See chapter by Bachstein/Badelt.

[16] See chapter by Strachwitz.

[17] Anheier/Romo.

[18] See chapter by Donoghue.

few foundations exist in France, and most of those that do are under relatively close state supervision.[19] Historically, however, foundations – or more precisely the Jacobin measures against them – constitute an important factor in the French state's development of sharp opposition to intermediary institutions it regarded as pre-modern relics of the *ancien regime* and bastions of church power. Rather than representing private institutions for the public good, the extreme Jacobin tradition sees foundations as unwanted special interests meddling in the democratic relationship between free *citoyens* on the one hand and the state as their true and only representative on the other.[20]

In neighbouring Switzerland, however, such ideologies would have found little support. Within the country's highly decentralized federal system, foundations have played, and are playing, a significant part in Swiss economic and political life. In fact, the Swiss welfare system could not function without foundations: health insurance schemes, pension schemes and many health and social service providers are organized as foundations.[21] Further to the South, we find a different situation yet: Italian foundations, despite their long history in welfare provision, are largely a product of the late 20th century.[22] Italy, as is the case in Spain[23] and Portugal,[24] has a pronounced church presence among foundations, reflecting the long-standing institutional influence of Catholicism, whereas secular foundations are of far more recent origin. Likewise, the foundation communities in Greece and Turkey contain two different components: a set of foundations that are part of the dominant religion (Greek-Orthodox Church or Islam respectively), and the other a modern, secular set of institutions that are often either linked to the emerging business elite or state action.[25]

Add to this diverse picture the emergence or re-emergence of foundations in the former socialist countries of central and eastern Europe, as Pinter shows in The Role of Foundations in the Transformation Process in Central and Eastern Europe. Largely supported by outside funding from other European and American foundations, and with

---

[19] See chapter by Archambault; Pomey.

[20] Archambault, *The Nonprofit Sector in France*.

[21] See chapter by Steinert; Wanger.

[22] See chapter by Barbetta/Demarie).

[23] See chapter by Olabuénaga.

[24] See chapter by Monjardino.

[25] See chapters by Tsakraklides and Aydin.

the aid of EU programmes, foundations are being introduced and re-introduced in a region which itself varies considerably in political culture and level of economic development. What the countries of the region share in common, however, is a 50 to 60 year hiatus and disruption in foundation history. Not surprisingly, and with the exception of Hungary, foundations remain relatively few in number throughout and many continue to rely on external funds from the United States and Europe. Yet in most central and eastern European countries, foundations played an important role in the initial transition and consolidation period of the 1990s, and they are likely to play a similar role in the accession process toward potential EU membership and the implementation of the *acquis communautaire*.

Clearly, as this Cook's tour has demonstrated, foundations in Europe reveal a great variety in form, purpose, and activity. Their historical development is as different as the current role foundations play across European countries that themselves vary in legal tradition, history, and form of government, economy and culture. Of course, at one level it is hardly surprising that an institution as old as the foundation comes with a complex terminological layer of definitions, meanings and uses, particularly when viewed cross-nationally. From a comparative perspective, therefore, applying some kind of conceptual order to achieve at least some minimal level of comparability across countries represents the first task of this chapter, to which we now turn.

2 Definitions and types

The rich tapestry of foundations in Europe speaks to us in different languages and uses a highly complex, sometimes confusing, terminology. At one level, *foundation, fondation, fundacion, fundacao, fundazzione, Stiftung, stichting, stiftelse, ιδρυμα* or *wakf*, share a common image: a separate, identifiable asset (the root meaning of *fund, fonds*) donated (the root of *stift*) to a particular purpose, usually public in nature (implying the root of philanthropy). But this is where commonalties end. The various legal traditions and systems in Europe define and treat foundations rather differently;[26] and registration, legal practices and oversight regimes vary accordingly, sometimes even within the same country, as is the case in Germany[27] or Switzerland.[28]

---

[26] See van der Ploegh as well as Section IV in this volume.

[27] Bertelsmann Stiftung/Maecenata Institut.

[28] Reimer.

The end result is a complicated terminological tangle: what is defined as a foundation in one country may not qualify as such in another. The Swedish 'company foundations' like the *Knut och Alice Wallenberg Foundation* and the Norwegian 'commercial foundations' would find it difficult to get past the English Charity Commission, the independent public agency overseeing voluntary associations and foundations; likewise many English foundations could not exist as such according to French law, nor would the Charity Commission itself for that matter. The Austrian 'private foundation' and the Liechtensteinian family foundation could hardly expect the approval of the Belgian Ministry of Justice; and many Danish foundations would expect long-drawn out and uphill legal battles in Italian courts, should they ever decide to re-establish themselves south of the Alps. In contrast, they would receive a much warmer welcome in Spain or the Netherlands.

What is more, not all organizations labelled 'foundation' are in fact foundations. Even though most legal systems incorporate the ancient Roman law differentiation between foundations based on some core asset (*universitas rerum*) and associations (*universitas personarum*), prevailing reality seems less clear-cut. In Poland and Hungary and other central and eastern European countries, many foundations are *de jure* and *de facto* either membership associations or some form of corporation, usually in the form of a limited liability company. The German political foundations like the *Friedrich-Ebert-Stiftung* or the *Konrad-Adenauer Stiftung* are state-supported political party organizations with no significant assets of their own; their operating budgets are largely covered by annual subventions from government.[29] In legal terms, the party foundations are registered associations with leading party officials as members. In the Netherlands, the distinction between foundation (asset-based) and association (member-based) has become largely indistinguishable in the field of education and social services. In Switzerland some foundations are primarily investment trusts for families, pension schemes for corporations, or local sickness funds.[30]

---

[29] See Beise.

[30] See chapter by Steinert.

2.1 Definitions of foundations

The definition of a foundation varies from one country to another[31] not along one primary axis but frequently along several dimensions. There are legal definitions that reflect either common law traditions with an emphasis on trusteeship (UK), or civil law traditions (Switzerland, Germany) with the important distinction between membership and non membership-based legal personalities.[32] Other definitions bring in additional aspects such as type of founder (private or public), purpose (charitable or other), activities (grant making or operating), revenue structure (single or multiple funding sources), asset type (own endowment or regular allocations), and the degree of independence from either the state or business interest.

To cut across this terminological tangle, this chapter adopts an approach that has proven fruitful in a closely related area, the comparative study of nonprofit organizations.[33] The adapted working definition is based on a slight modification of the structural/operational definition developed by Salamon and Anheier (1997). Accordingly, we define a foundation as an asset, financial or otherwise, with the following characteristics:

1 **Non membership-based organization.** The foundation must rest on an *original deed*, typically signified in a charter of incorporation or establishment that gives the entity both intent of purpose and relative permanence. Other aspects include some degree of internal *organizational structure*, relative persistence of goals, structure and activities, and meaningful organizational boundaries. What are excluded are *ad hoc* and temporary funds and other assets that have neither real organizational structure around them, nor relatively permanent identity and purpose. Also excluded are membership-based associations and owner-based organizational forms. Thus, a foundation is not only a financial or other type of asset, but also an identifiable organization.

2 **Private entity.** Foundations are institutionally separate from government, and are 'nongovernmental' in the sense of being structurally separate from public agencies. Foundations can be created and set up by government, can receive significant government support and can even have government officials sit on their boards. Yet they cannot be instruments of government whether

---

[31] See Anheier/Toepler, pp. 11–14 .

[32] Van der Ploegh.

[33] Salamon/Anheier, *The Emerging Nonprofit Sector.*

international, national or local. Therefore, foundations do not exercise governmental authority and are outside direct majoritarian control.

3 **Self-governing entity.** Foundations are equipped to control their own activities. Some private foundations are tightly controlled either by governmental agencies or corporations, and function as parts of these other institutions even though they are structurally separate. Self-governance implies that foundations must have their own internal governance procedures, enjoy a meaningful degree of autonomy, and have a separate set of accounts in the sense that assets, expenditures and other disbursements must not be part of either governmental or corporate balance sheets.

4 **Non-profit-distributing entity.** Foundations are not to return profits generated by either use of assets or the conduct of commercial activities to their owners, members, trustees or directors. A foundation may accumulate surplus in a given year, but the surplus must be applied to its basic mission (depending on the pay-out requirements stipulated in the relevant tax laws), and not be distributed to owners or their equivalents. In this sense, foundations are private organizations that do not exist principally to generate profits for owners, either directly or indirectly, and that are not primarily guided by commercial goals and considerations.

5 **Serving a public purpose.** Foundations should do more than serve the needs of a narrowly defined social group or category, such as members of a family, or a closed circle of beneficiaries. Foundations are private assets that serve a public purpose. The public purpose may or may not be charitable or tax-exempt in the relevant laws of a country, what is important is that the purpose be part of the public domain.[34]

This definition serves as a common reference point only, and provides a framework against which we can position the types of foundations in the various European countries. Let's look at each criterion in turn.[35]

---

[34] The criterion 'serving a public purpose' is not part of the structural/operational definition. Instead, Salamon and Anheier use 'voluntary' as a criterion. 'Serving a public purpose' is used to distinguish between funds and assets established to serve a closed, and relatively narrow, group of beneficiaries, and foundations serving a larger public.

[35] Unless otherwise indicated, reference to country-specific material and information in this and following sections is based on the individual country chapters included in this volume.

The criterion 'non membership-based' and the emphasis on foundations as a non owner-based organizational form are typically reflected in the legal statutes of both common and civil law systems. In a common law system like Britain or Ireland, a foundation is a charitable trust whereby an asset is entrusted to trustees who administer the asset for the benefit of the third parties, the beneficiaries. In contrast to private trusts, the founder gives up all ownership rights over the asset, and the trustees, in turn, gain fiduciary rights but do not assume ownership as such. In civil law countries like Austria, France, Germany, Greece, Switzerland and the Netherlands, a foundation is a legal personality, established by notarized deed, to administer an asset set aside by the founder for some specified purpose. For example, the Dutch Civil Code stipulates that a foundation is a 'legal person, created by a legal act, which has no members and whose purpose is to realize an object stated in its articles using capital allocated for such purposes.'

The requirement that foundations be 'institutionally separate from government' and the direct agencies of the state addresses the complex borderline between the public sector and foundations. Turkey and France are the countries whose governments possess the clearest discretionary control over the establishment and operations of foundations. Similarly, Belgian foundations require the approval of the Ministry of Justice, and foundations in Luxembourg must seek approval of their articles by ducal decree. Germany, Austria, Italy, Portugal and Greece have a somewhat lighter 'control mechanism' whereby government scrutinizes the basic legitimacy of the foundation. In what is called the concession system, the government (here: local authority-like municipality or county where the foundation is seated) grants the right of establishment to applicant foundations on a case by case basis, although the screening process is largely limited to formal legal requirements. In contrast to associations, most countries attach more requirements to the creation of foundations. In the Netherlands, however, other than registration no other governmental involvement is required. Thus, countries vary from an explicit hands-on to an explicit hands-off approach in how the state deals with the governance of foundations.

As Smith and Borgmann show in Foundation in Europe: the Historical Context, and as we will argue further below, the governance regimes of foundation reflect the way in which the conflict between foundations and the emergent nation state was resolved in the 19th and early 20th century. Fears of the *main morte* in *camaraliste*

France, questions about the emergence of independent power centres outside the state in Germany (von Savigny), anti-clerical policies in Italy during the *rissorgimento*, and concerns about the role of foundations in democracy in Scandinavian countries – all these are examples of the tensions that have characterized the relationship between foundations and the European states for much of the last 200 years.

The public foundation in civil law countries, however, shows that states themselves saw foundations as a useful tool to further their objectives.[36] Public law foundations are set up by government either through executive decision, act of parliament or equivalent legislation and placed under public law. They are typically established to meet some recognized public purpose that requires some special attention in approach, expertise or skills that could not easily be fitted into the regular apparatus of public administration. Moreover, putting such foundations under public law ensures close state supervision and control, while keeping them politically at arms-length. Most public law foundations would be excluded from the definition proposed above, as they ultimately represent state institutions.

Countries vary in the extent to which they make use of public law foundations: about 5% of German foundations are public law entities, although their relative share seems to have decreased over time, indicating a less active role of the state in the use of the foundation model.[37] By contrast, Greece has a sizeable and growing number of public law foundations that are either based on property the Greek Orthodox Church could no longer afford to maintain, or private law foundations whose endowment has depleted to a level that threatened the viability of the institution. Italy has seen the opposite movement since 1996, whereby public law institutions like opera houses and orchestras are transformed into private law foundations. Finally, about 10% of the foundations in Turkey are under public law. This includes nearly 1000 'social assistance and solidarity' foundations set up by cities and municipalities.

The role of religious institutions is of special interest in considering the public-private borderline. In all European countries, the Catholic Church, the Protestant Churches, and other dominant religions like the Greek Orthodox Church or Islam in Turkey had been the major founders of foundations until the 18th century, and well into the 19th century in some cases. While faith-related foundations

---

[36] Feddersen.

[37] Anheier/Toepler.

declined overall in numbers and importance, particularly in the 19th and 20th centuries, the emerging patterns of how this was effected are rather different across Europe. In France, religious foundations have been insignificant ever since the French Revolution and its aftermath, whereas in the Netherlands, Italy and Germany the church-related and church-owned foundations managed to maintain considerable importance.

In Germany, for example, church foundations are institutions established under canon law, which is constitutionally equivalent to public law. The estimated 35,000 church foundations[38] form a parallel universe next to other foundations, and are not regulated by public authorities but by internal church structures, for example at the diocesan level. Most of the German church foundations, which typically hold church property, real-estate and parish funds, would be excluded from the definition used here on the grounds that they represent quasi-state church institutions. To the extent that religious or church-related foundations are established under private law, however, they would be included.

The criterion of self-governance is important for a number of reasons. First, even when foundations have been established as separate legal entities, a third party other than the trustees or board may administer them. For example, municipalities from Istanbul and Madrid to Hamburg and Amsterdam administer many smaller endowments or dependent foundations in the language of civil law. Likewise, other government institutions (counties, ministries and departments) house private foundations. In Norway, municipal authorities administer about one-third of the total foundation assets held in the country. In Sweden, some estimates suggest that 39,000 foundations are managed by either the government, municipalities or, until recently, the state church. In Greece, and also in countries like Germany and Italy, municipal officials may treat older endowments, whose assets may have depleted over the years, as quasi-public funds in official accounts. As a result, many more foundations may exist across Europe than appear in foundation registers or official statistics.

Moreover, in several countries umbrella organizations administer and manage other foundations, typically those with smaller endowments. The *Fondation de France*, itself established by government, serves as an umbrella organization for nearly 500 foundations; the *Fondation Roi Baudoin* in Belgium manages 40 separate funds, and the

---

[38] Krag, p. 228.

Stifterverband für die deutsche Wissenschaft in Germany includes several hundred separate foundations. A variation of the umbrella foundation is the community foundation (see below) whereby separate endowments are pooled to form larger assets to serve local needs either through grant making, direct service-delivery or both. Community foundations, modelled after the American community chest[39] are of fairly recent origin in Europe, and most prominent in Britain and Germany.[40]

The requirement that foundations be nonprofit in the sense of not returning profits generated to the trustees or directors generally applies across Europe. The various laws and tax regulations establish foundations as nonprofit-distributing entities.[41] At the same time, there are a number of exceptions that bring the foundation form in close proximity to the profit motive. The most prominent cases are as follows:

- The commercial foundations in Norway and industrial foundations in Sweden which, next to charitable aims, also represent the founder's interest in maintaining control over separate company holdings. These holdings become assets in foundations, with the founder and family members as trustees. Examples are the Wallenberg, Johnsons and Kempe foundations. Such foundations – and the families behind them – have been criticized on the grounds that they use the foundation form for 'dynastic' control of the Swedish economy.[42]
- The family foundations in Liechtenstein and Switzerland, and to a lesser extent in Germany. These foundations are typically set up to benefit a closed circle, usually a family, in the attempt to create and protect some form of dynastic endowment. Switzerland has over 10,000 family foundations, which in their nature come close to investment funds. Liechtenstein has about 30,000 family foundations in a country of as many inhabitants. Many of these trusts, however, are set up by non-residents with the primary purpose of serving as offshore investment funds given the country's favourable tax laws. To counteract the outflow of capital to Liechtenstein, the Austrian government passed the Private Foundations Act 1993, which allows for the establishment of

---

[39] Hall.

[40] Feurt.

[41] See chapter by Gallop.

[42] See chapter by Wijkström.

foundations for basically non-charitable purposes. Within six years (i.e. between 1993 and 1999) over 1000 'private foundations' had been established. As a result, 'private foundations' now outnumber charitable foundations in Austria.

Finally, and related to the previous criterion, the definition stipulates that foundations serve a public purpose. Most countries make explicit references to the purposes foundations can serve, which are typically charitable in nature. However, the range of such charitable purposes varies across countries in terms of inclusivity and exclusivity. For example, Belgian foundations (*établissement d'utilité publique*) must address one or more of the following objectives or purposes: philanthropic, religious, scientific, artistic and educational. This is an exclusive list, and other purposes must remain incidental. Contrast this to the Spanish Foundation Act of 1994 which states in Article 2 that foundations should promote 'the general interest in fields like: social welfare, civil rights, education, culture, science, sports, healthcare, co-operation for development, environmental protection, economy, research, volunteering, and any other similar field'.[43] Similar inclusive purposes for foundations exist in Britain, the Netherlands and Germany, and other countries like Denmark, whereas Switzerland or Liechtenstein place virtually no restrictions on foundation purposes and activities.

In summary, as with any comparative definition some problems remain at the 'edges' and in what could be called 'grey zones'. Specifically, there are three major areas where the definition proposed here encounters difficulties:

- where foundations come close to markets and change into primarily economic actors
- where foundations become instruments of the state, and
- where they are dynastic means of asset protection and control.

Generally, however, the proposed definition that defines foundations as an asset-based, private, self-governing and nonprofit-distributing and public-serving organization captures a common set of institutions across the different countries and regions. With the definition at hand, we can now take a closer look at the different types of foundations that exist in Europe.

---

[43] Quoted in chapter by Olabuénaga.

2.2 Types of foundations

Europe has a rich morphology of foundations. Grant-making foundations are usually regarded as the prototype of the modern foundation, which is largely a reflection of the United States' experience and post-war dominance in the field of philanthropy.[44] Yet the majority of foundations in Europe is either operating, or pursuing objectives by combining grant-making activities with the running of institutions, programmes and projects. Historically, of course, foundations were primarily operating institutions (e.g. hospitals, orphanages, school, universities), although many did distribute money (alms-giving) and contributions in kind (food, wood), as shown in Smith and Borgmann, Foundations in Europe: the Historical Context. By contrast, the sharp distinction between grant-making and operating foundations emerged much later historically, and is for both the United States and Europe largely a product of the 19th and early 20th century.[45]

A look at three countries can illustrate the rich morphology of foundations in Europe. According to the Swedish foundation law 1220/1996, there are two major types of foundations in Sweden: grant-making foundations (*avkastningsstiftelse*) and operating foundations (*verksamhetsstiftelse*). In addition, there are special types: the fundraising foundation (*kollektivavtalsstiftelese*) and the pension foundation (*tryggandestiftelse*). This legal classification coexists with more traditional forms like the church foundation and the family foundation. German foundations can fall into three basic legal categories (public law foundations, civil law foundations, canon law foundations) and are further classified by purpose (grant making, operating, corporate), and organizational form (limited liability company, etc.), yielding a complex typology.[46] Finally, Turkish foundations are divided into pre-Republican or 'old' foundations in the tradition of the Islamic *waqf* system, and Republican or 'new' foundations, with each category being further refined according to founder, purpose and legal form.[47]

Behind the complexity of forms, nonetheless, are several basic categories that allow us to group the most common types of foundations across Europe according the the type of activity and type of founder.

---

[44] Toepler, *Operating*.

[45] Katz/Karl; McCarthy; Bulmer.

[46] See Hof.

[47] Yediyeldiz.

A Type of activity

- **Grant-making foundations** i.e. endowed organizations that primarily engage in grant making for specified purposes. Examples include the Leverhulme Trust in Britain; the Volkswagen Foundation in Germany; the Van Leer Foundation in the Netherlands; the Carlsberg Foundation in Denmark.
- **Operating foundations** i.e. foundations that primarily operate their own programmes and projects. Examples include the *Fondation Pasteur* in France; the Pescatore Foundation in Luxembourg running a home for senior citizens; the Home for the Blind in Greece.
- **Mixed foundations** i.e. foundations that operate their own programmes and projects and engage in grant making on a significant scale. Examples include the the Gulbenkian Foundation in Portugal; the BBV Foundation in Spain; the Bosch Foundation in Germany.

B Type of founder

- **Individual** i.e. foundations founded by an individual, group of individuals or family whereby donors bring their private assets into the foundation. The nature of the assets can be stock and other shares in business firms, financial, real-estate, patents, etc.
- **Corporate foundations** come in several subtypes. The most prominent type is the company-related or company-sponsored foundation. Corporate foundations vary in the extent to which they maintain close links with the parent corporations in terms of governance and management. Examples include the IBM Foundation; the Cartier Foundation in France; the BBV Foundation in Spain; the Agnelli Foundation in Italy; the Wallenberg Foundation in Sweden.
- **Community foundations** i.e. grant-making organizations that pool revenue and assets from a variety of sources (individual, corporate, public) for specified communal purposes. Examples include the *Stadtstiftung Gütersloh* or the *Bürgerstiftung Hanover* in Germany; the various community foundations in Britain under the umbrella of the Community Foundation Network.
- **Government-sponsored or government-created foundations** i.e. foundations that fit the definition but are either created by public charter or enjoy high degrees of public sector support for either endowment or operating expenditures. Examples include the Federal Environmental Foundation in Germany; the *Fondation de France*; the Government Petroleum Fund in Norway; the public foundations in Turkey.

Table 1 classifies foundations by founder and basic form, and illustrates in broad terms the diversity of foundations in Europe, ranging from grant-making foundations established by individuals to corporate foundations and government creations. Individuals create most foundations: in Britain virtually all foundations are set up by individuals; in Switzerland, individuals founded 95% of foundations under federal jurisdiction, of which 5% are primarily grant making, with the great majority either operating or of a mixed type. In Germany, likewise, the great majority of foundations are founded by individuals, followed by public authorities and corporations. There is a general trend for governments to make less use of foundations, either under public or private law. For corporations, data in France, Belgium, Britain, Germany, and Switzerland suggest the opposite trend. In France, for example, 44 corporate foundations were established after 1990 – in a country of less than 500 independent private foundations.

Table 1.1 Major types of foundations in Europe

Founder or type of endowment	Grant making	Primary purpose: Operating	Mixed
Private individual(s)	Nuffield Foundation, Britain	*Inselspital*, Switzerland	*Koningin Wilhelmina Fonds*, the Netherlands
Corporation(s)	Carlsberg Foundation, Denmark	Agnelli Foundation, Italy	BBV Foundation, Spain
Public sector	Federal Environmental Foundation, Germany	Social Help and Solidarity Foundation, Turkey	*Fondation de France*

Of course, many foundations are mixed types (i.e. engage in grant-making) initiate their own projects, and operate their own institutions, but in most cases one area of fund disbursement or use dominates.

3 A profile of foundations in Europe

How many foundations are there? Unfortunately, we cannot give a precise answer to this apparently simple question. This is due in large part to the lack of available statistics and other relevant information on foundations in most European countries – a problem that, as we have seen, is amplified by the diversity of definitions and types across Europe. Nonetheless, it is possible to come up with some initial estimates, however rough, about the number of foundations in each country covered in the chapter.

3.1 Size

As Table 1.2 shows, European countries show a great variation in the number of foundations, ranging from a high of 20–30,000 in Sweden and 14,000 in Denmark to a low of 30 in Ireland. Taken together, the data suggest that the existence of around 80–90,000 foundations among the countries listed in Table 1.2, or about 4–4500 per country. Were central and eastern European countries included, the number of foundations would increase to between 110–130,000, with 20,000 from Hungary alone. However, given the data situation in that region, and the tendency to define as foundation what are truly associations, it seems best to treat the relatively high number of central and eastern European foundations with great care. At least as defined here, it is probably safe to assume that the number of foundations in that part of Europe is still lower in relative and absolute terms than in most other countries of the continent.

According to the structural/operation definition introduced above, we had to exclude certain types of foundations in most countries included in Table 1.2. In Austria, 'private foundations' numbering over 1000 are excluded, and similarly in Liechtenstein, Norway, Sweden and Switzerland. The numbers of foundations excluded, and the assets associated with them are sizable: in the case of Liechtenstein the 35,000 family foundations own a significant portion of the CHF90 billion (€58 billion) deposited in the country's banks. In Switzerland, the 11,300 personal pension funds, set up as foundations, had assets of over CHF216 billion (€139 billion).

The Netherlands is a special case. On the one hand, the country has 131,395 foundations, mostly operating foundations in the field of health, social services, education and culture. The distinction between foundation and association, while clear in civil law, is sometimes difficult to make in reality, and is overlain by historical path dependencies.

Table 1.2 Foundations in Europe

Country	Absolute number	Relative share of grant-making foundations	Relative share of operating foundations	Mixed type	Other types/notes
Austria	803			majority	excludes 1097 private foundations
Belgium	310	few		majority	excludes 40 funds managed by *Foundation Roi Baudoin*
Britain	~8800	100	0*		* only 12 foundations were identified as operating
Denmark	~14,000				mostly small funds; only 3 foundations with assets >$140million
Finland	2522	50%	30%	20%	
France	404		majority		excludes 487 foundations administered by *Fondation de France*
Germany	8312	~50%	~25%	~25%	excludes ~35,000 church foundations
Greece	~500	few	majority	few	
Ireland	30	27%*	70%*	3%*	* absolute numbers 8, 12 and 1 respectively
Italy	~1300	15%	39%	43%	excludes unknown number of church foundations
Liechtenstein	~600		majority		excludes ~40,000 private foundations
Luxembourg	143		majority		
Netherlands	~1000	majority			excludes ~131,000 nonprofit organizations labelled foundations
Norway	2989			majority	excludes ~6300 commercial foundations
Portugal	664		majority		
Spain	~6000	5%	95%		excludes ~1100 church foundations
Sweden	~20,000–30,000				excludes ~7000–37,000 smaller foundations with assets <SEK350,000
Switzerland	~8000	5%	majority		excludes ~11,300 pension funds
Turkey	9326			majority	excludes 1005 public foundations

For example, most Catholic primary schools are foundations, whereas most of their Protestant counterparts are associations. In either case, both are fully integrated in the public education system and largely indistinguishable from each other as well as from state-run schools. The same would hold for the fields of health and social services. For these reasons (i.e. to avoid seemingly artificial divisions) the over 130,000 operating foundations have been excluded, leaving somewhat fewer than 1000 *fonds*, most of which are foundations in legal terms, although some are, for historical reasons, associations.

The Dutch example points to the complex borderline between grant-making and operating foundations in highly organized welfare states. Depending on where we draw the boundary for statistical purposes, the number of foundations in the Netherlands would range between 1000 and 130,000. The Swedish case is different in the sense that it highlights the complexity of a highly differentiated foundation sector; estimates for 1976 show 51,000 Swedish foundations, of which some 10% were family foundations; 60% were administered by state authorities, 10% were extensions of corporations, and around 11,700 foundations were managed by an autonomous board. Only the latter would qualify according to our definition, although many grey areas remain. More recent estimates indicate that the number of Swedish foundations has increased: in 1998 over 13,000 foundations had assets exceeding SEK350,000 (€42,000), suggesting that the total number may range between 20 and 30,000.

Other foundations excluded from the data presented in Table 1.2 are church foundations. In the case of Germany alone, this meant that some 35,000 foundations belonging to either the Catholic or Protestant churches are not counted. This does not mean that church-related or faith-based foundations are excluded as such. The exclusion applies only to foundations established under ecclesiastical or canon law, due to their public sector status. Spain, too, has a sizable number of foundations organized under canon law, reflecting the historical hegemony of the Catholic Church. Including church foundations would increase the number of foundations in Spain by 17% to just over 7000.

Finally, public sector foundations are also excluded, most notably in the case of Turkey, where about 10% of the total number of foundations are state institutions. Similarly, the approximately 500 foundations operating in Greece includes some public sector foundations; their actual number, however, could not be specified. Virtually all countries have foundations, funds or quasi-foundations located just on the state side of the public and private borderline: this includes the Austrian Science Foundation, the National Lottery in Britain, the National Insurance Scheme Fund in Norway or the Foundation of Prussian Cultural Heritage in Germany. These institutions were generally excluded from the data presented here.

For some countries it has been possible to collect information on the relative share of foundation types. As Table 1.2 shows, only British foundations are almost exclusively grant making, followed by Finland and Germany with about 50%. The Dutch foundation sector, as defined, is also primarily grant making, but the great majority of foundations in that country are operating institutions (see above). Overall, however, only in four of the countries included in Table 1.2 would operating foundations represent a majority, as they would most probably in central and eastern Europe. In most other countries we find that the majority of foundations are of a mixed type. They are both operating institutions and grant making, thereby combining service-delivery with philanthropic giving. This would apply to many British charities as well: three out of four operating grant makers had a grant-making function, and the 11 largest made grants in excess of £250 million in the mid 1990s.[48]

Clearly, the economic function of running institutions, programmes and projects tends to be more important than the actual grant-making activities. For example, estimates of the 1995 employment in German grant-making foundations ranged between 3–5000 employees, whereas operating foundations employed over 90,000.[49] The majority of German foundations, however, employ no staff at all: nine out of ten foundations are run and managed by volunteers only. In Scandinavia, we would find similar results: all but a few of Denmark's 14,000 foundations have paid employment at all, and only eight of the over 2500 Finnish foundations have more than ten full-time staff.

Of course, the raw number of foundations says little about their actual importance. For this purpose, it is useful to draw in additional information such as expenditures, employment, grants disbursed and assets. Unfortunately, complete information is available for none of the countries included; nonetheless, in most cases, we can at least take one additional 'sounding' of foundation sector size. Table 1.3 shows again the wide range and diversity of foundation sectors across

---

[48] Pharoah.

[49] See footnote 8 on the French case, which illustrates the significant difference in economic importance of foundations depending on whether or not operating foundations are included.

Europe; looking at the number of foundations per 100,000 population, we find a range from one in France to over 1900 in Liechtenstein. Foundation expenditures on gross national product vary from a low of 0.06% in Belgium to a high of 1.5% in Germany. Similarly, paid employment is lowest in Austria, with less than 1% of nonprofit sector employment, and a high of 14.3% in Sweden. Grants disbursed as a share of total nonprofit sector revenue range from 0.7% in Ireland to nearly 3% in Britain.

Asset estimates are the most difficult data to obtain on foundations, especially cross-nationally given the influence of different valuation measures and techniques. The asset figures in Table 1.3 should therefore be interpreted with great caution and taken as rough markers only. Using country-specific data on assets *per capita*, we observe significant differences across Europe. The German foundation assets are €354 *per capita*; the figure is higher for Britain, yet over €1000 for Italy, Sweden and Switzerland. Finally, the highest *per capita* assets are reported for Liechtenstein with a stunning figure that exceeds €12,000.

The German figures, even though they are lowest among the countries reporting assets, reflect the remarkable comeback of the country's foundation sector in recent decades, reaching two-thirds of the British asset figure in relative terms. The high number of *per capita* assets for Italian foundations is a function of the privatization of the banking sector in this country (Law 218/1990, or Amato law). Most public savings banks were quasi-public, 'nationalized' nonprofit organizations and changed to stock corporations as a result of the 1990 reforms. The shares in the privatized banks became the endowment for the new 'foundations of banking origin', which not surprisingly have significant assets ranging between €50–75 billion combined.

Given the data situation, it is not possible to construct a strict and consistent ranking of countries in terms of foundation sector size. Yet taken together, the various size indicators suggest three groups or clusters, and even such an admittedly crude classification involves some qualitative judgements. As Table 1.4 shows, Europe's foundation sectors can be grouped into three classes: small, medium and large, whereby the middle group can be further divided into subcategories.

Table 1.3 Relative size indicators of foundation sectors in Europe, by country

Country	Number of foundations per 100,000 population	Expenditure as % of GDP	Employment as % of total nonprofit employment	Grants disbursed as % of total nonprofit revenue	Assets per capita (in Euros)
Austria	10		0.20		
Belgium	3	0.07			
Britain	16			2.81	536
Denmark	272				
Finland	49				
France	1	0.15	3.00		
Germany	10	1.50	6.43	1.80	354
Greece	5				
Ireland	1			0.74	
Italy	2				1340
Lichtenstein	1911				12,258
Luxembourg	34				
Netherlands	5			2.11	
Norway	68				
Portugal	7				
Spain	15	0.60	0.61		
Sweden	200		14.30		1500
Switzerland	111				1389
Turkey	16				

Table 1.4 Foundation sector ranking by size

Relative size of foundation sector	Country
Small	Austria, Belgium, France, Greece, Ireland, Luxembourg
	Central and eastern European countries
Medium–small	Portugal, Spain, Turkey
Medium–large	Britain, Denmark, Finland, Germany, Netherlands, Norway
Large	Italy, Liechtenstein, Sweden, Switzerland

3.2 Areas of activities

Yet what do foundations do? In what areas do they work or operate, and what are some of the commonalties and differences across countries? Table 1.5 presents a breakdown of foundation activities by major field, following the International Classification System of Nonprofit Organizations (ICNPO), developed by Salamon and Anheier.[50] The unit of analysis differs somewhat across countries; while expenditures would in fact represent a more valid measure of foundation activity, in most cases only the number of organizations working in any of the ten fields is primarily available. Table 1.5 reveals three major results.

1. Two fields clearly dominate the profile of foundation activity: education and research, with an average of 30%, and social service (25%). Together, both fields account for over half of foundation activities so measured. In fact, education and research, and social services are the main categories in 8 of the 15 countries reporting. Adding healthcare, with an average of 17% of foundation activity, pushes the total share up to 71%. In other words, two-thirds of foundations operate in just three fields, the same fields that also dominate the nonprofit sector at large.[51]

2. The field of art and culture accounts for the third largest share of foundation activities. It is the most important field in Spain, with 44% of all foundations, and is relatively prominent in Finland, Germany, Italy, Portugal and Switzerland.

3. Some countries show clear concentration in one field particularly; this is the case for healthcare foundations in France, housing foundations in Ireland, international activities in the Netherlands, and

---

[50] Salamon/Anheier, *Defining the Nonprofit Sector*.

[51] Salamon *et al.*, *Global Civil Society*.

Table 1.5 Foundations in Europe: activities by field

Country	Arts and culture	Education and research	Health	Social services	Environment	Housing/development	Advocacy	International	Religion	Other	Unit of analysis
Austria	11	36	8	34	1	1	1	0	4	4	foundations
Belgium	16	46	17	16	–	–	–	–	5	1	foundations
Britain	10	41	12	15	5	2	1	–	9	4	grants value
Finland	23	47	–	12	2	–	4	–	1	11	foundations
France	1	14	56	23	–	2	–	–	–	5	employees
Germany	21	57	12	55	6	3	2	4	6	8	all purposes; multiple answers
Greece	4	41	5	39	1	2	–	–	6	2	foundations
Ireland	13	18	30	1	1	37	1	–	–	–	expenditures
Italy	20	36	8	23	–	5	–	1	4	2	foundations
Netherlands	11	10	25	25	4	1	6	14	3	1	funds
Norway	5	21	1	43	3	1	1	–	–	26	foundations
Portugal	29	14	6	43	1	1	2	1	3	–	foundations
Spain	44	20	26	–	–	–	–	–	–	10	employees
Switzerland	20	30	10	30	5	5	–	–	–	–	foundations
Turkey	6	21	5	26	2	6	2	–	12	–	foundations

cultural foundations in Spain. Such concentrations are the result of specific historical developments, for instance urgent demand for affordable housing in early 20th century Ireland, or institutional effect, such as the prominence of large healthcare research foundations in France (*Institut Pasteur, Institut Marie Curie*).

4 From history to current political context

Yet, one might ask, why is it important to know about foundations in the first place? What do their numbers and activities indicate? What do we learn, by looking at foundations, about modern Europe that we did not know before? These questions point to the theoretical and policy implications of the empirical information presented above. While we will return to wider conceptual issues further below, it may be useful to recall some of the major historical developments involved, even at the risk of gross oversimplification.

As Smith and Borgmann[52] suggest, the role and *raison d'être* of foundations in Europe underwent several dramatic changes between the 16th and the 20th century. The Reformation era did away with the medieval ideal of community and triggered the complex process of state building, in which foundations were no longer part of a *res publica christiana*.[53] Instead, foundations had to compete for space in an increasingly secular public sphere. Only some foundations succeeded in this task, and many, if not most became victims of secularization and state expansion. At the same time, new foundations emerged, fuelled by the interests of the crown, landed elite and the emerging middle class, particularly urban merchants and craftsmen.

As the nation state developed, the role of foundations changed from that of a traditional, religion-based charitable institution to a somewhat more pluralist provider of quasi-public goods, used by and for special groups and interests. The numerous guild-based and trade-related foundations in the growing cities of the 17th and 18th century are perhaps the best example to illustrate how foundations became a private tool for serving public needs. This re-positioning, however, implied that throughout the 19th and early 20th century the role of foundations continued to be challenged to the extent that the consolidated nation state assumed responsibility for and over other parts and groups of society.

---

[52] See Foundations in Europe: the Historical Context.

[53] Turkish foundation history is substantially different and shows more continuity from the Middle Ages to the early modern period.

In much of the 19th century, the development of foundations depended on the political solution, if any, that could be found between the aspirations of an expanding, and frequently struggling, nation state on the one hand, and the interests of a more pluralist civil society on the other. The latter included, in particular, the new economic elite, the urban middle class and the professions as the major force in the establishment of foundations. From a supply-side perspective, the development of foundations also depended on the extent to which the proceeds of market transactions could be transformed into philanthropic assets. In other words, even where public 'space' for foundations existed, countries and regions differed in terms of philanthropic entrepreneurship, whereby public-minded merchants, industrialists or professionals set up foundations.

While the potential supply of founders is difficult to estimate, the 19th century growth of foundations in Britain, Scandinavia and the Netherlands, and even in countries with autocratic regimes like Germany, the Austro-Hungarian Empire and Italy suggest that the supply-side considerations were much less of a constraint than restrictive state policies. Much of the growth in the number of foundations under aristocratic regimes was supported by the urban middle class at the local level. Most foundations remained local in character, often with well-defined circles of beneficiaries. For example, the foundation directory for the city of Vienna from the late 19th century lists 2148 foundations, the great majority of which serve highly special and localized needs ranging from welfare provisions to education support.[54]

In other countries like France, however, the state succeeded in establishing itself as the primary representative of the public will and in keeping foundations at bay under the umbrella of anti-clerical, anti-liberal policies.[55] Yet not all nation states were as successful as France in establishing a hegemonic regime across and against diverse political and cultural interests. More frequently, the emerging nation state remained weak, failed in its attempt to consolidate power, and had to forge political compromises with existing power bases and their institutions. As a result, traditional foundations remained strong (Italy, Spain) and many new ones emerged (Switzerland, Germany).

In other cases, early forms of private-public partnerships began to emerge between state and foundations, with Sweden and the

---

[54] Markhoff.

[55] Archambault, *The Nonprofit Sector in France.*

Netherlands as prime examples, leading to a general expansion and consolidation. Only in Britain, however, did the formation of a relatively independent set of foundations develop without too much state interference. The 19th century philanthropists and industrialists provided welfare services, supported the arts and even championed causes overseas, for example the anti-slavery society.[56]

Two key insights emerge from this overview of European foundation history.

1. At least since the reformation period, foundations have operated at or close to the major 'fault lines' of society: secularization in the 17th century, republicanism and political liberalization in the 18th century, industrialization and the social upheavals of the 19th and early 20th century. Depending on the sustainability and extent of the political compromises that were found or that emerged, foundations occupied more or less public space, either flourished or declined in numbers and importance, and either helped shape the social order or moved to more marginal positions. The country rankings in Table 1.4 reflect in part the long-term positioning of foundations in this context.

2. Throughout this historical development certain patterns or path dependencies emerged that accounted for more or less distinct national or regional traditions. Britain and France offer perhaps the best examples of the extreme range of persistent policy patterns across Europe. In the British case, the Statute of Charitable Uses of 1601 has functioned for 400 years to delineate the purpose and limitations of charity even though its actual definition and legal application continues to be shaped by prevailing practices and common law traditions. The Protestant gentry of the 17th century found the Statute appealing for its philanthropic aspirations, as did the industrialists of the 19th century who wanted to support educational institutions to improve the living standards of the poor. In France we find a different pattern that essentially sought to prevent the development of foundations as a modern tool of civil society. The *Loi de Chapelier* of 1791 established state monopoly over the public interest, which meant that foundations lost their legal status altogether; it was only at the end of the 19th century that foundations regained some ground, albeit under strict state supervision.[57]

---

[56] Leat, *Trusts in Transition.*

[57] Archambault *et al.*

In most European countries, foundations were caught in a complicated political conundrum, which few foundation sectors managed to escape unharmed. It would have taken a consolidated state, a self-confident middle class and an enlightened elite, in addition to the increasing economic prosperity of the 19th century, to bring about a full renaissance of foundations. Concerns over the *main morte* remained (France, Belgium, Luxembourg), as did social democratic rejections that saw foundations as undemocratic (Finland, Sweden), paternalistic instruments of the Victorian age (Ireland, Britain). Yet whatever patterns and path dependencies had developed until the early 20th century, nothing could have prepared European foundations for the upheavals that two world wars, economic crises, the Holocaust, and the establishment of communist regimes in the central and eastern parts of the continent would bring to most countries.

Of course, foundations in some countries such as Switzerland or Sweden were spared the devastation, but unknown numbers of foundations across the continent did not manage to survive confiscation, destruction, capital depletion, loss of property, and many faced legal and frequently illegal dissolution. In other words, the variations of foundation sector size (Table 1.3) and composition (Table 1.5) reflect not only long-term developments but significantly also the impact of the two major wars in the last century. It is no historical accident that of the four countries classified as possessing a large foundations sector, three escaped the destructive force of World War II, namely Sweden, Switzerland and Liechtenstein.

The impact of war was perhaps nowhere greater than in the central and eastern parts of the continent. The philanthropic elite and much of the middle class that had been central in building and maintaining foundations in the late 19th and early 20th century were displaced and often killed. The Stalinist and state socialist regimes that followed saw no need for foundations, and with few exceptions, confiscated the remaining foundation property that war and Nazism had not destroyed. It is therefore not surprising that much of the impetus to create and re-establish foundation communities in this part of Europe relies on external support, capital and know-how, at least initially, and perhaps for some time to come.

Western Europe shows a different and more varied post-war development. The foundation community in some countries such as Austria and perhaps Greece stagnated and never fully recovered from the events of the first part of the 20th century. In others like Italy, Spain and Germany, it took several decades before new, significant growth in number and importance could take place. In Scandinavia, foundations resumed close links with government but nonetheless assumed a distant second position to state efforts as the welfare state developed more fully after 1950. In either case, the aftermath of the two world wars meant greater state reliance and vastly expanded state responsibilities, first during the reconstruction period of the 1950s, and then under the umbrella of welfare state policies in the decades that followed. Throughout this period, foundations and their roles and contributions were hardly mentioned, if at all, and remained largely off the public agenda. Tellingly, some of the most influential works on the European welfare state such as Esping-Anderson (1993), Flora and Heidenheimer (1981) and Quadagno (1990) do not mention the role of foundations.

Yet by the late 1980s public, academic and political interest in foundation was rekindled and seems to have regained momentum since then. Indeed, foundations in most European countries appear to be experiencing some kind of a renaissance, which follows the first of the high Middle Ages, and the second of the industrialization period of the late 19th century. In several European countries, new foundation laws have been put in place, and are being considered. The basic thrust of the recent and current legal initiatives is to make the establishment and operation of foundations easier than under past regulations, and to provide greater incentives to potential founders for the creation of foundations. Examples are the Swedish Act on Foundation 1996, the Austrian Act on Private Foundations 1993, the reform of the bank foundations in Italy (law 218/1900), the Spanish Foundation Act 1994, and the current reform of foundation law in Germany.[58]

4.1 The revival of foundations

Of course, the reasons for the revival of foundations are varied. Important factors are the prolonged periods of political stability in most western European countries, the democratization of previously autocratic regimes (Spain, Portugal and Greece), and, importantly, levels of economic prosperity and social wellbeing unmatched in Europe's modern history. Wealth lost between 1914 and 1945 was not only replaced but surpassed, and this to such an extent that individual and corporate assets have never been higher. By the 1980s, political stability and economic prosperity in northern, western and southern Europe coincided with the rise of neo-liberalism as the postmodern

---

[58] See Bertelsmann Stiftung/Maecenata.

ideology against state dominance, and the lingering crisis of the welfare state in meeting growing demands and obligations. In addition, the fall of communism and the profound economic changes in eastern European countries have brought foundations back to the political and cultural agenda. There are three underlying reasons why foundations have become more attractive in recent years.

- **Politically**, they appear more acceptable to governments that seem to have become less certain about their own roles and ambitions, and are willing to allow institutions like foundations to play their part. In contrast to previous historical periods, the state seems less challenged by foundations – on the contrary, national governments and international organizations alike welcome foundation involvement in a broad range of activities and fields.
- **Economically**, foundations seem an appropriate vehicle to solve a number of corporate challenges. For the German or Swiss *Mittelstand*, foundations are one way to solve the succession problem for owner-managers of medium-scale enterprises, and to help provide stability in terms of ownership and control. For large international corporations, foundations are a tool to express corporate citizenship and concerns for the public good. And for government and corporations alike, foundations may be both a more economic and politically a more neutral way to handle specific problems and issues (e.g. assets held by holocaust victims in Swiss banks).
- **Culturally**, because a largely expanded middle class in all European countries seems to have regained the self-confidence and trust it lost during the first half of the 20th century. There appears to be a greater acceptance of private actors in the provision of public goods and quasi-public goods. At the same time, the state is no longer expected to be the sole provider of social security, culture, education and many other areas that have previously been lodged with the public sector.

Of course, the factors and reasons behind the revival of foundations are not born out equally across Europe. They seem more pronounced in Britain, Germany, Scandinavia and less in France, Belgium or Greece. How, then, are these changes reflected in the recent development of foundations across Europe?

4.2 Growth patterns

It is in the larger historical context described above that the expansion of foundation sectors in Europe assumes its true relevance. As Table

1.6 shows, there is a general trend among the countries for which overtime data are available, that more foundations were created in the last two decades than in the three decades before, and that more foundations were established after 1950 than prior to that date. In other words, in terms of number of foundations, the European foundation world is essentially a product of the post-war period generally, and of the last three decades in particular. Two out of three foundations were established after 1970.[59]

However, Table 1.6 reveals that countries vary in their growth rates. Three growth patterns seem to emerge.

- **High growth countries like Italy, Spain, Turkey or Portugal.** With the exception of Turkey, these are countries in which foundation law underwent a major reform (Italy: law 218/1990; Spain: Foundation Act 1994; Portugal: Law 460/1977), with the proven effect that foundations increased sharply in number. In Portugal, where 56% of all foundations were established after 1980, and Spain (over 90% for cultural foundations and 70% for educational foundations), the rapid growth could also be a delayed effect of the democratization in the 1970s, when both countries shed their autocratic regimes. The high growth is also a reflection of the rapid economic development of these countries of Europe's south, in particular Portugal, Spain, and Turkey.
- **Medium growth countries like Britain, Finland, Germany, Switzerland or Greece.** With the exception of Belgium and Greece, these are countries with already sizable foundation sectors, and recent growth rates of 20 to 30% per decade add to a relatively high base. Britain, Finland, Germany and Switzerland are high-income countries with stable political systems. We can assume that the foundation boom of recent years is in large measure a function of political stability and economic prosperity, amplified by a more self-confident middle class. Greece has a small foundation sector, and the expansion is probably the result of increased economic prosperity and greater political stability. But in contrast to the high growth countries, the absence of legal reform and the impact of continued fiscal crises has prevented an even greater expansion of Greek foundations.
- **Low growth countries like Austria, Belgium and France.** All three countries have small foundation sectors. Although they did

---

[59] Growth trends based on new foundations alone have to be treated with great caution as they do not include any information on the 'fate' of existing foundations in terms of persistence, expansion, merger or dissolution.

Table 1.6 Development of foundations, by country, in %

Country	pre 1900	1900–10	1910–20	1920–30	1930–40	1940–50	1950–60	1960–70	1970–80	1980–90	post 1990
Austria		23			11	7	6	10	10	15	19
Belgium	9				25			40			
Britain	5	1	1	2	2	3	9	26	26	21	4
Finland			9			10	20	14	12	20	15
France	28		22			13		24		13	
Germany	20	2	3	3	3	2	5	8	11	23	20
Greece				15				24	33	28	
Italy								20	8	26	46
Portugal	2	1	0	3	0	17		22		56	
Spain				3					3	36	58
Switzerland	2			17		6		14	22	26	12
Turkey		2					49			50	

expand, they did so at a much lower level. In contrast to high and medium growth countries, French foundations are older on average, with half predating the post-war period, and with fewer foundations being established during the current expansion period since the 1980s. Similarly, growth rates have changed little in Austria and Belgium over the last four decades, even though a slight upward trend is discernable. The reasons for the slow growth are legal and procedural, as the establishment of foundations in France or Belgium is highly regulated and complicated, providing relatively few incentives for potential founders. There are also political and cultural reasons, if we recall the historical distrust of the French state concerning foundations. While some of this suspicion may have lessened, its impact is still felt in terms of lower growth rates. Indicative of this is that the increase in the number of foundations under the auspices of the Fondation de France, from 326 in 1990 to 487 in 1998, is somewhat higher than the overall growth of the French foundation sector during the same period (393 to 468).

Table 1.7 combines the growth patterns with the scale of foundation sectors in each country. Among the relatively smaller foundation sectors only Greece is on a modest expansion course. However, with both legal reforms and the consolidation of public finance much needed, the maintenance of recent growth levels is uncertain. The other countries with smaller foundation sectors nonetheless have a well-developed nonprofit sector, indeed Ireland has some of the largest nonprofit sectors in Europe. It is likely that in France, Belgium and Ireland, other nonprofit forms may act as the preferred organizational form for foundation-type activities. Given that the establishment of foundations in these countries is typically complex,

Table 1.7 Foundation sector scale and growth pattern

| | | Scale | | |
		Small	Medium	Large
	Low	Austria, Belgium, France	[Ireland]	
Growth	Medium	Greece Most other central and eastern European countries	Britain, Finland, Germany	Switzerland
	High	Hungary	Portugal, Spain, Turkey	[Italy]

time consuming and therefore relatively expensive, potential founders might opt for other organizational forms even if a foundation would ultimately offer the more appropriate vehicle.

None of the medium- and large-scale foundation sectors fell behind in relative terms by revealing low growth rates over the last three decades. Notably, Italy's foundations have expanded in numbers and in asset size, fuelled primarily by the Amato reform of its banking industry. For similar reasons, but also with the added momentum of democratic reform and economic development, Portugal and Spain saw their foundation sectors expand at relatively high rates.

5 Functions and models

Whatever the outcome of current policy developments, they invite us to reconsider some of the basic aspects of foundations. Why do they exist? What functions do they serve? And what are their functional alternatives?

Several answers have been suggested in the literature.[60] Foundations, like all nonprofit institutions, exist for several basic reasons. At the most general level, they provide a vehicle for philanthropic values and deeds, that is a circuit for long-term and large-scale donations. More specifically, foundations exist because markets and government may fail, as Hansmann and Weisbrod have pointed out. Under conditions of demand heterogeneity, markets can fail to supply some public and quasi-public goods in efficient and equitable ways because of moral hazard problems inherent in such transactions.[61] Such goods cannot be supplied by the state because of government failure; correcting for such failures would run into conflict with the inherent constitutional doctrine of limited state inference in liberal democracies. In other words, diverse societies have needs that neither market nor state can provide at reasonable costs and risks.

Such reasoning may apply to most types of nonprofit organizations, and the question therefore arises as to what the special role or function of foundations might be? Anheier and Toepler have suggested a number of special functions served by foundations, which have found

---

[60] See Anheier/Toepler for an overview.

[61] Anheier/Ben-Ner.

their clearest expression in Prewitt.[62] Although the extent to which foundations actually fulfill these functions remains a matter of disagreement,[63] they serve nonetheless as useful markers to gauge the role of foundations in modern society. According to Prewitt, foundations can fulfill four basic functions.

- **Redistribution,** i.e. foundations channel funds from the better-off to the less affluent sectors of the population, thereby either directly or indirectly adding to the redistribution efficiency of the taxation system in place.
- **Efficiency,** i.e. foundations offer services and allocate philanthropic funds more efficiently than markets and government agencies could. Cost-to-benefit ratios are better for foundations than for alternative forms.
- **Social change,** i.e. foundations, unbound by market considerations and the constraints of the political process, can trigger and support desired change processes.
- **Pluralism,** i.e. foundations promote diversity and differentiation in thought, approaches and practice of advocacy, service provision and 'search procedures' looking for causes and solutions to a variety of problems and issues.

What, then, can we say about the extent to which foundations in Europe perform the functions suggested by Prewitt? Prewitt suggests that only the pluralism argument could withstand closer empirical scrutiny for serving as the 'legitimating theory' of foundations. Whereas foundations may create and preserve pluralism, and thereby increase the problem-solving capacity of societies, they may not be redistributive, efficient and change-oriented (or only to some limited degree). To explore Prewitt's functions, we have grouped the various countries into relatively distinct models.

As Table 1.8 indicates, Europe's foundation sectors represent several relatively distinct models.[64] These models differ in the importance and role of grant-making and operating foundations, as well as in their respective relations or borderlines with the state and the business sector.

---

[62] Prewitt.

[63] Leat, *British Foundations*; Frumkin; Clotfelter; Letts *et al.*; Toepler, *Das gemeinnützige Stiftungswesen.*

[64] The model presented here is informed by the work of Esping-Anderson; Salamon/Anheier, *Defining the Nonprofit Sector.*

Table 1.8 Classification of foundations in Europe

Model	Countries	Overall importance	Characteristics: Operating foundations	Grant-making foundations	Borderline
Social democratic model	Sweden, Norway, Denmark, Finland	High	Larger operating foundations integrated in public welfare service delivery	Many smaller foundations set up by individuals; large company foundations; social movement	Complex borderline between business and foundations
State-centred model	France, Belgium, Luxembourg	Low	Close supervision of foundations by state; emphasis on public utility	Few grant-making foundations, primarily operating, quasi-public umbrella foundations	Complex borderline between state and foundations
Corporatist model	Germany, Netherlands, Austria, Switzerland, Liechtenstein	Medium	Operating foundations part of welfare system, close state links, subsidiarity	Grant-making foundations somewhat less prominent, many mixed foundations	Complex borderlines between state and foundations, and foundations and business
Liberal model	UK	High	Fewer operating foundations	Prominence of grant-making foundations; long history of independence	Relatively clear boundaries, indirect state involvement

Table 1.8 *Cont'd*

Model	Countries	Overall importance	Characteristics:			Borderline
			Operating foundations	Grant-making foundations		
Peripheral model	Ireland, Greece	Low	Foundations are service-providers to compensate for public sector short-fall	Few grant-making foundations		Complex historical links to dominant religion, patriarchy, immigration patterns
Mediterranean model	Spain, Italy, Portugal, Turkey	Medium	Long history of operating foundations linked to dominant religion, parallel to public welfare provision	Delayed development of grant-making foundations; rapid recent development after autocratic experience		Complex relationship with state/religion
Post-statist model	Central and eastern Europe	Medium	Delayed development; operating foundations dominate, parallel to public welfare provision	Very few domestic grant-making foundations; rapid recent development		Complex borderlines between state and foundations, and foundations and business

- In the **social democratic model**, foundations exist in a highly developed welfare state. As part of a well-coordinated relationship with the state, operating foundations either complement or supplement state activities, although in absolute and relative terms their service-delivery contributions remain limited. In addition, large corporate foundations like Wallenberg provide a counterweight to hegemonic tendencies of the state. As a result, borderlines between foundations and large businesses are complex and fluid.

- In the **state-controlled model**, foundations are ultimately subservient to the state. Restrictive laws, complicated administrative procedures, and extensive oversight establish a relatively tight control regime for foundations. As a result, foundations are few in numbers and remain much less important than in other parts of Europe. Their grant-making activities are relatively minor, and as operating institutions they are dwarfed by the scale of state provision.

- In the **corporatist model**, foundations are by and large in some form of subsidiarity relation with the state. Operating foundations are part of the social welfare or educational system, and many combine grant-making and operative dimensions. Foundations are important as service-providers, and less so in terms of their overall financial contributions.

- The **liberal model**, represented by the United Kingdom, has a highly pronounced grant-making function, whereas operating foundations are less active as a whole. Boundaries with the state and the business community are relatively well established and unambiguous. Next to the social democratic model, the liberal foundation sector ranks high in terms of overall importance.

- The **peripheral model** refers to foundation sectors that for a variety of historical reasons such as colonialism and external domination have either not fully developed at all, or have, until recently, experienced long periods of stalemate or stagnation. This situation was helped, in part, by the peripheral location of these countries, and their delayed social and economic development. Foundations are primarily operating and compensate for shortfalls in public sector supply in social services (Greece) and housing (Ireland).

- The **Mediterranean model** refers to the southern countries of Europe that have experienced a significant expansion in their foundation sector in recent years. They share a long history of hegemonic religions, and delayed economic development when compared to the social democratic, corporatist and liberal model above. The massive expansion of the Italian foundation sector through the establishment of the bank foundations adds a new element to the future development of foundations in this region.

- Finally, foundations in the **post-socialist model** are primarily operating in nature and supported by outside funds, forming part of a political, though highly complex and ambiguous, agenda of public sector reform in a region that prepares for its second major social and economic transition in as many decades.

Of course, the models, represented in a more simplified version in Table 1.9, are relatively distinct from each other and some overlap exists among them. They are not meant to serve as strict archetypes but merely as descriptive markers to point to similarities and differences across European countries in terms of the four roles or functions suggested by Prewitt.

Table 1.9 Foundation models in Europe

Relative size of foundation sector	Are operating foundations important?	Are grant-making foundations important?	Model
Large	Yes	Yes	Social democratic
	No	Yes	Liberal
Medium	Yes	Yes	Corporatist
	Yes	No	Mediterranean
Small	No	No	State-centred
	Yes	Yes (international)	Post-socialist
	Yes	No	Peripheral

The redistribution function would apply primarily to grant-making foundations. It may also apply to operating foundations with large donations or other payments from the higher income groups for services provided to lower income groups disproportionately and at a lower price. As we have seen, only a minority of foundation sectors in Europe has a sizeable grant-making component, with the exception of Britain and perhaps Germany as well as Italy. Moreover, the revenue structure of an operating foundation tends to rely more on either public sector funding or direct fee-for-service income than on donations from high income groups. While foundations may add at the margin to the redistribution efficiency of countries, they do so, if at all, on a relatively small scale that may be insignificant in the context of the wider taxation system in place.[65]

At the same time, arguments could be made for the negative impact of family foundations and some types of corporate foundations in the social democratic and liberal regime. 'Dynastic capital' in the form of family foundations may be worthwhile for many purposes, even charitable ones, but such institutions are rarely redistributive in operation. Moreover, while many operating foundations serve the poor and address the concern of excluded populations, they may not do so disproportionately more than the state and even some market providers. Ultimately, the redistributive role of foundations remains an empirical question, and available evidence does not allow us to pass more than a preliminary judgment.

The efficiency function suggests that foundations offer services and allocate philanthropic funds more efficiently than could markets and government agencies under conditions of information asymmetry. This would apply primarily to situations where foundations supplement, complement or fill in for state provision in social services, health, education or housing, as they do in the corporatist, peripheral and Mediterranean model. Again, generally, it would seem to be an empirical question to explore whether foundations have better cost-to-benefit ratios than public or private sector providers, particularly so in highly regulated and somewhat standardized fields such as health, social service and education. It is a different question, however, if foundations offer services that would not be provided otherwise, that is where comparative efficiency questions are secondary to availability of some service-delivery mechanism in the first place. It would seem that foundations play a larger role in that regard in peripheral countries like Greece, and certainly in central and eastern Europe, where a general undersupply of services prevails.

It is in the post-socialist and the Mediterranean model that the social changes initiated and facilitated by foundations come out most clearly. Indeed during the transition period, foundations triggered and supported desired change processes, and contributed to the modernization and democratization of society. Of course the actual contribution of foundations is difficult to measure with any degree of certainty, but they have undoubtedly contributed to the consolidation of democratic reform in Spain and Portugal, and the development of a wider civil society in transition countries.

---

[65] Margo.

In corporatist, social democratic and liberal models, the social change argument is less pronounced in its net impact as there are probably many countervailing factors and checks and balances that come into play. Simply put: to the extent that some foundations support change, others may not, and either actively or passively seek to counteract developments in one way or another. This points to the role foundations play in public debate, particularly in the liberal, social democratic and corporatist countries; they can pick up themes and invite debate about social, economic, cultural and political issues of all kinds. By doing so, foundations help identify problems and give 'voice' to a greater variety of positions than would otherwise be the case.

This ultimately brings in the pluralism function, which Prewitt believes to be the true *raison d'être* for foundations. While some of the other functions appear to be model-specific in the sense that they apply more, if at all, to some types rather than to others, foundations promote and preserve diversity, and add to the institutional variety of societies regardless of whether they are liberal, social-democratic, Mediterranean or post-socialist. They counter balance the hegemonic tendencies of the welfare state in Sweden and Norway, and preserve the cultural identity of minorities in Finland. They add a relatively independent force to the subsidiarity structures in corporatist regimes in terms of service delivery and funding streams. Foundations give voice to a more diverse public sphere in Mediterranean countries, and they help influence the political agenda in Britain, particularly in the field of social and educational policy.

Of course, not all foundations perform the pluralism function to an equal extent. The important point is the aggregate effect foundations create toward greater diversity rather than the impact of each individual foundation alone. This aggregate effect can lead to a greater capacity for problem solving in the society as a whole – added capacity next to those of governments and markets. In this sense, foundations initiate additional, different 'search procedures' in addressing the social, political, economic and cultural problems of our time.

6 Conclusion

This chapter began with a look at the rich tapestry of foundations in Europe, and the complex terminology surrounding them. Until now, comparative knowledge of foundations in terms of size, functions, and activities has been largely nonexistent for virtually all European countries. Little was known about the larger political economy in which European foundations operate, their relationship with the state, future patterns or current trends. Even though this chapter could provide little more than initial answers to some of the basic questions about foundations in Europe, they can be summarized as follows.

- Defining foundations as asset-based, private, self-governing and nonprofit-distributing and public-serving organizations draws in a relatively coherent set of institutions, but also points to many important borderline cases such as family foundations in Sweden, church foundations in Germany, state foundations in Turkey or the so-called private foundations in Austria and Switzerland.
- The size of foundation sectors varies significantly across Europe. Three clusters emerged: those countries where foundations are few in numbers and play virtually no pronounced role; those countries with a sizeable foundation sector; and those where the foundation world is relatively large and important both economically and politically. France represents the clearest example of a country with a small foundation sector, Germany and Britain for the medium-sized sector, and Italy and Sweden for the third group.
- Most foundations in Europe are operating, though many combine service delivery with some form of grant-making activities. Countries differ in the relative weight of grant-making and operating foundations, although only Britain, Germany and Italy (and depending on the definition used, the Netherlands) have a relatively high proportion of grant-making foundations.
- Two fields clearly dominate the profile of foundation activity: education and research, although country-specific profiles seemed to emerge, for example culture in Spain or housing in Ireland.
- European foundations are clearly a product of the post-war period, and a veritable foundation boom seems to have set in beginning with the late 1980s. However, this growth is not evenly spread across Europe: in one group of countries, the foundation sector expanded little in terms of numbers; in a second group they grew considerably and added to an already high base, whereas a third group of high-growth countries were primarily found in the Mediterranean region. In absolute terms, the foundation sectors of Germany and Italy have expanded most in recent years, and they are moving into positions that equal the prominence of foundations in Britain and Sweden, and – of course much less so – the situation in the United States.

[66] Bulmer.

- Europe's foundations seem to cluster into particular types and models, with the social democratic, corporatist, Mediterranean and post-socialist models as the most frequent ones; other models includes the state-centred and peripheral one. The liberal model, which comes in many ways closest to the US-influenced image of the modern world of philanthropic foundations, could be found only in Britain among the European countries covered, although important differences exist between the two.[66]

- Against the background of the significant growth in foundations in most European countries, it is important to keep in mind that the development and longevity of foundations need some minimum level of political stability as well as economic prosperity to enable them to emerge and survive in larger numbers. While foundations may contribute to more wealth and greater stability, they are the product rather than the producer of these conditions.

It is because of this political stability and economic prosperity that foundations in Europe appear to be experiencing some kind of a renaissance. This foundation boom follows, after a hiatus of nearly 100 years, the previous foundation boom during the industrialization period of the late 19th century. Many things have changed since then, of course, and the conditions that led to the growth in the number and importance of foundations a century ago are different today. Yet as in previous eras, but in a radically different context and with different actors, persistent policy options and dilemmas have come back onto the political agenda. And it is in the context of these policy options and dilemmas that our knowledge about foundations matters. It is here that their numbers and activities reflect the impact of choices societies make or allow. In other words, by examining the role of foundations we are looking though a specific prism to see how modern Europe addresses fundamental questions about the constitution of economy and society. Among these questions are the following.

- **Who can decide on the use of wealth?** From 18th century *camaraliste* fears about the negative impact of the *main morte*, which was seen as capital withdrawn from the economy that could otherwise have been used more productively, to current concerns about taxation and equity issues, foundations figure prominently in similar debates today. Should the fate of fortunes, large and small, be left primarily to individuals, or does government, as the representative of society, have some moral or political priority over the use of wealth?

- **Who is responsible for delivering public and quasi-public good?** If governments no longer see themselves as the party solely, let alone primarily, responsible for social security, welfare, education, culture or many other fields, who, and under what conditions, has legitimacy to act in the public interest? Again, the future role of foundations will be decided by the answers European countries and the EU find to this question.

- **To what extent can governments allow private interests to influence the political agenda?** Both autocratic and democratic regimes and government in all the foundation models presented above face the same dilemma: independent actors like foundations can create alternative power centres. In autocratic regimes, this fear is obvious, but it is subtler in democracies. Ultimately, foundations, unlike democratic governments, are not answerable to the electorate, which creates profound accountability problems. And unlike interest and lobby groups, foundations are typically not answerable to specific members and stakeholders who might control or own them.

Of course, to some extent, the answers to these dilemmas and questions depend on the relevant policies and laws in place in the various European countries, but they are also shaped by the prevailing political climate. Across Europe, this climate currently favours a reduced role for government and greater responsibility lodged with individuals – a process amplified by the EU across a wide range of fields.[67] It is in this wider political context that the future of foundations in Europe will be decided, and which will lead to a continued re-positioning and redefinition of their role in the 21st century.

Bibliography

Anheier, H. K., 'Das Stiftungswesen in Zahlen: Eine sozial-ökonomische Strukturebeschreibung deutscher Stiftungen', in: Bertelsmann Stiftung (ed)., *Handbuch Stiftungen*. Wiesbaden, Gabler, 1998, pp. 47–82.

Anheier, H. K. and BenNer, A., 'The Shifting Boundaries: Long-term Changes in the Size of the Forprofit, Nonprofit, Cooperative and Government Sectors', in: *Annals of Public and Cooperative Economics*. 68(3), pp. 335–354.

Anheier, H. K. and Romo, F., 'Foundations in Germany and the United States: A Comparative Analysis', in: H. K. Anheier and S. Toepler (eds), *Private Funds and Public Purpose, Philanthropic Foundations in International Perspectives*. New York, Plenum Publishers, 1999.

---

[67] European Commission.

Anheier, H. K. and Toepler S. eds, *Private Funds and Public Purpose, Philanthropic Foundations in International Perspectives*. New York, Plenum Publishers, 1999.

Archambault, E., Bloumendil, J. and Tsyboula, S., 'Foundations in France' in: H. K. Anheier and S. Toepler (eds), *Private Funds and Public Purpose. Philanthropic Foundations in International Perspectives*. New York, Plenum Publishers, 1999, pp. 185–198.

Archambault, E., *The Nonprofit Sector in France*. Manchester, Manchester University Press, 1996.

Badelt, C. ed., *Handbuch der Nonprofit Organisationen*, Stuttgart, Poeschl, 1997.

Beise, M., 'Politische Stiftungen', in: Bertelsmann Stiftung (ed.), *Handbuch Stiftungen*. Wiesbaden, Gabler, 1998, pp. 205–224.

Bertelsmann Stiftung and Maecenata Institut eds, *Expertenkommission zur Reform des Deutschen Stiftungsrechts*. Gütersloh, Bertelsmann Foundation Publishers, 1999.

Bulmer, M., 'The History of Foundations in the United Kingdom and the United States: Philanthropic Foundations in Industrial Society', in: H. K. Anheier and S. Toepler (eds), *Private Funds and Public Purpose. Philanthropic Foundations in International Perspectives*, New York, Plenum Publishers, 1999, pp. 27–54.

Clotfelter, C. ed., *Who Benefits from the Nonprofit Sector?* Chicago, University of Chicago Press, 1992.

European Commission, *Communication from the Commission on Promoting the Role of Voluntary Organisations and Foundations in Europe*, COM 97/241, Luxembourg, Office for Official Publications of the European Communities, 1997.

Esping-Andersen, G., *The Three Worlds of Welfare Capitalism*. Princeton, Princeton University Press, 1990.

Feddersen, D., 'Stiftungen als Träger öffentlicher Aufgaben', in: Bertelsmann Stiftung ed., *Handbuch Stiftungen*. Wiesbaden, Gabler, 1998, pp. 269–94.

Feurt, S., 'Gemeinschaftstiftungen: Stiftungsarbeit von Bürgern für Bürger', in: Bertelsmann Stiftung (ed.), *Handbuch Stiftungen*, Wiesbaden, Gabler, 1998, pp. 239–68.

Flora, P. and Heidenheimer, A. eds, *The Development of Welfare States in Europe and America*, New Brunswick, NJ, Transaction, 1981.

Frumkin, P. 'Three Obstacles to Effective Foundation Philanthropy', in: J. Barry and B. Manno (eds), Giving Better, *Giving Smarter: Working Papers of the National Commission on Philanthropy and Civic Renewal*, Washington, DC, National Commission on Philanthropy and Civic Renewal, 1997.

Hall, P. D., 'The Community Foundation in America, 1914–1987', in: R. Magat (ed.), *Philanthropic Giving: Studies in Varieties and Goals*, New York and Oxford, Oxford University Press, 1989, pp. 180–99.

Hansmann, H., *The Ownership of Enterprise*, Cambridge, MA, Harvard University Press. 1996.

Hof, H., 'Zur Typologie von Stiftungen', in: Bertelsmann Stiftung (ed.), *Handbuch Stiftungen*, Wiesbaden, Gabler, 1998, pp. 943–72.

Karl, B. and Katz, S., 'Foundations and the Ruling Class', in: *Daedalus* 116(1), 1987, pp. 1–40.

Kendall, J. and Knapp, M., *The Nonprofit Sector in the United Kingdom*, Manchester, Manchester University Press, 1996.

Krag, H., 'Kirchliche Stiftungen: Tradition mit Zukunft', in: Bertelsmann Stiftung (ed.), *Handbuch Stiftungen*, Wiesbaden, Gabler, 1998, pp 225–38.

Leat, D., *Trusts in Transition. The Policy and Practice of Grant making Trusts*, York, Joseph Rowntree Foundation, 1992.

Leat, D., 'British Foundations: The Organisation and Management of Grant making', in: H. K. Anheier and S. Toepler (eds), *Private Funds and Public Purpose. Philanthropic Foundations in International Perspectives*, New York, Plenum Publishers, 1999, pp. 121–40.

Letts, C., Ryan, W. and Grosman, A., 'Virtuous Capital: What Foundations can Learn from Venture Capitalists', in: *Harvard Business Review*, 2, 1997, pp. 36–44.

Lundström, T. and Wijkström, F., *The Nonprofit Sector in Sweden*, Manchester, Manchester University Press, 1997.

Margo, R., 'Foundations', in: C. T. Clotfelter (ed.), *Who Benefits from the Nonprofit Sector?* Chicago, University of Chicago Press, 1992, pp. 207–34.

Markhof, C. F. and Mautner, Ritter von, *Die Wiener Stiftungen. Ein Handbuch*, Vienna, Carl Herold's Sohn, 1895.

McCarthy, K. D., 'The Gospel of Wealth: American Giving in Theory and Practice', in: R. Magat (ed.), *Philanthropic Giving: Studies in Varieties and Goals*, New York and Oxford, Oxford University Press, 1989, pp.46–62.

Odendahl, T., *America's Wealthy and the Future of Foundations*, New York, Foundation Center, 1987.

Pharaoh, C., 'The growth of community trusts and foundations', in: CAF (ed.), *Dimensions of the Voluntary Sector*, West Malling, CAF, 1996, pp. 70–73.

Pomey, M., *Traité de fondation d'utilité publique*, Paris, P.U.F., 1980.

Prewitt, K., 'The Importance of Foundations in an Open Society', in: Bertelsmann Foundation (ed.), *The Future of Foundations in an Open Society*, Guetersloh, Bertelsmann Foundation Publishers, 1999, pp. 17–29.

Quadagno, J., 'Theories of the Welfare State', in: *Annual Review of Sociology*, 13, 1987, pp. 109–28.

Reimer, H. M., 'Die Stiftungen. Systematischer Teil und Kommentar zu Art. 80–89 bis ZGB', in: A. Meier-Hayoz (ed.), *Berner Kommentar. Kommentar zum Schweizerischen Privatrecht. Band I. Einleitung und Personenrecht, 3. Abteilung: Die juristischen Personen*, Bern, 1981.

Renz, L., Mandler, C. and Tran, T., *Foundation Giving. Yearbook of Facts and Figures on Private, Corporate and Community Foundations*, New York, Foundation Center, 1997.

Salamon, L. M. and Anheier, H. K., *The Emerging Nonprofit Sector*, Manchester, Manchester University Press, 1996.

Salamon, L. M. and Anheier, H. K. eds, *Defining the Nonprofit Sector: A Cross-National Analysis*, Manchester, Manchester University Press, 1997.

Salamon, L. M., Anheier, H. K., List, R., Toepler, S. and Sokolowski, W. eds, *Global Civil Society: Dimensions of the Nonprofit Sector*, Baltimore, The Johns Hopkins Institute for Policy Studies, 1999.

Strachwitz, R. Graf, 'Foundations in Germany and their Revival in East Germany after 1989', in: H. K. Anheier and S. Toepler (eds), *Private Funds and Public Purpose. Philanthropic Foundations in International Perspectives*, New York, Plenum Publishers, 1999, pp. 219–31.

Toepler, S., 'Operating in a Grant making World: Reassessing the Rope of Operating Foundations', in: H. K. Anheier and S. Toepler (eds), *Private Funds and Public Purpose. Philanthropic Foundations in International Perspectives*, New York, Plenum Publishers, 1999, pp. 163–84.

Toepler, S., *Das gemeinnützige Stiftungswesen in der modernen demokratischen Gesellschaft*, Munich, Maecenata, 1996.

Van der Ploeg, T., 'A Comparative Legal Analysis of Foundations: Aspects of Supervision and Transparency', in: H. K. Anheier and S. Toepler (eds), *Private Funds and Public Purpose. Philanthropic Foundations in International Perspectives*, New York, Plenum Publishers, 1999, pp. 55–78.

Vincent, J. and Pharoah C., *Patterns of Independent Grant making in the UK*, West Malling, Charities Aid Foundation, 2000.

Wagner, A., 'Der Nonprofit Sektor in der Schweiz', in: C. Badelt (ed.), *Handbuch der Nonprofit Organisationen*, Stuttgart, Poeschl, 1997, pp. 35–50.

Weisbrod, B., *The Nonprofit Economy*, Cambridge, MA, Harvard University Press, 1988.

Yediyeldiz, B., *The place of the wakf in the Turkish cultural system*, Istanbul, Foundation of Turkey, 1996.

Ylvezaker, P. N., 'Foundations and Nonprofit Organisations', in: Walter Powell (ed.), *The Nonprofit Sector: A Research Handbook*, New Haven, Yale University Press, 1987, pp. 360–79.

Country Reports

The country reports treat the foundations sector in the respective country according to the following table of contents.

1 **Introduction**
2 **Historical background**
3 **Legal issues**
4 **A profile of foundations in the country**
5 **Current trends and conclusion**

▼ Werner Bachstein and Christoph Badelt

Austria

1 Introduction

In Austria foundations play only a minor economic and social role. Although previous research and available data on foundations are limited, certain aspects of Austrian history suggest possible reasons for this situation. On the collapse of the Austro-Hungarian Empire, and under the Nazis in particular, foundations suffered severe setbacks. Moreover, the Vienna stock market crash (1873) and the worldwide depression in the 1930s had a negative impact on attitudes toward long-term investment of capital. More generally, Austrian public opinion has been unsympathetic to the notion of creating a strong financial alternative to the public sector.[1]

For Austrian foundations in general, no comprehensive statistics were previously available. Virtually all the data cited in this article were gathered specifically for it and are published here for the first time.[2] A range of types of foundations now exists, highly influenced by Austria's federal structure and tending to concentrate on social services, education and research activities. Their steady but slow rate of establishment since the 1950s indicates the difficulty foundations have had in recuperating from historical setbacks.

In contrast, so-called 'private foundations' whose primary aim is to reduce liability to investment and inheritance taxes, thus falling outside the definition of foundations in this chapter, have grown rapidly in number and status over the past five years. Their development completely overshadows that of charitable foundations. Meanwhile public authorities continue to see their role in charitable foundation development in terms of regulation rather than the promotion of growth, and charitable foundations do not seem concerned with making their

---

[1] Matis, 1972.

[2] As part of primary research, numerous interviews were conducted with the responsible provincial foundation officials. The authors wish to thank Ms Mraz and Mr Grafl for their extensive support in conducting empirical research.

situation a public issue. The opportunity for charitable foundations to serve corporate or public policy has not yet been exploited, and would conceivably require a change in public awareness toward the contributions and potential of foundations in Austrian society.

2 Historical background

In Austria the origins of modern foundations are found in Roman, Germanic and Church Law.[3] Foundations, in the sense of institutions with a distinct legal personality, first appeared with the rise of Christianity, inspired by the idea of Christian brotherly love. The earliest foundation hospitals were established around the year 1000. In Austria they were first recorded in the 12th century, reaching their zenith in the 14th; one example is the municipal hospital foundation at Eggenburg, set up in 1299. The first Viennese foundation, the Eternal Light Foundation, was established in 1306 in support of the Magdalene Chapel in St Stephen's Cathedral. It was only with the legislation of the Emperor Ferdinand I (1555–64) and his successors that foundations ceased to be governed by Church Law. The administrative reforms of the Empress Maria Theresa (1740–1780) brought foundations under state control, and towards the end of the century her son Joseph II dissolved many (Church) foundations.[4] Following these setbacks, the foundation concept gradually regained recognition only after the Congress of Vienna in 1815.[5]

Under the Austro-Hungarian Empire, Austrian foundations lacked a universally valid legal framework. Instead, they were subject to a plethora of regulations dating from various eras and introduced by a wide range of different authorities. Yet it was precisely in this period that they experienced their golden age; the philosophical notion of the foundation was not only recognized but highly valued. Thus by 1900 approximately 62,000 foundations – some 54,000 religious and 8000 secular – were established in the province of Lower Austria, Austria's largest, alone.[6]

Following the Empire's collapse in 1918, Austrian foundations and funds were forced to adapt to the country's greatly reduced dimensions. Where previously they had stretched from Lvov (in the

---

[3] Beinhauer.

[4] Böhler.

[5] Stammer.

[6] Böhler; Stammer.

Ukraine) and Prague to Trieste and Merano (in Italian South Tyrol), their scope became limited to the area of present-day Austria. Moreover, under the Treaty of St Germain signed in 1919, the new Austrian Republic was obliged to place at the disposal of the victorious Entente all endowments, stipends and foundations established for subjects of the Empire, in their pre-war condition. In the inter-war period currency reforms and inflation caused many Austrian foundations to be merged or dissolved, and led to a further sharp reduction in their individual and collective capital. By 1938 only some 5700 foundations and funds remained in the country.

Nazi rule represented another blow. After Austria's incorporation into the Third Reich, numerous foundations – above all Jewish ones – were liquidated and their assets confiscated. Not less than 2400 foundations and funds were dissolved. Those few foundations which did survive into the post-war era were required to pay the so-called 'contribution to Austrian reconstruction', often resulting in a loss of more than 25% of their wealth. The financial capacity of Austrian foundations was thereby severely constrained and weakened.[7]

The first attempt to right such wrongs occurred in 1954 with the Foundations and Funds Reorganization Act, which enabled some foundations to recover their legal status. Yet they were few in number compared to those dissolved under the Nazis. And from the 1950s onward, there has been only a small increase in the rate at which new foundations have been established, both at provincial level and Austria-wide. The slow development of the foundation sector generally is related to the extreme youth of the legal framework governing Austria's foundations following the many setbacks suffered by foundations historically. Foundations entered a more rapid growth period after 1993, but this occurred only among private foundations as result of the Private Foundations Act 1993.

3 Legal issues

Under the Federal Constitution Act 1996, legislative and executive powers are divided between the federal government and the provinces, thus the legal basis of contemporary Austrian foundations is set out in various different pieces of federal and provincial legislation. Of these, the most wide-ranging and relevant – for foundations generally and according to the definition used in Anheier:

---

[7] Böhler, 1996.

Foundations in Europe: a Comparative Perspective – is the Federal Foundations and Funds Act (*Bundes-Stiftungs- und Fondsgesetz*) of 1974.[8] Those foundations whose aims are confined to a single province are governed by provincial legislation. Finally, private foundations are regulated by the Private Foundations Act 1993 (*Privatstiftungsgesetz*), known as the PSG.[9]

The characteristics of foundations vary as a reflection of the different legal frameworks they fall under; the greatest distinction between foundations occurs between those with private and those with non-private status.

- **Establishment**
  Whether under the Federal Foundations and Funds Act, the various provincial laws or the Private Foundations Act, a foundation can be established only by a private law deed. It involves a unilateral declaration on the part of the founder. For both federal and provincial foundations the Federal Foundations and Funds Act stipulates that the deed must take written form, that is, be signed by the founder and witnessed by a court officer or notary public. The Private Foundations Act requires private foundations to be established by notarial deed. Under the Federal Foundations and Funds Act a foundation comes into being on approval by the appropriate public authority; under the PSG this occurs on entry in the companies' register.

- **Purpose**
  The purpose of a foundation is of fundamental importance to its establishment, since under Austrian law a foundation exists only to achieve a particular objective over a period of time not terminated by the founder's death. The question of what constitutes a valid objective is regulated differently by the various relevant acts, and so differs for private and non-private foundations. Thus the Federal Foundations and Funds Act permits only charitable or benevolent purposes, while the Private Foundations Act recognizes all 'allowable' objectives with the exception of 'commercial activities'. Essentially, non-private foundations may serve only the common good whereas private foundations have no restrictions as to their beneficiaries.

---

[8] The Austrian *Arbeitsstiftungen* (Labour foundations) are not foundations in the legal sense of the word. Labour foundations are instruments of labour market policies to improve the job chances of employees who are threatened by layoffs; see Köberl.

[9] Beinhauer; Stammer.

- **Capital**

  The Federal Foundations and Funds Act specifies no minimum value for the capital of a non-private foundation; capital must merely be 'sufficient' to achieve the stipulated purpose. However, capital must be maintained intact, (i.e. only the returns on capital may be used for the foundation's ends). In contrast, the Private Foundations Act requires private foundations to have a minimum capital of ATS1 million (€72,670), but includes no preservation requirement, permitting both capital and returns to be disbursed.

- **Duration**

  Under the Federal Foundations and Funds Act 'unlimited duration' is assumed; no limitation on the foundation's life is possible. The provisions of the Private Foundations Act are much more liberal, permitting all conceivable forms of termination, such as a pre-set time limit, dissolution or revocation.

- **State supervision**

  All Austrian foundations are subject to state regulation. In the case of charitable and benevolent foundations, the Foundations Authorities ensure that capital is preserved and that resources are used only to achieve the stipulated purpose, as well as proper management practices. Private foundations are regulated by the courts, which designate auditors to examine the annual report of their governing boards.[10]

- **Tax regulations**

  For the purposes of taxation and other duties, the foundation constitutes one possible legal form of nonprofit organizations along with associations, funds, etc. Like these, it is not legal form but charitable status (for which application must be made to the tax authorities) that leads to favourable tax treatment. In Austria such advantages are in any case strictly limited. For example, only academic institutions with charitable status are entitled to offset donations against tax. Charitable institutions repeatedly demand that this privilege be extended to them.

4 A profile of foundations in Austria

With a population of just over eight million Austria is a relatively small country that nonetheless has a strongly federal structure. This is reflected in the fact that charitable foundations can be established

---

[10] Beinhauer; Böhler.

either at federal level or in one of the nine provinces. In mid-1999 there were over 200 federal and approximately 600 provincial foundations, giving a ratio of some 10,000 inhabitants per charitable foundation. The absolute number of charitable foundations has risen constantly since 1945 (see Figure 1.1).

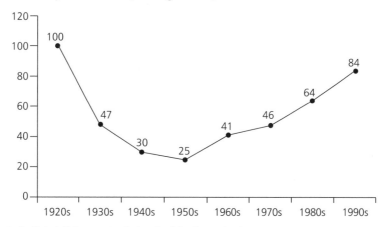

Figure 1.1 Establishment of charitable foundations
Source: Authors' research with the Foundations Authorities (mid-1999)

However, this trend should not be exaggerated. Compared to 1100 private foundations in existence only since 1993 (Table 1.10), the establishment of some 80 charitable foundations over the last decade marks relatively slow growth.[11]

Table 1.10 Private foundations, by province

Province	Number	Relative Share
Burgenland	11	1.0%
Carinthia	51	4.7%
Lower Austria	73	6.7%
Upper Austria	161	14.7%
Salzburg	82	7.5%
Styria	72	6.6%
Tyrol	30	2.7%
Vorarlberg	54	4.9%
Vienna	563	51.3%
Austria – total	**1097**	**100%**

Source: Authors' research with the Foundations Authorities (mid-1999)

[11] Czoklich, *Handbuch zum Privatstiftungsgetz.*

The rapid growth of private foundations made possible through the Private Foundations Act 1993 overtook that of charitable foundations which had been possible for more than 100 years.

Foundations in Austria (both federal and provincial) are concentrated in the education and research sector and the social services, and to a lesser extent in culture and recreation, and health and religious activities (Table 1.11). Together these areas account for almost 94% of federal foundations and nearly 88% of provincial foundations, with only religious activities being slightly higher at the provincial level.

Table 1.11 Foundations (federal and provincial), by main field of activity

ICNPO-Category	Number	Relative share
Culture and Recreation	89	11.1%
Education and Research	295	36.4%
Health	61	7.6%
Social Services	271	33.8%
Environment	6	0.8%
Development and Housing	7	0.9%
Law, Advocacy and Politics	5	0.6%
Philanthropic Intermediaries Voluntarism Promotion	0	0.0%
International	3	0.4%
Religion	33	4.1%
Business and Professional Associations, Unions	1	0.1%
Not Elsewhere Classified	32	4.0%
Total	**803**	**100%**

Source: Authors' research with the Foundations Authorities (mid-1999)

However the distribution of charitable foundations, both in number and by particular fields of activity, is uneven across provinces (Table 1.12). This corresponds in part to population and economic activity concentration, but more importantly to Austria's federal structure. The economically active population of more than 3.8 million is concentrated in just four provinces: Vienna, Lower Austria, Upper Austria and Styria.[12] Vienna, Lower Austria and Styria all rank in the top four for foundation concentration, joined by Tyrol.

---

[12] ÖSTAT, 1999

Table 1.12 Distribution of foundations, activities and population, by province

Province	Population	Foundations	Foundation activities			
			Culture & recreation	Education & research	Health	Social services
Burgenland	3.4%	1.3%	3.4%	2.0%	1.6%	0.0%
Carinthia	7.0%	1.6%	2.3%	0.3%	3.3%	2.6%
Lower Austria	19.0%	11.2%	3.4%	3.1%	16.4%	25.1%
Upper Austria	17.1%	2.5%	2.3%	2.4%	1.6%	1.9%
Salzburg	6.3%	3.1%	6.7%	2.4%	4.9%	2.2%
Styria	15.0%	4.4%	4.5%	3.1%	4.9%	5.5%
Tyrol	8.2%	6.5%	7.9%	4.8%	8.2%	4.8%
Vorarlberg	4.2%	4.0%	4.5%	0.7%	11.5%	5.5%
Vienna	19.9%	65.5%	65.2%	81.4%	47.5%	52.4%
Austria – total	**100%**	**100%**	**100%**	**100%**	**100%**	**100%**

Source: ÖSTAT, *Statistisches Jahrbuch für die Republik Österreich 1998*, and authors' research 1999

But Upper Austria ranks only seventh out of the nine provinces for foundation concentration (2.5%) despite its high population. Moreover, the distribution of foundations among the most populous provinces is quite wide. Vienna, which contains only 19.9% of the country's population, houses almost two-thirds of all charitable foundations (65.5%). Lower Austria contains 19.2% of the population but houses only about one-sixth (11.2%) the number of Vienna's foundations; and Styria has 15% of the population and less than half the foundations (4.4%) of Lower Austria. This reflects the division of powers between the federal government and the provinces, which emerges particularly in main areas of foundation activity in each of the provinces.

Looking at the four fields with the greatest activity (Table 1.12), we see that Vienna houses 65.5% of foundations specializing in cultural and recreational activities, while most other provinces house less than 5% and two are under 10%. Vienna also houses the lion's share of foundations focusing on education and research – over 80% – reflecting the capital's disproportionate importance in the education sector. By contrast, the more even distribution of foundations concerned with health and social services reflects the fact that these are provincial responsibilities in Austria. Those foundations located in Vienna include not only the city's own – provincial – ones, but also many which operate throughout the country. According the data available, Upper Austria has one of the lowest proportions of health and social service activity, explaining its low foundation number generally. Yet this is still surprising considering that Upper Austria is among the top four provinces in terms of population.

5 Current trends and conclusion

In the Austrian media, coverage of foundations is restricted almost exclusively to private foundations. It is concerned mainly with information for potential founders and with proposals to increase the tax privileges available to this type of foundation. The role of charitable foundations in political debates is even more minimal. Research among stakeholders – including both the public authorities and foundation representatives – showed a general picture of lack of interest. This is probably the most revealing statement on Austrian attitudes toward foundations.

At federal level, the establishment of large charitable foundations reflects above all the corporate strategies and public relations efforts of banks and other financial institutions. In the federal authorities' view, the main motive is to promote research (e.g. through provision of grant and financial support for medical research).[13] That, in turn, must be seen in connection with the favourable tax situation of non-profit organizations which, although not general in Austria, does apply to the areas of science and research. Pressure groups concerned with promoting foundations often point out that charitable foundations could also benefit indirectly from advantages of this nature.

This picture of foundations in Austria as a whole is reflected, with minor differences, in most of the provinces. The responsible public authorities see their role above all in terms of legal regulation, rather than contributing to a policy of actively promoting foundations.[14] Thus at present there exists a sort of harmony of interests between the authorities and the foundations themselves in that neither side is concerned with bringing the subject to public attention. In general, private charitable foundations are also rather sceptical about making their capital or their activities more transparent. This defensive attitude contrasts starkly with that of charitable foundations in the English-

---

[13] Interview with Dr Fischer.

[14] Interviews with the responsible foundation officials of the provincial Foundation Authorities (in particular Dr Häusler, Mag. Karven, Dr Orthofer, Dr Skorscheni).

speaking world. The gradual growth in the number of foundations in Austria reflects not any coherent policy, but the activities of particular individuals or organizations. Due to the historical setbacks foundations suffered, and the general lack of political will among the public and foundations themselves, the foundation sector continues to play only a minor social and economic role in Austria.

Bibliography

Badelt, C. ed., *Handbuch der Nonprofit Organisation. Strukturen und Management*, Stuttgart, 1999.

Beinhauer, G., Das österreichische Stiftungsrecht, in: *Österreichische Juristen-Zeitung (ÖJZ)*, 1972, No. 14/15, 378.

Böhler, E., *Die Stiftung in Österreich*, Master's Thesis, 1996, Wien.

Czoklich, P., *Stiftungen: ein Praxisleitfaden*, Wien, 1993.

Czoklich, P., *Handbuch zum Privatstiftungsgesetz*, Wien, 1994.

Doralt, W., Nowotny, Ch. and Kalls S., *Privatstiftungsgesetz*, Wien, 1995.

Ettel, M. and Nowotny, Ch., 'Rechtliche Gestaltungsgrundlagen für NPOs', in: C. Badelt, ed., *Handbuch der Nonprofit Organisation. Strukturen und Management*, Stuttgart 1999.

Feil, E., *Privatstiftungsgesetz*, Wien, 1994.

Köberl, A., *Die Arbeitsstiftung*. Diplomarbeit an der Wirtschaftsuniversität, Wien, 1996.

Matis, H., *Österreichs Wirtschaft 1848–1913 – konjunkturelle Dynamik und gesellschaftlicher Wandel im Zeitalter Franz Joseph I*, Berlin, 1972.

Österreichisches Statistisches Zentralamt, ÖSTAT (1999): *Statistisches Jahrbuch für die Republik Österreich 1998*.

Stammer, O., *Handbuch des Österreichischen Stiftungs- und Fondswesen*, Eisenstadt, 1983.

Seifart, W. ed., *Handbuch des Stiftungsrechts*, München, 1999.

Interviewees

Dr Burmeister, Vorarlberg Provincial Archive; Dr Fischer, Federal Ministry of the Interior, Foundations Section (Director, Federal Foundations Authority); Dr Häusler, Provincial Government of Vorarlberg; Mag. Karbel-Herzog, Provincial Government of Salzburg; Mag. Karven, Department 62, Vienna City Council; Mag. Mayerhofer, Provincial Government of Upper Austria; Neuner, Provincial Government of Tyrol; Dr Orthofer, Provincial Government of Lower Austria; Mag. Philipp, Provincial Government of Burgenland; Mag. Rieger, Provincial Government of Carinthia; Dr Skorscheni, Provincial Government of Styria

▼ Michel Marée and Sophie Mousny

Belgium

1 Introduction

The notion of foundations in Belgium is somewhat ambiguous as it commonly refers to two different organizational structures:

- public utility institutions (*établissement d'utilité publique*, or EUPs)
- nonprofit associations (*association sans but lucratif*, or ASBLs).

Those recognized under law as EUPs correspond closely with the notion of foundations described by Anheier in Foundations in Europe: a Comparative Perspective. An EUP is an institution established by a deed or will, through which 'a private person assigns all or part of his or her possessions irrevocably to the creation of an organization carrying out works of public utility' (law of 27 June 1921). It has legal personality, and must have a nonprofit-making purpose that is philanthropic, religious, artistic, scientific or pedagogic in nature.

Because the expression 'public utility institution' is rarely used in everyday language, there is some confusion between foundations (EUPs) and associations (ASBLs). The latter sometimes use the term foundation and are set up for purposes similar to those of foundations, but do not fall within the legal definition and are not subject to the same restrictions. In fact, EUPs are closely regulated, difficult and expensive to establish and consequently rarely used, whereas the creation and operation of ASBLs is far less restrictive. This explains in part why only 310 EUPs have been set up in Belgium since 1921 while ASBLs number over 10,000.

The majority of foundations pursue philanthropic or scientific purposes. In most cases, the founder is a natural person. Unlike other countries, Belgian corporations set up very few foundations. But in recent years new 'company funds' have developed through existing foundations that manage funds made available to them by private companies. These are part of a larger trend whereby foundations are taking on the management of new funds on behalf of individuals, associations and companies. Currently this trend may prove one of the most significant for the future development of the Belgian foundation sector, as recent proposals to amend the law on foundations seem unlikely significantly to alter the restrictions on establishing foundations.

2 Historical background

Before the French Revolution, Roman law and canon law provided a legal system for foundations. But the situation was reversed at the end of the 18th century as result of the French Revolution. The revolutionary legislation distrusted associations and all other groups of persons, and was favourable to neither foundations nor corporate bodies. This led in particular to the suppression of all religious foundations, and of the right of private persons to set up foundations.[1]

At the beginning of the 19th century, only legal entities set up under public law were authorized to provide charitable services. People wishing to donate their assets for public purposes could do so only by donations *inter vivos* or by will in favour of governmental bodies.

Belgium's independence was key to the legal recognition of foundations. Freedom of association was incorporated in the constitution in 1831 and since then has been defined in various laws:[2] the law of 1894 on mutual benefit companies, the law of 1898 on professional unions and the law of 1919 on international associations. In the latter law, for reasons of state security the purposes associations were authorized to pursue were restricted. Finally in 1921 two laws were adopted:

- the law of 24 May guaranteeing freedom of association
- the law of 27 June on ASBLs and EUPs.

These laws finally introduced the legal system for corporate bodies pursuing a nonprofit-making purpose.

To date, very few modifications have been made to the law of 1921, none of which have affected the functioning of EUPs. However, currently under examination is a government bill to amend the law, which may introduce some important changes.

---

[1] Defourny, p. 23.

[2] t'Kint.

3 Legal issues

According to the law of 27 June 1921 EUPs have the following legal characteristics.

- **Founder**

  Public Utility Institutions must be formed by one or more natural persons, who must each contribute part of the capital. A legal person having legal personality (a trading company, an ASBL, etc.) can also set up an EUP, but as a rule such an initiative is prohibited for legal persons governed by public law.

- **Establishment**

  An EUP must be formed either by a deed drawn up by a notary public or by a will. Its articles of association must be approved by the Ministry of Justice, which then grants legal personality. If the EUP is established by a will, approval will only be given after the founder's death.

- **Purpose**

  An EUP cannot pursue a profit-making purpose. The law also obliges an EUP to be set up for one of the following purposes: *philanthropic, religious, scientific, artistic or pedagogic*. Sports, social, political or leisure purposes are only acceptable as incidental activities or if they contribute directly to the principal purpose. An EUP must also be of *public utility*, which means that the assets making up the capital cannot be used for private purposes.

- **Capital**

  In order to pursue its purpose, an EUP must have a fixed capital. Only the interest on this capital may be used to accomplish the foundation's objectives. The Ministry of Justice has recently introduced the requirement that upon establishment an EUP must have an initial capital contribution of not less than BEF 1 million (approximately €24,800). The more ambitious an EUP's objectives, the greater its capital must be. In addition to this minimum capital requirement, initial capital can be composed of personal property (archives, libraries, copyright, etc.) or buildings. However, the law only authorizes an EUP to possess buildings that it uses directly (head office, cinema or theatre or exhibition hall).

- **Management**

  A public utility institution has neither members nor a general meeting. It is managed by a board of directors which is chosen freely by the founder. However, the Ministry of Justice is entitled to examine the way in which an EUP is managed, in particular to ensure that the capital of the EUP is in fact used for the purpose for which the EUP was established. In principle, an EUP must thus submit its accounts and annual budgets to the Ministry of Justice every year.

- **Dissolution**
  The founder can indicate an expiry date in the articles of association. The EUP will then be dissolved *ipso jure* at that date. If no period is stipulated in the statutes, the EUP will be considered established for an indefinite period. The directors cannot dissolve it voluntarily. However, a civil court may, at the request of the public prosecutor's office, decide that an EUP should be dissolved if it is incapable of pursuing the purpose for which it was created. In this case, assets are transferred to the state which in turn allocates them to a purpose similar to that pursued by the original EUP. Since 1921, some 30 EUPs or about 10% of all EUPs have been dissolved.

- **Tax regime**
  Like ASBLs, EUPs in Belgium benefit from a preferential tax regime. For example, when they are not pursuing profit-making activities or operations, or when such activities are purely incidental to a stated nonprofit purpose, EUPs fall within the scope of the tax regime applying to legal persons, which is considerably more favourable than corporation tax. It is also noteworthy that no registration fees are due when an EUP is set up or dissolved.

4 A profile of foundations in Belgium

By the end of 1998 only 310 EUPs had been set up in Belgium. Accurate information on financial details such as assets, annual expenditure or income of foundations is not available. Despite their legal obligations, EUPs often fail to communicate their accounts on a regular basis. However the Ministry of Justice has carried out several evaluations since 1995 with a view to determining whether the capital of EUPs is today adequate to guarantee their viability.[3] Statistics collected on roughly a hundred cases reveal that the capital of EUPs varies quite considerably between €3000 and €40 million.

---

[3] The method used consists in comparing the amount of the current capital with the indexed value of the initial capital, taking into account changes in the consumer price index.

On the basis of another sample, we were able to determine the global amount of expenditure and income on an annual basis between 1995 and 1997. The estimated annual volume of activity of all EUPs is €150 million, compared to Belgium's Gross National Product of approximately €219 billion in 1997. The distribution of total annual expenditure across foundations is wide ranging, from almost zero to about €2 million.

The income structure of foundations (interest, sales, donations, subsidies, etc.) is generally unknown. However it is noteworthy that a fifth of EUPs in the sample have a negative balance between income and expenditure. This balance should not necessarily be interpreted as an operating loss, since financial data supplied by the EUP corresponds more to an annual cash position than the true accounting position.

The number of foundations established each year since 1921 is very low, as Table 1.13 shows.[4] In the last decade, only between five and ten EUPs have been established yearly. One reason for this low number is that administrative obligations in connection with the formation and running of an EUP are particularly tedious. For many

Table 1.13 Rate of EUP development, 1921–1998

Years	Number of EUPs established
1921–1945	26
1946–1970	73
1971–1989	121
1990–1991	11
1991	9
1992	7
1993	10
1994	7
1995	9
1996	8
1997	7
1998	2
Total	**290**

Source: Analysis of data provided by the Ministry of Justice

---

[4] For Tables 1.13 and 1.15, the total number of EUPs used in the analysis is 290 and not 310, on account of the lack of statistics.

founders, ASBLs are also a more attractive organizational form because they operate under a legal system with far less regulation.

The geographical distribution of EUPs is very uneven. As Table 1.14 shows, more than half of EUPs are located in the Brussels region where less than 10% of the population is located.[5]

Table 1.14 Regional distribution of population and EUPs

Location	Population (1/1/98)	%	EUPs	%
Wallonia	3,326,707	32.6	76	24.5
Flanders	5,912,382	58.0	72	23.2
Brussels	953,175	9.4	162	52.3
Total	**10,192,264**	**100**	**310**	**100**

Source: Analysis of data provided by the Ministry of Justice.

Types of EUPs may be classified by their founder or the nature of their endowment, and also their main function. Table 1.15 shows that by far the most EUPs are set up by individuals. Data on the relative proportions of foundations with different functions is not available, however like other countries Belgium has both foundations that provide grants for external projects (grant-making foundations) and foundations that manage their own projects (operating foundations). Often institutions have both grant making and operating capacities.

Table 1.15 Distribution of EUPs by founder

Founder	Number of EUPs	%
Individual	221	76
ASBL or EUP	47	16
Corporations	16	6
Public authorities	6	2
Total	**290**	**100**

Source: Analysis of data provided by the Ministry of Justice.

Foundations may also be classified by their primary purpose or field of activity. As Table 1.16 shows, the majority of EUPs are active in the scientific and philanthropic fields. This strong concentration may

---

[5] It is to be noted that this table is based on their statutory address and not on operating offices.

be partly due to the relatively wide-ranging scope of philanthropic and scientific purposes, whereas pedagogical and religious purposes are far more restrictive.

Table 1.16 Distribution of EUPs by field of activity

Legal purposes	Number of EUPs	%
Philanthropic	102	33
Scientific	101	33
Artistic	50	16
Pedagogic	37	12
Religious	17	5
Combination of activities	3	1
All EUPs	**310**	**100**

Source: Calculations based on data provided by the Ministry of Justice.

5 Current trends and conclusion

One important current trend in the foundation sector is a government bill currently being examined by Parliament. This bill would amend the 1921 law on foundations, replacing the term 'public utility institutions' with the term 'public utility foundations'. This would reduce the confusion between public utility institutions (EUPs) that are private in nature and established by a private individual, and public corporations, that is to say legal entities set up under public law.

The change would also bring the name into line with a new category of foundation being envisaged – the private utility foundation, more commonly known as family foundations. These foundations provide a channel for the so-called certification procedure for securities and successions, a practice that already exists in the Netherlands where it attracts numerous Belgian citizens. It is particularly attractive to persons with personal fortunes which they do not want divided among their heirs; heirs will only be able to use the proceeds of foundation assets, while assets will be managed by the foundation. Such foundations are not of public utility and their purpose is considerably different from that of EUPs and foundations as defined by Anheier. However the proposed bill also allows the transformation of a private foundation into a public utility foundation.

The proposed amendment would also widen the scope of possible public utility foundation activities to include cultural purposes. However, the conditions necessary for the creation of a public utility foundation, such as state approval and a minimum capital, will once again remain virtually unchanged as they have since the 1921 legislation on EUPs.

A more fundamental development over the last ten or so years is the management of new funds by existing foundations. The most striking example of this procedure is the *Fondation Roi Baudouin*, an EUP established in 1976 which has become one of the most important Belgian foundations. In addition to donations it receives directly, the *Fondation Roi Baudouin* also manages around 40 or so funds on behalf of private individuals ('named funds'), associations ('specific funds') or companies ('company funds'). Each fund is supervised by a management committee which makes decisions after consulting the founder(s).

Establishing a fund with the *Fondation Roi Baudouin* represents an interesting opportunity to circumvent the constraints applying to the establishment of an EUP, particularly administrative formalities, whilst at the same time enabling the management of funds to be centralized and benefiting from the larger foundation's moral guarantee. This trend is the most striking recent feature in the world of foundations in Belgium. The number of funds established in the last ten years by the *Fondation Roi Baudouin* alone represents more than 12% of all EUPs.[6] This development, combined with the fact that founding an ASBL (whose status is close to that of EUP) is easier than creating an EUP, is likely to favour ASBLs in the future.

The small number, slow growth rate and limited role of foundations in Belgium can be explained by the relatively stringent legal conditions imposed on foundation establishment and management, particularly when compared with ASBLs. This situation has remained relatively unchanged since 1921. The greatest exception to this growth pattern has been the recent development of foundations managing funds for individuals, associations and companies. Recently proposed amendments to the legislation on foundations may also help the sector overcome obstacles to growth in Belgium. But even more worthwhile might be future legislation that is more accommodating regarding the ease with which foundations can be established. Such changes could also be made to the benefit of international foundations, which could strengthen Belgium's foundation sector. With its position at the heart of the European Union, Brussels is well placed to attract foreign foundations wishing to establish their headquarters in Belgium.

---

[6] Data provided by the *Fondation Roi Baudouin*.

Bibliography

Agulhon, M., 'L'histoire sociale et les associations', in: *Revue de l'économie sociale*, Vol. 14, pp. 35–44.

Banmayer I. and Talbot C., 'Les fondations : état présent et idées de réforme', in: *Annales de Droit de Louvain*, 1998, No 1.

Buissart A., *ASBL*, Vander Éditeur, 1973.

Defourny, J., 'Histoire et actualité du fait associatif : quelques repères', in: *Les fonctions collectives dans une économie de marché*. Commission 4, Dixième congrès des économistes belges de langue française, Charleroi, CIFoP 1992.

Defourny, J. and Develtere, P.: 'Origines et contours de l'économie sociale au Nord et au Sud', in: J. Defourny, P. Develtere and B. Fonteneau, *L'économie sociale au Nord et au Sud*, Paris / Bruxelles, De Boeck, 1999.

European Commission. *Communication on the promotion of the role of associations and foundations in Europe*, Brussels, European Union, 1997.

Document de la Chambre 1854/9–98/99, Projet de loi modifiant la loi de 1921.

Établissement scientifique de l'État: Établissement d'utilité publique, *Vade-mecum Droit administratif*, No 8, 1992.

t'Kint P., 'La loi du 27 juin 1921, sa genèse, ses modifications et l'évolution de son environnement', in: *ASBL et sociétés à finalité sociale : quelques aspects juridiques et économiques*. Gand, Mys and Breesch publishers and Syneco, 1996.

▼ Gunilla Hellman and Jeppe Parving

Denmark

1 Introduction

In Denmark little research has been carried out on private foundations and public debate about their role hardly exists although there is in general a positive attitude towards them.[1] Consequently, no systematic statistical surveys on foundations in Denmark are currently available, and other information on their historical and legal development is very limited.

The positive attitude towards private foundations in Danish society is probably related to the close ties formed between the Lutheran church and crown during the Reformation in the 16th and 17th century.[2] This close relationship persisted through the centuries, and was even preserved in the development of the welfare state.

In Denmark there are some 14,000 private foundations.[3] Foundations are considered private when operating with a capital of private origin, supporting individuals and projects for the common good. One spectacular type of private foundation in Denmark is the corporate foundation, for example the Carlsberg Foundation established in 1876. Next to private foundations there are public foundations established by communities and the public sector.[4]

---

[1] Tamm, *Træk*, p. 11, i Justitsministeriets, Betænkning.

[2] The positive attitude towards foundations was especially shown by the autocratic king and the church in the 17th – 18th century. Primarily this stems from the fact that it was now seen as a task for the state to provide for the poor and helpless. And since the foundations already did this, the state tried further to centralize foundations under the state, without seizing their finances. Today the positive attitude towards foundations is most clearly seen in foundation taxation laws. The law is very favourable and over the last ten years only the taxation laws have been altered – every time to the advantage of the foundations. For further information about this topic, see Andersen and Nørgaard, p. 11 and Tamm, *Træk*, pp. 15–17.

[3] Civil Rights Directory.

[4] According to the Civil Rights Directory, app. 14,000 foundations exist in Denmark, and these include public, private, corporate, and commercial foundations. There are no separate figures concerning the different types of foundations.

2 Historical background

The origins of the Danish foundation system are rooted in the ecclesiastical law of church property, which was deeply influenced by Roman and German laws. The first divergences took place in the Reformation period when King Christian III proclaimed in his coronation charter of 1536 a will to decentralize the power within the ecclesiastical system and to allow it to administer a range of different foundations. This decision marks a paradigmatic shift in ideas about state responsibilities toward needy citizens of Denmark, such as the elderly, poor, ill and uneducated. This brought about the emergence of a new kind of foundation – the capital foundation (*kapitalstiftelser*).

Capital foundations very much resemble the private foundations of today; a certain amount of property was designated for charitable use but only the interest on capital could be used, thus preserving the capital. This made possible donations for purposes of any kind, unlike the canonical laws of the Middle Ages which recognized only pious wishes.

As the foundation system began to flourish, questions of regulation and legislation arose. After 1660 the crown announced various measures to regulate foundation activities and to establish more centralized control. It has been stated that this was done primarily to secure the activities of foundations, not in order to confiscate capital for the state.[5] In 1708 an agreement was settled under which the original instruments of all foundations were to be left untouched indefinitely.

In 1765 the first official encyclopaedia concerning foundations was published,[6] and in 1771 the first literary works discussing foundations appeared.[7] In *Om stiftelser*, a Norwegian writer under the pseudonym Philomusus (thought to be Rasmus Fleischer) discussed the importance of the permutation law for the first time.[8] According to

---

[5] Tamm, *Træk* p. 16.

[6] Hans de Hofman, *Samling af Publique og Private stiftelser, Fundationer og Gavebreve der forefindes i Danmark og Norge, 1755–1765*. Translation: Collection of public and private charitable institutions, foundations and deed of gifts in Denmark and Norway, 1755–1765.

[7] Philomosus, *Om stiftelse, 1771*. Translation: Concerning charitable institutions, 1771.

[8] The permutation law is stated in the 'law concerning foundations and certain associations' (§ 32). It generally concerns the inalterability of the foundation's instruments. It has been discussed a great deal over the years, but generally it has been agreed that the foundation's instruments should *to the greatest possible extent* be respected in order to secure the original idea with establishment of the foundation. See: Tamm, *Træk* p. 14 and Andersen and Nørgaardk, pp. 71–81.

Philomusus a given foundation should be altered if the government found it necessary. He also gave expression to the common belief that only achievements in the provision of the common good should be considered when judging whether or not a foundation had the continuous right to exist.[9]

While Philomusus ultimately anticipated the relationship between the emerging nation state and private foundations, the main provision for distinguishing between public and private foundations was formulated only in 1828. It stipulated that private foundations could be organizations with restricted purposes of a non-public character. They could still be both profit-making and of service to a general public interest.[10] At the same time it was discussed whether foundations did or did not constitute a legal person.[11] This status was subsequently reserved for corporate organizations and associations. It was not until 1985 that the first general law outlining the legal sphere for private foundations was implemented in Denmark.[12]

Characteristic of the Danish foundation sector since the 19th century has been the great variety of types of foundations, such as private, public, grant making, corporate and commercial. The state has also emphasized the possibility of alternating the stipulations in the law concerning foundations and other associations, (§ 32 – about permutation), in order to keep foundations up to date. A particularly important trend has been the emergence of numerous corporate foundations, many established only recently.

---

[9] This point of view was later acknowledged by the German philosopher Immanuel Kant in *Methaphysik der Sitten (1797) - Von den Rechten des Staats in Ansehung ewiger Stiftungen für seine Untertanen.*

[10] 'Stempelforordningen af 3 December 1828', it is referred to by Tamm, *Træk*, p. 20.

[11] In Denmark this was especially discussed by A. W. Scheel. He was greatly influenced by the German F. C. Savigny, who had discussed the matter of foundations status as legal persons in his 'System des heutigen römischen Rechts II '(1840), see Tamm, *Træk*, p. 21.

[12] Lov nr. 300 af 6 juni 1984 om fonde og visse foreninger, med de ændringer der følger af lov nr. 350 af 6 juni 1991 og lov nr. 187 af 23 marts 1992. Translation: Law nr. 300 from 6th of June 1984 concerning foundations and certain associations.

3 Legal issues

According to the 1984 law on foundations, private foundations in Denmark[13] must have assets amounting to a minimum of DKK250,000 (€34,000) when established.[14] The Minister of Justice is responsible for the supervision of all foundations, but in practice the Civil Rights Directory (*Civilretsdirektoratet*) undertakes this task in collaboration with fiscal authorities.

To register a foundation, its name must be declared (the word *fond* is obligatory) as well as the foundation purpose and the composition of its board. This information must be delivered to the Civil Rights Directory within three months of establishment. Foundations must also prepare an annual financial report with the assistance of an accountant and have it approved by all board members within six months. Its annual accounts must be sent to the fiscal authorities. The taxation of private foundations is in general fairly low, as administrative costs and given grants are tax deductible.

The fiscal authorities must provide, on demand, information about the purposes, accounts and boards of foundations. The charter describes the foundation name, purpose(s), assets, net capital, registered home place, advantages offered to beneficiaries, and board appointment procedures.[15] However, the question of how foundation charters are maintained and to what degree foundation purposes are fulfilled remains a dormant policy issue. But in 1992 a law came into force which abolished the rule of obligatory registration and made formal registration a voluntary act.[16]

4 A profile of foundations in Denmark

Approximately 14,000 private foundations exist in Denmark, including corporate foundations with philanthropic purposes.[17] *Kraks vejviser* is a guide book regularly published to assist grant-seekers.

---

[13] The law discussed in this chapter does not apply to profit-making corporate and commercial foundations, which are subject to another law, (*Erhvervsfondsloven*) even when their profit is used only for charity.

[14] Corporate foundations need to have assets amounting to a minimum of DKK 300,000 (€40,000).

[15] Certain individuals could for example be family members of the founder.

[16] This circumstance has made it much more difficult to compile systematic data on foundations.

[17] Estimate by the Civil Rights Directory.

From this book it can be seen, that the number of grant-making foundations has diminished in relative terms, mainly because of fusions and dissolutions.[18]

No official statistics exist on the assets and net capital of foundations. According to 1986 figures, only five foundations had a net capital exceeding DKK1 billion (€134 million).[19] This number is probably higher today and the assets of Danish foundations remain highly concentrated in a few large foundations.[20]

The following three foundations are described as case studies. All three represent well-established and influential grant-making foundations in Denmark: the Carlsberg Foundation, the Egmont Foundation and the Augustinus Foundation.[21]

- **The Carlsberg Foundation** was established in 1876 by the industrialist J. C. Jacobsen. The intention was to create a foundation supporting scientific research by linking the foundation directly to industrial capital. The mission of the foundation is both to support basic research in Denmark and to remain as the majority owner of the Carlsberg Brewery. The Carlsberg Foundation is governed by a board of five directors appointed by the Royal Danish Scientific Society. In 1902–03 a second foundation was established. The New Carlsberg Foundation supports the arts, in part by maintaining the New Carlsberg Glyptotek, an outstanding collection of antique and contemporary art.
- **The Egmont Foundation** was established in 1920 by Egmont Harald Petersen and is a part of the Egmont Group, an international media group. It aims to improve living conditions for children and young people in Denmark and Lithuania. In recent years it has developed a proactive agenda in order to find new ways to improve the social environment of children and young people.
- **The Augustinus Foundation** was established in 1942 and is today the only shareholder of Chr. Augustinus Fabrikker A/S. The purpose of the foundation is to support the humanities, charitable purposes, arts and science.

---

[18] Berit.

[19] Weber.

[20] Weber.

[21] Information concerning the three foundations are taken from their respective annual reports from 1998–1999.

With its net capital of DKK1.9 billion (€255 million), the Carlsberg Foundation is one of the biggest foundations in Denmark. Its expenditure far exceeds that of the New Carlsberg Foundation, the Egmont Foundation and the Augustinus Foundation combined (Table 1.17). The newer foundations, while smaller, tend to diversify their interests including a greater focus on social welfare issues complementing state activities.

Table 1.17 Net capital and project expenditure of four Danish foundations

	Year	Net capital (million €)	Project expenditure (million €)	Projects
Carlsberg Foundation	1999	255	13.5	Scientific
New Carlsberg Foundation	1998	37	1.5	Scientific, art, social
Egmont Foundation	1998	unknown	2.5	Scientific, art, social, children
Augustinus Foundation	1998	unknown	5.2	Scientific, art, social

Source: Annual Reports, Carlsberg Foundation (1999), Egmont Foundation (1998), Augustinus Foundation (1998)

5 Current trends and conclusion

Private foundations in the Nordic countries have traditionally played a much more unobtrusive role than well-established democratic associations and popular movements. As a matter of fact the 'non-existent possibilities of democratic control' of foundations have often been pointed out as a weakness by politicians and journalists. This has been subject to criticism, not least in the public debate during the 1960s.[22]

It has often been stated in Denmark, as in other Nordic countries, that foundations play a critical role in guaranteeing a rich variety of supported projects and arrangements. This support to cultural, educational and scientific projects given by private foundations is in general considered a useful supplement to the government-subsidised infrastructure.

However, this role should not be exaggerated, as the amounts spent are low compared to public expenses. Rather, their importance lies in the fact that they offer alternatives to public spending: multiple

---

[22] Weber.

sources of financing allow different criteria to be taken into account when supporting projects, with a positive effect on the creative and innovative cultural climate in general.[23] For many years the Egmont Foundation has initiated cultural projects for children and young people in collaboration with municipalities, and projects have gradually been transferred to them. This is an innovative way of making cultural policies.

Danish foundations can find important new niches for their work, and are in a position to develop agendas and programmes of their own without serious interference from the authorities. Foundations have therefore shifted away from their historical fields of action and occupy small but important niches in society.

There are good reasons to believe that foundations will play an active and crucial role in tomorrow's society. In spite of strong and unanimous opinion among Danish citizens in favour of a continuing welfare society, the public sector will probably continue to decrease and new sources will be needed for collaboration and partnership.[24] The general law on foundations in Denmark is comparatively liberal and leaves room for a range of activities and future growth, which also requires greater openness and transparency. However, for the time being, foundations do not act in fully transparent environments, and the continuing lack of statistical data makes assumptions about them difficult to verify. But it is apparent that while foundations in Denmark flourished in number during the 20 years from 1960–80, they are currently increasing in size, mainly due to mergers.[25] This however has not meant that the number of foundations has decreased overall, since there are now 14,000 foundations compared to approximately 9000 in 1980.

Due to the generally favourable economic situation, foundations have never been able to spend as much on grant making and support as they are today. On the other hand, to a great extent, foundations in Denmark still work reactively rather than proactively. On the other hand, if they are to be considered serious and valuable players in tomorrow's society, foundations need to take a more active role as financial instruments and as providers of social risk capital.

---

[23] Andersson, Hårsman, Linzie.

[24] Duelund.

[25] Weber.

Bibliography

Andersen, Lennart Lynge and Nørgaard Jorgen, *En fondsbestyrelses arbejde*, [Translation: The work of a foundations committee], Copenhagen, Bikuben, 1994.

Andersson, Å. E., Hårsman B. and Linzie, J. *Universitet-region framtid*, Stockholm, Institutet för Framtidsstudier, 1988.

Bikuben, *News about foundations*, Copenhagen, Bikuben, 1989–98.

Berit, Jylling, *Vejviser til legater og fonde*, Billesø & Baltzer forlagsanpartsselskab, Copenhagen, 1998.

Duelund, P., *Den danske kulturmodel*, Klim, Forlaget, 1995.

Fondsregistret, *Fonde, en undersøgelse af 8852 fonde*, 1984, Copenhagen, Fondsregistret, 1984

Heide, S., *Ikke-erhvervsdrivende fonde – kapital og årsregnskab*, Copenhagen, Bikuben, 1986.

Justitsministeriets, Betænkning om Fonde, No. 970,1982.

Kraks, *Kraks fonds og legatvejviser*, 6th edition, Copenhagen, Kraks forlag, 1998.

Tamm, D., *Betænkning om fonde – Indledning*, Copenhagen, Justitsministeriet, 1984.

Tamm, D., *Træk af dansk stiftelsesrets historie*, 1982.

Weber, L., *Hvem ejer Danmark*, [Translation: 'Who owns Denmark], Copenhagen, Forlaget fremad, 1988.

Law material:

Lov nr. 300 af 6 juni 1984 om fonde og visse foreninger, med de ændringer der følger af lov nr. 350 af 6 juni 1991 og lov nr. 187 af 23 marts 1992. Trans: Law nr. 300 from 6th of June 1984 concerning foundations and certain associations.

▼ Kjell Herberts

Finland

1 Introduction

The Finnish foundation culture is in many respects similar to that of other Scandinavian countries. As in Denmark, Norway and Sweden, the word 'philanthropy' is not widely used due to the role of the welfare state; the need for philanthropic work tends to be regarded as a sign of failure in a society responsible for the welfare of human beings. Yet foundations engaging in philanthropic public work are not uncommon, and can be traced back to the 14th century when Finland was under Swedish jurisdiction. Later, Finland was part of the Russian Empire for more than a century, in part explaining why its legislative framework for foundations differs somewhat from other Nordic countries. Finnish legislation introduced a political culture of government control. After Finland gained independence in 1917 its foundation sector continued to develop under fairly strict state control.

Although foundations in Finland must be registered nationally, little information can be obtained from the authorities and we can therefore only rely upon very fragmentary statistics.[1] As a whole the definition of foundations suggested by Anheier in Foundations in Europe: a Comparative Perspective, very much applies to Finnish foundations, which are commonly considered an amount of property functioning as an independent legal person and used for a special purpose defined by the founder.

Currently about 2600 foundations are registered, but many small local funds which are very similar to foundations may be registered as associations. From an international perspective, Finnish foundations are rather small in terms of assets and expenditure. Many also have very small target groups according to their statutes. They mainly support education and research, including most foundations in the health

---

[1] The most relevant data collection is a Foundation Guide including 500 grant-making foundations with open policy. About half of the foundations do not offer open access for the public, only through the institutions they are maintaining.

field, but are also strong in cultural activities, science and arts. They are marked by religious homogeneity (the Lutheran church) and ethnic heterogeneity stemming from the presence of a minority Swedish population. To date the vast majority of foundations have been established by private individuals or small interest groups, and very few by the public sector. More recently foundations have been gaining increasing respect, and their importance looks likely to grow in the light of Finland's declining public economy. President Martti Ahtisaari (1994–2000) gave public support several times to the Finnish third sector.

2 Historical background

The first foundation in Finland was established in June 1329 when the Kraknäs limestone mountain was donated to the Cathedral of Turku.[2] At that time Finland was a part of the Swedish Kingdom and until the Reformation was deeply influenced by the Catholic Church. Royal letters on donated funds were used to identify funds dedicated to special purposes. These letters can be regarded as precursors of Finnish legislation on foundations. Notably, one royal letter issued in 1788 emphasized that the manager of donated funds must comply with the donor's purpose and will.

Between 1809 and 1917 Finland was a part of the Russian Empire, as a Grand Duchy. During these years foundations could be established only with permission of the Russian Emperor. According to an Imperial Declaration issued in 1848, private societies and associations must apply for permission to establish entities serving charitable or other purposes. Behind this declaration was an obvious mistrust of associations and all kinds of collective activism that might be considered a threat to political stability. Some of the oldest extant foundations in Finland received official permission from the Emperor, while others obtained a confirmation of their by-laws from the Senate or the Governor in Helsinki.

When Finland gained independence in 1917, the President of the new-born Republic took responsibility for granting permission to establish foundations. Specific legislation for foundations was soon under preparation and the first Foundations Act was enacted in 1930. That Act concerned only independent private foundations, excluding public as well as independent foundations, savings banks and all other types of collected property.

---

[2] Haarmann.

Most foundations established before the Foundation Act were supported institutions like schools and hospitals. When these institutions were overtaken by the public sector the whole purpose and structure of foundations changed. Many tasks were transferred to the state and the municipalities, and foundations took on new tasks to replace the old ones. After the wars, especially in the late 1940s, many foundations were established to support those who had suffered from the war. The Ministry of Justice took over the supervision of foundations in 1930, including maintaining the Foundation Register. Since 1955 pension foundations have been under special legislation. Amendments to the Foundation Act in 1964 increased the supervision of foundations, especially regarding their use of funds, and restricted the possibility of using a foundation as an organizational vehicle for economic enterprises.

The role of Finnish foundations has been under discussion in the past few decades. In the 1970s a state committee put radical changes on the agenda. Several members of the committee were quite suspicious of foundations, which they considered 'undemocratic bodies with far-reaching tax exemptions'.[3] A proposal was made for the state and municipalities to take full control of foundations, but no legislative changes occurred.

Amendments in 1987 made possible the merger of foundations and since 1995, when the latest amendment came into force, the National Board of Patents and Registration has been responsible for the registration and supervision of foundations.

3 Legal issues

There are two common forms of privately organized charitable entities in Finland:

- the association (in Finnish *yhdistys* – in Swedish *förening*)
- the foundation (*säätiö* or *stiftelse*).

The Foundation Act applies only to independent private entities, without members or shareholders, thereby excluding companies and associations. There is no exact definition under the Foundation Act, but a foundation is commonly considered to be a dedicated property functioning as an independent legal person and used for a special purpose defined by the founder.

---

[3] *Säätiölaitoskomitean mietintö* (State Committee of Foundations).

Under Finnish Law, any one or more private or legal personalities may establish a foundation, either through a deed or written will. However, permission must first be granted by the National Board of Patent and Registration, which upon registration grants a foundation an independent legal personality. A foundation is required to have a minimum initial capital of FIM150,000 (€25,050). Permission may be denied if the endowment of the foundation is so small that it appears unlikely to meet the purpose. If the purpose is to establish a foundation after the death of a person, such provisions must be included in a written will. Once established, a foundation is governed by its own by-laws. The only mandatory administrative body is its board of trustees, which attends to the proper management of foundation affairs and ensures secure and profitable investment.[4]

Foundations are exempt from taxation according to the Income Tax Act 1992, which states that any organization is eligible for tax exempt status if it operates:

> solely and directly for the public benefit/general good in a material, mental/intellectual, ethical or social sense.

Initial donations and donations to existing nonprofit organizations are free of taxes. Grants made by foundations are not subject to taxation if the annual amount does not exceed FIM75,000 (€12,600), the normal gift tax being 30–40%.[5]

An organization is liable for state income tax at a rate of 28% on commercial income not referred to in its by-laws and not supporting a nonprofit purpose. However, nonprofit organizations may apply for special clearance from the National Board of Taxes. Thereby a foundation will not pay tax on its business income if considerable amounts are used for charitable activities not causing disadvantage to other entities with similar business activities, and if the organization covers the whole of Finland. On the other hand, if commercial activities exceed the annual turnover of €8,400 the organization must pay VAT. Income-producing activities such as lotteries, games and small-scale business are excluded from normally taxable business income.

---

[4] The chairman of the board and at least one additional member must be residents of Finland. The remaining trustees must reside in the European Economic Area unless the Ministry of Trade and Industry grants an exception.

[5] Corporations have the right to income tax deductions for monetary donations made to promote the maintenance of Finnish cultural heritage, science or art. The minimum deductible donation is FIM5,000 (€840), the maximum 150,000 (€25,050) in any taxable year. Private individuals are not entitled to the same possibility for tax deduction, related to initial donations.

Municipal real-estate tax does not apply if property is used for non-profit purposes.

In 1997 the state auditor's office questioned whether nonprofit organizations should be given tax exempt status, considering that the state and the municipalities bear most of the responsibility for social and health care, while the business activities of nonprofit organizations are further distorting competition. The borders between the philanthropic and commercial activities of foundations are not quite clear and need, from the taxation point of view, to be clarified. A committee was also formed to study the taxation status of athletic and other similar organizations. Changes in the income and VAT treatment of non-profitable organizations were proposed, but have not yet led to legislative amendments.

4 A profile of foundations in Finland

It is difficult to provide a comprehensive overview of foundations in Finland. More than half are relatively closed entities without open access to the public, serving relatively limited target groups. Another difficulty lies in the ambiguity between foundations and associations. At present, about 2500 foundations, compared to 100,000 voluntary associations, exist in Finland. However, closely related to foundations are tens of thousands of small local funds, many of which are registered as voluntary associations. This creates some confusion, particularly as funds are sometimes linked to large umbrella foundations; for example, the Finnish Cultural Foundation has about 600 such smaller funds. As a rule a foundation is much larger than a fund, but both act in similar ways and their total impact, both from economic and cultural points of view, should not be underestimated.[6]

Rate of establishment, and dissolution

From 1931 to 1998 altogether 3340 foundations have been registered. Analysis of data from the National Board of Patents and Registration reveals an average annual rate of about 50 registrations, from a low of 14 in 1943 to a high of 97 in 1998. The rate of foundation establishment has risen steadily since the mid 1940s except for a slight decline between 1975 and 1984. It hit its peak in the 1990s, a trend which looks likely to continue in the future. Also from 1931 to 1998, 568 (or

---

[6] Work on the reorganization of the data processing system at the National Board of Patents and Registrations has taken place and a new system was expected to be in use in the year 2000.

17%) of foundations were removed from the register. These were in many cases companies' pension foundations which since 1955 have been under the supervision of the Ministry of Social Affairs. Another 230 had changed names and been re-registered. Since the 1987 legislative amendments, 20 foundations merged. Based on these numbers we can assume that in 1998 a total of 2522 foundations were active in Finland. Almost 60% are registered in the capital region of Helsinki which is home to around 20% of the country's population. This is because most foundations are nationwide and must therefore be registered in the capital.

Founders and types of foundations

Finland has roughly equal representation of grant-making and operating foundations; however the former frequently operate their own programmes and projects as well. The vast majority of all foundations, about 80%, are founded by individuals or voluntary associations, whose roles are thus quite crucial for foundation establishment in Finland. While in the 1930s and 1940s the majority of new foundations were established by private individuals, in the 1980s and 1990s most were established by institutions and associations. This includes a growing number of different community-based projects – about 10% of foundations – on the initiative of voluntary groups or associations. Another 10% of foundations are established by corporations. The public sector is involved in a few larger foundations (i.e. the Film Foundation and the National Opera), however its role in foundation establishment is almost invisible.

Most foundations established by private individuals tend to be grant making, while those established by associations tend to be operating (Table 1.18). Foundations established by corporations usually operate special programmes or maintain institutions. Community-based foundations often have both grant-making and operating purposes.

An interesting aspect on the profile of foundations in Finland concerns their distribution among ethnic groups. Finland is an officially bilingual country with two national languages, Finnish and Swedish. While the Swedish-speaking population constitutes only 5.7% (about 300,000) of the population, 11.5% of foundations are monolingual Swedish, and 11.5% are bilingual, indicating that minority activity is very important and that the Swedish-speaking minority has resources in these matters.[7]

[7] Foundation Register, 1999, classified by the author.

Table 1.18 Percentage distribution of basic types of foundations

Founder or type of endowment	Primary purpose	
	% grant making	% operating
Private individual(s), voluntary association(s)	50	30
Corporation(s)	–	10
Community	–	10
Public sector	–	–
Total	**50**	**50**

(Foundation Guide 1995, classified by the author, n=554 foundations)

Fields of activity

Foundations in Finland have always especially supported cultural activities, science and arts. The oldest foundations tended to promote education and medical care, but as these tasks were increasingly transferred to the state and the municipalities, foundations have taken on new fields of activity. The distribution of primary fields of activities among grant-making foundations (not by necessity smaller operating foundations) is presented in Table 1.19, based on a representative sample

Table 1.19 Percentage distribution of grant-making foundations by field of activity

Activities (by ICNO categories)	%
Culture and recreation	23
Education and research	47
Health	12
Social services	-
Environment	2
Development and housing	–
Law, advocacy and politics	4
Philanthropic intermediaries, voluntarism promotion	1
International	–
Religion	1
Business and professional associations, unions	10
Total	**100 (n=554)**

of foundations surveyed by *Säätiöpalvelu-Stiftelsetjänst* (Foundation-service) for the Finnish Cultural Foundation.[8]

The largest field of foundation activity is education and research, of which research (sometimes connected to higher education) is the most important. Many foundations support medical research and are quite specific, focusing on specific diseases suffered by the donor or the donor's family members. The second largest field of activity is culture and recreation – culture and the arts are preferred and as a result there are very few sports foundations. When it comes to social services, development and housing it is clear that these sectors are covered by the social welfare system. Foundations focusing on health tend to support research and healthcare for certain diseases.

Foundation size

With a very few exceptions Finnish foundations are very small with only a few larger administrative bodies. According to the 1992 survey[9] most of the foundations are run on voluntary basis, with only one out of four having paid staff, often on a part-time basis. Only one out of ten foundations employs more than two persons.

One exception is the Invalid Foundation, which with 450 employees is by far the largest foundation. It was founded in 1940 by the Ministry of Social Affairs and other public sector institutions. The largest of the more 'typical' foundations (when it comes to purpose) is the Finnish Cultural Foundation, registered in 1939 to advance cultural life in Finland. In 2000 it distributes over €12.1 million in grants and scholarships. The Jenny and Antti Wihuri Foundation is another very important foundation serving research with €5.4 million in 1999. For the Swedish speaking community the Swedish Cultural Foundation connected to the Swedish Literature Society is very important; it distributes €5.4 million in 2000. In 1999 the 34 largest foundations and members of the Foundation Service distributed €49 million to culture and research.

---

[8] This sample is based on over 1000 responses to a questionnaire sent to registered foundations in 1992 (at that time 1,776). About half of responses (554) were foundations that deliver scholarships on a regular basis. These constitute a representative sample of foundations with an open policy regarding access to and from the public. (Palotie).

[9] Palotie.

5 Current trends and conclusion

In Finland, foundation culture has historically been shaped by traditions inherited from the Russian Empire, combined with strong welfare state tendencies after World War II. The religious homogeneity (the dominating Lutheran church) and the ethnic heterogeneity (Finnish-Swedish bilingualism) are also reflected in the special profile of Finnish foundations.

Today, state control of foundations remains somewhat strict reflecting the Tsarist tradition of keeping collective activities under the control of the state. But the freedom for foundations is satisfactory; state control is more formal than real and largely regulates tax exemption in a country with a rather high taxation level.

Foundations have tended to concentrate on education and research, and cultural activities – domains not satisfactorily covered by the public sector. In the past decade, as Nordic welfare states have experienced crises, the role and importance of foundations has grown. The well-organized health and social security system was anchored to a growing economy; economic recession, taxation ceiling, and the adoption of European Union standards led by necessity to reductions in the public sector. In a society where people were used to public caring there arose growing request for voluntary action and voluntarism in the fields of education, health and social care as well as culture. Thus foundations have increasingly been regarded as bodies supporting specific needs in society. The rate of foundation establishment has increased and within larger umbrella foundations are many funds that could be independent foundations as well.

Today foundations are accepted as small yet important counterparts to the public sector. Their activities and policies are at last becoming known, in part thanks to the Foundation Guide published by the Finnish Cultural Foundation, although much remains to be done.[10] For example, many foundations are very small and cater to specific target groups, and these continue to remain quite invisible to the public.

The overall attitude toward foundations has changed from one of suspicion to one more realistic and demanding. Expectations are high and foundation resources are welcomed by all partners in a declining public economy.

---

[10] Foundation Guide 1995 (see Palotie).

Acknowledgements

Special thanks to Mr Jouni Varpelaide, Finnish Cultural Foundation and Mr Jyrki Ahdeoja, National Board of Patents and Registration.

Bibliography

Foundation Register, Helsinki (Unpublished lists of foundations).

Haarmann P-L., *Foundations in Finland*, 1995.

Halila H., 'Säätiöoikeuden tutkimuskysymyksiä', [Translation: Research Issues of the Foundation Rights] in: *Lakimies* 1/1998, pp 18–35.

National Board of Patents and Registration in Finland, Annual reports.

Palotie E.L. ed. *Säätiöluettelo* [Translation: Foundation Guide], Apurahoja jakavia säätiöitä, Suomen kirjallisuuden seura , Helsinki, 1995.

Säätiölaitoskomitean mietintö, [Translation: State Committee of Foundations], Helsinki, 1975.

Säätiöpalvelu, [Translation: Foundation Service], www.skr.fi/spalvelu/neuvottelukunta.htlm.

Säätiörekisterityöryhmän muistio, [Translation: Expert Group for Registration of Foundations] Helsinki, 1993.

Varpelaide J., 'Country Report Finland', in: C.S. George, *International Charitable Giving: Laws and Taxation*, loose-leaf publication, Washington, Kluwer Law International, 1998.

▼ Edith Archambault

France

1 Introduction

Among European countries France has no doubt a relatively less developed foundation sector, contrasting markedly with its vibrant and dynamic associative life. Currently there are fewer than 500 state-approved or RUP foundations (*fondations reconnues d'utilité publique,*), 44 corporate foundations (*fondations d'entreprise*) and some 450 endowments or non-autonomous foundations (*fondations abritées*) sheltered by the Fondation de France. They are small foundations, under the minimum asset requirement of FF5 million (€762,200).

These few French foundations meet the criteria offered by Anheier (in Foundations in Europe: a Comparative Perspective) as a common definition. In France, as a civil law country, a foundation is a legal person subjected to rights and obligations. All foundations are non-governmental, as public authorities cannot create them, and self-governing in that they are not instruments of other entities, governments or corporations. Up to one-third of RUP foundation board members may be government officials, leaving a majority of private administrators, while corporate foundations are structurally separate from their funders. Finally, to be authorized or renewed by public authorities a foundation must be nonprofit-distributing and serve a public purpose.

Why are foundations so scarce in France?

- **Historically,** in a country deeply rooted in Jacobin tradition the state has always been suspicious of foundations. The state holds the monopoly on public services and views foundations as inefficient competitors secluding mortmain property from productive economic flows. Foundations have played virtually no role in France for over 200 years.
- **Juridically,** foundations have until recently suffered heavy restrictions on their creation and activities, particularly compared to associations. The first laws on foundations were enacted in 1987

and 1990, and the process of creating a foundation remains long and complex, often resulting in failure.

- **Sociologically**, the average French person seems ignorant about foundations while the wealthiest do not intend to create them. Individual and corporate charitable giving is low, oriented toward associations.

Foundations continue to have an ambiguous relationship with the state, which both encourages and restricts their growth. The inclusion of foundations in umbrella organizations of the social economy, according to the 1998 European definition, could aid the development of these foundations in France. While the forecast for corporate foundations is good, that of state-approved foundations is dependent on a number of developments that remain uncertain.

2 Historical background

Throughout the Middle Ages foundations developed in France much as in other continental European countries. They mostly took the form of hospitals and asylums under the auspices of the Catholic Church. The Church and monastic orders such as the Benedictine and Franciscan successfully acquired bequests and donations, both in kind and in money, for the creation of foundations. Accordingly under the *Ancien Régime* many poorhouses and student hostels existed in France, alongside magnificent abbeys, churches and schools in foundation form.

However, the wealth that some foundations acquired through legacies and donations began early to arouse state suspicion of the accumulation of inalienable property and power beyond its direct control. Soon suspected by the French monarchs as a means of evading royal taxes, Louis XIV and Louis XV began restricting the rights of existing foundations and prohibiting the creation of new ones.[1] The negative attitude toward the creation of large patrimonies at that time is perhaps most clearly expressed in Turgot's entry in the Great Encyclopaedia edited by Diderot:

> A founder is a man who wants to eternalise his will [...] No man-made work is everlasting. As foundations, multiplied by vanity, would absorb in the long run all funding and individual property, it is necessary to destroy them.[2]

---

[1] Pomey.

[2] Quoted in Pomey, p. 35.

The fight against foundations was reinforced with the Le Chapelier Act 1791, which proclaimed the state's monopoly on activities in the general interest. The law was directed primarily against foundations as well as corporations, guilds and other forms of intermediate entities. The ensuing struggle between state and church had further substantial consequences for the foundation field, as properties of the clergy and church-related foundations were seized and many schools and charitable institutions had to close, while hospitals were nationalized. Foundations lost their legal status and virtually disappeared until the end of the 19th century.

The *Institut Pasteur* was among the first and most notable foundations to mark a limited reappearance of the foundation idea in the late 19th century. Following Pasteur's lead, a select number of other operating foundations were created before World War I, including the still existing *Fondation Thiers* (1893), the *Musée social* (1894) and the *Institut Océanographique* (1906). Others, such as the *Fondation Curie* (1921), *Rothschild* (1921), *Deutsch de la Meurthe* (1922), followed in the inter-war period. However, the endowments of many of the institutions that emerged in this first period of renewal proved vulnerable to prolonged inflationary trends. Consequently, interest in this institutional form ceased until the mid-1960s.

After 1965 some foundations were created in the field of culture such as the RUP foundations *Belem*, *Cziffra*, *Louis Voulard*, and *Maeght*. More recently, some large corporations have created company-sponsored foundations in new fields such as the environment, sports or arts and culture. In this last field, foundations mainly support exhibitions or artistic creation, particularly painting and cinema. The recent emphasis on the arts is in part due to the activities of Jack Lang, Minister of Culture in the Socialist governments of the 1980s, who extended available resources for arts through the promotion of *mécénat*, or private sponsorship. Very favourable tax exemptions for individuals or corporations giving to film production are the roots of vitality in the French cinema industry, the second in the world after the USA for number of new films. Conversely, the Minister of Culture's 1995 proposal to create a Heritage Foundation, inspired by the British National Trust, was a failure.

3 Legal issues

Until 1987 foundations were governed by general regulations applicable to a range of nonprofit organizations. They were eligible for state recognition as a matter of administrative practice, but did not exist as a specific legal form and did not enjoy separate legal status. Thus legislation on foundations is still in the first phases of implementation. Currently foundations are governed by the law of July 23, 1987 and the law of July 4, 1990. The 1987 law aims at foundations established by individuals, providing the first legal definition:

> the legal act through which one or several individuals or legal entities decide the irrevocable allocation of estate, rights or resources for a nonprofit making activity of general interest.

The 1990 law spells out the specific conditions under which corporations may create foundations.

In contrast to other countries, the term 'foundation' is now legally protected in France and can only be used for organizations covered under either of the two laws: the *fondation reconnue d'utilité publique* (state-approved foundation) or the *fondation d'entreprise* (corporate foundation). However, non-autonomous foundations – those lacking legal personality distinct from that of the organization that administers or 'shelters' it –exist as a hybrid form.

State-approved foundations

The establishment of a state-approved foundation (*fondation reconnue d'utilité publique*, RUP) is a lengthy, complicated and centralized process involving the highest state authorities; founders must seek authorization from the Prime Minister and the Ministry of the Interior. Legal personality is then granted through a decree issued by the *Conseil d'État*[3] (State Council) and published in the Official Journal. The *Conseil d'État* has the power to impose by-laws and to determine whether a foundation's endowment is sufficient to pursue its aim in addition to the minimum required endowment of FF5 million (€762,200). Initially a RUP foundation could only be established *inter vivos*, but since 1990 it has been possible to create such a foundation by will.

Generally, the legal treatment of state-approved foundations is much stricter and provides considerably more controls than do laws governing other types of nonprofit organizations, particularly associations which, according to the Act on Associations 1901, may simply register in a *Préfecture* and are not required to invite public authorities to join their board.

---

[3] The *Conseil d'État* is the highest court in France, ruling on the interpretation of legislation.

On the other hand, state-approved foundations enjoy a number of special privileges. Firstly, they enjoy a much wider legal capacity. Associations can only own buildings or real-estate if directly used for their operations, while foundations face no such restrictions. Foundations may also receive gifts and legacies, although certain transactions are subject to state supervision. Secondly, RUP foundations enjoy privileged tax treatment. They may engage in commercial activities (although profits are subject to regular taxation), while activities directly linked to the foundation aim are generally exempt from VAT or corporation tax. Individuals making donations to RUP fondations and registered associations that hold intermediary accounts with such foundations are entitled to a tax credit of 50% of the contribution, up to 6% of the donor's taxable income (law of June 24, 1996). Legacies are exempt from inheritance tax. Private companies can deduct donations up to 0.325% of their annual business turnover.

Corporate foundations

Corporate foundations (*fondations d'entreprise*), according to the 1990 Act, can be founded for nonprofit activities of public interest by one or more private or public corporations, cooperatives or mutual societies. While corporate foundations also need administrative authorization, the process is less demanding than in the case of RUP foundations. A corporate foundation receives legal personality either through explicit authorization by the state administration or through tacit consent in case of administrative silence within a period of four months after preliminary application.

In contrast to private, state-approved foundations, corporate foundations are initially authorized only for a five year period, after which authorization may be repeatedly renewed. Corporate foundations must be established with a minimum endowment of approximately one-fifth of projected programme expenditures for five years, which must amount to a five-year total endowment of at least FF1 million (€152,000) (Article 19–6, law of July 23, 1987 as amended by law of July 4, 1990). The governing board must include at least two employees of the founding corporation. The legal capacity of corporate foundations is as limited as that of declared associations, meaning that they can only own real-estate used to carry on their activities. According to the law of June 24, 1996, the founding company can deduct endowment payments from corporate tax for up to 0.225% of annual business turnover. Corporate foundations cannot receive donations and legacies.

Non-autonomous foundations

Non-autonomous foundations are 'sheltered' or hosted by other institutions rather than having their own legal status. About 1000 non-autonomous foundations are administered by the *Institut de France*[4] as a result of specific bequests. With very few exceptions, such as the Kodak and Fiat Foundations, the endowments of non-autonomous foundations administered by *Institut de France* are negligible. Those that have economically significant endowments tend to be 'sheltered' by the *Fondation de France*, which administers about 450 non-autonomous foundations. The advantage of non-autonomous foundations is that neither minimum endowments nor annual funding commitments are required by law. The disadvantage is dependence on a host institution. Non-autonomous foundations can be created by individuals – *inter vivos* or by last will – or by corporations. Indeed, about 50 corporate foundations are administered by the *Fondation de France*. It is questionable whether non-autonomous foundations are self-governing; they have their own boards including a minority of host institution representatives who decide on grants and operations, while the host institution manages foundation assets.

4 A profile of foundations in France

Due to the Jacobin tradition of favouring a state monopoly over the public interest, foundations have remained rare organizational forms in France. The small percentage of recent foundations in France shows that, compared to Germany and the US, France missed the recent foundation renewal (Table 1.20).[5]

Despite the recent legislation the French foundation sector continues to show no signs of accelerated growth, as Table 1.21 indicates in the case of state-approved foundations. Since 1989 RUP foundations grew from 383 to only 486 in 1998, a rate of about nine foundations per year. No doubt the legal environment continues to underlie the under-development of foundations in France, with its lengthy authorization and approval process and high minimum endowment requirement.

---

[4] The *Institut de France* is not a foundation itself, but a state-approved public institution created in 1795 that houses the five academies (the French academy, science, letters, arts and moral and political science).

[5] Table 1.20 compares the 358 RUP foundation founding periods to the German and American ones (see Anheier and Romo), calculated on 2799 German foundations and 16,221 American foundations.

Table 1.20 Classification of French,German and US foundations by founding period

	French RUP foundations	German foundations	US foundations
	%	%	%
Before 1918	28	22	1
1919–1945	22	11	5
1946–1968	13	16	30
1969–1982	24	21	14
1983–1992	13	30	50
Total	**100**	**100**	**100**

Source: author's calculation following GAFA 1995, Germany and US in Anheier and Romo, 1999.

Table 1.21 Number of *fondations reconnues d'utilité publique*, 1989–98

Year	1989	1990	1991	1992	1993	1994	1995	1996	1997	1998
Number	383	393	402	417	430	438	445	454	466	468
Creation		10	9	15	13	8	7	9	12	2

Source: Unpublished data provided by the Ministry of Interior

The development of corporate foundations has been even more stagnant. Only 44 have been created since 1990, and some of those are not really new as they are reorganized associations or quasi-corporate entities established prior to the 1987 law on foundations.

Non-autonomous foundations administered by the *Fondation de France* grew by 43% between 1990 and 1998 (Table 1.22). This is twice the rate of state-approved foundations in the same period, indicating that the high level of minimum endowments required for the latter might indeed discourage potential founders, whether individuals or corporations.

The localization of foundations in France reflects its high level of centralization: half of all state-approved foundations are in the Parisian area which holds only one-fifth of the French population. North-western, north-eastern and south-eastern France each have 13 to 15% of foundations. Another 8% are in south-western France, which is more consistent with the French population distribution.

Table 1.22 Number of foundations sheltered by *Fondation de France*, 1990–98

1990	1991	1992	1993	1994	1995	1996	1997	1998
326	351	358	364	395	404	420	466	487

Source: *Fondation de France*

Foundations constitute only a very small part of the French nonprofit sector. According to our tentative estimates, total operating expenditures of the foundation sector in 1995 may amount to some FF10 billion (€1.5 billion), that is 4% of the operating expenditure of the French nonprofit sector as a whole.[6] Overall, the impact of the *Fondation de France* on the French foundation field is most significant. Its total assets amount to about FF2.5 billion (€381 million). Annual grant expenditures totalled more than FF400 million (€61 million). Another noteworthy grant maker is the *Fondation pour la recherche médicale*, which reported an annual revenue of more than FF127 millions in 1993.[7]

Foundations also tend to be small in size, as seen in their employment at less than 3% of the whole employment of the nonprofit sector. The SIRENE file[8] from January 1996 recorded 404 foundations that ran a total of 735 establishments, with a total of 38,821 employees. This compares to 1,390,000 employees of 288,500 associations recorded in the SIRENE file. Most foundations have no employees or one or two employees; these are typically grant-making foundations. Foundations with 20 or more employees are usually operating foundations, the largest being hospitals with over 1000 employees, and the *Institut Pasteur*.

Table 1.23 breaks down the distribution of foundations and employment by fields of activity. There is an average of 1.8 establishments, or local units per foundation, with little variation by activities. Foundations contribute most activities in the fields of health and social services. More than half of foundation employment is in the

---

[6] Archambault.

[7] *Guide Annuaire des Fondations et des Associations*, 1995.

[8] SIRENE is the main register of economic activity in France: every enterprise, upon creation, receives an identification number which is referred to at every administrative operation; in this way, the register is automatically kept up to date. SIRENE data cover name and address, legal status, economic activity category, and number of employees. For nonprofit organizations, SIRENE records only those that have employees, pay VAT or are subsidized by the central government.

health sector, mainly in hospitals created before 1950 which are generally large organizations with an average of 235 employees. Foundation employment is also one quarter of foundation employment in social services. The extremely small proportion of foundations devoted to arts and culture contrasts with most other European countries,[9] probably due to the dominance of government in the cultural area, which recent legislative encouragements have not yet changed.

Table 1.23 Distribution of foundations and employment in 1996 by activities

	1		2		2:1	3		3:2
Sector	Total no.	%	No. of establishments	%		No. of employees	%	
Culture	25	6.2	35	4.8	1.4	162	0.4	4.6
Tourism/housing	33	8.3	79	10.7	2.4	701	1.8	8.9
Research	27	6.7	35	4.8	1.3	3,308	8.5	94.5
Education	30	7.6	70	9.5	2.3	2,029	5.2	29.0
Health	44	10.3	92	12.5	2.1	21,584	55.6	234.6
Social services	134	33.3	276	37.6	2.1	8,992	23.2	32.6
NEC	111	27.6	148	20.1	1.3	2,045	5.3	13.8
TOTAL	**404**	**100.0**	**735**	**100.0**	**1.8**	**38,821**	**100.0**	**52.8**

Source: Author's calculation following SIRENE file 1996

These concentrations of activity are reflected in grants distributed by the largest grant maker, the *Fondation de France*. As a multipurpose grant maker it distributes about 50% of its annual grants to social services; about 17% to health, 16% to culture and arts, 13% to research and education, a rising purpose, and around 5% to international activities and the environment.

5 Current trends and conclusion

Despite their limited number, foundations are now coming to the forefront in France as in many European countries. However, the attitude of the government toward foundations remains ambiguous.

---

[9] Strachwitz and Toepler.

On the one hand the foundation revival has been encouraged by the central government beginning with the creation of the *Fondation de France* in 1969 on the initiative of General de Gaulle and André Malraux. The *Fondation de France* encourages philanthropy and shelters individual or corporate foundations. It initiated a completely new and sophisticated concept: a multipurpose foundation. Most foundations created in the late 1970s also departed from traditional sectors and became successful and reputable, but as they were limited in size and assets most relied upon periodic private or public subsidies.

In the 1980s the socialist government, particularly the Ministry of Culture, accelerated the development of foundations in France. Unexpected attention was paid to corporate involvement in public interest topics, particularly arts and culture. This was promoted by the law of 1990. Of the 44 corporate foundations established since then some concentrate on arts and culture totally (Cartier, *Caisse des Dépôts*, GAN) or partially (*Gaz de France*, Air France), while others support first sports, the environment and (more recently) services for the most deprived. Generally, public corporations or formerly public enterprises, recently privatized, were the first to create corporate foundations, as were cooperative banks. However, socially responsible citizen enterprise culture in the French business sector is not yet widespread, and private for-profit companies follow shyly.

On the other hand, in contrast to government encouragement of corporate foundations, public authorities are constantly suspicious of their principal competitors, state-approved foundations. Through the 1987 law, the French administration continues to restrict foundation management and sometimes foundation activities. An unabashed belief in the superiority of governmental provision for public needs, and a distrust of independent privately-controlled institutions, continues to hold sway. Confronted with an administrative culture that has not yet fully adapted to the complex reality of philanthropy, foundations find themselves at a crossroads.

The suspicion harboured by Jacobin civil servants against foundations could have been reduced through the work of community foundations, but these were forbidden by law in 1987. However, the *Fondation de France* has many characteristics similar to those of community foundations. Another example is the *Fondation Agir contre l'exclusion* created in 1995 by Martine Aubry, former Minister of Labour; it gathers public and private money and employs corporate and official volunteers to help long-term unemployed to re-join the labour market.

One setback has been that umbrella organizations of the social economy – such as the *Comité national de liaison des activités mutualistes, coopératives et associatives* (CNLAMCA) or political agencies such as *Délégation interministérielle à l'économie sociale* (DIES) – have excluded foundations because they have no members and are not therefore democratically managed. This situation may change through the European channel, as the 1998 European definition of social economy includes cooperatives, mutuals, associations and foundations (CMAF).

In 2000, the touchstone of the relationship between foundations and the state administration will be the application of the September 1998 fiscal Act. This act suppresses the automatic tax-exemption of associations, foundations and congregations and binds these organizations to the three business taxes (VAT, corporate tax, local tax) if they produce services with the same price and publicity and for the same public as do standard businesses. The application of this new fiscal law may incite foundations to come out of the shadows, as all existing foundations are likely to become tax-exempt.

What may be the future of foundations in France? The concentration of corporations nowadays affords larger resources for corporate giving, and globalization disseminates the pattern of corporate foundations. Therefore corporate foundations, now still on the starting blocks, may progress rapidly and be part of the nonprice competition between large corporations.

The forecast is less easy for RUP foundations. They might need more flexible legal status, lower minimum endowment, more democratic governance, greater cooperation with government as well as association umbrellas and the cooperative bank network to become as substantial as in other European countries. But if these conditions are not fulfilled they will be in a stationary state, regarded as strange aristocratic institutions coping with last century's human needs. The development of community foundations linked to local governments will be another major issue. The creation of a 'council of foundations', an umbrella which would be a partner of public and European authorities, is another challenge.

Bibliography

Alfandari, E. and Nardone, A., *Les associations et les fondations en Europe: régime juridique et fiscal*, Second Edition, Brussels, Librairie Européenne-Juris-Service, 1994.

Anheier H. and Romo F., 'Foundations in Germany and the US. A Comparative Analysis' in: H. Anheier and S. Toepler, (eds), *Private Funds, Public Purpose: Philanthropic Foundations in an International Perspective*, New York, Plenum Press, 1999, pp. 79–118.

Archambault, E., *The Nonprofit Sector in France*, Manchester, Manchester University Press, 1997.

Archambault, E., Boumendil, J. and Tsyboula S., 'Foundations in France' in: H. Anheier and S. Toepler, (eds), *Private Funds, Public Purpose: Philanthropic Foundations in an International Perspective*, New York, Plenum Press, 1999, pp.185–98.

Castro, S., 'France', in: L. M. Salamon, *The International Guide to Non-profit Law*, New York, John Wiley & Sons, 1997.

Courtois, G., *Les fondations en France*, Paris, Guide annuaire des fondations et des associations, 1995.

Debbasch, C. and Langeron, P., *Les fondations*, Paris, PUF-collection, Que-sais-je, 1992.

Delsol, X., *Mécénat et parrainage: guide juridique et fiscal*, Lyon, SA2 – Juris-Service, 1991.

Dupuy, R-J., 'Le droit des fondations en France et à l'étranger', in: *Notes et études documentaires*, 4879, La Documentation Française, 1985.

Fondation de France, *Rapports d'activité*, years 1990 to 1998.

GAFA, *Guide Annuaire des Fondations et des Associations*, Paris, SA2, 1995.

Perrin, A., 'Cultural Sponsorship – 150 Years in the Service of Creation', in: *Alliance – Critical Journal of Corporate Citizenship Worldwide*, 2, pp. 10–15.

Pomey, M., *Traité des fondations d'utilité publique*, Paris, P.U.F., 1980.

Strachwitz, R. and Toepler, S., 'Traditional Methods of Funding: Foundations and Endowments', in: L. Doyle, ed. *Funding Europe's Solidarity*, Brussels, Association for Innovative Co-operation in Europe, 1996, pp. 100–08.

▼ Rupert Graf Strachwitz

Germany

1 Introduction

In Germany the concept of a foundation is a very old one. Two currently active foundations can trace their history as far back as the 10th century, and a number of church foundations may be even older. This may well be true for a number of European countries, but it is particularly striking in the light of Germany's history of political turmoil and strife, changing territorial divisions and allegiances, and breaches in societal development. Religious reformation and political upheaval have changed the map as well as the concept of society. Despite these odds, foundations in Germany have survived both as a concept and in concrete form – in fact as one of the most stable ingredients of an organized society. After a significant growth period in the number of foundations the legal framework is now under review, reflecting increased recognition of foundations as an element of civil society.

2 Historical background

The oldest currently existing foundation in Germany came into being around the year 917, when the small township of Wemding was given assets in perpetuity for the building and upkeep of a hospital. Similarly, Emperor Otto I founded the church in Quedlinburg around 936, declaring that the management of the legal entity he had established should be looked after by members of his own family or, should this no longer be possible, by the king.[1] These developments were in the Roman tradition and influenced by the early Church. Assets were devoted to *piae causae*, describing all philanthropic purposes which were seen exclusively in the context of salvation through good works. Over the centuries, towns, religious communities and universities have become trustees of numerous foundations. Indeed, by this general pattern assets with a distinct legal personality (*univer-*

---

[1] Coing; Liermann.

sitas bonorum) are handed over to an associative body (*universitas personarum*) which retains the actual incorporation. What is more, grant-making and operating foundations have existed side by side as far back as foundations can be traced.[2]

From around the 12th century, when Roman law increasingly replaced Germanic legal traditions, the foundation became recognized as a way of disposing of assets for the benefit of others. In particular, this was true for urban communities where foundations became an increasingly important part of the civic structure. Deeds of creation surviving from that period show that an adherence to standard principles was matched by a huge diversity in organizational regulations. From the late Middle Ages onward foundation purposes widened in scope to include arts, social services, religious and other activities.[3]

The first great breaches in continuity were incurred through acts of secularization inflicted upon church property by some of the Protestant princes in the 17th century. This move was prompted by the notion of the power of the temporal ruler over all matters within his realm, including church affiliation (*cuius regio, eius religio*), but may also be seen in the context of an emerging theory of the monopoly of power invested in the sovereign. The relationship with government became and has continued to this day to be a central issue for the development of foundations.

The period of political reshuffle prompted by the Napoleonic Wars presented the opportunity to consolidate state powers, quite often at the expense of old foundations. Between 1815 and 1848 a legal framework was devized that is still relevant for the German foundation community today. Friedrich Carl von Savigny developed a theory of foundations that became prevalent throughout Germany.[4] He interpreted Hegel's philosophy of the state as superior to society to mean that there was still scope for inferior organizations, albeit under tight state control. This became the dominant outlook on foundations in the 19th century. Around this time, secular goals increasingly replaced religious goals, giving rise to new types of foundations, for instance for the preservation of art.

---

[2] Liermann.

[3] See *Maecenata Institut/Bertelsmann Stiftung*. The Maecenata Institute for Third Sector Studies (*Maecenata Institut für Dritter-Sektor-Forschung*), Berlin, keeps a database and documentary centre of German foundations, based on a continuous effort of collecting data since 1990. The data are based on information provided voluntarily by the foundations and on public sources. All data in this article are from this database. Extracts are available on the internet at www.maecenata.de.

[4] Richter.

Strangely, only autonomous foundations bearing their own legal personality were the focus of law-makers' attention, while non-autonomous trusts remained more or less unregulated, as did the general use of the word, leading to widespread usage outside the traditional legal framework. Regulatory bodies were established to supervise the behaviour of autonomous foundations. In practice, these bodies often control and interfere with the policy decisions of foundation boards and directors. The most drastic regulation made it obligatory for foundations to obtain the consent of the government in order to acquire legal personality.

Despite this move towards uniformity and particularly towards curtailing traditional autonomy, foundations were not unpopular. The number of foundations established rose considerably in the course of the century.[5] After 1871 the number of foundations increased considerably. Symbols of patronage were considered a mark of respectability and a living memorial to oneself. The most famous one, however, is an exception. Ernst Abbe, an academic who had become Carl Zeiss' partner in forming one of the largest industrial corporations at that time, genuinely believed he owed something to society and that his heirs were not entitled to the huge inheritance they might have expected. After Zeiss' death he founded the *Carl Zeiss Stiftung* which exists to this day and still – as a complete anomaly – not only owns but actually operates the company. Due to Abbe's later work on behalf of factory workers, foundations became the object of profound suspicion among conservatives, showing that contrary to popular perception foundations were not accused of perpetuating traditional structures, but of being hotbeds of leftwing activities.[6]

Just before World War I, foundations encountered the first in a series of events that were to become decisive for the fate of many. Increasing government demand for funds led to regulations imposing government bonds on foundations (and others) as preferred investments. Most small foundations not owning real-estate thus became invested exclusively in this form of assets. After the war, hyperinflation in 1923 reduced the value of these bonds – and the asset value of foundations – to nil. Foundations managed by local communities, churches and universities were wiped out by the thousand, a blow that the foundation community has not recovered from to this day.

Only a few years later, Hitler's ideology was anything but favourable to autonomous organizations equipped with assets;

---

[5] *Maecenata Institut/Bertelsmann Stiftung*

[6] Strachwitz, *Die großen Stifter.*

under such circumstances it is surprising that many foundations remained untouched. Jewish foundations, however, did see their assets confiscated by the government. A sharp decline in new foundations was also an obvious result of government policy. The general turmoil of 1945 again dealt a blow particularly to foundations managed by public bodies.

In East Germany foundations were basically barred until 1989 except in a few very special cases affiliated to the churches. In West Germany foundations again began to gain popularity in the 1950s, resulting in a growing number of new foundations. However, the last 50 years have seen very little discussion on foundations and their role in society. They have tended to be seen as contributors to an overall corporatist structure, including the various levels of the public and the nonprofit and private sector, dominated by government. Only since the early 1990s has the scope of public debate widened.

3 Legal issues

Creating a new foundation today implies considerable preparation, as neither the term nor the legal framework are immediately apparent. The German Civil Code of 1900 (*Bürgerliches Gesetzbuch*) restricts its legal definition to specific autonomously incorporated legal persons, characterized by assets, destined to serve a specific statutory purpose in perpetuity as laid down by the founder(s), and granted legal personality without members or owners by an act of government. But in practice there are a number of other structures that can legitimately claim to be types of foundations.

While the existence of assets destined to serve the statutory purpose is essential for any foundation (even when assets are minimal), other characteristics may vary. Foundations under public law and by definition considered part of government, are formed and terminated by an act of parliament or government. Non-autonomous foundations, comparable to trusts in Anglo-Saxon law, do have legal owners, their (usually sole) trustee. This form is usually characteristic of comparatively small foundations. Associations, another legal form described in the Civil Code, occasionally bear the name *Stiftung* and, if they behave like foundations in that they adhere to their original purpose, have assets and possibly give grants, are generally considered to be part of the foundation community. The same goes for corporations (usually limited companies) bearing the name *Stiftung*.[7] Most of the foundations affiliated to political parties, a German peculiarity, are incorporated as associations.

Private individuals in any number, business corporations, associations and public bodies may establish a foundation. Only the foundation itself is precluded from doing so, which creates some problems especially when it comes to creating endowments for the benefit of universities. Although those established by individuals still dominate, foundations established by corporations and associations as part of a restructuring programme have increased considerably in recent years. The relationship between a foundation and a business company may be two-fold. A foundation may have been founded by the corporation as part of its overall communication strategy, or it may have been founded by owner(s) and entrusted with the (part) ownership of the corporation as such. One increasing debate concerns whether public bodies should be permitted to remove assets or management under parliament control, to a foundation dependent on government grants.

No uniform regulations for foundation governance and accountability exist other than the obligations of good stewardship. However, as in the business community, it has become common practice to distinguish between the director(s) and a supervisory board such that the former may not be part of the latter. Newly created foundations will usually have two directors and a board of five to seven members. Founders are commonly members of the board for life, or even directors of their own foundation, although foundation assets are kept entirely separate. Like associations, but unlike major business companies, foundations are not accountable to the general public. They present annual reports to the relevant government agencies, but these are not brought to public knowledge.

The federal fiscal code and a host of other fiscal regulations are relevant to the tax status of foundations, apply to all recognized charities and only contain a few items specific to foundations; specifically foundations may accumulate assets whereas associations, with few exceptions, may not. The revenue from such assets and any other donations a charitable foundation may receive in one year must be spent within the following year. Unlike the US, the real income rather than a fictitious percentage of the investments – be it more or less – must be spent. Just two exceptions to this rule make a minimum allowance for reserves to save for projects and to offset devaluation.[8]

---

[7] Of the largest foundations in Germany, some (e.g. the *Bertelsmann Stiftung*) bear a specific legal personality, while others (e.g. the *Robert Bosch Stiftung GmbH*) are incorporated as limited companies.

[8] Strachwitz, *Handbuch*.

4 A profile of foundations in Germany

Number and types of foundations

Over 96% of the 8312 German foundations identified in the Maecenata database[9] are recognized charities. This entails exemption from income, inheritance and gift tax (but usually not from VAT), and also grants tax benefits to donors (including the founder). It also makes them eligible for a number of government grant programmes open exclusively to recognized charities. German foundations today are not restricted as to the investment of their assets, provided the investment yields a revenue or the assets themselves serve the statutory purpose of the foundation. Quite a number of foundations, including some of the largest, are majority or sole shareholders of major business corporations. Twenty eight percent own and manage charitable businesses closely related to their statutory purpose, for instance hospitals, homes for the aged and disabled, museums, libraries, etc.

Foundations established for private purposes, which have a long tradition in Germany, often have a charitable purpose as well, but because such charitable purposes do not dominate their activities, these foundations cannot be recognized as charitable. These are taxed like corporations. On the other hand, charitable foundations may give up to one-third of their annual revenue to founders or their heirs without endangering their charitable status.

Foundations not established by private individuals have given rise to some new types of foundations, in some cases to solve complex legal problems. For example the ownership dispute between federal and state government in the case of Volkswagen was settled by establishing a foundation with the proceeds of the shares sold to the general public. This was the first of many foundations set up by government for a variety of reasons. Large nonprofit organizations have also established foundations, either as an asset-holding body separate from their operations or as a fundraising body. Finally, community foundations have begun to enrich the German foundation scene through their new approach that aims at combining the sustainable asset-holding feature of a foundation with democratic elements traditionally reserved for associative bodies.[10]

---

[9] Editor's note: recent survey data of different sources published by the *Bundesverband Deutscher Stiftungen* in autumn 2000 indicate that the total number of foundations existing in Germany may be close to 10,000. See *Bundesverband Deutscher Stiftungen*, p.5.

[10] Brummer/Ruprecht.

About one-third of all foundations are in some way operating foundations. In addition to managing institutions, this may include operating projects or giving awards. Grant-making foundations may support institutions (quite often those to whom their management is entrusted), fund projects, assist people in distress personally or give scholarships (see Figure 1.2).

While over 50% of foundations operate or make grants at national level and over 20% at regional level, less than 7% have an international scope of action. This is related to the relevant fiscal framework which does not generally favour tax-exemption for bodies whose activities do not directly benefit the German tax-payers or indeed the German government's resources.

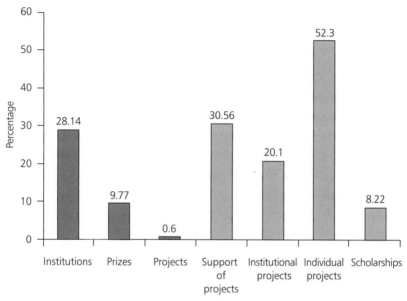

Figure 1.2 Pursuit of purpose by foundations (n=5680 foundations)

Source: *Datenbank der Deutschen Stifungen*

Assets and expenditures of foundations

An interesting aspect of foundations in Germany is their employment. While just over 10% employ any paid staff, (90% are managed entirely by volunteers, outside institutions or experts), the total number of staff employed is approximately 90,000, mostly of course in institutions. This reflects the enormous diversity in the size of foundations (see Figure 1.3).

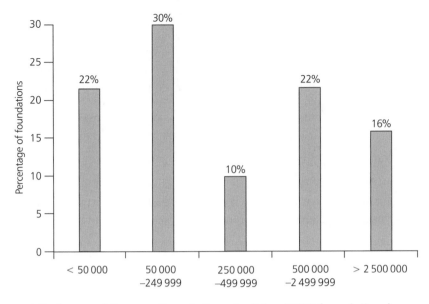

Figure 1.3 Assets of German foundations in € (n=2276 foundations)

Source: *Datenbank der Deutschen Stifungen*

Though it is certainly true that the average German foundation is small, figures have to be interpreted with caution. No generally accepted principles of valuation exist. Moreover, because foundations are not required to publish relevant data, less than 30% actually provide the documentary centre with the necessary information. Thus their estimated assets of DM28 billion (€14.5 billion) pertain only to those foundations who publish their data and whose expenditure amounts to DM10 billion (€5.1 billion). Total expenditure of approximately DM35 billion (€18 billion) per year must also be termed a rough estimate. It must also be noted that income corresponding to this expenditure is derived from revenue, services, donations, government grants and other sources.

Activities of foundations

Figure 1.4 classifies foundation activities by the ICNPO system. Over 50% of German foundations are involved in care for the needy in the broadest sense. This includes personal aid as well as operating services and grant making to social services. Education, research and sciences combined are included in over 50% of foundations' activities, while arts and culture only attract 20% of all foundations. It should be noted that larger foundations are usually active in several fields, while smaller foundations commonly restrict their activities to one field.

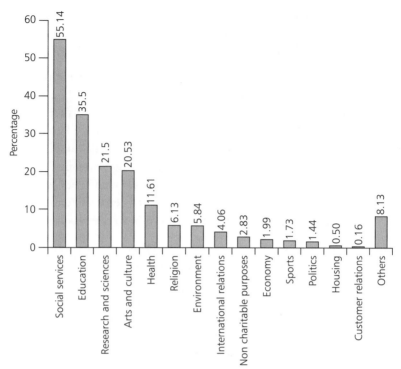

Figure 1.4 Purpose of foundations (n=6717 foundations, 11901 responses, approx. 2 purposes per foundation)

5 Current trends and conclusion

Since 1990, when data on foundations were first collected, more information has been made available to the public than ever before, and local directories are now quite frequent. However, it is still the case that less than 10% of foundations publish an annual report and no more than 8% have printed information available, while only 6% ever issue press releases. So while foundations are widely recognized as doing good in some way – to the extent that the term *Stiftung* is actively sought by fundraising organizations to improve their marketing value – very little is known about their impact. The general public does not have much opportunity to appreciate or indeed critically to discuss the work done by individual foundations or the role and potential of foundations generally, and there still exists a lack of research, be it historical, economical, or in the social sciences.

However, it is evident that the importance of foundations is growing. Since the 1980s, the rate of foundation establishment has soared, primarily due to a substantial increase in private wealth. Today, over 50% of all existing foundations are post-1945, 30% post-1985 creations. These new creations have brought to the foundation community new active founder personalities whose entrepreneurial attitude has produced new types of pro-active asset-holding members in the third sector.

Increasing strains on government budgets have also impelled law-makers to scout around for alternatives since neither public opinion nor the constitutional court were prepared to tolerate a further increase in taxation. In 1997 a bill was introduced by the Green Party in parliament (then in opposition) with the express aim of encouraging wealthy citizens to establish foundations, making their wealth available for the public good. However, it was quite clear that there was more to the issue than that.[11] Foundations may have been used to move forward the issue of reforming all legislation relevant to the third sector.

Since the change of government in 1998, changes in the law have been part of the programme agreed upon by the coalition. A number of proposals have been made, both by parties in power and by those in opposition, centring around deregulation balanced by publicity requirements on the civil law side and additional tax relief on the fiscal law side. Government permission to establish a foundation would be replaced with some form of registration, and the publication of annual reports would become mandatory. The tax authorities might be replaced with a new body of mixed composition.[12] This last change strikes at one of the prime issues at stake: whether law-makers may broadly define the public good at long intervals, leaving its intermittent development to tax authorities who may be the least able interpreters since it is their function to collect taxes, not to waive them.

In a European context, this argument is of particular importance. Trans-national tax-deductible giving, which is urgently demanded by donors and organizations, is adamantly rejected by the tax authorities as it would open the door to other trans-national tax issues. Furthermore, the difficult issue of competition versus nonprofit activity is not paid enough attention by national tax bodies who would sooner render NPOs taxable than bear in mind their share in society.

While foundations themselves are happy to have some additional tax relief, social scientists and an increasing number of political decision-makers see the reform process as part of a fundamental change in civil society.[13] Foundations have a specific and needed role within this

---

[11] Vollmer.

[12] *Maecenata Institut/Bertelsmann Stiftung.*

[13] Anheier/Toepler.

framework. Their long-term adherence to their governing principle balances the continuing and most necessary process of democratic decision-making, thus rendering them stable and reliable contractors. They may also act as capital market for the third sector while at the same time being in a unique position of autonomy and self-reliance that enables them to act decisively and free from outside intervention.[14]

As a first step towards a new legal framework a law was passed in July 2000 reforming the fiscal rules governing charitable foundations as of January 2000. With the aim of enhancing giving to charitable foundations (as distinct from other charitable organizations such as corporations or associations) and promoting the idea of philanthropy, the law introduces a flat deductibility of DM600,000 (€300,000) to be carried forward over nine years upon establishment of a new foundation and of DM40,000 p.a. for donations to existing foundations. These measures apply in addition to the previous rules of a 5% to 10% deductibility of taxable annual income. In addition foundations are allowed to increase reserve allocations to one-third of the surplus from endowment management per year.

Throughout history German foundations have reflected the relationship between state and citizen. Increasingly they were at the hand of the state and their original diversity and autonomy gave way to uniformity and a subservient role. Today there is a call, albeit moderate, for their liberation and for a restitution of their autonomous and pluralist state.

Thus, foundations in Germany are heading for a new chapter in their long history. After a period of state supervision, it seems inevitable that they will enter a phase of new autonomy, and indeed of providing valid alternatives and filling societal gaps. Newly found NGO activities in international development, in ecology and human rights have paved the way for this new understanding of third sector activities over the past 25 years, and a number of German foundations have become active partners in developing these issues. It is from them that the rest of the foundation community will possibly adopt a new attitude. This might consist in a shift from passive grant making to more pro-active programme development and foundation policy, and from a corporatist 'trying to fit in' attitude to a strong self-esteem based on close relationships with other equally strong subsections of the non-profit sector. To move in this direction, German foundations will increasingly have to help the general public and policy-makers realize

---

[14] Deutscher Bundestag, Protokoll 1998; Deutscher Bundestag, Protokoll 1999.

that the merit of foundations lies not only in their financial contributions, but in their contribution to the development of a strong civil
society.

Bibliography

Anheier, H. K. and Toepler, S., 'Stiftungen: Eine international vergleichende
Perspektive', in: H. K. Anheier, *Stiftungen für eine zukunftsfähige
Bürgergesellschaft*, München, 1998.

Bertelsmann Stiftung ed., *Handbuch Stiftungen*, Wiesbaden, 1998.

Brummer, E. and Ruprecht, S., *Statistiken zum Deutschen Stiftungswesen*, München,
1998.

Bundesverband Deutscher Stiftungen e.v. ed., *Zahlen, Daten, Faliten zum deutschen
Stiftungsweren*, Berlin, 2000.

Coing, H., 'Geschichte', in: W. Seifart, and A. Campenhausen von, *Handbuch des
Stiftungsrechts*, München, 1999.

Deutscher Bundestag ed., Protokoll zur Anhörung von Experten am 16.06.1998
zum Thema Stiftungswesen, Bonn, 1998.

Deutscher Bundestag ed., Protokoll zur Anhörung am 22.03.1999 im Wasserwerk
zum Gesetzesentwurf der F.D.P zum Stiftungsreformgesetz, Bonn, 1999.

Liermann, H., *Handbuch des Stiftungsrechts, Band 1: Geschichte des Stiftungsrechts*,
Tübingen, 1963.

Maecenata Institut für Dritter-Sektor-Forschung and Bertelsmann Stiftung eds
Expertenkommission zur Reform des Stiftungs- und Gemeinnützigkeitsrechts,
Gütersloh, 1999.

Richter, A., 'German and American Law of Charity in the Early 19th Century', in:
R. Helmholz and R. Zimmermann, Itinera Fiduciae. *Trust and Treuhand in
Historical Perspective*, Berlin, 1998.

Strachwitz, R. Graf, *Stiftungen – nutzen, führen und errichten: ein Handbuch*,
Frankfurt, 1994.

Strachwitz, R. Graf, 'Ernst Abbe', in: J. Fest, *Die großen Stifter*, Berlin, 1997.

Strachwitz, R. Graf, Foundations in Germany and Their Revival in East Germany
after 1989, in: H. Anheier, and S. Toepler, *Private Funds, Public Purpose.
Philanthropic Foundations in International Perspective*, New York 1999.

Vollmer, A., Stiftungen im Dritten Sektor, in: R. Graf Strachwitz, *Dritter Sektor –
Dritte Kraft*, Duesseldorf, 1998.

▼ Sophia P. Tsakraklides

Greece

1 Introduction

In comparison to most western and central European countries Greece has a weak foundation sector. The almost 500 Greek foundations typically provide welfare services, handle small endowments, and are in most instances in close contact with the state.[1] The relatively small number of private foundations in Greece can be attributed to the traditional inclusion of church foundations in the public sector, the slow rates of Greek industrialization in the middle and latter parts of the 20th century, which prevented the growth of private initiative, and the overall dominance of the state over civil society. [2]

The weakness of the Greek foundation sector does not arise solely from the small size and number of its foundations – it is also a result of limited autonomy. Most foundations receive a significant percentage of their funding from government sources and it is common for founders to put the endowments of foundations at the disposal of relevant ministries. The latter allows the state to regulate specific foundations as well as the growth of the sector as a whole. Thus, with few exceptions, Greek foundations exist in close relation to the state while compensating for its deficiencies; as in the case of other European countries, the role of foundations in Greece was more vital

---

[1] The Greek word *ίδρυμα* (foundation) describes all self-governing, non-membership based, nonprofit endowed organizations, which serve public *or* private purposes. To keep in accordance with the definition employed by other authors in this volume, this chapter deals only with the private law foundations in Greece. State and church foundations operate under public law.

[2] For discussions of the hypothesis that the Greek state dominates over civil society see Mouzelis, Mavrogordatos, and Tsoukalas. Greek foundations are bearers of a long-standing tradition of private philanthropy allied with state initiative. During the Byzantine Empire, church and court jointly created and maintained philanthropic institutions on the Greek peninsula. In the 19th and early 20th centuries, powerful Greek merchants, the so-called 'Great Benefactors', instigated the expansion of the modern Greek welfare state. The presence of foreign NGOs on Greek soil since the end of World War I and the incentives provided by the European Union since 1980 have helped to modernize the Greek foundation sector.

before the advent of the modern welfare state. During periods of strife that weaken the centralized state, openings are created for the involvement of foundations in public affairs.

2 Historical background

The Greek word φιλανθρωπία (philanthropy) literally means love (φιλία) for men (άνθρωποι). While the city-state of ancient Athens was the first to promote philanthropic giving among its wealthiest citizens in the Greek peninsula, modern Greek private philanthropy has more in common with the institutions and practices established during the Byzantine Empire (324–1453 AD). Following the lead of the Orthodox Patriarchate, emperors, nobles and other prominent laymen contributed to the creation and maintenance of mostly welfare but also cultural and educational foundations all over the Balkan territories.[3] Archival research has shown the existence of various specialized institutions such as hospitals, hospices, homes for the elderly, orphanages and homes for the poor.[4]

While the continuity between the institutions of Byzantium and modern Greece is still widely debated by historians, Byzantium at minimum affected the development of the Orthodox Church and thus of an essential actor in modern Greek welfare. Byzantine foundations were the manifestation of the alliance of state and religious action. Due to the religious character of the Byzantine state, church and court activities were both considered public. The little room left for private action was taken up by the activities of prominent wealthy men who made donations to public institutions and occasionally funded their own. The bond between church and state during the Byzantine period promoted the diffusion of Christian doctrines of philanthropic giving throughout the Byzantine territories, including Greece. Public expectations concerning the role of the state and of the wealthy in the delivery of social services rose.

After Constantinople fell to the Ottomans in 1453, the Church continued to play a significant role in welfare provision but now had to pay its dues to the sultanate. Community councils of governors took charge of decision-making in health, education, taxation and justice issues.[5] Under such localized state control, private involvement in

---

[3] Constantelos, *Byzantine Philanthropy*, and Constantelos, *Poverty, Society and Philanthropy*.

[4] Thomas.

[5] *kodjabashis*; see Zakynthinos, ch. 4; Vacalopoulos, ch. 7.

social life became very difficult. Around 1700 Greeks belonging to the wealthy and powerful merchant class in Germany, Poland, Italy, England, France, Russia, Egypt, the Austro-Hungarian Empire and the territory of present day Romania created foundations to preserve the cultural heritage of Greece and unite ethnic Greeks against the Turks.[6] In the complete absence of a nation state, these 'Great Benefactors' became the bearers of a continuously growing Greek national identity and of a culture of philanthropy focused on private initiative in the economy, thus diverging from Orthodox and Ottoman traditions.[7]

The War of Independence (1821) gave Greece its long awaited political autonomy but it did nothing to alleviate the country's chronic welfare needs. Those who had the means emigrated in huge waves toward the growing Greek communities of Europe. From there, wealthy Greek emigrants began establishing private and public foundations in their native Greek towns. Thus, many of the first Greek private foundations developed in some of the poorest rural areas of Greece. Often these benefactors made donations to local authorities for the building of hospitals and other types of welfare institutions. This practice gave rise to city welfare institutions run by local governments but supported by private money.[8]

Once Athens was declared the capital of the newly founded Greek state, philanthropists directed much of their activities to the relief of Athenians. Meanwhile, women of mostly aristocratic background began founding their own philanthropic foundations and associations. Important voluntary associations such as the Merciful Company, (Ελεήμων Εταιρεία, 1864) and the historic Parnassos (Παρνασσός, 1872) were created during this period. The middle classes too began to compensate for the slow development of state welfare institutions, not only by making large donations, but also by forming and running service-providing institutions themselves. Private initiatives carried the main burden of welfare provision until the beginning of the 20th century. Soon after 1922 legislation was passed to ensure that such private donations were used according to the wishes of the original founders.[9]

---

[6] Papageorgiou, pp. 15–43.

[7] Kalliga, ch.1.

[8] Kalliga, ch. 10.

[9] Pelleni-Papageorgiou, pp. 77–78.

The Treaty of Lausanne 1923, in which Greece and Turkey agreed to an exchange of populations in order to ensure future peace, affected foundation development in several ways. When 1.5 million immigrants arrived in Greece in need of immediate assistance, international NGOs such as the American Red Cross and the Near Eastern Relief – many operating under the legal status of foundation – came to the forefront of philanthropic action.[10] These organizations and others similar to them (mostly led by Greek Americans) are still functioning in Greece today and in some cases have branched out to many different foundations.[11] The presence of foreign-born NGOs in Greece helped improve public attitudes toward foundations, because they displayed a type of voluntarism that had not been practised by the mainly grant-making foundations of the Great Benefactors. These organizations were also more professional than foundations of the previous century and operated independently rather than through contributions to the state.

Another result of the immigration wave was the creation of foundations by the immigrants themselves. The arrival of Greeks from Asia Minor coincided with, and even encouraged the development of, the Greek labour movement.[12] The establishment of workers' unions with specific welfare demands led to dramatic changes in public expectations toward both private giving and the welfare state. The new Greek working class, conscious of its social status in relation to the old aristocracy, quickly rejected notions of philanthropic giving and began to look at the foundations of the wealthy with distaste. Gradually, foundations gave way to membership associations, less controlled by the state, and philanthropy to voluntarism.[13] At the same time the moderate rise in the standard of living brought about during the period of industrialization following the end of World War II encouraged prominent citizens to become more involved in founding institutions concerned with neglected social groups.

At the end of the 1960s and the beginning of the 1970s numerous private foundations for the care of the physically disabled were

---

[10] Cassimatis.

[11] For example, some of the most important foundations for handicapped children in Athens were the result of American philanthropy at the time and are still administered according to the original founding acts, see Stasinos, p. 57.

[12] Liakos.

[13] Law 1111 of 1972 allowed a number of associations to be admitted in the legal status of philanthropic nonprofit association. This legal status was created in order to provide a means of separating public from private benefit associations and further institutionalize the state's position as the main supporter of public benefit associations.

founded.[14] During the 1980s Greek civil society experienced a growth of the voluntary sector, as well as the expansion of the already existing environmental and feminist movements and the birth of the anti-racist and human rights movements. As a result, Greek foundations have recently found themselves competing with the expanding population of associations for both EU and state funds. In doing so they have become more flexible in adapting new technologies and strategies.

3 Legal issues

In Greece a 'foundation' – '*ίδρυμα*' – can be a legal 'person' in either private or public law. Private foundations are nongovernmental organizations governed according to the provisions of the Civil Code (Articles 108–121). Public foundations are governmental organizations operating under a different set of rules. A significant number of public foundations are based on church properties or on private foundations whose endowment has been depleted or donated to the state. Public foundations fall outside the definition of foundations offered by Anheier in European Foundations: a Comparative Perspective; thus the following concentrates on the legal aspects of private law foundations.

To establish a foundation two legal acts are necessary:

- the founding act
- state approval of the stipulations of the founding act.[15]

Approval for foundation establishment becomes a law of the state and is published in the official journal of the government. However, the process of obtaining approval is discouragingly time-consuming. It often takes years to approve a foundation charter, even when the proposed foundation is of important size and value.

1 Purpose: the most crucial element of the legal definition of private foundations is the foundation's purpose. The only constraint set by Greek law is that the purpose of foundations should be specific and lasting.[16] The state evaluates how 'worthwhile' a specific cause

---

[14] A report published by KEPE in 1970 suggests that the overwhelming majority of homes for the elderly existing in the country in 1967 (67 out of 72) had been established by private initiative. About half of the private homes were regularly or non-regularly subsidized by the state but the rest were self-supported. Services to persons with disabilities were reported as also being overwhelmingly provided by foundations such as the Home of the Blind, established in 1946 and The National Society for the Deaf and the Dumb; see Stasinos, pp. 52–55.

[15] Article 108, Civil Code.

[16] Pelleni-Papageorgiou, pp. 19–27.

is and supports the foundation accordingly, but it is well known that there are often political disagreements on the worthiness of foundations' causes. Greek law distinguishes between 'general foundations' and 'public good foundations'. The latter serve goals that the state recognizes as distinctly crucial for public welfare, and subsequently receive special tax treatment. Traditionally, public good foundations have served philanthropic or educational purposes, but new nonpublic good foundations are emerging, for example the corporate foundation, tied administratively and financially to a corporation.

2 Endowment: the second important element for the existence of a foundation is the existence of an endowment.[17] The law does not specify a minimum endowment necessary to create a foundation, but a charter cannot be approved by the state unless it is evident that the foundation already has or will soon acquire means for the fulfilment of its purposes.

3 Organization: a third element of the legal definition of foundations concerns their organization. Foundations are not membership organizations but are organizationally defined by their administration. Their existence depends on the precise functioning of their administration, which must be described in their charter. Greek foundations are normally administered by a governing board. If the governing board does not follow the stipulations of the founder's charter, the state may appoint officials as members of the board, punish members of the board with expulsion, and order a state take-over of the foundation where resources are used unwisely or have been depleted.[18] However, there are laws protecting foundations from state practices that could change the original purpose of a foundation or lead to a state take-over.

4 Taxation: once established, a private public good foundation and its founder become exempt from property tax and tax on their endowments.[19] Until recently donations to foundations were not taxed but this law was changed because donations are often made to iconic institutions solely for tax evasion purposes. This measure has already proved to be an obstacle to the survival of small foundations.

---

[17] Article 95, law 2039/1939.

[18] Pelleni-Papageorgiou, pp. 85–98.

[19] Law 231/1975 and law 3843/1958.

4 A profile of foundations in Greece

There are currently 489 foundations in Greece, the majority of which are located in Athens (Table 1.24). This overwhelming concentration reflects the concentration of half of the Greek population in the city governments composing the metropolitan area of Athens, located in the municipality of Attici. However, one should point out that often foundations established in Attici benefit the whole of Greece, while many of the foundations spread throughout Greece only promote the development of their localities.

Table 1.24 Geographic distribution of foundations in Greece*

Geographic region	Number of foundations	% of total	% of population in region
Attici	221	45.1	29.9
Ipirous	56	11.4	3.3
Ionian Islands	44	8.9	1.8
Peloponnese	51	10.4	10.5
Macedonia	21	4.2	21.7
Sterea Ellada	28	5.7	12.2
Thessalia	17	3.4	7.1
Thrace	5	1.0	3.2
Aegean Islands and Crete	46	9.4	9.7
Total	489	*	*

* Does not total to a hundred due to the rounding of percentages at the first decimal.

Source: Data provided by the Greek Ministry of Economics; data on population provided by the Statistical Agency of Greece.

The majority of private law foundations in Greece are operating foundations that may also on occasion provide grants for specific purposes. Some grant-making foundations exist but their grants are small in scale. The endowment of foundations is usually small so many foundations are dependent on outside funding in order to carry out their operations. Community foundations do not exist and corporate foundations are rare but are becoming increasingly common.

Founding entities are almost without exception individuals; wealthy industrialists have founded some of the largest and most active foundations, for example Onassis, Bothosakis,

Vardinogiannis, Kokkalis, and Lambrakis. Important cultural and educational foundations have been established in memory of important politicians such as Karamanlis, Papandreou, and Merkouri. Another group of founders are members of the intellectual elite of the country.

It is hard to speculate on whether the number of private law foundations currently operating in Greece has grown significantly in recent years.[20] Surely it would be difficult to match the rate of foundation building at the beginning of the century; by 1938 researchers of the Greek Ministry of Economics had documented the existence of 4000 foundations around the country. However, many of those foundations actually referred to endowments donated directly to other public or private institutions.[21]

Table 1.25 presents the number of foundations established each decade since 1950 by primary area of activity. A progressive increase in the number of new foundations is evident in the 1960s and 1970s. This was followed by a small decrease during the 1980s, which might be explained by decreasing levels of industrial development and by the nationalization of many private law foundations. Additionally, after the mid-1980s EU programs designed to fund undeveloped areas of welfare and cultural activity in European countries encouraged the proliferation of membership associations, which sometimes formed in order to take advantage of the sudden influx of funds. Membership associations were less difficult to create than foundations, and benefited from the same tax exemptions as foundations while maintaining greater independence from the state.

Thus, overall these developments pushed up the rate of establishments in the public law foundation sector and among associations. The public sector seems to have absorbed not only a large section of the older generation private foundations, but also many religious foundations; while the Church continues to fund and run many philanthropic institutions, they are now often not only legally part of the public sector, but essentially regarded as governmental organizations due to increased state intervention.

The general decline in foundation establishment also corresponds to a shift in areas of foundation activities over time, particularly away from

---

[20] The ministry responsible for the monitoring of foundations in Greece is the Ministry of Economics. However, apart from a basic list of foundations this ministry is not in the position to provide any other information on foundation activity.

[21] Zakopoulos, p. 23.

Table 1.25 Rate of foundations established since 1950, by area of activity

Primary area of activity	1950–60	1961–70	1971–80	1981–90
	%*	%	%	%
Social Welfare	49.2	51.4	33.1	29.6
Health	15.9	4.6	1.9	3.1
Education	21.7	24.2	43.7	48.4
Science	5.7	7.4	0.6	3.1
Religion	4.3	7.4	9.2	3.1
Art	1.4	0.9	1.9	7.8
Folklore			1.3	
Environment	1.4	0.9		
Foundation Support		2.8	3.3	3.9
Public Works			4.6	
Total Number	69 [100%]	107[100%]	151 [100%]	128 [100%]

Source: Data collected by Pelleni-Papageorgiou, pp. 60–65.

*Percentage of the total foundations established that decade. Percentages do not add up to a hundred due to the rounding of numbers at the first decimal.

social welfare and religious activities.[22] Private law foundations appear to become involved in new areas of activity with greater ease than public law foundations, particularly in the fields of research and education.

5 Current trends and conclusion

Despite the small number, and limited scale of Greek foundations, there are indications that the foundation sector will play an increasingly important role in the Greek economy. In recent years Greek foundations have been entering more specialized areas of social provision that require innovative strategies and advanced technological know-how. A number have become interested in human rights, the environment, the development of rural areas, information technologies, and even philanthropic action outside the Greek borders. Often,

---

[22] In 1981, 40% of nursing homes were legal persons of private law, and 60% were run by the Church and other public institutions. 25% of all orphanages, 75% of homes for the elderly and 64% of centres for the chronically ill were also operating as legal persons of private law. Most were foundations, with some larger associations. On average, private nonprofit organizations providing services to children received 70.6% of their budget from government sources, those caring for the elderly 17.7%, and foundations servicing the disabled 35.6% (KEPE 1985).

as in the past, foundations pave the way for important changes and the state follows either by creating new institutions or taking over existing private foundations.

However, low rates of economic development over the past two decades seem to have affected the rate of foundation building as well as the expansion of existing foundations. There are too few industrialists willing to form foundations, and the state finds itself unable to support older foundations. It also appears unwilling to provide incentives for the expansion of the sector. Indeed, the state has created obstacles to foundation building by taxing donations and delaying charter approval procedures. Although the Ministries of Education, Welfare and Economics recognize the crucial role foundations play, and often exert pressure on foundations to provide more services, they also advocate the nationalization of private foundations in order to control welfare providers more effectively.

A significant recent development is that Greek foundations have been combining in pressure groups and are increasingly vocalizing their views on public policy issues. Meanwhile, pressure from the media, interest groups and the EU is forcing the state to institute more rational mechanisms for the efficient control of the foundation sector. Greek foundations may thus finally be given the chance to play an important role in the economy at a time when general disillusionment with the state speaks in favour of more private initiative.

Bibliography

Cassimatis, L., *American Influence in Greece*, 1917–1929, Kent, The Kent State University Press, 1988.

Constantelos, D., *Byzantine Philanthropy and Social Welfare*, New Rochelle, Caratzas, 1991.

Constantelos, D., *Poverty, Society and Philanthropy in the Late Medieval Greek World*, New Rochelle, Caratzas, 1992.

Kalliga, E., Η Πρόνοια Για το Παιδί στην Ελλάδα του 19ου Αιώνα [Translation: Welfare Provisions for Children in 19th Century Greece], Athens, Dodoni, 1990.

KEPE (Centre for Planning and Economic Research), Κοινωνική Πρόνοια, Εκθέσεις για το Πρόγραμμα 1983–1987 [Translation: Social Welfare: Reports on the 1983–1987 Plan], Athens, KEPE, 1985.

Korasidou, M., Οι 'Αθλιοι των Αθηνών και οι Θεραπευτές τους [Translation: The Destitute of Athens and Their Therapists], Athens, General Secretariat of Youth, 1995.

Krapsitis, V., Σύγχρονοι Ηπειρώτες Ευεργέτες [Translation: Contemporary Benefactors from Ipirous], Athens, Friends of Souli Association, 1987.

Liakos, A., *Εργασία και Πολιτική Στην Ελλάδα του Μεσοπολέμου* [Translation: Work and Politics in Mid-war Greece], Athens, Commercial Bank of Greece, 1993.

Mavrogordatos, G., *Stillborn Republic: Social Coalitions and Party Strategies in Greece, 1922–1936*, Berkeley, University of California Press, 1983.

Mavrogordatos, G., *Μεταξύ Πιτυοκάμπτη και Προκρούστη: Οι Επαγγελματικές Οργανώσεις στην Σημερινή Ελλάδα* [Translation: In Between Pitiokamptis and Prokroustis: Professional Associations in modern Greece], Athens, Odysseus, 1988.

Mouzelis, N., *Politics in the Semi-Periphery: Early Parliamentarism and Late Industrialization in the Balkans and Latin America*, London, Macmillan, 1986.

Papageorgiou, S., *Έλληνες Ευεργέτες* [Translation: Greek Benefactors], Athens, Papazisis, 1997.

Pelleni-Papageorgiou, A., *Το Ίδρυμα Ιδιωτικού Δικαίου* [Translation: The Private Sector Foundation], Athens, Sakoulas, 1993.

Stasinos, D., *Η Ειδική Εκπαίδεση στην Ελλάδα* [Translation: Special Education in Greece], Athens, Gutenberg, 1991.

Stasinopoulou, O., 'Voluntary Care in a Mixed Economy of Welfare: Present Trends – Future Prospects', in: *Review of Decentralisation, Local Government and Regional Development*, Vol. 4, 1996, pp. 64–73.

Stathopoulos, P., *Κοινωνική Προνοια* [Translation: Social Welfare], Athens, Ελληv, 1995.

Tsoukalas, K., *Κάρτος, Κοινωνια, Εργαοία στην Μεταπολεμικη Ελλάδα* [Translation: State, Society, Work in Post-War Greece], Athens, Themelio, 1986.

Yiakos, D., *Εθνικοί Ευεργέτες* [Translation: National Benefactors], Athens, Atlantis, 1969.

Symeonidou, H., 'Social Protection in Contemporary Greece', in: Martin Rhodes, (ed.), *Southern European Welfare States: Between Crisis and Reform*, London, Frank Cass, 1997, pp. 67–86.

Thomas, J., *Private Religious Foundations in the Byzantine Empire*, Washington D.C., Dumbarton Oaks, 1987.

Vacalopoulos, A., *The Greek Nation, 1453–1669: The Cultural and Economic Background of Modern Greek Society*, New Brunswick, Rutgers University Press, 1976.

Wood-Ritsatakis, A., *An Analysis of the Health and Welfare Services in Greece*, Athens, Centre of Planning and Economic Research (KEPE), 1970.

Zakopoulos, P., *Τα Εθνικά Κληροδοτηματα Και Αι Προς Αυτά Υποχρεωσεις Της Πολιτειας* [Translation: National Inheritances and State Obligations Toward Them], Athens, Library of Parliament, 1968.

Zakynthinos, D., *The Making of Modern Greece: From Byzantium to Independence*, London, Basil Blackwell, 1976.

Ireland

1 Introduction

An air of secrecy and possibly ignorance pervades the world of foundations in Ireland, with consequent implications for research on the area. Surprisingly, despite quite a vibrant nonprofit sector, Ireland's foundations are underdeveloped and very little information about them is available. Currently only 20 operating and grant-making foundations and trusts have been identified.[1] Most if not all of the foundations identified are relatively new, the oldest being not more than 25 years of age. However, this list of 20 is not exhaustive and furthermore includes only foundations that have agreed to release their details to the public; it is probable that there are other foundations in existence that are older. For the time being, the actual numbers involved, the support foundations give and the assets they hold are all difficult to gauge.

There are signs that this situation may change in the near future. In 1997 the government released a Green Paper that devoted some space to community foundations with the aim of:

- considering ways of funding the nonprofit sector through means that would not necessarily lead to greater reliance on state support
- emphasizing further the 'community' focus of the Green Paper.[2]

Other advances may emerge through recent research on the nonprofit sector. Data have begun to be rigorously collected and reported,[3] and as areas of the nonprofit sector come under increasing scrutiny and light is shed on its operation, the foundation world may also begin to be revealed.

---

[1] See CAFÉ.

[2] Department of Social Welfare.

[3] Salamon, Anheier and Associates; Donoghue, Anheier and Salamon.

2 Historical background

Ireland was colonized by Britain until 1922 when 26 of its 32 counties became an independent state. It had a limited industrial base until the 1960s and since then the Irish economy has been based on substantial external or overseas interest. In 1997 more than 10% of Irish GDP was repatriated in profits to foreign owners of multinationals in Ireland.[4] Until recently, among developed countries, Ireland has been perceived as a relatively 'poor' country. It has been a net receiver of EU structural funds since 1973, and until the last decade was known for its high unemployment and sluggish economic growth. In the 1990s Ireland's fortunes changed and it became one of the fastest growing economies among developed countries.

The nonprofit or third sector in Ireland has a long history and, as recent figures have shown, is one of the largest nonprofit sectors internationally.[5] Nonprofit provision has traditionally been particularly strong in the education, health and social services fields.[6] Religious orders have played an important part in such provision, a role that has only begun to wane in recent decades.

When the nonprofit or voluntary sector in Ireland is discussed, foundations are not generally assumed to be part of its ambit. If thought of at all, foundations are seen as a support rather than a component of the sector. Almost nothing is known about them historically and very little information is available on their activities currently. Research difficulties are enhanced by a lack of information on the Irish nonprofit sector generally. At national accounting and statistics level the nonprofit sector is not classified separately, nor there is there a central umbrella body representing it.

Apart from the general poverty of the nation, it is probably the case that those with money to endow either left it to their families or to the Church. Increasing secularization may mean that this is not as popular an option as it was previously. Whether our new-found wealth will lead to a growth in the number of foundations in Ireland, however, remains to be seen.

---

[4] Central Statistics Office.

[5] Salamon, Anheier and Associates; Donoghue, Anheier and Salamon.

[6] Donoghue, Anheier and Salamon 1999.

3 Legal issues

As for nonprofit or voluntary organizations, there is no one legal form that defines foundations in Ireland. Foundations can take different forms, but are most likely to be companies limited by guarantee holding no share capital. This legal status is also the form recommended in the government's Green Paper. Its advantages include offering an organization a separate legal personality, thus preventing member liability in the case of bankruptcy. However, this organizational form is not sufficient to qualify for exemption from certain taxes.

Thus nonprofit organizations, including foundations, apply to the Revenue Commissioners for 'charity numbers', making them exempt from income tax, corporation tax on interest, annuities, dividends and shares, rent on property, gifts, profits from trade or land owned. Some organizations may also be exempt from capital gains tax, deposit interest retention tax, government stamp duty on property sold, capital acquisitions tax and probate tax. Philanthropic organizations are further exempt from VAT.[7]

However, the granting of tax exemption does not entail charitable status, which does not exist in Ireland. Moreover, as several statutory nonprofit organizations have charity numbers it is not necessarily a sign of voluntary nonprofit status. Indeed, there is no statutory definition of what a charity is and although the Revenue Commissioners make such a decision when nonprofit organizations apply for charitable exemption, the final arbiter in all cases is the court. The definition currently used is derived from the Pemsel Case in 1891 based on English jurisprudence, and the Irish Income Tax Act 1967. The latter defines a charity as a body 'established for charitable purposes only', which does not clarify matters any further. The Pemsel Case is somewhat more helpful, as it offers four categories of activities which constitute charitable work: the advancement of religion, education, the relief of poverty, or 'other purposes' beneficial to the community.

The regulation of charitable bodies is still contested terrain in Ireland and continues in the absence of either charitable status or legislation for the charitable sector. There is no system of registration of charities and recent media reports have raised this matter in relation to the accountability of charitable organizations. Despite an investigation of the matter by the Department of Justice, resulting in the 1990 *Report on Fundraising Activities*, no legislative changes have occurred. It is in this state of limbo that charitable organizations, including foundations, continue to operate in Ireland.

---

[7] Article 13 of the EU 6th VAT Directive.

4 A profile of foundations in Ireland

The lack of clarity surrounding definition, boundaries, regulation and registration of foundations means that anything said about them at this stage can only be a tentative step toward a fuller profile. To begin to redress this situation, a sketch of Ireland's foundation sector was drawn by contacting the 20 foundations identified in CAFÉ's handbook on fundraising in Ireland. The following data are based on their annual reports and information communicated regarding assets, size and grant making in 1997. However, in some areas specific information was not provided, therefore even these figures must be treated with caution.

There are at least 20 foundations in Ireland, of which ten are grant making, nine are operating foundations, and only one represents a community foundation. No corporate foundations could be identified. Most grant-making foundations are not based in Ireland, in contrast to almost all operating foundations. Foundations based in Ireland are located in Dublin, although their grant-making activities or operations are not restricted to that region.

The total amount of grants given by Irish foundations in 1997 amounts to €27 million. From the information available it is not possible to examine the size of foundations in Ireland according to their assets and endowments. However, in 1995 there were 133 people employed in a full-time capacity in the foundation field.[8]

Irish foundations are active in a variety of fields as Table 1.26 shows through a breakdown of their expenditures.[9] Almost half of all expenditures went to development and housing projects. This concentration of funding reflects trends in the nonprofit sector generally which has seen a recent upsurge in community activity.[10] Other main areas of foundation funding activity are culture and recreation, health and education, at 15% each. Based on the limited data available, the total contributions made by grant-making foundations were minimal; roughly 98% of all funds were contributed by operating foundations.

---

[8] Donoghue, Anheier and Salamon.

[9] Information is based mainly on expenditure information provided by 11 of the 20 identified foundations. Two other foundations, which focus on Northern Ireland, did not provide funding to the Republic of Ireland in 1997.

[10] Donoghue; Ruddle and Donoghue.

Table 1.26 Foundation grants in 1997, by main fields of activity

Activities by ICNPO categories	Grants (£IR)	Grants (Euro)	%
Culture and recreation	3,695,113	4,691,826	16.7
Education and research	3,138,430	3,984,984	14.3
Health	3,632,071	4,611,779	16.6
Social services	341,869	434,084	1.6
Environment	379,500	481,866	1.7
Development and housing	10,530,670	13,371,192	48.2
Law, advocacy and politics	149,410	189,713	0.7
Total	**21,867,063**	**27,765,442**	**100**

Despite the highest economic concentration in development and housing, both grant-making and operational foundations undertook more activities in the education and research category than in any other, followed by development and housing. It is also possible that areas of activity such as social services may actually see more activity but may have been classified by foundations as falling under the development category.

5 Current trends and conclusion

Given the small size of the field and the current success of the Irish economy, it does seem that there is scope for growth in the number of foundations. It could well be the case, however, that secrecy will still prevail and it may continue to be difficult to ascertain the true extent of foundations operating in Ireland. There are two issues that should be focused on at this stage:

- learning from history
- policy and future government support.

Our history, and the data presented in this chapter, raise questions about the factors inhibiting the establishment of foundations and what conditions are conducive to their growth. Indeed, it is interesting to note that Ireland has been a richer country than Greece, Spain and Portugal for many years and yet these countries have far greater numbers of foundations. An economic answer is, therefore, not the only response worth considering. It appears that our past of financial penury has probably had some influence as has the role of the Catholic Church in attracting to itself whatever potential or actual endowments were available. Ireland is now more secular and a presumption can be made that the Church may no longer be as popular a choice for endowing one's fortune. And yet, although there are now fortunes being made in Ireland, such wealth tends to be kept within families.[11] Moreover, voluntary organizations seem unsuccessful in targeting the 'new money' to support their purposes.

Government support of the nonprofit sector in Ireland is substantial, although it is significantly smaller for the voluntary and community sector. Indeed, the government's Green Paper proposed the establishment of community foundations as a future source of funding for the voluntary and community sector in Ireland.[12] There appears to be a lack of will or management ability, however, to make use of government subsidies; the government has given £1 million (IR) for the establishment of a community foundation, but to date it sits languishing in a bank while the individuals responsible for managing it cannot agree on how to move forward. Moreover, there have been suggestions that government support may diminish in future years because of the change in Ireland's status within the EU and a consequent reduction in EU funds, which have been beneficial to the voluntary sector.[13] Thus despite Ireland's increasing economic wealth, a concerted effort needs to be made to foster the establishment of foundations of any size; there is clearly some way to go.

Bibliography

CAFÉ, *The Irish Funding Handbook*, Dublin, Creative Activity for Everyone, 1994.

Central Statistics Office, *National Income and Expenditure 1997*, Dublin, CSO 1998.

Department of Social Welfare, *Supporting Voluntary Activity. A Green Paper on the Community and Voluntary Sector and its Relationship with the State*, Dublin, Stationery Office, 1997.

Donoghue, F., Anheier, H. K. and Salamon, L. M., *Uncovering the Non-profit Sector in Ireland*, Dublin, Policy Research Centre, Johns Hopkins University, 1999.

---

[11] Everett.

[12] Department of Social Welfare.

[13] See Everett. Since January 2000 Ireland comprises two administrative regions, one the Border Midland and Western Region which is still an Objective One area; the other is the Southern and Eastern Region which has been classified as Objective One in Transition.

Donoghue, F., 'Defining the Non-profit Sector: Ireland', *Working Paper of the Johns Hopkins Comparative Non-profit Sector Project*, No. 28, edited by Lester M. Salamon and Helmut K. Anheier, Baltimore, The Johns Hopkins Institute for Policy Studies, 1998.

Everett, J., *Community Foundations: An Introductory Report on International Experience and Irish Potential*, Dublin, Combat Poverty Agency, 1998.

Report of the Committee on Fundraising Activities for Charitable and Other Purposes, Dublin, Stationery Office, 1990.

Ruddle, H. and Donoghue, F., *The Organisation of Volunteering*, Dublin, Policy Research Centre, 1995.

Salamon, L. M., Anheier, H .K. and Associates, *The Emerging Sector Revisited*, Baltimore, The Johns Hopkins Institute for Policy Studies, 1998.

▼ Gian Paolo Barbetta and Marco Demarie

Italy

1 Introduction

In terms of foundation endowment, Italy may well appear among the five top-ranking countries. This is a decidedly surprising accomplishment for a country whose foundations, while boasting a robust ancient tradition, have suffered a complex variety of adversities for much of the 20th century.

Since the 1980s different types of foundation have appeared on the Italian scene, all akin in name yet rather heterogeneous in history, governance, culture, number and resources. Although a strong foundation culture embedded in a modern civil society is still in the making, the current situation is promising in several respects and a new age for foundations in Italian society may be in sight. The evolving legal and fiscal framework in Italy will of course affect the prospects for foundations in the future.

2 Historical background

A comprehensive history of Italian foundations remains to be written. It would be a history of continuity and fractures, of relevance and disregard, of similarity and anomaly and no distinctive interpretation of this history exists. It is possible, however, to describe something of the changes experienced by foundations, their legal status, social impact and reputation over the centuries.

The role of the Catholic Church in developing Italian philanthropic traditions cannot be underestimated. Canon law formulated the concept of 'body corporate', and a variety of church-related entities devoted to religious and/or humanitarian goals has existed on the Peninsula from medieval times to the present day. However, many examples of secular institutions provided with an endowment can also be traced. From the beginning these primordial foundations, often linked to local communities, were characterized by a decided disposition to run service activities which, *mutatis mutandis*, became a permanent feature of Italian foundations.[1] Centuries of *piae causae*, *opere pie*, *misericordie*, *Monti di Pietà*, *confraternite* were to follow.

The role of charitable institutions was first politically challenged by the absolutist state and the Enlightenment movement, following the French example. In the second half of the 19th century foundations were among the losers in the creation of a united Italian state (1861). This period saw the centralist and anti-clerical Napoleonic model adopted to organize the emerging modern state. Enlightenment-derived mistrust toward mortmain risks, and liberal political suspicion toward social bodies interposing themselves between the individual and the state, were trends that brought about the irrevocable decline, if not outright disappearance, of foundations in Italy.[2] Long-established charitable institutions were nationalized by law in several bursts of activity, while very few new foundations were created.

Socialist, liberal and later fascist political currents were similarly uninterested or blatantly hostile to foundations. Traces of such attitudes were present after World War II, and are still present in today's Italy. Although the Republican Constitution (1948) – a compromise between Catholic, socialist and liberal principles – guaranteed 'social bodies' as a vital component of the social fabric, foundations continued to play a marginal role in Italy until very recently. But the historical weakness of foundations is a prominent trait in Italy's charitable sector; scholars tend to agree that associations (mutual aid societies, voluntary organizations and later also cooperatives) rather than foundations are the expression of Italian charitable and civic-minded action.[3]

Although Italy was exposed to American culture after World War II, not much room was created for modern foundations. From the 1950s to the 1970s no more than a handful of significant foundations were created. These worked mainly in the welfare and health fields and were often religiously inspired, or in social sciences research, looking very much like an Italian version of American think-tanks. Not surprisingly, both types of foundation were definitely 'operating' in kind. Reflecting the sector's legacy of weakness, however, its activities did not emerge onto the public scene although many small foundations were established and older ones continued to exist.

---

[1] See Zaninelli.

[2] See Ristuccia.

[3] See Donati.

A turn-around occurred in the 1980s and especially the 1990s. Like many countries Italy experienced the grass-root social dynamism and the fiscal and legitimacy crisis of the welfare state at the same time. The newly rediscovered principle of self-organization created new opportunities for the third sector, including foundations. This occurred in view of the conspicuous growth rate of new private foundations, and also because the very concept of foundation was taken up by public authorities as a tool for implementing specific privatization policies or establishing new partnerships with private (profit and nonprofit) entities. One use of foundations was in restructuring and privatizing the public banking system.

The role of banks

In Italy a few public banks were originally established as joint stock companies while most enjoyed the legal status of 'savings banks' (*cassa di risparmio*) or 'public law banks' (*istituto di credito di diritto pubblico*). Most Italian savings banks were set up in the first half of the 19th century with start-up capital provided by rich and enlightened personalities, sometimes (especially in Northern Italy) supported by far-sighted government authorities. The savings banks were used to stimulate savings of the middle and working classes. Savings were not a requisite for the accumulation of capital or acted as a catalyst of industrialization, they were a 'provident' project.

To win support and reveal their reliability savings banks were established as nonprofit organizations subject to a nondistribution constraint. A large part of their profits was distributed in grants and the remainder accumulated in reserve funds. As these banks grew in number and influence, lending activities were extended from sound public or private nonprofit institutions to small corporations acting at the local level. The banks thus discovered a vocation for supporting local economic development initiatives.

Over the years, and especially during the fascist era, savings banks were submitted to public control and became part of the public sector. This 'nationalization' was enforced both because of the banks' public purpose and because banking itself was considered an activity of public interest. In 1990, all savings banks were controlled by government and still represented a strange hybrid of profit (banking) and nonprofit (charitable) activity, the latter rather underdeveloped and oriented toward 'marketing' purposes.

The nonprofit status of public banks seemed both anachronistic and restrictive when new capital was needed in order to comply with EU directives on banking (89/199 and 89/647). The entrepreneurial nature of banking, and the idea that economic development can be better pursued through efficient banking than charitable activity, were both gaining ground. Moreover, it became necessary to regulate competition between private banks (that had to pay dividends to shareholders) and public ones.

Law 218/1990 allowed savings banks (incorporated as foundations or associations) to change their legal status. Thanks to substantial fiscal incentives, they could break up their banking activities and contribute to new joint stock companies. Consequently the old nonprofit banking institutions broke into two parts: a new for-profit bank (established as a joint stock company) able to compete on an equal footing with other private banks; and a nonprofit foundation (the majority shareholder of the new banks) concentrating on charitable, social and welfare activities. The shares of the new bank represent the endowment of the old foundations while the dividends received constitute the income used to pursue the philanthropic goals.

At first, the legal transformation and the more controversial privatization of the banks constituted quite distinct targets. The law did not allow the foundations to relinquish control of their banks, unless control remained within the public sector. Therefore, 'foundations of banking origin' were initially perceived as financial holding companies rather than charitable institutions, notwithstanding their grant-making activities. This decision was subsequently reversed. In 1993 the government declared it illegal for one person to work as an administrator both of a foundation and the bank it owned. In 1994 a new law freed the foundations from the burden of maintaining a majority share in the banks, while a law passed in June 1999[4] forced the foundations to sell their shares of the banks, although only over a six-year period and with some loopholes. Consequently, banking foundations will become private sector institutions, forced to diversify their financial portfolios and to concentrate on charitable activities.

This recent change in law was driven more by the desire to put public banks in private hands than to create a strong sector of philanthropic foundations. Similarly, a large sector of private nonprofit institutions will be created as a result of public regulation rather then private benevolence. Foundations have already been used to transform the legal nature and the workings of a wide range of organizations, from opera theatres to local welfare institutions nationalized long ago. Some of these may prove useful models for other public bodies in the future.

---

[4] d. lgs. 153/1999.

3 Legal issues

Provisions concerning foundations are rather numerous in the Italian legal and fiscal framework.[5] Of greatest relevance is the First Book (*Libro Primo*) of the Civil Code (*Codice Civile*, 1942) which contains a section on nonprofit bodies and describes the essentials of a foundation as a legal body.

A foundation is defined as a private nonprofit organization, established as a contract between living founders or through a testament, and provided with an endowment. The endowment must be used to pursue the foundation's goals as specified in its charter and cannot by any means be re-appropriated by the founders. Common good purpose is not expressly referred to by the Code as a binding foundation feature, but is taken for granted and considered inherent in the very nature of foundations. Together, the endowment and the charter are the foundation's essentials. The endowment also differentiates the foundation from the other main form of nonprofit organization, the association.

The creation of a foundation is carried out through a notarial deed. However, to attain the legal status of a corporate body (*personalità giuridica privata*) giving foundation administrators limited liability and granting fiscal advantages, a discretionary and formal decision by the state administration is required. The state assesses the features of the foundation, particularly whether its endowment or prospective income will be sufficient to fulfil the aims stated in its charter. There is no minimum figure as far as the endowment is concerned, but the relevant offices (at the ministry or regional levels) may set different minimum amounts; the highest minimum amount generally required by the ministries is about €100,000.

The governing body of a foundation is called the board (*consiglio di amministrazione*), whose internal functioning rules are stated in the charter. But foundations are subject to state surveillance even after becoming legal persons. The government must evaluate and authorize any proposals to change a foundation charter, and may inspect and intervene in the foundation's life and activities in case of misconduct or ineffectiveness. One way is by requiring foundations to submit financial and activity reports annually. While this controlling power

---

[5] This legal framework, together with minor provisions, applies to the most numerous 'common' or 'Civil Code' foundations. Special laws may apply to other types of foundations or quasi-foundations. As far as foundation of banking origin are concerned, e.g. the Civil Code provisions are integrated by special laws and regulations.

is rather wide and even invasive in theory, it is generally consigned to the status of a mere formality if not to outright neglect.[6] Similarly, a foundation can also be terminated by the state if it fails to pursue its goals, but this rarely occurs. More commonly foundations are dissolved for reasons explicitly specified in the charter, or when the foundation's goal has been accomplished or has become impossible to attain. Foundation funds may then be transferred to other bodies or appropriated by the state and transferred to bodies with aims similar to those of the original foundation.

The relative looseness and flexibility of the Civil Code has permitted some degree of innovation, for example allowing the implementation of the first Italian community foundations and the recently conceived *fondazioni di partecipazione* (which combine characteristics of foundations and associations to facilitate private-public cooperation, particularly in cultural activities and heritage management). This has been important for a country afflicted by excessive law-making. However, over the years many proposals have been put forward to modernize the system and reform Civil Code provisions concerning foundations. Generally they have aimed to limit the discretionary power of the administration, cut bureaucratic delays and provide the legal concept of foundation with a new general set of rules enhancing transparency, effectiveness and accountability. Although few substantial steps forward have been taken so far, several measures were recently introduced to speed up incorporation and approval of charter changes, and in 1997 the state's right to hold authority over foundation real-estate purchases was abolished.[7]

As to their fiscal treatment, foundations do not enjoy a particularly beneficial position as nonprofit organizations. Italian fiscal law is known for its intricacy; provisions relevant to foundations do not escape this reputation. Moreover, in general, the Italian system neither appreciates nor substantially encourages philanthropy through its fiscal framework. It was only in 1997 that a set of measures was passed in order to favour and promote, from a fiscal and administrative point of view, nonprofit organizations concerned with the socially disadvantaged and the needy (*Organizzazioni non lucrative di utilità sociale, Onlus*).

---

[6] This could change rather soon. Parliament is currently considering the establishment of an independent authority appointed by the government to inspect and apply sanctions to the nonprofit sector.

[7] See Barbetta.

Italian fiscal law provides some advantages for non-commercial activities and non-commercial bodies; commercial activity is however allowed if it does not dominate an organization's work. Foundations active in deserving areas such as education and welfare enjoy income tax reductions. But grants made to foundations are not considered part of the foundation's taxable income and they must pay VAT on purchases. For donors there is no particularly favourable treatment; only a limited share of any donation is deductible from the donor's taxable income, with different rules for individuals or corporate bodies. Further steps toward a more generous and liberal fiscal setting are expected, but may be hindered by the currently difficult condition of the Italian state budget.

4 A profile of foundations in Italy

Information on Italian foundations is pitifully poor.[8] Foundations are not included as such in general socio-economic statistics, no comprehensive public record of their assets and activities is available, and administrative sources are scarce. Most of what is known about foundations originates from field research.[9]

A reasonable estimate of the number of existing active foundations is in the region of 1200 to 1500. However the Italian foundation world is quite heterogeneous, and the figure becomes higher (a very tentative 2000 to 2500) when privatized IPABs (*istituzioni pubbliche di assistenze e benevolenza*) are included. Italy's foundation world is even larger if we include the recent transformation of public cultural institutions into private nonprofit foundations, as well as 'foundations of banking origin' which we know more about in terms of net assets and activities than numbers. These new types of foundations largely explain the lively pace of foundation creation which in the 1990s was almost half the total of foundations ever established in Italy.

The various types of foundations in Italy pursue their activities as either operating or grant-making organizations, both of which have various levels of financial independence (Table 1.27).

---

[8] An ambitious survey by Istat (Italian central statistical office) launched in 1999 may fill this gap.

[9] If not otherwise specified, the following tables are drawn from the data-set on Italian foundations built up by the *Centro di Documentazione sulle Fondazioni*, Turin.

Table 1.27 Types of Italian foundation, by mode of operation and financial independence

Financial independence	Mode:	
	Operating	Grant making[10]
Endowed	• A few private foundations • Ex-IPAB foundations	• Foundations of banking origin
Not fully endowed	• The bulk of Italian private foundations • Opera House foundations • Ex-IPAB foundations	• Private fundraising foundations • (exceptional) Community foundations

Two features of the Italian foundation world clearly emerge: the dynamism of 'private' foundations established under the Civil Code for private reasons, mainly philanthropic; and the growth of new types of organizations closely related to foundations as a legal tool for public-private cooperation (or cooperation between different public bodies) or as a way of privatizing public sector-controlled activities. In many cases the distinction between the two types is blurred.

Civil Code foundations

Italy possesses a handful of institutions of excellence, specializing as operating foundations and working in specific fields such as social research, medical research, health and welfare. There is also a large number of small foundations, some committed to traditional charitable purposes, others addressing new social demands in a more innovative way. The latter tend to be young, often created by committed individuals, interest groups or public bodies.

The scope of foundation activities is very wide. Focus tends to be on education, social services and research, but heritage and the arts are also fairly well represented (see Table 1.28).

One of the distinctive features of Italian foundations is the typically small size of their assets. Their endowments tend to be small, and financially rather frail. Almost 90% of foundations declare endowments of less than €5 million (see Table 1.29). With some notable exceptions,

---

[10] Notice: Foundations of banking origin, Opera House foundations, Ex-IPAB foundations are private entities yet created or transformed by special Acts. Foundations termed 'private' plus community foundations are created in the framework of the Civil Code: public bodies may be among the founders.

Table 1.28 Percentage distribution of foundations by fields of activity

Social service	22.9
Training and education	22.4
Cultural heritage and the arts	19.9
Research in the field of humanities and social sciences	10.9
Health and medical research	8.3
Community activities	5.0
Religion and ethics	4.0
Research in the field of hard sciences	3.3
Prize awarding	2.0
International co-operation	1.3
	100.0

Source: Non-stochastic sample of 949 cases (1997–8)[11]

revenues derived from endowments are by no means enough to support activities, particularly considering the low level of present day gross market returns.[12] Paradoxically enough, grant seeking is more common than grant making among Italian Civil Code foundations. They rely heavily on income derived from commercial or quasi commercial activities as well as *ad hoc* contributions or contracts, mainly from and with local authorities.

Table 1.29 Percentage distribution of Civil Code foundations by endowment size

€0 – €100,000	22
> €100,000 < €500,000	30
> €500,000 <= €5 million	36
> €5 million <= €25 million	11
> €25 million	2
	100

Source: Non-stochastic sample of 458 cases (1997–8)

[11] As in the following tables, the sample refers to the database of the Centro di Documentazione sulle Fondazioni at the Fondazione Giovanni Agnelli, Turin. Figures derive from individual data obtained through mail questionnaires directly from foundations.

[12] Somewhat amazingly, endowment is the first source of income for financially micro-foundations with very limited missions, e.g. for tiny primary or secondary school prize-awarding foundations.

Another major peculiarity of Italian foundations is that they predominantly act as operating foundations; they provide services and goods rather than make grants. This characteristic is not necessarily negative, however one consequence is that independent, philanthropic grant-making activity on a large scale (according to American standards) has been almost non-existent in Italy. This has significant effects on the development of a vital and innovative nonprofit sector.

Table 1.30 Mode of foundation activity (% values)

Grant-making foundations	5.3
Fellowship and scholarship grant-awarding foundations	10.0
Operating foundations	38.8
Mixed foundations	43.1
– mostly operating	33.3
– mostly grant-making	9.8
Unspecified	2.8
	100.0

Source: Non stochastic sample of 536 cases (1996)

The operating character of Italian foundations is not unusual in Europe. However, Italian foundations' operating character and small endowment size may be, along with other factors, a reflection of the limited number of legal tools available for the creation of nonprofit organizations, and the relatively low minimum capital requirement for a foundation to be granted legal personality. These conditions may have encouraged many 'social entrepreneurs' to choose the foundation form as a means to establish what elsewhere would be simply recorded as a 'nonprofit-organization' with no further similarity to a foundation proper. Whilst the association form requires some kind of internal democratic governance, the foundation structure allows for more managerial, business-like conduct. Additionally, a foundation is commonly perceived as durable and capable of commanding public confidence, therefore attracting private and public generosity. This opportunistic though by no means unlawful use of the foundation form may also partially explain the high rate of creation of Italian foundations in recent years.

Among 'Civil Code' foundations are IPABs (*istituzioni pubbliche di assistenza e benevolenza*). These were originally charitable institutions of mainly religious origin, some very old. They provided health, welfare, educational and vocational services. Following the unification of Italy (1861) these institutions have been through different waves of nationalization, enjoying a peculiar and hybrid status. In fact, although public in law, they enjoyed a significant degree of autonomy. This autonomy decreased in 1977 when the IPABs were placed under the control of local authorities. In 1988, a decision by the Constitutional Court allowed them to reclaim their original status as private charities. In the second half of the 1990s the privatization of IPABs gained momentum; more than 1000 IPABs, generally provided with an endowment, were formally transformed into private nonprofit bodies, mainly foundations.[13]

Foundations as a tool for privatizing public bodies

Banking

Foundations have also been used to privatize the Italian banking sector. 'Foundations of banking origin', or 'banking foundations', are a by-product of this transformation, initiated by law 218/1990. By the end of the 1980s a very high number of public banks existed in Italy; representing about 65% of all deposits of the Italian banking system in 1988. Compared to average Italian foundations, foundations of banking origin are very well endowed. The total net assets of the about 90 banking foundations amounts to about ITL50,000 billion (about €25 billion). Less conservative estimates put total net assets in the range of ITL120,000–150,000 billion (about €60–75 billion). These assets are concentrated in just a few foundations: three (3.5% all foundations) have individual assets greater than ITL5,000 billion (about €2.5 billion), accounting for about 45% of total net assets. A large number of small institutions (49 foundations or about 57%) with individual endowments of less then ITL200 billion (about €100 million) account for only 9% of total net assets.

Foundations of banking origin are concentrated in northern Italy. Over half (53% of the foundations, holding 66% of the total assets) are located in this region. Banking foundations in central Italy are relatively limited in number and small in size, and almost absent in southern Italy. This geographic concentration is quite significant considering the great needs of southern Italy, given the tendency for foundations to fund organizations and causes located in their areas.

Notwithstanding their large assets, banking foundations have distributed quite limited amounts in grants over the recent past (Table 1.31). This may be explained by two different causes: the low performance

---

[13] Ranci e Costa.

of the banks' assets on the stock market, and the conservative behaviour of bank managers to hold earnings in reserve funds.

Table 1.31 Income of 'foundations of banking origin', by most common income destination (€million)

Income destinations:	1993	1994	1995	1996	1997
Reserve funds	167	177	133	121	102
Internal costs	33	28	35	45	56
Grants made	120	122	142	198	304
Total income	**328**	**357**	**374**	**429**	**548**

Source: A.C.R.I., 1996, p.122; 1997, p. 164; 1998, p.181; 1999, p. 82.

Banking foundation endowments could generate large incomes to be spent on charitable activities. A rough estimate is that €1.5 billion could be devoted every year to nonprofit and public organizations acting in the fields of culture, health, social services, the arts etc. It is therefore interesting to consider who receives these grants. The single largest sector is art and culture, followed by social services, and education (Table 1.32).

Table 1.32 Percentage distribution of grants from foundations of banking origin, by field of activity

Sector:	1993	1994	1995	1996	1997
Art, culture and recreation	30	31	31	35	36
Education and research	20	19	20	20	19
Health	16	17	10	10	11
Social services	26	26	26	26	25
Environment	1	–	–	1	1
Development and housing	4	3	8	5	5
Other	3	4	5	3	3

Source: A.C.R.I., 1996, p. 153 154; 1997, p. 108; 1998, p.100 and 1999, p. 106.

Italian banking foundations show a strong preference for financing the purchase of capital goods, the construction and restoration of buildings and the conservation or restoration of art (Table 1.33); more than 50% of funds granted were for these purposes. Moreover, over the last five years, on average a good 25% of funds granted were for 'running costs' of organizations.

Table 1.33 Purpose of grants made by foundations of banking origin (% values)

Purpose of grants	1993	1994	1995	1996	1997
Purchase of capital goods	23	24	15	15	14
Construction and restoration of buildings	22	15	19	16	15
Conservation and restoration of works of art	15	16	14	16	13
General operating support	21	22	31	23	26
Cultural, scientific and sporting events	11	9	9	9	9
Research projects	5	5	3	3	4
Other	3	9	9	18	19

Source: A.C.R.I., 1996, p. 156; 1998, p. 107, and 1999, p. 114.

The opera/theatre model

Most recently, another use of foundations has occurred through law decree 367, involving the privatization of public bodies. Since the decree was passed in 1996, Italy's biggest opera houses and other 'concert institutions' in the public sector have transformed into private nonprofit foundations. In the long term this legal transformation aims to reduce the financial burden which these cultural institutions place on the state; while boasting an international reputation, many (such as the 'La Scala' in Milan) have turned in a poor economic performance. The new law therefore treats opera as an economic activity and encourages private entrepreneurs and institutions to fund it, aided by 'matching grants' from the state. The new private foundations are subject to many public controls as well as certain restrictions when formulating their charters. But they enjoy many advantages, fiscal and other. They are entitled to annual public funding (by the national Fund for the Arts), while donations aimed at endowment building are tax exempt and donors benefit from much larger tax deductions than usual.

5 Current trends and conclusion

It is obvious that the world of Italian foundations has started to change only in the last 10 to 15 years – but it has done so dramatically. Before the war years foundations were by no means non-existent but mainly consisted of charitable institutions with very limited, if any, social impact and visibility. There have been a handful of exceptions to this rule, especially since the late 1960s, though one could say that in the eyes of the general public these organizations – either welfare, heritage or research institutions – were exclusively relevant to their specific mission; their foundation status was hardly perceived as a distinguishing characterization of mission and purpose.

In the last decade the foundation world has become quite complex. Three trends are particularly evident.

1 The proliferation of small and medium-size operating foundations, generally insufficiently endowed, acting almost like nonprofit organizations in a variety of social and cultural fields.
2 The entry of a number of wealthy grant-making foundations as the outcome of a rather tortuous process of privatization of the formerly state-controlled banking system.
3 The assumption among public decision-makers that foundations can be a convenient tool for privatizing existing bodies or running and funding social and cultural activities, taking advantage of both civil law and the cooperation with private partners.

Of these three trends, the emergence of strongly endowed bodies specializing in grant making, before practically non-existent, could be singled out as the most salient.

However, the need to rethink the role of banking foundations is evident if the nonprofit sector is to benefit from their large assets. In addition to improving their grant-making skills, developing strategies of intervention and building up their role in society and public policies, Italian foundations establish more independence from public authorities. Many local administrations that appoint board members of banking foundations perceive these institutions as their own reserve of free cash. Consequently, foundations tend to adhere passively to the strategies, desires and orders of local administrations without developing their own vision of the 'public good'. As they replicate (or simply fund) public intervention, these foundations don't 'make a difference' in any field.

Banking foundations should also re-assess their role in financial markets and in the market for corporate control. Given the size of their endowment and the limited number of institutional financial investors active in Italy, many foundations play a crucial role in controlling some of the largest financial institutions of the country. Moreover, the investment strategies of many foundations are not driven simply by the principle of financial diversification, but rather by a relevant interest in influencing control of some corporations. This could prove to be a temptation difficult to avoid, with lamentable effects on the functioning of the Italian stock market. Similarly, foundations' priority-setting process, effectiveness as grant makers, and the social perception of their role might be badly affected.

The use of foundations described in the opera/theatre model above is also rather promising. However, it is too early to say whether this transformation will be successful and the new foundations will be able to survive, or to maintain the high level of their artistic productions with reduced public funding. Nonetheless, it is quite likely that in the future the model of the opera theatres will be followed for the privatization of other public bodies in the fields of culture, education, health and social services.

We may be witnessing the birth of a significant Italian foundation sector, but the scene is still blurred. It is unclear whether new operating foundations will survive medium-term mission and management challenges, and whether their establishment rate will stay high. The mutation of privatized bodies into independent and professional foundations will certainly take time, and may not be a linear process.

The formation of a foundation culture within Italian society will be a crucial condition for the sector to emerge and thrive. Much pragmatism, experimentation, cooperation and accountability will be needed within and among foundations. The spread of a political culture more sympathetic to social subsidiarity and more liberal legal and fiscal provision for private philanthropy would also be beneficial. Hopefully, current trends do foreshadow the formation of a multifarious foundation community, in which various groups or even individual foundations specialize in specific functions, yet are capable of talking to each other and to society at large.

Bibliography

A.C.R.I., *Primo rapporto sulle fondazioni bancarie*, Acri, Roma, 1996.

A.C.R.I., *Secondo rapporto sulle fondazioni bancarie*, Acri, Roma, 1997.

A.C.R.I., *Terzo rapporto sulle fondazioni bancarie*, Acri, Roma, 1998.

A.C.R.I., *Quarto rapporto sulle fondazioni bancarie*, Acri, Roma, 1999.

Barbetta G. P., 'Foundations in Italy', in: H. K. Anheier and S. Toepler (eds), *Private Funds, Public Purpose*, Kluwer, New York, 1999.

Donati P.P. ed., *La società civile in Italia*, Mondadori, Milano, 1997.

Fondazione G. Agnelli, *Per conoscere le fondazioni*, Edizioni Fondazioni G. Agnelli, Torino, 1997.

Galgano F., *Le associazioni, le fondazioni, i comitati*, Cedam, Padova, 1996.

Hansmann H., 'The economic role of commercial nonprofits: the evolution of the savings bank industry', in: H. Anheier and W. Seibel (eds), *The third sector: comparative studies of non-profit organisations*, de Gruyter, 1990.

Ranci C. and Costa G., Dimensioni e caratteristiche delle IPAB. Un quadro nazionale, mimeo, 1999.

Ristuccia S., *Volontariato e Fondazioni*, Maggioli Editore, Rimini, 1996.

Zaninelli S., 'Gli sviluppi storici', in: Gian Paolo Barbetta (ed.), *Senza scopo di lucro*, Bologna, Il Mulino, 1996.

▼ Markus H. Wanger

Liechtenstein

1 Introduction

Introduced in 1926 by the Persons and Companies Act, foundations have since become a significant factor in Liechtenstein's growing wealth: to date more than 40,000 foundations have been founded and these hold a large proportion of the CHF90 billion (€56 billion) administered by Liechtenstein banks. Up to CHF1 billion is held by charitable foundations and a much higher amount by non-charitable foundations.

Liechtenstein judges and lawyers are experienced in foundation matters, and Liechtenstein's Foundation Law has proven successful enough to serve as a model for Austria's 1992 *Privatrechtsstiftung*. Yet, as in many other countries, Liechtenstein has no precise legal definition of a foundation. However, its foundations possess many of the characteristics of foundations defined in Anheier: Foundations in Europe: a Comparative Perspective; they are established by one or more founders with the intention, formulated in a deed, to form a legal entity for a certain period of time in order to implement a certain purpose, by donating assets and providing an appropriate organization.

Perhaps the greatest difference between this definition and the one offered by Anheier is that foundations in Liechtenstein are not required to serve a public purpose. This may help account for the huge number of foundations in Liechtenstein, and also their wide range of types: public law foundations, ecclesiastical foundations, pure family foundations, mixed family foundations, company foundations, staff welfare foundations and charitable foundations. Most of Liechtenstein's 40,000 foundations are family or mixed family foundations, and only some 600 are declared charitable foundations in law.

Liechtenstein foundations are used both by foreigners and Liechtenstein citizens to devote assets to charitable purposes including holding art collections, caring for ill or disabled persons, skipping generations when distributing assets, or having assets administered by independent members of the foundation's council. The government's positive attitude toward charitable foundations is strengthening, with a new act possibly on the way which may enhance their economic and social position.

2 Historical background

The origin of foundations in Liechtenstein goes back to Roman law, Byzantine law and canon law, which was later overlaid by two German legal institutes. One, the *Fideikomiss*, referred to assets of feudal families held in trust by its head for the benefit of its present and future members. The *Fideikomiss*, restricted to the nobility, was abolished in Germany and Austria following World War I, and was formally replaced by foundations in the 1920s. The foundation became a proper legal entity able to hold estates. Like a corporation it was administered by a board, usually called a foundation council, but unlike corporations it had neither legal owners nor beneficial owners – only beneficiaries with no rights to the foundation.

Liechtenstein followed the Swiss example when setting up its regulations on foundations in 1926. The Persons and Companies Act introduces the notion of a trust which is further expanded in the Trust Enterprise Act of 1928. Supported by these laws, foundations over the last 70 years have primarily been vehicles for asset protection, estate and tax planning.

3 Legal issues

Legal character

In Liechtenstein, the foundation itself is not legally defined. However it is characterized by five main attributes: it is established at the intention of a donor, it has donated assets and an organizational structure, and is a private (institutionally separate from government) and self-governing entity. Foundations are not necessarily nonprofit distributing or serving a public purpose. Liechtenstein foundations can therefore be defined as self-governing legal persons established by a natural or legal (private, public or ecclesiastical) person with a permanent endowment for a specific purpose laid down in a deed filed with the public register. Purposes may be charitable, ecclesiastical, family or enterprise oriented, in any combination.

In Liechtenstein as in other German speaking countries, charitable and non-charitable status is a matter not of the relevant foundation law, but of tax law categories. Charitable foundations must be entered in the public register and supervised by government. They are subject to provisions in the Liechtenstein Persons and Companies Act (*Liechtensteinisches Personen- und Gesellschaftsrecht*) abbreviated as PGR.[1]

Establishment procedures

No government approval is required to establish a foundation, and any number of persons may establish a foundation. However, establishing a charitable foundation requires a minimum capital of CHF 30,000. Foundations must be entered in the public register ('registered foundation') with basic information regarding, for example, foundation purpose and board members. These details are announced on the notice board of the Liechtenstein Country Court (*Liechtensteinisches Landgericht*). Charitable foundations established in a last will must be registered after the death of the founder, and in the case of an inheritance contract, after the death of one of the founders if not otherwise provided therein.[2]

Foundation statutes must contain provisions on the domicile, purpose, minimum capital, administration appointment and removal procedures, procedures for disposal of assets in the event of dissolution, and for the appointment and removal of an audit body. Usually by-laws and/or internal regulations are also issued but not filed with the public register, which regulates details of foundation administration and benefaction.[3] Foundation book-keeping and auditing rules are the same as for commercial entities.

Taxation and cross-border giving

Given the large number of foreign foundations in Liechtenstein, tax issues are of particular importance. The Liechtenstein Inland Revenue has authority[4] to decide, at its discretion, on part or full exemption from taxation for private charitable organizations, in particular foundations. The charitable purpose is irrevocably laid down;

---

[1] In particular arts. 106–245 (general provisions) and 552–570 (foundations) with further reference to arts. 534–551 (establishments) and art. 932 a (trust enterprises).

[2] Art. 557 cl. 4 PGR.

[3] Arts. 552, 932 a PGR / § 10 Trust Enterprise Act, *Treuunternehmens-Gesetz*, abbreviated as *TrUG*.

[4] Pursuant Art. 32 para 1 lit. e Tax Act *Steuergesetz*, abbreviated as SteG.

any changes to it must be filed with Inland Revenue and the public register. Charitable organizations may only undergo change of legal status if charitable purposes are not altered.

The material requirement is that such an exemption is enjoyed if charitable purposes are pursued exclusively.[5] Purposes considered charitable are social (e.g. caring for the poor and the sick), religious (i.e. those of publicly recognized religions), academic and educational activities. Political and lobbying activities are excluded. Activities with relatively small distributions to charitable organizations will not be accepted. The charitable purpose must also be nonprofit oriented. A charitable organization must provide evidence of the charitable use of its assets by annually submitting its audited accounts to the Inland Revenue. Exemption from taxation can be revoked at any time if the use of foundation assets is not in compliance with charitable purposes or if assets are managed with very few distributions to charitable institutions.[6]

There are no general restrictions on the extent to which a foundation may conduct charitable activities and transfer assets for charitable purposes outside the country. To the extent that a foundation conducts activities or transfers assets (for charitable purposes) abroad and is in principle accepted by the Inland Revenue, its privileged tax treatment and that of its donors will not be affected, nor are there different reporting requirements.

Gifts (i.e. grants) by foundations to any third party (individual or organization) are subject to taxation if third parties do not themselves qualify for a tax exempt status. Tax deduction for individual or corporate donors, including foundations, only arises for gifts made to officially specified charities in Liechtenstein and Switzerland.[7] Donations from income, capital gains or bequests arising within Liechtenstein jurisdiction are subject to the tax laws of the country of the charities to which donations are made. Donors themselves may apply for a tax reduction, but the Inland Revenue might be reluctant to grant it when the donation is not directly made to such charities. The same tax regime applies to foreign charitable foundations conducting activities in Liechtenstein.

---

[5] Also pursuant Art. 32 para 1 lit. e *SteG*.

[6] Art. 32 para 1 lit. e *SteG*.

[7] These listed charities are not subject to the double tax treaties with Austria and the neighbouring Swiss Canton of St. Gallen, but rather to reciprocal administration rules and practice. Donations to any other charities, including those in Austria, are subject to double tax treaties that do not cover the tax treatment of donations to charities.

Supervision

The Liechtenstein government has authority to oversee charitable foundations but not ecclesiastical, family and mixed purpose foundations, or foundations with defined beneficiaries. The authority of the Inland Revenue to revoke tax exempt status constitutes another form of state supervision of foundations.

4 A profile of foundations in Liechtenstein

In Liechtenstein more than 40,000 foundations are registered in a country of about 30,000 inhabitants. Liechtenstein has a very wide range of basic types of foundations, however there are no statistics about their relative proportions. It is evident that the vast majority – at least 30,000 – are family or mixed family foundations. Some 600 foundations have declared themselves charitable/nonprofit foundations, and about 200 of these have been accepted as such by the Inland Revenue.

- **Pure family foundations**

  A pure family foundation is understood as one whose assets must continuously be used for the purpose of paying the costs of education and training, outfitting or support of members of one or more specified families or for similar purposes.[8] Most Liechtenstein professionals, trustees and industrialists have their own family foundation.

- **A mixed family foundation**

  This is understood as a family foundation whose assets should additionally serve other purposes, that is ecclesiastic, charitable. Often these foundations support people in need or preserve objects of cultural importance. There are more than 35,000 pure and mixed family foundations registered or deposited in Liechtenstein. A significant amount of the CHF90 billion assets administered by Liechtenstein banks are said to be deposited by Liechtenstein Foundations.[9]

- **Charitable foundations**

  Charitable foundations serve the welfare of the poor and the sick or the furtherance of faith, science, education or other nonprofit making or social purposes.[10] The 200 recognized charitable foundations

---

[8] Art. 553 Section 2 *PGR*.

[9] According to Liechtenstein bank statistic by December 31, 1998.

[10] Art. 32 Section 1 lit. e Tax Law.

in Liechtenstein administer assets of about CHF1 billion (€620 million). They tend to focus on art and culture,[11] education,[12] economic development,[13] politics and law[14] and health care.[15]

- **Ecclesiastical foundations**
  Liechtenstein law defines ecclesiastical foundations as those formed for ecclesiastical purposes.[16] The law does not define ecclesiastical purposes but the term is interpreted widely to include care of the sick, furtherance of faith, instructional or other benevolent purposes. The constitution itself guarantees religious communities the ownership and all other economic rights concerning foundations established for religious, educational and charitable purposes.[17]

- **Public law foundations**
  Although the law on foundations in Liechtenstein governs only private law foundations, public law foundations also exist. Foundations formed under public law have various features of public law, such as incorporation in the system of public administration and the performance of public tasks, and their foundation councils are appointed by the government or parliament. They are also subject to special regulations on their formation, amendment of statutes, dissolution and application of assets after dissolution, following the provisions of the relevant act under which the foundation is established. The government traditionally uses public law foundations in order to provide public services, particularly art and culture, with more professional expertise and less party political involvement. Such foundations include the Liechtenstein National Library, the Liechtenstein State Art Collection and the Liechtenstein National Museum.

- **Company foundations**
  A foundation associated with a commercial enterprise is defined as a company foundation. Such foundations may only pursue a com-

---

[11] VPBank / Kunststiftung; Lampadia Stiftung; Ars Rhenia Stiftung zur überregionalen Förderung von Kunst und Kultur; Wanger Kunst & Kultur Stiftung.

[12] Dr Legerlotz Stiftung.

[13] LGT Innovationsstiftung.

[14] Peter-Kaiser-Stiftung, Stiftung für Internationale Staatswissenschaften.

[15] Aidshilfe Liechtenstein; Alter- und Pflegeheime; Caritas; Familienhilfe; Frauenhaus Liechtenstein; HPZ, Heilpädagogisches Zentrum; Krebsliga Liechtenstein.

[16] Art. 553 Section 1 PGR.

[17] Art. 38 Constitution.

mercial trade that serves the pursuit of a nonprofit purpose, or if the nature and extent of holdings require a commercial operation.[18] Foundations that do not themselves pursue a commercial activity but hold shares in a company are also designated as company foundations.

- **Staff welfare foundations**
  A staff welfare foundation is formed when an employer makes payments for staff welfare or when employees contribute to super-annuation or health, accident, life, invalidity or whole life insurance.[19] There are about 50 registered staff welfare foundations which administer about CHF1.8 billion (€1.1 billion).

More detailed figures about the size of foundations, their activities and geographical distribution are not publicly available. Most foundations are represented by lawyers and professional trustees and are therefore subject to professional secrecy according to Liechtenstein law.

5 Current trends and conclusion

The government's general approach towards foundations has always been positive and continues to be so today. Because Liechtenstein foundations are not obliged to serve a public purpose, they have also become a tool for a mixture of private and charitable purposes. Government's attitude towards foundations and especially charitable foundations gives the donor security and fulfilment of his will. With more than 40,000 registered foundations already, and a wide variety of types of foundations, Liechtenstein is a leading foundation centre in Europe.

Currently, the government is planning to improve the supervision of foundations and to promote Liechtenstein as the seat of charitable foundations. A new Act on Charitable Foundations, which aims to improve the status of charitable foundations and their contributions to civil society, is under discussion.

---

[18] Art. 552 Section 1 PGR.

[19] The law has defined these staff welfare foundations in the (§ 1173 a Art. 37 ff, *Allgemeines Bürgerliches* Gesetzbuch, General Civil Code.

▼ Alex Bonn and Alex Schmitt

Luxembourg

1 Introduction

Foundations have never been a subject of public debate in Luxembourg, and little data on them exists. Their development and legal status have been shaped by the legal traditions and foundation development in neighbouring countries. The influence of French and Belgian law underlying state and public attitudes toward foundations may in part explain the stunted growth of Luxembourg's foundation sector. In 1999 fewer than 150 legally recognized foundations existed in Luxembourg.

The evolution of foundations (*fondations*) continues to be marked by this tension, making the future of the foundation sector in Luxembourg still somewhat uncertain. On the one hand encouraging trends have taken place, particularly the new foundation law of 1994. New types of foundations have been created which diversify the sector, mainly in the areas of culture and recreation, indicating a changing public attitude and interest in foundations. Government is supporting the creation of new foundations, and establishes foundations on its own.[1] On the other hand, more recent draft laws not only seek to enhance the importance of foundations in Luxembourg, but also to increase state control.

2 Historical background[2]

Little is known about foundations in Luxembourg prior to the independence of the Grand Duchy of the Luxembourg State in 1839. With the exception of some historical records, according to which

---

[1] E.g. the *Fondation Musée d'Art Moderne Grand-Duc Jean*, a contemporary art museum.

[2] Much of this section is inspired by Nicolas Majerus' authoritative work, *Les associations sans but lucratif et les établissments d'utilité publique au Grand-Duche de Luxembourg*, Luxembourg, 1930.

John of Luxembourg made donations to the Church for the establishment of cloisters, there is far too little information available to determine when the first foundations appeared. But it is clear that until 1928 there was no legal framework specifically for nonprofit associations or foundations. The state was the only entity with the authority to create nonprofit (mostly charitable) organizations with a designated legal personality. Under this arrangement individuals could make donations *inter vivos* or by testament to such entities only with special ducal decree.

These restrictions on foundations are in part due to popular opinion of the time, reflecting the basis of Luxembourg law in the French legal tradition. First, it was believed that everything given for public utility was a gift to the state which was 'by nature' competent to accept these gifts. Second was the fear of the *main-morte* inherited from the Napoleonic Code; it was felt that foundations might hamper economic development since their assets were in some way withdrawn from the economy (especially their initial endowment) and therefore no longer circulating between different economic agents. Third, on a more philosophical level, was the opinion that according to natural law a man could dispose of his property only during his lifetime. As the establishment of foundations often occurs beyond man's lifetime through last will or testament, foundations were thought to be against natural law.

However, *de facto* foundations and associations did exist, some with far-reaching goals and significant assets. But the absence of legal personality made it very difficult for such entities to operate efficiently. For example, these entities could not own property in their own name. It was therefore necessary to manage these organizations through intermediaries, creating problems such as joint ownership.

As some of these entities became increasingly important, they were granted legal personalities by legislators intervening on a case by case basis.[3] But this procedure was inconsistent and time consuming. Moreover it appeared increasingly unnecessary, as neighbouring countries demonstrated by passing workable foundation legislation. Thus in the 1920s politicians requested similar measures be taken in Luxembourg.[4] In 1928 a law on nonprofit associations and public utility establishments (*'Loi sur les associations sans but lucratif et les*

---

[3] I.e. the Pescatore Foundation recognized in 1963, *Fondation Cuvelier Wurth, Fondation Edemée Tesch, veuve Emile Metz.*

[4] *Séance de la Chambre des Deputés du 30 avril 1914*, C.R. 1914, p. 2392.

établissements d'utilité publique') was passed, drawing heavily from a 1921 Belgian law relating to foundations. The 'public utility establishment' as defined in that law is the basis of what are today referred to as foundations.[5]

The new legislation was a landmark for foundations; it enabled any individual to establish legally independent public utility establishments (*établissements d'utilité publique* – EUPs) following a legally defined procedure. However many restrictions on foundation establishment and management remained. The fear of the 'dead hand' did not disappear altogether. The state maintained authority over the legal process by which public utility establishments could be set up, requiring an individual's notarial deed or last will to be approved by grand-ducal decree. Public utility establishments were also prevented from possessing more real-estate than the state considered necessary for the achievement of a specified purpose.[6] Perhaps because of restrictions like these, Luxembourg's foundation sector grew very little over the next 70 years. It remained fairly constant in concentrating primarily on health and (to a far lesser extent) education activities.

In 1994 the law was amended and the word foundation ('*fondation*') replaced the public utility establishment. But its legal definition was only slightly changed. The stipulation that foundation work 'shall not pursue the aim to make material gains' was replaced by the wording 'the work shall be realized mainly by means of the funds given to the foundation since its creation or during its life'. The law was also adapted to European Community law, replacing references to 'Luxembourg nationals' with 'EU citizens'. Other important changes include the designation of the Ministry of Justice as the authority responsible for supervising foundations. And, in order to encourage donations to foundations, they were made tax deductible.

While it is still too early to determine the full consequences of these reforms, several trends have emerged. For one, the rate of foundation establishment has risen. What is more, these new foundations perform a wider range of activities beyond the health and education sectors. It is reasonable to expect this diversification to continue for some time.

---

[5] Art. 27 of the law of April 21, 1928 as modified by the law of March 4, 1994.

[6] Article 35 official law of 1928 as modified.

3 Legal issues

It is important to distinguish the public utility institution or foundation from the *'association sans but lucratif'* (ASBL) or nonprofit making association, which are both defined by the same law of 1928. While the former is defined as a *'universitas bonarum'*, the latter is considered a *'universitas personarum'*. This is the distinguishing feature of a foundation: the fact that it holds certain assets affected to serve a special purpose. Conceptually speaking, it is this patrimony that is recognized as a legal entity, whereas in associations the collectivity of persons involved is granted legal personality. Another significant distinction is that foundations can only be established with approval by grand-ducal decree, while associations do not have this constraint.

As modified in 1994,[7] Luxembourg law on nonprofit associations and foundations considers a foundation to be a personalized set of assets, devoted to a particular cause or objective, and administered by a board in accordance with the particular cause. It is recognized as a legal person; it can act and sign legal documents and it can hold property in its own name. It exists to fulfil objectives that are philanthropic, social, religious, scientific, artistic, pedagogic, sportive, or tourist and which serve the public interest. For these purposes it must use funds provided upon its creation or during its life. It can be created by any person who, either by authentic deed or by testament (will), assigns all or part of their assets to it for the particular purpose.

There are nevertheless still some significant constraints upon establishing foundations. The foundation acquires its legal personality only through the approval of its articles of association (i.e. the foundation's aims, proposed administrators and procedures for new appointments, and asset destination if the foundation is dissolved, for example if it is unable to accomplish its objectives) by a grand-ducal decree.[8] To achieve this, an application must pass the approval of the Ministry of Finance, the tax authorities, and the Ministry of Justice which has the first and last say on whether authorization will be granted. Furthermore, if conditions of the modification of the articles of association are not specified, modifications can only be made with the consent of the Minister of Justice and the majority of the administrators.

---

[7] Mem. A of May 5, 1928 p. 521, modified by law of February 22, 1984 (Mem. A, March 10, 1984 p. 260) and law of March 4, 1994 (Mem. A March 4, 1994 p. 300).

[8] Article 30 of the law of 1928 as modified.

4 A profile of foundations in Luxembourg

Giving a profile of foundations in Luxembourg is a difficult task. Although foundations must be approved by grand-ducal decree and supervised by the Ministry of Justice, there is almost no data available from the authorities.[9] In October 1999, there were 143 legally recognized foundations compared to 4219 *associations sans but lucratif*, (ASBL), that is nonprofit associations. National foundations (except those providing health care) tend to employ very few staff members.

With a total Luxembourg population of about 424,000, there is approximately one foundation per 3000 inhabitants,[10] compared to one association per 100 inhabitants. This may be explained in part by the lesser restrictions on setting up ASBLs, both regarding the aims of the association and the lack of any requirement for approval by grand-ducal decree to be legally recognized. Thus the legal framework for the ASBL is widely used in Luxembourg; most service clubs (e.g. Lions Club), sports clubs, leisure clubs, lobbies or pressure groups organize under this form.

Most foundations focus on health, for example hospitals (*Clinique d'Eich*), rehabilitation centres (*Fondation Emile Mayrisch*), research institutions (*Fondation Luxembourgeoise contre le Cancer*), or homes for senior citizens (*Fondation Pescatore*). More recently foundations have been widening their fields of activities to address, for example, sports (*Fondation Josy Barthe*), art (*Fondation Musée d'art Moderne Grand-Duc Jean*), culture (*Fondation Servais*) and environmental protection (*Fondation Oekofonds*).

Most foundations in Luxembourg are operating rather than grant-making foundations. For example, the Pescatore Foundation, recognized as a public utility institution in 1863, runs a home for senior citizens by drawing funds from the monthly payments of residents, from donations and from legacies, as well as the state. In contrast to grant-making foundations, funds are used to finance the functioning of the institution and its development, in other words the

---

[9] This is in part due to the recent appointment of the Minister of Justice as supervisor of the foundation sector. The state-run statistics service, STATEC, had no available information concerning foundations. Consequently it is impossible to compare foundation activities and spending with that of the state. Information can only be obtained through foundations themselves, yet many are reluctant to provide information. Therefore the following provides a general sketch of foundations in Luxembourg rather than extensive profile.

[10] Serge N. Schroeder in *L'imposition du organismes sans but lucratif*, rapport Luxembourgeois pour le congres de 'l'International Fiscal Association a Eilat' du 10 au 15 octobre 1999.

foundation's own operating needs rather than those of other entities or activities.

Endowment income and other revenue generated through foundation activities tends to provide only part of the funds needed to support operations (e.g. the Oekofonds, which among other activities carries out research on environmental protection). In fact, foundations sometimes produce losses, especially in the health sector. This explains the state's considerable financial involvement in foundations. Although foundations receive donations, legacies, or income produced by their initial endowment, their main funding derives often from state subventions. For example health care foundations attempt to finance themselves with income from services provided, but in the end the national health insurance system pays for most services. The Luxembourg government supports hospitals such as the *Clinique d'Eich*, and also other foundations like the Grand-Duc Jean Foundation, enabling them to achieve their aims; for these foundations the state provided an initial endowment and will continue to provide funding.

5 Current trends and conclusion

Over the last few years, there has been an increasing interest in foundations in Luxembourg. In recent years the number of newly established foundations rose sharply relative to their previous stagnation. And a number of recently established foundations have already achieved considerable public recognition in Luxembourg. These include the Josy Barthel Foundation, created in 1995, which financially supports athletes in their professional and educational endeavours; and the *Fondation Musée d'Art Moderne Grand-Duc Jean*, set up to run a museum of modern art currently under construction. A related development is the transformation of associations into foundations, as in the case of the Luxembourg Association Against Cancer. It operated for 69 years before becoming the Luxembourg Foundation Against Cancer. This indicates that over the last few years, foundations have become much more attractive than they used to be. But with the increase in numbers and importance of foundations, it has also become evident that the existing legal framework is inadequate to provide efficient state supervision of the sector. Accordingly, the Ministry of Justice is preparing the draft of a new law on foundations. The proposed law would provide greater means of supervision and control, particularly concerning foundations' accountability. The requirements for establishing a foundation would also be changed, namely a proposed foundation would have to possess the necessary financial means to assure its survival over the first few years. The required minimum capital would vary according to the aims of the foundation. This draft bill is not yet finalized and might in fact take years to become law.

Luxembourg foundations are nonprofit entities of public utility, heavily influenced by both French and Belgian law. The tensions arising between these two legal frameworks in part explain the slow growth and minimal role of foundations in society until very recently. For most of foundation history in Luxembourg, foundations mainly existed in the health sector and were strongly regulated and subsidized by the Luxembourg state.

The main factor influencing the recent development of the foundation sector is the 1994 amendment to the 1928 law on nonprofit associations and foundations, which changed the tax regime of foundations, making them more attractive to potential donors. These reforms have not yet compensated for the long history of constraints and slow growth, but recent developments seem encouraging. However, recently proposed legislation may – if enacted – not only enhance foundation status but also bring foundations under closer state control and make their establishment somewhat more difficult, echoing the constraints upon Luxembourg's foundation sector historically.

Bibliography

Majorus, N., *Les associations sans but lucratif et les établissements d'utilité publique au Grand-Duche de Luxembourg*, Luxembourg, 1930.

Schroeder, S. N., *L'imposition du organismes sans but lucratif*, rapport Luxembourgeois pour le congres de 'l'International Fiscal Association a Eilat' du 10 au 15 octobre 1999.

▼ Ary Burger, Paul Dekker and Vic Veldheer

The Netherlands

1 Introduction

The Netherlands has a huge number of foundations. As of May 11 1999 there were 131,395 foundations according to the CD–ROM database held at the Chamber of Commerce. There are historical and legal reasons for this internationally exceptionally high number. Historically one may point to the religious fragmentation ('pillar-structure') that has stimulated the development of an extended and diverse nonprofit sector, in which the foundation and the association are its basic forms.

Legally, it is easy to establish a foundation in the Netherlands. The legal definition of a foundation in the Netherlands, while fitting well into the definition offered by Anheier in Foundations in Europe: a Comparative Perspective, is fundamentally different in one respect: it does not necessarily serve a public purpose. Moreover, a foundation in the Netherlands is commonly understood first and foremost an organization rather than primarily an asset. Establishing a foundation is cheap and fast as there are no limitations or requirements regarding purpose or minimum capital. Subsequently, while foundations as such should be nonprofit they have proven to be a useful legal device for commercial transactions and coordination in the business world.

Most foundations with a public purpose – generally the foundations of the nonprofit sector – are operating foundations (schools, hospitals, nursing homes) financed mainly through tax money and social insurance.[1] More interesting in the Dutch case is the subset of foundations, the funds, which are established to provide money for particular groups or purposes.[2] A fund is primarily a financial asset.

---

[1] The story of Dutch foundations is at best an interesting one for lawyers, and that of public purpose foundations is already being told in The Johns Hopkins comparative nonprofit sector project (cf. Burger et al.; Veldheer and Burger).

[2] In Dutch, funds are fondsen and foundations are stichtingen. The word fundatie also still exists according to the Van Dale dictionary ('a foundation based on a fund for a certain purpose'), but it can only be found in centuries-old names of charitable and clerical courts of almshouses, schools, etc.

Most funds are grant making, but some are operating. As long as money given for public purposes, or raised to replenish assets, actually constitutes the core business of an organization it is considered a fund. In the Netherlands, this sector is fast growing and self-regulating. It has maintained a healthy distance from the state, and so far has coped well with the increasing internationalization of the market.

2 Historical background

The origins of contemporary foundations lie in charity.[3] Churches have long been the largest fundraisers, appealing for donations to support their mission and social welfare work. Many foundations in the Netherlands nowadays still have a religious connotation and have their roots in the Church.

In the second half of the 19th century, charity from individual members of the social elite gradually took on organized forms of aid. Institutions of benevolence were founded to raise money via public collections. Ultimately, the central government thought it necessary to formulate regulations for these public collections, resulting in the Poor Mans Law 1854, confirmed in the revized law of 1912.[4] In 1929 public collections were licensed by local government.

Other private initiatives that developed concentrated on the arts, science or religion. Rich businessmen and other wealthy people erected foundations or bequeathed their personal property to social or cultural activities, such as building museums or buying valuable artwork. Banks and large Dutch companies like Philips and Heineken created financial funds to support a wide range of social activities, such as sponsoring visual and musical art, stimulating social debate on key issues, training and educating talented artists and caring for cultural heritage.

After World War II funding expanded to meet increasing social welfare needs. A remarkable increase also occurred in institutions devoted to science and culture. The Prince Bernhard Foundation – today one of the largest funds in the country[5] – is one of the most prominent examples. It originated during World War II as an initiative of Prince Bernhard, the husband of the Dutch queen-to-be. In 1940, with the help of Shell and Unilever, he raised money for the

---

[3] Hoogerwerf.

[4] Bak.

[5] In 1999 nearly €14 million were spent on sciences, arts, cultural heritage, social welfare and the environment.

liberation of the Netherlands. The majority of the nearly NLG20 million raised during the war was spent on military planes and tanks. The former 'fund for the buying of Spitfires' was re-established in 1946 as a cultural foundation. In 1998 it spent approximately €14 million on sciences, the arts, cultural heritage, social welfare and the environment.

After World War II, government increasingly took responsibility for social welfare tasks formerly performed by private institutions: social security, health, education, housing, arts etc. However, in most cases the state did not take over the execution of tasks, but extended their public funding step by step. Thus the growth of operating foundations and other private organizations was part of the development of the 'pillar-structured' Dutch welfare state.[6] In many areas the old 'private initiative' evolved into strongly regulated and almost 100% publicly financed annexes of the welfare state.

Since the 1960s social welfare has remained an important field for foundations but funds have increasingly been directed toward projects in developing countries. Mass media has become an important fundraising tool for humanitarian aid – from aiding the hungry in India (1966) to helping Kosovan refugees and Turkish earthquake victims (1999). Such developments have contributed to the need for coordination, control and accountability in the foundation sector, but funds have managed to remain self-regulating.

Since 1925 the main regulating body has been the Central Archive, a private organization now called the Central Bureau for Fundraising (CBF). It stimulates responsible and sensible fundraising, and supports local government in order to exchange information on the trustworthiness of door-to-door collections. It publishes an annual report on revenues and expenditures of fundraisers and assigns 'CBF quality marks' for accountability and costs (which must be less than 25% of proceeds). The CBF also draws up a yearly schedule for national collections to prevent overlap. Other organizations for coordination, advice and lobbying have developed more recently. The Association of Funds in the Netherlands (FIN), an important umbrella-organization for grant makers, was founded in 1988. It now has about 150 funds as members and is an important platform for policy discussions and funding decisions. It also spots international developments and publishes a book on funding sources for grant seekers.

---

[6] Burger *et al.*

Since the 1950s the government has financially supported the regulation and supervision role of the CBF. Subsidies for the CBF from the Ministry of Welfare, Health and Culture increased since the 1970s, and in 1996 the Ministry of Justice became a subsidizer as well in the hope of encouraging better citizen protection and integrity of funding organizations, and to prevent crime. Members of parliament have also become increasingly concerned about developments in the world of charitable fundraising.

Organizations like CBF and FIN are an expression of the corporatist character of the fundraising sector in the Netherlands, which has been and still is to a high degree self-regulating. Several initiatives to regulate the sector by law have been proposed due to the enormous growth of collections, but never put into practice. This occurred for the first time in 1949 when proposals were made to regulate the collections, make a collection-plan, and found a central organ as a representative for the different religious circuits. But ultimately the Dutch parliament considered the sector capable of regulating its own affairs. In 1975 there was a short revival of discussion about the desirability of legal action, which again did not result in law. In 1983 a committee of civil servants from different departments was installed once again to consider state regulation, but its advice was negative and the corporate character was maintained. Recently the call to re-structure the sector, either by self-regulation or by legislation, was again heard in the Ministry of Welfare, Health and Culture, but again was not acted upon.[7]

3 Legal issues

The foundation (*stichting*) is one of the three basic types of nonprofit organizations in the Netherlands. The others are the association (*vereniging*) and the Church. Churches have no specific legal regulations (but they might be organized as associations or foundations). Foundations and associations are regulated in the Civil Code as regards their general characteristics, rules for establishment and dissolution, internal governance, accounting and legal representation. The main difference between foundations and associations is that associations have members and foundations do not. The other difference is that foundations can only be formal, whereas associations may be informal.[8]

---

[7] Brouwer.

[8] Informal associations are established without any formal action and no statutes are laid down in a notarial deed; inclusion in the Trade Register of the Chambers of Commerce is voluntary.

A foundation is defined in the Civil Code as 'a legal person created by a legal act which has no members and whose purpose is to realize an object stated in its articles using capital allocated to such purpose'. Foundations must be established by a notarial deed containing the statutes, and can be established by one person (even in his or her last will). Permission to establish a foundation does not depend on specific purposes of the intended foundation, and does not require the involvement of governmental bodies. Neither is it necessary for a foundation to possess 'capital' at the moment of its establishment. Traditionally, a foundation was primarily defined as an asset, as in most other countries. In the course of the 20th century foundations became more and more a device for other purposes than the administration of an asset, but founders were still required to deposit a pro forma capital (NLG10) at the notary's office. This requirement was skipped in the first formal legislation on foundations in 1956. Since that year it is sufficient that assets (i.e. money, labour, property) are available when needed. Tax regulation is an issue of public law, and depends on the goal or purpose of an organization, not its legal form. In general, 'public purpose' foundations are exempt from company tax and enjoy low tax rates on gifts and inheritances.[9]

These characteristics make the foundation a very easy and attractive legal form. It is less regulated than associations with membership rights and general assembly, and it is less regulated and cheaper than private companies which must have a minimum capital.[10] The main restriction on foundations is that their purpose cannot be to distribute profits to their founder(s) or to members of its organs (i.e. only to target groups that apply for benefits relating to the purpose of the foundation). However, the nonprofit-distributing condition is hardly a restriction because it applies only to profits that are made by the foundation itself. A foundation can distribute profits made by other organizations. Consequently, foundations are used for many purposes – from preserving family property and administering stocks (trust offices), to joint activities in the commercial sphere such as the promotion of goods, interest representation and services.

However, in the nonprofit sector the choice between an association or a foundation can still be difficult to make. The attractiveness of

---

[9] Burger *et al.*, p. 14–16, and Van der Ploeg for details.

[10] There are only minor legal obligations for foundations: an annual report has to be made but it is acceptable not to do so as long as interested third parties or the tax authorities do not ask for it. In some situations courts might become active and dissolve a foundation or adjust its outdated purpose. For further information on regulations see Van der Ploeg.

democratic procedures, the wish to generate a substantial amount of money on a regular basis, and the prospected need to adapt purposes to new circumstances, make associations more desirable. Features such as simplicity and the ability to protect organizational purposes or aims against external threats argue in favour of foundations. The choice of organizational form may also be linked to religious affiliation. For example, Catholic (nonprofit) elementary schools tend to be foundations, reflecting the Catholic idea of 'subsidiarity'. Protestant elementary schools tend to be associations, reflecting their establishment by parents and the Calvinist idea of 'circles of sovereignty'.

Foundations that are primarily concerned with transferring money ('funds' – see below) are self-regulating, as all other foundations. No state admission is required, nor are there any specific legal obligations for these foundations, but for door-to-door and on-the-street collections they need a municipal permit and the municipalities provide permits only on the basis of CBF quality marks. Lotteries are more regulated, as they are obliged by law to devote a minimum of 40% of their gross earnings to worthy causes (so the costs of prices and the organization may never exceed 60% of all revenues).[11]

4 A profile of foundations in the Netherlands

Most of the over 100,000 foundations in the Netherlands are operating foundations, active in the fields of culture, education, social services and health care. In the fields of health and social services they form the majority of nonprofit organizations; in the field of culture and recreation they are outnumbered by associations (Table 1.34).

Funds are a subset of foundations; they are primarily concerned with raising and donating money. The core business of funds is commonly understood as 'transferring money for public purposes'; thus almost all funds are foundations. In some cases the distinction between a fund and an operating foundation is somewhat arbitrary. Estimates on the number of funds in the Netherlands range from 4000 to 12,000. The following data is based on almost 1000 of the main public funds.[12]

---

[11] An important exception is the state lottery whose net revenues flow directly into the national treasury. Recently, an advisory commission of the government has proposed to drop the 'paternalistic' obligation of at least 40% for worthy causes.

[12] Our data do not include support funds for family members or specific institutions, such as museums or churches, or funds for closed circles of beneficiaries such as (social) funds for employees of companies or government organizations. Neither included are the huge pension funds.

Table 1.34 Foundations and associations by ICNPO field of activity, 1995

	Foundations	%	Associations	%
Culture and recreation	15,964	16	39,478	43
Education and research	5941	6	2387	3
Health and social services	27,263	27	10,575	12
Development and housing	3729	4	915	1
Environment, advocacy, philanthropy, international, religion and professional	20,644	21	34,483	38
Other	26,788	27	3529	4
Total	**100,329**	**100**	**91,367**	**100**

Source: KvK (1995)

Types of funds

A distinction can be made between funds that raise money and funds that do not. Among the fundraisers are first and foremost those that seek financial support from the population, government and/or businesses for their own purposes. There are about 300 of these funds. Among them are the larger and well-known funds, such as *Koningin Wilhelmina Fonds* (cancer prevention and research), *Hartstichting* (heart diseases prevention and research), and the local branches of international funds like Foster Parents Plan (international child aid), *Wereldnatuurfonds* (World Wildlife Fund) and *Artsen zonder Grenzen* (*Médecins sans Frontières*). Among the operative foundations that are called funds because of their fundraising activities are also several animal and environment protection organizations, Amnesty International, and *Vluchtelingenwerk* (refugee aid).

Lotteries are a special type of fundraising foundation. Some of the major lotteries in the Netherlands were either set up by specific funds or transfer their net receipts to them. For instance, the largest lottery (*de Postcodeloterij*) divides its net proceeds among the founders, which include *Stichting Doen*, *NOVIB* (international aid), *Natuurmonumenten* (nature conservation) and *Vluchtelingenwerk* (aid to refugees). Other large beneficiaries from lotteries are World Wildlife Fund, *Médecins sans Frontières*, *Prins Bernhard Fonds* (culture) and *Juliana Welzijn Fonds* (welfare).

The second main type of funds are grant makers that do not seek public support. In the Netherlands the majority of these funds are called trust funds. They manage the proceeds from assets. Most of these funds were set up by individuals, are very small in size and prefer to operate in anonymity. If their purpose is highly exclusive, for instance to support family members, they have no interest in revealing their existence. Other funds fear the administrative burden of high volumes of applications. As a result, relatively little is known about trust funds. They are not usually listed in the annual directory of The Association of Funds In the Netherlands (FIN), which provides information on purpose, board, assets, budget and how to apply to about 400 funds.

Among the grant makers are also various 'company-related' funds. Sometimes they are pure trust funds that hold company stocks. Well-known examples are the *Van Leer Foundation* (childhood education in developing countries) and the *VSB fonds* (a bank fund active in various fields). But sometimes these funds rely on regular payments from the company. Like the other trust funds, very little is known about company funds. The FIN Directory of Funds mentions less than a dozen. We were able to identify a few more, including the larger, well known and public funds, but some funds were reluctant to supply information and clearly preferred anonymity.

According to available data, funds operate mainly in the traditional fields of organized charity (Table 1.35). One-quarter are active in

Table 1.35 Funds by ICNPO field of activity, 1997

	Number	%
Culture and recreation	78	11
Education	66	10
Health	170	25
Social services	173	25
Environment	30	4
Development and housing	10	1
Advocacy	41	6
Philanthropy	4	1
International	99	14
Religion	20	3
Professional	0	0
Other	0	0
Total	**691**	**100**

Source: CBF (1996) and FIN (1997)

health (and health research) and another quarter are active in social services. Other important fields of activity are international aid, culture and education. These fields account for 85% of the surveyed funds. However, it should be kept in mind that while most funds are classified according to their dominant activity, many funds work in several fields, and choice of classification can be rather arbitrary. For instance, funds active in supporting medical research were put in the health field rather than research. Even more difficult to classify are funds active in international aid and development. These can be classified as international activities, health care, social services or economic development.

Fund expenditures and revenues

The combined expenditures of all funds in the Netherlands amount to about NLG2.7 billion (€1.2 billion). This figure can be broken down by type of fund and by field of activity. The active fundraisers are the largest spenders. They spend about NLG2 billion (€900 million). Lotteries raise about NLG 450 million (€200 million) for worthy causes, about half of which is transferred to fundraisers. Data on the expenditures of trusts and company funds was unavailable because most operate in anonymity. Non-money-raising funds (trusts) spend an estimated NLG140 million (€63 million) per year, or 5% of total expenditures by funds.

The data in Table 1.36 refer to fundraising organizations and lotteries, which together spend about NLG2.5 billion (€1.1 billion). The expenditures of trusts and company funds were very difficult to break down by field and the distribution shown in Table 1.36 should

Table 1.36 Expenditures of fundraisers and lotteries in 1995 (millions NLG), by field of activity

Field of activity	Expenditure	%
Culture and recreation	125	2
Health	519	22
Social services	702	26
Environment	305	13
Advocacy	107	4
International	784	34
Total	**2542 (€1154)**	**100**

Source: CBF (1996)

not be over interpreted. According to these data, distribution of expenditures of funds by field reveal that international aid is the largest single category, followed by social services and health (research).

Table 1.37 describes where the income for expenditures comes from. Whereas lotteries derive all of their income from ticket sales, fundraising organizations have a more varied revenue structure: several forms of their own income, government subsidies and revenues from lotteries. Less than half of the revenues are from private giving (i.e. legacies and donations).[13] Capital income and other revenues account for about 10%. The rest of their income comes from government subsidies and lotteries.

Table 1.37 Revenues of fundraisers and lotteries in 1995 (millions NLG)

Revenue source	Revenue	%
Fundraising income	1176	46
Capital income	123	5
Lotteries[a]	428	17
Subsidies	660	26
Other revenues	155	6
Total	**2542 (€1,154)**	**100**

[a] Sales minus costs of organization and prizes.

Source: CBF (1996)

The revenues of fundraisers and lotteries have grown very fast over the past few years. The net income of lotteries particularly has shown a spectacular increase, from NLG88 million in 1980 to 162 million in 1990, and to 428 million in 1995. Government subsidies increased even faster. This concerns mainly funds active in international aid, which receive nearly three-quarters of all government subsidies to funds. Finally, the fundraising income or own revenues rose by no less than 50% between 1990 and 1995.

---

[13] For a further analysis of donations, see Schuyt. According to his survey data, most money donated to churches and door-to-door collections is still the most important means of giving.

5 Recent fund developments

Growing private wealth, withdrawal of the state and stress on 'social responsiveness' in some social and cultural areas, and doubts about the benefits to recipients of huge inheritances (from a tax point of view) are factors given to explain a strong growth in the number of funds in recent years. The succession duty authority reported a growth of 3000 worthy-cause organizations with tax exemption for 1998.[14] An interesting trend is the rather explosive growth of 'funds-on-name' since the early 1990s. Individuals transfer the administration of their assets to a vested foundation with a specific use for annual profits. The Prince Bernard Foundation, for instance, administered 82 of these funds-on-name in 1998, with a total spending of €1 million.

The commercialization of fundraising has developed over a longer period. Funds have become more like business organizations, well aware of cost effectiveness, thinking in terms of market shares and using modern marketing techniques to approach the public. This has been influenced by growing competition among organizations, both because of the increasing variety of means for collecting money (i.e. TV lottery and TV fundraising), and because of the increasing penetration of the market by organizations from abroad. Foreign competition (i.e. American) poses new challenges for Dutch organizations; even though such competitors do not yet possess a substantial market share in the Netherlands, they do have an impact, stimulating the 'old organizations' to accommodate new ways of approaching the public using modern marketing techniques. These developments correspond with changes in the behaviour of givers; they are becoming more critical and flexible: in the 1990s the term 'chari-shopper' – a person who donates money to a different fund every year – has been used to describe modern donors.

A final recent trend is the strong growth of the assets of funds that are active in the stock market. Some funds have serious problems spending their growing amounts of money in a responsible way, and more and more money is kept in reserve. In the fall of 1999 there were some critical articles in the Dutch media about this issue: 'Charities are too rich', 'Why still donate?'. The fundraising branch is well aware of the importance of remaining trustworthy in the public's eyes. Funds take

---

[14] NRC Handelsblad, 8 November 1999.

much trouble to account for growing wealth and there is growing support for the idea of setting a maximum to the amount of property a fund may own as a condition of eligibility for the CBF quality mark.

In general, self-regulation has successfully inhibited the growth of government regulation thus far. The dominant role of government is still one of the stimulation or activation of fundraising through fiscal ruling and private initiative support.

6 Current trends and conclusion

In the Netherlands foundations are a very simple and cheap legal device that, while being nonprofit, can function well in a business environment. Foundations are everywhere and serve many purposes – from simple constructs to administrators of family assets, hospitals and schools, national lobbying and deliberative bodies.

Next to foundations, there are funds. After World War II, funding in the Netherlands expanded enormously from social welfare activities into other fields such as cultural activities, sciences, health, international assistance and the environment. This was in part due to the increasing role of the state in subsidizing social welfare, and to the new needs and preferences of the donating population.

Fundraising in the Netherlands has become increasingly professional, commercial and businesslike. The 'chari-market' is becoming more competitive, dynamic and international. But the funding sector is still strongly institutionalized and self-regulating, and thus far has succeeded in keeping control of its own affairs. The government watches closely, but stays apart.

The tradition of self-regulation can come under severe pressure from commercialization and internationalization, but it is too early to foresee the outcomes. Economists have often predicted the end of Dutch corporatism, and political scientists have analysed the decline of Dutch consensual policy-making, but in the 1990s the country celebrated the international success of its corporatist consensual 'polder model'. In this model, self-regulation of funds might well survive internationalization.

Bibliography

Bak, M., *Het particuliere initiatief*, [Translation: The private initiative], MA thesis, Amsterdam, University of Amsterdam, 1986.

Brouwer, B. A. C., *(Beleids) ontwikkelingen op het terrein van fondsen en fondsenwerving*, [Translation: (Policy) developments in the field of funds and fundraising], Rijswijk, Ministry of Welfare, Health and Culture, 1990.

Burger, A., Dekker, P., van der Ploeg, T. and van Veen, W., 'Defining the non-profit sector: The Netherlands', Baltimore, Johns Hopkins University (The Johns Hopkins comparative non-profit sector project, working paper number 23), 1997.

BF (Centraal Bureau Fondsenwerving), *Jaarverslag 1995*, [Translation: Central Bureau on Fundraising: Annual Report 1995], Amsterdam, CBF, 1996.

FIN (Vereniging Fondsen in Nederland), *Fondsenboek 1997/1998*, [Translation: Association of Funds in the Netherlands, Directory of Funds], Zutphen, Walburg Pers, 1997.

Hoogerwerf, P. ed., *Handboek Fondsenwerving en Sponsoring*, [Translation: 'Handbook fund-raising and sponsoring manual'], Alphen a.d. Rijn (NL), Samsom, 1995.

KvK (Kamers van Koophandel en Fabrieken), *Adressen en bedrijfsinformatie catalogus '95/'96*, [Translation: Chambers of Commerce, Information on enterprises and addresses], Woerden, NV Databank Kamers van Koophandel en Fabrieken, 1995.

Schuyt, Th. N. M. ed., *Geven in Nederland*, [Translation: Giving in The Netherlands editions of 1997 and 1999], Houten (NL), Bohn Stafleu Van Loghum, 1997 and 1999.

Van der Ploeg, T. J., A comparative legal analysis of foundations, in: H.K. Anheier and S. Toepler (eds), *Private funds, public purpose*, New York etc., Kluwer Academic/Plenum, 1999, pp. 55–78.

Veldheer, V., and Burger, A., 'History of the Non-profit Sector in the Netherlands', Baltimore, Johns Hopkins University (The Johns Hopkins comparative non-profit sector project, working paper number 35), 1999.

Wester, M. J., 'Central Bureau on fund raising and how is fund raising organised in the Netherlands', in: T. J. van der Ploeg and J. W. Sap (eds), *Rethinking the Balance*, Amsterdam, VU University Press, 1995.

Electronic sources (12 May 2000)

See http://www.kvk.nl/kvk/ for the database of the Chambers of Commerce.

See http://www.goede-doelen.nl/kern for funds and their umbrella-organizations.

Norway

1 Introduction

It is not entirely clear how many foundations currently exist in Norway. The over 9000 or so foundations registered with the public authorities in 1997 may not include many older foundations. One reason for this situation may be the only modest political interest in foundations shown by Norwegian society generally, reflected in the fact that the first legislation specifically addressing foundations was only enacted in 1980.[1]

Two trends are apparent in the history of foundations in Norway. First is a tension between the idea of foundations as autonomous entities and the right of the public sector to direct their activities. This can be traced back to medieval conflicts between the King and the Church. As the Church struggled to establish its own property and activities outside royal jurisdiction, hospitals and monasteries were created which became the precursors of modern foundations. Second, unlike its Nordic neighbours whose foundations tend to have been built on wealth and family fortunes, the foundation sector in Norway developed from a wider variety of donations primarily from the middle class. Reflecting these origins, Norwegian foundations have tended to be small, community-serving grant makers with philanthropic or religious aims.

In recent years the purpose and function of foundations has changed significantly, again contrasting with the experience of other Scandinavian countries. Norwegian foundations are increasingly established by public authorities and often for activities that are less locally, or even nationally, oriented. Such foundations may enjoy an element of independence administering activities otherwise under the responsibility of the state. However, the close ties between foundations and public officials more than ever call into question the autonomous nature of foundations. The imminent enactment of new

---

[1] Lov av 23 mai 1980 nr. 11.

foundation legislation in 2001 appears likely to encourage this trend of public sector engagement with foundations and to increase the resultant uncertainty as to the independence of foundations in Norway.

2 Historical background

The historical development of foundations in Norway contrasts with that of the other Nordic countries. Norway was under the Danish crown for almost 400 years. Being granted an independent constitution in 1814, Norway allied with Sweden under the Swedish crown until achieving full independence in 1905 under its own monarchy. Until comparatively recently Norway was a relatively poor country in the outskirts of Europe with a population of about four million inhabitants. The absence of a national nobility and the general lack of wealth in the population are reflected in the historical structures of foundations. Today, older foundations and legacies often have a limited or small basic capital, and grants are distributed essentially for local purposes. Relatively few foundations have a large basic capital or are products of larger private fortunes.

The first foundation grew out of a power struggle between the King and the Church in the 13th century. Archbishop Jon had established a hospital for the poor in the town of Trondheim. However the building of the hospital took place without the King's permission, and several years later was contested. Ultimately the King chose to abandon his claim to the property in order to avoid a confrontation with the Church. In 1277 through royal decree he donated the property not to the Church as such, but to 'Friends of God' within the hospital. In this way, the property rights were related to those who, at any time, were administering the hospital.[2] This establishment later came to be regarded as the first foundation in Norway.

Other monasteries and hospitals were subsequently established, particularly in the 15th century, which were regarded as belonging to the Church and were accordingly placed under Church law. During the Reformation these properties were again placed under the jurisdiction of the King, later creating some confusion about right of ownership. The hospitals continued their work through statutes established by the King and gained status as 'public foundations'. Many of these still exist, among them the original hospital in Trondheim.

---

[2] Grankvist.

In Norway, large private foundations have never dominated the financing of civil and philanthropic activities. Consequently, private foundations have not been considered part of the voluntary sector.[3] However, during the 18th century a large number of legacies were established in Norwegian society. Often they provided economic support to vulnerable groups, for the education of individuals, or simply for the basic necessities of life at local levels. The basic capital within these foundations was small and their objectives were usually restricted to helping 'needy' inhabitants of one community or parish, or one occupational group, reflecting good intentions and civil spirit rather than the wealth and fortunes of Norwegian society.[4] For example, the legacy from one former factory owner was intended for 'dignified needy men of the conditioned classes in Oslo, who have seen better days and due to illness, ageing or working accident are without possibilities of getting hold of an income that corresponds to their social position in society'.[5]

The Norwegian Constitution of 1814 referred to foundations and legacies in two paragraphs. Paragraph 106 states that foundation property may be used only in accordance with a foundation's stated intentions. Paragraph 108 declares a prohibition of hereditary family properties. This paragraph reflects the strong national sentiment from peasants and common people against nobility and upper classes after almost 400 years under the Danish crown. The prohibition also echoes the influence of the French Revolution and the French Constitution.

Until 1917 the majority of legacies were administered by the Magistrate, who represented the state in all larger towns. Later, administration was handed over to various local authorities such as the chief of police, mayor, city treasurer or county court judge. After World War II, legacies and foundations have been administered and controlled by the regional commissioner (*fylkesmann*) as the local representative of the state.

In the last 20 years the number of foundations has grown, an increasing number of which have been founded by public authorities to release specific state activities or interests from political control. But in some cases this independence may be illusory since government may influence the foundation activities by regulating their mandates.

---

[3] NOU 1988, p.17.

[4] Backe and Krøvel.

[5] Backe and Krøvel p. 53.

The state's right to spend public money in accordance with public and political goals may be conflicting with foundations' legally instituted right to pursue their own goals, specifically as enacted under legislation in 1980.

3 Legal issues

The Foundation Legislation Act 1980[6] was Norway's first legislation specifically to address foundations. Previously the legal norms of foundations were based on court practice and general legal principles, which remain relevant today.

A key element in the definition of foundations is the 'requirement of independence' which states that an object of economic value must be placed at the independent disposal of the relevant purpose for which a foundation is established.[7] No individual, legal entity or interest outside the foundation is allowed any legal rights or power to influence the foundation and its administration.

Foundation activities must rest upon a capital base (*grunnkapital*). In traditional foundations this capital base is the source of life and activities, enabling the distribution of money for specific purposes. Operating foundations that primarily carry out nonprofit activities also need to be established with a capital base, but in these foundations the capital base is more of a formal matter. Rather than distributing money for a specific purpose, these foundations also frequently distribute money originating from outside sources such as government transfers and finance from other public authorities, or income derived from activities of the foundation itself.

Legally, foundations must also be of some permanence because their purpose, and consequently activities, are not restricted in time. This requirement was highlighted in the 1980 legislation, which made altering foundation objectives very difficult. It also excludes activities such as mass meetings and campaigns, or money collected for a special purpose such as aid to earthquake victims, which are not on-going activities.

The Foundation Legislation of 1980 distinguishes between private and official foundations:

- an official foundation is controlled by an official (public) authority
- all other foundations are private.

---

[6] Stiftelsesloven av mai 12, nr. 11.

[7] Woxholt.

Both types may be established (but not controlled) by either public officials or private persons. The essential difference between private and official foundations is that the latter are subject to stricter governmental control.

4 A profile of foundations in Norway

Traditional foundations

These foundations, with their historical roots, have been characterized by a high degree of autonomy. Usually, their activities are financed by the returns on their basic capital, and they are not dependent upon incomes from sales, business transactions or grants from public authorities. Traditional foundations encompass units with small amounts at their disposal, family foundations and some larger foundations realizing common good purposes.

Modern foundations

These usually have a lower degree of autonomy than their historical counterparts. Many derive their income through public budgets or revenue, and in consequence have a different economic structure than that of traditional foundations. They are nevertheless subject to the same public regulations, suggesting that legal regulations have not been sufficiently adapted to the present development of foundations.

Modern foundations can be divided into three categories.[8]

1 **Common purpose foundations**, which include philanthropic activities such as international aid, kindergartens and cultural activities. In these foundations, management of basic capital is of less importance. Within this category one will find many family legacies with a limited basic capital, some larger family foundations, and some that distribute grants for specific purposes.
2 **Ideal, service-producing foundations**. These are distinguished by a small basic capital and common-purpose activities like museums, permanent exhibitions and other cultural activities. More often than not they are initiated by civil (private) actors, but public sector activities may also be included in this category of service production. The usual intention behind the public establishment is to secure a certain degree of autonomy for the activity involved, as is often the case for research foundations.

---

[8] NOU 1998 p.7.

3 **Commercial foundations**, which fall into two sub-categories. On the one hand are those that conduct commercial affairs for themselves. Here, production and sales are integrated parts, and the foundation is working as a nonprofit firm. The other sub-category comprises foundations where the capital is invested in other firms or economic activities, and the foundation does not hold any production of its own.

Unfortunately, official statistics are unavailable for a complete picture of foundations in Norway. Foundations established in recent years appear in a public register (*Enhetsregisteret*) which some early foundations may have escaped. Thus the data presented here should be treated with caution.

A national study from 1939 described 6094 legacies and foundations in Norway (Backe and Krøvel, 1940). In 1997, almost 60 years later, a total of 9330 foundations were registered, of which 929 were commercial foundations. Altogether 23,731 individuals were employed in these foundations in 1997. Little is known about the properties they administer. In 1975, approximately 6000 official foundations were registered by the Ministry of Social Affairs, with total assets of between NOK500 and 600 million (€62 to 75 million).

In Norway, the National Court of Protection administers a considerable proportion of the foundations and legacies. In 1968, approximately 30% of their assets amounting to NOK150 million (€19 million) came from official legacies and foundations. Of this last mentioned amount, NOK96 million or 64% were administered by the Court of Protection in Oslo and its neighbouring county Akershus alone.[9]

Foundations also differ according to their primary field of activity, or purpose. It is very difficult to obtain a picture of the current purpose of foundations in Norway. *Statistics Norway* classifies foundations according to industry; these categories do not correspond very well to the stated purpose of foundations. Neither are all foundations registered. But the distinction between commercial and non-commercial foundations is reflected in official statistics. It seems that approximately one-third of all present foundations fall into categories 1 and 2 above (common purpose, and ideal/service-producing types), while the rest are commercial.

---

[9] NOU 1975:63, p. 10.

In 1998, more than 40% of all non-commercial foundations concentrated on social service activities. The second largest activity, comprising approximately one-fifth of all foundations, is education and research (Table 1.38).

Table 1.38 Non-commercial foundations: numbers and grants, 1998

Purpose	Number	%	Grants	%
Culture and recreation	153	5	1277	2
Education and research	616	21	13,049	21
Health	28	1	32	<1
Social services	1286	43	34,252	56
Environment	81	3	238	<1
Development and housing	25	1	374	<1
Advocacy, supporting employees	182	6	1807	3
Not elsewhere classified	618	20	10,146	17
Total	**2989**	**100**	**61,175**	**100**

Source: Statistics Norway 1998

5 Current trends and conclusion

The Foundation Legislation Act 1980 was formulated primarily to regulate activities of traditional foundations, that is, foundations administering basic capital in a 'passive' way, in order to distribute returns according to the formal intentions. But in the last 20 years the number of foundations established by public authorities has increased. Institutions and activities such as museums, broadcasting, research, cultural affairs, expert organs and centres of competence belong to this category. These public foundations frequently lack basic capital and depend on current income, normally financed by the public sector. These funds may not be distributed, even to realize a foundation's purpose. As for official foundations, the Foundation Legislation Act 1980 requires that at least two representatives are elected to the executive committee, whereas economic foundations with a capital base of more than NOK100,000 are required to have three. The 1980 Act does not require that the capital base is of a certain minimum.

One outstanding example of a semi-autonomous public foundation is the National Insurance Scheme Fund established in 1966 to prevent the growing oil surplus extraction in the North Sea being absorbed by increasing public expenditure. The primary purpose of the Fund is to make an optimal contribution to national insurance through the accumulation of wealth. Regulations regarding the management of the Fund are stipulated by the *Storting* (parliament). The Fund is subordinate to the Ministry of Finance and headed by a board of nine members who cannot be instructed by the Ministry on individual matters. However board members are appointed by the King. The Board invests the Fund's capital in different types of securities, mainly commercial papers and shares in Norwegian companies, to secure the best possible returns. The portfolio's market value in 1998 was NOK108 million (€13.4 million).

Another example is the Government Petroleum Fund established by the *Storting* (parliament) in 1990. The intention was to safeguard long-term considerations in the application of central government petroleum revenues. This Fund is also managed by the Ministry of Finance. In 1998, the Fund's portfolio totalled NOK171 billion (€21 billion).

One concern is that, as the Office of the Auditor General pointed out in 1998, controlled goal-setting for public foundations may conflict with the basic requirements for autonomy and self-regulation referred to in the legal regulations of foundations.[10] This trend seems likely to increase through new legislation on foundations proposed by a government appointed committee of legal experts in March 1998. The proposals, expected to be enacted in 2001, abolish the distinction between official and private foundations and subject all foundations to official control and public approval. Common, non-profit foundations will also be required to have at least NOK100,000 (€12,500) capital base, and commercial foundations to have NOK 200,000 (€25,000), unlike the 1980 law which required no minimum. Only foundation income – not assets – may be distributed to achieve foundation objectives.

The roots of foundations in Norway can be traced back to the Middle Ages and conflicts between the King and Church. But in the 18th century foundations developed through donations from a great variety of sources, mainly within the middle classes, frequently based on philanthropic or religious values, and with the community as the frame of reference. These historical roots distinguish Norway from its neighbours, where large family fortunes have played an important role in foundations.

---

[10] Riksrevisjonen.

In recent years, foundations have become an institutional solution for the deregulation of certain types of publicly financed activities such as research and cultural institutions, and the management of national wealth. But the political needs to regulate the scope of foundation activities may conflict with the legal requirement that foundations be autonomous. This conflict is likely to intensify when new legislation is enacted in 2001 which will subject foundations to greater official control.

Bibliography

Backe, J. and Krøvel, A., *Legat - register*, Oslo, Cappelen, 1940.

Fondering av folketrygden, NOU 1998.

Grankvist, R., *Nidaros Kirkes Spital 700 år. Trondheims hospital 1277–1977*, F. Bruns Bokhandels Forlag, 1982.

Knudsen, G., *Stiftelsesloven, kommentarutgave*, Oslo, Universitetsforlaget, 1997.

Legater til utdanning i teoretisk og praktisk retning, Oslo, Universitetsforlaget, 1971.

Om stiftelser NOU 1988.

Riksrevisjonens undersøkelse vedrørende bruken av stiftelser i statlig forvaltning, Document nr. 3:6, 1998-99.

Stiftelser og omdanning, NOU 1975.

Woxholt, G., Stiftelsesrett, Unpublished manuscript, 1999.

▼ Carlos Monjardino

Portugal

1 Introduction

The existence of foundations in Portugal dates back to the early days of the monarchy. However their legal definition has remained somewhat ambiguous, leading both to flexibility and rigidity over the centuries. Generally, foundation characteristics recognized under Portuguese law are almost identical to those presented in the chapter by Anheier. Foundations in Portugal are self-governing, nonprofit-distributing and serve a public purpose. One special category is public foundations, which are created, financed and recognized by central or local authorities.

Traditionally foundations dealt with social needs issues. Today most foundations still pursue social aims, but cultural foundations have increasingly come to the forefront since the middle of this last century despite Portugal's years of isolationist policy and intense state control. After the 1980s, with mistrust and state-imposed difficulties overcome, rapid economic development and attractive tax incentives increased the rate of foundation establishment dramatically. At the same time, foundations have diversified their objectives considerably.

Today Portugal's foundation sector includes nearly 700 public or private institutions. They are mostly small operating foundations with limited resources compared to those of other European countries. Their increasing number and development has however led to a situation in which existing regulations and legal practices are no longer appropriate. The combination of on-going studies and new legislation due to be enacted in the near future should lead to greater understanding and use of this changing and growing sector.

2 Historical background.

As in other European countries the first foundations in Portugal appeared under the influence of the Catholic Church. The donation of property or inheritances to charitable and religious organizations has been practised since the early days of the monarchy, becoming particularly common in the Middle Ages and still continuing today. The creation of a foundation is attributed to D. Teresa (died 1130), the mother of Alfonso Henriques, Portugal's first king. The King's wife would later found another similar institution that survived until the 18th century.

Although the legal definition of foundations in Portugal only appeared at the end of the 19th century there are very early records of this type of organization. One of the oldest is the *Confraria dos Homens-Bons de Beja* (Brotherhood of Good Men of Beja), established in 1297. A lay organization, it was the first of many institutions that established the principles of what would later come to be known as mutual support.

The huge concentration of property owned by such institutions soon led monarchs to claim the right to inspect and hold jurisdiction over them. From the end of the 15th century, as part of their attempts to centralize government, some kings incorporated or merged many of these institutions. For instance all hospitals in Lisbon, many privately established, were merged to form one single institution. Other foundations, including their property and income, were incorporated into organizations like the *Misericórdias* (Houses of Mercy). The first *Misericórdia*, a charitable, church-run institution, was created in Lisbon on August 15, 1498. It became the model for many other institutions known as *Santas Casas* that soon spread throughout Portugal and into the overseas territories. Today they are public corporations included in what are called private welfare institutions.

The absolutism and anti-clericalism that characterized the 18th and 19th centuries limited the ability of foundations to acquire or own property. There were so many legacies benefiting foundations, both religious and secular that, in 1769, controls were imposed on people's freedom to leave goods to them. Coupled with an evident hostility towards the donation of goods in perpetuity, the new end-of-century ideological and philosophical concepts created the context for a series of laws that would be damaging to foundations.

The oldest foundation recorded in the Portuguese Company Records Office is the *Lar de Nossa Senhora das Dores e São José do Postigo do Sol* (Rest Home), created in 1825. However, the vast majority of the 664 foundations registered in Portugal were created after the 1950s.

This rapid growth is clearly linked to the Calouste Gulbenkian Foundation, the largest and most important foundation in Portugal, established in 1956. Encouraged by the Gulbenkian Foundation's influence and the major standing it acquired in all its fields of activity (particularly culture), Portugal has benefited from a favourable legal framework that allowed the sector to develop rapidly.

The consolidation of democracy in 1974, favourable economic conditions, and recognition of the failure of the comprehensive welfare state model among policy-makers, all contributed to a sharp increase in the number of foundations created by private initiatives and by the state. Civil society, either by choice or obligation, took upon itself duties that were formerly the domain of the state, and the latter in turn acknowledged that there were other ways of pursuing the common good.

3 Legal issues

There is no precise definition of a foundation in the Portuguese legal system. Currently, foundations are governed under the Civil Code, according to which a foundation is a nonprofit-making collective body with long-term aims and which is endowed with certain assets (Article 188). The flexibility of this general definition may be in part responsible for a surge in foundation creations in recent years; however it has also given rise to ambiguity and some confusion between different types of foundations and consequently will soon be changed.

Portuguese foundations may be either in the public or in the private interest. The designation 'in private interest' is applied when they carry out activities that benefit private groups only, or when they do not cooperate with the Public Administration despite having aims that are in the general interest. Foundations are 'in the public interest' when they act in the general interest and also cooperate with the state. This recognition of public interest is based on the principle that these entities provide relevant services to the community, often complementing the role of the state itself.

Public interest foundations, which are the vast majority, are administratively classified into two types: public legal entities acting solely in the public interest, and private social welfare institutions. Most Portuguese foundations are private social welfare institutions, that is they support children and young people, families, health initiatives, shelter for the elderly, job training, housing schemes and integration into society and the community. Foundations not classified as private social welfare institutions are considered public interest legal entities.

To establish a foundation a founder must designate assets to a particular long-term purpose, but the foundation acquires legal status only when government grants it recognition. Government recognition of public interest foundations is granted on an individual basis at the request of founders, their heirs or foundation administrators, except for foundations that pursue social welfare purposes in which case recognition is granted automatically according to standard administrative norms. Until 1987 only the civil government could recognize foundations. Since then it has, in principle, been the responsibility of the Portuguese Home Office. However, depending on its activities a foundation may also be recognized by the Ministries of Education or Social Welfare.

A foundation will only be officially recognized in Portugal if considered to be of long-term public interest and if it has sufficient resources and its own administration to pursue these aims. However, the law raises no objection to the creation of a foundation without any initial capital, provided activities are funded from some other source. Moreover, there is no legal definition of a minimal organizational structure for foundations, and no prescribed model of how foundations should be governed. Founders must define these foundation aspects, which consequently vary. Foundations may dissolve when (a) unable to pursue the aims for which they were created, (b) by-laws specify a situation calling for dissolution, and (c) a court decision of insolvency determines its defunct status.[1]

Government control over private social welfare institutions, whose aims are perceived as coinciding with government duties, is greater than for legal entities acting solely in the public interest. But in return private welfare institutions receive greater benefits. Therefore private social welfare foundations are governed by their own specific legal regime.[2]

Given their recognized status, public interest foundations enjoy a series of privileges and tax benefits whose values vary for private social welfare institutions and foundations operating solely in the public interest. All benefits are granted by established administrative norms or on an individual case basis depending on the tax in question, and all must submit their annual report and accounts for the financial year to the prime minister's office.

---

[1] Civil Code, Art. 192.

[2] The Regulation is contained in Decree-Law 119/83, 25 February.

All foundations recognized as being in the public interest are exempt from corporation tax. The Finance Ministry recognizes these exemptions and defines their scope when the parties concerned apply for tax exemption. VAT exemptions apply to foundations.[3] If so requested, foundations can also benefit from exemption from property sale and purchase tax, inheritance and donation tax, as well as exemption from local rates once approved by the relevant authority. Other benefits may also be granted, such as exemption from stamp duty and vehicle sale tax, benefits under the import duties system, and reduced electricity and water charges.

4 A profile of foundations in Portugal

There is no precise record of how many foundations exist in Portugal, in part because of their high rate of creation and in part because they may be recognized by different authorities. The following analysis is based on data from the Portuguese Company Records Office, the latest Portuguese *Foundations Guide* and a recent study by the Portuguese Home Office.

According to the Portuguese Company Records Office there were 664 foundations registered at the start of 1999. The oldest foundation dates back to 1825 but for over 100 years very few foundations were created, as Table 1.39 shows. This may be explained by Portugal's turbulent history during this period, characterized by several internal upheavals and also an unfavourable legal regime. In stark contrast, from the 1940s onwards the foundation sector changed dramatically.

Table 1.39 Rate of foundation establishment

Years	Number	%
1825–1900	12	1.8
1900–1920	7	1.1
1920–1940	17	2.6
1940–1960	115	17.3
1960–1980	143	21.5
after 1980	370	55.7
Total	**664**	**100**

Source: Portuguese Company Record Office

[3] They are established in the VAT Code and in the Decree-Law 20/90, 13 January.

Over 250 foundations were established between 1940 and 1980, and in the following 20 years this number was easily overtaken due to the stabilization of democratic life and a period of major economic development that encouraged the creation of foundations with less traditional aims, tax benefits and new interests in civil society.

Currently, the rate of foundation establishment is far from slowing: 48% of private foundations recognized by the Portuguese Home Office between 1987 and 1998 were created after 1995.

Foundations are geographically concentrated in the areas surrounding the two largest cities, with 50% of foundations in Lisbon and 22% in Oporto (Table 1.40).

Table 1.40 Geographical distribution of foundations

Region	%
North	18
Oporto region	11
Centre	24
Lisbon region	28
South	14
Madeira and Azores	5

Source: Portuguese Company Record Office

Data from the same source shows that geographical distribution was substantially even until the 1940s, and that uneven distribution became more pronounced subsequently. This is likely to be due to large-scale migration into urban areas.

Following the current legal framework, Portuguese foundations are generally incorporated with the minimum start-up capital. According to the latest Portuguese *Foundation Guide* (1996), more than 50% of foundations listed there were created with an initial fund of under PTE10 million (€50,000) while only 2% were created with funds in excess of PTE250 million (€1.25 million). Data provided by the Portuguese Home Office on trends between 1987 and 1998 show a similar pattern throughout the decade, with a slightly lower number of foundations (44%) having minimum start-up capital. This situation explains why the vast majority of Portuguese foundations are operating foundations, devoted to running small-scale programmes and providing services and goods rather than making grants. The number of grant-making foundations is not significant in Portugal, although they usually have large financial resources.

Historically Portuguese foundation activities were mainly of a social nature, but cultural activities have become increasingly important since the 1950s – particularly with the establishment of the Calouste Gulbenkian Foundation. Table 1.41 confirms that, even today, a large majority of these institutions aim to satisfy social and cultural needs: almost 50% of foundations are involved in social services and nearly 30% undertake cultural activities. However, in the last two decades foundations linked to education and research have grown at a healthy rate, reflecting new social needs. Other foundations with diverse objectives have grown equally.

Table 1.41 Foundation activities (%) by ICNPO categories, 1996

Culture and recreation	29
Education and research	14
Health	6
Social services	43
Environment	1
Development and housing	1
Law, advocacy and politics	2
International	1
Religion	3

Source: based on data from the Portuguese *Foundation Guide*

5 Current trends and conclusion

With their number growing to meet the needs of a changing society, foundations have unquestionably assumed a more important role in Portugal; their credibility is acknowledged both by society and the state. However, the existing legal regime has become outdated. The way forward must involve further study and a new legal framework that should be both clear and up-to-date.

In brief, the first step is for foundations to be clearly defined. The widespread confusion over the difference between public and private foundations, between foundations and private social welfare institutions, and the very concept of working 'in the public interest', needs to be addressed. Equally, the means of gaining legal status, the ways and means of creating foundations, the minimum statutory requirements and the organization and formation of the initial fund and assets should also be reviewed. Finally, the guiding principles governing action and recognition of foundations both need to be updated.

Foundations and public authorities should build a closer, more complementary relationship for public service provision. Under these conditions, without losing their autonomy, the short-term fall in foundation establishment should be matched by the growth of new foundations better equipped to meet the needs of Portuguese society in a time of radical change. There has never been such a great interest in these institutions as there is today. Foundations in Portugal are already recognized as trustworthy and competent organizations and have gained a vital position in Portugal's social economy. Their importance historically should also be fully acknowledged in order to promote a new period of stronger and more dynamic foundations.

Bibliography

Barroco, M. F., *Pessoas Colectivas e Solidariedade*, Livraria Arco-Íris e Cosmos, 1996.

Brás Carlos, A., *et al.*, *Guia dos Impostos em Portugal, Quid Juris?*, 1999.

Caetano, M., *Das Fundações*, Ática, 1961.

Freitas do Amaral, D., *Curso de Direito Administrativo*, Coimbra, 1987.

Ferrer Correia and Almeno de Sá, 'Algumas notas sobre Fundações', in: *Revista de Direito e Economia*, Ano XV, 1989.

Fausto de Quadros, das Fundações Públicas,- Polis. Verbo, 1984.

Ferrer Correia, 'Le Régime Juridique des Fondations Privées, Culturelles et Scientifiques en Droit Portugais', in: *Estudos vários de Direito*, 1982.

Guia das Fundações Portuguesas/Portuguese Foundations Guide, Fundação Oriente, 1996.

História de Portugal, Edição Monumental, Vol. IV, Portucalense, pp. 531-544, 1982.

Grande Enciclopédia Portuguesa Brasileira, Vols. XI and XVIII, Enciclopédia, 1960.

▼ José I. Ruiz Olabuénaga

Spain

1 Introduction

A foundation, in the Spanish context, is an organization whose main objective is the management of a patrimony or assets, intended by its founder for nonprofit-making purposes of general interest. Foundations have a long history in Spain, beginning in the Middle Ages and continuing to the present. This history is marked by a controversial relationship with the state, which has exerted considerable control over foundation establishment and management.

However, far from disappearing or losing social importance, foundations have acquired a new strength in modern Spanish society and are currently developing and diversifying. They have increasingly compensated for activities not covered by the welfare state, are relatively independent from the civil service and from the interests of the market, and yet have considerable influence in both those areas. The foundation sector is currently dominated by operating foundations working in the fields of culture and leisure, research and education, and welfare. Future amendments to the 1994 law on foundations could improve the currently increasing status and role of foundations in Spanish society.

2 Historical background

The beginnings of the nonprofit-making concept emerged with the institutionalization of the *traditio corporis et animae*, first introduced in the hospital of Bishop Masona from Mérida (6th century) and later extended to all Benedictine monasteries.[1] These were the beginning of a network of hospitals and hostels for pilgrims and sick people from urban areas. Later the ecclesiastical orders for the redemption of captives began to appear.

---

[1] The tradition of giving oneself in body and soul was a kind of covenant by which an individual joined a religious or monastic institution, committing both one's self and possessions to the institution during life and after death.

The tradition of Spanish foundations can be traced back to the Middle Ages when, *causa pietatis*, citizens started to make donations to churches and ecclesiastic authorities began to create cathedral schools, hospitals, hospices, orphanages and shelters for pilgrims and the poor. As it became popular among the early bourgeoisie to found welfare, educational and medical institutions, foundations spread. Families often chose to exert their influence on specific groups in need such as children, young girls, unmarried mothers, widows, or the elderly.

In these institutions initial patrimony was provided and later supplemented with alms, donations and contributions made by kings, lords, towns or individuals. This growing process led to an extraordinary flourishing of foundations in the 17th and 18th centuries. Around that time the rupture of the ancient regime brought a new social system that sought to increase the scope of state intervention, disapproved of church control over social welfare, attempted to free real-estate from the control of *main-morte* holders and demanded the development of a state welfare system.

The new system of land ownership introduced by the liberal revolution in Spain involved the abolition of the feudal estates, the break up of the feudal order and finally the selling of church lands. In 1798 King Carlos IV ordered the sale by royal decree of 'all the real-estate as well as the ground rents from those institutions and foundations' (see *Novisima Recopilación* where the decrees of Kings Carlos III and IV are codified). Twenty years later a new so called disentailment law (Spanish: *desamortization*) was added to the royal decree; it stipulated that all foundation properties were to be sold by the government. Specifically, by royal decree, King Carlos IV ordered the sale of 'all the real-estate as well as the ground rents from those institutions and foundations'. Disentailments, meaning that the assets of foundations were sold at public auction before the institution was dissolved, substantially reduced the number and economic importance of foundations but contrary to all expectations could not erase foundations from the social map.

According to the State Administrative Office there were 9107 foundations in Spain immediately before the King Carlos decree in the late 18th century. However, a number of trends subsequently contributed to a substantial decrease in foundation prestige and number.

First, a philosophical trend in vogue at the beginning of the 19th century claimed that the abolition of entailed estates (estates owned and administered by the institutions and foundations) was essential for the modernization of Spanish society. Entailed estates should be for sale on the free market, and foundations – considered a hindrance from the past – should disappear. The most immediate effect was the dissolution of existing foundations and the banning of new ones.[2]

Second, social pressure arose for the state to replace private welfare activities, thus meeting the new social needs generated by Spain's industrial revolution in the second half of the 19th century. Both the socialist ideologies and the corporatism of the Franco regime also demanded state rather than private intervention. With the development of the welfare state (although later in Spain than in the rest of Europe and only partial at that) foundations no longer seemed to have a purpose and their activities were considered unnecessary and superfluous.

The socio-economic success of social democracy, and its subsequent crisis, were also reflected in Spanish society later than in Europe. In the beginning this caused a period of national euphoria that, following the European crisis of the welfare state, promoted the presence of private nonprofit-making entities, once again including foundations. After almost two centuries of institutional hostility towards foundations, Spanish society witnessed a partial acceptance. This public approval was reflected in the Spanish Constitution of 1978, which explicitly acknowledges the right to create foundations. However, this acknowledgement was not completely free of an underlying distrust of foundations; almost 20 more years passed before a new law (1994) was passed to regulate the ordinary activity of foundations.

3 Legal issues

Before the Spanish Constitution, there was a legal tangle of a wide range of dissimilar regulations with more than doubtful legal force or even applicability. The Spanish Constitution established the right to create foundations (Article 34) and acknowledged the right of foundations to operate for the general interest. The Act on Foundations 1994 and Tax Incentives for Private Participation Activities for the General Interest 1994 effectively updated the legal definition of foundations, going beyond the traditional identification of foundations with their patrimony and instead considering them 'organizations'.

The Act on Foundations 1994[3] differentiates two kinds of nonprofit organizations: associations and foundations. The core element of

---

[2] Acts from 1823 and 1836.

[3] The exact denomination is 30/94 Act on Foundations and Tax Incentives for Private Participation in Activities for the General Interest.

foundations is their patrimony or assets (*universitas rerum*), whereas the core element of nonprofit associations is their membership (*universitas personarum*). Thus the main characteristic of a foundation is that its patrimony or assets, which may include 'all kinds of goods and rights liable to economic appraisal' (Article 17.1), must be intended for a particular purpose.

Foundations are legally defined as 'nonprofit-making organizations whose patrimony or assets, by their founders' wish, is intended permanently for purposes of general interest'. Purposes of general interest, according to Article 2.1, include 'fields like: social welfare, civil rights, education, culture, science, sports, medical care, co-operation for development, environmental protection, economy and research, volunteer work, or any other similar field'. This article stresses that foundations must not be used for fraudulent purposes or for the exclusive or preferential benefit of founders, their family or friends.

Thus foundations are private institutions for the public interest. This relationship between private property and public interest, and between the founder's wish and the law, requires a balance. Articles 1 and 2 stipulate that 'foundations are ruled by their founder's will, by their statutes', while Article 9 specifies that 'any provision in the foundation's statutes or statement in the founder's will contrary to this Act will be regarded as not included'.

The foundation's main governing and representative body is the board of trustees but it is further managed by the protectorate and the Foundations' Higher Council. The protectorate is a state body whose function is 'to see the effective fulfilment of the objectives of the foundation in accordance with the founder's will and bearing in mind the attainment of the general interest' (Article 32), and to safeguard 'the legality of the foundation's constitution and functioning' (Article 33).[4] The Foundations' Higher Council is a 'consulting body integrated by representatives of the State and of the foundations'.[5]

---

[4] The protectorate's specific functions are: a) to give legal advice to registered foundations and to those in the process of being constituted; b) to see to the effective achievement of foundations' aims; c) to ensure that foundations' economic resources are applied to achieve their aims; d) to give publicity to the foundation existence and activities; e) to provisionally perform the functions of the governing body of the foundation if for some reason all its members are absent (Articles 32 and 33).

[5] According to Article 39 the functions of the Higher Council are: 'a) to assess, inform and give opinion on any legal or statutory provision which directly affects the foundations, as well as to make proposals; b) to plan and propose the necessary actions for the promotion and encouragement of foundations, carrying out the required research; c) all other functions that the provisions in operation may assign it'.

According to the 1994 Act, foundations are eligible for several main kinds of tax exemption.

- **Corporation tax.** Foundations enjoy tax exemption on the benefits obtained by the activities constituting their specific social purpose or aim, or by the capital gains from purchases or transfers of properties or shares once obtained or done in the fulfilment of the specific aim of the foundation.
- **Economic activities tax.** Foundations are exempt from real-estate tax and from the economic activity tax on the activities that constitute their social aim.
- **Donations made by individuals.** Individuals may deduct from their personal income tax a maximum of 20% of the amounts donated to known foundations and associations.
- **Donations made by legal persons.** The law differentiates several types of donations made by societies to foundations and associations that fulfil the known requirements. Depending on the donation the deduction may be 10% or 30%.
- **Commercial and political activities.** Foundations may not participate, in any way, in commercial societies in which they should be personally responsible for the liabilities of those societies. There is no reference or legal limitation to political activities, in fact it is quite common to create foundations within the political parties themselves.

The Foundation Act 30/1994 is considered excessively interventionist and too controlling of the right to create foundations.[6] This alleged excess is thought to be an institutional reflection of Spain's historical suspicion toward foundations. Various institutions and foundations have made proposals to modify the regulations, usually focusing on the functions of the protectorate which is regarded as a mechanism of tutelage and control of foundations. However, the protectorate institution can also be seen as one that avoids both fraud and failures in the management of the foundations.[7]

---

[6] LEY 30/1994; Fundación BBV.

[7] Other proposals involve changing the Foundation Act to include a paid manager of foundations, and putting foundations and associations on equal footing regarding their liquidation. Currently if a foundation is dissolved the remaining capital is donated to entities with purposes of general interest, whereas upon the on the liquidation of an association, each member gets his or her share.

4 A profile of foundations in Spain

The Spanish foundation sector is rather heterogeneous. The Act on Foundations 1994 gives rise to a typology of foundations differentiated by their founder (public – created by the state and public entities – and private);[8] territorial area of action (national level and autonomous community level); aims (welfare, cultural, educational and work foundations); and patrimony (endowment foundations with initial patrimony or assets sufficient to fulfil their objective, and managerial or operating foundations whose assets are essential for their subsistence).

Today there are about 6000 foundations spread throughout Spain. More than 20% operate nationally, whereas the rest restrict their area of influence to one or several Autonomous Communities.[9] The social importance of foundations may be measured by comparing their number with that of nonprofit-making entities in Spain (Table 1.42). Of a total of 253,507 nonprofit-making organizations, 2.4% are foundations.

Table 1.42 Distribution of types of nonprofit-making organizations

Type	Number	%
Foundations[10]	5698	2.4
Associations[11]	174,916	70.0
Sport clubs[12]	58,085	23.0
Co-operatives	7822	3.1
Education centres	6392	2.5
Pension plans friendly societies	400	>1.0
Hospitals	144	>1.0
Savings-banks that fund charities	50	>1.0
Total	**253,507**	**100**

Source: Own calculations of the author (2000).

---

[8] In all cases, foundations regulated by the Act 30/94 on Foundations are private entities.

[9] Cabra de Luna.

[10] However, as a result of the historical hegemony of the Church civil law coexists with the canon law of the Catholic Church, which in the Spanish legal system maintains an important social presence in foundation issues. After extrapolating the figures for some Spanish dioceses, we estimate the total number of existing foundations is probably 17% higher than the number verified in the Foundations Registry.

[11] The figure corresponds to the listing provided by the Spanish Home Office dated 31/12/96, but it would be more accurate to apply it to the year 1995 given the bureaucracy gap between the recording of the data and the publication of the Register.

[12] Only competitive and federated sport clubs not transformed into Public Limited Companies (PLC) by the recent Spanish legislation are included.

The social and economic changes experienced by Spanish society are reflected in the evolution in the number and type of Spanish foundations. The rate of foundation establishment shown in Table 1.43 shows that more than 70% were created after Spain's economic development plans of the 1970s. Before 1970, the most important foundations were found in the welfare and social services sectors.

Table 1.43 Rate of foundation registration at the Ministry for Education and Culture (% of all foundations)

	before 1970	1970–79	1980–89	after 1990	Total
Cultural	2.8	2.8	36.1	58.3	100.0
Educational	16.2	10.6	19.2	54.0	100.0

Source: Cultural Foundations Official Register 1997

Cultural, educational and research activities experienced the greatest growth throughout the 1980s and 1990s. In general, Spain's recent economic success has made it possible for many individuals as well as corporations to donate assets to nonprofit institutions. On the other hand, the provision of social assistance by the welfare state has encouraged founders to promote cultural and research foundations rather than those oriented toward welfare.

Currently, most civil law foundations (80.5%) concentrate their activities in three sectors: culture and leisure, research and education, and welfare.[13] This is true across the foundation sector; a breakdown of foundation activities by the 11 sectors of the international classification of nonprofit organizations shows that 2002 foundations are active in education and research, 1450 in social services, 772 in health and 1140 in culture, sports and recreation. Less than 350 foundations are active in the remaining sectors.[14]

More than 95% of Spanish foundations are operating rather than grant making, mostly set up by private owners rather than by communities or enterprises. However, an increasing number of foundations are both grant making and operating, and an increasing number are created by local authorities.

---

[13] Source: Ministry of Labour and Social Affairs; Ministry of Education and Culture. Within the group the foundations are distributed in the following proportions: education and research foundations 35.9%, culture and leisure foundation 34.0%, welfare foundations 30.1%.

[14] Sources: Ministry of Labour and Social Affairs; Ministry of Education and Culture; Ruiz Olabuénaga.

Most foundations in Spain have only small assets. Relatively few are giant foundations that are economically powerful because of their patrimony. These typically have high quality modern management bodies and technology, whereas small foundations often have non-professional management and show institutional weaknesses that force them to make concessions to their patrons and benefactors. Most foundation presidents and directing board members are volunteers, who have little management experience.

The economic importance of foundations can be evaluated within the nonprofit-making sector generally and as a proportion of the Spanish GDP (Table 1.44). Their economic importance is higher (14.9%) than their number of entities (2.24%). The economic importance of foundations can be estimated as ESP418,820 million (€2.5 billion), equivalent to a 0.6% of the Spanish GDP. However it varies considerably across different fields of activity. Most foundation expenditures occurred in one of the top three fields of activity for foundations (culture; sports; recreation) and were lowest in fields provided for by the welfare state.

Table 1.44 Economic importance of foundations, by fields of activity, 1995

Activities	Total nonprofit sector expenditure (ESP)	Foundations		
		Expenditure (ESP)	% of the nonprofit sector	% of GDP
Culture, sport & recreation	491,417	270,270	55.0	0.39
Education & research	584,325	56,216	9.6	0.08
Social services	445,963	47,784	10.7	0.07
Health	370,764	25,730	6.9	0.04
Others	926,104	18,820	2.0	0.03
Total	**2,818,574**	**418,820**	**14.9**	**0.60**

Source: Own calculation (2000); Cabra

Foundations employed 64,332 people in full-time jobs in 1995, representing 13.5% of all jobs in the nonprofit-making sector (475,179) and about 0.6% of all non-agrarian full-time jobs in Spain.[15]

---

[15] Ruiz Olabuénaga, p. 150.

5 Current trends and conclusion

Despite hundreds of years of adverse treatment by the state, foundations have made an impressive comeback in Spain, particularly in activities not covered by the welfare state. The current crisis in the welfare state and the re-emergence of civil society as an alternative to state omnipresence suggest that the influence of foundations in Spanish social life will be even greater in the near future. Their number and size, far from decreasing, are likely to increase steadily.

Although some Spanish state institutions and intellectuals still retain something of the historical suspicion toward foundations,[16] it is obvious that foundations are increasingly gaining social legitimacy. In Spanish society a new idea is taking hold: that foundations, given their legal personality and tax treatment, are an attractive type of institution for promoting all kinds of social care, cultural and scientific activities. They successfully fill a gap that neither the state nor private enterprise can cover. In this sense, there is great pressure for the modification of present legislation so that foundations may be more independent of state supervision and control, particularly the protectorate. There is also a need for solutions that reflect the heterogeneous nature of the Spanish foundation sector.

Bibliography

Alberich Nistral, T., 'Aspectos Cuantitativos del Asociacionismo en España', in: *Documentación Social*, 1994, 94, pp. 53–74.

Alvarez Alvarez, J. L., *El Patronato y el Gobierno de las Fundaciones, La Ley 30/1994 de Fundaciones*, Ciclo de Conferencias de la Real academia de Jurisprudencia y Legislación, Madrid, Fundación Ramón Areces, 1996.

Anes Fernández, L., *Las Fundaciones de Asistencia y Enseñanza en la Asturia Rural de la Segunda Mitad del Siglo XVIII*, Madrid, Universidad Complutense, 1995.

Arias, M. D., *Las Fundaciones en el Impuesto sobre Sociedades*, Madrid, Marcial Pons, 1995.

Baiges, S., *Las ONGDs de desarrollo en España*, Barcelona, Flor de Viento 1996.

Beneyto Berenguer, R., *Las Fundaciones Benefico-Asistenciales de la Iglesia Católica en el Ordenamiento Jurídico Español*, Valencia, Universidad de Valencia, 1995.

Cabra de Luna, M. A., *El Tercer Sector y las Fundaciones en España. Hacia el nuevo milenio*, Madrid, Escuela Libre Editorial, 1998.

Casado, D., *Organizaciones Voluntarias en España*, Barcelona, Editorial Hacer, 1995.

Centro de Fundaciones, *Directorio de las Fundaciones Españolas*, Madrid, Centro de Fundaciones, Fundación San Benito de Alcántara.

---

[16] Perez Diaz; Fundacion BBV; de Lorenzo; Casado.

Confederación Española de Fundaciones, *Código de Fundaciones: Normativa Estatal, Autonómica y Fiscal Concordada*, Madrid, Confederación Española de Fundaciones, 1997.

Cortes Generales, *Ley de Fundaciones y de Incentivos Fiscales a la Participación Privada en Actividades de Interés General: Trabajos Parlamentarios*, Madrid, Publicación de las Cortes Generales, 1996.

De Lorenzo García, R., 'Las Fundaciones y el Sector No Lucrativo', in: *Documentación Social*, 103, págs. 217–28, 1996.

Fundación BBV, *Consideraciones sobre el Tratamiento Jurídico y Fiscal de las Fundaciones*, Bilbao, 1994.

Gomez Villa, J. I., *Intervención en la obra Consideraciones sobre tratamiento jurídico y fiscal de las fundaciones españolas*, Bilbao, Centro de Fundaciones, Documenta, Fundación BBV, 1994.

Jornadas sobre la Nueva Ley de Fundaciones, *Las Fundaciones: Su Nuevo Régimen Jurídico, Fiscal y Contable. Jornadas sobre la Nueva Ley de Fundaciones*, Madrid, Dykinson, 1995.

López Alarcon, M., *Las Fundaciones Eclesiásticas bajo el Nuevo Régimen de la Ley 30/1994, de Fundaciones e Incentivos Fiscales*, Murcia, Real Academia de Legislación y Jurisprudencia, 1997.

Ministerio de Asuntos Sociales, *Encuentro sobre Fundaciones*, El Escorial, Madrid, 1994.

Ministerio de Asuntos Sociales, *Las Fundaciones en la Acción Social: Directorio de Fundaciones y Establecimientos tutelados por el Ministerio de Asuntos Sociales*, Madrid, Ministerio de Asuntos Sociales, 1995.

Ministerio de Educacion y Cultura, *Directorio de Fundaciones Culturles*, 1997.

Nieto Alonso, A., *Fundaciones: Su Capacidad. Especial Consideración a la Realización de Actividades Mercantiles e Industriales*, Galicia, Universidad de Santiago de Compostela, 1995.

Piñar Mañas, J. L., 'El derecho de fundación como derecho constitucional', in: *Revista Derecho Privado y Constitución*, Núm. 9, mayo-agosto, 1996.

Rodriguez Cabrero, G., Montserrat Codorniu, J., *Las entidades voulntarias en España. Institucionalización, estructura económica y desarrollo asociativo*, Madrid, Ministerio de Asuntos Sociales, 1996.

Rojas Montes, L., *La Fundación: Instrumento privado de intereses generales*, Granada, Real Academia de Jurisprudencia y Legislación, 1996.

Ruiz Olabuénaga J. I., *El Tercer Sector en España*, FBBV, Bilbao, 2000.

Saenz de Miera, A., 'Las Fundaciones Españolas en el siglo XX', in: *Revista de Occidente*, 180, 1996, pp. 71–93.

Serra Rodriguez, A., *Las fundaciones: elementos esenciales y constitución*, Valencia, Editorial Práctica del Derecho, 1995.

Yuste Grijalba, J. L., y Del Campo Arbulo, J. A., 'Apuntes históricos sobre fundaciones en España', in: *Revista Situación*, Núm. 4, Bilbao, Servicio de Estudios del BBV, 1989.

▼ Filip Wijkström

Sweden

1 Introduction[1]

Foundations are sparsely researched and, in general, poorly understood actors in Swedish society, as seems also to be the case in the other Scandinavian countries. On different occasions estimates of the total number of foundations in Sweden have, for example, varied between 20,000 and 50,000. However, thanks to new legislation in 1996, requiring foundations of a certain size to register with public authorities, we can for the first time obtain a better picture of around 14,000–15,000 larger foundations.

Foundations represent a significant part of the Swedish nonprofit sector. In 1992, foundations accounted for 12% of the total operating expenditures of this sector, as shown by Lundström and Wijkström.[2] Foundations in Sweden are grant making as well as operating, and can be administered either by a board of their own or via the board of another organization, for example, a voluntary association or a municipality. The foundation definition suggested by Anheier fits the situation in Sweden quite well, where a foundation is a private, self-governed, non-membership-based and nonprofit distributing asset. However, foundations in Sweden are not required to serve a public purpose.

Foundations are important actors in Swedish society as a whole, particularly in areas such as scientific research funding or pension funds. Significant parts of Swedish industrial and business life are further controlled through stock kept in a number of private foundations. Within Swedish government, foundations have also been used, especially in the 1970s and 1980s, for example to promote regional

[1] The author is grateful to Mikael Wiman (the County Administration Board in Stockholm) for invaluable support, as well as to Dr Dan Brändström (CEO of the Bank of Sweden Tercentenary Foundation) and Professor Jan S. Nilsson (Executive Member of the Board of the KAW Foundation) for encouragement and comments on earlier drafts.

[2] Lundström and Wijkström.

development and cooperation between business and universities, at national as well as municipal level.[3] Many private foundations – some 30,000 as estimated in the late 1970s – are also administered under public auspices, mainly at municipal level.[4] Finally, new and interesting activities, in a recently re-opened borderland between the state and the private sphere, have in several cases been started as foundations by 'social entrepreneurs'.

2 Historical background

Foundations have a long and rich history in Sweden, a history that starts in the Middle Ages. When Statistics Sweden surveyed the 12,629 foundations existing in 1910, it was found that at least 70 were created in the 17th century or earlier.[5] Many were established by royalty or by the nobility, and some were even used as tools in the administration of the country prior to a clearly distinguished state apparatus or a separate public sector. Danviks Hospital in Stockholm, for example, was founded by King Gustav Vasa in 1533; in the 1620s, King Gustav Adolf donated large estates to Uppsala University, which as a result became self-sustaining for centuries.[6]

Early foundations were established mainly as orphanages or to provide relief to the poor. A shift toward higher education took place after the Reformation. Many older foundations were caught in a trap similar to that affecting the concept of charity. The concept has a negative connotation in Swedish and is today almost exclusively associated with private social welfare for the poor to the exclusion of art, culture and education.[7] Charity in Sweden was heavily dependent on a wealthy and paternalistic upper class, often inspired by a 'scientific charity doctrine', which held that the root causes of poverty and distress lay in the bad habits of the poor. The negative images of charity and philanthropy stem from a picture of poor and needy human beings, caught in pauperism and restricted to the limited capacity of eleemosynary and, at times, capricious arrangements for their very existence.[8] This picture does not sit well with a Swedish social-democratic tradition.

---

[3] RRV.

[4] Ds Ju, 1979.

[5] Reported in Frii, p. 12.

[6] Olsson, *Stiftelser*, p. 59; Brändström, p. 2.

[7] See Lundström and Wijkström, pp. 17–19.

[8] Lundström and Wijkström, p. 18.

In the late 19th and early 20th century, it was typically members of the aristocracy or the capitalist elite, the 'establishment', that created foundations. This practice can be seen as conserving existing power structures by lessening the worst effects of an expanding industrial society in order, not to promote a more equal distribution of wealth or an egalitarian society, but rather to tone down the most apparent distress and inequalities. Disadvantaged groups were prevented from revolting against more fortunate classes. Furthermore, in the early 19th century, official documents stated that if donations to foundations were accepted without constraints, there was a risk of concentrating greater wealth than necessary in foundations. It was also feared that 'if the right to establish new foundations would be unlimited, it would be possible to separate considerable property from private ownership only to satisfy personal whims or vanity.'[9]

These factors, a negative image of charity, a power conservation effect, and the 'vanity risk', help explain a generally suspicious stance toward foundations in Sweden. We can also understand why the idea of charity as well as private philanthropic foundations as part of the social welfare system has been contested in Sweden during most of the 20th century, and is still a burning issue when moving into the 21st century.

These fears also led to restrictions on foundations, for example a less favourable fiscal treatment compared to that of nonprofit (*ideell*) associations. By the mid-20th century, suspicion and hostility toward foundations surfaced again. The debate was refuelled, when it became increasingly apparent that a number of major foundations were being used to ensure a few families' extensive control over large industrial corporations – a control stretching over generations. Some of the largest industrial groups were, and still are, ultimately controlled by private foundations that own a substantial part of their stock.[10] In 1962, the leader of the Swedish Communist Party (VPK), C. H. Hermansson, published a book in which he identified the 15 most powerful industrial or business families in Sweden. In the book he specifically recognized foundations as an important tool of control used by these families.[11]

In an influential official report from 1968, this line of thought is followed up. The report identifies a number of charitable foundations

---

[9] *Förstag till Allmän Civillag* (1826), quoted in Hessler, p. 5, my translation.

[10] Sundin and Sundqvist.

[11] Hermansson, pp. 284–85.

that double as power tools for families such as the Wallenbergs. Part of their exceptionally strong control position in Swedish business life is due to the control of property belonging not to the family, but to the Knut and Alice Wallenberg (KAW) Foundation. Through this foundation, the family had a significant impact on the selection of board members in major Swedish corporations.[12] Other examples included in the 1968 report are the Axel and Margaret Axson Johnsons Foundation, the Åhlén Foundation, the two Kempe Foundations as well as both the Söderberg Foundations. Conclusion: 'With few exceptions, it could be assumed that foundations of this type have been set up to make it easier for the donating family to maintain the control of the concerned companies.'[13] The debate lead to increased demands for public control over private charitable foundations in the late 1960s.[14] As a result, a special law was introduced in 1982, giving government the right to assign one member to the board of a number of large, private tax-exempt foundations.[15]

A partly parallel debate resurfaced in the mid-1990s, but instead of focusing on certain families, it concentrated on how the capital rationale associated with some of the dominating actors (some of them using foundations) might harm the plurality and freedom of ideology in the press and perhaps restrict media diversity.[16] A sense of this negative attitude thus prevailed in the 1990s, as also noticed by several institutions (e.g., the Royal Academy of Science, the Nobel Foundation and the Beijer Foundation) in their comments upon a proposed new law for foundations.[17]

A power struggle over the use and control of foundations by different groups can be discerned in Sweden throughout the 19th and 20th centuries. Foundations are, by tradition, created by individuals and ideological interests leaning more to the right or conservative side of the political spectrum. However, as the major popular movements (e.g. temperance, labour movement and free-church movements) as well as other membership organizations grew stronger, the foundation form was increasingly used by them to secure taken ground.

---

[12] SOU 1968:7 (p. 118).

[13] SOU 1968:7 (p. 35) my translation.

[14] See Olsson, *Stiftelser*, pp. 269–71, for recent comments on this debate in Sweden, and Nielsen, or Ylvisaker, p. 361 for a similar development in the United States.

[15] Law 1982:315. Only foundations with assets surpassing SEK5 million (€585,000), and only ten foundations at a time, could be controlled in this way.

[16] SOU 1994:145 (p. 145).

[17] Ds 1992 (p. 21–9). See also Olsson, *Stiftelser*.

Important cases are the residential colleges (*folkhögskolor*), often incorporated as foundations, but most of the larger Swedish popular movement organizations have today a number of closely associated foundations through which a variety of important institutions are operated.

At the same time, though, foundations have been used by conservative interests to counterbalance these shifts of power occurring in society through the increasing influence of the popular movements and their organizations. This intention is clear, for example, in the will establishing the foundations behind one major local Swedish newspaper, *Upsala Nya Tidning* (UNT). Three foundations were created explicitly to preserve a liberal spirit and to save the paper from being edited in a social-democratic, temperance or free-church spirit.[18] Other, more recent, examples are many of the 'free-schools' (*friskolor*) established during the 1990s, at least partly to break up the earlier monopoly of the public sector in this field. Approximately 25% of the nearly 550 private operators running schools in Sweden today are foundations.[19] But, foundations have also deliberately been used to balance the institutions *both* of the market and the state: 'Through the foundation form, we strive to distance ourselves both from private capitalism and state ownership.'[20]

Despite the struggles and prevailing negativity toward foundations in Sweden, many foundations have managed to become successful and some have achieved high public esteem. This is especially so concerning foundations financing scientific research, which was added to the list of purposes granted tax exemption in 1942. Today, this is a major activity of Swedish foundations, at least in terms of their accumulated wealth. Three of the largest and most prominent Swedish foundations are the earlier mentioned Knut and Alice Wallenberg (KAW) Foundation, the Nobel Foundation and the Bank of Sweden Tercentenary Foundation.

The KAW Foundation, founded in 1918, is the largest and most important private contributor to research and higher education in Sweden,[21] with assets valued at SEK27.2 billion (€3.2 billion) in 1997. In the same year, SEK776 million (€90 million) were distributed for

---

[18] '... att tidningen redigeras i liberal, icke i förbudistisk, frireligiös eller socialdemokratisk anda', reported in Hirschfeldt, p. 13.

[19] Personal communication with Ms Saghi Partovi at the National Agency for Education (Skolverket) in March, 2000.

[20] Ds 1992, p. 71 my translation.

[21] Hoppe, Nylander and Olsson.

scientific research in the natural sciences. The Nobel Foundation is probably the best known Swedish foundation internationally. The first Nobel Prize was awarded in 1901, based on Alfred Nobel's will from 1895. The original donation of SEK31.5 million grew to some SEK2 billion (€234 million) by 1993. The Bank of Sweden Tercentenary Foundation was instituted in 1962 to promote scientific research through an endowment from the Bank of Sweden. Since 1965 it has awarded at least SEK2.5 billion (€292 million) in research grants.[22] At the end of 1997, its total assets were valued at SEK5.4 billion (€630 million), the original endowment representing SEK3.3 billion and the remainder comprised of a special endowment from the former Wage-Earner Funds received in 1994.

Foundations are thus important actors in the field of research and higher education in Sweden. As an example, the Stockholm School of Economics (itself an operating foundation with an annual turnover of SEK300 million) and the associated Stockholm School of Economics Association received some SEK50 million from four major grant-making foundations in the fiscal year of 1997–98. Grants or scholarships received by individuals or groups of researchers are not included.[23]

3 Legal issues[24]

The nonprofit sector and its organizations have received limited attention in research and policy work in Sweden. However, we can observe in the legal system, as well as in praxis, how the ideology of the welfare state towards nonprofit organizations is codified.

Until 1996 there was no foundation law in Sweden; their legal treatment was based on praxis and legal doctrine only. The only previous legal definition of a foundation is found in a 1929 law[25] on supervision and control, describing a foundation as an autonomously administered property set aside continuously to serve a specific purpose. Today, foundations are dealt with in two areas of Swedish legislation: fiscal laws dating back to the early 19th century, which determine foundation tax benefits; and, since 1996, in the corporate or associational legal system.

---

[22] Brändström, pp. 10–12.

[23] SSE Annual Report 1997/98, p. 11.

[24] Based on a review of the legal entities of the nonprofit sector by the author, published as Chapter 4 in Lundström and Wijkström, pp. 108-133. For further reading, please refer to the bibliography.

[25] Law 1929:116

According to the 1996 law, a foundation is created when it is given a name (including the word *stiftelse*), and when certain property has been irrevocably assigned to be managed autonomously in accordance with the written constitution of the foundation. This is, to a large extent, a codification of existing case law and legal doctrine. The difference lies in a stronger focus on the demand that the property really has been separated from the donor. Under the new law there are two major types of Swedish foundations: grant making (*avkastningsstiftelse*) and operating (*verksamhetsstiftelse*) foundations.[26]

The law, explicitly, does not cover church foundations or family foundations, but introduces two other special forms of foundation – the fundraising foundation (*insamlingsstiftelse*) and the collective-agreement foundation (*kollektivavtalsstiftelse*).[27] The new law also specifically recognizes a third type, the safe-guarding foundation (*tryggandestiftelse*), which is covered in a separate law from 1967 and refers to pension and personnel foundations. A pension foundation is created by an employer; the exclusive purpose being to safeguard a pension commitment to the employees.[28] Safe-guarding foundations are large capital owners and represent some 25% of all larger foundations. They control more than 40% of the total foundation wealth in Sweden, and a number of the largest pension foundations (e.g. the foundations associated with ABB, Volvo and Electrolux) have created an interest organization of their own, the 'Swedish Pension Fund Association'.

A fourth type of foundation was introduced (but not instated) in the proposals leading up to the new law: the appropriation foundation (*anslagsstiftelse*). This type of foundation has often been used by government or municipalities, and the assets of the foundations are spent each year, making the foundation dependent upon new annual appropriations to continue its work.[29] Foundations may further be classified by their type of administration, which according to the new law can take two basic forms: administration by a board of its own (*egen förvaltning*) or through linked administration (*anknuten förvaltning*), whereby the board of another organization is responsible.

---

[26] Proposition 1993/94:9 (e.g., pp. 40–41). See also Isoz (e.g., p. 19) or Olsson, *Stiftelser*, p. 73) for comments and discussions on the new law.

[27] Proposition 1993/94:9, pp. 52-59.

[28] Law 1967:531 (Tryggandelagen).

[29] See, e.g. RRV or Olsson, *Stiftelser*.

Fiscal law granted foundations favourable tax treatment by 1810, particularly for scholarship funds and some charitable foundations (*fromma stiftelser*). However, the current legislation dates back to 1942.[30] Foundations are traditionally less favoured than nonprofit associations in Sweden in terms of the range of activities for which they are granted tax-exemption, and because they are generally held to stricter standards and kept under tougher control.[31] For example, a government bill from 1942 explicitly repudiated the idea of expanding the range of tax-exemption for foundations to fields like theatre, music, the arts or sports, which would all be tax-exempt for nonprofit associations.[32]

To receive tax-exemption as a foundation in Sweden today, a foundation must belong to one of two main groups:

- the charitable foundations
- the 'Catalogue' subjects (see below).[33]

To be considered charitable, a foundation must comply with three prerequisites.

1 Its aim and purpose should be considered a 'qualified' public good purpose.
2 More than 80% of its income over five years should be spent.
3 Its main activity should be carried out along the aim or purpose stated.

'Qualified' purposes include health care, strengthening the national defence, furthering childcare and upbringing or education, relief work among the needy, promotion of scientific research (included in a revision in 1942), and furthering cooperation between the Scandinavian countries (included as late as in 1991).[34]

The 'Catalogue' (*katalogen*) lists 14 categories of legal entities (e.g. compulsory student unions) and 45 specifically mentioned organizations (e.g. the Nobel Foundation). The included foundations are only subject to tax on income from real property, and not, for example, on income from other business activities.[35]

---

[30] Isoz, p. 23.

[31] As noted by Lundström and Wijkström, pp. 122–3, 128.

[32] Proposition 1942:134, p. 48.

[33] SOU 1995:63, p. 219ff.

[34] SOU, 1995:63, p. 128.

[35] Law 1947:576 (7 § 4 mom). See also SOU 1995:63 for a good overview.

New legislation for foundation taxation was proposed in 1995.[36] The revision has met with criticism on the grounds that a drastically new situation would be at hand for some foundations – especially the grant-making type but also foundations with their assets in real-estate. This could, it has been argued, foster a negative attitude in the general faith in the legal system as far as future donations and foundations are concerned.[37]

4 A profile of foundations in Sweden

In the early 20th century, between 12,000 to 13,000 foundations existed in Sweden; by 1976 an estimated 51,000 foundations with a combined wealth of SEK23.7 billion (€2.8 billion) were found.[38] About 48,100 of these were classified as nonprofit or charitable (*ideella*) while the rest were considered family foundations, or personnel and pension foundations.[39] Pension and personnel foundations, as well as collective-agreement foundations, are important actors in the labour market field.

About 39,000 foundations in the 1976 survey (with total assets of SEK2.7 billion or €315 million) were managed under linked administration. Some 31,300 were found under public auspices (e.g. government, county or church municipality), while another 6600 were controlled by a nonprofit organization, and 1000 foundations were managed by the same board as a for-profit corporation. Finally, approximately 11,700 foundations, (combined wealth estimated at SEK21 billion or €2.5 billion) were managed by autonomous boards.[40] A later survey found that 16,169 foundations were registered with the tax authorities in 1990, and estimated that 1500 new foundations were created in the period 1982–88.[41]

To provide a more recent estimate of the number and wealth of foundations, a preliminary analysis of national data obtained from the County Administration Board in Stockholm has been carried out specifically for this chapter (see Table 1.45). According to the new

---

[36] SOU, 1995:63.

[37] E..g. Mutén, or Proposition, 1993/94:9, pp. 46–8.

[38] However, higher wealth estimates have also been provided and the estimated number of foundations has been questioned (see e.g. Frii , p.9, or Isoz, p. 11.

[39] Ds Ju, 1979:4.

[40] Ds Ju, 1979:4, pp. 3-4; 28–30.

[41] SOU1995:63, pp. 56–57.

law, all operating (*näringsdrivande*) foundations as well as foundations with total assets exceeding SEK350,000 (€41,000) must register with the County Administration Board. In total, more than 14,200 foundations – with assets of approximately SEK226 billion (€26.4 billion) – have been registered until May 2000.

Table 1.45 Preliminary estimate of distribution of Swedish foundations[42]

Type of foundation	Share (%)	Share of wealth (%)
Pension foundations	21.2	38.7
Personnel foundations	5.0	2.2
Fundraising foundations	2.3	0.2
Collective-agreement foundations	0.2	1.2
Operating foundations (*näringsdrivande stiftelse*)	12.2	15.0
Other foundations	59.1	42.6
Total number/wealth (SEK billion)	**14,213 [100.0%]**	**225.852 [99.9%]**

Source: The County Administration Board in Stockholm (May 12, 2000)

Some 37% of these larger foundations (controlling more than 75% of the total assets) are registered in Stockholm. Exactly the same share of Stockholm-based foundations was found in a 1992 study of all foundations with employees (approximately 2600).[43] An estimate of the maximum wealth of small unregistered Swedish foundations – another 35,000 foundations according to the highest estimate – is SEK12 billion, since none of these foundations has assets surpassing SEK350,000. The larger foundations thus represent at least 95% of the total foundation wealth, which amounts to approximately SEK240 billion (some €28 billion).

The number and wealth of foundations in Sweden is impressive, even more so when compared internationally, on a *per capita* basis. With some 10,000 larger foundations (excluding labour-market related foundations) with assets of about SEK130 billion (€15.2 billion), and a population of approximately nine million, this represents a *per capita* wealth of nearly US$1450. This is to be compared to the *per capita* foundation wealth in the US of US$673. In Germany, grant-making foundations held US$14-29 billion, giving a maximum *per*

---

[42] Preliminary figures only. A number of foundations still remain to be registered, but a qualified estimate is that less than 1000 remain. Personal communication with Mikael Wiman at the County Administration Board in Stockholm, May 2000.

[43] Lundström and Wijkström, p. 302.

capita figure of US$354, whereas in Sweden, a similar figure might roughly be US$1000 *per capita* (42.6% of US$22.6 billion and a population of nine million).[44] All of these calculations and figures must, however, be treated with great caution, as cross-country comparisons may very well be skewed by factors such as different legal definitions and data from different years.

Finally, a couple of notes on employment. In 1992, some 2600 larger private, nonprofit foundations employed 14,300 persons, out of approximately 100,000 employees in the Swedish nonprofit sector.[45] However, the total number of employees in Swedish foundations has been declining during the 1990s. In 1991, almost 58,000 persons were employed by a foundation, but in 1994 this figure had fallen to 23,126, and in 1997 it was down to 21,452. This development indicates a 63% decline over a six-year period, compared to a slight increase of 6% in nonprofit (*ideell*) associations during the same period – from 70,750 in 1991, to 72,441 in 1994 and 74,920 persons in 1997.[46] However, when figures are adjusted to account for the transformation between 1991 and 1994 of *Samhall* – (a large public sector operation, aiding impaired persons in the labour market, employing 34,000 persons) from a foundation to an incorporated stock company, the decline is not nearly as dramatic (approximately 10%).

5 Current trends and conclusion

One of the most important recent changes in the Swedish nonprofit sector and the population of Swedish foundations was the politically controversial transformation of the Wage-Earner Funds (*löntagarfonderna*) during the 1990s into private foundations aimed at supporting research. Another change is the transformation of the Church of Sweden from a state church, with a considerable share of its wealth in foundations or foundation-like arrangements to a private institution.

During the 1970s and the 1980s, foundations were increasingly created by government as well as municipalities. This is apparent in the use of appropriation foundations (*anslagsstiftelser*) in the cooperation between public institutions and various private interests (for example in the field of culture or in regional development). But it is also obvious

---

[44] Toepler.

[45] Lundström and Wijkström.

[46] Kulturdepartementet, pp. 60–1.

when, for example, real-estate owned by a municipality is transferred to a foundation.[47] Finally, new and interesting activities, in a re-opened borderland between state and private sphere, have in several cases been started as foundations by 'social entrepreneurs'. Salient examples are *Fryshuset* in Stockholm, a social youth project started in 1984; *Kvinnoforum* started in 1990 with the mission to increase women's influence in society; and *Noaks Ark – Röda Korset* – a centre for HIV/AIDS prevention and care development that opened in the 1980s. Two of the foundations have come to be connected to a couple of more established major Swedish nonprofit organizations. *Fryshuset* is associated with the Swedish branch of the YMCA and *Noaks Ark* is operating under the banner of the Swedish Red Cross.[48]

These changes run parallel to a continuous reformulation of the role and extension of the modern (welfare) state, as well as changes in the public–private borderland, re-defining what is public (state) and what is private. As a result, the borders between what is private and what is public are becoming blurred, and a number of foundations are central in this process, as actors in a civil society.

To sum up, a thoroughly critical stance towards foundations in Sweden has been identified and discussed. Part of the critique against the foundation as a form in Sweden appears to be misguided. In some instances, it seems as if it is not really the form but rather the purpose of the foundation that attracts criticism, as for example with elite schools. At other times, either the usage or the management of foundations complicates the picture. A foundation could wrongly be used to do what would be done better under another legal construction, or the foundation form could be used correctly (according to the intentions of the founder) when it is set up, but the current board and management (maybe decades or half a century later) have neither the required capacity nor the competence to manage a foundation. Instead, they strive to change or adapt the foundation form to fit other governance or management models, to make the foundation easier to manage and operate according to their present competence and experience.

We have discussed the idea of understanding foundations as 'ideology-bound pools of capital', and, as such, vehicles to counteract as well as to promote social change. This is perhaps most apparent in the fields of education and publishing, exercised by right- or left-wing as

---

[47] See, e.g., RRV, pp. 107ff or SOU 1994:147, p. 10.

[48] For good analyses of Noaks Ark, see Johansson or Olsson, L. E.

well as other ideological or religious interests, but it can also be found in the field of, for example, social welfare.

Foundations are involved in the redefinition of the role and scope of the modern welfare state, as well as in the challenging of traditional ways as they introduce and develop innovative practice in welfare-related fields. The foundation is thus – as an institutional form – at the forefront of a number of crucial changes in Swedish society.

However, we lack a critical and informed public debate on foundations and their role in contemporary Sweden. Although foundations wield considerable economic power, their importance in social, cultural, political or economic matters is seldom discussed.[49] Part of the explanation is probably a general lack of knowledge and understanding of what a foundation really is.[50] This is especially surprising, considering that private foundations cater not only for a substantial share in an area such as scientific research financing, but also increasingly so in the operation of educational, cultural and welfare institutions.

Bibliography

Brändström, Dan, 'Foundations in Sweden', in: *EUROMECUM*, December, 1993.

Ds Ju 1979:4, *Stiftelser. En statistisk undersökning utförd av statistiska centralbyrån på uppdrag av och i samverkan med stiftelseutredningen*, Stockholm, SCB, 1979.

Ds Ju., *Stiftelser. Sammanställning av remissyttrandena över departementsromemorian*, (Ds Ju 1987:14), Justitiedepartementet, Stockholm, Fritzes, 1992.

Frii, L., *Förvalta fonder och stiftelser*, (2nd edition), Stockholm, Norstedts Förlag, 1989.

Hermansson, C. H., *Monopol och storfinans*, Stockholm, Arbetarkultur, 1962.

Hessler, H., *Om stiftelser. Studier över stiftelseinstitutet i svensk rätt*, Lund, Berlingska Boktryckeriet , 1952.

Hirschfeldt, L., *De Johanssonska Stiftelserna*, Uppsala, AB Upsala Nya Tidning.

Hoppe, G., Nylander G. and Olsson U., *Till landets gagn*. Knut och Alice Wallenbergs stiftelse 1917-1992, Stockholm, KAW-stiftelsen, 1993.

Isoz, H., *Stiftelselagen. En kmmentar*, Stockholm, Norstedts Juridik, 1997.

Johansson, G., *Möta HIV, möta sig själv*, Stockholm, Sköndalsinstitutet, 1997.

Kulturdepartementet, *Social ekonomi – en tredje sektor för välfärd, demokrati och tillväxt?*, Rapport från en arbetsgrupp, Bilagor, Stockholm, Fakta Info Direkt, 1999.

---

[49] Represented in the US by authors like Nielsen, Margo or Ylvisaker.

[50] As argued by e.g. Olsson, *Stiftelser*, p. 450.

Länsstyrelsen, Statusrapport från stiftelseregistret (period: 960101-200512), internal report, Stockholm, Länsstyrelsen i Stockholms län, 2000.

Lundström, T. and Wijkström, F. *The nonprofit sector in Sweden*, Manchester, Manchester University Press, 1997.

Margo, R. A., 'Foundations' in: C. T. Clotfelter (ed.) *Who Benefits from the Nonprofit Sector?*, The University of Chicago Press, 1992.

Mutén, L., 'Stiftelsebeskattningen', in: *Svensk Skattetidskrift* (SvSkT), 10/95, pp. 745-51, 1995.

Nielsen, W. A., *The Big Foundations*, New York, Columbia University Press, 1972.

Nielsen, W. A. *Inside American Philanthropy. The dramas of Donorship*, Norman, University of Oklahoma Press, 1996.

Olsson, K., *Näringsdrivande stiftelser*, Stockholm, Nerenius & Santérus, 1996.

Olsson, L.-E., *Från idé till handling*, Stockholm, Almqvist & Wiksell International, 1999.

Proposition 1942:134, Förslag till lag om ändring i vissa delar av kommunalskattelagen, 1942.

Proposition 1993/94:9, Stiftelser, 1993.

RRV, *Stiftelser för statlig verksamhet*, Dnr 1989:422, Stockholm, RRV, 1990.

SOU 1968:7, *Ägande och inflytande inom det privata näringslivet*, Stockholm, Allmänna Förlaget, 1968.

SOU 1994:145, *Ägarkoncentration i dagspress och radio/TV – fem promemorior och diskussionsinlägg*, Pressutredningen, Kulturdepartementet, Stockholm, Fritzes, 1994.

SOU 1994:147, *Former för statlig verksamhet*, Finansdepartementet, Stockholm, Fritzes, 1994.

SOU 1995:63, *Översyn av skatteregler för stiftelser och ideella föreningar*, Slutbetänkande av Stiftelse- och föreningsskattekommittén, Stockholm, Fritzes, 1995.

Sundin, A. and Sundqvist, S.-I., *Ägarna och Makten i Sveriges Börs-företag 1998*, Stockholm, DN, 1998.

Toepler, S., 'Foundations and Their Institutional Context: Cross-Evaluating Evidence from Germany and the United States', in: *Voluntas*, Vol. 9, No. 2, pp. 153–70, 1998.

Ylvisaker, P. N. 'Foundations and Nonprofit Organizations' in: Walter W. Powell, (ed.) *The Nonprofit Sector: A Research Handbook*, New Haven, Yale University Press, 1987.

Switzerland

1 Introduction

Bernhard Hahnloser, head of the Confederate Foundation Supervisory Authority (*Eidgenössische Stiftungsaufsicht*) for 13 years describes Switzerland as a 'paradise for foundations'.[1] The number of organizations listed in the commercial register under the legal form foundation is indeed remarkable (about 21,000 in 1997)[2], even more so since the numerous church and family foundations are not included. This is best explained by the positive attitude which the state administration and courts have shown toward foundations, and subsequently Switzerland's rather liberal and flexible foundation law which guarantees the founder a large measure of freedom regarding purpose and organization.

However, the number of foundations in Switzerland should be put into perspective by examining the types of foundations differentiated in the Swiss Civil Code (*Schweizerisches Zivilgesetzbuch; ZGB*) of 1907. One type is the traditional foundation, which generally fulfils a charitable purpose with a more or less open circle of beneficiaries and thus fits the definition of foundations offered in the chapter by Anheier. Traditional foundations now play a very important role in the worlds of science, arts and culture, foreign aid, education, work with youth and also social welfare. With one traditional foundation for every 1000 citizens, Switzerland can indeed be seen as a paradise for founders.

All other types of Swiss foundations – the Church, family, corporate, and personal pension foundations – have either a closed circle of beneficiaries and therefore do not serve a public purpose, or are profit-oriented. Personal pension foundations are the most common category in Switzerland, managing funds slowly approaching the size of the Swiss GDP, around CHF250 billion. Consequently, only about

---

[1] Hahnloser, p.3.

[2] BFS (ed.), *Auszug aus dem Handelsregister*.

8000 of the 21,000 foundations in Switzerland fulfil Anheier's criteria for foundations. Traditional foundations are thus the primary focus of this article, but personal pension funds merit comment due to their sheer size.

2 Historical background

The Swiss conception of the foundation is rooted in classical Roman private law, according to which an individual could donate property during life or after death. The influence of the Roman Catholic Church later made such donations increasingly welfare-oriented, and the legal perception of foundations also changed. The foundation became a fund linked to a purpose with an independent legal identity. Churches also became regarded as public institutions and carried out an increasing number of charitable activities through such funds.

Foundations in Switzerland date back to the 12th century.[3] Examples of early church foundations are two *sine cure* foundations dating back to the years 1360 and 1367 which are mentioned in *Repertorio di Giurisprudenza patria*.[4] The most famous traditional foundation is the *Inselspital* ('island hospital') in Bern, established in 1354 and still in operation today.[5] One of the oldest foundations documented operated for the benefit of the poor, especially needy or sick travellers, in the village of *Münchenbuchsee* in the year 1188. The first family foundations – the *Berner Familienkisten* and the *Zürcherschen Familienfonds* – were not founded until around the year 1700.[6]

The first codification of foundation law can be found in the Civil Code for the canton Zurich (PGB).[7] It had a strong influence on the articles dealing with foundations in the future Swiss Civil Code (ZGB), which is the basis of today's foundation law. The ZGB (1907) came into effect in 1912 and contains 12 articles that grant founders a large measure of freedom and explicitly mention the traditional foundation as well as pension, family and church foundations. Since then foundation law has not been modified apart from additional provisions on pension foundations.

---

[3] Riemer, *Stiftungen*, ST N 558.

[4] Riemer, *Stiftungen*, ST N 557.

[5] Rennfahrt, p. 11.

[6] Riemer, *Stiftungen*, ST N 559.

[7] *Zürcherisches Pivatrechtliches Gesetzbuch.*

When the ZGB came into effect the number of foundations in Switzerland was estimated at about 200.[8] Encouraged by the liberal foundation law, new types of foundations appeared and until the 1980s the number of foundations continually rose. These included:

- the **church foundation**, which links a religious community and a religious non-charitable purpose
- the **family foundation**, which helps families with education, setting up home and general financial support.

Little is known about the development of family and church foundations because neither registration in the commercial register nor control through the supervisory board are required by law.[9] The presumable inherent purpose of a family foundation, tax evasion, became illegal with the introduction of the ZGB, therefore such foundations are nowadays mainly set up in the neighbouring country of Liechtenstein.

Among the new 'atypical' foundations that have developed are the following:

- **Personal pension foundations**, set up by employers under legislation requiring them to have an independent legal status. In fact one of the most important dimensions of the total increase in foundations stems from the commercial law (*Obligationenrecht*) of 1937, which encouraged employers to invest in pension funds for their employees; almost all of these funds have been registered as foundations.[10] Nowadays, pension foundations represent about 60% of all foundations.
- **Corporate foundations** which have a profit-making orientation, either a minor shareholding in one or more firms or a complete management control of a company. Although their legality is seriously questioned, they are still of major importance for Swiss business.[11]
- As for **traditional foundations**, we know that their numbers as well as their importance have grown in recent years. Foundations now carry out many duties formerly fulfilled by government. For example cultural policy is now administered by foundations such

---

[8] BFS (ed.), *Jahrbuch*, p. 63.

[9] ZGB, article 87.

[10] With the introduction of the A/H/V-law, the employer is obliged to do so.

[11] Examples are the Sandoz Family Foundation with shareholdings amounting to around CHF7,800 million and the Wilsdorf-Foundation which controls Rolex S.A.

as *ProHelvetia*,[12] and the major share of scientific research is funded by the Swiss National Funds which in 1998 invested CHF 355.1 million (€ 221 million).[13] Both foundations were founded by and receive most of their receipts from government. In recent years privately-established foundations have also become increasingly active in supporting research. A considerable part of foreign aid is also provided by foundations, including the Swiss Foundation for Foreign Technical Aids founded in 1959 which is mainly funded by the private sector. *Pro Juventute* (founded in 1912) and *Kinderdorf Pestalozzi* (founded in 1945) help young people and children. The most important relief organization for the elderly is the Swiss foundation *Pro Senectute* (founded in 1917).[14]

The number of international foundations that have chosen Switzerland for their headquarters has also risen, attracted not only by the liberal legal framework but also by the monetary and political stability in this country.[15]

3 Legal issues

The Swiss Civil Code ZGB constitutes the core of foundation law. There has been only a small number of relevant federal court decisions, but thousands of judgements and decisions by the supervisory authorities and other bodies that 'form a rather unusual case of a sort of Common Law for foundations'.[16]

To establish a foundation in the traditional sense, the ZGB[17] requires only three components (*essentialia negotii*)[18]:

- a **foundation will**, expressed by an individual or an organization, to set up a foundation
- a **foundation fund**, considered to be adequate for the foundation's purpose by the supervisory authority
- a **foundation purpose**, based on the foundation will and either set out explicitly in the foundation document or in a testament, or derived implicitly from the will.

---

[12] Neuhoff and Pavel, p.99.

[13] Source: SNF,1999.

[14] Source: Pro-Senectute 1999.

[15] Hahnloser, pp. 4–6.

[16] Hahnloser, p. 5.

[17] ZGB Article 80.

[18] Riemer, *Stiftungen*, ST N 19.

In accordance with the principle of foundation freedom, founders may arrange their will at their own discretion, expressing anything that is neither illegal nor immoral. The foundation is established by registration in the commercial register,[19] after which it comes under the supervision of public authorities – either federal, state or local in accordance with the foundation's sphere of activity.[20] The relevant supervisory authority must approve major changes in the foundation's organization and activity and can revise the foundation's organizational structure when necessary.[21] The authority can also order the liquidation of a foundation 'as soon as its purpose becomes unattainable',[22] but generally a foundation lasts 'indefinitely'.

The principle of the priority of the founder's will means that a foundation is, in effect, its own proprietor. A foundation can only dissolve itself if it fulfils objective criteria set out in the founding document.[23] Its organizational arrangement, executive body and management are not regulated by law but by regulations laid down by the founder. However, at least an executive body is mandatory in order to manage and represent the foundation,[24] usually the foundation board.[25]

International foundations must have at least one member of the board authorized to sign, with their main domicile in Switzerland. In addition the major part of foundation assets or funds must be administered from Switzerland.[26]

Regarding fiscal law, foundations are taxable in the same way as individuals. However if the foundation has a nonprofit status it may apply for tax-exemption, whereby donated funds are exempt from taxable income up to a certain sum or percentage.[27] To attain a nonprofit status, a foundation must act unselfishly and operate in the general interest.[28]

---

[19] ZGB Article 81, a registration for family and church foundations is not mandatory.

[20] Ruggli p. 36.

[21] ZGB Articles 85, 86.

[22] ZGB Article 88 and Manhart p. 16.

[23] Riemer, *Stiftungen*, ST N 24

[24] Riemer, *Stiftungen*, ST N 5

[25] Lanter pp. 26–30.

[26] Hahnloser p. 10.

[27] Depending on state law, the numbers vary considerably. Whereas in some cantons there are no restrictions whatsoever, others limit donations which are tax-exempted to between 5% and 20% of taxable income. Further information including a table specifying the individual cantonal law can be obtained at www.zewo.ch (Central Agency of Charitable Organisations).

[28] Maissen pp. 5–7.

Thus it must actively create benefits in favour of third parties with an altruistic and unselfish attitude, without demanding a *quid pro quo*. To attain tax benefits a foundation must also be deemed worthy of support by 'the respective authoritative public opinion',[29] and the foundation's circle of beneficiaries must, in principle, be an open one.

4 A profile of foundations in Switzerland

Switzerland has neither a central authority nor an organization that collects data on Swiss foundations in general, nor does it possess a complete register of tax-exempt foundations. It is therefore hardly possible to draw a complete picture of the sector and its activities. Additionally, Switzerland's data protection laws make inaccessible any information relating to financial situations except when published voluntarily. Data compiled by tax authorities is protected by tax-secrecy and not publicly available.

However, a number of existing statistical data collections offer a starting point for research.[30] The *Arbeitsgemeinschaft für gemeinnützige Stiftungen* AGES (Association of Nonprofit Foundations), a private association based in Basel, provides useful information on about roughly 500 foundations. The Federal Statistic Bureau (BFS) offers a complete register of organizations (*Betriebs- und Unternehmensregister, BUR*) from which the BFS conducts comprehensive surveys from time to time (*Betriebszählung, BZ*).[31]

Figure 1.5 presents the total number of nonprofit status foundations and their development since 1912. The total number of registered pension funds has been subtracted from the total number of organizations in the commercial register with the legal entity of a foundation (21,090), leaving about 8000 nonprofit foundations. However, this number includes corporate foundations as well as registered family

---

[29] Maissen p. 9.

[30] Blümle p. 39–45.

[31] Surveys were conducted in 1985, 1991 and 1995. More generally, the BFS register identifies foundations in general based on the 61 independent commercial registers in Switzerland but is not amenable to in-depth analysis of nonprofit foundations and will remain inaccessible until a centralized commercial register is online. The same problem exists with the *Nationale Buchhaltung*, (National Accounting) since their data are also based on the different commercial registers. Finally, the 27 foundation supervisory boards in Switzerland lack adequate computerized information on foundations, while inspection of their databases by researchers is not allowed at present. The federal supervisory authority does regularly publish a printed register on foundations under their control, but it is incomplete, as foundations are free to participate or not. For these reasons, only estimated data on the general characteristics of the Swiss foundation sectors can be presented.

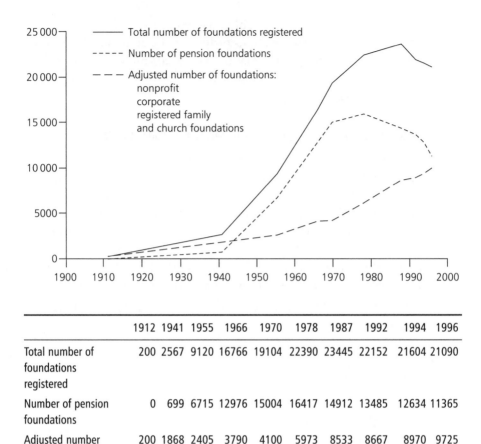

	1912	1941	1955	1966	1970	1978	1987	1992	1994	1996
Total number of foundations registered	200	2567	9120	16766	19104	22390	23445	22152	21604	21090
Number of pension foundations	0	699	6715	12976	15004	16417	14912	13485	12634	11365
Adjusted number of foundations; nonprofit corporate, registered family and church foundations	200	1868	2405	3790	4100	5973	8533	8667	8970	9725

Figure 1.5 Number of Swiss foundations and rate of development, 1912–96

Source: Data from the Federal Bureau of the Commercial Register and the Statistics on Pension Funds

and church foundations, whose number is unknown. Therefore the actual number is probably consistently 10% to 20% below the recorded data.

More generally, nonprofit foundations constitute about 3% of all registered organizations in Switzerland (298,000 in 1995). They have a ratio of about one foundation per 1000 Swiss citizens. The estimated assets of those traditional foundations are about CHF10,000 million, although this number is probably now closer to 11 billion.[32] They are supervised at different levels according to the activities they undertake. The following information is based on an analysis in a dissertation by the author, conducted with the financial support of the *Gebert-Rüf-Stiftung*.

Traditional foundations under federal supervision

The Federal Foundation Supervisory Authority is in charge of foundations whose activities reach beyond one canton or are international. Currently there are 1753 traditional foundations under federal supervision, 95% of which were founded by individuals, the rest mainly by corporations. Of the first group, approximately 5% are primarily grant making and 95% are operating. Table 1.46 classifies these foundations by major field of activity based on the ICNPO code, showing the highest activity in education and research, and social services.

Table 1.46 ICNPO classification of foundations under federal supervision

1 Culture and recreation	20%
2 Education and research	30%
3 Health	10%
4 Social services	30%
5 Environment	5%
6 Development and housing	5%
9 International	about 50% of the above categories are active internationally.

Source: Data provided by the Federal Foundation Supervisory Authority

The contribution of foundations in various sectors can be estimated from a study conducted by the *Federal Statistic Bureau (Bundesamt für Statistik, BFS)* in 1992, which compared the expenditures from public funds, industry, and foundations promoting culture in 1989.[33] Foundations with a cultural purpose constitute approximately 23% of all traditional foundations. Their expenditure on culture in 1989 amounted to around CHF60 million, while expenditure from corporations spent about CHF250 million, and public funding amounted

---

[32] Talks with: Riemer, H.M. (14.06.1999), Prof. for International Law, University Zurich, Substitute Judge at the Federal Court, author of the prevailing legal opinion on foundation law; Spring, A. (31.05.1999), head of the Confederate Foundation Supervisory Authority; Degen, C. (09.03.1999), Secretary of the AGES.

[33] Huber.

to CHF1500 million.[34] Thus, the financial promotion of Swiss cultural life by foundations amounts to 24% of that provided by corporations, and 4% of that provided by public funds. However this estimate changes when taking into account the fact that federal subsidies to foundations are considered public funds, not foundation funds. According to the same study, cultural foundations consist of about 500 operating foundations and 1000 grant-making foundations. Data on foundations in other sectors of activity are not available.

Traditional foundations under cantonal supervision

Switzerland consists of 26 autonomous cantons, which can be placed into three regions: German, French and Italian. Table 1.47 provides some data on regional differences in the foundation sector, clearly showing that Switzerland's heterogeneity is reflected in its foundations sector.

Table 1.47 Regional foundation differences

	German	French	Italian
Inhabitants	5,048,200	1,742,600	305,600
Income *per capita* in CHF	45,800	41,700	37,200
Total number of foundations	11,715	3643	565
Traditional foundations	3418	1819	392
Pension foundations	8250	1309	38
Inhabitants per foundation	431	478	541
Inhabitants per traditional foundation	1477	958	780
Inhabitants per pension foundations	612	1331	8042

Source: Data provided by the Cantonal Foundation Supervisory Authorities

Although the *Tecino* (Italian part) obviously has the lowest economic strength, it possesses 1.9 times as many traditional foundations as the much bigger and richer *Deutschschweiz* (German part). Even the *Romandie* (French part), which is also smaller and economically weaker, has more than 1.5 times the amount of traditional foundations compared to the German part. It may be that the establishment of foundations is of greater importance for the minority sections of the Swiss population, possibly as an opportunity to secure and support one's way of life and traditions.

---

[34] About 40% of foundation expenditures came from those under federal supervision, 40% from those under state supervision, and 20% from those under local supervision.

No coherent picture can be drawn of cantonal foundation founders, proportions of grant-making and operating foundations, or major fields of activity. However, data from nine cantons (with 1213 out of 5629 traditional foundations)[35] seem to suggest that the activities are in line with trends presented in Table 1.46.

5 Current trends and conclusion

The past few years have seen the establishment of foundations with considerable fortunes. For example, the *Gebert Rüf Stiftung* (funded with CHF220 million in 1997)[36] promotes research and development, and the *Albert Koechlin Stiftung* (funded with CHF500 million in 1997)[37] contributes to Switzerland's social and cultural life. More generally, the number and significance of nonprofit organizations has been continually growing but private funding has not yet reached the same level of importance as in the United States. Consequently a proposal for a comprehensive revision of foundation law – not modified since 1907 – was introduced in 1989. It aimed to ban profit-oriented corporate foundations, codify current legal practices and to confront controversial questions of supervisory practices.[38] However, to date the proposal has not been and probably will not be implemented since it has not yet been put into the legislative process.

Thus in 1999 a new discussion on basic principles of foundation law and tax law emerged.[39] The issues under discussion are:

- changes in the foundation purpose
- the restoration of foundation funds
- competitive salaries for administrators
- additional tax exemptions and their standardization at federal and cantonal levels.

The change in tax laws would be particularly welcome, as regulation has become increasingly strict. Agreement on tax harmonization has been reached, and additionally a general disclosure requirement has been introduced to address the lack of transparency in the foundation sector. However, a more comprehensive register is still necessary.

---

[35] Steinert, p.117.

[36] Gebert Rüf Stiftung.

[37] Lüscher.

[38] Riemer, *Revisionsbestrebungen*, p.15.

[39] Vontobel, p.15.

Swiss foundations are governed by a liberal legal framework, developed out of the Roman Catholic Church's foundation concept from which secular foundations sprang, and finally based on the ZGB in 1907. This has led to the establishment of some 8000 nonprofit foundations in Switzerland, active in a range of fields and with total estimated assets of more than CHF10 billion (€6200 million). Additionally, about 900 international foundations exist in Switzerland. Personal pension foundations constitute the greatest economic force in Switzerland's foundation sector.

Today's principal problems concern tax regulations, lack of research and lack of transparency. At a time when governmental benefits are being reduced in every aspect of public life, foundations and their activity represent an important potential. In accordance with the aims of Swiss foundation law, the establishment and expansion of nonprofit foundations acting in the general interest can still be seen as a priority for the future.

Bibliography

BFS ed., *Statistisches Jahrbuch der Schweiz*, 1917, Bern, 1918.

BFS ed., *Auszug aus dem Handelsregister*, 1996, Bern, 1997.

BFS ed., *Pensionskassenstatistik*, 1996, Bern, 1999.

Blümle, E.B. *et al.*, Statistische Erfassung der Organisationen ohne Erwerbscharakter, Fribourg, 1991.

Burckhardt, J.-L., 'Leitfaden für Stiftungen und die Funktion der Bank bei deren Errichtung und Verwaltung: unter Berücksichtigung des schweizerischen und liechtensteinischen Rechts', in: *Publikation der Swiss Banking School*, Nr. 129, Bern, Stuttgart, Wien, 1996.

Eidgenössische Stiftungsaufsicht ed., *Stiftungsverzeichnis*/Eidgenössische Stiftungsaufsicht, Bern, 1997.

Hahnloser, B., 'Die Stiftungsaufsicht', in: *Schriftenreihe der Arbeitsgemeinschaft für gemeinnützige Stiftungen AGES*, Basel, Frankfurt am Main, Heft 1,1989.

Huber, P. *et al.*, 'Öffentliche und private Kulturförderung, in: Bundesamt für Statistik', in: BFS (ed.), *Statistik der Schweiz, Fachbereich 16, Kultur, Lebensbedingungen und Sport*, Bern, 1992.

Lanter, M., 'Die Verantwortlichkeit von Stiftungsorganen', in: P. Forstmoser, C. Hegnauer *et al.* (eds), *Zürcher Studie zum Privatrecht*, Zürich, Band 41, 1984.

Laum, B., *Stiftungen in der griechischen und römischen Antike*, Aalen, 1964.

Maissen, S., 'Die Steuerbefreiung gemeinnütziger Stiftungen', in: *Schriftenreihe der Arbeitsgemeinschaft für gemeinnützige Stiftungen AGES*, Basel, Frankfurt am Main, Heft 3, 1992.

Neuhoff, K. and Parel U. eds, *Stiftungen in Europa. Eine vergleichende übersicht*, Nomosverlagsgesellschaft, Baden Baden, 1971.

Rennfahrt, A., 'Geschichte der Rechtsverhältnisse des "Inselspitals" der Frau Anna Seiler', in: *Sechshundert Jahre Inselspital*, Bern, 1954.

Riemer, H. M., 'Ist das Stiftungsrecht wirklich so reformbedürftig?', in: *Neue Zürcher Zeitung*, Nr. 104, 07.05.1999, p. 69.

Riemer, H. M., 'Aktuelle Revisionsbestrebungen im schweizerischen Stiftungsrecht', in: *Schriftenreihe der Arbeitsgemeinschaft für gemeinnützige Stiftungen AGES*, Basel, Frankfurt am Main, Heft 2, 1991.

Riemer, H. M., 'Die Stiftungen, Systematischer Teil und Kommentar zu Art. 80–89bis ZGB', in: A. Meier-Hayoz (ed.), *Berner Kommentar, Kommentar zum schweizerischen Privatrecht*, Bern, Band1, Einleitung und Personenrecht, 3. Abteilung: Die juristischen Personen, 3. Teilband, 3. Auflage, 1981.

Ruggli, C., 'Die behördliche Aufsicht über Vorsorgeeinrichtungen', in: K. Spiro, G. Stratenwerth *et al.* (eds), *Basler Studie zur Rechtswissenschaft*, Basel, Frankfurt am Main, Reihe B, Öffentliches Recht, Band 37, 1992.

Schaffer, K., 'Schweizerische Stiftungen im F&E-Bereich', in: Schweizerischer Wissenschaftsrat (ed.), *FUTURA* 4/96, Bern, 1996.

Schweizerischen Arbeitsgemeinschaft kultureller Stiftungen und Bundesamt für Kultur ed., *Handbuch der öffentlichen und privaten Kulturförderung in der Schweiz*, Zürich, 1997.

Steinert, M., *Schweizerische Stiftungen – Eine Analyse des schweizerischen Stiftungswesen unter besonderer Berücksichtigung der klassischen Stiftungen*, Dissertation, University of Fribourg, 2000.

Vontobel, H. *et al.*, 'Reformbedürftiges Stiftungsrecht', in: *Neue Zürcher Zeitung*, Nr. 38, 16.02.1999, p. 15.

Sources on the Internet

Lüscher, S., Ein einzig Volk von Stiftern, in: *Bilanz*, Mai 1999 (ed.), http://www.bilanz.ch/ 10.05.1999.

SNF ed., Schweizer Nationalfonds, http://www.snf.ch, 04.06.1999.

Pro-Senectute ed., Pro-Senectute, http://www.pro-senectute.ch, 04.06.1999.

Gebert Rüf Stiftung ed., Gebert Rüf Stiftung, http://www.grstiftung.ch, 14.06.1999.

Turkey

1 Introduction

In Turkey foundations have played a vital role in social, economic and cultural life throughout the country's history. Foundations developed under the Seljuk and Ottoman Empires to the point that they touched most aspects of individuals' lives. Today there are more than 10,000 foundations of various kinds serving many functions in Turkey.

As in other countries, the concept of 'foundation' in Turkey is used in different ways. According to the definition suggested in the chapter by Anheier, a foundation is an asset managed by an identifiable organization that is simultaneously private, non-membership-based, self-governing, nonprofit-distributing and serving a public purpose. Turkish foundations share many of these characteristics, but few meet all five criteria equally well. The Turkish foundation sector consists of those set up according to Islamic Law (hereafter referred to as 'old foundations'), public foundations, and private foundations established to avoid restrictions facing associations after 1980.

Taken as a social institution, in Turkey a foundation is historically and culturally understood as a corporate body possessing legal entity that confers legal status and perpetuity to the feelings of solidarity and philanthropy, thus contributing to the public good and moral value of a nation.[1]

In the 1990s Turkish foundations, like nonprofit organizations more generally, enjoyed a rediscovery. To continue in this direction foundations will need to benefit from a restructuring of both legal and administrative aspects. In particular, new legislation is needed to devolve more state responsibility onto private foundations and civil society.

---

[1] Güzel, p.1.

2 Historical background

In Turkey, foundations can look back over a history of three to four thousand years. The institution as such developed significantly after Turks had accepted Islam as their religion; however there is even earlier evidence of the existence of foundations. The first known document concerning Turkish foundations is *Türk Eti Vakfiyesi*, which was written before 1280 BC. It is now preserved in the Department of Oriental Arts in the Istanbul Archaeological Museum.

Many services today provided by the state – such as education, health, religious and social services, city-planning and local government – had been typical foundation activities for centuries.[2] These foundations also fulfilled many of the functions overtaken by private sector organizations today, such as management of properties and management of hotels and caravansarais.

Foundations contributed substantially to the establishment and growth of two great Turkish empires. The institution of foundations developed under the Seljuk Empire and was perfected under the Ottoman Empire. Foundations were found not only in all kinds of public services, but also in the administration of property holdings. In fact the majority of property holdings in Ottoman Istanbul were under the administration of foundations. In this respect, Istanbul was a city of foundations. In other cities of the Empire a significant proportion was administered in the same way. Subsequently, the foundation institution in the Turkish-Islamic legal system has been a unique model.[3]

As social, legal and religious institutions, foundations played an important role in the social, cultural and economic life of the Islamic world.[4] In the Seljuk and Ottoman period it became common practice for rich persons who wanted to please God to leave their movable or immovable properties to a foundation in order to provide religious, charitable or social services.[5] In the Ottoman era, the social and economic roles of the foundation were so highly developed that a person could be born and raised in a foundation house, receive nourishment from foundation properties, be taught in a foundation school, receive a salary from a foundation administration, and upon death be buried in a foundation coffin in a foundation cemetery.[6]

---

[2] Aydın, *Turkish Foundation System*, p.185.

[3] Baloglu, p. 8.

[4] Öztürk, p. 48.

[5] Yediyıldız, p. 42.

[6] Güneri, p. 22.

In the course of their long history foundations evolved into an important element of civilization, promoting historical consciousness, converting wealth into public services, providing a basis for economic, social and cultural institutions, and promoting integration through the establishment of ties of affection, social solidarity and mutual assistance among members of the community.[7] Beyond being social institutions, foundations also owned about one fifth of the whole Ottoman territory by the early 16th century.[8] The expansion of the foundation sector eventually led to a substantial decrease in government revenues, and finally in 1826 the government set up a Ministry of Foundations in order to control foundation development better.

During the Republican period the management and auditing of foundations was first given to the Ministry of Sharia and Foundations. Later this Ministry was replaced by the General Directorate of Foundations, which registers the establishment of foundations, audits their operations, administers their properties and engages in research on foundations to protect their historical and cultural works.

When in 1926 the Civil Code was adapted following the Swiss model, the foundation system in Turkey entered a new period. Law 903 passed in 1967 set out the regulations and principles of the organization and functions of new foundations. This law led to the establishment of many new foundations in fields such as education, culture, religion, health and the environment. Some of those operating for public benefit without distribution profit to members were granted tax exemption by the Board of Ministers.

3 Legal issues

In the Turkish legal system, the institution of foundation is defined and organized by the Turkish Civil Code. Article 73 (as amended) defines a foundation as 'the allocation of a property to a certain purpose on condition that it preserves its entity.'[9] The second item of the same Article states that the whole of a property or all kinds of realized or expected income or economic rights should be relinquished to a certain purpose.

---

[7] Öztürk, p. 48.

[8] Ercüment, pp.10–11.

[9] Oguzhan and Akyol, p.30.

For a foundation to come into being, three basic elements are required:

- property
- purpose
- allocation.

Any kind of income, assets, and any right having an economic value can be considered property. There is no limit on the amount of property that may be allocated for a foundation purpose, but there is a minimum requirement that it be sufficient to achieve the foundation purpose. It is essential that the foundation purpose be clearly defined. According to the Turkish Civil Code, it is forbidden to establish a foundation whose purpose contradicts articles of law, moral and national interests, or which is unachievable or supports a political viewpoint, particular race or member of a particular community. Apart from these restrictions, foundations can be established with any purpose in social, economic and cultural fields. The allocation element ensures property is linked to a stated purpose.

As for the establishment of a foundation, Article 74 of the Civil Code reads:

> A foundation is established by a formal, written document or the will of a person who leaves his property to the foundation which achieves its legal personality by the registration of his address at the court of first instance. [...] The court ex-officio notifies the General Directorate of Foundations about the registration.

This stipulation applies to all foundations.

4 A profile of foundations in Turkey

There are currently 10,331 foundations registered in Turkey. As we have seen, with respect to their historical development, two types of Turkish foundations can be distinguished: pre-Republic (or 'old') foundations and post-Republic (or 'new') foundations.

- Old foundations are the *Mazbut*, the *Mülhak* and the minority foundations. *Mazbut* (administered) foundations are managed directly by the General Directorate of Foundations, a state organization established further to develop, audit, direct and preserve old foundations. *Mülhak* (supervised) are managed by trustees, but supervised and audited by the General Directorate of Foundations. Minority foundations are established and managed by minorities (in Istanbul: Greek, Jewish, Armenian etc.) to meet their religious, social and cultural needs, but supervised and audited by the General Directorate of Foundations.

- New foundations can be public foundations and private foundations. Public foundations are set up according to a special law and operate as part of the public administrative system. These are organizations like the Foundation for Strengthening the Turkish Military Forces,[10] Social Help and Solidarity Foundations[11] and foundations for environmental protection.[12] These foundations are as defined by Anheier in Foundations in Europe: a Comparative Perspective, but form part of the civil service. Private foundations are set up by private individuals according to the Civil Code. They can be classified into two subgroups: social security foundations – which are similar to pension funds and insurance funds and are mostly established by banks and other financial institutions – and private foundations serving a narrower public purpose. The latter are registered with the General Directorate of Foundations.

The majority of today's foundations are old foundations (56.7%), but the rate of development of new foundations has been quite impressive. In just over 30 years 4705 new foundations were registered as Figure 1.6 shows.

Together public and private new foundations now comprise 43.3% of the foundation sector. Table 1.48 breaks down the number and percentage distribution of the different types of foundations.

Foundations in Turkey are generally operating foundations. There are no 'pure' grant-making foundations. Foundations operate in many fields. Activities of old foundations are indicated by their distribution of properties, see Table 1.49. Religious activities are clearly the highest concentration.

---

[10] The Foundation for Strengthening Turkish Military Forces was formed to develop the national military industry and to establish new branches of military industry. Founders of the foundation are the Defence Minister, the Deputy Chief of General Staff, the Secretary of National Defence Minister, the Head of the Administration of Developing and Supporting Defence Industry (12), see Law No. 3388 (dated 17.6.83) for the Strengthening of the Turkish Military Forces.

[11] These are the foundations formed in cities and townships with the purpose of helping the citizens in need and poverty in the framework of the Law of Social Help and Encouraging. The board of trustees is composed of the head of the civil service, the mayor, the head of the police and other local authorities, see Law for Encouragement of Social Help and Solidarity, Official Journal, 29.5.98, pp.1–3.

[12] Founders of these foundations are the governor, city health director, urban development director, city directors of education, culture, tourism etc.

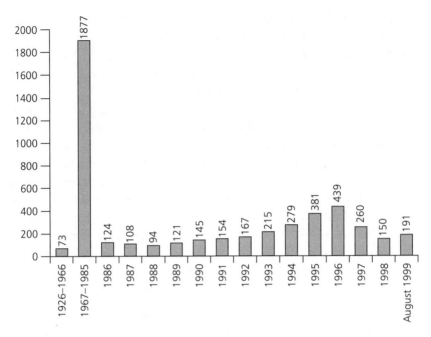

Figure 1.6 Number of foundations registered
Source: General Directorate of Foundations, 30 Sept. 1999

Table 1.48 Distribution of foundations by type (old, public, private)

	Total	%
Mazbut (administered) foundations	5376	
Mülhak (supervised) foundations	322	
Minority foundations	161	
Subtotal I: Old foundations	*5859*	*56.7*
Foundation for Strengthening Turkish Military Forces	1	
Social help and solidarity foundations	928	
Foundations for environmental protection	76	
Subtotal II: Public foundations	*1005*	*9.7*
Social security foundations	24	
Private individual foundations[13]	3443	
Subtotal III: Private foundations	*3467*	*33.6*
Total	**10,331**	**100**

Source: General Directorate of Foundations, August 1999

---

[13] 191 of them were granted tax exemption by the Board of Ministers.

Table 1.49 Distribution of properties of old foundations

Mosques	4949	Bridges	43
Churches/synagogues	70	Building complexes	9
Dormitories for students	62	Schools	174
Business buildings	135	Observatories	10
Hotels and Caravansarais	999	Houses for feeding the poor	35
Tombs	1234	Shipyards	37
Fountains and Sadirvans*	281	Mental health asylums	9
Bazaars (Bedesten)	42	Libraries	14
Other properties	1314	Thermal baths	7
		Total	**9424**

Source: General Directorate of Foundations, Sept. 30 1999
*Sadirvan is a kind of charitable foundation that is generally located next to mosques.

New foundations can be classified by major field of activity. Table 1.50 shows that social services, education and research, and Foundations of Social Help and Solidarity have the highest concentration.

Some education and research functions of new foundations are shown in Table 1.51.

Table 1.50 Number of new foundations by major field of activity

	Total	%
Culture and recreation	264	5.9
Education and research	939	20.9
Health	223	4.9
Social services	1165	26.1
Environment	95	2.1
Development and housing	274	6.1
Law, advocacy and politics	70	1.6
Religion	514	11.5
Subtotal	*3544*	
Foundations of social help and solidarity	928	20.7
Total	**4472**	**100**

Source: General Directorate of Foundations, August 1999

Table 1.51 Education and research activities of new foundations

Students supported by foundation grants (1998)	159,082
Dormitories operated	306
Dormitory capacity	25,187
Foundations with schools	44
Foundation universities	15
No. of students in foundation universities (1998)	17,052

Source: Aydın, Saglam Basar and Öztürk 1999.

5 Current trends and conclusion

Each society finds its identification in the culture it created. Institutions help sustain culture. As in the eras of the Seljuk and Ottoman Empires, foundations continue to play a crucial role in the creation of cultural values by fostering a feeling of public service and a sharing of public tasks. Over the past ten years, expectations of this role have increased as the belief in not taking everything from the state has increased, and demands for greater social solidarity and a more transparent economic and political system have arisen. In particular, with the catastrophic earthquake in 1999 Turkish society discovered once more the importance of the nonprofit sector, including foundations, as private voluntary organizations came to the forefront to provide help and support.

For the future of the Turkish foundation sector, the following aspects are on the agenda.

- A reform of General Directorate of Foundations to enable the development of Turkish foundations.
- The creation of more favourable legal conditions commensurate with the philosophy of foundations serving public purposes, and providing better incentives for the establishment of private individual foundations.
- The provision of training for managers and personnel of foundations.

At present, it is evident that efforts to rearrange and increase the income of foundations and properties should be intensified. In particular there is a need to transfer to private individual foundations more of the services conducted by the state in the fields of education, health and social services. Meanwhile, public foundations operating as a part of public management and financial systems should be more clearly separated from private individual foundations, and the distinction between foundations and associations should be clarified.

The aim would be to return to a view of the Turkish foundation sector expressed by a visiting Swiss professor in the 1920s, the early years of the Turkish Republic, in his farewell to Prime Minister İsmet İnönü:

> We see the Turkish foundations as the aim which Europe wants to achieve. It is appropriate to bring economic innovations to the foundation system without changing the strong contribution of your ancestors to national culture, social help and solidarity.[14]

Bibliography

Aydın, D., The Turkish Foundation System, Eskişehir Anadolu Üniversitesi, İktisadi ve İdari Bilimler Fakültesi Dergisi, Cilt 7, Sayı, 1 June 1989.

Aydın D., Saglam N., Baser, M., Öztürk, M., Vakıfların Mevcut Durumları Sorunları ve Çözüm Önerileri, Anadolu Universitesi, Eskişehir Ekonomik Araştırmalar Merkezi, Yayın No. 1999–2, Eskişehir 1999.

Baloğlu, Z., 'A new national approach in a land of age-old wakf tradition', in: *The Foundation of Turkey*, Istanbul, TUSEV, 1996.

Elif Matbaacılık, A., Kom. Şti. Ankara, 1986.

Ercüment K., Vakıf Müessesinin Mahiyeti ve Günümüz Değerlendirilmesi, I. Vakıf Şurası, December, 3–5, 1981, Elif Matbacılık A. Komandit Şirketi Ankara, 1986, pp.10–11.

Güneri, H., Türk Medeni Kanunun Açısından Vakıfta Amaç Kavramı ve Amaca Göre Vakıf Türleri, Sevinç Matbaası, Ankara, 1976.

Güzel, Ü., Vakıf Eski Eserlerin Korunması Hakkında Rapor, DPT, Mart 1982.

Law for the Encouragement of Social Help and Solidarity, *Official Journal*, 29.5.98, pp.1–3.

Oğuzhan, K., and Akyol, Ş., Medeni Kanun Borçlar Kanunu, Tatbikat Kanunu ve İlgili kanunlar- Tüzükler- Yönetmelikler, Fakülteler Matbaası İstanbul 1967.

Öztürk, N., 'The wakf: Its past and present', in: *The Foundation of Turkey*, İstanbul, TUSEV, 1996.

Yediyıldız, B., The place of the wakf in Turkish Cultural System, in: *The Foundation of Turkey*, İstanbul, TUSEV 1996.

---

[14] İskenderoglu, R.: his speech at the I. Vakıf Şurası, December, 3–5, 1985; in: Elif Matbaacılık, p.24.

▼ Diana Leat

United Kingdom

1 Introduction

In the UK the term 'foundation' is traditionally used to refer to endowed charitable bodies whose primary task is to give grants for charitable purposes. However, the terms 'trust' and 'foundation' may also refer to fundraising charitable grant makers. In popular usage, the defining characteristic of a foundation is that its primary business is making grants to other organizations or individuals for purposes which are charitable under charity law.[1] Thus the definition, development and operation of foundations in Britain is closely tied up with the definition, development and operation of charities in general.

Today foundations contribute only a small proportion – between 6% and 10% – of total voluntary sector income.[2] But foundation funds may be particularly significant as a source of innovation, especially in areas of the sector which lack popular or political support. The funds of foundations may also be viewed as significant irrespective of size because they are relatively secure and their distribution is free from market and political constraints.[3]

The story of British grant-making foundations is one of ambiguous formal and informal relationships with the state. In the last century at least, the role of foundations *vis-à-vis* the state in social provision has waxed and waned. The state has encouraged foundations with various fiscal incentives, but has also required some degree of control. England and Wales (but not Northern Ireland and Scotland) are unusual in having a formal supervisory body for charities (the Charity Commission) but the power and effectiveness of the Commission in regulating foundations is unclear.[4] Today, old

---

[1] There are some exceptions; see Siederer for a useful discussion of types.

[2] Posnett; Clare and Scott; Kendall and Knapp; Charities Aid Foundation; FitzHerbert, Adison and Rahman.

[3] O'Neill.

[4] van der Ploeg.

assumptions concerning foundations' formal and informal independence from the state are being upset by new government-created grant makers, questions about the sustainability of grants, and policy emphasis on cross-sector partnerships.

The data on foundations are patchy and largely restricted to the minority of relatively rich foundations which command the lion's share of assets and income. In addition to lack of systematic data there are also problems of double counting and of distinguishing between purely grant-making foundations versus operating charities that make grants in the course of their work. Furthermore, there are no registers of foundations for Scotland and Northern Ireland; estimates of numbers and known names are included in various guides but the data are obviously less robust than those relating to England and Wales.

2 Historical background

The historical development of foundations illustrates their changing and ambiguous relationship to the state. In the late Middle Ages social welfare was provided largely by lords of feudal manors who were obliged to provide the necessities of life for their tenants, by the merchant and craft guilds, by extended family and, most significantly, by the Roman Catholic Church. The Church also encouraged wealthy individuals to give charitably, and if a man died intestate one-third of his property was devoted to pious purposes by the ecclesiastical courts. However, the medieval Church's approach to giving was less about helping the poor than about making it easier for a rich man to enter the kingdom of heaven. By the 14th and 15th centuries the Church and the ecclesiastical courts were increasingly corrupt and inefficient in relation to philanthropic works. The Reformation and, in particular, the Tudor seizure of power from the Church radically changed the philanthropic landscape. Henry VIII dissolved the monasteries and strengthened mortmain provisions to prevent bequests of land to chantries and other ecclesiastical institutions. Later Edward VI confiscated the property of existing chantries.

At around the same time that feudal relations were breaking down social problems grew. In particular the problem of beggars and vagrants was exacerbated by the disbanding of armies following the end of the Wars of the Roses and the displacement of monks and nuns following the dissolution of the monasteries. Concurrently, major increases in foreign trade began to create a newly wealthy merchant class. While the landed aristocracy continued personal almsgiving, the new merchants and gentry practised secular philanthropy for municipal improvement, inspired by a mixture of motivations: Renaissance humanism, Protestant zeal for good works (a subject of many contemporary sermons), the desire to be viewed as good citizens, concern for the educational standards of the present and future labour force, and fear of rebellion by the masses of vagrant unemployed poor.[5] Interestingly, at the end of the 20th century these motivations for giving to foundations are probably equally relevant.

As the state became increasingly involved in social welfare provision for the growing number of vagrant and unemployed poor, it took various measures to encourage philanthropy. By the end of the Tudor period the Court of Chancery had taken over the role of judicial enforcement of charitable gifts previously regulated by the ecclesiastical courts. In part this fundamental change reflected the growing secularization of philanthropy but it was also related to the individualism of major Tudor philanthropists who preferred giving charitable gifts/endowments for particular specified purposes rather than outright gifts to charitable organizations.

The industrial revolution of the 18th and 19th centuries caused enormous social upheaval and amplified existing problems of social welfare, as well as adding new ones to the list. For reasons no doubt little different from those of the Tudor philanthropists described above, 19th century industrialists and other wealthy people contributed to social welfare at home and abroad (e.g. in the anti-slavery society) as well as to the arts and the environment.

In the 20th century foundation establishment has continued. In the light of the growing scope of statutory welfare provision, foundations have emphasized five key principles in their work:[6]

- doing what the state doesn't do
- pump-priming – small grants to attract further funding
- innovation
- unpopular causes and risk taking
- emergency funding.

These principles have gone hand-in-hand with traditional practices which stress being responsive rather than proactive; making smaller short-term grants; giving grants for specific projects rather than for

---

[5] Chesterman, p. 17.

[6] Leat, *Trusts*.

core funds and often for capital rather than revenue purposes. In this way, foundations have distanced themselves from the state and limited their responsibilities.

In recent years, as successive Conservative administrations have attempted to rein back the expansion of the state, 'doing what the state doesn't do' has become an increasingly unreliable defence against demands on foundations' over-stretched funds. Pump-priming works if there is a nearby well containing water, but in a terrain in which statutory funding has largely dried up pump-priming has increasingly been seen as an ineffective strategy. Foundations today are still grappling with defining their proper role, and especially their relationship with the state, in a continually changing context.

3 Legal issues

The legal treatment of foundations again highlights the twin themes of encouragement and control by the state. Very broadly, governance of charitable organizations in Britain takes three main legal forms:

- the unincorporated association
- the incorporated association
- the trust.[7]

In modern common usage the term trust or foundation is most likely to be used to refer to organizations which adopt the trust form, but there are exceptions (i.e. some organizations may be referred to as foundations or trusts but adopt other legal forms of governance). Conversely, some organizations that are legally trusts may not be commonly described or known as such. As noted elsewhere, the term 'trust' or 'foundation' is commonly reserved for organizations whose primary purpose is grant making for charitable purposes.

During the Tudor period the trust (or use) came to be the main way of bequeathing money for pious causes. The Court of Chancery recognized and enforced charitable use, helping it to become the main legal mechanism for philanthropic purposes. The legal privileges of charities were confirmed and enhanced and the Statute of Charitable Uses 1601 provided for appointment of commissioners to investigate the administration of charities, especially misuse of charity property. Tudor attempts to supervise charities were not the first but they were especially important. The preamble to the Statute of Charitable Uses

---

[7] Chesterman, p. 5; for details of regulation of charities in Scotland see Logan.

1601 listed the limits of the Statute's operation and formed the basis of the legal definition of charitable purpose today: the relief of poverty, the advancement of education, the advancement of religion and other purposes of public benefit. Various commentators have noted the close relationship between the definition of charitable purposes and the provisions of the state poor laws, but its actual wording allowed for purposes unrelated to poverty.

With the introduction of income tax the precise definition of what was charitable for income tax purposes became a matter of contention in the courts. In a landmark case between the Income Tax Commissioners and Pemsel (later known as the Pemsel case) in 1891, the House of Lords ruled that the definition of charitable purposes should be that of the 1601 preamble, that is that poverty is not a necessary condition. The general principle that charities – and thus charitable foundations – as defined by the 1601 preamble should be exempt from tax remains today, although it is once again increasingly contested.

With growing philanthropic activity in the 19th century, concern resurfaced about the lack of public scrutiny of charities (this lack of scrutiny was one of Gladstone's arguments for removal of tax exemption). A Royal Commission appointed to look into the administration of charities led to a succession of Charitable Trusts Acts in 1853, 1855 and 1860 and the establishment of a permanent Charity Commission. The Commission's major powers were:

- to exercise jurisdiction concurrently with the Court of Chancery in making schemes for the administration of charities whose purposes were not sufficiently spelt out, or (under a cypress scheme) whose purposes could no longer be fulfilled
- to appoint and remove charity trustees
- to investigate suspected abuse
- to require annual accounts
- to act as custodian of land and investments if trustees wished
- to keep a register of charitable trusts
- to give advice to trustees on administrative matters.

Thus by the turn of the century charities, including foundations, enjoyed a range of legal and fiscal privileges, but at the same time were required to submit to state supervision (however limited). The trust was preserved as a flexible legal form for establishing a charity, although charities could also adopt other legal forms such as the company limited by guarantee. Perhaps most significantly, as various taxes increased in number and size, the fiscal advantages of charity status increased.

All these advantages carried forward into the 20th century despite the advent of the welfare state. Charities were still encouraged and still expected to submit to supervision in return for fiscal and legal favours. In the 20th century there has been very little legislation altering the general position at the end of the 19th century. The Charities Act 1960 very broadly increased the powers of the Charity Commission. Its jurisdiction was extended to almost all charities and not, as before, restricting it to endowed charities. It was enabled to take remedial action in cases of misconduct (e.g. by freezing a charity's bank account), as well as to modernize the purposes of a charity. The Charities Act of 1992 and 1993 required foundations to publish an annual report (something relatively few foundations had previously done and to which some foundations objected) and to keep accounts in the form specified in regulations based on a recommended accounting practice (SORP 2). Even more radically, perhaps, foundations were required to make their accounts available to any member of the public who asks for them and pays a reasonable fee, and both annual reports and accounts were to be available for inspection at the Charity Commission. In addition the 1992 Act gave the Charity Commission statutory powers to demand information from charities and to hold formal enquiries, as well as legal authority to exchange information with other government bodies, including the Inland Revenue. The Act also strengthened the powers of the Commission in cases of mismanagement and made it a criminal offence to fail, persistently and without reasonable excuse, to fulfil the requirements of the Act. The 1992 Act also broadly increased foundations' freedom in handling their investments and income.[8]

These provisions of the Act concerning foundation accountability and openness marked a radical change in the requirements of foundations. In an important sense, they marked the end of an era of privacy for foundations. That said, foundations are still remarkably free, for example to pay high salaries to trustees acting as administrators, to pay high fees to a trustee's company for investment advice, and otherwise run up considerable administrative expenses (though it appears that very few actually do so).

4 A profile of foundations in the UK

An estimated 8800 charitable grant-making foundations currently distribute around £1.25 billion (€2 billion) each year in grants to

---

[8] Leat, *Grant-Making Foundations.*

other bodies. In addition, the National Lottery Charities Board alone gave £680 million (€1 billion) to nearly 12,000 projects between 1995 and 1997. Donations are further swelled by the contribution (around £280 million, €420 million, in total) of a dozen large operating charities which give grants in the course of their work, bringing the overall annual total to about £1.9 billion (€3 billion).[9]

Different types of foundation

- **Endowed foundations**
  By definition, endowed foundations make up the bulk of all charitable grant-making foundations. Endowed foundations vary radically in size and level of grant-making activity.

- **Corporate foundations**
  The category of corporate foundations overlaps with that of endowed foundations in two ways. First, some endowed foundations were originally established by companies but may have long since lost their original close ties with the founding company. Second, some modern corporate foundations are endowed. Other corporate foundations have no permanent endowment but rather receive regular transfers from the associated company. Five hundred or more (non-endowed) givers listed in the third edition of the *Guide to UK Company Giving* gave £240 million (€350 million) in charitable donations and a further £180 million (€260 million) in other forms of charitable support.[10]

- **Community Foundations**
  Although well developed in the US, community foundations are relatively new to the UK, first appearing in the late 1970s. By 1997 there were 18 fully active community foundations with another 20 under development.[11] Community foundations raise and manage a permanent endowment of charitable donations from which they make grants to local and community projects. They restrict their grant making and much of their fundraising to a specific geographical area. In a sense, community foundations are endowed foundations in the making and as such they straddle the boundary between the endowed and fundraising categories.

  In 1995–96, 17 community foundations distributed more than £3.7 million (€6 million) in grants to local community groups. Their

---

[9] Pharoah and Siederer.

[10] Smyth.

[11] Humphries, p. 73; C.S. Mott Foundation.

absolute grant-making capacity more than doubled in just two years rising from £1.6 million in 1993–94 to £3.7 million in 1995–96. Community foundation endowments grew by 60% from £19 million (€30 million) in 1994–95 to almost £31 million (€50 million) by 1995–96, average income grew by 61%, grant making by 57%, core costs by 23% and endowment by 28%. These are average figures and, as in so many areas of the foundation world, there is huge variation among community foundations.

- **Fundraising grant makers**
  Fundraising foundations are not new. Many of today's established foundations (e.g. the Kings Fund) were funded by public subscription. But fundraising foundations have grown in recent years. Data on them is patchy and the various guides tend to treat them erratically. Fundraising grant makers include broadcast appeals on radio and television, of which there is no comprehensive systematic record not least because their number varies from year to year, often in response to local, national and international crises.[12] A conservative estimate of the annual amounts given in grants from broadcast appeals might be £40 million (€64 million). The category of fundraising grant makers also includes the National Foundation for Sport and the Arts, funded from weekly subscriptions by football pools promoters, giving over £60 million (€96 million) in 1993. There are an unknown number of other such organizations.

- **Government-inspired grant-making foundations**
  Since 1995 the total amount given in grants by non-endowed charitable organizations has been increased by the recently introduced National Lottery. The projected total of grants by all five Lottery Boards to good causes over the seven year licence was £9 billion (€14.4 billion).[13] The effects of this level of grant making on grant recipients and on the level of demand for continuing funding (falling on foundations) may not become apparent for some years. In addition to the Lottery Boards there is a small but growing number of grant-making charitable organizations set up as a channel for the distribution of government funds.

- **Operating grant makers**
  An estimated 75% of the largest charities have a grant-making function.[14] The largest 11 operating grant makers made grants of

---

[12] Leat, *Fundraising*; Leat, *Broadcast*.

[13] FitzHerbert, Giussani and Hurd.

[14] Osborne and Hems.

£256 million (€410 million) in 1996–97 and had total income of £487 million (€780 million) and assets of £369 million (€590 million).[15]

Assets, grant making and foundation development

Size and distribution of foundation assets

Estimates of total assets of foundations are difficult to obtain partly because some foundations do not put a price on their assets and because those that do often rely on some degree of guesswork. A broad estimate is £30 billion (€48 billion).

In Britain, as in other countries, the assets and income of grant-making foundations are very unevenly distributed among the total population of foundations. Even within the top 500 foundations the vast majority of assets (total £12.5 billion, €20 billion in 1994), income and grant making is concentrated within the top 50 foundations. For example, of the top 500 foundations in 1991–92, the top 50 (10%) owned around 60% of the total assets, had around 60% of total income and distributed around 75% of the total value of grants.[16] A wide range in distribution of assets exists even among the very richest grant makers (Table 1.52).

Table 1.52 Distribution of assets among the top 20 grant-making trusts

Assets in 1995–96 (£million)	(€million)	Number of foundations
Over 500	Over 803	3
300–500	482–803	4
100–299	160–481	7
50–99	80–159	6
Total		**20**

Source: based on data in Pharoah and Smerdon, p. 94, 1997

Distribution of grant making according to activity

Distribution of grant making varies across the foundation sector according to the fields of activities in which foundations make grants (Table 1.53). Social care activities receive the highest proportion of grant expenditure, followed by health and education.

---

[15] Pharoah and CAF Information Unit, p.87.

[16] Saxon-Harrold and Kendall.

Table 1.53 Foundation activities by proportion and value of grants made in 1996–97

Activity	Value (£ million)	% of total grants expenditure
Social care	233	25
Health	174	19
Education	155	17
Arts/culture/recreation	95	10
Religious activities	76	8
Development/housing	42	5
Environment/animals	30	3
Philanthropy/volunteering	30	3
Science and technology	24	3
Civil society/law and advocacy	23	3
International	20	2
Social science	14	2
Subtotal classified	*916*	*100*
Uncoded to main subject	64	
Total	**980**	

Source: Vincent and Pharoah, p25, 2000

Geographical distribution of grants given

Foundation giving tends to be heavily skewed towards London and the south east, but it is not clear to what extent this is a function of the location of grant seekers' head offices. There are foundations which have a specific geographical remit and, more recently, some of the larger foundations have deliberately chosen to favour particular disadvantaged geographical areas.[17]

Foundation formation

Available data on the rate of foundation establishment shows a steady increase from 1900 to the 1950s, when rates began to increase dramatically. Foundation formation hit its peak during the 1960s and 1970s. The ACF Annual Review for 1996–97, commenting on the possibility of a review of charity taxation, suggests that general taxation levels are the key factors in foundation formation and growth. Relief from income and corporation tax has been undermined by progressive

---

[17] The Directory of Social Change also now publishes a series of regional guides to foundation giving. See also Vincent and Pharoah.

reductions in the rates of the taxes themselves, so reducing the income of investing charities and the value of the gifts to them. Although taxation levels are unlikely to return to the levels of the 1960s and 1970s, these were boom periods for the formation of foundations – mainly because tax-relieved funds were worth very much more when put in trust for charity than if kept (and taxed) for personal use.[18]

Table 1.54 Foundation formation over time

Year	No.	% of total	Income: % by category	Assets: % by category
Before 1900	154	5	9	13
1901–1910	31	1	3	5
1911–1920	43	1	4	3
1921–1930	62	2	7	10
1931–1940	60	2	9	2
1941–1950	98	3	23	4
1951–1960	270	9	13	18
1961–1970	824	26	15	24
1971–1980	829	26	7	13
1981–1990	663	21	8	7
1991–1994	113	4	2	1
Totals	**3147**	**100**	**100**	**100**

Villemur 1995 p. ix

Table 1.54 clearly needs to be treated with caution. The number of foundations does not come close to the total number of foundations in the UK and it raises a number of further questions concerning the high income proportions in 1940–50 relative to assets and establishment.

5 Current trends and conclusion

The creation of the government-inspired National Lottery Boards has radically transformed the charitable grant-making landscape. On the other hand, with the creation of an Association of Charitable Foundations providing foundations with a voice in lobbying parliament, foundations may be transforming their relationships with the state. Other recent developments include the creation of new founda-

---

[18] Association of Charitable Foundations, p. 30.

tions emerging from bank mergers and demutualization of the building societies, as well as the expanded PPP Healthcare Medical Trust, and the creation of the Diana Princess of Wales Memorial Fund.

More generally, the composition of CAF's top 500 table has changed by 10% over the last year with 50 new entrants to the table (and obviously the same number of exits). The total of new grant making entrants is higher than that of exits. But overall, a larger number of trusts reported a decrease in grant making than reported an increase, and many appear to have kept their grant making at the same level. In spite of some dramatic individual increases in grant making, there has been a very slight decline in real terms in grants and assets. This contrasts dramatically with the growth in income between 1994–95 and 1995–96 of 10% in real terms.[19]

The story of ambiguity in relationships between the state and foundations looks set to continue. The ambiguity of state-foundation relationships is most obviously highlighted in the growing value of fiscal favours and legal privileges on the one hand, and on the other, the state's growing demands for accountability and control. But there are other more indirect threats to the independence of foundations. These stem from wider policy changes including contracting out of statutory provision to voluntary organizations, as well as increasing emphasis on partnerships between the sectors in funding and provision of a range of services. One effect of these policies is to break down old boundaries between the statutory, voluntary and commercial sectors, creating tensions for foundations regarding who and what they are funding.

The introduction of the state-inspired National Lottery Boards and more recently the New Opportunities Fund may further threaten the autonomy of foundations. These funds, with their assets far exceeding those of foundations, their practice of requiring matching funding and their emphasis on short-term grants, place new demands on foundations as a whole.[20] The irony is that government appears to be turning the tables on foundations, acting in effect as innovator and pump-primer, expecting foundations to march to their tune.

---

[19] The figures may reflect the adoption of SORP and inclusion of incoming resources for endowment within the income figure, see Pharoah and CAF Information Unit.

[20] Unwin and Westland, Association of Charitable Foundations.

Bibliography

Association of Charitable Foundations, Promoting the effectiveness of UK grant-making trusts, *Annual Review 1996–97*, London, 1997.

Charities Aid Foundation, *The Directory of Smaller Grant Making Trusts 1998–1999*, West Malling, 1999. (Gives details of grant-making trusts with an income of £13,000 or less and therefore not included in the major Directory of Grant Making Trusts also published by CAF.)

Charities Aid Foundation, *The Directory of Grant Making Trusts 1999–2000*, Vol. 1, West Malling, 1999.

Chesterman, M., *Charities, Trusts and Social Welfare*, London, Weidenfeld and Nicholson, 1979.

Clare, R., and Scott, M., 'Charities contribution to gross domestic product', in: *Economic Trends*, 482, 1993.

FitzHerbert, L., Giussani, C. and Hurd, H. eds., *The National Lottery Yearbook*, 1996 Edition, London, Directory of Social Change.

FitzHerbert, L., Addison, D. and Rahman, F., *1999/2000 A Guide to the Major Trusts, Vol.1 The Top 300 Trusts*, London, Directory of Social Change, 1999.

Humphries, G., 'Community foundations in review, 1995–6', in: C. Pharoah and M. Smerdon (eds), *Dimensions of the Voluntary Sector*, 1997 edition, West Malling, Charities Aid Foundation, pp.73–5, 1997.

Kendall, J., and Knapp, M., Voluntary Means, Social Ends: Policy Issues for the UK Voluntary Sector in the 1990's, Canterbury, Personal Social Services Research Unit, University of Kent.

Leat, D., *Fundraising and Grant Making A case study of ITV Telethon '88*, West Malling, Charities Aid Foundation, 1989.

Leat, D., *Broadcast Charitable Appeals*, London, Directory of Social Change, 1990.

Leat, D., *Trusts in Transition: the policy and practice of grant-giving trusts*, York, Joseph Rowntree Foundation, 1992.

Leat, D., *Faith, Hope and Information: Assessing a grant application*, York, Joseph Rowntree Foundation, 1998.

Leat, D., 'Grant-Making Foundations: Policy Shapers or Policy Takers', in: *Proceedings of the XXth Anniversary Conference of the Centre for Voluntary Organisations*, London School of Economics, 1999.

Logan, B., 'The Regulation of Charities in Scotland', in: *Top Charities in Scotland 1998*, London, Caritas Data Ltd, 1998.

C.S. Mott Foundation, *In Focus*, Vol.2, 1, 1999.

O'Neill, M., *The Third America: The Emergence of the Nonprofit Sector in the US*, San Francisco, Jossey Bass, 1989.

Osborne, S. and Hems, L., Survey of the Income and Expenditure of Charitable Organizations in the UK: Summary of Findings, Birmingham, Public Sector Management Research Centre, Aston Business School, 1994.

Pharoah, C. and Siederer, N., 'Number, income and assets – new estimates', in: C. Pharoah and M. Smerdon (eds) *Dimensions of the Voluntary Sector*, 1997 edition, West Malling, Charities Aid Foundation, 1997.

Pharoah, C. and CAF Information Unit, *Dimensions of the Voluntary Sector*, 1998 edition, West Malling, Charities Aid Foundation, pp.87–105.

Posnett, J., 'The resources of registered charities in England and Wales – 1990–91', in: S. Saxon–Harrold and J. Kendall (eds), *Researching the Voluntary Sector*, 1st edition, West Malling, Charities Aid Foundation, 1993, pp.1–9.

van der Ploeg, T. J., 'A Comparative Legal Analysis of Foundations: Aspects of Supervision and Transparency', in: H. K. Anheier and S. Toepler (eds), *Private Funds, Public Purpose, Philanthropic Foundations in International Perspective*, New York, Kluwer Academic/Plenum Publishers, 1999, pp.55–78.

Saxon Harrold, S. and Kendall, J. eds, *Researching the Voluntary Sector*, First Edition, West Malling, Charities Aid Foundation, 1993.

Siederer, N., 'Independent Funding: the role of the charitable trust', in: C. Hanvey and T. Philpot, (eds), *Sweet Charity*, London, Routledge, 1996.

Smyth, J., *The Guide to UK Company Giving*, Third edition, London, Directory of Social Change, 2000.

Unwin, J. and Westland, P., *Local Funding: The Impact of the National Lottery Charities Board*, London, Association of Charitable Foundations, 1997.

Villemur, A. ed., *Directory of Grant Making Trusts 1991*, West Malling, Charities Aid Foundation, 1995.

Vincent, J., and Pharoah, C., *Dimensions 2000*, Volume 3: Patterns of Independent Grant Making in the UK, West Malling, Charities Aid Foundation, 2000.

▼ Frances Pinter

The Role of Foundations in the Transformation Process in Central and Eastern Europe

1 Introduction

This chapter explores the role of foundations in central and eastern Europe. Ten EU accession countries, Bulgaria, the Czech Republic, Estonia, Hungary, Latvia, Lithuania, Poland, Romania, Slovakia, and Slovenia are covered here. There is no reference to Russia and the CIS countries, nor to the countries of south-eastern Europe. Although these countries receive substantial funding from the same, primarily Western, foundations that are active in the accession countries, they fall outside the remit of this book.

The ten countries considered here are very important because their European Union membership will have a profound impact on Europe as a whole. Their landmass will represent a 33% expansion of the geographical territory of the EU. An additional 105 million people will comprise 28% of the total population. The aggregate GDP, even when adjusted to purchasing power, is only 9% of the EU with an average GDP equal to 32% of the EU average per head. The unadjusted figures of 4% and 13% respectively make for even grimmer reading.[1]

It is against this backdrop that foundations have come to play a significant role, firstly in the transition from communism to democracy and market economy, and secondly in the long journey down the road towards EU accession. This double transition places additional burdens on the countries.

---

[1] Avery and Cameron.

In this time of pervasive upheaval foundations have taken on a multiplicity of roles. They bring money and know-how. As they finance new innovative models of activity, introducing new patterns of governance, they enable the creation of the building blocks of civil society. The more people are offered opportunities to develop new relationships unhampered by the authoritarian structures of old, the easier it becomes to establish trust, take risks and create the social capital needed for a functioning civil society.

Much social transformation is occurring as the countries grapple with the requirements and implications of EU membership. Each country is required to bring its laws into line with the *acquis communautaire* or as it is now referred to the 'acquis of the Union'. Twenty thousand laws and regulations need to conform to EU standards. Membership of bodies such as the Council of Europe as well as association with NATO, OSCE and others have helped set standards to which these countries have committed themselves, thereby requiring substantial legislative and social reforms. Foundations support the development of independent perspectives on the nature of the changes to come.

The first decade of foundation activity since the collapse of communism has been dominated by foreign foundations. There are few corporate foundations concerned with the public good, and community foundations are in their infancy. However, governments are watching foundation activities and beginning to establish independent government-sponsored foundations as the benefits of such independence become increasingly evident. Most foundations are grant making and rely on third parties such as nonprofit organizations to undertake implementation. However the Soros Foundation network, the largest in the region, functions both as a grant-making and an operating foundation. This dual-capacity strategy was chosen to handle their rapid growth during the 1990s.

Foundations in central and eastern Europe are beginning to look more like those in the West but still maintain some persisting differences. Most are non-membership based and require some kind of charter. In most countries they are required to register with an official body. Some countries distinguish between public and private foundations although the former are institutionally separate from government. Nonetheless, the foundation sector discussed in this chapter is primarily private. The governance of these entities is prescribed by law and the principle of self-governance has been widely adopted, although in some countries there can still be informal governmental influence. On the whole foundations are not allowed to distribute their funds to their owners, but irregularities have certainly been more prevalent than in western countries. A continuing distrust of foundations as serving the public good has prevented them from gaining public confidence, irrespective of the fact that such objectives are now reflected in the new laws.

2 Historical background

The role of foundations (both public and private) in central European society cannot be divorced from the enormous upheavals of the past decade. With the sudden arrival of democracy there was little clear thinking on how to establish, maintain and encourage foundations that could work for the benefit of society. This was hardly surprising given their virtual absence between World War II and 1989. The origins of the new foundations determined the emergence of a very different relationship between foundations and their grantees. Most foundations were, and still are, governed by foreign funders.

Though the distinction is perhaps somewhat artificial one can divide the 1990s into two periods: the revolutionary moment when looming difficulties were understated due to the general climate of euphoria, and the post-revolutionary period when realism set in.

In the early 1990s foundations were primarily concerned with economic reform. The theory was pragmatic; for democracy to prevail a functioning market economy needed to be established. For various reasons activities were later broadened to encompass arts and culture, education and information, health and civil society development. By the end of the 1990s disappointment with institutional reforms had brought about a shift in emphasis toward public administration, legal reform and human rights.

The first wave of new laws in the early 1990s did little to promote the interests of foundations that were truly philanthropic. Loose wording encouraged less than scrupulous individuals to use foundations as tax avoidance shelters with no intention of ever promoting a public good. This diminished public confidence in the concept of 'good works' as corruption became visible on an unprecedented scale. In some countries foundations attempting to create social change were accused of social manipulation and, if foreign, were branded (sometimes with anti-Semitic tones) as agents of the 'imperial West'. Extremist political parties at both ends of the left-right spectrum attacked foundations to suit their purposes.

The parameters of acceptable activities for foundations are still taking shape. The political influence of foundations is probably considerably greater than in many other countries. In most western countries, to maintain tax privileges foundations must not participate in political campaigns or engage in activities to influence legislation. The very same foundations that adhere to these rules in the West are engaging in activities that have a very substantial political impact in the East. Even if not directly funding political parties, the mere fact that so much legislative and policy review as well as support for various forms of media comes from foundations (mostly foreign funded at that) puts a different complexion on their activities.

Assistance coming into central and eastern Europe from bilateral and multilateral agencies has influenced the directions taken by foundations. Although some argue that help from the West was insufficient, the money that flowed in did have an impact, though on occasions with attached conditions that were at odds with what local people wanted to achieve. While the European Bank for Reconstruction and Development focused on infrastructure development, their work could not be carried out without cadres of trained local economists, public administrators and functioning businesses. World Bank education loans concentrated on structural changes such as re-organizing the administration, computerizing facilities and streamlining delivery to accommodate dwindling state resources. Foundations worked to modernize curricula and balance the development of life skills with the knowledge-based education that had been core to education under communism. Western staff from these various bodies intermingled, sharing ideas and increasingly co-sponsoring projects.

After 1989 the countries of central and eastern Europe watched their economies spin into recession. With this came a total redefinition of the role of the state in every aspect of human activity. It was inevitable that dislocations in the supply of goods and services would occur while the governments, with their universally underpaid civil servants, re-defined their existence and reconstructed their sources of financing. Responsibility and power were shifting away from the centre, but to where exactly was not clear. Revolutions turned out not to take place overnight and transitions took even longer. 'Transitology' became an academic discipline. Only towards the end of the 1990s did 'consolodology' enter the picture, the study of which is likely to extend for at least another decade.

Concepts of power have very different roots in the post-communist societies. The idea of a positive relationship between strong civil societies and strong effective states was muddled to people whose experience with strong states was negative. Historically, the strength of a communist state depended on how strength was measured. Its ability to crush opposition by brute force was unquestionable, but it had long lost legitimacy. In the subsequent vacuum people lost the ability to identify with anything as subtle as a self-regulating civil society.

One major obstacle was the absence of trust, an element considered essential to the formation of a strong civil society and democracy. Without it there can be no social fabric. Marxist interpretations of society had little patience with the concept of trust given their preoccupation with conflict; trust as a precondition of social organization was considered a wishy-washy western concern. In post-revolutionary countries it was far from clear where, apart from family and close friends, one could place trust; even betrayal from the closest of relations was not unheard of, as revealed by Tina Rosenberg[2] and others. Its presumed absence historically does much to explain how central and eastern Europe responded to the arrival of idealistic western foundations.

In a perhaps excessively critical account of western aid to eastern Europe, Janine R. Wedel[3] argues that western foundations were naive in their approach and were seduced by recipients' abilities quickly to learn the art of grant applications. The importance of these grants, she contends, was far more than money – it was 'symbolic capital':

> … an individual's combined cultural, social, and financial power, which served to compound the power of the individual's group in the public arena – that could be leveraged both in and outside the region … Securing Western – sometimes specifically American – funds greatly enhanced one's reputation and lent legitimacy that could be leveraged internally to enhance symbolic capital and accrue further political, financial and social rewards. For this reason, even small sums of hard currency could be enormously life enhancing to the beneficiaries.

As states withdrew subsidies to softer areas such as arts and culture, foundations leapt in, eager to respond to requests and often creating a dependency which they would later find difficult to abandon. At the same time, western foundations had arrived with idealistic notions about goals that could be achieved and the time required to achieve

---

[2] Rosenberg.

[3] Wedel, p.91.

them. With a highly-educated population apparently eager to adopt democracy it was all too easy to believe that only a few crash courses in business and economics would be required. But 40 years of communism had created a population with values and priorities that were different, often antipathetic, to western ideals. The slow realization of these differences in the second half of the 1990s brought a re-evaluation of foundation roles in the transition.

With hindsight it is easy to say that the extent and depth of the transition had been underestimated. During the latter part of the 1990s much soul-searching was undertaken by western foundations as well as the liberal vanguard of the East who were trying to instil a sense of the civil into their societies. Everyone agreed that 'social capital', described by Robert Putnam[4] as 'features of social organization, such as trust, norms and networks, that can improve the efficiency of society by facilitating coordinated action', was in short supply. Former dissidents had assumed a latent civil society had been 'forced underground, shackled by apathy and fear, and thereby reduced to "the safety of the mousehole"'[5] and was now awaiting its renaissance. But there was simply too little understanding of the know-how required for this rebirth to occur. Politicians of the region needed skill not as 'ironfisted' leaders, but as 'skilled practitioners of the difficult art of unscrewing the lids of despotism and enabling the growth of civil society, mainly by forging new compromises between state actors and their subjects, and by withdrawing and retreating from unworkable positions'.[6] Such skills are acquired with practice that new politicians did not have.

Might there have been a different set of outcomes leading to a speedier transition? Looking at other countries' experiences it seems unlikely. For example Spain's transition to democracy actually took much longer than apparent to the casual observer. It involved three overlapping stages – transition, consolidation and institutionalization – the first of which Victor M. Perez Diaz argues cannot even begin without some prior beginnings of democratic tradition and practice from which to draw. Although these stages are:

> often understood as sequences that follow from critical choices made by elites, social groups, and the population at large [...] the fact is that only very rarely do these people face problem situations

---

[4] Putnam, p.167.

[5] George Konrad in Keane, p.22.

[6] Keane, *Political Quarterly*, pp.340–52 and Keane, 1993, p.43–4.

as rational choice makers, weighing the costs, benefits, risks and probabilities of success of several alternatives, in the short, medium and long run. More often they simply react to the situation at hand and to others' responses to it in the framework of previously existing traditions that shape their preferences and their definitions of the situation.[7]

Thus it is hardly surprising that when change is initiated more rapidly, it is more difficult for civil society to take root. Arguably, foundations can have an irreplaceable role in nurturing an emerging civil society if these lessons can be translated into better decision-making.

There were no models from the economic sphere that could show the way toward a more functional society. Growth through central planning clearly did not work. Trust and risk-taking, essential to democracy and a modern economy, had been crushed under communism. Deregulation and privatization did not have a proper environment in which to flourish. Francis Fukuyama defines trust as 'the expectation that arises within a community of regular, honest, and cooperative behaviour, based on commonly shared norms, on the part of other members of the community'.[8] As such, trust is a 'social virtue that creates social capital (passim) by allowing persons to organize and spontaneously associate with others'.[9]

Lack of trust stultifies the emergence of large complex enterprises. For example Fukuyama cites Latin America, with its preponderance of family run businesses, as a 'low trust' society. However in regions like central and eastern Europe where large enterprises were held together by authoritarian rule and there was little scope for even small-scale private enterprise, the transition starting point was considerably lower than zero. It was hardly surprising then that the economies fell into decline for several years, not just because of structural re-organization but also because of the massive change in mind-sets needed to implement the changes.

The need for greater transparency emerged in the second half of the 1990s. Western foundations felt betrayed as their funds failed to produce the changes that they had anticipated. Recipients did not understand this reaction, seeing little wrong with arbitrary and closed procedures still being used to allocate new funds to the 'right' people.

---

[7] Perez–Diaz, pp.6–7.

[8] Fukuyama, p.26.

[9] Fukuyama, p.48.

In western countries funds from foundations account for only a small amount of NGO income and activity. However, it is generally recognized that their impact far surpasses the relative size of resources, as foundations are able to fund innovative projects without political or other constraints. Much cutting edge thinking in education, culture and other spheres of social life comes from experimental pilot projects that only foundations are able and willing to support. This model was previously unknown in the East, which naturally used foundation funds to maintain essentials that were suddenly chronically under-funded by the state.

By the latter half of the 1990s the sustainability of foundation financed projects rose high into the agenda, as did the absence of any precedent for third sector engagement in income-generating activities. Newly-formed NGOs were reliant either upon the state budget or on foundations to finance their activities. In the early 1990s many of the countries of central and eastern Europe did not have adequate legislation enabling the third sector to free itself from centralized single source funding. So while NGOs flourished, nonprofit organizations that funded themselves through the sale of goods and services could function only after a second round of legislation was introduced in the late 1990s.

The development of professional know-how in both grant-making and operating programmes had to begin from scratch, as there was little tradition in philanthropic work. Decision-making processes within the organs of state that were previously responsible for much of what foundations now undertake were certainly not models to be emulated. Competition based on clearly-stated criteria and transparent evaluation and selection methods had been the exception rather than the rule. The introduction of this methodology was not easy; the previous social order came under attack, simple seniority and status (or party membership) could no longer ensure access to resources, and small cliques were forced to give up preferential treatment. In the early 1990s rules of governance were unclear. The intellectual elite, much revered as the vanguard of reform, now found their incomes decimated by inflation and their status in society equally diminished. Education followed arts and culture as candidates for drastic cuts. These were the areas through which foundations, particularly foreign, felt they could influence the development of democracy. The inevitable clash of perceptions, eastern Europe seeing foundations as a lifeline, and western Europe seeing them as a means of changing society, was widely debated over the decade.

With much of the fledgling NGO sector relying on foundation grants, it is interesting to see how governments have responded to the pressures to establish independent public foundations that operate transparently and are able to serve the needs of specific sectors. Much of the methodology for running new public foundations was drawn directly from the standards set by the larger foreign foundations.

Another fundamental impediment to implementing change was, and still is (at least for the older generation) the common attitude toward risk. Writing on the history of risk, Peter Bernstein points out interestingly that:

> the word 'risk' derives from the early Italian 'riskare' which means 'to dare'. In this sense, risk is a choice rather than a fate. The actions we dare to take, which depend on how free we are to make choices, are what the story of risk is all about. And that story helps define what it means to be a human being.[10]

He concludes that 'when the Soviets tried to administer uncertainty out of existence through government fiat and planning, they choked off social and economic progress'.[11] Accepting and taking calculated risks has been one of the most difficult and subtle adaptations necessary to the creation of a functioning civil society, democracy and market economy. With pivotal programmes that reward innovation and risk-taking, foundations have often played a crucial role in the transition of central and eastern Europe.

No historical summary can be complete without a word about the role of the Soros Foundation in central and eastern Europe. As shown in Table 1.55, page 295, the Soros Network of Foundations accounts for well over one-third of all support from international foundations to central and eastern Europe. As is well known, George Soros set out to open the world of closed societies as defined by the philosopher Karl Popper. Soros created a network of national foundations in central and eastern Europe which also worked with regional programmes that were established at his Open Society Institutes (OSI) both in Budapest and New York. Cumulatively, Soros has spent over $2 billion in central and eastern Europe and the former Soviet Union in the 1990s. The Soros model of operation is unique: in all cases national foundations are run by boards comprised of local citizens. Most staff are also local to the countries in which they operate, with the Budapest regional programme headquarters housing a multinational group of individuals

---

[10] Bernstein, p.8.

[11] Bernstein, p.8.

from both East and West. Also unique to the region (and the world) is such a large foundation operating with a single living donor. Soros's individual stamp is clearly on the foundations. His ear is close to the ground, enabling a fruitful dialogue between the founder and the national foundations to flourish.

The historical development of the role of foundations in central and eastern Europe could be said to have two distinct phases. In the first phase foundations were mainly concerned with economic reform. They found themselves also rapidly replacing the withdrawing state in traditional activities such as the arts. There was a quantitative emphasis during this phase. The persistence of some of the problems forced foundations to reconsider their role as they realized some of the more structural issues involved in the transition. Their concern turned to issues of transparency and sustainability and their support turned mainly to education and political development in particular and innovative approaches that reward risk-taking in general. It could be said that foundations too have undergone transformation.

3 Legal issues

The legal framework governing the establishment and functioning of foundations is currently going through a second round of adjustment since the changes of 1989–90. Although there are still some pieces of legislation dating from earlier periods they exist often more in theory than in practice. For example Slovenia still has intact the Kingdom of Yugoslavia's Law on Foundations 1930, which did not function under communism from 1945 to 1991. Similarly a few sections of Bulgaria's Persons and Family Act 1949 still serve to regulate some aspects of foundation activity.

While many of the countries operate under a civil code, Slovenia, for example, does not. The concept of a charitable trust, an Anglo-Saxon legal institution operating under common law, is non-existent as most legislation is based on the German tradition.

Countries vary significantly in the way they define a foundation. For example while Estonia distinguishes only between private and public foundations, Bulgaria also defines religious and non-religious institutions in its legislation. Hungary further distinguishes public and private foundations which can then be either public benefit organizations or 'special public' benefit organizations. Since January 1999 only those that qualify as public or special public benefit organizations are eligible for special tax considerations.

There are also differences in registration requirements. While state authorization is required in Slovenia this is not the case in Estonia. Hungarian foundations are required to register at the local county (Budapest) court and receive permission to do so only if their papers are in order. In Bulgaria any local court can determine an entity's right to register as a foundation.

The management and governance of foundations has proven difficult to prescribe in law. Laws are only beginning to tighten up regarding the abuse of foundations evident in the early 1990s. For example, Bulgaria recently adopted a new law governing legal persons with nonprofit purposes which attempts to prevent the problems that arose from a lack of regulations governing conflict of interest and self-dealing. The new law's provisions regarding self-dealing, however, might still require tightening up. In Hungary the supervisory or governing board only requires a minimum of two people, although in practice these tend to be composed of three to five people. Legislation in Slovenia dictates that persons (or their relatives) are not eligible to vote on particular decisions that might be to their personal benefit. On the other hand, Estonia has tried to assure accountability by insisting on separate supervisory and management boards.

With much of the funding for foundations initially coming from outside these countries it is interesting to note the nationality requirements of the governing bodies. Of the ten countries only a minority have any nationality or residency requirements. Estonia requires half of any foundation board to be residents of the country.

Policies on tax relief on donations have been cautious. This may be in part because there is little by way of tradition of giving, while tax incentives are not perceived as sufficient inducements. The range of deductible taxable income varies from 5% to 35%. Some countries distinguish between individual and corporate donations. In the case of Hungary the formulation appears overly complicated with various levels of deductible donations ranging from 20% to 33% while in Bulgaria founder donation tax exemption is limited to 5%.

While in the early 1990s foundations were often prohibited from engaging in commercial activities, by the mid-1990s legislative changes began to take a more balanced approach. Nonetheless, there are significant differences among countries. In Slovenia there are no proscribed activities but the strict state authorization process for registration and the tight tax regulations prevent foundations from benefiting their founders. In Hungary not more than 50% of a foundation's total income may be derived from commercial activities. The inherent distrust of commerce among people who engage in public good activity has actually been a greater hindrance to the development of nonprofit commercial ventures than has legislation. Such attitudes can easily be understood given the historical context.

In general it has been necessary for all the countries to create new legislation governing foundations. This appears to have been a two step process with the earlier laws of the first half of the 1990s subjected to revisions in the second half. Each country has its own traditions and concerns that need to be taken into account when creating new laws.

4 A profile of foundations in central and eastern Europe

General overview

It is again helpful to divide analysis of foundations in central and eastern Europe into the two time periods of early and late 1990s. By the end of the 1990s foundations were financing a broader range of activities than before. The shift from simple assistance in the economic reform process to a more complex web of activity both in grant-making and operating programmes has enhanced the role of foundations in the evolving third sector. As their benefits become clearer, laws governing foundation activities have been strengthened. The EU accession process itself has further galvanized efforts to strengthen their role.

The number of active foundations is difficult to ascertain. From the three sources cited in Figure 1.7 there appear to be relatively few. However, some local directories list additional organizations that probably have very limited impact and are quite small (and may indeed not be true foundations as defined by law). In a directory of nonprofit organizations in Bulgaria, for example, out of just over 1000 NPOs, 233 called themselves foundations.

Funding

The known financial contributions from major foundation sources to the accession countries during the 1990s probably approach close to $1 billion. Quigley[12] provides probably the most comprehensive statistics for the period of 1989–94. For the purposes of this chapter

---

[12] Quigley.

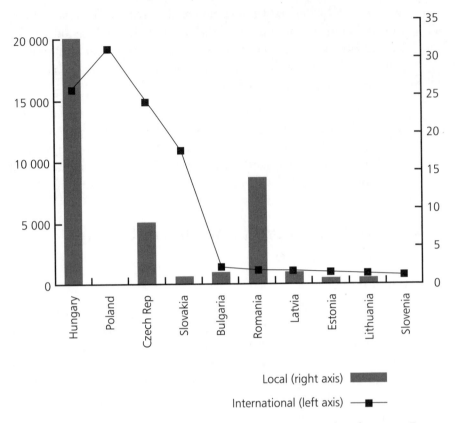

Figure 1.7 Number of foundations per country in central and eastern Europe

Source: Centre for European Foundations, Funders Online, and Quigley[13]

Quigley's data has been updated and expanded to include additional countries and activities.

A clear pattern can be discerned from Table 1.55. The main players are by and large the major US foundations with German foundations following in second place. Foundations from other countries such as France and Holland and Japan follow.

Activities

The interests of foreign foundations become evident when distinguishing between types of activities (Table 1.56). Using the International Classification of NonProfit Organizations code it is clear that the main preoccupation has been with education (23% of

---

[13] Centre for European Foundations (online database), Funders Online (online database), and Quigley.

Table 1.55 International foundation funding to central and eastern Europe by country US$000 1989–97

Foundations	Poland	Hungary	Czech Rep	Slovakia	Czechos.	Bulg et al.[14]	C. Europe	Interreg.	Total
Konrad Adenauer Stiftung	3890	3560	2160	280	1440			3220	14,550
Stefan Batory Foundation (Soros)	32,835							708	33,543
Bertelsmann Stiftung								3480	3480
Bosch Stiftung	9950						1930		11,880
Lynde and Harry Bradley Foundation	284		80		430		200	2041	3035
Carnegie Corporation of New York		25		300				12,776	13,101
Co-operating Dutch Foundations		2980	830	500	1250				5560
Central European University (Soros)		1500					53,889	3000	58,389
Civil Society Development Foundation			3050	370					3420
Friedrich Ebert Stiftung	8930	4300			4200			560	17,990
European Cultural Foundation								2055	2055
Fondation de France	1860								1860
Ford Foundation	15,500	1962	2317	568	1162		3722	12,537	37,768
International Media Fund	1460	1780	1130	900				1300	6570
German Marshall Fund of the United States	2322	345	445	223	341		879	610	5165
Alexander von Humboldt Stiftung	18,096	8309	1097	1134	4922				33,558
John D. and Catherine T. MacArthur Foundation	107		1300		2100		60	2371	5938
Andrew W. Mellon Foundation	11,763	8962	1223	1306	6456		9200	6143	45,053
Charles Stewart Mott Foundation	934	647	226	199	342		1553	4254	8155

Table 1.55 *Cont'd*

Foundations	Poland	Hungary	Czech Rep	Slovakia	Czechos.	Bulg *et al.*.[14]	C. Europe	Interreg.	Total
Friedrich Naumann Stiftung	2960	3390			1840			3220	11,410
National Endowment for Democracy	11,372	4550	618	1730	2442	4232	365	5419	30,728
Pew Charitable Trusts	3455	1145	85	315	1600		4840	19,640	31,080
Rockefeller Brothers Fund	1757	1489	996	110	470		5220	1003	11,045
Sasakawa Peace Foundation	250	100	70	150	132		4349		5051
Hanns Seidel Stiftung								8160	8160
Soros (Open Society) Network of Foundations	423	72,666	9537	11,471		115,800	45,870	219	255,986
Fritz Thyssen Stiftung	222	2351	99		39		412	104	3227
Volkswagen Stiftung	197	1109						21,726	23,032
Total	**128,567**	**121,170**	**25,263**	**19,556**	**29,166**	**120,032**	**132,489**	**114,546**	**690,789**

Source: Foundations' annual reports (data between 1995–1997) and Quigley (1997) (data between (1989–94)).

[14] Bulgaria, Latvia, Lithuania, Romania and Slovenia.

Table 1.56 Activities (ICNO code) supported in each country

	1	2	3	4	6	7	8	11	12	Inst. Build.	Unknown	Total
Poland	2634	28,741	1269	2403	18,235	9497	21,602	582	11,392		32,212	128,567
Hungary	4569	21,917	7560	12,656	6723	6934	11,594	1320	24,947	6940	16,010	121,170
Czech Rep	1227	2746	435	3051	1914	1940	3759		1701		8490	25,263
Slovakia	1668	4222	357	2055	751	2144	1208	321	2420		4410	19,556
Czechoslo		6221			5895	64	6046		2210		8730	29,166
Bulgaria	2484	1674	513	3102		7301		1690	26,841			43,605
Estonia	1254	3354	675	1086		1854		45	3249			11,517
Latvia	1455	570	111	3951		2296			3393			11,776
Lithuania	1611	740	438	6429		1021		797	4566			15,602
Romania	1149	2921	1170	4062		5665		1218	10,653			26,838
Slovenia	1461	360	645	3495		817			3916			10,694
C Europe		52,672			2538	3391	6277		3649	53,032	10,930	132,489
Interreg.		33,554			12,077	10,524	29,262		9189		19,940	114,546
Total	**19,512**	**159,692**	**13,173**	**42,290**	**48,133**	**53,448**	**79,748**	**5973**	**108,126**	**59,972**	**100,722**	**690,789**
% of total	3%	23%	2%	6%	7%	8%	12%	1%	16%	9%	15%	100%

Source: Foundations' annual reports for data between 1995–97 and Quigley[15] for data between 1989–94. Amounts in US$000. Activities corresponding to ICNPO code can be found below. 'Inst. Build.' stands for 'institutional building'.

[15] The description of foundation activity made by Quigley (1997) does exactly follow the ICNPO code, thus the following conversion was made: 'education and training' was interpreted as 'education'; 'technical assistance' was interpreted as 'development'; 'policy research' was interpreted as 'law, advocacy and politics'; 'institutional building' and 'funding for intermediaries' were interpreted as 'philanthropic intermediaries and voluntarism promotion'; 'Other' was interpreted as 'not elsewhere classified'. Quigley's work is one of the few with quantitative data on foundation activities in central and eastern Europe; however it is concerned primarily with funding for democracy and thus less interested in foundation activities such as arts or health. Since we draw extensively on Quigley's work for this chapter his bias towards activities related to democracy is probably still very strong in this chapter.

total). This is in line with recognition that at the heart of the transition process is a re-orientation towards the world, which can only be achieved through complete reform of the education process.

ICNPO classification code

1 –	Arts, Culture and Recreation	7 –	Law, Advocacy and Politics
2 –	Education and Research	8 –	Philanthropic Intermediaries
3 –	Health	9 –	International
4 –	Social Services	10 –	Religion
5 –	Environment	11 –	Business and Professional Associations
6 –	Development	12 –	Not Elsewhere classified

Whilst in the first half of the 1990s law programmes represented only 8% of expenditure, they grew substantially in the late 1990s and will increasingly be a focus of attention as corruption in society and rule of law become more significant issues. Law is tied with institution building, which received 9% of funding but has a much broader brief. Spending on philanthropic intermediaries and volunteerism promotion (21%) point toward the supportive role of foundations in strengthening local civil society and thus assisting the transition to a more transparent and democratic society.

Perhaps as revealing as what Figure 1.8 shows is what it hides. There was a relatively low level of funding for environmental issues by

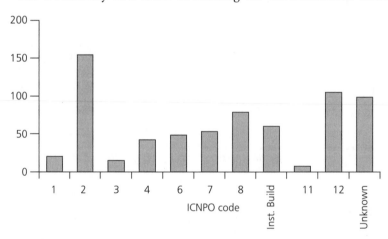

Figure 1.8 Foundation assistance per area of ICNPO activity code US$m 1989–97

Source: Foundations' annual reports for data between 1995–97 and Quigley for data between 1989–94.

foundations. There is a very large number of 'not elsewhere classified' and 'unknown' activities, reflecting the difficulty of obtaining detailed data and applying traditional classification systems to the activities in the region. This fact lends credit to the argument that foundations have been quite innovative and supportive of innovative activities in the region. Activities in areas such as women, information and ethnic groups escape more traditional classifications but constitute a very large part of foundation spending in the region, and highlight another important role foundations have in the transition process in the region.

From Table 1.57 we can see a remarkable similarity between foundation spending in central and eastern Europe and in Turkey. As a

Table 1.57 Comparison between central and eastern Europe foundation spending in proportion of amount spent and western Europe spending[16]

	CE Europe	UK	Germany[17]	Italy	Portugal	Turkey
Art, culture and recreation	3	9.8	22.3	35	29	6.3
Education and research	23	40.7	57	20	14	22.6
Health	2	12.1	11.6	10	6	5.3
Social services	6	15.3	55.1	26	43	20.5
Environment	<1	5.1	5.8	1	1	2.3
Development and housing	7	2.2	0.5	5	1	6.6
Law, advocacy and politics	8	0.4	1.4		2	1.7
Philanthropic intermediaries and volunteerism promotion	21	0.5				12.4
International			4		1	
Religion		8.9	6.1		3	
Business, prof. assns, unions	1	<0.1	2			
Not elsewhere	16	3.5		3		22.3
Unknown	15					

Source: Figures for CE Europe as Figure 1.8; figures for other countries taken from chapters in this book.

[16] Figures for central and eastern Europe, UK, Italy and Portugal refer to percent of amount spent in different activities. Figures for Germany and Turkey refer to percent of the number of foundations (not amount) dedicated to the different activities. It is hoped that both measures can be comparable as they both refer to the relative attention of foundations concerned with various activities in the different countries.

[17] The description of foundation activity in Germany does not exactly follow the ICNPO code. Here the figure for business, professional associations and unions is the sum of 'non-charitable purposes' and 'economy' in the German description.

developing nation Turkey is also undergoing a number of transitions and arguably faces some of the same challenges faced by countries in central and eastern Europe. Turkey also has large spending on 'not elsewhere classified' activities. In Turkey foundations strongly support civil society development by devoting a large part of their spending to philanthropic intermediaries and volunteerism promotion. However, low spending on legal and political activities may suggest that the transition in Turkey may be more economic than political in nature.

Foundations have very different spending priorities in central and eastern Europe compared to those in Germany or the UK, despite a common primary focus on education and research. Legal and political spending in both countries is minimal. This reinforces the idea that foundations in central and eastern Europe have an extraordinary role in supporting political transition in the region. Foundations in both the UK and Germany also have non-trivial spending on environmental and religious activities that do not appear to be priorities in central and eastern Europe.

Geographic distribution

The geographic distribution of foreign foundations demonstrates a greater interest in the stronger economies. Hungary was initially seen as the strongest, soon to be overtaken by Poland and Czechoslovakia. A few years after the creation of the Czech Republic economic growth slowed down. Hungary itself experienced a set-back in the mid-1990s, resuming growth only after an austerity package put in place in 1996 began to have an impact. While Poland, Hungary, the Czech Republic and Slovakia seemed like safe bets to most outside investors, the other accession countries had a rougher ride. Bulgaria only began to grow economically after a new government came to power in 1997. Romania's economy was still struggling at the end of the decade despite a promising government elected to office in 1997. Estonia's head start (with growth at one time rising to 13% primarily due to re-exports of Russian metal goods) slowed down significantly. None of the countries experienced continuous growth after recovery from the initial shock of the breakdown of communism which plunged economies into negative growth for the first few years.

As shown in Figure 1.9, Poland and Hungary have received over half of the total foundation support to central and eastern Europe since 1989. The reasons for this are complex and warrant some examination; factors explaining the allocation of foundation support to

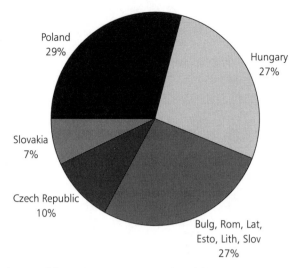

Figure 1.9 Share of foundation support by different countries

Source: foundations' annual reports for data between 1995–97 and Quigley for data between 1989–94

different countries in the region include the size of their population and economy, their attractiveness to foreign investment, their relative poverty and the amount of official aid received. The following analysis relating to Table 1.58 through Table 1.60 and Figure 1.10 through

Table 1.58 Foundation support and population numbers for selected countries

	Population 1998(m)	Foundation support (1989–97) US$m
Hungary	10.116	121.170
Poland	38.718	128.567
Czech Republic	10.282	25.263 (43.346)
Slovakia	5.377	19.556 (30.639)
Bulg, Rom, Lat, Esto, Lith, Slove	40.350	120.032 [all 6 countries]

Source: population figures from UN[18] and foundation support from foundations' annual reports for data between 1995–97 and Quigley for data between 1989–94.[19]

[18] United Nations, Department of Economic and Social Affairs, Population Division: 'World Population 1998', New York, 1999.
http://www.undp.org:80/popin/wdtrends/p98/fp98.htm.

[19] Figures in brackets include the attribution of US$29.166m in donations to Czechoslovakia. This was added to donations to the two countries after 1993. The addition maintained the proportion between donations to the Czech Republic and Slovakia (i.e., 62% to the Czech Republic and 38% to Slovakia).

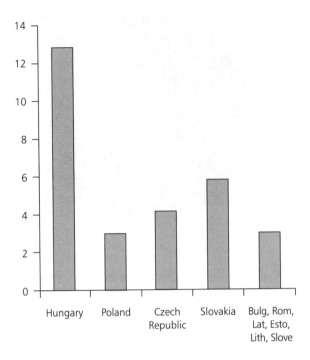

Figure 1.10 Foundation assistance *per capita* in US$ 1989–97

Source: Foundations' annual reports for data between 1995–97 and Quigley for data between 1989–94[20]

Figure 1.14 is restricted to four countries due to the difficulty of obtaining data on the other countries. The four countries covered in Table 1.58 had considerable variance in GNP.

Although Poland and Hungary receive similar total assistance from foundations, the picture changes dramatically when considered on a *per capita* basis (Table 1.58). Hungary is the clear favourite, as Figure 1.10 illustrates, with just over US$12 *per capita*. It receives as much as Poland although it has only one quarter of Poland's population. Poland, on the other hand, received only US$3 *per capita* – as much as Bulgaria, Romania, Latvia, Estonia, Lithuania and Slovenia combined. Foundation giving is therefore not directly related to population size. Countries with a larger population seem to receive more money (e.g. Poland) than countries with less population (e.g. Slovakia) but Hungary is a clear exception to this rule.

Could the size of the economy be responsible for attracting foundation support? A look at Figure 1.11 shows that as GNP grows foundation support also grows with a remarkable fit. The notable

---

[20] As per note 19.

Table 1.59 GNP, foreign direct investment (FDI) and foundation assistance in selected countries

	GNP US$m 1997	FDI US$m 1995	Foundation support (1989–97) US$m
Hungary	45,800	4540.35	121.170
Poland	138,900	3370.55	128.567
Czech Republic	54,000	2294.86	25.263 (43.346)
Slovakia	19,800	166.17	19.556 (30.639)

Source: GNP data from UNDP.[21] FDI data from UNDP.[22] Foundation support data from foundations' annual reports for data between 1995–97 and Quigley for data between 1989–94 [23]

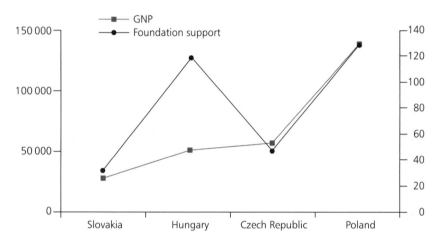

Figure 1.11 GNP 1997 (US$m) and foundation support 1989–97 (US$m)
Source: see Table 1.59

exception is again Hungary, receiving proportionally more foundation assistance for its size of the economy than would be expected according to trends in the other countries.

Could investment attractiveness as measured by net foreign direct investment be a good predictor for foundation support in central and eastern European countries? Looking at the evidence it could be said that by and large the answer is yes. Figure 1.12 shows a correlation

[21] United Nations Development Program: 'World Development Report –1999', New York, 1999. http://www.undp.org/hdro/report.html.

[22] Foreign direct investment figures from multiplication of two UNDP indicators: GNP figures (http://www.undp.organization/hdro/iectrends.htm) and net foreign direct investment as % of GNP (http://www.undp.organization/hdro/ifinance.htm).

[23] As per note 19.

between falling FDI and falling foundation assistance. There is a somewhat less good fit in each individual country when looking at size of the economy, but Hungary no longer stands out as an exception. Indeed the fit between FDI and foundation assistance in Hungary is better than for any other country, suggesting that much

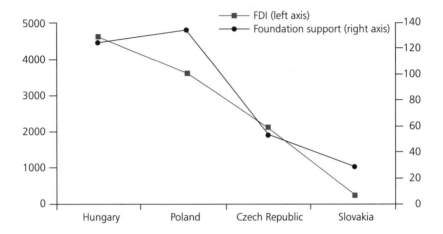

Figure 1.12 Foundation support US$m (1989–97) and FDI US$m (1995)

Source: FDI data from UNDP.[24] Foundation support data from foundations' annual reports for data between 1995–97 and Quigley for data between 1989–94[25]

Table 1.60 GNP *per capita*, FDI *per capita* and foundation support *per capita* for selected countries

	GNP *per capita* (US$) 1997	FDI *per capita*[26] US$	Foundation Support *per capita* ('89–'97) US$
Hungary	4510	448.82	12.70
Poland	3590	87.05	3.13
Czech Republic	5240	223.19	4.21
Slovakia	3680	30.90	5.70

Source: GNP data from UNDP.[27] Foundation support data from foundations' annual reports for data between 1995–97 and Quigley for data between 1989–94[28]

[24] As per note 22.

[25] As per note 19.

[26] FDI *per capita* obtained from dividing total FDI by the countries' populations presented on Table 1.58.

[27] As per note 21.

[28] As per note 19.

foundation assistance to Hungary could be explained by the FDI it attracts. On the other hand, the very large funding of the Hungarian Soros Foundation may distort this fit.

Do foundations give more to poorer countries? Evidence indicates that foundations give less to the poorest countries. Figure 1.13 demonstrates that as income *per capita* grows (from left to right in the chart) foundation assistance *per capita* also increases. Perhaps foundations concentrate more giving (*per capita*) on countries that have already achieved a minimum level of wealth. However, as countries achieve a higher level of wealth foundation giving is reduced, possibly because it becomes less necessary. That is the case of the Czech Republic. Part of the explanation might be that as state functions are increasingly taken over by the private sector there is less need for the state to subsidize activities of foundations. Another factor not to be underestimated is the political climate of each country.

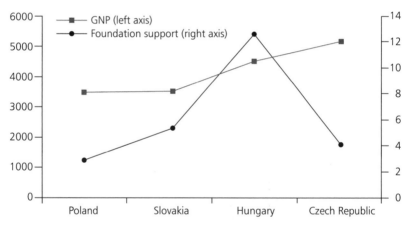

Figure 1.13 Comparison between foundation giving *per capita* (US$) and GNP *per capita* (US$). Countries in ascending order of GNP *per capita*.

Source: GNP data from UNDP.[29] Foundation support data from foundations' annual reports for data between 1995–97 and Quigley for data between 1989–94[30]

Foundation assistance followed a pattern remarkably similar to official assistance from bilateral and multilateral donors, as comparisons in Figure 1.14 show. Aid resource flow has been the best predictor of foundation giving in the countries examined. Foundation giving is equal to about 1% of aid resource flows. From 1990 to 1996 aid flows

---

[29] As per note 21.

[30] As per note 19.

totalled US$62,470m (OECD, 1999) while foundation assistance from 1989 to 1997 was US$690m. Foundations also appear to have responded to major structural transitions such as entry into the EU, which determines much of official aid.

The poorer countries attracted less attention for a number of reasons. In the eyes of many they were less attractive financial investments. They have weaker human capacity actually to deliver programmes and fewer contacts to build on from the pre-1989 days.

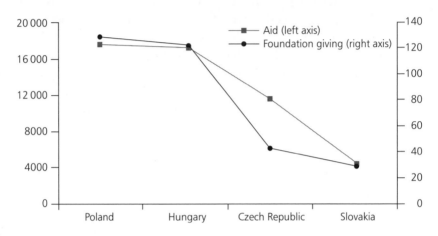

Figure 1.14 Aid resource flows US$m 1990–96 and foundation support to central and eastern Europe US$m 1989–97

Source: Aid – OECD;[31] foundation assistance – foundations' annual reports for data between 1995–97 and Quigley for data between 1989–94[32]

The striking correlation between aid and foundation assistance may be related to the need to find delivery channels that rely on the same types of people to implement projects. The result is that foundations are not complementing official aid (at least quantitatively), rather they are following the same structural patterns. Countries less attractive to aid are left without the alternatives that perhaps organizations from civil society such as foundations should provide. This trend is confirmed by the above mentioned close fit between foundation giving, FDI and size of the economy. Foundations appear to be giving more to countries that are already receiving more from other sources.

---

[31] OECD: Aid and Other Resource Flows to the Central and Eastern European Countries and the New Independent States of the Former Soviet Union, Development Co-operation Directorate, 1999. http://www.oecd.org/dac/htm/pubs-foc.htm.

[32] As per note 19.

The same analysis is true on a *per capita* level. Here too foundations appear to be giving more *per capita* to countries with a higher income *per capita* at least until they reach a certain level of income *per capita*. It is beyond the scope of this chapter to estimate the impact this might have on the speed of transition but the question is clearly of significance.

Regional initiatives

Alongside the bilateral activity of government programmes such as USAID, the British Know How Fund and other programmes, as well as help from regional authorities such as the German Länder, the programmes of the EU such as Phare, Tempus, Socrates, Tacis, Leonardo and Bistro play an important role.

Regional initiatives funded by Soros include the Constitutional and Legal Policy Institute (COLPI) which currently focuses on legal reform and human rights. A separate Roma Programme was developed and a Women's Programme augments the national foundations' initiatives. Established in 1998, a new Institute for Educational Policy develops demonstration models with a view to larger-scale funding coming in at later stages (e.g. from the World Bank) once the effectiveness of a model is proven. The Higher Education Support Program (HESP) founded in 1991 aims to support higher education institutions and academic centres that show potential for excellence and set examples of innovation.

In the area of information provision Soros has been active on a regional basis through programmes such as the Network Media Program, the Network Library Program and the Centre for Publishing Development. Extensive internet infrastructure building was a priority in the mid-1990s, but now that the backbone has been established there is a greater focus on content creation and information dissemination. The East-East programme funds local initiatives that involve more than one country, thus contributing to transfer of know-how and improved communication between countries.

One issue that transcends borders everywhere is that of the environment. Although perhaps not so heavily funded, numerous foreign foundations have supported research and NGO activity in this area. One well-known enterprise is the Regional Environmental Centre (REC) located in Budapest, which after a rocky start in the early 1990s found its role coordinating funding from a variety of sources, including the German Marshall Fund, the Rockefeller Brothers, the

Charles Stewart Mott Foundation and a host of smaller foundations with specific agendas aiming to support local NGO development. The Regional Environmental Centre played an important role in harmonization required for EU expansion and in the Environmental Partnership for Central Europe (originally initiated by an OECD task force). Foundations interested in environmental issues tend to cluster together providing joint support for programmes. The REC is an interesting example, bringing together finance from both public and private foundations, and working with a variety of international NGOs.

Country profiles

Due to space constraints the country illustrations below are indicative only of the range of activities and issues rather than a comprehensive review.

Bulgaria

Bulgaria's foundations receive over 95% of their income from contributions originating from outside the country. They co-exist with associations and cultural centres as the three main types of non-governmental organizations. None are corporate foundations. Statistics on the number of foundations are hard to come by and vary from 250 to 850. Their activities reflect the priorities of the post-communist era with a concentration of foundations funding science, education, research and arts and culture.

While the legal basis of foundations is favourable, strict attention is paid to enforcing the tax regulations after a period of abuse in the early 1990s. Foundations are not prohibited from carrying out business activities and are only obliged to pay taxes on profits. There is some tax incentive for juridical and physical persons wishing to make donations.

The Czech Republic

The Czech Republic began changing the laws it inherited from Czechoslovakia in 1993. Foundations were required to re-register and some loop-holes evident in the earlier laws were tightened. As in other countries there is still some suspicion concerning foundations. However, the new Republic continued with obligations taken on in 1992 to begin funding Czech foundations with a portion of the proceeds from the privatization programme. In 1999 $13 million was allocated for distribution to foundations with another $45 million earmarked for 2000–01. Only about 200 of the 5000 registered foundations are grant-making foundations. The rest are operational, falling into two categories: foundation funds, which do not require endowments and have no tax benefits; and public benefit corporations that can provide fee charging services.

Foundations fund the activities of numerous NGOs. Despite lack of support from Prime Minister Vaclav Klaus in the mid-1990s, foundation law and NGOs' activities have steadily matured in the second half of the 1990s. Early financial assistance was, as elsewhere, focused on economic reform. Under Klaus, the Czech Republic sought to wean itself off foreign aid much earlier than the other countries of central Europe. Foreign foundations followed the footsteps of the aid agencies and turned their attention elsewhere.

Nonetheless, important educational establishments such as the Centre for Economic Research and Graduate Education (CERGE) affiliated with Charles University in Prague received substantial assistance from foundations. Following the pattern of western higher education CERGE pioneered the idea of uniting teaching and research and presented an alternative model to the existing status quo. The idea of doing so as part of a public institution while retaining enough autonomy to function independently proved highly challenging. Foundations such as Mellon, PCT and Soros with USAID co-financed CERGE and eventually larger sums of Czech public funding provided support as well.

Foundation support has played a large part in providing access to information and training in NGO management. Despite criticism of western approaches, much of the methodology has been adopted to good effect.

Estonia

Foundation activity in Estonia is limited. There are only 150 foundations – relatively few even for a country as small as Estonia with its population of 1.5 million. While governed by the Foundations Act 1996 a revision of the Commercial Act in 1998 triggered a re-registration process which revealed 50 independent foundations, a few corporate foundations and a majority of government-linked or fundraising foundations. Activities most heavily supported include arts and culture, education and some social welfare and environmental issues.

The most active foundation has been the Open Estonia Foundation, but as EU membership draws closer it will transform itself into a policy studies institute. The National Culture Foundation is the most important body making grants with money from private donations.

Hungary

Hungary has a long history of foundations, the first established 1000 years ago. There was a preponderance of church foundations until the 1848 Revolution, after which secular foundations began to grow. In 1998 there were almost 20,000 public and private foundations. A number of regional initiatives such as the Environmental Partnership for Central Europe have located their main offices in Budapest.

This growth is related to the potential for reform, which Hungary demonstrated even before the revolutions of 1989. This ensured that considerable investments were being made in the country by the early 1990s; it received over 40% of all investments in central Europe despite the fact that it represented only 16% of the population. Its attraction to foreign foundations was equally strong. George Soros, a native of Budapest, established his first central European foundation in Hungary in 1984. His strategy was to support the local intellectual elite, a model followed by others after 1989.

The local Hungarian Soros Foundation (SFH) reported a 1999 budget of $12 million (down from $19 million in 1998). Again the view is that with EU accession around the corner others need to take on the burden of financing the third sector; the SFH2000 budget was cut to $5 million. Downsizing was achieved by concentrating on social protection issues, particularly concerning minorities, and continuing smaller arts and culture and education programmes.

Latvia

Latvia has over 500 foundations registered under the Law of Public Organizations. Other foundation-type bodies are registered under other provisions. The largest foundation is the foreign-funded Soros Foundation Latvia (SFL). The priority areas for SFL are promoting civil society and education. Joint sponsorship with the King Baudouin Foundation has promoted projects fostering ethnic tolerance between Russian and Latvian language groups. The Children's Fund sponsors childcare programmes, and the Latvian Cultural Fund promotes arts and culture.

Lithuania

Foundations in Lithuania register either with the Ministry of Justice or with local municipalities. There are over 300 national foundations, about 100 local ones and 30 governmental foundations. Most foundation funding still comes from abroad, the Soros Foundation long being the leading actor, although its role is diminishing. However local foundations are also emerging; for example the largest daily newspaper *Lietuvos Rytas* has established a foundation.

A large number of foundations concern themselves with the handicapped, the elderly and others who have fallen out of the increasingly fragile social services net. Other foundations support the traditional areas of arts, education, science and sporting activities. While charitable donations to these foundations are tax-free, foundations do pay a 5% profit tax. Moreover they are not permitted to engage in business activities. These impediments hinder self-sustainability.

Poland

Poland, the largest central European country, has extensive contacts with foundations outside its borders. An interesting example is the influential Foundation in Support of Local Democracy (FSLD), established primarily to work on local government issues. Founded by members of the Lech Walesa Civic Committee, many of whom have held high-level positions in and out of post-communist governments, this body is governed by its Council of Founders which is assisted by the board of management. The Council of Founders is also assisted by a Council of Directors consisting of directors from affiliated regional training centres and colleges of local government and public administration. Quigley describes this 'overlapping jurisdiction without clear lines of authority', observing that:

> this structure also suggests a problem common to many independent organizations in Poland and other parts of central Europe. That is, although many of their programmes are quite successful, their organizational structure and administrative arrangements are not very sophisticated. One explanation for this lopsided development is that much of the external assistance was devoted to programme development, and relatively scant attention was paid to governance and management issues.[33]

Much funding for FSLD came from foreign foundations anxious to make an impact.

Without a history of open public policy debate, Poland and other countries received considerable assistance in promoting such discussion. This was achieved in part through the establishment of

---

[33] Quigley p.49.

think-tanks. One particularly influential organization is the Centre for Social and Economic Research (CASE) established by Leszek Balcerowicz (currently Poland's Finance Minister) and his wife Ewa.

In the last ten years, foundations in Poland have spent over $250 million on what could loosely be described as education. Leaders in the field are Humboldt, and the *Bosch Stiftung*.

Following these German foundations, the next most active was the Stephan Batory Foundation established by George Soros in 1988. Like other foundations it diversified its sources of financing towards the end of the 1990s. In its 1997 report Batory listed seven foreign donors (apart from Soros) making up 7% of their budget. Thirteen domestic donors were cited as having contributed 3% of the total budget, which was just over $10 million. Their grant-making programmes amounted to six times the expenditure of their operating programmes.

The trend is moving towards consolidation and reduction of funding from Soros. As the EU accession process gains momentum the Batory Board has narrowed its range of activities. For the first few years of the new millennium it will prioritize strengthening democratic institutions and values, promoting international cooperation, advancing educational development and supporting culture.

The foundation landscape in Poland also includes a long tradition of foundation-like activities undertaken by the Catholic Church. Since the liberalization of its activities in the 1990s it has resumed a more important role in social services generally.

Romania

Romania is the second largest country within the EU aspirants' group, with a population of over 22 million. It is also a deeply scarred nation living with the legacy of one of the most brutal regimes in south-east Europe. In 1998 8000 registered foundations were accounted for. With a large Hungarian minority in Transylvania a larger than usual proportion of foundation activity is devoted to ethnic and minority issues. The Foundation for an Open Society supported a wide range of programmes until 1997 when, following a promising election, it chose to concentrate on legal reform, public administration, education and public health. A number of initiatives have been spun off to become separate income-generating entities, such as the Internet Centre in Bucharest.

Slovakia

Over 400 foundations are now registered in Slovakia. After a shaky existence under the Meciar government foundations are now playing a more active role in supporting the development of civil society. Education is the most popular area of activity, with 150 foundations set up by schools with healthcare. Culture follows in popularity. A Law on Foundations was passed in 1996 and the re-registering procedures brought greater clarity to the types of organization eligible for foundation status. There are about 30 corporate foundations.

Slovenia

Slovenia has made a remarkable transition with a GDP three times that of the other most developed central European countries. The third sector has made considerable strides with foundations playing a significant role particularly in education, arts, and culture. There are about 60 foundations functioning in Slovenia. Their finances derive primarily from domestic sources, an encouraging development down the road to self-sufficiency.

5 Current trends and conclusion

The role of international foundations in the next ten years is uncertain. These donors are showing less interest than in the heady days of the 1989–90 'revolutions'. Some feel their mission has been accomplished and it is now time for the EU and local foundations to take over the role of funding third sector activities. The attitude of the Mellon Foundation is not atypical:

> We are continuing to phase down our grant-making in eastern Europe, largely because many of our original objectives have been accomplished. As always, there is more to be done, and we do not intend to terminate our support of programmes in eastern Europe in an abrupt fashion; but we do believe that the Foundation must always be ready to re-deploy its resources in response to changing needs and new opportunities. Thus, in 1996 we concentrated our grant making in eastern Europe on sustaining and institutionalising the most promising of the initiatives funded in earlier years (Andrew W. Mellon Foundation, 1996).[34]

Nonetheless, it will take many years before the region is wealthy enough to produce enough benefactors to generate a critical mass of 'self-sustainable' local foundations. In the meantime many activities

---

[34] http://www.mellon.organisation/arpr96.html#rn9.

previously funded by western foundations are now seen as the domain of the EU. The PHARE programme has expanded its initiatives from Poland and Hungary to other accession countries. The EU established the separate directorate of DG1A to deal entirely with accession issues. By the end of the 1990s programmes such as Tempus, Socrates, Tacis, Leonardo, Bistro and others all had accession country components. There is recognition that adoption of the Aquis of the Union is likely to be a much longer process than in the case of more recently accepted western Europe member states. This 'double' transition has put a significant financial burden on the accession countries, but one they are choosing to bear. However, the cultural differences are in evidence and can often be a greater barrier between East and West than financial ones. Here foundations have a role to play in helping the people of each country understand that they have choices to make. Many foundations are now working in the policy area, helping officials gain confidence in their mastery of complex issues as they prepare for accession.

While EU funding will increase, a number of western foundations are turning their attention to pressing concerns in the Balkans and other regions of the world. The Charles Mott Foundation has made this explicit in its 1999 report, and at the end of the decade the Soros Foundation was re-examining its activities in south-eastern Europe. Many foundations will collaborate with each other to a far greater degree than in the past.

Increasingly foundations are beginning to recognize their power to exert leverage on state resources. This has been particularly evident in information programmes where foundation initiatives lead to an increase in government commitment to invest in infrastructure, for example providing the possibility of internet connection to schools.

The differences in legislation governing foundations described above is only one part of the story of extensive diversity between the nations. Their legacies may all be of communism, but the forms practised between Romania and Hungary for example were marked by different heritages. The brutalization that occurred in Romania continues to hamper the development of trust and this in turn makes the functioning of civil society difficult. It will take several generations to achieve the realization that democracy is not just about voting, but about maintaining a dynamic if delicate balance between the myriad forms of social organizations without construing every situation as a zero-sum game. Accountability and transparency in these circumstances is of paramount importance.

However, the relevant laws are changing and becoming more favourable for the establishment of foundations working towards a public good rather than a few individuals' pockets. Issues of corruption are being given far greater attention than in the past. New governance strategies will take longer to achieve transparency and accountability, but here again huge strides are being made.

Engagement with western Europe will set certain procedures in place. For example, with the emphasis on cross-border collaboration most EU programmes require applications to be made by two or more institutions, at least one from an EU member country. This has significantly increased cross-border travel between East and West and has opened up many educational opportunities for young people from central and eastern Europe.

As initial enthusiasm for the transformation of politics and policies in central Europe gave way to pessimism and finally a more balanced sense of realism, donors of all kinds began looking for a *modus operandi* to provide improved results. In the early days relatively few programmes were co-funded by a multiplicity of organizations. Now reformers are looking to ensure maximum 'buy-in' not only in financial terms but also in terms of human commitment. As the new millennium unfolds, foundations are counting on broader consensus building around concepts of 'public good' as a tactic to achieve their aims.

The next ten years will probably be a time when foundations shed their public image as an additional department of the state bureaucracy and develop purposes clearly different from those of government. Working out which functions should be performed by the third sector and which by the state remains one of the main preoccupations of the transition process. As governments come and go different models are tried, and power shifts occur as attempts are made to find an efficient balance.

The foundation landscape in the EU accession countries of central and eastern Europe has undergone a rapid transition during the first ten years since the fall of the communist regimes. Following the lead of foreign foundations, new local foundations of both a private and public nature are beginning to find their niches. As societies become more comfortable with the rise of the third sector, foundations will have an increasing role in funding NGOs, which in turn will have to find ways of ensuring their viability.

Sustainability has become a major issue as NGOs grapple with the implications of funding cuts by initial funders. Foundations are wary of particular sectors becoming excessively dependent on their hand-outs – a relationship likely to become a focal point for policy-makers over the next decade. Entrepreneurship will no doubt be injected into programmes and projects. Sharing financial responsibility amongst a number of donors is one option, but increasingly both NGOs and foundations are looking for independent means of income generation through the sale of goods and services as in the West.

The laws that were first hastily drawn up in the heady aftermath of 1989 are undergoing revision and harmonization with standards set by the EU. As that process is completed and economies improve, foundations with ambitious and complex agendas are likely to play a more active role in society even if funding levels decline. Nonetheless, countries should look toward a time when funding no longer comes primarily from the West, and engage in serious discussions about the role of foundations in their societies.

Foundations in central and eastern Europe fulfil a very different function to those of western Europe. While each country can claim evidence of foundation existence of some kind or another before World War II, the very concept was antipathetic to the ideas of communism. Thus there was little immediate tradition to draw upon as new democracies were born. The last ten years have been characterized by a very specific type of foundation working in the transition environment.

Foreign foundations have been the major source of funding for innovative civil society activities. Their agendas were to assist the shift to democracy and market economies, rather than become a replacement of the socialist state. But due to the drastic decline in state budgets, many found themselves taking on quasi-state responsibilities in areas such as arts, culture and education. Toward the end of the 1990s they increasingly turned to law, public policy, minority issues and accession to the EU.

The importance of foundations cannot be underestimated despite the undeniable fact that early efforts were not entirely successful. The 'double transition' from communism to democracy, and from outside to inside the EU has been a double challenge for the accession countries. But as foundations act less as supplements to the state and move towards becoming leaders in innovation and experimentation and providers of funding for seed and demonstration projects, other resources will have to be better utilized for government and non-government activities in all areas of social and economic life. The impact of well-trained young people who understand and value the third sector is demonstrated by the rapid growth of NGOs. Further maturation will be necessary early on in the new century; it will remain important to look comparatively at others for models of governance and practice. The role of foundations continues to be an important part of the debate on the role of the state and its relations with its people.

Acknowledgements

I would like to thank Nuno Themudo for his assistance in assembling the data and his perceptive comments as the text developed.

Bibliography

Alexander, J. ed., *Real civil societies: the dilemma of institutionalisation*, London, Sage Publications Ltd, 1998.

Avery, G. and Cameron, F., *The Enlargement of the European Union*, Sheffield, Sheffield Academic Press, 1998.

Bernstein, P. L., *Against the Gods: The Remarkable Story of Risk*, New York, John Wiley and Sons, 1996.

Croft, S., Redmond, J., Rees, W. and Webber, M., *The enlargement of Europe*, Manchester, Manchester University Press, 1999.

European Foundation Centre, *European foundation fundamentals: a portrait of the independent funding community in Europe*, Brussels, EFC, 1999.

Freeman, D., *The handbook on private foundations*, New York, The Foundation Center, 1999.

Fukuyama, F., *Trust: the social virtues and the creation of prosperity*, London, Hamish Hamilton, 1995.

Hall, J. A. ed., *Civil society: theory, history, comparison*, Cambridge, Polity Press, 1995.

Harvard Business School, *Harvard Business Review on Nonprofits*, Cambridge, Mass., HBS Press, 1999.

Keane, J., *Civil society: old images, new visions*, Cambridge, Polity Press, 1998.

Keane, J., 'Politics of Retreat', in: *The Political Quarterly*, Vol 61, No 3, 1990.

Misztal, B., *Trust in modern societies: the search for the bases of social order*, Cambridge, Polity Press, 1996.

Pérez-Díaz, V., *The return of civil society: the emergence of democratic Spain*, Cambridge, Mass, Harvard University Press, 1993.

Putnam, R., *Making democracy work: civic traditions in modern Italy*, Princeton, N.J, Princeton University Press, 1993.

Quigley, K. F., *For democracy's sake: foundations and democracy assistance in central Europe*, Washington DC, Woodrow Wilson Center Press, 1997.

Rosenberg, T., *The haunted land: facing Europe's ghosts after communism*, London, Vintage, 1995.

▼ John Richardson

Foundations in the Public Arena: the European Foundation Centre

1 Introduction

At the fifth European Conference on the Social Economy, held in Seville in 1995, European Union Commissioner Christos Papoutsis noted that organizations comprising the social economy have contributed solidly and consistently to the welfare of the peoples of the European Union. Foundations, as an integral part of the social economy, have made, and are making their contribution to the benefit of the peoples not only of the EU, but across the broader Europe – indeed, the world.

The social economy in Europe is comprised of foundations, associations, cooperatives and mutuals. Of these four groups, foundations may be the fewest in number, but they exert the greatest influence on the workings of the social economy. Foundations contribute the venture capital for a host of citizens associations and other nonprofit endeavours. Particularly because they are few in number, they cooperate with these organizations – either through direct grant making or, for operating foundations, through implementation of their own programmes with local players as partners. Thus, by their very nature, foundations are interested in cooperation to further their work within the broader social economy.

This chapter concerns international cooperation by foundations and it largely focuses on the work of the European Foundation Centre (EFC). Though cooperation is not new to the foundation field, an additional impetus has been provided by the real changes brought about by the New Europe – particularly the single market, the re-emergence of civil society in central and eastern Europe, and an increased awareness of the importance of European citizenship. Throughout this chapter these points will be highlighted.

2 The European Foundation Centre (EFC)

2.1 An overview of the EFC

The EFC was established in Brussels on 9 November 1989 by seven of Europe's leading foundations. The EFC is a knowledge-based membership association, dedicated to strengthening organized philanthropy in Europe and internationally. Today, the EFC provides benefits and services to some 200 independent funder members and associates active in Europe and to around 30,000 associated and affiliated organizations linked through networking centres in 35 countries.

EFC Membership is open to individual grant-making and operational funders, that is European foundations and corporate funders, and global funders with European interests. There are two categories of EFC membership – members and funding members. At the discretion of the Membership Committee and subject to approval by the Governing Council, provision is made for EFC Guests. This category is underwritten for central and eastern European foundations by support from the Charles Stewart Mott Foundation.

EFC Members come from 28 different European countries. As noted above, EFC membership is open to global funders with European interests. Accordingly, EFC membership includes many of the leading foundations in the USA and Japan. The EFC is governed by its European Foundations Council, which is comprised of representatives from foundations or corporate citizenship programmes from 16 different European countries and from the USA. As a membership-led and membership-funded organization, the Centre's fundamental commitment is to serve the interests of its members.

2.2 EFC areas of activity

To serve its members, the EFC focuses on three core service areas, elaborated below. These three service areas are:

- representing member interests to national goverments, the EU and EU Institutions, the Council of Europe, the UN and the World Bank,
- convening at European level to promote good practice and common projects, and
- providing communication and information services that underpin funding.

2.3 Representation

At EU level, the EFC represents an expanding membership by building its capacity to monitor and interact with the European Institutions. The EFC maintains close contacts with European Commission services across a broad spectrum of EU interests, such as the environment, culture, education, central and eastern Europe, the Mediterranean region, trans-atlantic relations, and the social economy in general.

The European Commission and European Parliament have repeatedly acknowledged the representative role of the EFC and now view the EFC as a first point of reference in matters relating to foundations and grant making. There are three typical instances where the EFC has been instrumental in the effective representation of its membership at EU level. The first concerns inputs to the proposed European Statute on Associations and Foundations. The second was a major contribution to European Parliament initiatives in respect of patronage and sponsorship in culture and sports, and the third was decisive action on proposals for the future self-regulation of foundations in Europe.

On 4 June 1997, the European Commission adopted, at the initiative of Commissioner Christos Papoutsis, responsible for Social Economy, the long-awaited paper on associations and foundations in the form of a *Communication on Voluntary Organisations and Foundations*. The primary purpose of the Communication is to raise consciousness and understanding of the association and foundation sector and to commend voluntary organizations and foundations to policy-makers as bodies whose social and economic importance has hitherto been underestimated. The contribution of voluntary organizations and foundations will, in the future, be of increasing importance for the development of Europe.

The Communication describes the legal and fiscal environment of voluntary organizations and foundations in the different member states, their range of activities and their economic importance as well as their contribution to social and economic problems. It illustrates the growing importance of the sector in Europe, but also the challenges and problems it currently faces, in particular in developing its trans-national European work. Finally, the Communication proposes a series of specific measures at European level as well as at member states level, with a view to strengthening the development of the sector in Europe and improving its capacity to meet future needs and maximize its contribution to European integration.

As part of its representation role, the EFC assisted in several ways in the development and impact of this Communication. Firstly, the EFC helped design the survey instrument that the European Commission used to gather information, and provided contacts across Europe for the survey mailing. Secondly, the EFC provided the names of leading foundation and corporate funder contacts across Europe. The Commission used these contacts for in-depth interviews, which supplemented survey data. Finally, on the release of the Communication, the EFC released a document informing its membership of the importance of this Communication, ensured that members had access to it, and were able to respond if they so wished.

The EFC, as the European umbrella organization of independent funders, is committed to playing a leading role in developing the social economy. Therefore, the EFC is involved in the European Consultative Committee for Cooperatives, Mutual Societies, Associations and Foundations that was set up by the Commission in March 1998. The EFC plays an active role in it, thereby ensuring that independent funders have concrete input into the implementation of the Committee's work programme and an expanded role as negotiating partners with the Commission.

Also, as part of its representation activities, the EFC is involved in close contacts with the European Parliament. The primary focus of these contacts is with the European Parliament Social Economy Intergroup, due to be relaunched during the 1999–2004 parliamentary term. The Intergroup aims to increase understanding and awareness of the social economy, to monitor critical issues affecting foundations and corporate funders at the European level, and to promote EU initiatives on the social economy whilst improving access to funding.

The representational role of the EFC also extends beyond Europe. This role is acknowledged at the international level, not only by the European Institutions but also by the World Bank, the United Nations, and intercontinental nonprofit sector initiatives such as the Johns Hopkins Comparative Nonprofit Sector Study and CIVICUS, the international alliance dedicated to strengthening citizen action and civil society throughout the world.

Concerning the World Bank, the EFC helped a chapter of members to initiate a new dialogue with the Bank, whose current organizational and policy changes now include a formal commitment to cooperate more proactively with foundations – particularly on initiatives which relate to poverty reduction. This cooperation is with a view to setting up possible operational partnerships, exchanging know-how and expertise, and promoting the development of foundation-like organizations to work with the Bank on development issues.

Regarding the United Nations, the EFC assisted with the benchmark Foundations Forum, held during the Second UN Conference on Human Settlements (HABITAT II) in Istanbul, Turkey in June 1996. This meeting gave rise to the Istanbul Declaration uniting foundations in a new focus on the Mediterranean region, which is discussed below in section 2.4.

CIVICUS is an international alliance dedicated to strengthening citizen action and civil society throughout the world. CIVICUS is dedicated to pursuing a world in which voluntary citizen action is a predominant feature of the political, economic and cultural life of all nations.

CIVICUS divides the world into six regions, of which Europe is one. The EFC has acted as CIVICUS regional convenor in Europe, and the EFC Director serves on the CIVICUS Board as Treasurer. Europe's commitment to CIVICUS was demonstrated by its hosting of the Second World Assembly, in Budapest, Hungary in September 1997.

Finally, the Johns Hopkins Comparative Nonprofit Sector Project is the first major examination of the scope, structure, financing and role of the private, nonprofit sector throughout the world, using a common framework and approach. Phase One of the project included 12 countries, of which five were in Europe, whilst Phase Two included 22 countries, of which 12 were in Europe. A chapter of EFC members contributed to both Phase One and Phase Two. The EFC co-hosted, with Johns Hopkins University, the European Parliament, and the European Commission, the world launch event of the results of Phase One of this project, summarized in *The Emerging Sector*. The results of Phase Two were launched in Europe at the EFC's 1998 Annual General Assembly and Conference in Turin.

2.4 Convening role

A second part of the core services of the EFC is its convening role at European and intercontinental levels to promote good practice and common projects.

Before the establishment of the EFC, the Hague Club was the only organization to convene European funders on a regular basis. Established in 1971, the Hague Club is an association of individuals. Its purpose is to facilitate discussion and cooperation between the chief executives of leading foundations in Europe, as well as prominent persons involved with foundations. One of the major differences between the EFC and the Hague Club is that the membership of the club is restricted to individuals. The majority of the founder members of the EFC were, and remain, Hague Club members.

The major convening function of the EFC is its annual conference, which is the largest gathering of international donors in the world today. Since 1990, the EFC has traditionally held its Annual General Assembly and Conference (AGA) on November 9, the anniversary of the day on which the Berlin Wall came down and – by no means coincidentally – the day on which the EFC was founded. Each year, the EFC annual meeting brings together some 400 to 450 representatives of foundations and corporate funders to exchange experiences and work together on common projects.

Each annual meeting includes plenary sessions where chief European or world philanthropic leaders address participants – for example George Soros addressed the 1999 Berlin conference. The AGA also includes a host of specific breakout sessions grouped into four types – organizational capacity building; trends; issue groups; and civil society dialogues/regional interest groups. Each AGA is approximately two days, with a full programme of satellite events bringing this to a total of four or five days. EFC members also meet regularly within the framework of conferences, seminars and *ad hoc* working groups to exchange views on funding practice, to monitor developments which impact on grant making, and to develop replicable model programmes and projects. A list of these ongoing meetings would include:

Programme area networking

- Health
- Youth
- Immigration
- Multicultural issues and minorities
- The arts
- Social inclusion
- Employment and job creation
- Education and training
- Science and technology
- Environment and sustainable development
- Awards and prizegiving

Good practice and networking

- Funding and resourcing
- Operational project management
- Cross-frontier grant making
- EU institution monitoring
- Legal, fiscal and regulatory trends
- Code of Practice for independent funders
- Corporate citizenship
- Voluntarism
- Community foundations
- Social economy research

Regional networking

- Central and eastern European issues
- Trans-atlantic funding
- Mediterranean funding
- Europe-Asia funding
- Intercontinental cooperation

The EFC's success in convening can be highlighted by briefly looking at four specific initiatives. These are the Grantmakers East Group, the Trans-Mediterranean Civil Society Dialogue (TMCD), Corporate Citizenship Europe (CCE) and the Community Philanthropy Initiative. A more detailed look at anther initiative, the Trans-atlantic Donors Dialogue (TADD), is provided in 3 below.

Grantmakers East Group

The Grantmakers East Group is the largest group of funders that the EFC helps to convene. Grant makers interested in central and eastern Europe collaborate within this group. The group, comprising over

200 representatives, is led by a steering committee of funders who meet regularly to provide direction.

In 1998, just prior to the EFC annual meeting in Turin, a Grantmakers East meeting catered exclusively for donors active in the region. This meeting attracted over 100 independent funders and representatives from the European Commission, the United Nations, the US State Department, and the World Bank. Some 30 countries were represented. In 1999, a similar meeting was held just before the EFC AGA in Berlin.

Trans-Mediterranean Civil Society Dialogue (TMCD)

The Trans-Mediterranean Civil Society Dialogue (TMCD) parallels the successful Funding East Programme developed by the EFC Orpheus Programme to support civil society initiatives in the emerging democracies of central and eastern Europe. It will thus represent a major EFC initiative in the years ahead.

The TMCD reflects various initiatives taken by European and North American foundations to evaluate shared interests in the region and assess prospects for collaboration. Chief among these initiatives were the Funding South think-tanks hosted by the Oriente Foundation and the Luso-American Foundation in Lisbon and Seville in cooperation with the Council on Foundations of the United States, and the Foundations Forum, discussed above. A key success of the TMCD has been the compilation and publication of *Mediterranean Funding* (1999). This volume provides a map of funders active in the region and should act as a catalyst for developing cooperation at a Mediterranean level.

Corporate Citizenship Europe (CCE)

The EFC also lays considerable emphasis on facilitating the development and integration of corporate citizenship and community involvement in Europe. A special Corporate Citizenship Europe (CCE) Committee has been developed as a partnership of community and public affairs executives from leading EFC corporate citizens and corporate foundation members. The Committee is committed to the promotion of partnership and collaboration with the foundation community for more active solidarity between corporate philanthropies and the societies in which they operate. In addition to the EFC core services to its members, the CCE Secretariat provides specific information and support relative to corporate philanthropy of benefit and interest to corporate citizens and corporate foundations. The CCE also publishes a quarterly newsletter, *efc partners europe*.

To achieve its objectives, the EFC interest group 'Partners in Philanthropy', formerly known as the CCE Intermediaries Project Network, recognizes the valuable role intermediary organizations can play in the promotion and development of corporate philanthropies across Europe. These organizations act as catalysts and as effective bridges between corporate citizenship programmes and the independent funding sector in Europe. The objective of the network is to forge a pan-European alliance of established intermediaries further to promote effective corporate community involvement at national and European level. The network is present in 13 European countries.

Other CCE initiatives include European-level conferences on corporate citizenship and a series of benchmark publications: 'Company Giving in Europe', 'Promoting Corporate Community Investment in Europe', and 'Transnational Giving: An Introduction to the Corporate Citizenship Activity of International Companies Operating in Europe'.

Some EFC members playing a key role in CCE Committee activities are: Allied Zurich; American Express; Amway (Europe) Ltd; Deutsche Bank; Diageo; IBM Europe; Johnson & Johnson; Levi Strauss & Co; Microsoft Europe; Nike; Philip Morris Corporate Affairs Services; Shell International and SmithKline Beecham.

Community Philanthropy Initiative

Finally, the Community Philanthropy Initiative was formally launched in 1997. The purpose of the Community Philanthropy Initiative is to foster the development of community-based philanthropic mechanisms in Europe. These vehicles attract, manage and distribute funds for social purposes at the local level. They include, among others, community foundations, United Ways, and locally-oriented funding intermediaries.

The community foundation concept is a particularly promising mechanism, and is the primary focus of the EFC's work. Currently, community foundations exist, or are under development, in at least 17 European countries or regions. The EFC is providing, or collaborating with, other in-country organizations on a range of services including information, research, technical assistance and training, networking, outreach and education, and resource development.

Specifically, the Community Philanthropy Initiative seeks to:

- strengthen existing community philanthropy organizations and facilitate establishment of new ones
- build the capacity of emerging and established national community philanthropy support organizations and informal networks
- increase awareness, knowledge and understanding about issues, trends, needs and opportunities affecting community philanthropy organizations
- promote and advocate on behalf of the community philanthropy movement to key target audiences in Europe
- build a strong and sustainable European-level network of community philanthropy organizations, national support centres, funders and other interested groups.

An additional aspect of the convening role of the EFC is its important work with national associations of foundations and cooperative agreements signed with such associations on other continents.

Links to national associations of foundations

A major objective of the EFC Philanthropy Network Project has been to develop mutually-empowering relationships among the national associations of foundations in Europe. This relationship should be beneficial to organized philanthropy in Europe and intercontinentally. The Philanthropy Network Project is part of the EFC Orpheus Programme, discussed below.

Across Europe there are some 17 distinct national associations serving foundations, such the *Bundesverband Deutscher Stiftungen* which provides services to German foundations. These also include the Association of Charitable Foundations in the United Kingdom, the Portuguese Foundation Centre, and a number of new 'Donors Forums' – specifically dedicated to assisting funders – across central and eastern Europe.

Since 1996, the EFC has convened an annual meeting of national associations of foundations in Europe. The meetings looked at a number of topics of interest to associations such as technology, training programmes for members, the promotion of philanthropy, the organizational mandate and communication techniques.

In addition to these meetings, the EFC plays an active role in the International Meeting of Associations Serving Grantmakers (IMAG). Initiated by the USA Council on Foundations, IMAG held its first meeting in Mexico in February 1998. Designed for associations of nonprofit organizations that include grant makers in their membership, the meeting convened 82 people representing 26 different countries. The meeting explored how these associations can increase their capacity to serve their grant-making members and, through them, strengthen the nonprofit sector around the world.

EFC cooperation agreements

The EFC has also signed numerous cooperation agreements with associations of foundations on other continents. By these agreements, both organizations recognize each other as colleague organizations cooperating in the encouragement of, and support for, the growth of philanthropy in Europe, in the respective country of the counter signatory, and in the wider world. Each organization formally undertakes to:

- make its conferences, seminars and workshops available to representatives of the other;
- exchange newsletters and general mailings
- make publications reciprocally available at member rates.

Cooperative agreements have been signed with the following.

Asia Pacific Philanthropy Consortium – Asia
Cámara de Fundaciones de Paraguay (CAFUPA) – Paraguay
Centro Brasileiro de Fundaçoes – Brazil
Centro Colombiano para la Pilanthropia – Colombia
Centro Español de Fundaciones – Spain
Centro Mexicano para la Filantropía – Mexico
Confederación Española de Fundaciones – Spain
Council on Foundations – USA
Federación de Fundaciones Argentinas, FEDEFA – Argentina
Japan Foundation Center – Japan
Philanthropy Australia – Australia
Southern Africa Grantmakers Association (SAGA) – South Africa

The EFC also has a long-standing and mutually beneficial relationship with the Foundation Center (USA). A staff member initially detached from the Foundation Center was instrumental in the setting up of the EFC Orpheus Programme, discussed below.

2.5 Information services

The third core service area of the EFC is information services. This is perhaps the most important area of service, for without fundamental information – on the legal and fiscal environment for independent funding in Europe, and on the programme interests of private funders – the EFC could neither represent nor convene with full professional standards. The EFC's information is on two fronts. Firstly, the EFC provides members with a stream of current awareness publications on a regular basis. Secondly, under the EFC Orpheus Programme, the EFC provides long-term information services that underpin the foundation and corporate funding community in Europe.

2.5.1 Current awareness information services

Current awareness information services include the publication, on a regular basis, of key documents and newsletters. These include the following.

- **Conference reports** providing extensive coverage of major networking events, including the Annual General Assembly.
- **Newsline**, a membership newsletter reporting quarterly on EFC activities.
- **Alerts** pinpointing sector and issue-specific developments relating to the activities of EFC Interest Groups and Committees.
- **Codex** reporting on developments relating to the EFC Code of Practice.
- **Communiqués** on issues of regulatory and operational concern to members.
- **Annual Reports** offering an overview of developments within the Centre in the year under review and summarizing emerging trends.

Specific EFC projects also release newsletters – *efc partners europe* (see above); *efc bookshelf* and *LINK-s* (see below).

Members also benefit from two additional information services.

1 The EFC provides members with information on demand, and incoming requests have ranged from potential funding partners and contacts in their programme areas, to legal and fiscal issues and assistance on convening meetings on specific programme areas, such as social inclusion.
2 Eurobriefings are a new EFC information initiative. To ensure that EFC Members are fully apprised of developments at the EU level, it is planned to complement the provision of information on European developments by developing issue-specific Eurobriefings in the form of one-day information status report meetings on European programmes and initiatives. A Eurobriefing has already taken place on education issues.

2.5.2 The EFC Orpheus Programme

The EFC Orpheus Programme serves grant makers, grant seekers, the EU institutions, researchers and the media by providing a public record and a public information service on foundations and corporate funders active in Europe. As a special project, Orpheus is grant-funded separately from the main EFC budget.

Orpheus facilitates a decentralized network of centres throughout Europe and operates a broad range of:

- publications
- library, information and database services
- network support and training
- issue-specific research.

For the projects and activities noted below Orpheus has been generously supported by the Bernard Van Leer Foundation, Charities Aid Foundation, Charity Know How, Charles Stewart Mott Foundation, *Compagnia di San Paolo*, European Cultural Foundation, *Fondation de France*, The Ford Foundation, Evkaf Foundation, *Freudenberg Stiftung*, *Haniel Stiftung*, King Baudouin Foundation, Luso-American Development Foundation, Microsoft Europe, Open Society Institute – Budapest, *Robert Bosch Stiftung*, *Stifterverband für die Deutsche Wissenschaft*, and the European Commission.

1993 saw the launch of the Orpheus Programme and it is a continuing initiative. Major accomplishments of the programme to date include a broad range of information tools and services. A prime achievement of the programme has been the development of a network of cooperating information centres across Europe. These network centres contribute information to the programme, and they make Orpheus Programme information services available at a national level. In cooperation with the network centres, the EFC developed the Orpheus database on private funders in Europe.

From this database, the programme has delivered a number of important publications. These include an introduction to the European independent funding community; directories of EFC members; a bibliography on foundation and corporate funding literature; a European Grants Index; and directories of funders working in central and eastern Europe, the Mediterranean, culture, education and the environment. The bibliography is updated regularly by the quarterly publication of the *efc bookshelf* newsletter.

Another key achievement of the programme was the development of the first *Typology of Foundations in Europe*. The *Typology* presents the most common foundation types in Europe, grouped initially into four generic categories as follows:

- independent foundations
- corporate foundations
- governmentally-linked foundations
- fundraising foundations.

Orpheus has also provided numerous training and professional development opportunities to the network centres participating in the programme. The EFC convenes annual training workshops for information officers and documentalists. The 1999 event, held in Sofia, Bulgaria, looked specifically at the Internet and electronic information provision. Additional workshops for the centres have been on subjects including strategic planning and media / public relations.

Current Orpheus Programme projects and initiatives include the following.

- **Youth Project**
  This project provides information services on foundation and corporate funders active in the youth sector in Europe. A directory on youth funding will be launched at the EFC's 1999 Annual General Assembly in Berlin. The Youth Project builds on and complements the work of the Education Dossier, which published *Education Funding in Europe* in 1998.
- **European Foundation Fundamentals**
  This project has just published *European Foundation Fundamentals*, a user-friendly guide to the foundation and corporate funding community in Europe. Profiles of the independent funding communities of more than 30 European countries are included, along with a guide on how to approach funders.
- **Funders Online**
  In conjunction with ARIES (Social Economy Online), this service is building Europe's philanthropic community by delivering and facilitating access to funding information provided via modern technology, specifically the Internet and the World Wide Web.
- **Information Network Project**
  This project will help organizations in central and eastern Europe and the newly independent states promote effective and collaborative philanthropy in a wider European context through

strengthening the philanthropic information infrastructure. It is also helping build the European network of associations of grant makers referred to above.

- **Social Economy Documentation Centre**
  Ongoing creation of this specialized information service and library, which will bring together, in one house, information relating to foundations, associations, and cooperatives in Europe. The EFC is collaborating with Euro-Citizens-Action-Service (ECAS) on this project.

- **Civil Society Project**
  Launched in 1994, the Orpheus Programme Civil Society Project develops and sustains indigenous information and support centres serving foundations and associations in central and eastern Europe, the newly independent states and the Baltic republics. The Civil Society Project builds on the centres' initial capacities, focusing on management training, information and communication, funding from foundations and corporate citizenship programmes, the advocacy of a positive legal and fiscal environment, and the promotion of self-awareness of the social economy.

  A total of 25 centres, from 15 different countries in the region, participate in this decentralized network. The Civil Society Project has provided fruitful ground for improving existing services and developing new programmes and partnerships.

  As a special project, the Civil Society Project is also grant-funded separately. Support from the Charles Stewart Mott Foundation has been instrumental to the project. Additional support has been generously provided by the Charities Aid Foundation, Charity Know How, the *Fondation de France*, the Stefan Batory Foundation, International Renaissance Foundation, and the European Commission.

  Significant achievements of the Orpheus Civil Society Project include the following.

  - **Select Legislative Texts and Commentaries Central and East European Not-for-Profit Law (1995)**
    The project covers foundation and association law in six countries. It was accomplished in collaboration with the International Center for Not-for-Profit Law, the European Foundation Centre and the Union of Bulgarian Foundations. First of its kind, this research and publication contributed greatly to the understanding of the legal and fiscal environment in the developing democracies in central and eastern Europe.

- **A review of the Slovak Bill on Foundations**
  The EFC was selected by the European Commission to coordinate and present a review and recommendations on the draft Slovak Bill on Foundations. The legal advisors to the EFC, Loeff Claeys Verbeke, lent their considerable expertise on European law governing foundations and associations to produce this document.
- **Social Economy and Law (SEAL) Journal**
  SEAL has been developed by the Orpheus Programme Civil Society Project. It aims to enhance the effectiveness of social economy law reform process in Central and Eastern Europe by improving the knowledge of current legal developments throughout the region, and to develop indigenous capacity to collect, analyse, publish and disseminate legislative and fiscal material on regional scale. Four issues have so far been published.
- *LINK-s* **is the Civil Society Project's newsletter**
  The resource centres publish this quarterly network newsletter on a rotating basis. *LINK-s* is available in print and electronically on the Internet.

2.5.3 ARIES

In today's world, rapid access to information is becoming increasingly important. That's why the EFC, in order to develop and strengthen its information services to its members, had a commitment to expand ARIES (Social Economy Online) in cooperation with associations, cooperatives, mutual societies and the European Commission.

Thanks to ARIES, Europe's social economy has its own electronic information network. ARIES brings together foundations, cooperatives, mutual organizations and nonprofit organizations throughout Europe, together with their federations, development agencies and umbrella organizations. ARIES offers on-line information on a wide and growing range of topics specific to the social economy, including details of funding opportunities, tenders, media review, seminars and conferences.

3 The Trans-Atlantic Donors Dialogue (TADD)

The EFC supports the Trans-Atlantic Donors Dialogue (TADD) programme as a facilitator and convenor.

Background

At their Madrid Summit in 1995 the EU and the US adopted the New Transatlantic Agenda. This Agenda has as one of its major goals the 'building of bridges' across the Atlantic, to ensure that future generations will be committed to the development of full and equal partnerships through improved communications in business, science and education. Already, this Agenda has brought renewed vigour to the relationship between the EU and the US, creating opportunities and initiatives to meet future challenges, and deepening social, commercial, cultural, educational and scientific ties among its peoples.

In May 1997, the New Transatlantic Agenda took a significant step forward through a two-day conference jointly organized by the Commission of the European Communities and the US Department of State. The Trans-Atlantic Conference, held in Washington, brought together prominent Europeans and Americans to look afresh at four areas:

- civil society
- education, culture and youth
- electronic exchanges
- building partnerships in the global economy.

The European Foundation Centre co-chaired the civil society working group of this conference, along with the American Federation of Teachers.

The Trans-Atlantic Civil Society Dialogue (TACD) was one of the key proposals to emerge from the Trans-Atlantic Conference. During the conference, delegates recognized that Europe and America face many challenges that threaten the mechanisms of democracy. These challenges include crime, alienation, marginalization and social exclusion. Delegates expressed a need for renewed efforts to strengthen and sustain civil society through people-to-people links, to develop and support practical initiatives involving closer cooperation between government, business, foundations and citizens' associations.

In March 1998, representatives of European and US donors met in Berlin and decided to re-launch the TACD and make it into an informal forum for independent funders interested in trans-Atlantic funding issues. The renamed Trans-Atlantic Donors Dialogue (TADD) would complement the activities of the Trans-Atlantic Business Dialogue (TABD), established in the aftermath of the EU-US Madrid Summit. Both the Business Dialogue and the Donors Dialogue would act as effective catalysts for progress in EU-US social and economic partnerships.

The TADD contributes to greater donor effectiveness and efficiency by facilitating communication, interaction and cooperation among private and public funders in Europe and the US, and by developing and implementing programmes that enhance the capacity of civil society players to address a range of social, cultural, economic and sustainable development issues in the two regions.

The Dialogue is an informal network of US and European private and public donors who actively support the goals of promoting the growth and development of people-to-people links and strengthening civil society on both sides of the Atlantic. It forges closer links between Europe and the United States by promoting partnerships and cooperation at the level of foundations, citizens' associations, government and business in these two world regions.

The Dialogue is spearheaded by the Luso-American Development Foundation of Portugal and the German Marshall Fund of the United States.

3.1 TADD programme objectives

The broad objectives of the Dialogue are to provide access to information on trans-Atlantic funding and to foster the growth of philanthropy in Europe and in the United States with a focus on trans-Atlantic funding.

The Luso-American Development Foundation (Portugal) and the German Marshall Fund of the United States, both EFC Members, have committed their support to the continuation of the TADD. They also co-chair the Working Group. The EFC will provide support to the TADD as facilitator and convenor, and underpin the Working Group through a secretariat function reporting through the EFC Director to the co-chairpersons of the Working Group. The TADD Programme will comprise several phases over a renewed two-year period.

3.2 TADD programme of initiatives

The programme objectives are met by alerting existing and potential donor organizations to the most effective mechanisms and models available to effect resourcing and to help them learn from, and strengthen links with, similar organizations.

Specific research objectives are met by:

- **documenting** the state of play with respect to the trans-Atlantic funding activities of European and US donors as identified via existing databases complemented by surveys and research studies
- providing **strategic analysis** of resourcing trends and resource programme management to pinpoint mechanisms for effective trans-Atlantic grant making
- promoting **networking** and **communication** between donors across the Atlantic by convening seminars, encouraging staff exchanges, organizing study visits, fostering the transfer of knowledge and know-how, and building synergies with respect to issues of common concern.

The results of the Dialogue are documented in a series of reports on trends, management practice, staff exchanges and study visits. These reports are circulated to all Dialogue participants and made available to interested third parties both in hard-copy format and electronically via the ARIES social economy online initiative and TIES, the Trans-Atlantic Information Exchange Service. Further information on the TADD Programme, as well as on all EFC activities mentioned in this chapter are available from the EFC.

Bibliography

All titles published by the European Foundation Centre (EFC).

European Foundation Centre Annual Reports, Brussels, 1991–98.

European Foundation Centre Conference Reports, Brussels, 1990–98.

Codex – EFC code of practice task force progress report, Brussels, January 1996

Principles of Good Practice, Brussels, January 1996

Education Funding in Europe, Brussels, 1998

Environmental Funding in Europe, Brussels, 1998

European Foundation Fundamentals, Brussels, 1999

European Grants Index, Brussels, 1998

Independent Funding – A Directory of Foundation and Corporate Members of the EFC, Brussels, 1998.

Mediterranean Funding, Brussels, 1999

Youth Funding in Europe, forthcoming

EFC Communiqués, Brussels, no. 1–150

Typology of Foundations in Europe 1995/1996 version, Brussels, 1996.

▼ Section II ▼

Mission, Governance and Organization

▼ Kenneth Prewitt

The Foundation Mission: Purpose, Practice, Public Pressures

1 Introduction

This chapter examines the nature of a foundation's mission – how it is formulated, altered, and implemented. The emphasis is on large-scale, private foundations as they emerged in the US in the late 19th century and then spread in number, size, and social influence throughout the 20th century. Although foundations have antecedents that predate this period and can today be found in many parts of the world, it is in the US over the last century that professionalized philanthropy has been developed on a vast scale.

A naive reading of how the modern foundation selects its mission would suggest that a donor transfers his or her wealth to the foundation (which often carries the donor's name), stipulating in the process the mission to be advanced. Trustees and officers then translate the donor's preferences into specific grants. However, this reading is an incomplete, even seriously inaccurate, guide to the history of foundation practice. It is especially inaccurate in its suggestion that the mission is static. An historical perspective indicates otherwise.

1.1 A century-long perspective

A century-long perspective matters for three reasons. First, leading American foundations include a few that began in the earliest decades of the 20th century, and which now have an institutional history sufficiently deep to make this history itself a factor in understanding their respective missions.

Secondly, if individual foundations have a history, so also does the foundation sector more generally. From a base of fewer than 100 in 1900, there are today nearly 40,000 foundations distributing more than $11 billion yearly in grant funds. In the 1980s alone, more than 3000 new foundations were established. The current annual growth rate of new foundations is 3%. With this growth in numbers and in grant-making power has come professionalization and institutionalization of the sector itself. There are membership organizations that assemble foundations for joint planning, to publicize foundation accomplishments, to battle against unwanted regulations or taxes, and to attempt to set standards for the sector. The foundation sector is itself a target of grant making, and in a few instances foundation funds are used to start up other foundations. Foundations operate in a professional environment composed of other foundations, and their practices now include shared agendas, complementary grant-making strategies, efforts at cross-leveraging, and even formal partnerships. Missions are neither formulated nor implemented in isolation. The peer community matters.

Thirdly, the vaunted independence of foundations notwithstanding, they are not indifferent to social expectations. Changing social expectations redefine acceptable practice and thus the philanthropic mission. Not surprisingly, foundations today are subjected to much greater public scrutiny than they were during the first half of the century: a foundation that never even thought to issue an annual report of its activities in the 1930s will today publish, and distribute widely, glossy annual reports that rival the best of the corporate sector. This small but telling example points to a broader change that has taken place across the century. Whereas early foundation mission and practice essentially reflected the viewpoints of donors, trustees, and officers, more recent developments have heightened the influence of interested parties external to the foundation. The state is one such party, which in its legislation and tax policies sets boundaries to the grant-making practices of foundations. Foundations, having been investigated more than once by congressional committees, are on the alert for practices, or missions, that might bring the state investigatory powers to bear. Beneficiaries constitute another interested party, reasonably successfully insisting that it be heard as foundations select their programme strategies. The independent foundation is not immune from demands that it be publicly accessible and politically accountable, an issue discussed later in this chapter.

If expectations have altered across time, so also have the conditions in which foundations operate. To note obvious examples: the sizeable investment by American foundations in area and international studies, language training, and student exchanges is a product of post-World War II conditions; the rise of environmental consciousness in the 1970s decidedly altered grant-making priorities; the collapse of communism suddenly opened up opportunities in eastern Europe and the former Soviet Union to which foundations were quickly responsive. Such examples could be multiplied over and over, indicating that the foundation mission, and especially how it expresses itself in grant making, is not rigid but rather adapts and evolves as the social environment changes.

In conclusion, the mission of a foundation is historically and socially constructed – and the way in which this construction has come about in the US can be used to illustrate a more general account of why foundations of the late 20th century conduct their affairs as they do.

Before turning to this analysis, we note that this chapter pays little attention to the thousands of American foundations whose annual grant budgets are less than $1 million, and who operate mostly at the local level. In 1994, there were 38,807 foundations, but only about 1500 whose grant making exceeded $1 million and only 163 with grant budgets of at least $10 million. Except as they share general traits with the independent foundation, this chapter also ignores corporate foundations (14.3% of the total) and community foundations (6.5% of the total).[1]

The emphasis is on the largest independent foundations – those with grant budgets of at least $25 million and which employ professional staff to manage programmes on a national or even an international scale. There are approximately 50 such foundations, the largest of which have assets of $8 billion and the smaller of which have assets of a half-billion. Because grant-making budgets are normally 5% of the asset base, the range is from grants of approximately $400 million a year to $25 million a year.

---

[1] Foundation Giving.

1.2 The American context

The wealthy donor inclined to philanthropy as a way to perpetuate his or her name and social influence is not a recent phenomenon. Plato bequeathed property so that his Academy would continue after his death, and in fact the Academy lasted nearly a millennium, from 347 BC to 529 AD, until it was deemed unchristian and dissolved by the Emperor Justinian. Popes and princes became patrons of the arts to enhance their esteem in the public eye. The royal gift, especially to provide a health or educational service, is known across history and across royal regimes from China to India, Egypt to England. More than a millennium of Islamic philanthropy built libraries, universities and mosques. Commercial wealth has generated philanthropic endeavours across the centuries, and not just since industrial capitalism. The famous Hotel Dieu in Burgundy was established in 1443 when the benefactor donated a highly-valued vineyard. The University of Uppsala was similarly endowed with a gift of productive land. Philanthropy as reflected in the royal gift, papal patronage, and even the private endowment formed the background to US philanthropy towards the end of the 19th century. This earlier philanthropic practice was not, however, a blueprint.

Late 19th century industrial wealth became the basis for a new type of philanthropy – the private foundation. Those foundations aim to achieve more than the one-time gift to endow a hospital or centre of learning. Philanthropy expressed through the private foundation, a legally immortal institution, extends the bequest and its purposes into the distant future: rather than endow an institution the philanthropic act endows the foundation itself. As shown below, this permits a flexible mission that can be altered as social conditions change. Modern philanthropy represented a break from Victorian era charity, which focused on the immediate relief of suffering and poverty. Philanthropy intended to do something about the deeper causes, the 'root causes' in the metaphor favoured at the time, that led to suffering in the first place.

There are a number of reasons for this institutional innovation, one being the sheer magnitude of the private fortunes gained by controlling a key industry (oil, steel, banking, transport) during the unregulated and largely untaxed decades of the late 19th and early 20th centuries. The amassed wealth was too large to be absorbed by a single beneficiary. For the moderately wealthy, Leland Stanford for example, endowing and naming a university might suffice, but the immoderately wealthy could not so easily dispose of their fortunes.

Although John D. Rockefeller donated what in today's dollars amounts to more than half a billion dollars to the University of Chicago, giving even at this spectacular level could not keep pace with his growing fortune. In a famous passage his early partner in philanthropy, Frederick T. Gates, argued to Rockefeller that:

> Your fortune is rolling up, rolling up like an avalanche! You must keep up with it! You must distribute it faster than it grows! If you do not, it will crush you and your children and your children's children![2]

Similarly, Andrew Carnegie, who by 1911 had managed to give away $180 million (approximately $2.6 billion in 1990 dollars), came to see that he would still not honour his proclaimed principle that it was sinful to die a wealthy man without transferring a further and significant part of his fortune to a private foundation that would continue to disperse funds long after his death. The private foundation, then, is a place to park wealth too substantial to give away in one's lifetime.

Viewed from an historical perspective, that the late 19th and late 20th centuries have in common a sharp increase in the transfer of privately-held wealth to the privately-managed foundation is not surprising. The late 20th century wealth gained through such new industries as electronics, information, media and entertainment is on a scale comparable to those 19th century fortunes made in oil, steel, and railroads. It occurs in a period when the rules of the economy allow, and even encourage, the accumulation of inordinate wealth in private control. If wealth redistribution through public policy was not in favour in the 1880s and 1890s, neither was it in favour in the 1980s and 1990s. The private foundation becomes, then, a means to recycle some of this wealth, though on terms largely set by the individuals who control it.

Of course the private foundation is by law and custom obliged to benefit those other than the holder of the wealth and his or her family and friends. The foundation must serve what is commonly understood to be a public, not a private, purpose. A serviceable definition of the American foundation is an institution that privately manages private funds in pursuit of a public good. This is so whether the philanthropic activity is social service (a clinic, an orphanage), patronage (an art museum, a university), broad education (public television, subsidized publications), or public policy (policy analysis and advocacy).

---

[2] Fosdick, p. 3.

Understood as private funds linked to public purpose, the private foundation is a social invention consistent with a political culture that prefers a weak state. This weak state tradition dates to the nation's founding period. Following a revolution to overthrow a tyrannical regime, the early architects of the American government created a weak state by distributing power horizontally across the judiciary, legislature, and executive branches, and vertically through federalism and decentralization, giving taxation and police powers to local authorities. This fragmented power system was further constrained by constitutional prohibitions on the exercise of power such as are embedded in the Bill of Rights. The American state was born of a deep suspicion that an unchecked government will sacrifice individual liberty and entrepreneurship in the drive to expand public authority; better to let the private market and private institutions deliver the goods than to grow a government bureaucracy.

This weak state tradition in the American political culture helps to account for the rise of the private foundation. If wealth accumulated is too substantial to be consumed or given away in one's lifetime, and thought to be too great to bequeath to family members, there are a limited number of ways to dispose of it. Furthermore, if the political culture as well as law and taxation policy invite the wealthy to create private institutions that can function as an alternative to the state, there is much satisfaction to be gained by creating a foundation. In the 20th century, then, the private foundation has become one of the major mechanisms by which large-scale, privately held capital memorializes the donor, endows his or her charitable inclinations, and substantially reduces tax obligations. As noted below, in some instances it also serves to keep control of a business enterprise in the hands of a founder's family and descendants.

2 The mission as purpose

What could be easier than describing the foundation mission? Is it not the broad goal clearly stated by the foundation, which is then translated into programme guidelines and implemented in grant making? This is a partial answer. Foundations take pride in announcing their missions, often citing the philanthropic intentions of their donors and the founding documents – charters, wills, bequests – that brought them into being. We start the analysis, then, by considering donor motives and founding statements.

2.1 The donor motive

Looking over a list of the 50 largest American foundations, it is noticeable that nearly all carry the name of their founding donor: Carnegie, Ford, Getty, Johnson, MacArthur, Mellon, Packard, Rockefeller, and so on. Based on this simple indicator, it is tempting to conclude that the major motive for establishing a foundation is vanity – the desire of the wealthy to secure public recognition across the decades and centuries to come. While vanity no doubt plays a part, a number of other motives have been claimed by the donors and their close associates or been assigned by those who have studied the creation of foundations.

The attributed motives fall into two general categories:

- altruistic, benign and charitable
- protectionist and self-interested, venal and manipulative.

In the first category the attributed motives are variations on a theme set forth in Andrew Carnegie's famous 1889 article 'The Gospel of Wealth'. This essay advanced an analysis of capitalism consistent with social Darwinian theories favoured by 19th century industrialists and their apologists. Carnegie noted that industrial capitalism was providing more and more benefits to ever greater proportions of the population, but acknowledged that its workings inevitably generated substantial surplus wealth under the control of the few.

> We accept and welcome, therefore, as conditions to which we must accommodate ourselves, great inequality of environment; the concentration of business, industrial and commercial, in the hands of the few; and the law of competition between these, as being not only beneficial, but essential to the future progress of the race.[3]

But if the laws of competition result in vast surplus wealth in the hands of the few, how should it be disposed of? Carnegie forcefully argued that the wealthy few have a deep moral obligation to direct their surplus wealth to charitable ends.

> The millionaire will be but a trustee for the poor, intrusted for a season with a great part of the increased wealth of the community, but administering it for the community far better than it could or would have done for itself, [concluding with his oft quoted declaration] The man who dies thus rich dies disgraced.[4]

---

[3] Carnegie, p. 3.

[4] Ibid., p. 12.

For Carnegie and other philanthropists at the turn of the century the 'stewardship of wealth' derived from their religious principles, 'to whom much is given will much be required', as framed in the Judeo-Christian tradition. In explanations of Rockefeller's philanthropy much attention is given to his practice of tithing as a young man, long before his rapid accumulation of wealth. The tithe was an integral part of his strong Baptist upbringing and much of his early philanthropy did concentrate on Baptist causes. As summarized in a history of early foundation practice: 'no one who examined closely the beginnings of many modern foundations is likely to escape one conclusion: most of the founders were seized by a social vision which stirred them deeply, and which was in many instances a modern expression of religious feeling'.[5]

It was Max Weber, in *The Protestant Ethic and the Spirit of Capitalism*, who gave sociological depth to the association between Protestant asceticism – with its emphasis on discipline, secular engagement and deferred gratification – and the thrifty, hard-working business ethic that shaped modern capitalism. The Protestant ethic stressed the greatest possible productivity, but frowned on the luxurious enjoyment of the wealth so earned. If work is to manifest God's glory, the profits of work are to be re-invested in that which is productive and socially beneficial. To do good works in this life is a sign of grace. Not that salvation could be earned by good works, but doing good as well as being good was to be expected of wealth. This was a convenient doctrine for men, Rockefeller and Carnegie notably among them, who were both devoutly religious and wealthy beyond measure; it is comforting to know that one can dedicate oneself to acquisition and yet be virtuous.

Although explicitly religious motives are not often cited in today's more secular culture, the Protestant ethic retains its hold. The notion that one is a 'steward' of surplus wealth still appears in explanations of philanthropy, as do echoes of the belief that good works in this life signal moral worth. Late 20th century billionaires speak of an obligation to repay society for having been so good to them. They are in this respect reflecting the notion, a particularly American notion, that the wealthy, because they are wealthy, are obliged to be philanthropic. Inherent in wealth is the responsibility for the public good that one's wealth can promote.

---

[5] Harrisson and Andrews, p. 23.

The attribution of benign motives is echoed often in commentary drawing on Andrew Carnegie's stewardship theme, though more recently Carnegie's social Darwinism has been discarded. Frederick P. Keppel, a long-time president of the Carnegie Corporation, accepted that:

> the donor may not be averse to the publicity attending his gift. He may not be blind to the conveniences attending exemption from taxation [...] But the dominating reason [for the creation of a foundation], I believe, is the recognition of the 'stewardship of surplus wealth'.[6]

Nearly half a century later, another ex-foundation president reached a similar conclusion:

> But let it be recorded now as one man's opinion that the most widely prevalent reason for the establishment of foundations has been the decent philanthropic urge on the part of the donor.[7]

Most students of foundation history acknowledge that religious sentiments and charitable inclinations play some role in the establishment of many foundations, but few would accept that analysis can stop at this point. There are simply too many instances where self-interested motives, in one form or another, come into play. Of Rockefeller it is claimed that he invested heavily in charitable work as a way to counter the greedy and grasping person he had become in the public imagination, that is, publicly to redeem his self-image as a good and charitable man. Of Ford it is noted that though he may have been charitable, it was no accident that the complex way in which the Ford Foundation was charted protected the family's control over the Ford Motor Company, and in a manner that avoided heavy taxation. Of the Duke Endowment it has been pointed out that its founder, the tobacco and utility magnate James Buchanan Duke, managed to direct its grants to areas served by the Duke Power Company, thus securing favourable publicity for his business interests.[8] More generally, with the establishment of progressive income taxes and inheritance taxes, except in the rarest of cases the motivation to escape heavy taxation is certainly a factor in the generation of so many foundations in the US. This motive is not limited to the American business community: Reinhard Mohn, founder of the Bertelsmann Foundation in Germany, writes of the 'burden of inheritance taxation' and further

---

[6] Keppel, p. 18.

[7] Cuninggim, p. 15.

[8] MacDonald, pp. 42–4.

notes that the establishment of the Foundation derived from 'the wish to secure the continuity of the corporation'.[9]

No doubt, then, each of the motives thus far cited – stewardship, charitable impulses, vanity, guilt, business interests, tax avoidance – are present if in different mixtures for different donors. But even were we to have a precise measurement of the proportion of each of these motives present in any specific case, it would not explain what the funds actually do. The commonly attributed motives do not shed much light on how the mission is formulated.

We now turn to a different line of reasoning, one that does relate motive and mission. Though normally denied by those who create foundations, there is a long tradition in the US of seeing in the establishment of foundations the motive to exercise lasting political-economic-social control. The very wealthy did not earn their fortunes without exercising economic control – of an industry, a marketing strategy, a scientific innovation, a new product. Nor have these individuals been indifferent to how policies, regulations, tariffs, and taxes can help or hinder the acquisition of wealth. It is not much of a leap from these facts to presume that transferring private wealth to a private foundation is a way to extend political-economic influence. The philanthropic motive that matters is not social betterment but social control.

This charge surfaces in the earliest congressional investigations into private foundations. The Walsh Commission (1915–16), named after its chairman, observed that industry and wealth in the US had come under the control of a few very wealthy persons. The Commission alleged that this small group intended to continue and extend this control by establishing 'enormous privately managed funds for indefinite purposes'.[10] Here, then, is coupled the late 19th century anxiety about the concentration of economic power with the fear that private foundations would perpetuate the dominance of business interests in American political and social life.

It is a theme repeated often. In the 1930s, for example, a study into the purposes of the large private foundation concluded that:

> Philanthropic and business interests are not merely complementary, they are identical. Just as you can't run a steel mill without machine guns, so you can't run a capitalist democracy without a pretence of philanthropy.[11]

---

[9] Mohn, p. 25.

[10] US Congress, Senate, Vol. 1, p. 18.

[11] Coon, p. 276.

By the 1980s the argument that foundations exist to perpetuate American business interests had been extended to explain its overseas grant making; the phrase 'cultural imperialism' appears in the title of one work, a Marxian influenced account of foundations as instruments of capitalist exploitation of Third World countries.[12]

This critique from the political left found its mirror image in a critique from the political right. A mid-century congressional investigation, named after its chairman B. Carroll Reece, charged foundations not with extending but with undermining capitalism. Chairman Reece was convinced that certain foundations 'support efforts to overthrow our government and to undermine our American way of life'.[13] This critique, which is echoed in the conservative press down to the present, frequently adds the argument that it is subsequent generations of trustees and officers who have deflected the foundation from the purposes intended by its original donor. Cited as evidence is the resignation of Henry Ford II, grandson of the founder of Ford Motor Company, from the foundation that bears his name. His letter of resignation noted that the Ford Foundation existed only because of capitalism, but that it 'was hard to discern recognition of this fact in anything the foundation does'.

The critique of the left and of the right come to a similar conclusion in this sense: the reason that persons of wealth establish foundations is to perpetuate the political-economic system under which they accumulated that wealth in the first place. The motive and the mission come together, whether the conclusion is that the mission is being carried out or that it has been thwarted.

In matters of motive, convincing evidence is not easy to come by. On the claims of religious sentiment and charitable impulses as motivating factors, the evidence relies on little more than testimonials. On the claim of vanity, evidence is found in the names that foundations carry forward into history. On the claim of tax avoidance, the evidence is more convincing because the work of lawyers and accountants leave records and these records document, time and again, the effort that goes into minimizing estate taxes. However, as suggested earlier, this array of motives might tell us why the foundation was established, but not what it will do.

The motivation to perpetuate an economic system or doctrine is, of course, a motive that is also a mission. How much weight to assign to

---

[12] Arnove, also Berman.

[13] Congressional Record, Vol. 99, No. 141, p. 10188.

this motive would require analysis well beyond the scope of this essay. Summarizing the current literature is not satisfactory; it draws heavily on conspiracy theories. Whether it is asserted that foundations are a plot to protect and extend capitalism; or, conversely, a plot to replace the market with socialism and government bureaucracy, the arguments too often proceed from assertion to anecdote rather than from evidence to assertion.

This author believes that careful historical analysis would reach two conclusions regarding the hypothesis that social control, more than charity, is the donor motivation. First, donor motives, if not exclusively, certainly include a strong preference that the foundation they establish will enhance particular political and economic doctrines. Given the social location of persons wealthy enough to establish a foundation, it is not surprising if the doctrine of choice is private enterprise and market capitalism. Perhaps there is an irony in the fact that the American foundation results from the accumulation of substantial private wealth and yet in instance after instance declares that its mission is to improve the lot of the poor and powerless. It goes about that mission by helping to lower the barriers to upward mobility, by working to ensure basic civil and political rights or by contributing to education and health for the poor. It does not go about that mission by calling into question the political-economic arrangements that allow for unequal wealth acquisition in the first place, despite the oft repeated claim that foundations will find and eliminate the 'root causes' of poverty, discrimination and illness. It is not the task of this essay to determine whether the root cause might include the rules that govern wealth acquisition. But it is clear from the historical record that whatever their motives, the donors established foundations that have largely left this issue unaddressed.

There is a second likely conclusion: the ability of donors to influence the long-term mission of the instrument they establish is seriously constrained in a number of ways, not least of which is the vagueness of mission statements and the inevitable attenuation of donor influence with the passage of time.

2.2 The founding charter

Donors do leave imprints on the foundations they establish. Legally this occurs when the foundation secures its charter, which in the US is provided typically at state and not federal level. In the case of a bequest that comes into force only with the death of the donor, this charter will incorporate the purpose of the foundation as set forth by the donor in his or her will. As suggested below, the purpose so set forth is often designed to permit considerable flexibility of interpretation and implementation. In many instances, however, the donor establishes a foundation during his or her lifetime. In such circumstances the donor will usually see to it that the charter identifies the philanthropic purposes to be pursued by the foundation, and will often live long enough after the creation of the foundation to remain an active presence. There is also the presence of the donor's close associates or children, who carry on the founding mission after his or her death. Of course all these factors can come together, and sometimes have, but over the long term it is clear that there is an inevitable attenuation of the donor's influence.

That this would not only be so, but should be so was a matter of principle among those who pioneered the creation of the modern American foundation. Both Andrew Carnegie and John D. Rockefeller Sr were sensitive to the possibility that the philanthropic institution carrying their name through history could stagnate and become socially irrelevant if its mission were restrictively framed. They elevated to self-conscious principle the proposition that there should be no 'dead hand' of history constraining successor generations of trustees and officers.

Carnegie's will is explicit on this matter. He assigned to the trustees of the Carnegie Corporation 'full authority to change policy or causes hitherto aided from time to time, when this, in their opinion, has become necessary or desirable. They shall best conform to my wishes by using their own judgement.' As a matter of fact, by the time Carnegie shifted the bulk of his remaining fortune to the Carnegie Corporation in 1910 he was exhausted with philanthropy and only too glad to rid himself of the burden of responsible giving.

The Rockefeller story is a similar one of founding charter flexibility though he did not, of course, withdraw from the foundation(s) he charted. In the immediate years prior to the establishment of the Rockefeller Foundation (1913), Rockefeller organized his giving through a number of charitable trusts, including the Rockefeller Institute for Medical Research (later to become Rockefeller University), the General Education Board, and the Rockefeller Sanitary Commission. In each instance the actual grant-making activities were entrusted to independent trustees, selected from among persons experienced with the subject matter at issue. These trustees and the officers they selected were then given a free hand in carrying out the work. As Rockefeller himself commented:

I have not had the hardihood even to suggest how people, so much more experienced and wise in those things than I, should work out the details even of those plans with which I had the honour to be associated.[14]

This permissive principle took concrete expression when the Rockefeller Foundation itself was established. It is most clearly stated by the attorney responsible for the incorporation of the foundation, when he expressed Rockefeller's sentiments as follows:

The charities of the fourteenth century are not the charities of the twentieth century. The charities of the twentieth century will not be the charities of the twenty-first century, and it is eminently desirable [...] that the dead hand should be removed from charitable bequests and that the power to determine to what specific objects they should be applied should be left in the hands of living men who can judge of the necessities and of the needs in the light of the knowledge which they have as contemporaries, and not that they shall find their hands tied by the will of the man who is long years dead. The wisdom of living men will always exceed the wisdom of any man, however wise, who has long since been dead.[15]

The community foundation movement in the US, which dates from 1914, further institutionalized the flexibility principle. A community foundation is designed so that unrestricted charitable gifts can be left to benefit a particular community. The donor is expected to take the broad view but is assured that the foundation will remain under the control of local community members and that it will be dedicated to community improvement. It is said that the founder of the first community foundation, Frederick Goff, a Cleveland banker, was motivated by anecdotes of how narrow interests led to irrelevant bequests, for instance that of a London benefactor who in 1626 left his estate to finance the recovery of captives taken by pirates, or the St Louisian whose 19th century bequest was intended to benefit those who guided the western territories pioneers in their wagon-wheel caravans.

US courts have generally sided with the donor intent when disputes have occurred over how narrowly or broadly to interpret those intents. A narrow, constructionist view by courts has lent its weight to the tendency by many donors to articulate broad and permissive guidelines.

---

[14] Fosdick, p. 11.

[15] Ibid., p. 17.

The Mellon Foundation announces that its purpose is to 'aid and promote such religious, charitable, scientific, literary, and educational purposes as may be in the furtherance of the public welfare or tend to promote the well-doing or well-being of mankind'. For the Robert Wood Johnson Foundation, established in 1972 on the basis of wealth acquired from the world's largest medical supply company, Johnson & Johnson, the mission is simply stated as: 'to improve the health and healthcare of all Americans'.

Even such broad guidance as this is sometimes omitted. The Nathan Cummings Foundation, established with a $230 million bequest, specified no areas of concentration – leaving to the donor's children the setting of foundation goals. In a defiant mood, the reclusive John T. MacArthur left his insurance billions to a foundation with the cryptic comment: 'I figured out how to make money, let them figure out how to spend it'.

MacArthur was an exception, and not only in his indifference to the goals of the foundation that would bear his and his wife's name; unlike most wealthy donors whose fortunes and names became institutionalized as a foundation, MacArthur had not engaged in charitable activity prior to his death. In the process of wealth accumulation, it is far more common for donors to begin to make large-scale charitable gifts during their lifetimes. And this pattern of giving can suggest the terms under which a subsequently established foundation will operate. Rockefeller's early gifts that established the University of Chicago and the medical laboratories that were to become Rockefeller University set directions for the foundation that bears his name.

Wealthy individuals will often establish the foundation while they are still alive, remain actively engaged with it until their death, and then leave a large bequest to perpetuate its work. Eighteen years is the average elapsed time between a foundation's establishment and the death of its founder. For those donors less wedded to the flexible principles expressed by Carnegie and Rockefeller, this time provides an opportunity to set directions. The Alfred P. Sloan Foundation comments that its founder:

> looked upon the Foundation as an extension of his own life and work, including his philanthropic interests. Although Sloan recognized the inevitability of change that might dictate a different course, he expected that the Foundation would 'continue as an operating facility indefinitely into the future [...] to represent my accomplishments in this life'.[16]

---

[16] Annual Report, Alfred P. Sloan Foundation.

As chief executive officer and chairman of the board of General Motors for more than a quarter of a century, Sloan was closely engaged with science, technology and industrial productivity. During his lifetime his giving reflected those interests. Today they are central concerns in the grant activities of the Sloan Foundation.

The Ewing Marion Kauffman Foundation has gone to unusual lengths to perpetuate the presence of its founder. Kauffman had been actively involved with the Foundation for the ten years before his death in 1993. During this period he videotaped his vision of the foundation's mission, tapes which are now obligatory viewing for all new employees as a means of instructing them in the founder's values and beliefs. Presumably this is to guard against the tendency for successive waves of officers gradually to redefine the mission in a manner that might not be welcomed by the donor. Other foundations, even when they take up causes and projects not anticipated in the will or the founding mission statement, nevertheless insist that they are adopting new goals that would have been adopted were the founder still alive. The Pew Charitable Trusts, founded in 1948 by Joseph N. Pew on the basis of his Sun Oil fortune, initially focused on the arts, health, education, and religion. Today protecting the natural environment is one of its largest programmes, an area of giving not envisaged in 1948. The Pew Board, eight of whose members are descendants of the founder, deliberated and reached the conclusion that protecting the environment would have been adopted as an area of giving by Joseph Pew had its importance been recognized when he was alive.

As the Pew case suggests, immediate family members, especially children, have often ensured a degree of continuity between donor interest and grant-making strategies. A number of key directions set in the early years of the Rockefeller Foundation, on whose board the founder's son was active for many years, continue to this day, most notably being the long-standing funding of medical research and public health. The Rockefeller Foundation has sustained a major international portfolio: Rockefeller felt that his wealth having been augmented through business interests overseas it should be equally international when applied to philanthropic endeavours and this was an interest strongly shared by his son. Other foundations whose board members include children of the founder include the Pew Charitable Trusts, as noted above, the McKnight Foundation and the Packard Foundation. In the latter two cases, family members constitute a majority presence on the board and the foundations are commonly referred to as 'family foundations'. The Packard

Foundation is presently organizing itself in terms of programme interests reflecting the different priorities of the children of the donor. Its 'mission' has become the collection of differing and loosely coordinated charitable interests of family members ranging from children's welfare to marine research, from population issues to environmental conservation.

The strongest measure to ensure donor influence occurs when the donor is willing to expend principle as well as income, thus greatly magnifying the reach of the foundation in the years when the donor is still alive. The Annenberg Foundation is one such example, as are the several foundation instruments being established by George Soros, though in each case it is too early to know whether the magnitude of the fortune might not yet result in a large-scale, permanently endowed foundation.

Some donors have resorted to a time-limited foundation, in which the specified life of the foundation more or less corresponds to the life-expectancy of the donor. A time-limited foundation is one in which the principle as well as income is allocated on a fixed schedule. One of the earliest foundations in America, the Peabody Education Fund, was established in 1867 by a Baltimore banker, George Peabody. For 50 years the Fund was to carry out innovative and courageous work improving education in the South, with a special emphasis on Black education. Peabody felt that the foundation would not improve with ageing, and after half a century of work it should be liquidated. The Julius Rowenwald Fund, also devoted to Black education, was set up to expend its principle and income over 25 years, and closed its doors in 1948. More recently, the New York based Aaron Diamond Foundation expended its $200 million asset in the decade ending on the last day of 1996. Irene Diamond led the foundation across its entire history. The Joseph J. Jacobs Foundation is following a similar strategy, but has set 2028 as its terminal year because that date is estimated by its founder to coincide with the death of the last of his three daughters. These are interesting but isolated cases. In denying the common expectation that a foundation allocates only earned income each year and thus operates in perpetuity, the time-limited model is unlikely to be widely adopted, however much individual donors may wish to ensure that their preferences are honoured into the distant and unforeseeable future.

In practice, the history of 20th century American philanthropy can only be understood by recognizing how much, not how little, foundations adjust strategies and redefine missions as social conditions change. It is safe to assume that the older the foundation the more likely it is to have reformulated its mission in ways that would not, except at the most abstract level, be easily recognized by the donor. Could Rockefeller, the founder of the Standard Oil Company, have imagined that the foundation which bears his name would today fund a sustained attempt to reduce the dependence of the world on fossil fuels, including especially petroleum? Or that the Foundation would be funding scientific work dedicated to the discovery of a male contraceptive? Such programme goals can be made consistent with the broad mission statement – the 'well-being of mankind throughout the world' – but they are clearly late, not early, 20th century definitions of what the Rockefeller Foundation should be about.

Even more so with the Ford Foundation, which started life in 1936 as a small philanthropy focused on the Detroit-area interests of its founders, including the Detroit Symphony, the Henry Ford Hospital, and a local museum housing trolley cars, buggies, steam engines and, of course, automobiles. Not until the late 1940s, following the death of Edsel Ford (1943) and Henry Ford (1947), did the Foundation come into the enormous assets it enjoys today. Its mission then derived from a 1949 report prepared by a consultant, Rowland Gaither, who recommended five programme areas: the establishment of peace; the strengthening of democracy; the strengthening of the economy; education in a democratic society; and individual behaviour and human relations. It is noteworthy that these areas bore no relationship to the local charitable interests of Henry and Edsel Ford and that they themselves have not been sustained in the form expressed in the 1949 report. The Foundation's programme emphases have been periodically redefined, often following changes in senior management. At present the Ford Foundation organizes its grant making under three broad headings: asset building and community development; peace and social justice; and education, media, arts, and culture. In all three areas there is a persistent concern with poverty. Moreover, the Foundation spends 40% of its grant dollars through 16 regional offices spread around the world, hardly an arrangement that bears resemblance to the pre-1950s foundation or even the one that took shape in the 1950s. Not that this is surprising; the 1949 report itself recommended that the Foundation should re-appraise its aims every five or ten years to ensure that the Foundation would be responsive 'to new opportunities created by changed conditions'.

Though donor intentions are not irrelevant to the unfolding mission of any given foundation, especially in its earlier years, it should now be clear that enquiry into how foundations determine their mission needs to go beyond the necessarily time-limited vision of their original donors. Indeed, it is necessary to shift the frame of reference, turning from the 'mission as purpose' to the 'mission as practice'.

3 The mission as practice

What is it that foundations actually do? Foundation practice involves three separate, though inter-related, dimensions:

- subject-matter emphasis
- strategic choice
- instruments used.

3.1 Subject-matter of grant making

It is commonplace to refer to a foundation's mission by describing the areas of its primary grant making. A foundation is what and who it funds. It sees itself, and is seen by others, in terms of the social conditions with which it engages. This is a reasonable definition of strategy, though not one that avoids ambiguities. One difficulty arises from the obvious fact that many foundations are engaged with a number of social sectors and thus following a subject-matter definition can only lead to describing them as multiple-mission foundations.

Based on statistics it collects from thousands of private foundations, the New York based Foundation Center uses a ten-part classification to report grant making by subject-matter:

- arts and culture
- education
- environment
- health
- human services
- international affairs and development
- public/society benefit
- science and technology
- social science
- religion.

As would be expected, the larger foundations offer grants across this array. The Ford Foundation has programmes in all ten areas. Kellogg, Pew, MacArthur, Mellon, Rockefeller, or Packard may skip one or two areas, but have seldom limited themselves to fewer than half a dozen sectors. Of the large foundations it is generally the operating foundations which tend to be less dispersed in grant making – the Getty Foundation in the arts and the Howard Hughes Foundation in biomedical research.

One might expect that what is true of the largest foundations would not be true for the smallest, that is, that the very small foundation would select one arena in which to be active so as to maximize its influence. But the small foundation is normally a local foundation. And it finds that there is no easy way to contribute to the local museum but not to the after-school programme for disadvantaged children, or to make a grant to the homeless shelter but to ignore nature conservation. Small, community-based foundations are no less likely to pursue multiple-purposes. It is in the mid-range that one most often encounters what are sometimes called 'niche foundations', that is institutions which concentrate in one sector. An example is the Spencer Foundation, which spends approximately $18 million a year exclusively on educational research.

This absence of fit between foundation size and number of pro-gramme areas does not prevent us from defining the foundation mission with reference to subject matter. But it does imply that for a majority of foundations active in many sectors this definition pro-duce an uninformative list. To say that a foundation's mission is to advance the well-being of mankind by working through arts, culture, environment, health, population, education, human services, and reli-gion is to say little more than that the foundation wants to do good in a large number of ways.

A subject-matter definition of mission is even problematic for those foundations that concentrate in one or two sectors. Of the large, non-operating foundations, the Robert Wood Johnson Foundation is perhaps the most narrowly focused. It restricts its grant making to the US and is active primarily in the health field. But the health field is a vast terrain. Robert Wood Johnson does not fund medical research, believing even its $300 million or so grants budget to be too small compared to that of federal government. Nor, except in a few limited cases, does it support medical training and fellowships. In fact, Robert Wood Johnson has only three goal areas: providing access to health care at reasonable cost; improving services to those with chronic health conditions; and reducing substance abuse. To under-stand this foundation's mission, then, is to ask how these three foci came to be selected and how they are pursued.

Taking a broad perspective it could be said that the Carnegie Corporation's mission has been reasonably focused across its history, reflecting the terms of its charter: 'to promote the advancement and diffusion of knowledge and understanding among the people of the United States.' But the foundation's interpretation knowledge advancement and its dissemination has in fact varied across the decades. An early interpretation of the mandate led the Carnegie Corporation to fund and help found such elite scientific institutions as the National Research Council and the National Bureau of Economic Research. It sponsored studies that resulted in influential books such as Gunnar Myrdal's *An American Dilemma*. The same mandate, however, was viewed as consistent with a long-standing interest in pre-school education. The Carnegie Corporation charter has also been viewed as permitting investment in the Mexican-American Legal Defense and Educational Fund and the Legal Defense Fund of the National Association for the Advancement of Colored People (NAACP). In short, across its 80-year history, the Carnegie Corporation has funded a wide range of projects, from basic scientific research to public advocacy.

The geographic focus of a foundation is a further complicating factor when attempting to use subject-matter to define mission. We noted that smaller foundations tend to concentrate at the community level. Larger foundations operate at regional, national, and, increasingly, international levels. In some respects it tells us more about a foundation to learn that it operates internationally than to learn about its subject-matter emphases. For example, Ford and Rockefeller maintain a high profile internationally. From this perspective, their missions are similar, more so in fact than are the missions of the Rockefeller Foundation and the Robert Wood Johnson Foundation, although both institutions are heavily engaged with the health sector. The health programme of the former is (at present) exclusively international and that of the latter is (at present) exclusively domestic; they therefore share no grantees and no grant-making strategies. To compare, then, Ford, Rockefeller, and Robert Wood Johnson in terms of subject-matter is less instructive than to know that the former two operate overseas and the latter does not.

The subject-matter approach to mission is complicated by another dimension. One of the ways in which foundations differ is in the proportion of their grant dollars given to provide general support or fund capital campaigns as against that given for specific programmes and projects. Some foundations have strong policies that prohibit contributions to building projects, capital campaigns, or endowments; these tend to favour programme and project grants over general support. Other foundations – Kresge is an example – dedicate practically all their grant dollars to capital projects, usually in a highly leveraged fashion by requiring that matching funds are secured by the grant recipient. Among the largest foundations in the US, programme and project grant making absorbs approximately 60% of their grant funds, with capital projects attracting approximately 22% and general support about 13%.

To conclude, knowing the subject-matter foci of a foundation does not involve understanding how it goes about its business. And it is through an understanding of how it does its business that we can get closer to a foundation's operating philosophy.

3.2 Strategic choices of grant making

Foundations make a choice about the most effective way to advance their goals. This strategic choice is revealed not by the social conditions being worked on – peace, justice, health, inequality, culture – but by the approach or course of action brought to such conditions. Choice is revealed in the grantees typically funded: universities and scientific laboratories, advocacy organizations and grass roots groups, service delivery agencies.

A strategic choice gives operational meaning to the 'theory of change' adopted (even if implicitly) by a foundation. Does the foundation operate on the assumption that ideas drive history; or that technologies do; or social movements, market incentives, government interventions, moral exhortation? If ideas drive history, invest in intellectual efforts; if government interventions drive history, invest in policy analysis and advocacy; if exhortation drives history, invest in public education. Or, to use a term much favoured by foundations, grant making should seek out the point of 'leverage' judged to be most productive of desired social change.

This is not to suggest that a foundation need be guided by just one theory of change. Just as a foundation can be active across a number of subject areas, it can simultaneously pursue a number of basic strategies. And of course an effort to identify particular strategic choices must recognize at the outset that the categories are imprecise, the boundaries overlapping. This caution voiced, we offer a number of approaches.

3.2.1 New knowledge

Foundations in the US have made major investments in universities and in research institutions, equipment, and personnel, as part of a broad strategy to advance human understanding in nearly every field of study imaginable: anthropology, astronomy, biology, chemistry, economics, history, medicine, music, physics, political science, and psychology, to name only the most obvious. These investments have, at times, been sustained over long periods, for instance the Rockefeller Foundation's century-long involvement with medical science. For some foundations, over certain periods of their history, the search for new, fundamental knowledge defined what they took to be their vocation. The Howard Hughes Foundation (an operating foundation) is largely focused on ground-breaking research in bio-medical fields. The Russell-Sage Foundation has been closely associated with the search for new knowledge in social sciences. The 'new growth theory' currently being advanced in economics offers a rationale for philanthropic engagement with advancing knowledge, for this theory argues that economic growth results from new ideas as much as from the traditional factors of labour, capital, and resources.

3.2.2 New knowledge applied

Closely linked to the pursuit of new knowledge has been the systematic attempt to see it used in socially beneficial ways. An example is investment in the public health profession, viewed as a means to ensure that discoveries from biomedical science will reach the broadest population possible, and especially those groups that might otherwise be ignored. There are many other examples: new knowledge in learning theory being coupled with school reform efforts, new knowledge in plant physiology leading to the development of higher-yielding food crops and their dissemination in poorer countries.

3.2.3 Policy analysis

American foundations have had a long, close relationship with studies and publications that seek to inform public policy. This can be seen in the heavy investment in policy research institutions such as the Brookings Institution, the Rand Corporation, the American Enterprise Institute and hundreds more. It has been argued elsewhere that the rise of the independent policy institute and the independent foundation are not only intricately linked, but are responsive to the same deep pulse in American political culture that prefers the private to the public sector.[17] Foundation funding of the social sciences, which started before the turn of the century, has generally been motivated by the quest for improved public policy. The close relationship between foundation funds and public policy analysis in the US underscores the fact that privately held philanthropic resources attempt to advance public purposes. This relationship has been a complicated one, attracting its share of sharp criticism from both the political left and political right. The task here is not to judge but to point out that the production of policy analysis has certainly been one of the consistent philanthropic strategies motivating American foundations. So it is elsewhere. The German-based Bertelsmann Foundation defines one of its primary goals as providing new concepts and models for the social market economy and for public administration.

3.2.4 *Policy advocacy*

American foundations have funded a seemingly endless number of organizations dedicated to fighting for or against particular public policies: in human rights, equal opportunity, school reform, nuclear disarmament, environmental protection, free speech, children's welfare, and so on. Although already a dimension of philanthropy early in the century,[18] such funding gained momentum in the post-World War II period as the federal government became increasingly active in areas long of interest to the philanthropic sector. If foundation funds could stimulate the government to adopt the 'right' policy in civil rights or social welfare, the impact would be far greater than that accomplished with foundation funds alone. From this emerged the notion that if government, through its regulatory and taxation powers, influences private expenditure patterns, philanthropy can reverse the direction of influence by spending private funds on policy analysis and advocacy that will change government spending priorities. In earlier years, the policy advocacy groups supported by foundations largely focused on the US. In recent years, however, attention has broadened to include the international arena and international actors; so that policies of the World Bank or the World Health Organization or multinational corporations are targets for internationally organized advocacy groups, especially in the fields of environment and human rights. The post-1989 preoccupation with what is often, if not very precisely, described as civil society funding is a combination of policy advocacy and the next strategy to be discussed, social movement philanthropy.

---

[17] Prewitt.

[18] Sealander.

3.2.5 *Social movements and social empowerment*

Though overlapping with policy advocacy, social movement philanthropy is sufficiently different to merit its own category. Broad-scale social movements are about more than policy change. In recent decades, the major beneficiaries have been social movements organized around equality for women, environmental protection, and civil rights for racial and ethnic minorities. Although each of these social movements originated outside philanthropy, foundation dollars rather quickly led to their stabilization and professionalization. Support for social movements is largely a post-World War II phenomenon, stemming from the activism that characterized the 1960s. This type of funding has also been internationalized, as worldwide organizations have formed to advance environmental protection or women's rights or children's welfare. What foundations refer to as support for grass-roots organizations, or community groups, is often an element of social movement philanthropy.

Closely associated with such funding is an emphasis on social empowerment. This term refers to the direct empowerment of individuals, especially the traditionally powerless or disenfranchized social groups. An example is micro-credit lending, which is designed to put resources directly in the hands of the powerless poor. Social movement and social empowerment philanthropy are linked in that the former has the dual purpose of empowering its adherents and changing the social landscape. But direct empowerment need not be part of an effort to create a social movement. The beneficiaries of a micro-credit lending programme or a female education strategy are not viewed as members of a movement in the same way that feminists or ecological activists are. Social empowerment, of course, is a close cousin to charity – the direct relief of suffering – but distinct from it in that empowerment seeks to change the condition of the disenfranhised permanently and as such is a strategy of professional philanthropy.

3.2.6 *Social service delivery*

The philanthropic approach which most resembles charitable work is grant making focused on the direct delivery of social services, e.g. youth development, housing, healthcare, special education, legal aid, or employment training. What distinguishes service delivery philanthropy from direct charity is that the former, as a foundation project, is normally justified as testing out a model or promoting an innovative strategy that can then be adopted elsewhere. A large proportion of community foundation grant making falls into the service delivery category, as does grant making by smaller foundations. Social service philanthropy accounts for approximately 20% of grant activity in the US.

Conclusion

This discussion of foundation strategies offers an analysis of how a foundation might see its mission, rather than simply analysing it on the basis of subject-matter. Subject-matter analysis tells us something about the issues of importance to a given foundation, but very little about how the foundation will design programmes and grant making to confront those issues. Foundations which share a philanthropic vocation – that are engaged in policy advocacy or service delivery – have more in common, even if active in different sectors, than do foundations which share a sector but bring to it quite different theories of change.

3.3 Instruments of grant making

If a foundation's theory of change is its strategy, the kinds of grant-making instruments deployed are its tactics. These include, for instance, demonstration projects, training programmes, public commissions, endowment contributions, networking grantees, public education campaigns and institution building. Though the distinction between 'strategic choice' and 'instruments' lacks precision, it helps us see that one instrument can be used in different strategies. Training, for example, is an instrument favoured by foundations that otherwise differ widely in their strategies. Foundations award fellowships to advance scientific careers and thus new knowledge, to train leaders for policy advocacy work and social movements, and to offer in-career training opportunities to staff of social service organizations. The fact that the same instrument is used across subject-matters and strategies suggests the usefulness of treating it as a separate dimension of foundation practice. Certain instruments co-vary with particular strategies however – demonstration projects are usually associated with service delivery philanthropy; public education is often part of policy advocacy funding; commissions are used to study and report on social problems.

The foregoing suggests that every foundation could be described in a three-dimensional space:

- its subject-matter foci
- its notions about social change
- the instruments it tends to use.

A foundation so described could be studied over time, to see how it shifts along one dimension or more. Such analysis would also permit comparisons among foundations, and could even provide classification of foundation practice. Such an effort is beyond the scope of this essay. The account is not yet complete, however.

4 The mission as response to public pressure

Over the last quarter of a century the issue of public accountability has begun to alter how foundations define their priorities. There is now uneasiness over the traditional notion that a foundation is accountable only to its donor, its trustees, its self-defined mission. The fact that foundations are accountable to the broader public because they are chartered by the government and engage only in practices authorized by statute has not reduced this uneasiness. By some this is thought too limited a conception of public accountability and that there should be some measure of accountability to the groups and interests that foundations fund and promote.

The origins of this viewpoint can be traced to the 1960s, when notions of participatory democracy gained currency. Participatory democracy claims were most clearly voiced in student activism and the anti-war protests, but they echoed across the civil rights and feminist movements. The 1960s also saw the sharp decline of public confidence in the major institutions of American society – government, media, corporations, unions, even religion. Foundations were not immune to this public disenchantment with elite institutions. And one of the ways they tried to reposition themselves so as to secure public approval was to disavow their elite status. This they could best do by being more open, accessible, responsive. If this need for better communication with the public influenced foundation practice, the immediate stimulus to change was a long-drawn-out congressional investigation that spanned the 1960s.

Responding to real if scattered instances of financial abuses by foundations, as well as to grants that were judged too close to partisan politics, the US Congress held public hearings on the grant making and general practices of foundations. The hearings were to continue for eight years, under the strong leadership of Congressman Wright Patman, a populist democrat from Texas. The legislative result was the Tax Reform Act 1969. Its provisions were modest – constraints on self-dealing by foundation officers and trustees; no more than 20% of the portfolio could be invested in any single corporation; a number of disclosure requirements; a 6% annual payout requirement (subsequently reduced to 5%); and an excise tax on net investment income. More draconian measures were considered, but dropped, including a clause that would have required all foundations to expend their assets in 40 years, that is, to become time-limited organizations. Despite widespread foundation outcry at the time, and fears that private philanthropy was being destroyed, the Act as passed did not seriously threaten foundations. However, it was influential in ways unanticipated by both its promoters and detractors.

During the congressional hearings, there was near-panic among many foundation leaders, and a pervasive if exaggerated fear that foundations were endangered. Organizations dedicated to protecting foundations – the Council on Foundations, The Foundation Center and the National Council on Philanthropy – stirred themselves to action, most importantly in the appointment of a special Committee on the Foundation Field.

The line of defence adopted by the Committee was to insist that foundations were publicly misunderstood. The attack mounted in the Tax Reform Act could never have happened if the public had known of the vast number of good works that resulted from foundation grant making. The remedy was to become more public, even self-promotional. As usefully summarized by one scholar:

> [prior to 1960 private foundations] often operated discreetly, avoided public controversy, and had as their mission the pursuit of the private philanthropic interests and values of wealthy donors. [From the 1970s and beyond], foundations emerge as profoundly public institutions, open and accountable to all, that work hard to build better relations with grant applicants and the public.[19]

Responding in part to peer pressure, as voiced through the Council on Foundations, nearly all American foundations now routinely publish annual reports, newsletters, guideline brochures, and, of course, provide information through websites. Awards are given for the best annual reports, which now are glossy, expensive publications. Most major foundations have public information offices, and a few call press conferences to announce new grant-making criteria.

But there is more to the shift in foundation practice than is represented in public information efforts and public relations campaigns. The working vocabulary of many foundations is much more constituency-

---

[19] Frumkin, pp. 1-2.

sensitive than it was in the first half of the century. The terminology is suggestive, as foundations frequently insist that they are demand – rather than supply – driven. Grant making, it is often asserted, should be 'bottom up' rather than 'top down'. Being responsive to the 'grass-roots' is an endlessly repeated, although seldom defined, aim. Such vocabulary reflects the view that grantees have a wisdom and experience that should be taken into account as foundations set priorities and even define missions. This is an important shift in the self-definition of foundations. Citing the work of the Council on Foundations, one scholar writes that:

> the Council's principle concern following the Tax Reform Act 1969 was to open up foundations to the public and to instill in foundation workers the belief that foundations *were really public trusts* to be operated for public purposes.[20]

Insofar as foundations have accepted this formulation, they are moving away from the historical understanding of foundations as 'private money privately managed' for public purposes. The notion that a foundation is, or should be, more like a public trust is not embedded in law so much as in public expectation. It is an idea that entails a shift in the relationship with the grantees, that would share 'ownership' of the foundation with its intended beneficiaries. Worried that they will be charged with elitism or aloofness, foundations speak now of partnerships with grantees, of working side-by-side in the nonprofit sector. Of course the partnership is unequal, but this does not distract from the sincerity with which foundations lay claim to it. When the next congressional inquiry into foundation practice occurs, as is inevitable, foundations are determined to have grantees at their side. But if grantees are expected to be proponents, it is not surprising that they want their say in the priorities and practices of foundations. Carried to its logical conclusion this results in representatives from the grantee community serving as trustees, and this of course now occurs.

It would be seriously misleading to conclude that foundations now conduct their affairs as if they were public trusts. The mission of foundations has not been turned over to outside constituencies, nor is it likely to be. In fact some of the most visible foundation activity in recent years still resembles that of a century ago. A strong donor presence is clearly evident in the Soros Foundations, as it is in the Annenberg Foundation. And across the foundation world, independent trustees and professional officers, their rhetoric notwithstanding,

---

[20] Ibid., p. 9. (Italics added).

set programme directions and write guidelines. Consultation takes place, but except in rare instances final authority rests with those who control the money, and not with those seeking it.

Yet there has been a shift in the culture. The foundation mission is more negotiated than it was in the first half of the century. It is certainly more public. This has probably improved the reputation of foundations with the general public. Although most Americans (61%) would like foundation trustees to be more accountable, they nevertheless overwhelmingly (95%) believe that foundations play an important role in bettering society. And citizens are not concerned that foundations have too much influence on social policy (fewer than one in ten express this concern). Nor does the public want the government to increase its regulation of the private foundation (only 7% express this view).[21]

The important question is whether the greater openness and the resulting improvement in public reputation since the Tax Reform Act 1969 has led to more effective grant making and through that to greater social achievement. Scholars have yet to take up the task of assessing the social achievement of foundations in terms that would permit comparison of styles and strategies that worked in the 1920s with those that are demanded in the new millennium.

5 Conclusion

The mission of a foundation cannot easily be traced to a single source. It is private in the way it honours the charitable preferences of its donor; it is public in the way it prudently anticipates the interests of the state and, more than this, in how it responds to signals from the larger society. Nor is the foundation mission a fixed and unchanging point of reference. For any given foundation and even more clearly for the foundation sector as a whole, what is considered an appropriate mission will shift as opportunities and constraints change. It is often said that foundations have neither shareholders nor voters, and thus are unusually free to set their mission and pursue their goals as they see fit. There is truth in this saying, but it is not the whole truth. Foundations are social institutions, well aware that the tax-free funds they dispense are theirs only as long as the public, and its instrument, the state, tolerate the arrangements which permit them to exist in the first place. Their missions are crafted accordingly.

---

[21] The Chronicle of Philanthropy, Vol. 14, May 1, 1997, p. 14.

Bibliography

Alfred P. Sloan Foundation, *Annual Report 1995*, New York, 1996.

Arnove, R., ed., *Philanthropy and Cultural Imperialism: The Foundations at Home and Abroad*, Boston, G. K. Hall & Co., 1980.

Berman, E., *The Influence of the Carnegie, Ford, and Rockefeller Foundations on American Foreign Policy: The Ideology of Philanthropy*, Albany, State University of New York Press, 1983.

Carnegie, A., 'Wealth', in: *North American Review*, CXLVIII, June, 1889, pp. 653–64, and CXLIX, December, 1889, pp. 682–98.

Carnegie, A., *The Gospel of Wealth and Other Timely Essays*, New York, Century Company, 1900. Reprinted in Dwight F. Burlingame (ed.), *The Responsibilities of Wealth*, Bloomington, Indiana University Press, 1992.

The Chronicle of Philanthropy, Vol. IX, No. 14. May 1, 1997.

Congressional Record, Vol. 99, No. 141, July 27, 1953.

Coon, H., *Money To Burn: What the Great American Foundations Do With Their Money*, New York, Longmans, Green & Co., 1938.

Cuninggim, M., *Private Money and Public Service: The Role of Foundations in American Society*, New York, McGraw-Hill Book Company, 1972.

Fosdick, R., *The Story of the Rockefeller Foundation: Nineteen Thirteen to Nineteen Fifty*, New York, Harper and Brothers, 1952.

Foundation Giving, Yearbook of Facts and Figures on Private, Corporate and Community Foundations 1996 Edition, New York, The Foundation Center, 1995.

Frunkin, P., 'Private Foundations as Public Institutions: Regulation, Professionalization, and the Redefinition of Organized Philanthropy'. Conference paper presented at 'Philanthropic Foundations in History: Needs and Opportunity for Study', New York University, 1996. To be published in a collection edited by Ellen Lagemann.

Harrisson, S. and Andrews, F. E., *American Foundations for Social Welfare*, New York, Russell Sage Foundation, 1946.

Keppel, F., *The Foundation: Its Place in American Life*, New York, Macmillan Company, 1930.

MacDonald, D., *The Ford Foundation: The Men and the Millions*, New York, Reynal & Co., 1956.

Mohn, R., 'Objectives of an Operating Foundation', in: *The Work of Operating Foundations: Strategies-Instruments-Perspectives*, Gütersloh, Bertelsmann Foundation Publishers, 1997.

Prewitt, K., 'Social Sciences and Private Philanthropy: The Quest for Social Relevance', Indiana University Center on Philanthropy, *Essays on Philanthropy*, No. 15, 1995.

Sealander, J., *Private Wealth & Public Life: Foundation Philanthropy and the Reshaping of American Social Policy from the Progressive Era to the New Deal*, Baltimore, John Hopkins Press, 1997.

US Congress, Senate. (Walsh) Commission on Industrial Relations, *Final Report and Testimony*, 64th Congress, 1st Session, Senate Document No. 415, Vol. 1, Government Printing Office, Washington, 1916.

Weber, M., *The Protestant Ethic and the Spirit of Capitalism*, Translation by T. Icott Parsons, Los Angeles, Roxbury, 1996.

▼ Joel L. Fleishman

Public Policy and Philanthropic Purpose – Foundation Ownership and Control of Corporations in Germany and the United States

1 Introduction

Germany and the US have a great deal in common with regard to their respective laws governing charities, charitable contributions and foundations.[1] There is, however, one area of law relating to charities in

---

[1] I am grateful to many for their help with this chapter in one way or another. Among those to whom I am most indebted are my long-time friends and sometime colleagues Professor Harvey Dale, Professor John Simon, Professor Boris Bittker, Elizabeth Boris, Professor Charles Clotfelter and Thomas Troyer, from all of whom I have learned a great deal over the years. In addition, I wish to express special thanks to Rupert Graf Strachwitz for his most helpful comments on aspects of German law and practice regarding foundations, as well as to Dr Carl-Heinz Heuer and Dr Volkmar Loewer. Let me acknowledge also the superb research and editing assistance given me by my research assistant David James. Needless to say, any errors which may be found herein are solely mine.

which the practices of the two countries are dramatically different – regulation of the ownership or control of operating businesses by charitable foundations.

In Germany, public policy has evolved to facilitate the establishment of foundations as a legitimate means of maintaining continuity of ownership and management of business corporations.[2] Under German law, a foundation may own as much as 100% of the voting or non-voting stock of a corporation. In the US, the tax code has since 1969 permitted a private foundation to own only a small percentage of an unrelated business enterprise and has required divestiture of any 'excess business holdings' within a statutorily prescribed time.[3]

The differences between these two sets of public policies dealing with the same subject matter are so striking that one cannot help but wonder how they have come to exist and what consequences they have on the establishment and enlargement of foundations, as well as on the performance of both the foundations which own the corporations and the corporations which are owned by the foundations. The aim of this chapter is to explore the differences, with the hope that scholars, public policy-makers, donors, corporation directors and foundation trustees in both Germany and the US may learn something of usefulness from the laws and regulatory schemes of one another's country.

In the US, there is direct and indirect evidence to suggest that, had the Congress not so sharply limited the ability of foundations to own a controlling interest in corporations, as well as intermittently circumscribed the tax deductibility to donors of gifts of appreciated securities to private foundations, many more large foundations would have been created or enlarged over the last 30 years than has been the case.[4] Although most of the reasons given for the prohibition of excess business holdings do not seem compelling (since many

---

[2] Wössner, pp. 42–7.

[3] Internal Revenue Code Section 4943. See BALLAN for an authoritative exposition of relevant US tax code provisions and subsequent Internal Revenue Service and Tax Court decisions.

[4] Over the past decade, Congress has enacted temporary provisions permitting full fair market value deduction for gifts of appreciated stock by individuals to private foundations. In 1999, such deductibility by individuals for gifts of what the Internal Revenue Code calls 'qualified appreciated stock' was enacted as a continuing provision of the Code, no longer requiring periodic re-enactment. It is important to understand, however, that such deductibility is available only for gifts of stock for which market quotations are readily available on an established securities market. Gifts of closely-held, non-publicly-traded appreciated stock are not eligible even now for tax deductibility in any amount higher than their cost to the donor. See IRC Section 170(e)(5)(B)(I).

of the harms that that section is intended to prevent are effectively discouraged by other sections of the Internal Revenue Code), there are legitimate concerns about both the risks of over-concentration of foundation assets in the securities of a single holding, and the need to put in place governance structures for foundation-owning corporations that minimize the likelihood of abuses.

In Germany, there do seem to be very good reasons to guard against *de facto* corporate control of foundations which in turn own the corporation's shares. It is also important to ensure that corporations which are owned by foundations be required to pay to their foundation owners a return on investment that is reasonably commensurate with the return expected by other shareholders, as well as sufficiently adequate to serve the public interest purposes that made possible the tax-favoured creation of such an arrangement in the first place.[5] The latter might, for example, require a foundation to pay out annually for public purposes some minimum percentage of the fair market value of its assets, rather than merely the income, or some percentage of the income, it receives in the form of dividends, as the present law provides. Before dealing with these issues in depth, however, some background on the nonprofit policy framework and tax policies of the two countries would be useful.

---

[5] It is essential that readers understand some of the major differences between the underlying purposes of German law facilitating foundation-creation and -regulation, and those in the US. In the US, the aim of the laws is to encourage the devotion to public interest purposes in the here and now of as much foundation income as is financially prudent with regard to the long-run viability of the foundation, the aim in Germany is quite different. As observed by Dr Volker Then, Director Foundations and Philanthropy of the Bertelsmann Foundation, in the Summer 1999 issue of *Social Economy and Law*, published by the European Foundation Center, 'The prime interest of foundation law as it was codified in late 19th century was to guarantee the founder's intentions and will for eternity'. In a letter to this author of 5 October 1999, Dr Then elaborated the implications of this difference, as follows: 'From all these fundamentals of German foundation law you can gather that the German system is not primarily concerned with any dynamics of the contributions to the public good but rather with its strategic function on behalf of the original donor. Introducing any alterations to the system which would stipulate payout-requirements and anything like excess business holding rules would require more fundamental changes than just introducing respective clauses [...] [B]eyond reforming the legal situation of payout, reserves, and growth of a foundation, a change in the system would require major systematic changes in civil law regarding the establishment of the foundation and role which the state plays in this process'.

2 The nonprofit public policy framework

In Waldemar Nielsen's book *Inside American Philanthropy: The Dramas of Donorship*[6] the second chapter is entitled 'In the Beginning Is the Donor',[7] and therein lies the basic truth – and glory – of large foundation philanthropy. Often, it is the donor's motivation that brings the foundation into being in the first place, it is the achievement of the donor's objectives which dictate the framework of the foundation, and it is the donor's values that constitute its soul of the foundation and that impart particular substantive content to its agenda and priorities. In some foundations, the donor's personality, vision, hopes and goals are so vividly stamped on the philanthropy he or she created that successive generations of foundation decision-makers have a clear reference to guide them in adapting policy and programme to the changing needs of the times. Yet the worldwide record of foundation creation is full of examples to illustrate that donor motivations are usually complex, multifaceted and frequently in conflict with one another, or even hasty, sloppy, haphazard and ill-conceived; that foundation governance structures are not always designed well enough to achieve donor objectives; and that donor values are rarely spelled out with sufficient precision to serve effectively as guides to trustees and directors.

One thing is clear: 'governance' implies a governor – an individual, a board, or a collection of boards in some relationship embodying the checking and balancing of one another. While 'governance' provides a structure of governing, it cannot alone supply the substantive values necessary to determine the foundation agenda. The governors, of course, can use their own values in creating the foundation agenda, and frequently do so whether or not the donor has specified the values he or she wishes to control the foundation, but where the donor – individual, family, or corporation – has specified values, goals and programme objectives for the foundation, 'governance' implies some degree of fidelity to those guides and procedures. Where the donor has made clear his or her intentions and hopes, the trustees of many foundations do seem to strive to be faithful to them, even if often adapting those intentions to the changing needs of the times.

In addition to the values and objectives specified by the donor, foundation governance must operate within the context of constraints created by law and public policy. Laws and public policies governing

---

[6] Nielsen.

[7] Nielsen, pp.10–19.

foundations vary of course from country to country, but they deal, unsurprisingly, with many of the same issues.

1 Laws specify the purposes which a foundation may – indeed must – serve, such as educational, social, scientific, cultural, or artistic ends, among others, frequently prohibiting certain kinds of activity, such as partisan political actions.
2 Laws specify the forms in which foundations can be embodied as legal entities – independent legal associations – corporations in the US – and trusts, among others, and the forms of governance which they may employ. Laws also frequently regulate the relationships among foundation governing boards, any corporations which are closely related to the family of the donor or the stock of which is a major holding of the foundation, and the families or personal holdings of the donor.
3 Laws usually specify the ways in which foundations must operate procedurally in order to maintain their privileged tax status, such as with respect to financial dealings between foundation directors and officers and the foundation itself, or between the foundation and any related corporations. Frequently, laws specify the required foundation annual pay-out in grants and limit the amount of administrative expenses.
4 Laws frequently specify the tax and other consequences of particular actions by the foundation's donor in relation to the foundation, whether at its creation or subsequently.

In some countries, especially in the US, private foundations are subject to a set of regulations and a level of supervision that are much more stringent than those governing any other form of nonprofit organization. It is not at all clear why they are so singled out. What is said to justify such restrictive laws regulating foundations? Usually it is argued that a foundation, being perpetual in existence and not answerable directly to any constituency with any power to hold it accountable other than its own self-perpetuating board of trustees or directors, warrants close scrutiny by the public whose law and public policy enabled it to be created in the first place. Lack of effective accountability may well accurately describe foundations, but it also describes most other nonprofit organizations, which are not subject to such stringent supervision in the US. It is argued that foundations are allowed to accumulate their earnings free of any tax, but that, too, is true of other organizations in the US nonprofit universe. Perhaps the concern is that foundations, unlike other nonprofits, have no ongoing operational activities that demand specified annual outlays, unless required by law. The lack of such continuing claims on revenue, in theory, would permit them to accumulate tax-free earnings perpetually. That is one of the reasons given for the annual mininum percentage of assets pay-out requirement which was imposed on US foundations in 1969.

A final point of concern arises from the deferral of benefits to the public from the gifts establishing the foundation. The argument is that assets given to foundations, encouraged by tax benefits to donors, are usually intended to be invested, and some portion of the annual return on those invested assets will be paid out in the present. It is therefore only a portion of the total return on such investments that will reach the public beneficiaries in the near future, even if such benefits are to continue forever. But that is true of all endowments of any kind – universities, schools, hospitals, museums, and the like – and tax benefits to US donors do not discriminate between gifts for endowment and gifts for operating costs.

It seems that these points of concern add up to the proposition that US foundations are required to accept stringent legal and policy constraints on the ways they operate in order to compensate for:

- their substantial freedom from meaningful accountability
- their primary mission of distributing with substantially unlimited discretion some amount of money to others who generally have no claim on it[8]
- the incommensurableness between the size of the tax-favoured gifts which created them and the social benefits they confer on the contemporary generation.

All these distinctions between foundations and other nonprofit organizations are differences of degree rather than kind. The only one that seems to me persuasive in justifying more stringent scrutiny of foundations in exchange for the tax benefits is the essentially unfettered discretion possessed by foundations to decide what and what not to do, unconstrained by either ongoing operations or recipient claims.

---

[8] It is important to underscore that foundation pay-out requirements, absent quantitative minimum pay-out requirements under law, could vary widely. In Germany, a foundation is required to pay out only a minimum specified proportion of the dividends actually received – usually two-thirds with no more than one-third retained as reserves, without any relationship to the value of the assets it owns. In the US, however, the minimum pay-out is based on a percentage of the assets, in part because US foundations invest for total return under prevailing diversified asset investment policies, and do not seek to maximize dividend and interest income. Foundations rarely receive sufficient dividend income to satisfy the pay-out requirement, and therefore instead sell assets to meet the requirement.

The tax benefits are considerable. It is primarily those tax benefits which enable foundations registered as charities to exist in perpetuity, and to accumulate large asset bases: they can grow steadily larger without ever being subject to taxes on their increase.[9] The tax benefits vary from country to country, but they are similar in nature even if not in extent. Foundations are usually exempt from property taxes on their assets, and they generally do not pay income tax on their annual income.[10] Perhaps even more important than the taxes from which the foundation itself is exempt are the tax preferences given to individuals as an incentive to them to create and endow a foundation in the first place or to augment a foundation's assets. The primary tax benefit is exemption from estate and gift taxes for bequests and gifts to foundations, as well as, in some countries, a deduction from income tax for gifts to foundations. It is these benefits that encourage controlling stockholding individuals and families to give large blocks of stock to foundations, thereby avoiding any tax on the appreciated value of the stock and any tax that would have been required had the stock remained in the donor's estate.[11] Indeed, it is the avoidance of estate and gift tax which has frequently been cited by donors themselves as one of their main motivations to establish, endow and enlarge foundations. By creating a foundation with stock in a publicly-held corporation, a donor can preclude the likelihood of the corporation's being sold at his or her death in order to pay taxes. At the same time, the donor's family or those who control the corporation can retain the power to deploy the wealth represented by the stock by governing the foundation to which the stock has been given.[12] In addition, in Germany, foundations so created are permitted to pay up to one-third of their income to members of the donor's family through the second generation after the donor.[13] Such income paid by foundations to family members is, of course, subject to normal income taxes paid by those who receive it.

---

[9] In Germany, foundations must be registered as charities in order to be relieved of taxation. Foundations not so registered are subject to taxation.

[10] While it is generally not regarded as an income tax, the 1%–2% excise tax now required under US law is essentially that.

[11] Since the latest reform act of June 2000, any gifts can be made free of taxation in Germany as well (before, donors were taxed on appreciation against book value when making the gift).

[12] The limitation to 'stock in a publicly-held corporation' applies specifically to the US. Such a restriction seems to be rare elsewhere.

[13] That is not to say that donors in the US or elsewhere cannot achieve the same objective; they certainly can do so by using a different form of a gift. For example, in the US

Aside from tax benefit considerations, there are other public policy rationales that are used to justify the constraints under which foundations operate. Those rationales grow out of the nature of foundations as essentially unaccountable institutions. Foundation trustees and directors do not have voters, as political officials do, to turn them out of office. They do not have stockholders, as for-profit corporations do, to look over their shoulders and question their decisions. They do not have members, as many nonprofit organizations do, who can provide a check on the power of the directors. Moreover, the press, which provides effective scrutiny of organizations forced to operate in the public view, is not especially effective in disciplining foundations because they rarely operate in full public view, conducting most of their business and making most of their decisions in private. In essence, foundation directors are not accountable to anyone else for their decisions, and that fact seems to many to warrant some restrictions on their power, as well as close monitoring by government authorities.[14] Indeed some countries, such as France, routinely insist on public representation on foundation boards, from the national and local levels, so as to get a foot in the door. Whether that is an effective method of public accountability remains to be seen. All too often, one would surmise, the public representatives can easily be coopted by the donor's family foundation directors, and end up being part of the problem rather than a means of solving it.

Most civil law countries impose a fairly rigorous pre-screening and certification process on nonprofit organizations before awarding tax-exempt status, but, after certification, give the nonprofit directors a fairly free hand. Most common law countries, reflecting a strong

---

it is a frequent practice for individuals to make gifts to charities while reserving a life interest in the income for themselves, or an interest in the income or some specified yield for designated others, such as surviving spouses or children for some period of time, after which the charities enjoy the full income. Reversionary interests can also be given during life or bequeathed at death to foundations in the US. What is unusual about the German provision is that the foundations themselves, after they have been established and endowed, are permitted to pay out of their income some amount to the donor or his successors, if so provided for expressly in the legal instruments creating the foundation. The US law differs, too, in that that part of a charitable remainder trust that generates payments to family members or other non-charitable recipients is non-deductible as a charitable gift. In Germany, the entire gift is excludable from taxation even if part of it will benefit the family of the donor.

[14] Of course, both in Germany and the US, the taxing authorities have the potential to hold foundation directors accountable, but the supervision is so light that, in effect, there is little real accountability. If violations are discovered, however, the penalties in both Germany and in the US are severe. Whether one would want to rely on the taxing authorities as principal accountability enforcer is a different matter. Self-regulation by the nonprofit sector itself, augmented by nongovernmental watchdog organizations, would be much more desirable.

commitment to freedom of association, tend to stand back at the point of creation of nonprofits, but bind the directors' hands during the post-creation regulatory regime.[15]

3 Tax benefits for charitable gifts in Germany and the US

Both Germany and the US generally encourage the creation of non-profit organizations designed to serve the public good, and provide generous tax incentives for contributions to such organizations. The details of such tax incentives vary between the two countries. In both countries, gifts to charities are exempt from inheritance and gift taxes, and real property owned by charities, if used for the primary purposes for which the charity was created, is exempt from property taxes.[16] In both countries, the income of charities is exempt from taxes which other, non-charitable, organizations are required to pay. The tax deductions for contributions to charities available to individuals are still more generous in the US than in Germany, at least for very large donations.

- Germany
  Tax deductions are available to individuals for up to 5% of one's income for gifts to general charitable or religious purposes, or 10% of one's income for scientific, cultural, and specific charitable purposes, with one year carry-backward and five year carry-forward provisions for amounts greater than DM50,000.[17] The reform act of June 2000 has added an additional tax allowance of DM40,000 per year (in addition to the 5 to 10% of taxable income allowance) as well as an additional deductible allowance of DM600,000 for initial donations upon the creation of a foundation.

---

[15] I am indebted to Stefan Toepler of Johns Hopkins University for this insight. See Toepler, *Myths and Misconceptions*, p.19.

[16] In Germany, any gift to a charitable foundation during life or at death is exempt from gift and estate taxes. Indeed, according to Section 29 of the German Estate Tax Law, any estate tax which had been levied on heirs will be cancelled, will full retroactive effect if, within 24 months of the passing of the estate, the heirs choose to donate all or part of the estate to a charitable foundation. The same objective can be accomplished in the US, in effect, by the heirs if they donate their inheritance to a charitable foundation, and then take a deduction for its value from their inheritance tax base. See IRC Section 2055. Moreover, as of 1 January 1997, there are no longer property taxes in Germany.

[17] Corporate donors do not enjoy the carry-backward but do have a six year carry-forward.

- **United States**

  Tax deductions are available for up to 50% of one's income for gifts to organizations classified as public charities if the gift is not in appreciated property, or up to 30% of income if the gift is in appreciated property; up to 30% of income for gifts of non-appreciated property to a private foundation, or 20% if appreciated property is given. Contributions in excess of 50% to public charities may be carried forward and deducted, subject to the same 50% limit, over five years; contributions to private foundations in excess of 30% of income may similarly be carried forward five years.[18]

Both countries define the public good in much the same expansive way so long as the public good served is within the national borders. Both countries withhold tax deductions for charitable gifts by individuals to organizations outside their boundaries unless an affiliated organization is created and registered within their boundaries.[19] Such 'friends of' organizations, as they have come to be called in the US, are not necessary in order for private foundations to make grants to organizations outside the US because these foundations do not need to claim charitable deductions for their gifts; domestic deductibility is the primary reason for having 'friends of' organizations, affording German and US individual and corporate donors a comparatively simple way of making tax deductible gifts to qualified organizations outside their borders.[20]

4 Foundation-controlled corporations in Germany

Foundation ownership of corporations is considered unexceptional throughout northern Europe; in fact, some of Europe's most successful companies have long been associated with foundation control. In Sweden, foundations own a controlling interest in rubber-products manufacturer Trelleborg and in furniture-maker Ikea; in Denmark,

---

[18] IRC §§170(b)-(e). In Germany, there is no difference between individual and corporate tax-payers in this regard. Both can deduct only those donations given to a German-based, nationally-approved charity. The 'friends of' model is occasionally used to overcome this difficulty.

[19] In Germany, nonprofit organizations may distribute funds outside Germany provided this power is expressly included in their organizing instruments. The German Internal Revenue Service is particularly strict in approving provisions of this kind when granting charitable status.

[20] Dale, *Foreign Charities*.

the Carlsberg brewery and pharmaceutical company Novo Nordisk are both controlled by foundations. In Holland, packaging manufacturer Royal Packaging Industries van Leer was owned, until 1999, by the van Leer Group Foundation with an entity governed by three totally separate, self-perpetuating boards composed of the same people. That arrangement changed in 1999.[21] In Holland, Jan and Paul Baan, the founders of Baan Software, established the Oikonomos Foundation, which, with about 43% of outstanding shares, effectively has a controlling interest in Baan Software.[22] In Italy, the decade of the 1990s saw an explosion of bank-owning foundations as a result of a the enactment of Law 218, called the Amato law, which enabled semi-public-sector banks to transform themselves into either joint stock companies or companies with affiliated grant-making foundations. As a result, there are now about 80 foundations in Italy which effectively control affiliated banking institutions.[23] In Britain, foundation-controlled corporations have included the Wellcome Trust, Britain's largest grant-making foundation and, until recently, the world's wealthiest foundation in terms of assets, which formerly owned a controlling interest in the Burroughs Wellcome Company, now part of Glaxo Wellcome; the Baring Foundation, which owned the non-voting stock in the ill-fated Barings Bank; and the Nuffield Foundation which formerly owned a controlling interest in British Leyland.[24]

The prominence of foundation control in Germany is especially notable. The dramatic growth of foundations in Germany in the years between 1983 and 1991, when about 30% of today's existing

---

[21] In 1996, in order to expand the capital base of the RPIvL, it was permitted by the foundation to sell additional shares in the equity markets, and became a company listed on the Amsterdam Stock Exchange (see Bernhard van Leer Foundations, p.8). In August 1999, the Bernard van Leer Foundation agreed to sell all of its Royal Packaging Industries Van Leer NV stock to facilitate a merger between RPIvL and the Finnish packaging company Huhtamaki, in which entity, Huhtamaki Van Leer, the Foundation took a 14.6% interest. In a special shareholders agreement with the Finnish Cultural Foundation, a major owner of Huhtamaki, the Van Leer Group Foundation received the same financial and voting rights as FCF, along with the right to appoint two representatives on the Board of the new corporation. See Bernard van Leer Foundation letter to the public of September 1, 1999.

[22] Hutheesing, p.113.

[23] At some point the foundations are required to reduce their voting interest on such banks to less than 50%. For a thorough description of the Italian foundation picture, see Prof. Gian Paolo Barbetta's *Foundations in Italy*, published by the Universita Cattolica del Sacro Cuore and the Instituto per la Ricera Sociale, in Milan, November 1996. I am indebted to Rupert Graf Strachwitz and Dr Volker Then for leading me to this information.

[24] Dale, *US Law Affecting Foundations*, p.65; Thomsen, p.212.

German foundations were established,[25] suggests at least some public policy encouragement of foundation creation.[26] Many of those foundations – certainly some of the largest in assets – were created by successful business entrepreneurs and endowed with controlling stockholdings in the corporations they built, although the structures of foundation governance they adopted tend in some instances to obscure the fact of control, even if not the effectiveness with which it is exercised.

In earlier periods, the birth rate of German foundations was much slower.[27] From 1949 to 1960, new foundation establishment in Germany hovered around 20 per year; from 1960 to 1977 it increased to between 20 and 40 per year, and from 1978 to 1981 to between 40 and 60 per year. In 1988 alone, however, 140 new foundations were established, and, since 1992, it is estimated that about 200 foundations have been created every year. In the years since 1951, therefore, some 4200 – about one-half – of Germany's 8000 foundations came into existence.[28] This surge in the creation of foundations in Germany coincided with the 1980s' and 1990s' robustness in business enterprise in both Germany and the US, which has created a great deal of new wealth in both countries and thereby provided the assets with which to create new foundations. In addition, the 1980s and 1990s constitute the period in which the post-war generation of Germans began retiring from their money-making careers and started, in large numbers, to plan for the distribution of their wealth.

In the US, the new foundations created by corporate entrepreneurs since 1969 have had to be substantially divorced from the companies the entrepreneurs controlled, but, in Germany, the foundations have sometimes served explicitly as the means of ensuring the continuation and preservation of corporate control by owners, their descendants, and corporate managers.[29] At the present time, around 200 of the largest corporations in Germany are thought to be related by significant ownership interests to foundations.[30] Among them are such well-known names as the *Carl Zeiss Stiftung*, established in 1889 and the oldest of such foundations (though not a nonprofit foundation), the *Bertelsmann Stiftung*, *Robert Bosch Stiftung*, *Gemeinnützige*

---

[25] Anheier, p.19. See also Maecenata.

[26] Toepler, *Myths and Misconceptions*, p.9, citing Karpen.

[27] Toepler, *Distant Relatives*, p.113.

[28] Maecenata.

[29] Mohn, Wössner.

[30] Geinitz.

Hertie-Stiftung, *Alfred Krupp von Bohlen und Halbach Stiftung*, and *Körber Stiftung*, all of which were, as of 1996, among the top ten German foundations in asset size.[31] It is important to emphasize that the assets of foundations represented by interests in closely-related operating businesses are not usually reported at present fair-market value but at an arbitrarily chosen amount at some point on the scale between book value and true market value. If market valuations were used instead, all of the above-mentioned foundations would report assets at much higher levels. When Reinhard Mohn transferred his stock to the Bertelsmann Foundation, it was widely estimated to be worth DM10 billion, but the book value is only DM1.2 billion.[32] It should be noted that the Volkswagen Foundation, also one of the ten largest in Germany, is totally divorced from the Volkswagen Corporation, and does not own a significant stock interest in the Volkswagen Corporation.[33]

The governance structures of German foundation/corporation relationships vary widely. Rupert Graf Strachwitz puts the situation as follows:

> There are no standardized rules of governance for German foundations, except that they have to be adequately managed, so practices vary quite considerably. More often than not, foundations adapt to standard corporate procedures, i.e. a board of directors with responsibility for management and legal representation, and a supervisory board with responsibility for appointing the board of directors, approving accounts, etc.

The number and kinds of boards, and their appellations, are totally within the discretion of the foundation-establishing donors. Some arrangements feature only two boards – one for the foundation and one for the corporation. Others have three or more boards – one for the foundation, one for the corporation, and one, sometimes called a curatorium, which serves as the formal legal representative of the foundation to the state.

---

[31] Anheier, table 3. The *Hertie-Stiftung* sold its 90% interest in Hertie in 1996.

[32] The DM10 billion estimate was publicly acknowledged by Bertelsmann CEO Mark Wössner in 1996. It should be noted that, in Germany, there are as yet no standardized accounting procedures for foundations; the comparison of asset valuations is consequently unreliable.

[33] In the US, company-affiliated foundations – not the kind of affiliations referred to above with regard to German corporate-foundation affiliates – generally do not own stock in the companies with which they are affiliated, and most have no endowment, receiving annual gifts from their companies. The Ford Foundation is now totally unrelated to the Ford Motor Company. See section 5.1 below for other US examples.

Gifts of stock to foundations are exempt from inheritance and gift taxes whether the stock given is voting or non-voting, and whether it constitutes a controlling interest or not.[34] A frequent practice in Germany (though not, however, a legal requirement) is to separate stock ownership from the right to vote in matters subject to stockholder vote.[35] The foundations governed in that fashion usually hold the non-voting stock, while the voting shares are held by a separate entity with a separate board, which usually includes persons who also hold positions on the corporate and foundation boards. The reason usually given for such tripartite governance structures is to build what appears to be a wall between corporation and foundation, because nonprofit corporations become subject to taxation if they exercise what is regarded as 'considerable influence' on the executive board of a corporation.[36] That is why, according to a newspaper article,[37] some large nonprofit foundations do not accept voting rights in the corporation. As Carl-Heinz Heuer puts it in a letter to the author:

> any entrepreneurial influence in excess of a mere shareholding is occasionally considered by the tax authorities to be a commercial operation, [which] leads to a delimitation between the tax-exempt asset management and the commercial operation of a not-for-profit corporate body.[38]

To take an extreme, perhaps singular, example, the *Robert Bosch Industrietreuhand KG*, which owns only 0.01% of the stock in Robert Bosch GmbH, also controls all the voting rights for all the shares held by the Robert Bosch Foundation, which amounts to 92% of the outstanding shares of Robert Bosch GmbH. The Bosch Foundation, despite its name, is not in fact a *Stiftung* or 'foundation' in form but a nonprofit GmbH, or corporation.[39] It has a board of

---

[34] As we will see below, it is only voting stock which causes the problem in the US.

[35] The donor can achieve that separation, for example, either by donating non-voting stock to the foundation or by giving to a separate entity a proxy to vote the shares of voting stock given to the foundation.

[36] US Internal Revenue Code Section 4943 seems to have been targeted at preventing donors from using the foundation form to help them exercise control over their corporations, while the German 'considerable influence' rule seems aimed at preventing the foundation staff from influencing the corporation. In the view of this author, the German provision is aimed at the wrong problem. Much more serious than foundation attempts to influence the management of the related corporation is the great danger that the corporation may seek to influence, if not control, the foundation. We will return to that subject below.

[37] Geinitz.

[38] See letter quoted under footnote 40.

[39] It is not clear to this author whether this arrangement uses a proxy mechanism or non-voting stock.

directors and an advisory board. It regards its board of directors as primarily responsible for keeping the donor's intentions alive.[40] Bertelsmann, which is a nonprofit foundation in form, offers yet another example. As Reinhard Mohn, the donor of the Bertelsmann Foundation, said:

> For managerial reasons, the voting rights were not transferred, as the premises for corporate management differ from those necessary in the establishment and management of a foundation.[41]

The stock Reinhard Mohn has already transferred is non-voting stock – approximately 71.1% of shares outstanding. In addition, as of 1 July 1999, the voting rights on these shares as well as the remaining outstanding voting stock of the Mohn family – 92.5% of all voting rights – have been transferred to a GmbH with six members, one of whom is to be a representative of his family's ownership interests in the corporation, another a representative of Bertelsmann Corporation's workers, and the others the chairman and vice chairman, and past chairman and past vice chairman of the Corporation. The Carl Zeiss Foundation is the sole owner of the Foundation Corporation Carl Zeiss (Oberkochen) and *Schott Glasswerke* (Mainz), neither of which has other stockholders or partners. It is because the Carl Zeiss Foundation is not legally separated from the corporation that it does not have charitable status.[42] The Hertie

---

[40] Bosch is a singular case. As the Bosch entities are incorporated as a charitable GmbH and as a *Stiftung*, respectively, they are subject to the binding governance regulations of a GmbH, requiring both a board of directors and a supervisory board composed of the legal owners. The latter are private individuals who are owners in name only, since the charitable status prevents them from exercising the rights of ordinary ownership. This matter is elaborated well in a letter to this author from Carl-Heinz Heuer as follows:

'The Robert Bosch Foundation is, in effect, not at all a foundation but a nonprofit GmbH. Unlike a foundation, which could be regarded as an independent estate, the nonprofit GmbH has an ownership, namely the shareholders in the nonprofit GmbH. Why we are nonetheless able to refer to the Robert Bosch Foundation as a foundation can be attributed to a rather incomprehensible decision of the Higher Regional Court at Stuttgart which is in stark contrast to the principle of truthfulness of a company's name otherwise adhered to in Germany. The reason for selecting the organization form of a nonprofit GmbH was as follows: In Germany, foundations are subject to government control and Robert Bosch in his capacity as a liberal Swabian entrepreneur was adverse to such control. Moreover, the nonprofit GmbH also enables the family to exert its influence on events for the simple fact that there are shareholders. In the case of a foundation, all this would be impossible. The fact that Bosch is referred to as having a board of directors instead of a board of trustees (curatorium) is of minor significance in this connection: A foundation may very well also have a board of directors; in Germany, this is a matter of discretion with the choice of term completely irrelevant.'

[41] Mohn, p.25.

[42] Bertelsmann Foundation, p.95.

Foundation owns 29.4% of Karstadt AG, making it the largest single stockholder, as well as other investments. The Charitable Hertie Foundation has a sister non-charitable foundation, mainly invested in real-estate, that used to exercise the voting rights when Hertie Corporation was still owned by the Foundation. The Körber Foundation owns all the shares of Körber AG. The Alfred Krupp von Bohlen und Halbach Foundation owns 50.02% of the stock of Friedrich Krupp AG Hoesch-Krupp. The Else Kroner Fresenius Foundation owns a majority of the shares in Fresenius AG.

One is tempted to wonder, given the frequency of substantial overlapping membership among the foundation and related corporation boards whatever their number, whether such formal distinguishing among separate legal entities might in fact be distinctions without differences so far as actual control is concerned? Who is controlling whom – the foundation the corporation or the corporation the foundation? This issue is discussed below.

5 Foundation-controlled corporations in the US

As I have noted, US public policy affecting such matters is substantially different to that in Germany although, as we shall see shortly, it has only become so within the past 30 years. Today, in general, private foundations are permitted to own no more than 20% of any corporation's voting stock, and, for purposes of calculating the permissible 20%, any voting stockholdings in the same company retained by the donor to the foundation, or by his or her family, must be included.[43] In effect, the 20% limit on foundation stock ownership gets reduced by the shareholding of family members, what the Internal Revenue Code calls 'disqualified persons'. Altogether, the total may not exceed 20%. If the foundation owns no more than 2% of the voting stock, it is not subject to the restrictions of Section 4943(c)(2)(A), no matter how large the stockholding, whether voting or non-voting, by the donor or his family members may be.

It is important to note that these restrictions affect only private foundations, and that other nonprofit organizations, such as educational and medical research institutions, are not barred from owning controlling interests in corporations. We will return to this matter below. For the

---

[43] IRC Section 4946 describes persons whose shareholdings – mainly the donor and his family – must be lumped together with those of the foundation as 'disqualified persons'.

moment it is enough to point out here that, for example, educational and medical research institutions are permitted to own interests of any size in corporations, including entire businesses. Such businesses, of course, pay income and other taxes just as do all other for-profit corporations. For example, the Poynter Institute of St Petersburg, Florida, owns both the *St Petersburg Times* and *Congressional Quarterly*, as well as other major media properties. As an educational institution that focuses on providing training for the media it is tax-exempt.

Under US law, there is no limit on the percentage of a corporation's outstanding non-voting stock a foundation may own, so long as the 20% aggregate limit on voting stock in the same corporation described above is not exceeded. If 'disqualified persons', however, own 20% or more of the voting stock of a corporation, the foundation cannot own any of the non-voting stock, which hardly makes sense.[44]

5.1 The US before 1969

US law has not always been so hostile to the ownership by foundations of controlling interests in corporations. Indeed, the history of such foundation/corporation arrangements in the US is a long and illustrious one, including some of today's leading names in philanthropy. The Duke Endowment owned 57% of Duke Power Company common stock and 82% of the preferred stock. The Kellogg Foundation and the Kellogg Foundation Trust – a tripartite arrangement – owned 51% of the W.K. Kellogg Company common stock and 45% of the preferred stock.[45] The William Randolph Hearst Foundation owned 54% of the value of all shares of the media conglomerate Hearst Corporation in non-voting stock. The Lilly Endowment owned 45% of the voting common stock of drugmaker Eli Lilly and Co. The Ford Foundation owned 46% of all classes of Ford Motor Company stock. The John A. Hartford Foundation owned 33% of the common stock of the Great Atlantic and Pacific Tea Company, then one of the largest supermarket chains in the US. The Pew Memorial Trusts owned 21% of the Sun Oil Company common stock. The Hershey Trust – an educational institution, not a foundation – still owns 76.1% of the voting stock of Hershey Foods

---

[44] I acknowledge my special debt to my colleague Prof. Harvey Dale, who first pointed out this inconsistency to me. He describes this provision as simply 'bad drafting'.

[45] By 'tripartite', I mean three boards – the corporation's board, the foundation's board, and the asset-holding Foundation Trust board. This arrangement is similar to the one introduced by the Körber Foundation after Mr Körber's death, except that it is only one legal entity (the Foundation) with three separate boards plus the corporation's own board of directors.

Company.[46] And these are but the best-known names. Indeed, according to Yale Law School Professor John Simon, most of the largest American foundations were created with gifts of appreciated securities or controlling interests of corporate stock:

> As of the time of the 1969 Act, approximately 80 per cent of [US] foundations with more than $10 million in assets had been endowed with corporate control stock or appreciated property or both. A study conducted by the Council on Foundations and the Yale Program on Nonprofit Organizations (Odendahl, 1987) revealed that, of all foundations with more than $100 million in assets in 1982, 50 per cent had been formed with gifts of shares in non-publicly-owned companies, and 34 per cent had been started with gifts of shares of stock that represented voting control of the companies involved. Either type of gift would be likely to fall foul of the 'excess business holdings' rule if made after October, 1969, and the appreciated property rule as well.[47]

5.2 The unconvincing rationales offered to justify Section 4943

In view of the large number of high-profile company/foundation combinations that were created in the early and middle 20th century and the significant asset bases then controlled by each such arrangement, it should be no surprise that government policy-makers and elective officials began to express serious concern about the abuse of the foundation form. That concern gradually led to Congressional hearings, and, in turn, ultimately to legislation in 1969 that imposed stringent controls on both the extent to which such combinations would be permitted to exist at all and also on the transactions that could legally be undertaken between those in the foundations and those in the related corporations.

It must be said that if the founders or builders of corporations wish to establish a foundation, whether for purely philanthropic or mixed philanthropic/managerial continuity reasons, the government surely needs some powerful public policy reasons for resisting their wishes. What might such reasons be? In the 1965 Treasury Department report, which was an important basis for the 1969 Act, the following arguments were given.[48]

---

[46] US House of Representatives, pp.97–9.

[47] Simon, The Regulation of American Foundations, p.249, citing Odendahl and Boris.

[48] See US House of Representatives; see also the summary of arguments made in the Treasury Department report in Dale, US Law Affecting Foundations, p.61–3.

1 The competitive advantage which tax-exempt foundation owner-ship allegedly confers on businesses owned as against businesses not so owned. The unfair competition argument focuses not only on any competitive advantages that may be thought to arise from a foundation-owned corporation's immunity from taxation, but also on 'sweetheart', non-arms-length favourable, terms which the foundation might choose to give to the related corporation on loans or other dealings, which could have the effect of disadvantag-ing competition with the foundation-owned corporation. After the 1950 enactment of the Unrelated Business Income Tax provi-sions (UBIT) which have applied to many nonprofit organizations, including foundations,[49] and the 1969 enactment of the prohibition on self-dealing by officers and directors of private foundations, which applies also to related corporations,[50] both aspects of the argument are now significantly weakened. It would seem, therefore, that the unfair competition argument is not per-suasive and should carry little weight.[51]

2 The 1965 Treasury Report argues that the burden of dealing with corporate matters will divert foundation trustees' and executives' attention from their primary mission of social benefit.[52] As Bittker and Simon both argue, however, the 'diversion of attention' argu-ment is clearly a straw man, because foundations have to hire people to manage their investments under all circumstances any-way, and can surely hire someone to run the business or (the most frequent occurrence) create a separate board of directors for the corporation and let that board do the managing. It is also hardly clear that requiring someone to do only one thing at a time will yield the most effective performance.[53]

3 The 1965 Treasury Report makes a great deal of the danger that the foundation vehicle might possibly be used as a means of enabling

---

[49] IRC Sections 511 *et seq.*

[50] IRC Sections 4941(d)(1)(B) and (d)(2)(B).

[51] On this point see Bittker, p.150–4; Simon, *The Regulation of American Foundations*, p.250; and Simon, *Testimony*, p.1636. The 1965 Treasury Report disagrees: see US House of Representatives, p.31. Also see IRC Sections 511–5. It should be noted that Prof. Simon believes that, even with the combination of UBIT and IRC Section 4941, there is still some latitude for sweetheart deals.

[52] US House of Representatives, pp.35–6.

[53] As Rupert Graf Strachwitz points out, however, there is a school of thought in Germany that doubts the availability of officers with experience and skills in both managing a nonprofit organization with grant-making programmes and supervising a commercial company. This is the case, he says, especially if the foundation and com-pany are comparatively small, thereby putting responsibilities for both functions, to a large extent, in the hands of one person.

the donor or his family to continue benefiting materially from substantial personal stockholdings which, together with those of the corporation, would constitute control.[54] The issue of personal material benefit by the donor and his family, however, is an entirely different issue from that of foundation ownership of corporations, because personal benefit by donors to foundations can occur in connection with any of the assets, whether of related corporation stock or of any other assets, held by a foundation on the board of which a donor or members of his family may sit, and, in any event, will now often be punished under the separate 'self-dealing' provisions enacted in 1969.[55]

4 Concerns were raised about inadequate dividend income. When considering how best to dispose of corporate earnings, shareholder-owned corporations engage in a balancing process, in which the need for the corporation to re-invest its earnings in new capital acquisitions or for research and development purposes is balanced against the desire of shareholders to realize a reasonable return on their investment in the form of dividends. Indeed some institutional investors have a policy against investing in corporations which do not pay dividends. On the other hand, many investors prefer not to receive dividends from their investments because dividends are taxed as ordinary income, and they would rather earnings were retained and reflected in higher stock prices. The risk to be avoided here is that corporations substantially controlled by foundations may not feel any pressure, which many broadly-based, shareholder-owned corporations do, to pay out a reasonable return in earnings as dividends. If, for example, the foundation donor or his family members continue to own stock in, and exert control over the management of, the corporation, it may well be in their personal interest to retain earnings in the corporation rather than pay a reasonable return in dividends either to themselves or to the foundation. In the absence of stock market pressures to pay dividends, managers of corporations are likely to have a strong preference for retaining earnings, even in slow-growth corporations which have less reason to retain earnings than high-growth companies, rather than paying them out in dividends. Over the long term, any such policy of holding dividends down would tend to result in a diminution of the size of the foundation's corpus because, assuming any reasonable pay-out requirements,

---

[54] US House of Representatives, pp.37–45.
[55] IRC Section 4941(d).

assets would have to be sold in order to pay grants at the level of the minimum pay-out requirements.[56] As Simon points out,[57] the Section 4942 distribution requirement, now pegged at 5% of asset market value, 'exerts pressure on a foundation to insist that the business in which it holds control stock produce dividends at about this level' – or much more.[58]

Mandatory minimum pay-out requirements on corporations might be regarded as an effective method of compelling them to provide their foundation stockholders with sufficient current income to avoid endowment erosion, although it must be said that placing such a restriction on the discretion of corporate managers' governance decisions would definitely not be sound public policy. Young and research-intensive firms in industries such as biotechnology and microelectronics, for example, will always have a much greater need to re-invest earnings than older firms or those with established brands and predictable revenue flows. For example, investors in Microsoft have, since its founding, been perfectly happy to forego substantial dividends in return for steady equity appreciation, and continually give Bill Gates a hearty vote of confidence by running up the price of its stock, on the assumption that he has proved able to create more value from Microsoft's retained earnings than stockholders might expect to make elsewhere from any dividends that could otherwise have been paid.

A totally separate danger faced by a foundation with a concentrated investment in a single corporation is that the foundation might witness a decline in the value of its assets over time (even if growing in nominal dollars) compared to what its investments might have been worth had the foundation allocated them more widely over several asset classes and a diversity of securities. While many of the large US foundations have indeed diversified their investments out of the corporations founded by their donors, some notable ones have not. The Lilly Endowment, as of the end of 1996, had more than 99% of its assets invested in Eli Lilly and Company common voting stock, and the Robert Wood Johnson Foundation, at the end of 1995, had 80% of its assets invested in Johnson & Johnson common voting stock. In neither case did their holdings exceed the permissible 20% of the respective company's outstanding voting stock; the Robert Wood

---

[56] It is also true that other strategies for meeting minimum distribution requirements are available, such as by borrowing.

[57] Simon, *Testimony*, page 1636–7.

[58] In Germany the problem is different in that foundations are not required to pay out a percentage of assets, but rather two-thirds of earnings received.

Johnson Foundation's holdings constituted 5.37% of Johnson & Johnson, while the Lilly Endowment's share of Eli Lilly and Company was 16.74%. It happens that both of those companies have done extremely well, and the value of their stock has soared. Others have produced the opposite result.[59]

In summary, as Ballan noted:

> A review of the legislative pronouncements made at the time section 4943 became law suggests that many of the ills section 4943 was aimed at correcting were actually addressed by other statutory means. Things causing concern in the late 1960s included: unfair competition with taxable businesses, for instance by financing with tax exempt dollars; neglect of charitable purposes and activities by board members preoccupied by the need of the for-profit business; failure of the foundation to receive adequate dividends; the purchase of businesses as potentially non-income generating investments and resulting lack of diversity in a foundation's investment portfolio. These ills have been, for the most part, addressed by the on-going refinements in the UBIT rules, the section 4941 self-dealing rules, the section 4942 minimum distribution requirements, and the 4944 jeopardy investment sanctions.[60]

As mentioned above, another fundamental defect is the reasoning which led to the singling out of foundations as the only form of non-profit organization prohibited from owning a controlling interest in a business.[61] Any of the alleged abuses foundations were accused of by Representative Patman and the Treasury could have been, and could still be, committed by other charitable and educational organizations.[62] The Poynter Institute's control of the *St Petersburg Times*, and the Howard Hughes Medical Institute's one-time controlling

---

[59] Under IRC Section 4944, failure to diversify assets can subject a private foundation to penalties for what the Code calls 'jeopardizing investments', that is investments that place the foundation's endowment at inordinate risk. Foundations are generally required to diversify their investments under this provision, but there are exceptions, including where the original donor stipulated in the gift instrument that the stock donated should not be sold. Moreover, one can have an asset allocation policy of, for example, 40% in large capitalization stocks, 30% in small capitalization stocks, 20% in bonds, and 10% in emerging markets, and still have only one security in each class, which could consist of one single corporation. On the need for asset allocation in trusts, see Dale and Gwinnell; see also American Law Institute.

[60] Ballan, pp.6–19.

[61] On this point, see especially Bittker.

[62] Representative Wright Patman was an influential Member of Congress from Texas who, during the 1960s, held a number of hearings believed by many to be designed to generate as much criticism of foundations as possible.

interest in Hughes Tool, would be permitted under current law. Discerning a coherent, persuasive rationale for this discrimination against foundations would tax even those who spend all their waking hours thinking only of the recondite world of taxation. While such an exercise might yield an understanding of Congressional intent circa 1969, it would serve no other useful purpose.

We arrive at what seems to be an inescapable conclusion, therefore, that the US excess business holdings provision in its present form was, simply put, a wrong-headed idea, unevenly applied. In other words, it probably shouldn't have been enacted at all.

5.3 The deterrence of new foundation creation

Had the excess business holdings provision of the 1969 Act not been in place, it seems likely that many more large foundations would have been created in the US over the last three decades. The best evidence for that conclusion is not only the comparable foundation birth rates in Germany but also some recent data reported in survey research on the attitudes of potential donors:

> A number of disincentives to foundation formation were also mentioned by study participants. The most often cited were federal rules, including limits on allowed gifts, 'excess business holdings' and the paperwork. Several people said that their lawyers had dissuaded them for these reasons, which all stemmed from provisions introduced as part of the 1969 Tax Reform Act. However, most of the wealthy informants were not familiar with the technicalities of the law.[63]

America's Wealthy and the Future of Foundations gives data supporting the conclusion that the larger a foundation is, the more likely it was to have been formed by the donation of a controlling interest in the stock of a single corporation. Elizabeth Boris reports as follows:

> Thirteen percent of [more than 1000] responding foundations did divest business holdings to comply with the regulations, but this divestment pertained primarily to the larger foundations. Almost one-third of those with more than $5 million disposed of 'excess' business holdings, but only 12 percent of smaller foundations did so. The proportion that have disposed of 'excess' holdings increased with the size of the foundation. Of those with assets over $100 million in 1982, 47 percent have divested of such holdings.[64]

---

[63] Odendahl, p.237.

[64] Boris, p.72.

The explosive growth in the numbers of new foundations – particularly larger foundations – in other Western countries, such as Germany, is also highly suggestive. While economic conditions have varied considerably between the US and Germany over the last 30 years, enough similarities have existed to make broad comparisons valid. When making such comparisons, one is struck first by the differences in scale; Stefan Toepler found that while there were 35,000 private foundations of all sizes in existence in the US in 1993, there were only 6500 in Germany at around the same time; if only the larger foundations[65] are compared, the disparity more than triples, with 9424 in the US and 478 in Germany.[66] Given this different base, relative rates of formation are more instructive. Toepler found that, in the decade 1950–59, larger foundations increased 140% in the US and less than 20% in Germany. In the decade 1960–69 there was a further increase of about 50% in both countries. After the passage of the Tax Reform Act 1969 in the US, however, foundation formation in Germany has substantially out-paced that in the US. In the 1970s, for example, there was a 60% increase in the number of large foundations in Germany, but only a 20% increase in the US; similarly, in the 1980s Germany's 70% increase was matched by an increase of about 50% in the US.[67] When foundations of all sizes are considered, the recent experience in Germany has been even more pronounced; while 30 to 40 new foundations a year were formed in the 1970s, the annual numbers increased nearly every year in the 1980s to well over 100 per year.[68] That German foundations are permitted to own and control closely-held businesses seems to have been a strong incentive for foundation creation. It must also be noted that the lack in Germany of any significant requirement for public disclosure of financial data about the foundation's investments presumably acts as an additional – and powerful – incentive for foundation creation.

6 Some possible reasons for the difference between the US and Germany

What might account for this stark policy difference between Germany and the US? Perhaps Germany's friendly policy towards the continuity of corporate management is a consequence of what

---

[65] Those with assets of more than $1 million or DM1 million, respectively.

[66] Toepler, *Distant Relatives*, p.111.

[67] Toepler, *Distant Relatives*, p.114.

[68] Anheier, Figure 1, p.29.

some scholars have called the German neocorporatist culture,[69] a culture which has admiration for concentrated corporate power and sees its strengthening as being in the national interest. To the extent that neocorporatism is an accurate description of German public policy, that interpretation would partially explain why German law has given generous incentives to families that control corporations to donate stock to foundations. Those incentives enable donors to avoid the otherwise inevitable inheritance tax on transfer of stock at death from one generation of owners to the next; failing this foundation recipient option, an amount of stock would have to be sold by the heirs in order to pay these taxes, thereby causing the loss or diminution of founder family control. It would also explain why German law looks kindly on the unusually cosy, at least by American standards, relationships permitted between the corporations and the foundations which own them. It would not necessarily explain, however, why German policy-makers chose to use foundation ownership of founder family stock as the means to facilitate continuity of ownership and management. A much simpler means would have been to reduce or eliminate the inheritance tax on the stock of certain classes of corporations, but that, of course, would have been vulnerable to political criticism as unjustifiably favouring the rich and powerful.

One might speculate, too, that a reason the foundation vehicle was chosen is that German policy-makers perceived a lack of foundations on the German nonprofit landscape, and deliberately decided to encourage the growth of foundations in that fashion.[70] Certainly, the German political and intellectual elite, in their determination to create durable democratic institutions in Germany following World War II, became increasingly familiar with the rapidly growing nonprofit sector, including foundations, in the US. They might well have concluded that the fostering of a multiplicity of nonprofit power centres, (part of what political scientists call the system of 'polyarchy', as contrasted with unitary, centralized authority in the former system of powerful monarchy), with authority to take initiatives in solving a variety of problems in the public sphere, would be an important means of strengthening post-war German democracy. While it would have been

---

[69] Siebel, pp.205–29.

[70] I know of no hard evidence for this speculation, but, considering German post-war history and the commitment to building a democratic society, it seems to me a reasonable inference to make. There are many public statements by politicians to this effect, although there is scepticism about the sincerity of such, especially when viewed against the background regulatory practices at the administrative level. In addition, one has to keep in mind that in Germany tax law is federal law, but administrative regulations are state law.

comparatively easy for German law-makers to craft a number of legal provisions to facilitate the continuity of corporate ownership/management without resorting to the foundation vehicle, whether charitable or not, it would not have been possible to facilitate the rapid growth of large foundations without channelling into them the recently accumulated wealth locked up in corporate stock owned by persons and family members with finite life spans. On the other hand, however, to have permitted very wealthy stockholders to avoid inheritance taxes for gifts to charitable foundations without some justification of public interest, and aside from a general public policy in favour of managerial continuity, would surely have violated the general sense of equality that is fundamental to most modern democracies, including Germany. By choosing the charitable foundation vehicle as the means to ensure managerial continuity of corporations, policy-makers are able to claim, with some justification, that the taxes foregone by the German government are offset by the social benefits to be conferred by the new foundations and that German corporate managerial continuity will be served as well.

As between foundation-creation and managerial continuity-strengthening, which has been the end and which has been the means? That is not easy to say, although it would be a knowledgeable bet that corporate managerial continuity has been the end sought and foundation-creation the means.

Subject to the reservations expressed below, it would seem that the German socio-cultural, educational and charitable landscape is much better off with the current policy, whatever its motivating forces, than without it. It is likely that the charitable instinct alone, without the carrot of managerial control-preservation, would not have been effective in producing the large number of new foundations that have in fact been created. The combination of inheritance tax avoidance and insider/family control preservation has, is appears, been an irresistible incentive for foundation creation in Germany. It is of course possible that, even without the carrot of insider/family control preservation, some large foundations might have been created from the recent growth of great wealth, as the post-1969 US experience suggests. However, the important question is whether the trade-off between the harms that potentially grow out of the foundation-controlled corporation arrangement and the polyarchy-serving advantages of a proliferating number of foundations is beneficial to German society on balance. Perhaps any disadvantages of the arrangement might be justified, in either the short or the long term, by the clear social benefits arising from the existence of foundations.

It is, however, necessary to ask whether the clearly beneficial policy of jumpstarting the creation of a multiplicity of nonprofit power centres in the public sphere in the short term remains, in the light of the potential disadvantages, a wise policy in the long term. It is one thing to encourage donors to create new foundations which start out with controlling corporate stockholdings, and quite another thing to permit virtual guarantees of the preservation of that control in perpetuity. Such arrangements, which are perpetual because they are essentially unchallengeable by external influences, could possibly result in serious harm to the nonprofit sector in Germany.

On the operational side, what about the comparative profitability and efficiency of corporations owned by 'friendly' foundations? To what extent do such corporations have competitive advantages or disadvantages, because of their potential perpetual control by related insiders, over competitors either within or outside Germany which have broad-based ownership, enjoy unlimited access to the capital markets for equity investments, are subject to investor/stockholder pressure, and are vulnerable to takeover in the event of unsatisfactory performance? On this point, see Steen Thomsen ('Foundation Ownership and Economic Performance' in *Corporate Governance*), who found, in fact, that Danish companies owned by foundations displayed no significant differences in profitability or growth as compared with companies owned either by individuals or by dispersed stockholders.[71]

What about corporate policies, for instance on wages and benefits, in foundation-controlled corporations? Perhaps it is the case that foundation-controlled corporations are less able or less willing than those not so governed to resist worker demands for more generous packages, thereby diminishing their competitiveness with other corporations in Germany and abroad? It is entirely possible that foundation ownership of corporations has no measurable effect on the success or failure of corporations, but research is needed to provide answers to these and other questions.

From the foundation side, do comparably-sized foundations, in Germany or elsewhere, which are not related to corporations, have a higher or lower pay-out as a proportion of the fair market value of their assets? In other words, does a close relationship between foundation and corporation directors reduce the amount of money which the corporation pays over to the foundation in dividends to use for the public purposes which, in reality and under law, the foundation

---

[71] Thomsen, pp.212–21.

was created to serve? How is it possible for directors and trustees of closely-related corporations and foundations to reconcile corporate interest with foundation interest, and to decide on preference when the two interests conflict? Moreover, how can a foundation's directors reconcile their obligation to serve the public interest by diversifying, if necessary, the foundation's investments through the sale of corporate stock to others, with the business interest of the related corporation in keeping its large stockholding in friendly hands? The law regulating the investment policies of all charities, including foundations, especially in the US and UK, seems to be moving in the direction of preferring broad asset allocation of investments over concentration, and towards discouraging excessively 'conservative' investment policies.[72] Creators of foundation-owning corporations in Germany have been explicit about their dual motivation of preserving, strengthening and assuring the managerial continuity of their corporations while at the same time serving the public interest by creating foundations to which to transfer their ownership interest. Among the reasons given by Reinhard Mohn for the establishment of the Bertelsmann Foundation, for example, was 'the wish to secure the continuity of the corporation', since 'for many companies, the burden of inheritance taxation is too great to bear'.[73] It is noteworthy that, in Germany, such a dual motivation is not considered troubling or in any way shameful but rather legal, moral and honourable. Perhaps it is Americans' exaggerated sensitivity to conflict of interest that is peculiar rather than Germans' seemingly casual acceptance of the ambiguity of dual, conflicting loyalties. There is no question that this difference in attitude in part grows out of Americans' longstanding fixation on purity of motive with regard to the ethics of obligation, which some regard as too simplistic a view of ethics. Perhaps Continental Europeans in general, and Germans in particular, are not troubled by conflicting loyalties or singularity of motivation because the ethical theory by which they act is more nuanced and complex than Americans' narrower ethical focus on pure motive?

Other reasons have been given for the differences in posture between Germany and the US. One of the most trenchant is that offered by Volker Then.[74] He emphasizes that the dominant aim of German foundation law is to ensure that foundations remain meticulously

---

[72] See Dale and Gwinnell, pp.65–94.

[73] Mohn, p.25.

[74] See his article and letter cited above in footnote 5.

faithful to the will of the establishing donors, including their intentions about corporate control, and that foundations guide their asset management primarily so as to preserve capital. He notes that most of the recent discussion about foundations in Germany has emphasized those objectives. In the US, however, the substance of the discussion is very different. For the first time in recent years, there has been a growing chorus of critics urging that the minimum foundation payout be raised from its present 5%, arguing that, at a time when foundation assets are growing at a double-digit rate, it does not serve the public interest for foundations to continue to pile up endowments when many present-day needs of charities are going unmet.

7 Balancing competing interests within the nonprofit form

Notwithstanding the foregoing, the legal and ethical problems are significantly exacerbated, even by German standards, when the foundation itself can be effectively controlled by officers or past officers of the corporation which it owns. Whatever may be said in mitigation, the domination of a foundation by the interests of its captive corporation has to be regarded as a fundamental violation of the purposes and interests that nonprofit organizations are created by law to serve. The integrity of the nonprofit sector is undermined even by the more nuanced, flexible conflict-of-interest standards of Germany. A corporation controlled by a foundation (or another closely-related corporation) should not therefore be allowed, in turn, to control the foundation.

Moreover, to the extent that corporate interests are able to dominate foundations' interests, they thereby violate generally accepted rules, including those in Germany, that prohibit the use of foundations as instruments for obtaining private, personal gain for the benefit of any interested parties. It seems clear that, if the interests of the foundation are subordinated to the interests of the corporation, the managers of the corporation are using their power in the foundation to benefit themselves in impermissible ways. The basic principle of social benefit, which is the justification for the tax-favoured treatment permitting the establishment of the foundation, would seem inherently to be violated where corporate managers influence the decisions of the foundation to serve the interests of the corporation. As we have seen, this conflict of interest is inherent in such basic decisions as whether the foundation can, if it wishes to do so, diversify its portfolio of investments. With regard to decisions about how much to pay out of the corporation to the foundation in dividends, the corporate interest may well lie in minimizing pay-out so as to use cash generated for purposes of research and development, growth of the corporation, or for acquisitions.

When a foundation owns a corporation whose managers in effect control the foundation, and seem likely to do so in perpetuity, the governance arrangement might appear a recipe for mutual disaster. Because such a foundation is inextricably wedded to the fortunes of a single corporation, the foundation cannot single-mindedly focus its energies on the goal of serving the public. Moreover, because its financial welfare is interlocked with that of the corporation, it stands to suffer if the corporation suffers, and has no way of abandoning such an arrangement. Because the corporation, through its managers' dominance of the foundation board, is able to use the foundation control of its stock to insulate itself from any serious threats or pressures, its leadership might regard itself as having an advantage over its publicly traded and publicly controlled competitors; in the long term, however, that insulation seems to me likely to subject the corporation to potentially enervating complacency. The combination of those two dangers – to corporation vibrancy and discipline and to the ability of the foundation to focus single-mindedly on fully serving the public's interest – should be seriously troubling to many public officials.

The corporation/foundation combination presents a large aggregation of capital, with significant operations in both the for-profit and the nonprofit sectors, which is essentially unaccountable to, and unchallengeable by, anyone. It offers possible competitive advantages on the for-profit side, and the potential to exercise significant unchecked power in matters of social policy on the nonprofit side. No wonder that some governments – the US first and foremost – have imposed stringent rules regulating such corporate/foundation relationships.

If the US were to change its law so as to permit foundations to control corporations, therefore, it is essential that governance mechanisms designed to ensure genuine foundation independence be put in place. It was undoubtedly some vague sense of the importance of independence that led Congress, in crafting the 1969 Act, to permit foundations to own as much as 35% of the outstanding voting stock of a corporation, provided that the stock is vested in a genuinely independent entity.[75]

---

[75] It is this provision under which the Kellogg Foundation is permitted to own 35% of the voting stock of the W.K. Kellogg Company.

Aside from the problem of corporate control of the foundation in principle, there are troubling ancillary problems. Once a donor takes advantage of tax-favoured giving to create a foundation, the public has some considerable interest not only in the total return on the foundation's investments and in how the income from the endowment is spent, but also in ensuring that the foundation's purchasing power is maintained. Permitting foundations to concentrate their holdings in the stock of a single corporation forever, no matter how blue chip an investment it may seem at the time, seriously risks significant erosion of value over time. One can say 'well, that's too bad, but it was the donor's wish to stay concentrated', or one can say, 'once the gift is made, the public acquires an interest in seeing that the benefits it expects to accrue from the tax revenues that are foregone are not significantly diminished over time, and that precludes the continuation of concentration in a single asset over a long period of time'. In a sense, that was part of the rationale of US policy, as articulated in the jeopardizing investment provisions of Section 4944, but there are enough exceptions to the requirement that foundations diversify their investments to enable foundations to avoid the rule if donors plan carefully.[76] In other words, the percentage of outstanding voting stock a foundation may own is limited by the 1969 Act, but not the percentage of a foundation's investment represented by a particular stockholding, at least if the foundation remains invested in the originally-donated stock and the donor has so instructed it. As we have seen, some of the largest US foundations – Robert Wood Johnson and Lilly – have virtually their entire portfolio in the stock of the company of their founders, as did the Wellcome Trust in the UK. While many of those foundations have prospered along with the companies in which their investments are concentrated, there are other examples – the John A. Hartford Foundation, the Kellogg Foundation and the Dewitt and Lila Wallace/Readers Digest Funds in the US and the Baring and Nuffield Foundations in the UK – whose assets have been seriously diminished because of business reverses suffered by the companies in which their investments were concentrated.[77]

It is generally believed that such foundations are themselves significantly disadvantaged when their own financial security is tightly bound to the financial success of a single corporation. Usually, the

---

[76] See Treasury Regulations Section 53.4944-1(a)(2)(I).

[77] It must be underscored that, looked at over the long run, the assets of the Kellogg Foundation and the Wallace/Readers Digest Funds have appreciated greatly. It is only in the window of the past two years that their assets have declined significantly from earlier highs.

governance structure makes it difficult, if not impossible, for the foundation's trustees to sell much of the corporation's stock in order to diversify its holdings and thereby reduce its dependence on any single asset, as in the case of The Duke Endowment. The Trust Indenture creating The Duke Endowment requires unanimous consent of the trustees to sell any shares of Duke Power Company, and when the late Doris Duke, the daughter of the donor, was still alive, she refused to vote for any motion to sell, except on one occasion. Even under governance agreements which permit the foundation's trustees full discretion in making investments, the overlap of trustees/directors between corporation and foundation creates severe conflicts of loyalty, thereby significantly reducing the likelihood that diversification of holdings will in fact occur.[78]

Prudential foundation investment policy would strongly argue for a gradual phasing down of a foundation's concentration in a particular stock arising from a gift by a donor. This is perhaps the only way in which a modern foundation would find itself with so large a concentration of stock in a single company; diversified asset allocation is increasingly the policy by which foundations shape their portfolios.

8 Some afterthoughts

As we have seen, the policy culture and legal treatment of foundations vary significantly between the US and Germany. The differences between the two legal systems – civil law and common law – have led to major differences in public policy toward the creation of new foundations, particularly with regard to endowments consisting of stock in a corporation. Since the 1960s, German law has encouraged a remarkable process of growth in the foundation sector and the establishment of numerous new foundations, while in the US, the birth of new foundations slowed considerably for a while, with the growth rate falling below that of Germany. Because sustained economic growth over long periods is a precondition to a growing foundation sector, it was possible for Germany to develop a significant foundation population only after World War II, the first long period in modern Germany in which large fortunes might be accumulated undisturbed by cataclysms such as inflation and war.

The slower rate of emergence of new US foundations prompts the question of the extent to which US donors may have found it prudent to resort to establishing philanthropic activities 'offshore', that is

---

[78] Fabrikant, p.1.

under the law of another country. An understanding of the dynamics of foundation creation cautions us to consider whether alternative venues or forms of establishing philanthropic and other nonprofit enterprises can have been utilized to escape regulations that restrain donors from realizing their intentions.

After all is said and done, empirical data on long-term foundation activities in Germany is still in the making, because a number of the largest foundations date from a very recent period of growth, and most of the foundation-owned corporations (with the exception of the Robert Bosch Foundation) are of fairly recent origin. It seems all the more difficult, therefore, to make a reliable comparative assessment of the consequences of the German situation. For example, because of the recency of most foundation creation in Germany, it is too early to say whether the long-term business and social interests of a corporation are in fact hampered by being owned by a foundation or whether the charitable interests of a foundation are likely to be damaged by the fact that its endowment consists of concentrated holdings in a single corporation's stock. The long-standing and telling example of the Bosch Foundation has hardly proven to be a case of harm – either to the foundation or to the corporation – and the Scandinavian and UK experience does not suggest any cause for concern. This should be kept clearly in mind when weighing the consequences of globalization and international competition on foundation-owned corporations.

Comparison between the German and US legal and foundation cultures also suggests that attitudes prevalent in the capital markets are having consequences for the investment of foundation capital. While US culture favours a diversified policy of portfolio investment in the public stock market, and also legally enforces it, German attitudes clearly favour closely-held, inter-related institutional investors. The existence in Germany of many large banks, insurance firms and industrial corporations holding large blocks of stock in one another is reflected in the relationships between foundations and corporations; it is not regarded as a conflict of interest for a German foundation to hold the majority of stock in a corporation.

The German corporatist philosophy of the relationships among these institutions grows out of a corporate culture that involves a delicate system of checks and balances. Labour law and labour co-determination (*Mitbestimmung*) in corporate governance are mechanisms that strongly encourage corporate boards to seek consensus and to balance interests in their strategies rather than sharpen conflicts. In that system of checks and balances, the relationship of a foundation to a corporation it owns, and vice versa, is only one element among the many checks and balances. Moreover, that system of checks and balances, so far as foundation-owned corporations are concerned, is maintained by reasonably close supervision of foundation operations on the part of official regulatory authorities. Both the foundations and the corporations understand that the charitable status of a foundation, as well as its possible loss, depends in large part on strict obedience to the expressed will of a foundation donor, which is the major definition of the public good so far as such arrangements are concerned. This is so even in a structure which does not treat corporation and foundation as completely independent entities with competing interests managed by totally different individuals.

In addition to the continuous monitoring and control of all foundation activities by the regulatory authorities to ensure that their activities are fully in accord with the requirements of legal charitable status, foundations in Germany are subject also to an ongoing supervision by the German states, or *Länder* (*Stiftungsaufsicht*). In order to enable the responsible authorities effectively to control the conduct of foundation practices, the various regional laws enacted by the German *Länder* contain a variety of regulations which require foundations to provide a financial account of, and other information on, their activities. For special transactions, the foundation laws require the approval of the legal authorities. Such approval-requiring transactions include, for example, the re-alignment of portfolio assets, which might impair the capability of a foundation to fulfill its mission, or legal or financial transactions of foundation managers with themselves as representatives of third-party interests, such as the foundation-owned corporation. To enforce their decisions, the legal authorities are empowered to issue orders that revoke or modify decisions made by the foundation officers and directors.[79]

In contrast, the US regulatory scheme, despite all its policy stringency towards foundations in principle, is notably irresolute in practice. Only the federal government has any substantial power over foundations through the Internal Revenue Service and, until recently, the IRS had no power to impose any sanctions on foundations or their directors or officers other than to revoke their tax-exempt status. Except in outright fraud and self-dealing, the states have played little role in supervising foundations. Moreover it is still the case that IRS audits are extremely rare, and that both the IRS and state attorney general offices are woefully under-staffed.

---

[79] See Then article cited in footnote 5 above.

In summary, the implications of the differences between Germany and US policies and practices with regard to foundations and foundation-owned corporations can hardly be said to be clear. Those differences do suggest the importance of closely tracking the behaviour of each country's foundations and corporations over a longer period in order to discern whether policy changes are desirable, either toward the US model or towards the German.

Bibliography

American Law Institute, Restatement of the Law (Third), Trusts, Prudent Investor Rule, St Paul, Minn., 1992, pp. 3–101.

Anheier, H., *Foundations in Numbers: A Profile of German Foundations*, manuscript dated June 16, 1997, p.28.

Ballan, J., 'Private Foundations. How the Excess Business Holdings Rules Work in 1995 and Beyond', in: *Proceedings of the New York University 24th Conference on Tax Planning for 505(c)(3) Organizations*, Matthew Bender, Albany, New York, section 6.01–6.06.

Barbetta, G. P., *Foundations in Italy*, Universita Cattolica del Sacro Cuore and Instituto per la Ricerca Sociale, Milan, November 1996.

Bernard van Leer Foundation, *Annual Review* 1995, p. 8.

Bernard van Leer Foundation, *Letter To Whom It May Concern*, 1 September 1999.

Bertelsmann Foundation, 'Reports from the Workshops. Workshop I: Governance and strategy of foundations', in: Bertelsmann Foundation (ed.), *The Work of Operating Foundations. Strategies-Instruments-Perspectives*, Gütersloh, Bertelsmann Foundation Publishers, 1997, pp. 89–96.

Bittker, B. I., 'Should Foundations Be Third Class Charities?', in: F. F. Heimann (ed.), *The Future of Foundations*, Prentice-Hall, Englewood Cliffs, New Jersey, 1973, pp. 132–62.

Boris, E., 'Creation and Growth. A Survey of Private Foundations', in: T. Odendahl (ed.), *America's Wealthy and the Future of Foundations*, The Foundation Center, New York, 1987, pp. 65–126.

Dale, H. P., 'Foreign Charities', in: *The Tax Lawyer*, Vol. 48, No. 3, 1995, pp. 657–63.

Dale, H. P., 'Reflections on Inurement, Private Benefit, and Excess Benefit Transactions', in: *Tax Forum*, No. 520, 1997, pp 1–46.

Dale, H. P., 'U.S. Law Affecting Foundations and Their Ownership of Businesses', in: Bertelsmann Foundation (ed.), *The Work of Operating Foundations. Strategies-Instruments-Perspectives*, Gütersloh, Bertelsmann Foundation Publishers, 1997, pp. 57–68.

Dale, H. P. and Gwinnell, M., 'Time for Change. Charity Investment and Modern Portfolio Theory', in: *The Charity Law & Practice Review*, Vol. 3, Issue 2, 1995/96, pp. 65–96.

Fabrikant, G., 'Cultural World Gets Painful Lesson in Finance', in: *New York Times*, August 26, 1997, Section A, p.1, and Section D, p.4.

Fishman, J. T. and Schwarz, S., *Nonprofit Organizations. Cases and Materials*, Westbury, New York, The Foundation Press, 1995, pp. 667–71.

Geinitz, C., 'The Generous Grin of Capitalism', *Frankfurter Allgemeine Zeitung*, 8 July 1997.

George, C. S., *International Charitable Giving. Laws and Taxation*, London/Dordrecht/Boston, Graham & Trotman/Martinus Nijhoff, 1994, p.9.

Hutheesing, N., 'Auto-Baan', in: *Forbes*, October 6, 1997, pp. 109–13.

Karpen, U., *Gemeinnutzige Stiftungen im pluralistischen Rechstsstaat – Neure Enwicklungen des amerikanischen und deutschen Stiftungssteuerrechts*, Frankfurt/Main, Metzler, 1980.

Maecenata Management GmbH, *Dokumentationszentrum Deutche Stiftungen*, 1996.

Mohn, R., 'Objectives of an Operating Foundation', in: Bertelsmann Foundation (ed.), *The Work of Operating Foundations. Strategies-Instruments-Perspectives*, Gütersloh, Bertelsmann Foundation Publishers, 1997, pp. 24–32.

Nielsen, W., *Inside American Philanthropy. The Dramas of Donorship*, Norman, Ok. and London, University of Oklahoma Press, 1996.

Odendahl, T., 'Wealthy Donors and Their Charitable Attitudes', in: T. Odendahl (ed.), *America's Wealthy and the Future of Foundations*, New York, The Foundation Center, 1987, pp. 223–46.

Odendahl, T., *America's Wealthy and the Future of Foundations*, New York, The Foundation Center, 1987.

Seibel, W., 'Government – Nonprofit Relationships in a Comparative Perspective. The Cases of France and Germany', in: McCarthy, Hodgkinson, Sumariwalla and Associates, *The Nonprofit Sector in the Global Community*, San Francisco, Jossey–Bass, 1992, pp. 205–29.

Simon, J. G., 'The Regulation of American Foundations. Looking Backward at the Tax Reform Act of 1969', in: *Voluntas*, Vol. 6, No. 3, December 1995, pp. 243–54.

Simon, J. G., *Testimony, U.S. House of Representatives, Committee on Ways and Means, Hearings on Tax Rules Covering Private Foundations*, June 27–29, 1983, p.1626–47.

Then, V., 'Legal Reform to Promote Foundation Growth in Germany', in: *European Foundation Centre, Social Economy and Law*, Summer 1999 issue.

Thomsen, S., 'Foundation Ownership and Economic Performance', in: *Corporate Governance*, Vol. 4, No.4, Oxford, England, Blackwell Publishers Ltd, 1996, pp. 212–21.

Toepler, S., 'Distant Relatives. A Comparative Analysis of the German and U.S. Foundation Sectors', in: *1995 ARNOVA Conference proceedings*, 1995, pp. 111–4.

Toepler, S., *Myths and Misconceptions? Evaluating the Govern/Foundation Relationship in Germany Against the American Experience*, Johns Hopkins University Institute for Policy Studies, Center for Civil Society Studies Working Paper, No. 14, 1997, pp. 1–19.

Wössner, M., 'Foundations as Guarantors of Entrepreneurial Continuity and Social Responsibility', in: Bertelsmann Foundation (ed.), *The Work of Operating Foundations. Strategies-Instruments-Perspectives*, Gütersloh, Bertelsmann Foundation Publishers, 1997, pp. 42–7.

US House of Representatives, *Committee on Ways and Means, Treasury Department Report on Private Foundations*, Washington, US Government Printing Office, 1965, pp.30–7, 97–9.

▼ Luc Tayart de Borms and Emmanuelle Faure

Transparency and Accountability

1 Introduction

'Transparency' and 'accountability' are related concepts which are today invoked with increasing frequency. The two concepts continue to be hotly-debated issues and remain at the centre of an increasingly large body of academic research both in the private and in the non-profit sector. To many, the two concepts are synonymous with sound management, an appropriate response to the expectations of the public, the regulatory authorities and an organization's immediate stakeholders. They are also seen as important management tools to combat improprieties and abuse.

Most successful corporations now acknowledge that transparency and accountability are essential elements of good corporate governance and the sustained conduct of business. That these principles are relevant not only to corporations but also to foundations would appear self-evident. It might be useful to ask the following questions:

- Are transparency and accountability, in themselves, a warranty of sound management?

- Should they be imposed from without or is the task of applying these concepts better left to those who are in the front line of management?
- Can the two approaches be combined?

This chapter addresses these issues from a practical standpoint, the aim being first to highlight reasons why transparency is important and, second, to examine how transparency can be achieved administratively in the case of foundations with limited human and financial resources. Experiences at national and, above all, European level are described and evaluated.

2 Transparency and responsibility

The concept of transparency is essentially simple. It encompasses the dissemination of any and all information that the public at large has a legal right to access at a given moment. This entails a genuine communication policy, including the publication of detailed reports which set out an organization's financial position and financial management principles, and disclose internal decision-making structures, operational methodologies, and details of ongoing and proposed projects and initiatives.

Accountability is a more complex notion, although it is essentially the process of the 'due and proper rendering of accounts'. In the case of foundations, three areas of accountability are most commonly cited.

- **Fiscal** accountability, which relates to the foundation's financial integrity.
- **Process** accountability, which demonstrates that the foundation has achieved what it set out to achieve.
- **Programme** accountability, which confirms that the foundation has acted in accordance with its objects clause.

As a result, the concept of accountability is notionally more restrictive and more judicial in nature than the concept of transparency as a whole. However, it can be said that between them the two concepts of accountability and transparency encompass all the regulatory, statutory and ethical content of the information provision process; further, they serve the goal of efficiency and efficacy.

On the other hand, defining the two concepts in this way without explaining a specific ethical context is not completely satisfactory. Regulatory and statutory prescriptions are readily identified by reference to the letter of the law and are automatically applied, subject only to questions of interpretation. By contrast, ethical content is neither universal nor absolute; it is arguable that ethical content can in practice vary as a function of an organization's size, the resources it administers or the source of those funds.

It is also arguable that if ethical content is absent, the organization in question will quickly become the object of public opprobrium. Transparency and accountability are therefore essential but by no means exclusive determinants of sound management practice. They are there above all to ensure openness at all levels throughout the organization.

3 The need for transparency

The need for transparency is due to a number of factors.

- **The information society**
  First and foremost, are the challenges arising from the emergence of the information society. Today, there is nowhere to hide; communication is almost instantaneous. Additionally, staff and consultants come and go to different jobs yet modern management insists on an 'open-book' approach which implies that when they leave, they take with them quantities of information which they can eventually 'use'. Further, foundation boards are sometimes large, with members coming from disparate backgrounds and remaining for a limited time. When they leave, they too take relevant, possibly even confidential, information with them.
  We live in a knowledge society and foundations are knowledge corporations which depend upon obtaining relevant information to conceptualize their projects. However, one can only access relevant information if there is trust and if one also provides relevant information.

- **Political considerations**
  There are also political reasons which underpin the need for transparency. Most foundations maintain relations with public authorities, government bodies and the public at large. This is for a variety of reasons – because they manage funds from private individuals (donations, legacies, lottery monies, etc.) or because the funds managed attract favourable fiscal treatment by the respective government, for example. If for no other reason than this, the public at large has a legitimate interest in, and right to obtain information on, foundations.

In addition, most foundations not only tackle the symptoms of society's problems, they also attempt to bring about social change. To achieve this, foundations frequently work together with private or public partners or try to influence public players. Exerting this influence or forging partnerships implies trust. And trust is created, among other things, when the respective parties feel that nothing is being hidden from them.

- **Strategic considerations**
  Not least, there are strategic reasons for transparency. Sadly, there is no reason to believe that foundations are less vulnerable to fraud or corruption than other members of society. As experience in the US has shown, a scandal involving a major foundation can inflict damage on the foundation sector as a whole.
  Because of their role, foundations tend to have a good name; if that good name is lost or tarnished, the consequences can be dramatic, particularly in the light of the leverage role foundations seek to play in society. Accordingly, foundations need to be vigilant in their efforts to prevent and anticipate scandal, not least given the climate of suspicion which increasingly attaches to major social institutions such as political parties, the Church, trade unions and the like. Foundations are often perceived as being part of this establishment, and it is becoming clearer with every passing day: for foundations, it is no longer enough to do good, it is also essential to do good *well*.

3.1 Accountability and new philanthropy

Two trends in society are important for the foundation sector and for the concepts under discussion here:

- the approaching transfer of wealth to a new generation
- the emergence of new donors with a more social venture capitalist-oriented approach.

In the years immediately ahead, much of the wealth generated and accumulated after World War II will pass to a new generation. Because of a lack of heirs or for other reasons, people will consider creating foundations. Wealthy new donors are beginning to initiate philanthropic programmes during their own lifetime, frequently adopting a distinctly hands-on approach and contributing resources that are sometimes larger than the annual budgets of some sovereign states. Such generosity is however the exception rather than the rule and tends to be viewed with jealousy and suspicion; in a democracy, it raises important questions about the influence of such donors on public life if democratic control is not exercised rigorously.

In the light of these two trends, it will be increasingly important to explain what foundations do and how they do it. In other words, there will be a call for even greater transparency and accountability. Over and above ethical and legal obligations, these fundamental considerations should be taken into account by those – whether inside or outside the foundation world – who question the importance of developing proactive attitudes to transparency.

The great majority of organizations operating outside the commercial sector are already aware of the importance of transparency, and they have at their disposal a large number of instruments which enable them to disseminate information objectively. Among these is the annual report which reviews activities and programmes throughout the year and presents a financial statement. This document is not mandatory but its use is becoming increasingly widespread. Many organizations also publish promotional or explanatory brochures, write articles for sectoral journals, contribute to publications targeted at specific audiences, and organize frequent meetings with the media to maintain the flow of information to the public.

Further, in certain countries (see below), individual organizations have come together to elaborate codes of good practice or codes of ethical conduct designed to set out a general framework for their activities. Transparency, and the concrete compliance it implies, are generally accorded top priority in such codes.

Fears expressed by foundations relate less to the doctrine of transparency *per se* than to the specific disclosures that may be imposed as a result. There are several major considerations in this respect, the principal one probably that the particular demands of specific sectors often go unrecognized by those entrusted with the drafting of regulations. The result is often a defensive reaction on the part of the foundations concerned.

4 Voluntary or imposed regulation

In a publication entitled *L'argent du cœur*, Xavier Descarpentris of *Médecins sans Frontières*, France, asserts that 'it is up to the state to assume responsibility for regulation of humanitarian organizations'.[1]

---

[1] See Dufourcq.

In his view, organizations based on the principle of self-regulation must be ambiguous *per se*: they have no reason to exercise strict control over one another in the absence of mechanisms that provide for strict sanctions or exclusion. He goes further, calling into question the credibility of any self-regulation by associations; for him, no sector can moderate and regulate itself.

Nevertheless, it can also be argued that excessive external regulation is harmful to effective citizen participation, and that it is precisely when associations operate under conditions of active citizenship participation that they are more likely to operate on sound management principles. If this logic is followed, then foundations should be left to organize themselves and to take those measures they deem appropriate to accommodate the legitimate expectations of the citizens they exist to serve.

Aside from an intuitive resentment of interference by a public authority, what are the arguments that can be advanced in favour of one approach or the other? A number of organizations may oppose stricter external controls because they rely exclusively on their own resources and make no demands on public funds. It is perhaps only to be expected that these organizations resent the glare of publicity and wish to be no more constrained by regulation than comparable commercial entities. Other organizations, with lesser means, express fears at the high cost of compliance implicit in stricter external regulation and argue that they have do not have the resources, financial or human, to achieve it.

At this point it should be noted that regulations are universally applicable, whereas no one can be forced to adopt or comply with a code of good practice. That said, externally imposed regulations frequently result in reluctant and formal compliance, whereas a series of principles articulated by the sector itself will ultimately stand a better chance of being accepted and implemented.

It would seem inopportune for society, in its anxiety to ward off potential abuses, to deprive itself of the dynamism and creativity of a host of smaller organizations, stunting their imaginative and flexible nature by imposing a series of constraints which they are in no position to respect. All the more so, since there is no guarantee that these constraints will prove genuinely effective.

No one approach is perfect. That said, the most adequate response would certainly appear to be a process adopted at national and European level, whereby a number of independent foundations with sufficient resources and a clear sense of what is at stake have set up (frequently under the approving gaze of public authorities) networks and/or committees to elaborate codes of practice. In the initial phase, compliance with these codes is limited to those who contribute to their elaboration; subsequently, the codes operate as systems of accreditation. But the overall objective is to provide non-costly guidance and support for smaller organizations by helping them comply with the provisions of the code in question. This process is progressive and the foundation variant has progressed in some countries more quickly than in others. Accordingly, it is important to look at experiences both positive and negative and to ask what can be done to refine these codes and promote their adoption.

5 Experiences at the national and European level

The codes and charters developed over the past ten years by and for associations and foundations in Europe, Africa, America and Canada respond to a dual rationale.

- On the one hand they 'reassure' donors – since the relationship of transparency between donors and the voluntary sector is at the core of the doubts raised by a number of scandals in both Europe and the US in recent years – and more generally to reassure public authorities in order to prevent the sector from coming under supervision and being subjected to administrative controls that would undermine its dynamism and flexibility.
- On the other hand, they demonstrate a concern for the good management and effectiveness of nonprofit sector interventions, which might be said to correspond to the kind of initiatives launched when quality circles were created in the business world.

Codes and charters establish a number of principles and rules, which, while for the most part referring to the statutory regulations imposed on the nonprofit sector, actually go a step further than this. The implementation and credibility of such self-regulation initiatives call for the following stages:

- consultation
- development and acceptance of principles of good practice by the sectors concerned
- introduction of a formal or informal accreditation system
- establishment of a mechanism and body for ensuring compliance with such practices and for imposing sanctions.

Below we examine some aspects of these stages.

5.1 American experiences: promoting good practices; multiple initiatives

The nonprofit sector's self-regulation systems have for the most part been inspired by North American experiences and models. In order to preserve the public trust from which the sector benefits, a wide range of initiatives have emerged in the US to promote good practices, guarantee the transparency of accounts and prevent any type of fraud or abuse. Initiatives such as these which have been developed in different sectors of activity are generally considered to have been useful in forestalling the regulation[2] of foundations and associations. Various nongovernmental organizations have drawn up such principles, notably InterAction.[3] Others include those established by the National Charities Information Bureau (NCIB), which relate mainly to matters of administration, public information and the sector's responsibility, and the principles of the Charitable Advisory Service of the Council of Better Business Bureau, which promote good fundraising practices. The above organizations regularly publish reports on the bodies that apply these principles and those that fail to abide by them.

There are other initiatives aimed specifically at independent fund-providers. In 1980, the National Committee for Responsive Philanthropy (NCRP) drew the attention of the public and the sector to a study on the information practices of the major American foundations and proposed a series of recommendations on the type of key information all foundations should provide to the public.[4]

At the same time, the Council on Foundations adopted its 'principles and practices for effective grant making' in June 1980. This contains a list of provisions on the commitment of fund-providers:

- to define their programmes and objectives clearly
- to re-examine their validity periodically
- to establish a decision-making body responsible for defining this strategy
- to inform the public and organizations seeking funding about their programmes, procedures and criteria for awarding funding.

---

[2] At federal level, responsibility for regulating foundations in accordance with the 1969 Tax Reform Act falls to the Internal Revenue Service (IRS) and at state level to the attorney general's office.

[3] See InterAction-American Council for Voluntary International Action.

[4] See National Committee for Responsive Philanthropy.

Finally, they encourage fund-providers to work with other national and regional charitable organizations and with other organizations in the nonprofit sector to promote private initiatives aimed at serving public needs and interests. Since 1983, adhesion to these principles has been a prerequisite for membership of the Council on Foundations. Furthermore, the application of certain provisions proposed by the Council on Foundations is studied in advance by the Council's affinity groups (working parties), such as the Grantmakers Evaluation Network (GEM), which strives to promote the development of practices and models for evaluating charitable activities.

The adoption by independent fund-providers of these principles of good practice is the culmination of consultations and discussions which started ten years ago with the aim of allying pluralism, the foundations' individual priorities and the shared mission of all independent fund-providers, whilst at the same time demonstrating that public authority intervention was neither necessary nor desirable. In 1970, a Council committee set out to examine how to promote good practices among independent fund-providers, taking into account the diversity of the sector and the need to set up information and training services to encourage foundations not only to comply with the regulations, but also to apply sound and efficient management and ethical conduct. The issue of whether and to what extent the Council ought to promote these principles also led to a wide-ranging debate. It has been demonstrated in practice that Council membership constitutes de facto approval by the Council which, in fact, stands as a guarantor of public confidence. On this basis, the Council has, over the past ten years, developed a complete information and advisory service for the staff and administrators, not only of the various member foundations and corporate fund-providers, but also of other charitable organizations. Awards of excellence have also been created to reward the efforts of fund-providers in disseminating information to the public or to distinguish exceptional leadership.

In 1994 another milestone was crossed with the creation of a study group which set out to redefine the Council's role and function in the promotion of and compliance with the principles of good practice adopted in 1980.[5] The group also examined whether the Council's terms of membership and the mechanisms for responding to alleged or manifest violations were sufficient to safeguard the interests of the Council and of the public. Concluding that the cases of breach of public trust were isolated, the study group nevertheless recommended

---

[5] See Council on Foundations.

that the Council should improve the sector's self-regulation capability, step up its mission to provide information and education on good practices, increase its efforts to examine new topics and reach out to a wider audience. One of the group's key recommendations was to set up procedures for a preliminary enquiry and a more in-depth investigation into alleged or evident cases of fraud or abuse, whether legal or ethical in nature. This new mechanism would be based on the creation of an advisory body comprised of five to seven members, the Advisory Panel on Public Accountability, to advise the Council on action to be taken and, where required, to work in coordination with the regional associations of independent grant makers (RAGs). The report also provided for a series of sanctions, ranging from withdrawal of the benefits conferred by Council membership to exclusion from the Council, or even, subject to a decision by the board of directors, to public communication of the alleged offences, whether or not the alleged perpetrators are members. These recommendations were adopted by the Council on Foundations in November 1995.

The Council is not itself a regulatory body, but an organization committed to protecting and safeguarding public confidence by encouraging the sound and ethical management of national and local charitable organizations in association with the RAGs.

Apart from the above-mentioned initiatives on good practice and transparency, notable work has been carried out by the Independent Sector[6] – a national forum comprised of some 800 foundations, corporate fund-providers and associations whose primary objective is to encourage philanthropy, volunteer work and other voluntary initiatives – and we would like to underline the crucial role played by the Foundation Center of New York and its five bureaux throughout the country in the matter of transparency and in disseminating information about foundations. The latter collects precise and objective data about foundations and makes it available to people seeking funding and other interested persons in the form of publications, indices and databases. It supplies the public with information notified to the central government (the Internal Revenue Service's form 990-PF on private foundations) as well as with other information drawn from various studies.

---

[6] See Independent Sector.

5.2 Towards a quality label: the collective self-regulation system of France's Charter Committee

In the battle to retain donor loyalty, transparency in the accounts and activities of the nonprofit sector has become a fundamental strategy. Concerned for their credibility and anxious to forestall public authority regulation, in 1989 France's largest social and humanitarian associations created the Charter Committee on Professional Ethics (*Comité de la Charte de Déontologie*). Inspired by the American model, the Committee's fundamental purpose is to strengthen professional ethics and self-discipline: by undertaking to comply with common rules, foundations and associations aim to provide donors with better information about their tasks and how they use the funds raised. The basic guidelines relate to financial transparency, the quality of measures and messages, the rigour of fundraising methods and monitoring compliance with their commitments. Some members of the Charter Committee have embraced this rationale within their own organizations; for instance, in 1990, *Médecins du Monde* set up a donors' committee both to evaluate and report on the use of funds raised.

Any organization wishing to join the Charter Committee is subjected to a rigorous admission procedure. It must supply a number of documents, including administrative and accounting documents as well as documents giving evidence of public fundraising campaigns. After examining the latter, the Committee accepts or rejects the applicant organization; if it is accepted, the organization receives a label to display on its fundraising documents identifying it as a member. It will then be subjected to an annual in-depth assessment of the transparency of its accounts and of all aspects covered by the Charter, to determine whether or not it can continue to benefit from membership of the Committee. This assessment is undertaken by:

- an independent auditor, appointed for three years to each member organization, who is responsible, on behalf of the Committee, for establishing an annual report on the organization to which he has been appointed
- the Monitoring Committee which advises the Committee on membership applications, on the decisions to be taken in the light of periodic reports and on the possible withdrawal of approval from a member organization.

At present, there is no doubt that Committee members benefit from their 'quality label' and that this label has tended to influence donors.

Membership of the Committee involves voluntary compliance with the principles stated in the Charter. The Committee today includes around 40 organizations and, apart from Committee members, other organizations appealing for generosity have now decided to publish their accounts, whereas they did not do so previously. To date, the Committee has not excluded a single member, a fact for which it has been criticized. However, it has admonished a number of its members on the issue of financial transparency. A number of French organizations, deeming that no sector can effectively monitor itself and that the Charter Committee cannot be both judge and be judged, want responsibility for monitoring to be handed over to the central government. No doubt the real issues are the Committee's greater resources and greater professionalism. Can and should the Committee be open to everyone and monitor all organizations that appeal for public generosity, even the most modest? On the basis of the 1991 and 1996 Acts giving the national audit office (*Cour des Comptes*) the possibility and right to monitor organizations appealing to public generosity, advocates of increased central government control highlight the limitations of the Charter Committee's voluntary membership concept. Nevertheless, it is necessary to be realistic about the national audit office's ability to intervene. How many audits is the office really in a position to conduct per year?

Future changes will no doubt hinge on the role of the state itself, deciding whether it should encourage and support voluntary efforts or, by virtue of its still highly radical tradition, whether it should perpetuate an arbitration approach involving administrative supervision. Some believe that a mixed approach should be developed, that is a number of statutory obligations defined by the public authorities in consultation with the sector, supplemented by the self-regulation of foundations and associations and other professional ethics initiatives. Between 1996 and early 1997, joint public administration/voluntary sector working groups examined the issue of the financial transparency of nonprofit-making organizations and came to the conclusion that greater transparency was needed. With respect to the issue of monitoring, the report considered the current legal framework to be adequate but felt that the various players involved had to become more familiar with it. With regard to organizations appealing to public generosity, the group asked the public authorities to encourage them to be accountable to their donors and to support inter-association entities such as the Charter Committee.

The activities of the Charter Committee provide only one example among many in Europe of the sector's self-regulation. Such systems have been developed by a number of nongovernmental organizations in Austria, Germany, the Netherlands, Norway, Sweden, Switzerland and the UK, as well as in the US and Canada. In 1990, the latter banded together as the International Committee on Fund Raising Organizations (ICFO), based in the Netherlands, and adopted a series of common criteria for increasing the transparency and reliability of the nonprofit-making sector in their respective countries.

5.3 What's new in central and eastern Europe?

In a 1994 report on the voluntary sector in eastern European countries, Ewa Lés pointed out that one of the most pressing challenges facing the sector was the need to deal with the weakness of regulation and public control mechanisms for foundations and associations, and of the sector's self-regulation procedures.[7] Moreover, she stated that many analysts and managers in the sector were calling for efforts to be concentrated on developing a number of standards for the sector's transparency and responsibility in the areas of finance and services, and for re-inforcing its organizational, administrative, internal management and planning capabilities.

The debate on ethics and good practice in the nonprofit sector that has developed in eastern Europe over recent years should be seen in the context of the revival and growth of foundations and associations. The legal, regulatory and fiscal framework is in the midst of being overhauled and developed, and the relationship between nonprofit sector and public authorities is being redefined. This debate has given rise to a series of initiatives (consultations, working parties, seminars, etc.), both at national level and at the level of the entire eastern European region, some of which are yet to be fully defined.

In a 1994 declaration, the Czech Republic's nonprofit sector set out the sector's basic principles and its role in the creation and development of civil society.[8] The declaration stated that legislation should provide for the formation of various types of nonprofit organization and for the introduction of a suitable legal and fiscal framework to regulate the sector and to support and encourage its growth. That same year, the Sinaia conference in Romania brought together representatives from 13 countries in the region to examine a list of

---

[7] Lés.

[8] Declaration of the Non-Profit Sector of the Czech Republic, Karlovy Vary, May 7, 1994.

principles relating to nonprofit sector responsibilities in the area of administration, management, fundraising and communication, as well as the role of organizations representing the sector. More recently, a series of seminars on ethics in the nonprofit sector has also been held in the New Independent States, notably in Ukraine in 1999.

Furthermore, a number of codes of professional conduct or charters of good practice have already emerged in several countries (see below), in some cases aimed at independent fund-providers, but the vast majority aimed at voluntary sector organizations as a whole.

The Union of Bulgarian Foundations and Associations (UBFA), created in 1992, introduced a code of professional ethics as an appendix to its statutes. The code lays down a series of principles of good practice relating to transparency and responsibility and urges the UBFA's 103 voting members to 'be accountable' with respect to their programmes and objectives, funding practices, and performance. The UBFA monitors compliance with these principles based on the information sent to it annually by its members, since the UBFA's statutes also stipulate that any member in breach of these principles will be excluded from the Union.

In 1995, the Forum of Polish Foundations (PFF) organized a brainstorming seminar in Madralin, Poland, on self-regulation of the sector, with the participation of the committee of the European Foundation Centre (EFC) in Warsaw. Since then, discussions on self-regulation have been extended from the PFF to the Association of the Forum on Non-Governmental Initiatives (*Forum Inicjatyw Pozarzadowych* – FIP), which relaunched the debate based on a reference dossier developed by the EFC. These discussions resulted in the introduction of a 'Charter on the operational principles of non-governmental organizations', adopted in 1996 at the first National Forum on Non-Governmental Initiatives in Warsaw. The principles of the Charter cover:

- compliance with legislation
- respect for human rights and personal dignity
- the independence of organizations
- the separation of administrative and management functions
- the rational use of resources in line with the statutory aims of organizations
- financial transparency.

The Charter's adoption was followed by the introduction of a series of programmes to enhance sector managers' understanding and application of the ethical and legal principles and standards required to increase not only the efficiency but also the credibility of organizations in the voluntary sector. These programmes launched by the FIP are aimed first and foremost at educating the leading federations and coalitions of nongovernmental organizations in Poland, whilst at the same time promoting the transfer of skills from these organizations to their respective members. Since September 1999, the FIP has monitored compliance with the principles of the Charter by the organizations concerned. This work, carried out on the basis of questionnaires sent to nonprofit sector organizations, enables the FIP to vary its activities and programmes in line not only with needs and weaknesses but also with the progress achieved.

Another more recent initiative has emerged in Belarus. In November 1999, some 25 nongovernmental organizations jointly signed a series of principles, proposed by United Way Belarus, governing not only their working practices but also cooperation between organizations in the nonprofit sector. These principles underline the importance not only of openness, transparency and organizational integrity but also of solidarity and dialogue within the sector.

5.4 A European initiative: the Draft Principles of the European Foundation Centre (EFC)

The Draft of Principles of Good Practice[9] adopted by the members of the European Foundation Centre (EFC) in November 1995 emerged from the concerns of independent fund-providers, especially in central and eastern Europe, about the improper use of the term foundation and about cases of abuse or fraud in their respective countries. This concern led to the Prague Declaration being drawn up and adopted by the EFC and its members at their annual general meeting in Prague in November 1993. This declaration was an important milestone in affirming the objectives and responsibilities of Europe's community of independent fund-providers. The Prague Declaration proved of immediate usefulness to western Europe when, in 1993, the European Parliament proposed the creation of a code of good conduct for foundations, accompanied by recognition of their usefulness to Europe. This is a sort of quality label, valid only for a limited period but periodically renewable after review. It is awarded, after consultation with the Parliament, on the basis of a foundation's declared plans and the results achieved. The Parliament's doubtless well-intentioned but ill-considered proposals called for a series of

---

[9] See 6, pages 426–430

measures to be introduced for harmonizing and regulating foundations' activities. Following prolonged negotiations with the EFC and its members, the Parliament agreed, one year later, that the nonprofit sector should be responsible for promoting good practices and transparency by developing a voluntary code based on the Prague Declaration. The EFC went on to develop its Draft Principles of Good Practice on this basis, endeavouring not only to promote transparency in the sector but also to preserve foundations' organizational and operational independence.

The work on researching and writing the Draft Principles was carried out by a task force comprised of members of the EFC, legal experts, representatives of national associations, independent fund-providers and ICFO (see above). Formulating the Draft Principles was, and is, a continuous process, the first stage of which was jointly to define a number of key principles to take into account not only diversity in the types of foundation and their modes of operation, but also diversity in the regional and national systems and cultures from which they spring. In addition, the EFC set out to examine initiatives in progress in a number of countries, such as the UK, which in 1997 was developing its 'Guidelines for Funders of Voluntary Organisations', jointly drawn up by the Association of Charitable Foundations, the Charities Aid Foundation, the Corporate Responsibility Group, the National Lottery Charities Board, the public authorities represented by the Department of National Heritage and various local authority associations.

The EFC's Draft Principles of Good Practice relates to the responsibilities and requirements for transparency and accountability in the internal management of foundations and in the latter's dealings with the general public, the individuals and organizations which they support, and the public authorities. Without examining in detail all the Draft Principles, it is nevertheless possible to draw from them a number of implications.

- The importance of recognizing not only the plurality and diversity of independent fund-providers, but also their collective commitment to helping to set up and promote effective and flexible responses to the socio-economic, cultural, scientific and environmental, health and education challenges facing today's society.
- The importance of the participation of fund-providers in the development of a lasting, fair and pluralist civil society by contributing their funds and/or by running projects in a concern for openness, transparency, integrity and responsibility.

- The issue of the administration of foundations and the importance of a responsible and independent decision-making body to take care of the organization's smooth operation and the safeguarding of public confidence in both spirit and letter. The involvement and participation of a board of directors dedicated to pointing the way forward, establishing priorities, monitoring and examining progress, and evaluating and reviewing its choices.
- Responsibility towards the public and the dissemination of information, that is the importance of providing information and of 'being accountable' as an essential prerequisite for transparency. Providing information on and accounting for their objectives, activities and programmes, revenues and expenditure, by developing a policy of openly disclosing information to third parties, either through annual reports or other information media, listing their activities and presenting a comprehensible and audited annual financial statement.
- The principles and practices of allocating funds. Not only to provide information about the policies and practices applied in allocating funding, but also to ensure the prompt and objective selection and processing of applications, as well as clear evaluation procedures appropriate to the type of support provided.
- Finally, good internal management, responsible investment practices and use of resources and a concern for effective interventions, which involves monitoring and evaluating the activities and funds deployed.

The Draft Principles, which have been translated into several languages in order to ensure wider dissemination at national and regional levels, are periodically reviewed. The work of promoting the Draft Principles has also taken the form of a series of information measures aimed at the members of the Centre and other charitable organizations, in particular putting together a reference dossier on self-regulation initiatives developed to date in the voluntary sector. The Centre also regularly organizes working parties on key aspects of the Draft Principles, such as:

- the role and responsibilities of programme leaders and donor-organization administrators
- means of public communication and information
- investment practices
- evaluating the programmes and activities of such organizations.

A study was carried out in conjunction with *Compagnia di San Paolo* (Italy) on the evaluation methods of Europe's foundations.

The development of the various self-regulation systems initiated by independent fund-providers, as well as by associations, relies on the premise that self-regulation is likely to be more acceptable to the sectors in question than rules imposed by a third party (i.e. the public authorities). Nevertheless, principles of good practice and other codes of professional conduct are credible and effective only if they are respected by the players concerned. Moreover, they must be seen by the public and the public authorities to have been respected. The various European initiatives on the matter are relatively recent and further initiatives should be encouraged. However, they testify to recognition by the European nonprofit sector of the need for transparency and professionalization and of the role that the collective and representative organizations in the sector can and must play in promoting good practice. With regard to transparency, the EFC's experience, not only during its negotiations with the European Parliament, but also in its day-to-day activities, testifies to the importance of gathering detailed information about the role, operation, practices and activities of independent fund-providers in their various areas of activity, and of making such information available to a wide public. This research and information role, which has been developed by many organizations at national level and, in 1993, at European level, with the creation of the EFC's Orpheus communication programme, is crucial to providing better knowledge and understanding of the independent fund-providers' sector, as well as to greater transparency.

6 EFC Code of Practice Task Force: Revised Draft Principles of Good Practice

The **Draft Principles of Good Practice** set out in the following mark a further step in a process launched during the 1994 Annual General Meeting (AGM) of the European Foundation Centre (EFC) and further revised at the 1995 AGM in Seville, Spain in November 1995. They provide a basis for open and ongoing dialogue among independent funders by building on the EFC **Prague Declaration**, a statement of principles and reciprocal commitments for independent funders. The **Draft Principles** are subject to further review and modification.

The **Draft Principles** were developed by the European Foundation Centre (EFC) Code of Practice Task Force. They constitute a general recommendation to reinforce good practice, openness and transparency in the European independent funding community. As such, they are intended to be of application both within the European Union and in the context of the wider Europe. **It is expressly noted that independent funders encompass an uncommonly broad variety of organisations with not only diverse structures, cultures and activities but also disparate concerns and policies. Accordingly, these Draft Principles cannot aspire to accommodate the approach of every individual funder, nor will they be fully applicable in all instances. It is hoped, however, that funders will respect the spirit in which they are drafted to the extent that individual circumstances and operating procedures permit.**

Preamble

Independent funders are committed to the development and promotion of innovative, flexible, and effective responses to specific social, cultural, environmental, educational, scientific, health and economic challenges in today's society.

Independent funders acknowledge the importance of operating in accordance with the wishes of founders who provided initial capital or, in the case of foundations and corporate philanthropy which are dependent upon multiple donations, the wishes and concerns of such donors.

In fulfilling their role in helping build a just, sustainable and pluralistic civil society by providing resources and undertaking operational projects, independent funders acknowledge the importance of openness, transparency, integrity, accountability and self-regulation.

Independent funders also recognise the value of diversity and the need to avoid unnecessary duplication in the use of resources and the exercise of good stewardship.

In subscribing to these principles, foundations and other independent funders should act for public benefit according to the law in democratic societies as follows:

Towards the public at large

a Policy and programmes

Independent funders should define a clear set of basic policies specifying their mission, objectives, goals and related programmes and review these on a regular basis.

Independent funders should ensure open communication with the public at large by disclosing aims, and objectives, procedures and programme interests.

b Governance

Independent funders acknowledge the importance of an identifiable decision-making body (hereinafter 'the board'), whose members and successors should be nominated in accordance with established principles and procedures.

Independent funders also recognise the need for obligations of their board, including decision-making procedures within the organisation, to be clearly defined, and for provision to be made where applicable for delegation of competence and authority.

Independent funders should ensure public record availability of their statutes and the composition of their board.

c Finance

Independent funders should maintain accounts in accordance with standards and practices obtaining in their respective countries and, further, should observe transparency with respect to income, expenditure and assets.

d Annual reporting

Independent funders undertake to inform the general public on a regular basis by means of periodic reports, including annual reports or equivalent information packages available on request which include:

- an explicit narrative of funder purpose and activities in the fiscal year of record such as to enable direct year-on-year comparisons
- a descriptive summary of principal sources of revenue and information on revenue generation
- a descriptive summary of expenditures
- a descriptive summary of grants awarded to other institutions and organisations, as appropriate; and
- a list of board members.

Towards those supported

Independent funders should function transparently with regard to activities supported and related results.

Independent funders that have a grant-making activity should disclose appropriate information regarding their grant-making practices, including geographic and policy limitations and procedures for making grant decisions.

Decision-making procedures should be appropriate and objective.

Applicants should be notified of decisions within a reasonable period of time.

Requirements for monitoring and evaluation should be appropriate to the funds awarded and should be made known at the time of award.

Grants should not be withdrawn or terminated once awarded, other than in exceptional circumstances and for well-founded reasons.

Towards authorities

Independent funders should:

- comply with statutory obligations and restrictions in the jurisdiction(s) in which they operate; and
- ensure disclosure of and access to information concerning their organisation's statute, support activities, income and expenditures, and board members.

Towards self

Independent funders are committed to promote efficient organisation and work while ensuring prudent and sustainable management, investment strategies and procedures, and use of resources.

With a view to promoting and executing sound management policies according to objectives and goals set by their board, they should choose and implement the measures most appropriate to attain those objectives and to achieve those goals.

To this end, the institution board and executive staff should ensure that management practices and resources are commensurate with the needs of activities and programmes supported.

Independent funders should ensure appropriate internal control of resources, carry out internal monitoring, evaluation of programmes supported, and long-term planning measures of performance (monitoring) and outcome (evaluation) should be established in a way that is appropriate to the level of activity and services, and/or to the support and funds provided.

Bibliography

Council on Foundations, *Report of the Task Force on Grant Makers and the Public Interest*, Washington DC, 1995.

'Declaration of the Non-Profit Sector of the Czech Republic', Karlovy Vary, May 7, 1994.

Dufourcq, N., *L'argent du Coeur*, Paris, Hermann-Editeurs des Sciences et Arts, 1996.

Independent Sector, *Ethics and the Nation's Voluntary and Charitable Community: Obedience to the Unenforceable, Everyday Ethics: Key Ethical Questions for Grantmakers and Grantseekers*, Washington, 1991.

InterAction-American Council for Voluntary International Action, *Inter-Action Private Voluntary Organisations (PVO) Standards*, Washington DC, 1993.

Lés E., *The Voluntary Sector in Post-Communist East Central Europe, Regional Report*, Washington DC, CIVICUS, 1994.

National Committee for Responsive Philanthropy, *Foundations and Public Information: Sunshine or Shadow?*, Washington DC, 1980.

▼ Craig Kennedy, Dirk Rumberg and Volker Then

The Organization of Foundations – Management of Human Resources

1 Introduction

The purpose of this chapter is to examine the development and management of human resources within a foundation. This includes not only its staff, but also its board, volunteers and consultants. How this cast of characters with their wide range of motives, incentives and interests is organized into an effective team is of crucial importance to the foundation sector. Unlike many other institutions in society, foundations do not operate in a competitive environment which would allow their performance to be measured and their success or failure in structuring and deploying human resources to be judged. Moreover, in Europe, where the staffed foundation is still an exotic creature, special attention needs to be paid to this aspect of foundation management.

Why should the reader care about this subject? The easy answer is that human resource management will have a greater influence on the effectiveness of a foundation than any other single factor. Occasionally, people of wealth have decided that the expense and bother of having a staff can be avoided because good ideas and people will naturally gravitate towards money. Unfortunately, these do-it-yourself philanthropists almost always fail in their missions because the philanthropic enterprise – even in its most simple form of charity – is sufficiently complex to require good cooperation between trustees, staff, volunteers and others.

An additional reason for paying attention to this topic is that foundations have one large cost centre: people. With the exception of foundations that operate laboratories and other capital intensive enterprises, most philanthropic institutions spend the bulk of their administrative budgets on people. Yet spending on administrative costs has to be scrutinized with care. This is especially so in Europe where operating foundations are common and the allocation of staff cost to either overhead or project budgets may be difficult. Without supervision and thought, staff and internal resource costs can grow rapidly without a concomitant contribution to the foundation or its mission.

What are the elements that influence this human dimension of foundations? Many external and internal factors can determine the size, shape and nature of a foundation's human resources. Several of these are especially influential and worth noting.

1 **The foundation's mission** can be a major determinant of its staffing needs. Foundations with narrow or highly technical missions will almost certainly require human resources – staff,

volunteers, board members and outside expertise – with a certain level of sophistication and knowledge in that area. Of course, foundations with vague or diffuse missions may also employ similar staff because of programme choices and related decisions. But, in the first case, a decision to build a foundation around cancer research, a collection of great art, or the advancement of chemical engineering will have a direct impact on later human resource decisions.

2 **Strategic choices** – decisions on the fundamental operating style of the foundation – will also have a major effect. If a foundation chooses to be an operating institution and conduct most of its programmes internally, a staff of sufficient size and expertise to undertake the work becomes essential. And, with that staff, there will also be a need for more complex and sophisticated management structures to ensure that foundation resources are being effectively and economically deployed.

3 **The size of a foundation** will be an important element in these choices. For foundations of modest dimensions, the management options are multiple. As noted below, paid staff may not even be necessary if trustees and other volunteers are interested and motivated to undertake the task of allocating the fund's resources. However, for large endowments with significant budgets, this 'all-volunteer option' is generally closed. Some paid staff are inevitable and, more than likely, a substantial corps of consultants, programme officers and other professionals will be employed.

4 **History**: foundations are often developed with one goal in mind and then, at a later stage, try to shift missions or strategies. If the move is from a lightly staffed organization to one requiring more human resources, the problems are few. However, a move in the other direction is very difficult. There are very few cases of foundations that have significantly reduced their staff, even among those suffering a dramatically declining resource base. Entrenched interests, lack of external pressures and a host of other forces all join together to make 'downsizing' a foreign word in the foundation business. As a result, it is necessary to keep in mind that early decisions about staffing may be difficult if not impossible to reverse later.

2 Role of boards

Foundation boards provide a vital supervisory function and, in some cases, serve as an important source of expertise in developing and evaluating projects. For smaller foundations, boards may provide the only staffing that is needed to pursue the foundation's mission. In other cases, board members may support both the work of professional staff and the foundation's goals by becoming actively involved in ongoing projects. The challenges are:

- to ensure that boards can continue to serve the legally necessary supervisory function
- to ensure that conflicts do not develop between professional staff and trustees.

2.1 Board as supervisory mechanism

The supervision of a foundation's operations is the most important function of a board of trustees. While the exact structure and name for this body may vary, all European countries provide for its authority and, in essence, expect it to ensure that a foundation's resources are being used for legally acceptable public purposes.

That supervisory function requires a broad knowledge of the foundation's financial and programme operations. In the US, the Council on Foundations has prepared an extensive 'check list' of the types of information necessary for trustees to be familiar with in order to fulfil their legal and ethical responsibilities. The European Foundation Centre and other European foundation associations have also addressed this issue because these supervisory boards play a key role in maintaining the public credibility and legitimacy of foundations in modern society.

Simultaneously serving as a member of the operational team of an institution may however compromise a trustee's ability to provide supervision. For example, if a board member is heavily involved in implementing a large, but troubled, project, can he or she also be expected to provide objective judgements on further investments in this venture? Similarly, if a board member is placed in charge of selecting investments for the foundation's endowment, can he or she then assess the effectiveness of those choices?

These potential conflicts can be resolved in many different ways including the creation of special outside advisory groups and the exclusion of an affected trustee from certain supervisory decisions. The important point is to be aware that combining staff and supervisory functions can raise serious ethical and legal questions.

2.2 Board as source of staffing

Foundation boards can serve as staff in a wide variety of situations. In some cases, directors may have primary responsibility for programme management. In other instances, the board works side by side with professional staff and consultants. Besides the legal and ethical issues raised above, the biggest constraint on the use of directors as staff members is simply time. As a foundation grows or its mission becomes more complex, it is difficult to find directors who are willing to find the necessary time.

When trustees have more than a supervisory role, it can provide them with an added sense of involvement in, and knowledge of, the foundation's work. However, these benefits may be more than offset by conflicts between trustees and professional staff. The latter may find it difficult to perform their duties in an open and objective way when there is substantial trustee involvement in the actual evaluation process. One solution is to place staff in a clearly subordinate role in the review process so that they are subject to the interests and judgements of the directors. However, this approach makes it much more difficult to recruit and keep highly skilled professional staff.

An alternative is clearly to proscribe the role of trustees in day-to-day operations. For example, trustees may serve on review committees that vet proposals and new projects before the whole board acts. Similarly, directors may be included in site visits and other information-gathering trips but with a clear understanding that the professional staff have primary responsibility for project review.

The following three examples illustrate the conditions under which trustees can assume staff functions.

2.2.1 Small foundations

The most common case is when a foundation's assets are modest and directors believe that paid staff cannot be justified. In the US and Germany, the vast majority of all foundations fit this description and are staffed by trustees.

At what point should a foundation consider professional support? There are no easy answers to this question. If a foundation makes a few large grants to institutions that are well known to the trustees, staffing may never be necessary. However, if the fund directors want to have a more public image, make many small grants to institutions or undertake labour-intensive activities like fellowship programmes, professional support from staff or consultants may be essential even where the foundation is small.

2.2.2 Specialized and technical foundations

A second situation where trustees commonly serve as staff is when the foundation has a highly specialized mission that requires a board with sophisticated knowledge of the field. Typical examples are institutions that support medical or other types of scientific research as well as funds that provide fellowships to artists and musicians. While a professional staff may solicit applications and perform initial evaluations, the trustees of such foundations often have a very active role in reviewing applications and interviewing potential recipients.

The rationale for this approach is that it would be difficult to recruit a full-time professional staff with the same experience, stature and knowledge that one could recruit for a part-time board. A Nobel Prize winner or an award-winning writer may be willing to serve as a director and even devote a good deal of time to the foundation's work as long as they are free to pursue their own independent research and projects.

As with small foundations, the primary constraint on this approach is time. The concept of an expert board is an attractive one but it may prove unworkable in practice if more than a few proposals have to be reviewed. Some trustees inevitably find it difficult to attend review meetings and perform their staff functions as demands increase. As a result, the fund's effectiveness begins to deteriorate or professional staff take on broader and more important roles.

Another limitation is the potential for conflicts of interest when practitioners in a field are also making grant decisions concerning their peers and subordinates. While rules of conduct can be imposed to minimize this risk, the fact is that few people are able to leave their loyalties and prejudices at the board room door when they are awarding lucrative fellowships or making major research grants. These conflicts can potentially diminish the credibility of a foundation and almost always create tensions between professional staff and trustees. Nonetheless, one can point to several prominent and highly regarded institutions that make heavy use of trustee expertise and also maintain a strong reputation for fair and effective grant making.

2.2.3 Limitations on administrative costs

Finally, for a third group of foundations, trustees play a strong staff role out of necessity because there are formal or informal limits on the fund's administrative costs. The founders of the great American foundations often had an aversion to large staffs and high overhead costs. In some instances, this emphasis on frugality ceased with the death of the donor or his immediate family. But, in other cases, fiscal austerity becomes part of the foundation's culture and utilizing trustees as staff is one way to honour this tradition.

As a foundation's assets grow, staffing austerity will have a strong impact on its operations. If the administrative cap is honoured, then the fund must narrow its focus, make ever larger grants and/or perform less rigorous evaluations of each new request or project. The alternative is to break with tradition and take on more staff. In general, the latter course is most common. However, an increasing number of foundations are finding ways to keep their personnel and administrative costs low and still be effective philanthropic institutions.

2.3 Determining board structure

The structure of a foundation's governing board is a crucial element in the design of the organization. The US and Europe offer a variety of models in terms of board functions, size and operations. National and local laws often set a basic framework for board structure. However, other considerations including privacy, control and public accountability play a role in the specific choices that foundations make.

2.3.1 Board composition and roles

One of the initial questions that faces every foundation is who should belong to the endowment's governing body. Should the board be limited to the donor's family and business associates or should a wider group of individuals be considered? Should the donor and his associates have a special status on the board, with different terms or legal responsibilities, or should all members be treated alike? Will committees be given special rights to approve budgets and oversee financial investments, for example, or will most major institutional decisions be made by the board as a whole?

These choices are sometimes technical, but almost always have major implications for the foundation's future operation. For example, in the US, it is not unusual to have two classes of board members, one group with permanent positions and a second group serving specific terms or being re-elected each year. The former group is usually reserved for the donor and those closest to him and the latter for 'outsiders'. Similarly, executive committees are often given extraordinary authority to approve budgets and make grants, with the larger board serving in a more passive supervisory role. Of course, some foundations avoid these machinations and simply have small boards comprising the donor, his family and business associates.

In the US, many believe that foundation boards should have substantial outside representation and that these outsiders should be treated equally with other members who have a closer relationship to the donor, his family and their business. The American emphasis on public accountability of foundations means that small, closely-held boards, and those with different board classes or functions, are generally seen merely as mechanisms for allowing the donor and his family to exert undue control. In practice, most of the largest foundations follow this path of openness by drawing on outsiders for board membership. However, many other endowments have boards that are largely comprised of family members and business associates with few if any outsiders.

The European foundation tradition is different and so are the standards of conduct; while Americans have tended to emphasize the public nature of foundations Europeans have kept them firmly within the private sphere and, in most countries, allow close connections to the donor's business interests and family. As in the US, many of the largest foundations do have outsiders on their boards. However, the use of diverse and independent governing bodies is still not a common practice in Europe.

2.3.2 Board size

The issue of board size is a difficult one. Most observers would agree that boards should be large enough to accommodate a range of skills, interests and perspectives on the foundation's mission and operations. Yet there is also general agreement that large boards are difficult to manage and susceptible both to internal conflicts and staff manipulation.

Several criteria can provide guidance to the golden mean between these two points.

1. Optimal board size is partially a function of the foundation's complexity. To provide adequate supervision of a fund's work, the board must include some individuals who are knowledgeable in its fields of endeavour and particular strategies. For example, a small foundation that makes grants to a limited number of institutions in one city may be able to ensure sufficient supervision with a three or four person board while a substantial foundation with an international agenda in many fields will need a much larger supervisory body, drawing on individuals from different disciplines.

2 Board size is also determined by the operational style of the foundation. Large boards can be unwieldy due to the logistical difficulties of scheduling busy people. They also present challenges in creating a common culture and a sense of commitment among a large number of people with different motives and interests. If a foundation board needs to meet often or has the capacity to make expeditious decisions, then a small board may be necessary. If a board is expected also to act as staff and work closely together in developing projects, a smaller number of directors may be necessary simply to have the level of cohesiveness and collegiality demanded by the fund's operating style.

3 A third consideration is credibility and accountability. Some foundations need large, diverse boards for reasons of public image and validity. For example, community foundations customarily have large boards with representatives from different segments of their local constituency in order to demonstrate their responsiveness to community interests. Other foundations with public policy agendas may also have large boards including distinguished experts in order to legitimize their recommendations to government. Advisory boards and review panels can achieve some of these same ends. However, board membership is generally viewed as a more effective mechanism for securing public approval and legitimacy.

2.3.3 Terms of service

Board tenures is another difficult issue. Should a foundation have specified terms of service for its directors and should there be limits on how many terms a trustee can serve? Should there be a mandatory retirement age and should it apply to all board members including the donor?

The process of answering these questions often causes considerable tension within a foundation board especially when it is dominated by a founder and his associates. Terms of service and of mandatory retirement both force changes in board membership and disturb comfortable working relationships. In the US, the majority of foundations have no fixed terms of service and add new members only when death, disease and voluntary retirement make it necessary.

Nonetheless, there is a trend toward limits on tenure. For some foundations, fixed terms of service become a way of revitalizing boards by including new members who bring new perspectives and needed expertise. In other cases, terms of service are a relatively humane means of ensuring that older members with declining energy can be replaced. Finally, a board may be more willing to experiment and take chances with different kinds of trustee when board membership does not carry with it lifetime tenure.

As with board size, the choice of board terms is partially a function of size, complexity and a fund's need for public credibility. For small endowments, the time-consuming task of identifying new members and the disruption to board continuity may present costs that far outweigh the benefits gained from a regular renewal of the governing body. Conversely, for a community foundation or any other large and visible endowment, terms and mandatory retirement ages may be essential for long-term institutional effectiveness.

2.3.4 Committees

A key issue of board structure is the role of committees. Under what conditions does a foundation board need to devolve some authority to specialized committees? What kinds of committees are most needed and appropriate for the proper management of a foundation?

The need for committees is linked with many of the factors that have already been discussed. The size and complexity of a foundation's operations, however, may be the best determinants of a need for board committees. As an endowment grows in size and complexity, an investment committee may be necessary in order to provide adequate monitoring of the foundation's financial health. If the board is large and has fixed terms, there may be a need for a nominating committee dedicated to identifying and screening new trustees. If the board is closely involved in the screening of applications for support, separate trustee committees for specific programme areas are a common addition.

In the US, most large foundations have at the minimum an audit and an investment committee. An executive committee is sometimes added as a mechanism for overseeing top management and making major decisions between regular board meetings. Nominating committees are also becoming more common as more boards do adopt terms of service.

In the end, there is no absolute rule on board committees. If every board member is competent to supervise the financial and programme components of a foundation and has the time and energy to do so in an appropriate manner, there may be no need for committees of any kind. However, most medium and large foundations will find a need to devolve some authority onto committees.

2.4 Identifying and recruiting board members

A sound and effective board is one of the most important elements of a successful foundation. The identification and recruitment of trustees is a crucial part of creating or maintaining a quality board. For many years, foundation boards reflected largely the friendships and business associations of the donor and his successors. However, as the size and importance of foundations has increased, as well as the level of public scrutiny, most established foundations do something more than simply tap their friends when there is a board vacancy. Indeed, in the US, the composition and competence of foundation boards is increasingly a topic of much discussion. The choice of a chief executive is still the most important job of a trustee body. However, the selection of new trustees has quickly become another major responsibility.

2.4.1 Criteria for trustee selection

Whether a new board is being formed or an existing body is being renewed, the key questions are the same. What competencies are needed to perform the board's responsibilities? Which constituencies need to be represented in order to ensure the board's credibility in its fields of endeavour?

As with many topics in this section, the answers to these questions have changed dramatically over the past decade within the foundation community. Twenty years ago, the principle quality sought in recruiting a new trustee was loyalty to the founder and his family, business and philanthropic interests. Today, very few American foundations and a declining number of European foundations would have such narrow requirements. Loyalty is still an issue, but competency and representativeness are equally if not more important.

How does one determine the competencies needed by a foundation board? The grant making and operational programmes of the endowment should first be examined. While trustees do not have to be experts in every area of interest, a certain level of knowledge and understanding is essential if the proposals of staff and fellow trustees are to be evaluated in a thoughtful manner. It would be irresponsible to allow a foundation devoted to medical research to operate without trustees possessing the ability to judge the need for, and quality of, its work. Similarly, a foundation focused on Asia or Latin America needs board members who know those regions and have a sense of the types of programmes that will be most effective.

A second area of competency is foundation management. A board needs people who can supervise the investment of endowment resources and the administration of other business interests. It also needs a few members with the interest and skill to serve on audit committees and other board bodies that ensure the wise deployment of foundation resources. These tasks include the assessment of executive compensation, legal expenses and other large costs associated with the philanthropy.

The question of representativeness also arises when developing boards. In the US, it is commonly accepted that the trustees of a foundation should reflect to some extent the constituencies affected by its programmes. At a minimum, that entails attention to the number of women on a board and, depending on the foundation, it may also make minority representation highly desirable.

However, the issue of representativeness is not simply one of being politically correct. It is also an issue of being politically effective. A board can be a powerful tool in implementing a foundation's programmes. For example, if a foundation is focused on public policy, the presence of respected politicians on its board will add credibility to its work. These representatives may also bring knowledge about the fund's chosen fields. But, their endorsement of the foundation's work may be a more important reason to have them as members.

Emphasis on credibility can carry risks. It is possible to end up with a highly credible board comprised of people who have little time for or knowledge about the foundation's actual operations. The need for core competencies always has to be the first priority. However, faced with two equally knowledgeable trustee candidates, it is prudent to select the one who will also provide the greatest external credibility.

2.4.2 Methods of recruiting trustees

Once the criteria for new trustees have been set, the next challenge is to find suitably qualified individuals with an interest in serving on a foundation's board. This task is not necessarily an easy one. While foundation boards are highly attractive positions, the right people may not have the time or experience for the supervisory functions that are normally the province of trustees. Compatibility, personal style and general disposition are crucial considerations in the selection of new trustees, yet these are highly subjective qualities.

One or more of three means are generally used to recruit new board members.

1 Most commonly, the networks of the existing board members are tapped for possible candidates. This avenue can often guarantee a high degree of compatibility. However, if the foundation needs people with competencies or constituencies different to those already present on the board, this path may not be productive. When only existing trustees are used as recruiting sources, there will be a tendency to develop an ingrown board with a high sense of togetherness, but a lack of contrasting perspectives.

2 Another common method is to solicit nominations from outside experts who understand the foundation's mission. This approach may broaden the search substantially, but it also has its risks. The most obvious is that these expert nominators may have their own self-interest in mind especially if they are current recipients of foundation support. They may suggest colleagues who will support their ideas or at least support a particular programme strategy. Similarly, they may see themselves as possible candidates and use the opportunity to push their own qualifications forward. Interviews with experts and with colleagues in the foundation business can be a good means of identifying board candidates as long as these risks are borne in mind.

3 An outside firm can be hired to conduct a search for new board members. While only a minority of American foundations use this approach, it is much more common today than it was ten years ago. In using a search firm for this task, a foundation can cast a much broader net and be assured of some level of objectivity in identifying possible candidates. The limitation is that few search firms will have sufficient knowledge of a board to judge a candidate's compatibility with his or her fellow trustees. If there is the active involvement of a nominating committee in the search process, this weakness can be greatly reduced.

2.5 Board orientation

The final step in the board development process is integrating new members into the existing structure. Integration is fundamentally an education process that gives the new trustee the information that he or she needs to function effectively. This information falls broadly into three categories.

1 **People – both fellow trustees and key staff.** In many cases, new trustees will have met their board colleagues during the recruiting process. But only rarely will they have existing relationships with key staff members. Some foundations make a point of inviting new trustees to meet with staff before their first board meeting. Others

use a less formal mechanism. However, in all cases, new trustees should be given a list of key personnel, information on their duties and appropriate biographical information.

2 **Administration and programmes**. New trustees should have information on the foundation's financial condition, major financial commitments and liabilities and other management issues that are relevant to their duties. Similarly, the new trustee should be introduced to the foundation's major projects and external programme commitments. This may simply entail providing them with a copy of the fund's most recent annual report or it can involve a detailed briefing by staff and fellow trustees on each of these topics.

3 **Basic framework governing the trustee's relationship with the foundation**. This topic includes rules on expenses, board–staff contact and conflicts of interest. In the former case, there should be a clear written statement of what the foundation will cover in terms of the trustees' travel and other board-related expenses. In the second case, the board chairman or chief executive officer should make explicit the rules governing board–staff interactions. For example, should board members call programme staff directly if they have a question about a project or should the enquiry be routed through top management? Lastly, the new trustee should be provided with a clear statement of the foundation's rules on conflicts of interest. This statement should cover situations where the trustees are direct beneficiaries as well as instances where they serve on the board of an institution that receives money from the foundation.

Many foundations provide limited orientation to new trustees and when the fund is small and its operations are relatively transparent there may be little need for this process. However, for most mid- and large-sized foundations, this type of introduction to the people, projects and rules is absolutely essential to the smooth operation of the institution.

3 Role of staff

3.1 Staff Size

3.1.1 Operational or grant making?

Next to the size of the annual budget the strategic decision about an operating or grant-making working method has the greatest impact on the number of staff employed. This is evident if one considers the major operating foundations which run hospitals, medical research centres, museums or educational institutions. But it also applies if a founder has decided to establish a think-tank producing public policy advice or strategic studies.

When a new foundation is created the strategic decision about the operating style clearly has a considerable impact on the rate of growth that the institution can manage in a productive way. The more operational a founder intends the institution to be, the more resource management restricts what can be successfully achieved within a short period of time after establishment. Operational foundations require a high level of in-house expertise in their chosen field. They need to create internal management structures to control the institution and to choose and develop their operational resources with care if they are to set high standards for their work. The governing structure of such a foundation needs to be entrepreneurial in the true sense of the word, and this in itself is likely to lead to success.

3.1.2 *Operational foundations*

The minimum requirement for setting up an operational foundation is that it must have sufficient financial resources to employ permanent staff. Whereas a grant-making foundation can mobilize voluntary leadership and the participation of volunteers in running its programmes, an operational foundation would not come into being if it relied on voluntary work only or contracted out its permanent tasks. However, outside resources and capabilities can always help to increase outreach and productivity.

Yet the working method of a foundation does not altogether determine its staff requirements. There are several options for running the desired programmes at varying levels of in-house staff. Operating foundations can still contract out specific tasks and this can both enlarge staff capacity and enhance staff capabilities. To put it another way, operating foundations rely on outside resources in the sense of buying in services rather than granting financial support to outside institutions. The division of labour between internal and external resources allows the institution to maximize productivity. Yet cooperation with outside partners can also be considered a training programme for inhouse staff which develops internal resources for the future. From this perspective, the application of outside resources is part of a learning organization and helps to accumulate skills and human capital in the foundation. Needless to state that this process of organizational learning can also include transfers of staff from other institutions into the foundation to internalize what used to be external resources.

Obviously, what a foundation can achieve by relying on internal resources is also related to the complexity of projects and programme areas. The more varied the management tasks, the more numerous are the staff involved in the project. In this sense, the Rockefeller Foundation's Bellaggio Conference Center is certainly a less demanding task than the Robert Bosch Clinics or the Paul Getty Museum in California. Building up a think-tank institution such as the Bertelsmann Foundation requires a more sophisticated strategy for recruiting expertise in various fields and in linking it in an interdisciplinary way than building up an operational foundation active in only one field (such as medicine, the fine arts, care of the elderly, the performing arts). An institution that focuses on political and economic problem-solving must meet high standards of innovative interdisciplinary work if it is to leave a real mark on public debate and influence decision-making.

Even an operation as small as a local youth centre, a small community museum or research in only one highly specialized field (such as the ecology of housing construction), management requires a diversity of staff qualifications and probably therefore several members of permanent staff. In very large operating institutions, certain services like financial control could be contracted out to ease the burden of supervision. In general, the number of staff required is a function of the level of involvement in operating projects, ranging from strategic decision-making at one end of the spectrum to building up a team of highly qualified experts to do most of the programme work in house at the other.

Staff requirements depend not only on the nature of programmes but also on criteria such as level of complexity, supervision, size of organization and working methods in general. It is obvious that developing and coordinating a research programme is a totally different task from organizing an international students' exchange or a further education scheme. These again are different from acting as a convenor or from running a vaccination programme in Third World countries.

In some cases staff may be required in only one location, in others it is advisable to set up field offices. The nature of programmes also dictates whether or not staff need to be organized in special programme departments supported by common service units (e.g. media relations and communications, computing).

Whatever an operational foundation does, its founders must clearly be aware of the challenges of careful internal resource management and the need to decide on internal resource allocation as well as outsourcing.

3.1.3 Grant-making foundations

The process of making grants to applicants can be achieved without any staff at all; a small number of grants, and only one or two programmes, can be handled by the board or a few volunteers. However, if applicants for grants are to be thoroughly screened, consultants or agents must be brought in to assist. Where a programme is to run for several years, there are advantages to the employment of permanent staff. Information on previous applicants and their performance can be collected and processed by them and over the course of time a network of grantees can be built up on a database. Permanent staff can help a foundation build up its own expertise and develop sophistication in running in programmes. As a result it may then consider introducing operational elements into its programme work.

The number of staff required to expedite grant making depends on the size of the individual grants and therefore on the grant to budget ratio. Foundations experiencing rapid growth tend to increase the average size of their grants. It is certainly more demanding on staff time to run a programme which has many individuals as grantees and to which thousands of individuals may apply than to make few large grants to university institutes; whereas in the latter case it may be sufficient to organize a system of peer reviews by respective fellow academics, the former case will require considerable man hours simply to check applications for completeness let alone for suitability.

Foundations develop their own cultures in terms of the type and size of grants they make. Some handle institutions seeking nonprofit and private funding whereas others handle large numbers of individual grantees with considerable skill. The Körber Foundation, for example, has developed a good reputation for its national and regional competitions and awards, which attract applications from hundreds or thousands of individuals. In the case of programmes aimed at a wider public, foundations frequently arrange for their professional staff to work side by side with volunteer review teams or reviewers serving on an honorary basis. The primary task of the professional staff members in this case will be to ensure that the programme meets clear and distinguishable social or public needs and that it reaches its target groups.

Staff requirements do not, however, result exclusively from the number of grants or their size. Working with institutions in academia, the arts, social welfare or charity, education, politics, the Third World or the local community requires totally different skills from working with individuals. Grant making involves elements of professional cooperation: to be a successful grant maker to institutions means not just allowing grantees to find outside financial resources for their own interests, but also influencing their programme priorities. To achieve this, the professional skills of the foundation staff need to match the professional standards of the institutions to be granted funds. Staff must be sufficiently qualified to be competent to conduct peer reviews.

Grant making involves decisions as to the degree to which applicants or the success of programmes are to be reviewed. The level of evaluation envisaged dictates the number of staff involved and the outside resources to be applied to the task: foundations can call for applications, choose their grantees and simply transfer the funds to them. On the other hand, they can decide to monitor grants and their use during the whole duration of the project supported. This may mean staff attending site visits, meetings, running steering groups and conducting interviews. The contribution by Joseph Breiteneicher and Melinda Marble in this book shows the variety of options that strategically oriented grant making has.

A last and special case is the supervision of international grant making or cross-border giving. This covers both international exchange programmes and grants to institutions to conduct projects in international cooperation. The operation of such programmes may include the need to open field offices or to commission agents to take responsibility for parts of the programme abroad. In such cases, major benefits can be gained from appropriate forms of cooperation with other foundations or institutions. Foundations choosing to run international programmes on the basis of their own resources have to employ staff with international working or academic experience, a very good command of the appropriate language and a thorough knowledge of the country concerned. Smaller foundations may only invest in international grant making if this is a core part of their mission or if the programme is small and manageable by a limited staff.

Foundations have to face a long list of options regarding size and qualifications of their staff. The scale can range from a single professional programme manager to organizations of several hundred staff members. A foundation has to find its own balance between resources allocated internally and those contracted for externally. The possibility of relying solely on honorary board members and for volunteer contributions for running the programmes should not be ignored: however the level of professionality and strategic scope may be compromised. As soon as members of staff are employed, their appropriate selection and competence become key concerns. Contrary to US experience, a labour market of professional foundation managers does not really exist in most European countries. Therefore any choice always involves judgements as to the relevance of skills and qualifications gained in other institutions. And while foundations in the US can rely on professional consultants with experience of making these judgements on their behalf, this option is rarely available in European countries. What should European founders then look for in staff to get their venture going at all?

3.2 Types and level of expertise and competence

3.2.1 Technical versus general expertise

Philanthropy is driven by the desire to produce a tangible impact on the life of society. It is based on a mission. The actual operations have therefore to command both highly general management skills and very specialized knowledge in programme areas. Depending on the financial structure of a foundation, asset management, fundraising and the actual programme departments will have to be distinguished. Foundations that rely on a large endowment need to be concerned with asset management, general administration and programme work. Foundations that rely heavily on current income need skilled fundraisers, administrators and programme officers. The communication strategies of two such foundations may be totally different: whereas the former type has to make public the services that it renders to society, the latter has to mobilize support and demand involvement (or funding) from the public. In short, it is clear that foundations may require four groups of staff members: financial experts, administration experts, programme experts and communication talents. If the organization is very small, it has to be decided which of the four is the easiest to contract out and which can possibly be performed by a combination of staff members.

Since no labour market exists for programme experts, we can only give a range of options from which founders or boards may chose. First of all, most programme officers are academically trained people who have had research or other working experience before joining the foundation. They need scientific, medical, political, economic or other knowledge and they have to be able to apply this to the particular task of managing knowledge rather than researching it. They have to possess understanding of the fine arts, of the performing arts or of any other field without being able to perform or to paint or to be active members of these communities. Primarily, such members of staff have to be information scouts and communicative talents. In some cases they will be forced to be their own PR officers, financial controllers and publication editors at the same time. Their theoretical basis of training and profession may vary from case to case; they nevertheless have to bridge the gap between academia and practicality. In many cases, they will have to command good political skills in their own negotiations or be good mobilizers of whatever support the programme needs. The longer the list of potential skills required by programme managers gets the clearer it becomes that all the qualifications are rarely available in one person. They either have to be collected together through a division of labour or recruited, at least partially, from outside.

3.2.2 Technical expertise
In-house or external expertise

In creating an organization the board members or the founders have to decide on the required scale and scope of in-house expertise. Budget constraints and quality standards determine what degree of first class in-house expertise a foundation can afford. From the beginning it must be quite clear that the option of building up in-house expertise requires substantial and continued investment in staff and their salaries as well as their continued qualification as experts in certain areas or communities. Therefore small foundations may find it more practicable to rely on contracted or volunteer services. Even this option will provide a considerable challenge in appropriate management and coordination.

Having opted for in-house staff, a foundation must be aware of labour market and legal situations. Staff can be hired on a permanent or a temporary basis, however this decision is dependent on the level of qualifications desired. This in turn has a serious impact on the innovative potential of programme work: programmes which can only be successful by building up relationships of trust and cooperation with other institutions and which are most effective when a foundation has built up a reputation of excellence in the field, are difficult to manage with temporary staff. Fluctuation of staff may endanger the stock of embedded knowledge that is available in the organization and therefore such projects will to a large extent depend on permanent staff working over years.

On the other hand, foundations with permanent staff lack flexibility when they wish to change programme areas or abandon programmes to engage in fields which they find more innovative or more effective in fulfilling their mission. As a minimum requirement organizations should take care to maintain some flexibility in the programme responsibilities of their officers. This can be achieved by allowing or encouraging programme officers to be involved in more than one programme field or by structures of interdisciplinary cooperation which to some degree spread the available knowledge within the organization rather than confining it to single individuals.

In addition to programme-related and organization-based considerations foundations have to assess their relative position in the labour market. In making the decision to employ in-house expertise they have to be clear that they can afford competitive salaries to attract the people they would like to recruit, and to decide on salary levels a foundation has to identify its preference scale of desired qualifications. As a result the founder or the board members may find that their target group should be young members of academic research centres or young business professionals. They may find that they have to compete with salary levels of journalists or of activists of other NGOs.

In some cases, corporations or business owners establish their foundations and then recruit from their existing organizations. The same is true in the case of politically inspired foundations. Yet a foundation may still be faced with a considerable span between what a trainee of a business corporation would expect and what a young teacher could earn.

In the absence of professionalization in foundation management, the building up of in-house expertise has to be based on careful decisions as well as the mission of a foundation.

Methods of using outside expertise

Outside expertise may be required to perform specific analyses in specific fields of knowledge. But it may also be required to provide practical experience in any given field of work in society. Outside expertise is contracted for by involving independent experts for specific tasks. They can be requested to provide studies, perform research analyses, do surveys, provide material or data, search for methods of best practice or identify benchmarks in a field. Outside experts can contribute to the definition of new programmes, they can be commissioned to perform programme management, they can be hired as consultants for internal work, they may do evaluation and they can serve as scouts for new promising activities in a programme area. They can also serve on committees, be appointed members of advisory boards or members of award or competition juries, assist in communicating programme results to target groups, or implement programme suggestions. In any case it is the crucial task of the foundation to set the goals for what it wishes to achieve by involving outsiders. It is also a prime in-house responsibility to organize the employment of outside experts in such a way as to retain the foundation's autonomy. Ensuring the independence of outside interests is key when choosing advisors, programme experts or other consultants.

Appropriate experts may be identified by holding competitions, calling for proposals, cooperating with competent institutions, running selection processes on the basis of in-house expertise, doing feasibility studies, applying methods of systematic evaluation, running programmes on a trial basis, doing pilot programmes or studies, or – after some period of its existence – relying on experts from previous programmes.

The involvement of experts may be organized on a temporary basis (for a particular meeting, a conference, a programme period, one year, one call in a competition or award), or foundations may wish to build up networks of longstanding partners on whose contributions they rely in many regards and for many years. Where this is the case it will be necessary to ensure the impartiality of programme work and to prevent the programmes from becoming stagnant for lack of new ideas.

Methods of building inside expertise

There are a number of key routes to grow the expertise of foundation staff:

- experience
- exchange among staff
- outside contacts
- the rotation of tasks and duties
- formal training.

Whatever programme is carried out the members of staff responsible for it are acquiring valuable new experience. No matter whether the programme in question was successful or not, in both cases it is crucial to have established mechanisms of assessing success and drawing conclusions. Systematic approaches will build up communication structures among members of staff with different duties. This can involve various programme fields but it can also involve different types of expertise (conference organization, publications, PR, network programmes, education schemes, etc.). As previously noted, this approach ensures that expertise is spread around the organization rather than being concentrated in single individuals who may leave and cause serious ruptures. A foundation should always keep in mind that the participation of their staff in conferences and seminars of other institutions is part of a permanent learning process and this should be budgeted for.

Changing the responsibilities of programme managers may also contribute to capacity building. Through working for different programmes foundation managers have a chance to acquire various competences and compare the requirements of programmes so that they develop general management skills. When a foundation has been working for several years with a well established organizational structure, it can also use formal training to enhance the skills of its staff. This training can encompass a wide range of skills, from language qualifications to project management seminars, from protocol training to marketing know how. Whatever the foundation's approach, the prime field of expertise of its staff will be decision-making – staff should be encouraged and trained to make constant decisions when managing programmes.

Access to research facilities and time devoted to systematic learning in their programme areas will also contribute substantially to staff qualifications. Do resources and time allow for sufficient reading, researching, following reviews in journals and browsing CD-ROM databases? Can the foundation afford to subscribe to major publications, newspapers, and other periodicals? A foundation may not aspire to become an academic research institute but its governing bodies must be aware that the qualifications of their personnel may become outdated at a considerable pace if not refreshed. Measures in this area are the more crucial, the more active and operational a foundation wishes to be.

3.3 Organizational style

3.3.1 Continuum: centralized versus decentralized

When building a foundation organization, founders do not have to do without any models. There are basically two options available:

- the corporate or business organization model with its bureaucratic principles and centralized structures
- an academic model which implies a more decentralized structure.

The scale of operations is important in the first model and in the process of growth tendencies towards decentralization may in fact appear; the larger a foundation grows the more it will have to resort to building divisions or departments with relative autonomy, leaving only crucial decisions to be taken by the central governing bodies of the institution. This process is known from corporate history as the development from personal entrepreneurship to a functional, departmental organization and further on to a divisional structure.[1] But before going into details regarding the processes of growth we should examine both the centralized and decentralized models in more detail.

3.3.2 *Centralized model*

Any centralized organization requires common goals and a mission, both of which determine the activities in the institution. All members of staff at any level of the hierarchy look to them for orientation of their work. In a foundation of this type the goal-setting and strategic decision-making capacities of the board and any members of the governing bodies are of the utmost importance since it is their initiative which makes the whole institution move. According to this perception of foundation work staff are implementers of a shared strategy and have only limited scope for their own initiative. In such a foundation, it is the governing bodies which decide whether it will perceive of itself as a player in public policy-making or as a convenor, to name but two examples. The staff will then have to design and implement the appropriate programmes.

Obviously in such a foundation the demands made on decision-making and strategy-setting qualities of the governing body will be taxing and the involvement of staff in these areas relatively modest. Indeed, to involve staff in strategy-setting in such an institution may simply provoke competition for resources rather than fostering a spirit of cooperation. The foundation may face the danger of being split into factions rather than making the most productive use of its resources. Centralized types of foundation organization are in fact dependent upon the fairly homogeneous views of their founders or governing bodies as to their primary targets. They rely on the initiative and

---

[1] Vgl. A.D. Chandler, Strategy and Structure ...; ders., Scale and Scope, ...

innovative capacities of top management and channel programme initiatives top down.

The decision to operate a foundation along these lines requires the board to have a vital interest in monitoring the performance of projects against the targets set. From this it follows that the level of investment in instruments of monitoring and control, and the manpower devoted to it, are relatively high. Simultaneously, management interpretations of mission and targets have to be communicated to everyone in the organization, and staff perceptions of these in implementing programmes, as well as the results of programmes, have to be reported back to the board. Such a model can only be efficient as long as the targets are relatively few in number and do not require too complex a cooperation between different competences. Otherwise the institution will be overburdened with opinions and communications and its innovative and decision-making capacity will be restricted.

A centralized foundation will require some members in its governing body to devote all or a major share of their time to its work. It will act like a large corporation in a traditional industrial market and will concentrate on a small number of 'product lines'.

To stay with the comparison, a highly innovative corporation which will easily explore new markets, develop a continuous flow of innovative products, and diversify into different markets will require a fairly decentralized and responsive organization. It will be dependent upon a high degree of information processing regarding customer demands. Innovative and inventive staff capacities will be essential for success. Therefore the corporation will either be organized in product or in geographical divisions, both of which are characterized by a relatively high degree of autonomy in their actions and market strategies. The divisions will be linked by their efforts at mobilizing synergies, managing know how, and optimizing the investment of funds available. This model holds for foundations as well and therefore they may opt for a decentralized model of organization.

3.3.3 Decentralized model

A decentralized foundation is distinguished from its centralized counterpart by regarding common goals and its mission as a framework within the boundaries of which the organization is free to act. This means that staff will be encouraged to initiate and design strategic programme approaches. Mission and goals in this case exist as incentives rather than standards against which the activities of everyone in the organization are measured and monitored. The quality of programme work and the innovative potential of the decentralized foundation will be largely dependent upon the expertise and competence of its staff. Such an organization could possibly develop and successfully manage several 'product lines', that is programme areas, which may vary considerably in scale and scope. One of them could be a research programme, another an education scheme and a third could be a forum for international exchange and understanding. The success of the respective efforts will to a large extent depend upon skilled and qualified staff, who need to be well connected, have a reputation among experts in their field and enjoy autonomy to be most effective in managing programmes.

Top management in a decentralized foundation should resist getting involved in details of programme work and limit itself to governing and taking general decisions as to resource allocation and the exploration of new programme areas including recruiting appropriate staff. There is great scope for success in this model, in which governing bodies and board members perceive themselves as coaches and guides rather than agenda setters.

Such an organization has a high potential for innovation at least in theory; in practice it depends more than most on staff recruitment and personnel management. It can be very responsive to social needs and it has the chance to open up new programme areas in a flexible way. It may be easier for such foundations to work in community-oriented or social welfare programmes which depend upon thorough knowledge of the social situation to be improved and upon a good spirit of cooperation with other community institutions. A decentralized organization may also be helpful when working with specific groups such as the homeless or the elderly, of whom top management or board members may have little experience.

The advantages of decentralization are balanced by challenges: it will be difficult to maintain an adherence to common goals and to develop some sort of corporate identity in such a foundation. In the public eye the foundation will probably be associated with some of its most successful programmes rather than with an overall corporate identity. Public relations staff will have a difficult job to do in conveying some general view of what the foundation sees as its mission and its prime goals. It will even be difficult to establish a common corporate design that makes programmes identifiable as an initiative of the foundation. The renowned activities of the *Körber Stiftung* in Germany provide an example of foundation work characterized by well-known 'programme brands' like the *Bergedorfer Gesprächskreis* or the *Schülerwettbewerb*

Deutsche Geschichte which are less well known for originating from the same foundation. Nevertheless experience shows that these minor difficulties (which also depend on the view which a founder or a board takes of an institution's public appearance) can be overcome.

More serious checks on the effectiveness and the success of a foundation may result from the way in which competition among its divisions and programmes is handled. Even where there is a high degree of autonomy divisions should share information in a spirit of cooperation and undertake programmes of an interdisciplinary nature. Competition for limited resources should not end in internal battling but rather in joint exploration of promising fields of activity. Here the coaching and encouraging capacities of the board are of the utmost importance and can develop into the primary task of top management. Understanding the importance of this strategic action on the part of governing bodies is crucial for the foundation's internal organizational culture – it also prevents the foundation from competing in an inefficient way for scarce external resources such as expert knowledge, prominent public figures or institutional partners. The entrepreneurial task primarily includes creating a climate of exchange, a culture of openness and know how management.

Different models of organizational structure involve different levels of expertise from different groups of staff and different perceptions of the tasks and time devoted to foundation governance. When setting up a foundation, its mission, strategic field of interest, mode of operations, size of venture and many other factors all have to be taken into account; the following paragraph makes an overall comparative assessment of the respective models.

3.3.4 *Points of choice*

Foundations working in a field requiring highly specialized staff with high levels of competence are bound to be organized in a more decentralized way. It helps them to attract appropriate staff and allows these people to use their skills in the most effective way. Such foundations have either decided to devote their work directly to knowledge production or they are working with grantees or partner institutions which are active in knowledge production. Obviously programme work in such fields could not be competently directed by any board or top management if they were not composed of such experts. The more specific the single programme areas and the more widespread the overall activities of a foundation in terms of scope and scale of programmes, the more decentralized will be the organizational structure.

The clearer the mission of a foundation and the more definite its objectives, the more readily a centralized structure can handle them. However, even in this case the governing body cannot ignore the fact that highly competent and at times specialized staff will still be required. As staff numbers grow and individuals become involved in specific sub-cultures the pressure to establish an autonomous and decentralized structure will increase. The information processing capacity of any given board inevitably limits its monitoring and directing capabilities.

Whatever programme areas and missions founders or governing bodies decide to focus on, they need to avoid dogmatism about organizational structures and address the question of what structure will deliver the most effective method of working.

3.4 Coordination among divisions and programmes

3.4.1 Two dimensions of coordination

Growing foundations are processing an ever-increasing flow of information and its management requires efficient coordination. To be a productive philanthropy, a foundation must be able to handle the large amounts of information upon which its competence depends. Whatever programmes it may have chosen, continuous communication between its various programme departments and staff departments is essential. The two major aspects of coordination within a foundation organization are:

- coordination between staff and programme departments
- coordination among programme departments.

3.4.2 Coordination between staff and programme departments

Larger foundations in many cases comprise a number of staff departments. How can they be made into efficient and helpful instruments to support successful programme work? The development of public relations activities, for example, is important for foundations which wield no executive power to change society and are dependent on their communication skills in civil society. Whenever programme activities are to be successful in making a difference to the world, disseminating information to the public, communicating to other institutions, presenting model cases as solutions to social problems or honouring social contributions of citizens or other institutions all become essential. A public relations department is therefore among the first staff departments to develop in a foundation. The work of such a department may be concentrated on information to be given to the media, but it may also include the production of foundation-edited media to provide information to the public. In its most extended version this department may even include a nonprofit publishing house.

Of course, a foundation also needs administrative and financial departments from the beginning. This includes both the administration of the endowment and capital accounts of a foundation and the processing of all financial and contractual obligations arising from programme work. Among these administrative functions, which may best be described as services to the organization as a whole, are computer or internet applications. Any such services may both serve in-house staff, outside communication and the requirements of particular programmes.

Foundations with extended conference activities – especially on an international scale – may find it helpful to develop a conference department which assists programme departments with organizational tasks and allows them to concentrate on content when preparing for a conference.

The following paragraphs describe how to link staff departments to programme work in the most efficient ways.

First, public relations tasks that are regarded as integral to programme work will be assigned to programme officers, whereas PR tasks that are regarded as part of corporate public relations for the whole foundation will require the involvement of a special department. Of course, between the extremes of all-corporate and all-programme PR there are any number of possible approaches depending on target groups, programme-related experience of addressing the public, pre-existing personal or institutional relationships, and the level of expertise required to give competent information on a programme. A more corporate approach offers the chance of linking programmes in the presentation to the public; a more programme-oriented approach allows for continuous and deepened relationships with specific target groups.

In any case, the organization has to ensure that both staff and programme department meet and communicate at regular intervals. This can be done on a systematic annual, half-annual or quarterly basis as well as by holding *ad hoc* coordination meetings. However, it has to be kept in mind that coordination is not only bilateral between staff and programme departments, but also has to take into account the plurality of programmes. In the assignment of tasks therefore the respective capacities of the departments involved must be accounted for. In the case of very large programmes, it may be necessary to regard PR work as integral to the project. A special PR officer may even be hired for the programme itself.

Mistrust and suspicion are the enemies of coordination between departments. The longer a programme and a staff department have been in cooperation, however, the more mutual experience and trust should contribute to their joint effectiveness.

The cooperation between staff and programme departments can be enhanced by allowing programme departments to outsource services needed. As long as they have the option of having programme results published by outside publishing houses or as long as conferences or events can also be organized by external agents, the services and contributions of the internal staff departments can be regarded as efficient if they can compete with external offers.

A similar approach to enhancing cooperation is to allocate services by staff departments to the programmes through an internal market. A programme demanding support from staff departments then has to justify allocation of resources against other programmes' demands. Each programme has to prove that its own particular task is the most effective way of applying foundation resources in manpower and in money. Two levels of competition can emerge as a result:

- the programme department without staff support can turn out to be as successful in its work as others
- the staff department can prove to be more effective in working for one programme than another.

Ultimately, where sufficient resources are available and the organization is large enough, the most effective method of ensuring coordination between departments seems to be the formation of project teams which involve everyone concerned right from the beginning. For instance, programme officers can meet with conference organizers and editors of the foundation's publishing department to coordinate an international conference and its documentation. In this kind of teamwork clear statements of responsibilities and checklists of tasks to be performed by those involved have proven to be very helpful in avoiding ill-coordinated work.

3.4.3 Coordination between programme departments

Academic experience indicates that the most challenging type of cooperation is that between different disciplines. However, innovation and progress increasingly require coordinated input from different sources. A foundation – an operating foundation in particular – develops competences and acquires knowledge which should not be allowed to remain in isolation embedded in its staff. With the increasingly interdisciplinary nature of social problems that it tries to address, a foundation may also discover that overlaps develop between its departments and coordination is required to approach outside partners effectively. There are at least three modes of effecting such coordination:

- using the budget process and allocating common funds to interdisciplinary programmes
- using staff management and allocating members of staff to project teams
- creating mega-programmes or programme focuses to ensure collaboration within a common framework.

The most far-reaching example of the first case is provided by the sustainable-forestry programme of a number of major American foundations guided by the initiative of the Rockefeller Brothers Fund. In this case, the common financial resource includes funds from different foundations which have been pooled to allow for more effective use of larger amounts of money than any individual foundation could have afforded. From this pool a steering committee allocates resources to individual programme steps. A similar procedure can be established within the boundaries of a foundation which in turn allows for more effective methods of integrating project partners, requires joint steering bodies involving the internal departments and possibly external expertise.

Coordinating programmes by establishing teams is another promising way of bringing together expertise which the foundation may have acquired over many years of programme work. Substantial forces of resistance may defend the seemingly independent work of departments, but on the other hand rotating responsibilities for directing a programme can also offer staff development opportunities. It should become quite clear to all that, depending on the nature of a programme, the expertise of one department is vital for success and that therefore this department should take the lead, with the others contributing. For the next programme, the lead may lie with another department.

Finally mega-programmes will demand a strategically designed framework for decentralized, but coordinated action by several programme departments. For instance, in a major foundation which is involved in education work in many different areas, a coordinated education scheme could include elements from civic to media education, from alphabetization programmes to reading competitions, from developing school organization to awarding prizes for innovative model cases, from supporting training for NGO-initiators to encouraging university research by young scholars.

3.5 Recruitment and development of staff

It is obvious that much of the knowledge and the competence of a foundation is embedded in its staff members. Since the recruitment of programme managers and other staff cannot rely, in most European countries, on an established labour market for professional foundation work, the choice of professions from which staff will be drawn largely depends on the idiosyncrasies, mission and programme focuses of foundations. They will first of all have a preference for candidates who can make decisions. Shaping society according to one's own visions and having an impact on the life of society requires many decisions for which there are not always models available.

With a growing culture of cooperation in philanthropy, staff exchanges, staff fellowships in other foundations and joint efforts at qualifications are becoming increasingly attractive. In-house formal training is organized side by side with external qualification programmes. Funders or foundations may associate for certain programme interests or form alliances according to shared visions and missions. Ultimately, foundation staff can develop its competence by returning to universities for periods of research, teaching and re-qualification; both universities and foundations profit from this exchange. All this primarily applies to large foundations and the more so the more operating they are. Quite a different strategy – and sometimes related to programme goals – is that of involving volunteers in foundation work. Starting a foundation is already a step of volunteer action and very often, the foundation could not come into being without its first steps being supported by volunteer activities.

4 Role of volunteers

Foundations are institutions active in civil society. In many cases, they combine gifts of assets and gifts of time. This points to the importance of volunteers in establishing and managing foundations, not the least in the European environment which is characterized by a relatively small proportion of foundations employing professional staff.[2] Volunteers in Europe play a vital role in bringing philanthropic institutions into existence. The following section will examine the role of volunteers focusing on the development and management of human resources.

4.1 Volunteers as staff

The first question to address when engaging volunteers to work with a foundation is: why exactly do we want to involve a volunteer for this particular purpose? Is it to save money? Is it to utilize commitment? Is it to gain specific expertise? Is it demanded by the legal structure?

The degree to which volunteers are involved in a foundation largely depends upon the type of foundation, its assets and its annual outgoings. The founders' investment in time and assets defines the initial proportion of volunteer activity. In the course of institutional development, the decision for professional staff or for volunteer governance and management depends on the character of a foundation; certain goals can be better achieved if both professional staff and volunteers are involved. So how do volunteers fit into the hierarchy, how do you find them, train them, how do you evaluate their work as compared to the work of professional staff?

Most foundations do not have staff on their payrolls at all. The people who work for them are solely those who are volunteer members of the governing bodies. In the long term, however, such a strategy is probably only possible for small foundations with a limited range of interests. Once programme areas become diverse or the structure – and with it fiscal and legal issues as well as those of evaluation – becomes more complex, professional staff are likely to be brought in. However, even in foundations with professional staff employed, a good deal of the work – especially in strategic decision-making – could still be done by voluntary governing bodies.

4.1.1 Board as staff

Once a founder has made the decision that they or their families cannot handle the work to be done alone, some additional or volunteer board members may be regarded as a sufficient solution. If the board is enlarged, a clear division of labour is essential if it is to work effectively.

---

[2] Only about 10% of German foundations employ salaried staff. See Elisabeth Brummer and Silvia Ruprecht (eds), *Statistiken zum Deutschen Stiftungswesen 1998*, Arbeitsberichte des Maecenata Instituts für Dritter-Sektor-Forschung, München 1998, especially pp. 11, 31–2.

4.1.2 Volunteers as reviewers

No foundation which has to rely on extensive review processes can do without volunteers. That is true for grant-making foundations which rely on peer reviews just as much as it applies to foundations which award prizes. In Germany the *Volkswagen Stiftung* and the DFG (*Deutsche Forschungs Gemeinschaft*) probably have the most elaborate system of peer reviews for grant applications. The challenges for the volunteers – in this case mainly university professors and researchers at non-university institutes – is professional (in terms of time) and ethical (in terms of fairness and intellectual copyright). For professional staff the main challenge is to identify the best, most efficient, most fair and reliable reviewers and to coordinate their work.

Similar efforts – though not peer reviews in many cases – have to be made by foundations awarding prizes. The Körber Foundation in Hamburg for example has for almost 30 years been running a student essay competition on history: *Schülerwettbewerb Deutsche Geschichte um den Preis des Bundespräsidenten*. Jurors at regional and federal levels are required to read all the work which is handed in (in some cases more than 1300 papers – some of them rather books than essays) to select the prize winners.

If selection processes involve special knowledge or very great numbers of people, the project will frequently involve volunteers. All foundations which give scholarships to students at any level need large selection committees composed of volunteers. In Germany probably the most sophisticated system in this respect has been developed by the *Studienstiftung des deutschen Volkes*.

In all these cases the reason for including volunteers in philanthropy are the following.

- They provide expertise which a foundation could not afford on a professional basis.
- The contribution of expertise is only needed for a limited period during the year, but the need is regular.
- A large number of people are required to process applications.

4.1.3 Donor-grantee relationship

In many cases it can be of mutual benefit to both sides if there is a continued exchange between donors and grantees. Volunteer work may result from this where representatives of grantee organizations develop a close relationship to the donor foundation and are subsequently asked to serve on its advisory board. Former award winners or grantees in personal grant programmes may later in their careers return to work for a foundation as a volunteer. Foundations providing support to self-help groups in crisis situations may request volunteer help in return.

4.2 How to identify volunteers

The strategies used to attract and recruit volunteers to philanthropy again depend on the purposes and programme philosophies of individual foundations. In certain cases, foundations serving social, health or community-oriented purposes attract voluntary engagement by the very nature of their work; grant recipients can be required to give assurances of 'matching schemes' – matching gifts in funds by gifts in kind or time.

In the case of juries or selection committees, a foundation needs to attract specific (frequently academic, artistic or political) volunteer expertise. High reputation individuals can be invited to serve on programmes which, having established a public reputation, will then be successful in attracting other high-profile volunteers. Membership of appropriate bodies may be attractive to the best minds, not the least because many programmes involve identifying promising talents with whom committee members may have a chance to work in their own profession. Altruistic motivations to join and work for the public good join notions of self-interest in many of these cases.

A strategy frequently found is the recruitment of former grant recipients, representatives of institutions in the field which is to be supported (which excludes their organizations from receiving funds), or career professionals who themselves profited from foundation grants earlier in their lives. All these approaches involve investment of time and planning on the part of the foundation and often cannot be completed effectively without professional staff support.

4.3 Training and development

The simplest reason for involving certain volunteers is that they already bring along the expertise needed for a programme. In that case, the professional standard of their activities should be corroborated by their experience. Such people need only be introduced to the mission, goals and regulatories of a programme. Sometimes, they have even been involved in designing exactly this framework.

Very different is the situation where volunteers are involved in all kinds of community activities, because their services frequently compete with professions or commercial businesses providing similar services which are not, however, available to all. One of the purposes of a programme may be to train the trainers or to build capacity among multipliers who will then contribute to improving the living conditions of the community. This training might be provided by both volunteer and professional specialists. Social capital building is key in many such cases and that does not require professionalism – fundraising, or writing articles for the local newspaper, for example, can be learned by training on the job.

Training becomes more and more important with growing responsibility, expertise or specific knowledge. Notes of caution should be added however.

- The requirement for training should not be allowed to put off people who want to contribute – especially in the social sector.
- Training should not be too time consuming.

For some volunteers training and personal development do serve as incentives. The very fact that a foundation is willing to invest in their training shows them that they and their work are valuable to the community.

4.4 Relationship with professional staff

The clearer the division of labour and responsibilities the more effective the cooperation of volunteers and staff can be. The relationship of a board composed of volunteers with a professional management has already been addressed in 2, 'Role of boards', in this chapter. Frequently volunteers and full-time staff do the same or comparable jobs (e.g. care for the elderly, youth, disadvantaged people) and can feel themselves to be in competition. A great deal of service sector voluntary work has however been carried out over the last decades by professionals. This is particularly true for the large welfare associations that support the German system of subsidiarity in organizing the welfare state. It is still difficult to predict the legal obligations of charities active in fields in which goods provided are no longer public goods due to market failure but private goods deliverable (at least in principle) by commercial activity. However, political interests in many European countries have the goal of re-invigorating civil society on their agendas and volunteer involvement is the key to success in all kinds of civic projects.

4.5 Limitations and risks of using volunteers

The essential risk of involving volunteers is that quality and effectiveness will be compromised. Poor quality delivery can endanger an organization's credibility and legitimacy. It will also discourage other volunteers. This issue is therefore both a matter of motivation and of evaluation.

To avoid problems the most important rule is not to give work to volunteers which really requires – because of its content, the time or the continuity required – the permanent attention of professional staff. Do not overburden volunteers who have a full-time job, a family to care about and probably further commitments. Where volunteers are early-retired, retired, or spouses of professionals who have another, independent source of income, this may not be the case. Some of these volunteers may be willing to devote as much time to the task as a member of staff. They may regard volunteering as one of the purposes of their lives and an enrichment. In many cases the environment they are working in and the foundation they are volunteering their time to will also provide their most important social contacts.

Respecting the time restrictions of volunteers and managing their division of labour is the key professional challenge faced by governing bodies or staff of any organization. They will also have to account for the legal requirements regulating certain services and charities.

5 Role of consultants

5.1 Scope of consultant involvement

In most European countries there is as yet no professional market for consulting services in the field of philanthropy. There are a very few organizations offering specialized advice to the sector and a somewhat greater number of others who provide specific know how on legal, financial, fundraising or personnel issues. However, the philanthropic advisor in the US mould who can also offer assistance in defining a charity's purpose, in developing an organization and in creating and managing programmes, is still to emerge. What, therefore, can consultants currently contribute to the overall availability of human resources in a foundation? What is their relationship with other groups?

A distinction needs to be made between the establishment of a foundation and its later operations.

- Establishing a foundation requires legal advice and frequently involves discussion with business friends, family members or other philanthropists about their values, missions and operations. This process will help to formulate and design the governing documents and structures of a foundation. This process centres around the interests of the donor.
- Contributions to the running of existing foundations can consist of expertise that is lacking in-house: specific knowledge, evaluation, communications, personnel recruitment, new venture designs, restructuring foundation programmes or simply providing an outside view to help in the making of decisions. Consultants may also offer the help of an extra pair of hands when workloads temporarily threaten to overwhelm permanent staff.

5.2 How to identify consultants

Consultants might be drawn from business or family contacts (lawyers, accountants, personnel consultants). They can usefully be addressed even where their experience is in the business rather than the nonprofit world.

There are also systematic ways of identifying the few specialized sources of advice in the field of philanthropy.

- Donors can search for information and guidance from support organizations and associations in the field, for example the European Foundation Centre, the *Bundesverband Deutscher Stiftungen* or the Council on Foundations. They all have websites on the Internet providing further information. Their offices may help in identifying specific assistance.
- Some specialized institutions such as the Maecenata Institute for Third Sector Research and its Resource Centre as well as the Consulting Branch Maecenata Management in Germany or the Charities Aid Foundation in the United Kingdom may provide helpful information.
- The Internet provides both national and international advice, for example, on community foundations in Germany (*www.buergers-tiftungen.de*).
- Another valuable source of reference is existing foundations which have programme interests in promoting civil society or even philanthropy. Foundations are developing an increasing awareness of the value of professional exchange – of serving as mutual consultants.

5.3 Relationship with professional staff

Situations where there is cooperation between professional staff and consultants are still the exception, and these are limited to large foundations. In many cases, small foundations are completely managed by advisors (frequently lawyers). A potential for conflict therefore only arises in cases where large organizations are employing consultants and find their contributions unsatisfactory. A clear division of labour at the outset can help to avoid obvious sources of conflict. It is the responsibility of foundation staff to specify the services required of advisors clearly and to stipulate these in a written contract.

Where a foundation wishes to explore a new area of activity the initial involvement of consultants in programme design or strategic development will allow time to understand the competencies and capacities required of new staff before attempting to hire them.

The services of a consultant can also be called upon to restructure an ill-managed institution.

5.4 Limitations and risks of working with consultants

Working with consultants involves costs. This is true in a basic sense of fees, but it also has the effect of inhibiting the development of skills within an organization. Knowledge and information are primarily processed externally rather than internally. In addition, there may be the risk of advisors not familiarizing themselves sufficiently with their client foundation or learning more in the process of cooperation than the foundation.

Nothing involves more mutual trust and confidence than consulting people on the use and allocation of their personal wealth, a process which is always involved when establishing and managing a foundation. However, trusted advisors may not in fact be those able to offer the best quality services ideally suited to philanthropic institutions. Donor autonomy and advisor professionalism do not always match. In the worst case advice may be provided that is not without a certain degree of self-interest.

Consultant services should therefore always be judged against their capacity to offer references to good practice examples in existing philanthropy. Do not expect a consultant to drive your philanthropy – the driving force behind any engagement in projects designed to better society and our world is the personal values of those who live them and are convinced that they should give expression to them in public.

Bibliography

Anheier, Helmut K. and Toepler, Stefan eds, *Private Funds, Public Purpose, Philanthropic Foundations in International Perspective*, New York, Plenum Publishers 1999.

Bertelsmann Foundation ed., *Handbuch Stiftungen*, Wiesbaden 1998.

Brummer, Elisabeth, and Ruprecht, Silvia eds, *Statistiken zum deutschen Stiftungswesen 1998*, München, Arbeitsberichte des Maecenata Instituts für Dritter-Sektor-Forschung, 1998.

Chandler, Alfred D. jr., *Strategy and Structure, Chapters in the History of the Industrial Enterprise*, Cambridge, Mass., MIT Press, 1962.

Chandler, Alfred D. jr., *The Visible Hand, The Managerial Revolution in American Business*, Cambridge, Mass., Belknap/Harvard UP, 1977.

Chandler, Alfred D. jr., *Scale and Scope, The Dynamics of Industrial Capitalism*, Cambridge, Mass., Belknap/Harvard UP, 1990.

Clotfelter, Charles T. and Ehrlich, Thomas eds, *Philanthropy and the Nonprofit Sector in a Changing America*, Bloomington, Indiana UP, 1999.

Krüger, Wilfried and Homp, Christian, *Kernkompetenz-Management, Steigerung von Flexibilität und Schlagkraft im Wettbewerb*, Wiesbaden, Gabler Verlag, 1997.

Lagemann, Ellen Condliffe, *Philanthropic Foundations, New Scholarship, New Possibilities*, Bloomington, Indiana, 1999.

Salamon, Lester M., Anheier, Helmut K. *et al.* eds, *Global Civil Society, Dimensions of the Nonprofit Sector*, Baltimore, MD, The Johns Hopkins Center for Civil Society Studies, 1999.

▼ Section **III** ▼
Programme Selection and Management

▼ Thomas K. Reis and Stephanie J. Clohesy

Unleashing New Resources and Entrepreneurship for the Common Good: a Philanthropic Renaissance

1 Introduction

In this era of unparalleled economic growth and its corresponding economic disparity, a new generation of entrepreneurs is becoming increasingly committed to using market-based approaches to solve social problems. The combined trends of wealth creation, wealth transfer and openness to intersectoral and market-based approaches for social change are attracting and unleashing an unprecedented level of new financial resources and human innovation within philanthropy. These changes in philanthropy and society appear to be marking a significant – and almost sudden – societal shift.

To most people, change often does seem to be sudden; but societal shifts actually happen gradually as small changes accumulate. The lily pond can serve as an illustration. Several days before the pond is completely covered by lily pads the water is only half covered. And a week before that it is only a quarter covered. And the month before that only an eighth covered. So, while the lily pads grow imperceptibly all summer long, only in the last part of the cycle do we notice their 'sudden' appearance. This is often referred to as the 'tipping point' phenomenon.

In the 'law of tipping points' – a biological change theory – significance precedes momentum. In other words, important changes are happening before momentum is apparent. The 'tipping' metaphor of the lily pond provides valuable insight into the changes occurring now in philanthropy and the social service/social change arena. Many changes are happening now, but it is difficult fully to perceive and understand their importance until they accumulate and achieve recognizable critical mass.

The extraordinary mass of financial capital produced by the late 20th century economy along with the creative force of a new generation of innovators has formed a wellspring of new ideas for philanthropy. With an entrepreneurial focus on the common good and a desire for partnerships among the commercial, public and nonprofit sectors, emerging social innovators are pushing philanthropy to a tipping point of change.

Traditionally, philanthropy – as legislated and practised in the United States – has served as a way for citizens to hold otherwise taxable resources in the private domain but allocated for the public good. Individual and institutional philanthropy has provided a means for people to help others according to their own perceptions of needs and possibilities. Philanthropy has been a process of redistribution of resources as those in need make their case for assistance to those with money and time. Depending upon its level of formality, philanthropy varies from simple charity at one end of the spectrum to highly strategic, system changing investment at the other.

New wealth creators and new social innovators are bringing to philanthropy market-based models that emphasize equity and ownership; measurable results; fiscal sustainability; and capitalization to scale. Such market models, defined through language like 'venture philanthropy' and 'social entrepreneurship', are expanding the boundaries of traditional philanthropy. Some of the most zealous proponents of venture or market-based philanthropy believe that the new models should displace and replace much of 'old' philanthropy. Yet it seems more reasonable to value the new models as enhancers of current organized philanthropy, adding options in philanthropic approach to the spectrum of societal challenges and opportunities.

In this chapter we will:

- describe the major waves of change affecting philanthropy in the US
- discuss social entrepreneurship, venture philanthropy and Internet-based philanthropy as drivers of change within philanthropy
- map the key ideas, groups and players who are catalyzing changes in philanthropy
- outline a scenario for action to capitalize on these changes and inherent opportunities underway in the US.

The original data for this chapter was collected in 1998–99 by the W. K. Kellogg Foundation with two different research efforts. The first dealt with the emergence of market models in philanthropy and social change work and their potential for unleashing new resources; and the other documented and categorized the rapid growth of Internet-based or 'e-philanthropy' and 'e-volunteerism'. Both of these reports were born out of an emerging societal shift to a more entrepreneurial focus on the common good – resulting in new partnerships among the commercial, public and nonprofit sectors. Attributes of this shift include those listed below.

- A blurring of traditional sectoral boundaries.
- The opportunity to balance an increasingly powerful market sector with a commitment to public responsibility.
- The phenomenon of wealth creation. The late 20th century is a time of unprecedented wealth creation, both through earned wealth and the transfer of wealth from one generation to the next. At the same time, however, persistent poverty and inequality – especially among women, children and people of certain ethnic groups – is bringing about a growing gap in wealth distribution. New wealth creators and their ideas about balancing market and public responsibility may provide new resources and innovations to improve significantly social and economic change-making and help narrow the wealth gap.

This shift also reflects the larger significance of the profound economic revolution that is occurring as we move from a production-based industrial economy to a new knowledge-based network economy. Organizations of all sectors need to learn how to operate within this fast-paced network economy. Rapid and turbulent cycles of change are the norm as innovation produces knowledge that changes the environment and then requires more innovation.

1.1 Assumptions and language

To understand the situation in the US and the related insights conveyed in this chapter it is important to share the starting assumptions. These assumptions attempt to clarify the significance, implications and possibilities of change of this societal shift affecting philanthropy. The assumptions include those described below.

- The transfer of wealth to the baby-boom generation in the US is providing an unprecedented opportunity for resources to flow into philanthropy and nonprofit ventures. That wealth, estimated now to encompass a minimum of $41 trillion over the next 55 years will include approximately $6 trillion for philanthropy. Current organized philanthropic assets in the US total approximately $500 billion. The sheer size of the transfer of wealth – as well as the anticipated distribution of this transfer into thousands of small and medium-sized funds – will change the face of philanthropy.
- New wealth creators are earning fortunes at younger ages than the previous generation resulting in many of them moving earlier in life to devote time and resources to philanthropy.
- Society's intractable social and economic problems are not solvable through fragmented, single-sector programmes – all sectors need to work together, exchanging and sharing traditionally accepted roles.
- The rapid adaptation of entrepreneurial solutions for sustainability of innovations and financing require systems for developing and maintaining services at a scale proportionate to need.
- A critical mass of readiness and momentum for new kinds of social investing is emerging and can be catalysed for greater impact and effectiveness.
- Without systematic intervention to accelerate and improve what is happening, substantial numbers of new donors and social entrepreneurs could be discouraged, turned off and lost from philanthropy and social change work.
- Experienced funders are needed as partners with new funders to create bi-directional mentoring that leads to a deeper appreciation of lessons learned from previous experiments as well as to new ideas, learning and action opportunities for old and new funders.

- A useful intervention into this evolution of philanthropy and social development needs structure and leadership that is formed collaboratively and 'owned' by many stakeholders: it cannot be owned and led by one entity.

Language and terminology are important in this climate of change within and around philanthropy. Some people believe that the ideas of emerging social entrepreneurs and new wealth creators are only semantic differences – new words for old ideas. For others, the social entrepreneurs/social innovators and wealth creators are creating a powerful revolution of ideas and practice in the worlds of philanthropy, the nonprofit sector and social change.

Some scholars and practitioners are trying now to get agreement on many of the terms in order to build a shared dialogue among funders, investors and actors. The following is a glossary of some of the emerging language.

- **Social entrepreneurs**
  Play the role of change agent in the social sector by: relentlessly pursuing opportunities to create and sustain social value; applying innovative approaches in their work and their funding; acting boldly without being constrained by the resources currently in hand; and exhibiting a heightened sense of accountability to the various constituencies they serve (communities and investors) for the outcomes they create. (Greg Dees)

- **Nonprofit enterprise**
  A revenue-generating venture founded to create jobs or training opportunities for very low-income individuals, while simultaneously operating on a sound financial basis. Nonprofit enterprises are variously known as social purpose businesses, community-based businesses, community wealth enterprises, etc. (New Social Entrepreneurs, Roberts Foundation)

  Beyond enterprise specifically created for economic development there are also income-producing enterprises developed by non-profits primarily for their income streams. Some examples of these include: museum stores, eco-tourism and co-branding of products. (Greg Dees)

- **Venture capital**
  Builds an investment model through which innovative ideas and capable organizations can gain access to markets.

- **Venture philanthropy**
  Strong leaders with bold ideas plus a venture approach produce effective community organizations. The venture approach includes funding social entrepreneurs in organizations with scale-up potential. Support is long term and the funder makes substantial commitments to a few rather than smaller commitments to many. Support includes board participation, team building and a resource network.

- **Intersectoral**
  The blending of two or more sectors working collaboratively and using their resources, inherent perspectives, experience and management tools to achieve common goals.

- **New profit sector**
  A new sector of the American economy composed of individuals, foundations, corporations and other entities that straddle both the existing nonprofit and for-profit sectors. (New Profit, Inc. business plan)

- **Social capital**
  Social capital begins with human capital; the development of self-sufficient individuals who are mutually supportive and have the generosity and skills to create the structures, organizations and resources needed for healthy and equitable communities. Ultimately, the ability of social structures and systems to help people achieve their goals for the common good is perceived as 'social capital'.

- **Socially responsible business**
  The practice of integrating ethical behaviour and proactive positive concern and action for the public good by private sector entities whose main purpose is the creation of enterprise and profit.

- **Wealth creators**
  Individuals with substantial financial resources and powerful networks to leverage. They are steeped in a set of values and beliefs about market-based approaches to solving problems, entrepreneurism and outcomes-oriented thinking.

- **The common good**
  The aspiration that society's essence needs to be imbued with fundamental values of generosity and civic participation – that all people have a common stake in caring for each other and their communities, resulting in a mutually responsible and just society.

1.2 Five waves of change

There are five waves of change that are producing what some are calling a renaissance in US philanthropy and social change work. Briefly summarized they are as follows.

1 **Social entrepreneurs** are changing civic and human services, leadership and institutions to encompass market-based approaches for appropriate scale, impact and sustainability.

2 **Business and social responsibility**. Business leaders are moving from a one-dimensional charity method to multi-dimensional methods of achieving corporate citizenship.

3 **Philanthropy as social venture capital**. Philanthropists – traditional and emerging – are building on a generation of social investment experiments to devise market-driven and venture capital concepts to add to the philanthropic tool box and to intensify partnerships and shared responsibility with funders and social action organizations.

4 **Women, communities of colour and youth**. New philanthropic values and habits are emerging out of new social and economic demographics. Women, communities of colour and youth are changing philanthropy by creating new institutions and devising innovative solutions to problems closest to their own lives.

5 **Internet-based philanthropy and social change**. Internet and e-commerce models are catalysing e-philanthropy and e-volunteerism by and for social entrepreneurs, philanthropists and the nonprofit sector. An open and accessible process facilitated by technology has the potential to change traditional giver-receiver relationships and may hold possibilities for a more open, problem-solving environment in which philanthropists and social entrepreneurs work together on equal footing. In addition, the ease and efficiency of Internet-facilitated giving could lead to 'everyperson'/ubiquitous philanthropy.

2 Social entrepreneurs

Social entrepreneurship is driven by two strong forces. First, the nature of the desired social change often benefits from an innovative, entrepreneurial or enterprise-based solution. Second, the sustainability of the organization and its services requires diversification of its funding streams, often including the creation of earned income streams or a partnership with a for-profit organization.

In response to these different but interrelated forces, nonprofit organizations and their leaders make critical decisions to invent or expand into entrepreneurial models to do their work. These two forces driving the shift into nonprofit social entrepreneurship are best illustrated by observations from the Roberts Enterprise Development Fund and from Professor J. Gregory Dees of Stanford Business School:

> We cannot escape from the fact that you do not service people out of poverty. At its core, the ability to exit poverty is a question of employment, asset accumulation and wealth creation.

> Roberts Enterprise Development Fund, 'Social Purpose
> Enterprises and Venture Philanthropy in the New Millennium'

> Faced with rising costs, more competition for fewer donations and grants, and increased rivalry from for-profit companies entering the social sector, nonprofits are turning to the for-profit world to leverage or replace their traditional sources of funding. In addition, leaders of nonprofits look to commercial funding in the belief that market-based revenues can be easier to grow and more resilient than philanthropic funding.

> Dees J. Gregory, 'Enterprising Nonprofits, What Do You Do
> When Traditional Sources of Funding Fall Short?' Harvard
> Business Review, Jan/Feb 1998, 55–67

Throughout the US, nonprofits are increasingly using entrepreneurial models and language to design their services, organizations and partnerships. They are creating organizational structures to link an array of nonprofit and for-profit entities. There are hundreds – and perhaps thousands – of examples throughout the US of organizations that are experimenting with enterprise or market-based approaches for solving problems. Many of these are based within traditional organizations such as Goodwill, the Salvation Army, Boy and Girl Scouts, community food banks. Some are new organizational models such as New Profit, Inc. and Share Our Strength that are weaving together profit-making activities with social change purposes.

With social entrepreneurship activity increasing, new networks are forming. A second national gathering of social entrepreneurs took place in April 2000 and was structured to help participants give greater definition to the needs of social entrepreneurs and to offer workshops for practitioners in specific skills need for social enterprise work and social entrepreneurship. The organizers reached out to 4000 identified social entrepreneurs and funders/supporters of social entrepreneurs.

Another new network, SEA Change, is being organized to link social entrepreneurs and social change investors in an active learning process with each other. In a recent survey of more than 200 social entrepreneurs the SEA Change organizers learned that the most pressing need of most social entrepreneurs is gaining access to potential investors and a loan fund for social purpose ventures. In addition they said they needed help in finding contacts and developing partnerships with other for-profit and nonprofit social purpose ventures. They are also looking for technical assistance with organizational development and access to technical *pro bono* resources.

The *Chronicle on Philanthropy*, the main newspaper of the nonprofit sector in the US described the new organizations and their new leaders in this way:

> A new guard of non-profit leaders is emerging that will shape the charity world in the next century [...]; even the language that these young leaders use is different from that of preceding generations. Terms like activist, social worker and community organizer have been replaced by social entrepreneur. They seek new ways to blend non-profit, government and corporate work that will generate quick, quantifiable improvements to problems.

> Gray, Susan, 'Entering Another World, More People are Leaving Charity Work to Start Socially Responsible Companies', *The Chronicle of Philanthropy*, April 9 1998

With all the optimism and hope that surrounds market approaches to social needs, it is tempting to think of market ideas as a panacea. However, many social issues will require complex solutions that blend market approaches with direct charitable and educational services. J. Gregory Dees, in his 1998 article, 'Enterprising Nonprofits' cautions nonprofit leaders that:

> The drive to become more business-like, however, holds many dangers for nonprofits. In the best of circumstances nonprofits face operational and cultural challenges in the pursuit of commercial funding. In the worst, commercial operations can undercut an organization's social mission. To explore the new possibilities of commercialization and to avoid its perils, nonprofit leaders need to craft their strategies carefully.

In sum, social entrepreneurs create social value through innovation and leveraging financial resources – regardless of source – for social, economic and community development. The expectations for non-profits to provide services and achieve social change on a larger scale, while also diversifying funding resources, are motivating social entrepreneurs to invent organizations that are hybrids of nonprofit and for-profit structures. The innovations of social entrepreneurs and the organizational models they are creating require new perspectives and responses from traditional philanthropy.

3 Business and social responsibility

Pressures from an active and vocal civil society, along with enlightened corporate leadership, are motivating many businesses to reconsider how they can be responsible about their business and the communities in which they work and serve their customers. Such responsibility has been shown to lead to increased corporate marketability and profitability.

This perspective is creating new opportunities and incentives for the commercial sector to partner with philanthropies, other nonprofits and government. For example, American Express Financial Advisors teamed with South Shore Bank to bring investment products – like stocks, bonds and life insurance – to South Shore's largely African-American customers in Chicago. This new alliance is one of the most significant partnerships between a Fortune 500 company and a neighbourhood development organization. In addition, there are hundreds of long-standing school-company partnerships, with new partnerships emerging every day. One of the newest is the Welfare to Work partnership which in two years gained the participation and support of 7000 corporations.

In its Summer 1998 issue *The American Benefactor* criticized private industry as a whole for allocating only 1.3% of pre-tax earnings for charitable purposes. However, the journal found some positive trends in the making. Companies that advertise heavily tend to give more than the average. Women entrepreneurs are especially generous, contributing an average of 5.2% of pre-tax profits to charity. Family-led firms make a strong philanthropic commitment. And, in large public corporations, there appears to be a trend toward more strategic philanthropy to align self-interest with the larger public good.

The *Business Ethics Journal* monitors corporations for more comprehensive approaches to responsible business. Increasingly, companies are reporting efforts to understand and improve their overall impact on society and in the environment. For example, Monsanto has created a new environmental accounting system that enables the company to track and report on the impact it has on the environment. British Petroleum America has announced that it will publish its first 'social report' showing the company's new policy statements on environment, employees, relationships and ethics. Many companies are engaging in ethics and social responsibility audits to determine the overall impact of their policies and practices.

Business coalitions in the US such as The Conference Board, The Council on Economic Priorities and Business for Social Responsibility are actively engaging in facilitating new dialogues on the meaning of corporate citizenship and the balance of market pressures with public responsibility.

The next generation of business leaders is also taking on the challenge of doing well by doing good in society and in their communities. Ethics is now an accepted and usually required part of the curriculum in most business schools. The organization Net Impact has emerged in recent years to inspire and facilitate the commitment of business school students to a future as responsible business leaders.

Many of the renewed efforts relating to socially responsible business have been sparked by the growing awareness of the blurring of sectoral roles and the increasing need for intersectoral partnerships to solve thorny problems. But the disappearance of strict sectoral boundaries is sparking another trend in the commercial sector as increasing numbers of private sector entities, such as industrial giant Lockheed Martin, are entering the traditionally nonprofit business fields of direct human care and service. In effect, traditional businesses also are engaging in social entrepreneurship.

The privatization of healthcare in the US represents the largest transition of business from nonprofits and government to for-profit institutions. Other fields, such as youth services, are also beginning to see a transition towards privatization. For-profit corporations are creating their own philanthropic schemes. Financial services such as Fidelity's Charitable Gift Fund and Merrill Lynch's and Vanguard's donor services are similar to donor-directed funds that have been developed by community foundations. Fidelity's fund has grown rapidly since it was established in 1992, and is now the fifth largest recipient of all charitable contributions in the United States (nearly $457 million in 1999). These new mechanisms enable the individual to centralize their banking, financial investments and social investments.

For-profits becoming or creating nonprofits; nonprofits becoming or creating for-profits; new organizations emerging as hybrids – these are structural evidence that those dedicated to positive social change are trying to do the work differently and better.

4 Philanthropy as social venture capital

In the May 1998 issue of *The Economist*, an article titled 'The Challenge for America's Rich', said:

> For if 1900 marked the high point of one era of wealth creation, with enormous riches for those who seized new national markets just then opening up, 2000 may mark another with the opportunities flowing this time from globalization, new technology and corporate restructuring. America at the last count, had 170 billionaires compared with 13 in 1982.

In addition to the 170 billionaires, *The Economist* also noted that the US boasts 250,000 decamillionaires and 4.8 million millionaires. Observing that today's new rich have the opportunity to be benefactors of extraordinary generosity and to shape the US – and the world – just as profoundly as Carnegie and Rockefeller did in their time, the article also notes that few of the new rich are yet fulfilling their potential as philanthropists.

At the same time other publications regularly track a steadily emerging stream of philanthropists from among the new wealth creators. The Entrepreneurs' Foundation issued a late 1999 report listing 58 members. Organized over the past two years, the Entrepreneurs' Foundation is a collaborative venture capital and social responsibility process that engages young start-up companies in the philanthropic process. The young companies pledge stocks and/or other cash/human resource donations early on in their start-up phase to provide venture capital for nonprofit social change ventures with potential for significant financial resources if these start-up firms later go public or are bought out.

Many of the philanthropists who are emerging from the new fortunes define themselves as social entrepreneurs. They want to solve defined problems in a specific way. They do not want simply to earmark money for 'some vaguely benevolent purpose'. They focus on performance. They try to make projects self-sustaining. If the manufacturing of products has been part of their wealth creation, they often make these products part of their giving (e.g. Apple Computers). They believe strongly that equipping people with tools and investing in them to go out and create 'wealth' is a vital part of their philanthropy. Their interpretation of the age-old equity and access challenge revolves around information and knowledge as the new currency and driving equalizer. While this may smack of naïve optimism based on their own success, these wealth creators want their philanthropy to come out of the paradigm of a 'hand up ... not a hand out'. Rightly or wrongly, they do not want to hear about the have-nots and the negativity associated with dependency syndrome. Their philanthropy is often targeted to broad economic and educational improvement first, with the belief that other forms of social and spiritual wealth will follow.

'Through high-tech computer and biotech industries, entrepreneurs have had a transformative impact on the economy and on the society', said Catherine Muther, who created a women's foundation using a venture model. 'When these entrepreneurs turn their attention to social issues and philanthropy, nothing less than transformative social change is expected'.[1]

Muther's philanthropy, the Three Guineas fund, has a highly focused strategy to help women develop new technology ventures. She has decided not just to spread money throughout the systemic issues that affect women and their access to opportunities. Instead, Muther is choosing to work explicitly on modelling a venture capital process that would provide access to needed resources for women who are high-tech innovators in the for-profit world. She believes if these women entrepreneurs succeed in the for-profit world they will, in turn, apply some of their wealth to the public good and contribute to society in general as high producers.

The Roberts Enterprise Development Fund (REDF) is another bold example of a funder with a targeted focus (wealth creation and economic development for homeless) using a social venture capital practice with social entrepreneurs to achieve impact. The practice of using a concept like 'social venture capital' requires a new language to describe this blended approach of both business and community constructs. In a Stanford Business School case study about REDF, the shift from old language to new includes terms like:

---

[1] From a personal conversation between the author and Catherine Muther.

Old	New
Grants	Grant equity
Funder	Investor
Grantee	Investee
Evaluation	Measurement
Grant proposal	Business plan

In mid-1999 the Triangle Community Foundation in Research Triangle Park, North Carolina, started the Entrepreneurs Venture Fund which enables local entrepreneurs to pledge stocks and funds and to work with the Community Foundation to help solve local problems. At about the same time the Community Foundation of Silicon Valley held its first meeting for young entrepreneurs, venture capitalists and other professionals to donate to the community foundation and to function as a committee to learn and to make decisions together. Both of these efforts – along with The Entrepreneurs Foundation mentioned above – typify the flow of new money from relatively young entrepreneurs into new partnerships and new forms of philanthropy.

In their article, 'Virtuous Capital' Christine Letts, William Ryan and Allen Grossman propose that recent traditions of philanthropy have been based on 'programme efficacy' and that new approaches to philanthropy are more focused on 'organizational capacity'. New approaches to philanthropy are moving away from an emphasis on demonstration programmes as solutions, towards an investment model for innovative ideas and solid organizations that can get the innovations 'to market'.

Roots for this venture approach to philanthropy are not totally new. Foundations and individual donors have experimented steadily over many years with market style ideas and the need for organizations to sustain themselves and to put good ideas into practice. Using grants, loans and programme-related investments, private funders have helped to create breakthrough economic concepts for social development: charitable organizations like the Salvation Army and Goodwill have a long history of selling products both to generate revenues and provide benefits to their target clients. The Grameen Bank micro-loan programme has revolutionized global thinking about micro-enterprise development. Women's World Banking has opened resources and set new standards worldwide for community banking, while dealing with deep-seated opposition to extending credit to women and women's economic development.

What is new about the emerging generation of philanthropists is their potential size and number (there will be many more small and medium-sized foundations in the future); and the values, beliefs and approaches they bring to the field. An analysis by the Kauffman Center for Entrepreneurial Leadership in Missouri found that more than 300 of the people on the Forbes 400 list of wealthiest Americans are first-generation entrepreneurs who – as the researchers put it – 'started with little or nothing and built a major enterprise creating enormous wealth'. Another recent survey of 200 members of the Young Entrepreneurs' Organization was recently conducted by New Ventures in Philanthropy, a national initiative of the Forum of Regional Associations of Grantmakers. The research revealed that 50% of those surveyed are already significantly involved in nonprofit or philanthropic work. When asked to pick the characteristics of business leaders they knew and respected, 83% said they most admired leaders who could create good organizational cultures and who were willing to lead, mentor and give back to their communities.

This wave of philanthropy as social venture capital has the potential to be enormous in both size and influence. Belief in the value of wealth creation in addressing social change along with the principles of venture capital investment is influencing the practice of emerging philanthropists among the new wealth creators as well as women's, youth and diverse ethnic groups' new philanthropy ventures. The practices of these new philanthropists are challenging more experienced leaders in philanthropy to think about changing roles and relationships with grantee partners, using new tools and approaches that stretch philanthropy beyond traditional grant making and into more opportunistic and market-based models.

5 Women, communities of colour and youth

Embedded within the data about the imminent transfer of wealth in the US are demographics that reveal a changing picture of the US population and its power structures. Only a decade or two into the next century the US is expected to shift to a population in which white Caucasians are the minority and the combined numbers of people of colour (African Americans, Hispanics, Asians, Native Americans) are in the majority.

As these populations grow in numbers they will continue to grow in influence and resources. In the 21st century the philanthropy of women, communities of colour and youth are likely to have a substantial influence on traditional philanthropic institutions. Already these populations have created new philanthropic institutions and networks that more closely resemble their social/ethnic cultures and that attempt to solve issues they consider to be of most importance. Yet for women and communities of colour there is an unsettling dichotomy. On the one hand are trends showing significant wealth accumulation for some within these population groups. On the other hand are the frightening and paradoxical statistics of women, Hispanics and Blacks being the poorest of the poor with little public support.

There are at least three highly identifiable areas of action and strategy for organized philanthropy among women and communities of colour:

- engaging the world of mainstream philanthropy to respond to the inclusion of women and communities of colour in the field of philanthropy and to respond appropriately to their needs
- developing individual philanthropies and philanthropic institutions—both public and private—for women and communities of colour
- research, documentation and knowledge building about philanthropy within these population groups.

5.1 Women

Women's philanthropy in the US has grown out of the women's movement which was catalysed through the larger movements for social justice, human rights and civil rights. Within the women's movement, philanthropy is one of many strategies and institutions for social change. Services, rights and justice advocacy, economic development, civic engagement and empowerment, personal development, academic research and history and theology all have been pathways for achieving the full and equal participation of women in society. Philanthropy is also one of those pathways.

Women's organizations as well as other nonprofits are beginning to see the first indications of the 'women's' transfer of wealth as women's focused endowments are being built and as bequests begin to flow for the first time to the women's institutions founded in the late 1960s and 1970s. The potential size of women's philanthropy – whether directed towards mainstream institutions or towards women and girl-focused services – makes it an inevitable major trend and change-maker for 21st century philanthropy.

5.2 Communities of colour

While communities of colour in the US have long and strong traditions of generosity and charitable work, they have conducted their philanthropy informally and with few institutions to leverage the power of personal contributions. For example, one form of philanthropy – often overlooked in formal studies but widely practised – is the remittance of a portion of earnings back to the country of origin to help relatives.

The Hispanic Federation's 1999 Latinos and Giving survey indicated that two-thirds of all Hispanics contributed to a charitable cause: 48% gave to churches and 38% gave to a nonprofit. When asked why they give, they noted a commitment to self-sufficiency, a desire to rely less on government, and a recognition of the value of nonprofits in communities. As income and education increase, giving to nonprofits and charitable causes also increases, suggesting that there is much room for growth in philanthropy among Latinos.

Data about African Americans in the US show not only a 200-year history of 'philanthropy among friends' but also show rates of giving that equal or exceed that of whites. Other examples of African Americans using the public power of philanthropic activity to create social change include the civil rights movement in the US between 1957 and 1968 and the creation of new institutions in the last two decades: United Negro College Fund, Black United Fund, and Associated Black Charities. In the last decade, as more individual wealth has been created by African Americans, more visible private and family foundations are emerging.

As with many other ethnically identified communities in the US, the most vibrant traditions of giving and volunteering within the Asian American communities are the informal and indigenous forms of giving to and helping each other through mutual aid societies, self-help groups, family and neighbourhood arrangements. In recent years, some Asian Americans have stepped forward to formalize their philanthropy for mainstream American institutions, as well as for emerging organizations serving the social and economic needs that are growing with increasing Asian immigration to the US. Data about Asian-American philanthropy shows that second and third generation donors are likely to give to social justice and civil rights causes and are interested in pan-Asian and collective, united or federated fundraising efforts.

Native Americans have strong traditions of caring for and giving to each other as well as to those outside their immediate communities. Until recently, Native Americans have not participated extensively in formalized US philanthropy. Now, however, formalized giving by Native Americans is increasing and the tools of organized philanthropy are providing a useful addition to traditional ways of giving. Some examples of how Native Americans are now using formal philanthropy include:

- establishment of tribal foundations, designated through tribal law, as a way for Native people to protect their sovereignty and independence and contribute to services and infrastructure needs
- emergence of new forms of philanthropy from the increasing profits involved in reservation-based gaming
- the participation of Native Americans in allied philanthropic and social change organizations working for social and economic change.

Several major US foundations have recently agreed to partner with some of the emerging philanthropic institutions in communities of colour to expand their use of institutional philanthropy with the objective of increasing the leverage and impact of existing indigenous resources.

5.3 Youth

Although philanthropy appears to be a deeply entrenched social and ethical practice in the US it is a voluntary act that occurs only when individuals believe that personal generosity – unified with the generosity of others – can help solve social and economic problems. For the ethic of giving to transfer from one generation to the next there is a need to cultivate the habits of giving early on with young people.

Developing young people as givers of both time and money is a process that relies on a fundamental belief that youth are resources for the society – not problems to be fixed. Most youth-serving organizations already challenge youth to be responsive to their communities by giving time and effort. And major efforts are underway in the US to attract young people into community service (e.g. service learning programmes in schools and in after-school organizations).

Currently in the US, community foundations of all types (e.g. community funds, women's foundations, population or cause-based funds) are beginning to include young people in the philanthropic process both to build their habits of giving while also gaining insight and help from them as leaders in the community. Results documented so far through programme evaluations show that the youth philanthropy efforts successfully give young people the opportunity to contribute to community decisions and allow them to recognize the impact every individual has upon building an effective community.

6 Internet-based philanthropy and social change

During the past year the existence and importance of online philanthropy and volunteerism in the US has moved from being hardly noticeable to national visibility. While much was going on in terms of idea generation and early website development, it was for the most part out of the mainstream. Interactive sites (that enable the user to do something) began coming online in the spring off 1999 and were a mix of nonprofit, for-profit and hybrid enterprises. In addition, Guidestar, a nonprofit, was completing the work of digitally capturing all form 990s (nonprofit organizational information statements filed annually with government). New applications were also being developed and refined to facilitate volunteerism (e.g. Impact Online) and diffusion of applied good practice (e.g. Handsnet).

In July 1999 the W. K. Kellogg Foundation conducted a brief scan of Internet philanthropy and volunteerism to discover new interactive sites and to cluster those sites by type and function. The July report revealed the rapid development of Internet-based options for giving time and money and documented some of the promising active on-line sites, approximately 45 at that time. The e-philanthropy and volunteerism landscape, however, is evolving rapidly.

In September and October 1999 several new enterprises of great potential significance went live. Cisco Systems and the United Nations Development Program initiated NetAid – a technology and rock concert model for raising funds for international Third-World development. The Tides Foundation opened www.e-grants.org, an electronic market-place for donations and grants for progressive social change organizations. And, with much public visibility, the AOL Foundation launched its new philanthropy and volunteerism web portal as part of America On Line's services to its subscribers. The AOL venture is a partnership with Benton Foundation, Impact Online, Guidestar, Points of Light Foundation, Independent Sector and Urban League. It is designed to provide technology information and mentoring, access to volunteering opportunities and an electronic donation process.

Even for those sceptical of the Internet's potential for the nonprofit sector it does appear that the use of Internet technology by non-profits and foundations is literally exploding. Despite the technology gap (hardware, software, human capacity) experienced by many nonprofits, there are thousands setting up websites to communicate with members, provide information and to raise funds. Some of the more innovative/early adopter nonprofits are offering interactive services. Impact Online places volunteers, Innonet helps nonprofits to do evaluation, CompuMentor advises organizations, Benton Foundation connects citizens to action opportunities to serve youth and the Markle Foundation has made Internet-based technology the centre of its grant-making strategy.

For-profit corporations and venture capitalists are also adding to the array of services and applications for online giving. Many online sites for selling books, toys, drugs, food and services of all types offer charitable contributions as part of the purchase price. For-profit providers of traditional fundraising services are selling their services online to nonprofits. And venture capitalists and commercial entre-preneurs are looking to build services and information to and about nonprofits and giving opportunities as a new arena for e-commerce. Charitableway.com, for example, is capitalized and funded by Softbank and Benchmark Capital and has established a full-service site to enable direct donations, profit sharing for social causes through merchant partners, facilitation of non-cash contributions, outreach to corporate partners, etc.

Categories of e-philanthropy and volunteerism sites include the fol-lowing.

- **E-commerce profit sharing**
  E-commerce sites that provide either direct or registered shopping and offer their shoppers the opportunity to give by allocating a small percentage of the purchase price or profit to charity. The for-profit sites earn their revenues with advertising and/or taking a slice of the giving transaction for services rendered. (See list of Internet-based philanthropy, volunteerism and social change web-sites given in the Bibliography to this chapter.)

- **Fundraising and donor services**
  The more commercial of these sites have a narrow focus of directly facilitating the giving process for donors and/or enabling nonprofits

to do direct fundraising. Several sites like the Red Cross are single source fundraising sites. There are also a number of sites that are less commercial and provide more education, networking and connecting services for donors.

- **Knowledge and capacity development**
  These sites provide space for dialogue and discussion along with access to information about the philanthropy and social change-making. Some sites provide technical assistance related to non-profit organizational effectiveness.

- **Volunteering and service**
  These sites have a very focused mission to facilitate the placement of volunteer time and talent in nonprofit organizations.

- **Events and auctions in communities and online**
  These sites promote barter, auctions and local fundraising events run by volunteers and/or nonprofits in community-based settings.

- **Full spectrum of services**
  These sites offer a portal or one-stop shopping approach to a variety of services including: information and knowledge sharing, connections to volunteer opportunities, online donations or guidance in making donations.

6.1 Needs and opportunities

In all phases of the original research underlying this chapter, leaders, social entrepreneurs and philanthropists were asked to identify needs and opportunities that are part of the future evolution of these new trends in philanthropy and social change. The needs were expressed in numerous ways; nevertheless, they can be synthesized into three groups:

- **Knowledge management**
  Capturing, archiving and using knowledge and learning for innovation.

- **Human capacity development**
  The development of people and the tools they need for leadership, organizational, financial and planning challenges.

- **Deal-making**
  Coordinated opportunities for finding funding/co-investment partners.

6.2 Knowledge management

Knowledge management needs include those listed below.

- New philanthropists and social entrepreneurs want to learn from each other, from technical experts and from more established foundations and institutions. They want and need new networks that they have helped to create.
- Assessment, evaluation and dissemination are needed so that many can learn from the experiences of others. This will require conceptualizing new ways of capturing, archiving, tracking, synthesizing and diffusing information.
- Investment is needed in technology platforms that can be used to organize and facilitate the use of information.
- Funders need realistic exit strategies and social entrepreneurs need to devise more options for sustainability.

6.3 Human capacity development

Human capacity development needs include those listed below.

- New organizational models and structures demand new leadership, organization building, management and financial development solutions.
- Individual innovators, leaders, funders and other holders of resources in all sectors need opportunities to get to know each other and to discover common interests and goals.
- New tools are needed for more sophisticated capital markets leveraging as well as better measurement of social return on investment.
- Consultants, trainers and outsourcing partners are needed to work effectively with these new tools and entrepreneurial approaches.
- Nonprofit leaders and social entrepreneurs need more sophisticated capacity in financial capital structures; conversely commercial entrepreneurs need more expertise in the literature about social change and the civil society.

6.4 Deal-making

Deal-making needs include those listed below.

- New philanthropists need opportunities to collaborate and co-invest (when appropriate) with each other and with experienced philanthropists.
- New financial and human resources need to be connected to new social innovators. This will require connecting mechanisms, mentors

and role models. The work requires one-on-one opportunities that develop trust and credibility.

- Opportunities and resources are needed for incubating ideas and networked activities.
- Internet-based philanthropy and volunteerism – whether profit or nonprofit in structure – need to serve the public good and should be guided by vision and values that are compatible with the altruistic and social change ideals of the nonprofit sector.

In summary, while great promise can be seen within the many different solo creative efforts of social entrepreneurs and emerging philanthropists, the biggest need at this point is to connect these new waves of change, these many 'tidal pools' of knowledge, resources and innovation. They need to become a 'tidal basin' of synergy that catalyses activities to new levels of productivity and impact. Currently, there are few places to connect streams of innovative thinking and action. More shared knowledge about the available pools of capital for new ideas, the inclusion of new populations, the use of new technology and more access to specialized technical assistance for these new challenges is vital.

7 Action scenario

The following is an attempt to provide the beginnings of a conceptual framework for action based on knowledge gained from the two different research projects conducted by the W. K. Kellogg Foundation, along with experience from recent programme studies. It is being offered in the spirit of stimulating creative dialogue.

7.1 Vision

To unleash and leverage new resources dedicated to social development, driven by a blend and balance of market mechanisms and public responsibility.

Implicit in this vision statement is the desire to reach and inspire donors – large and small – who are experimenting or who want to try new partnership and market approaches to philanthropy. Within this aspiration is a picture of the future in which the meaning of wealth is leveraged to include social, spiritual and community capital – all of which are resources necessary for developing and sustaining the common good.

7.2 Implementing mission

Create a collaborative mechanism to catalyse and enrich the current critical mass of market-model activities. This would be done by connecting these activities, creating shared learning, building the collective capacity to innovate and create social value and identifying opportunities to fund collaboratively.

7.3 Principles/values

The principles and values underpinning the action scenario include those listed below.

- An effort to build on the work of both existing and new organizations if they are meeting, or have the potential to meet, critical needs and opportunities. (Don't re-invent the wheel!)
- A commitment to experiment with market and entrepreneurial models while balancing common good, equity and access with market efficiency.
- A desire to create social investment partnerships.
- A commitment to quality practice, efficiency and mentoring; a humility in learning; a hunger for discovery; and a willingness to share ideas.
- A commitment to redefining and expanding the meaning and application of wealth and to working with organizations – old and new – that can produce effective models for social development.

7.4 Proposed activities

The following activities are proposed to fulfil the mission statement.

- Create a knowledge management system to capture, archive, use and diffuse information (via technology and person-to-person mentoring). Both successes and failures need to be understood and used.
- Create peer-learning opportunities.
- Develop and share prototypes and models that work.
- Find and recruit staff, board members, advisers and consultants to assist donors and social innovators.
- Provide mentoring, technical assistance and apprentice-style learning.
- Foster connections, deal-making, co-investing.
- Map, track and diffuse good practice.
- Disseminate the story of evolving philanthropy and social development practices.

- Share assessment and impact measurement processes and approaches.
- Trade and barter 'know-how', management expertise and products.

7.5 Ideas for structure/design

The core purpose of a new collaboration would be to promote, facilitate and invest in more effective approaches to social development. It may be that a new entity or mechanism is needed for this purpose. Like those it intends to convene and serve, this entity could be formed and function as a market place for investors/funders and social innovators/social entrepreneurs from the public, nonprofit and commercial sectors. The investors/funders would be a partnership of current and emerging stakeholders including national and regional philanthropic associations; private, community, corporate and family foundations; and individual philanthropists.

As a community of entrepreneurial developers, investors, partners and learners, the market place should be easy to access, explicit about its goals, accountable and transparent to its stakeholders and, most importantly, a 'hothouse' and a 'magnet' for innovation. At one level, the market place would fulfil the rigorous needs of learning from each other, sharing best practices, disseminating information to others – in other words, producing and using knowledge. It could also be a place to co-invest in specific social change efforts that are more sensibly done in a collaborative fashion (such as large-scale, systems-change efforts requiring significant assessment costs and multiple site locations). Different investors and social innovators could partner and sponsor sites based upon their local desires and priorities and yet reap added value from being part of a larger systems-change effort. Although investors and innovators might not sit at the same table all of the time, the inclusion of both could enrich the learning and begin to model a new 'collective investment philanthropy' that represents a more seamless exchange between money and action.

At another level, the market place could open opportunities for participants to act on policy or regulatory issues collaboratively. For example, partners might want to work together to develop new capital market financial instruments that would require government and commercial sector cooperation, or even policy change.

Like any market place, the decision-making process of choosing to partner, collaborate in a group effort, or 'go solo' would be self-determined, and would vary depending upon the opportunity at hand.

Over time, with the building of relationships, trust and a sense of identity, the market place could evolve into an open guild – analogous to the craft associations of the Middle Ages, but open to all interested parties in the proposed activities and principles of the collective effort. This organizational architecture is once again re-emerging in the knowledge age with its networked economy.

8 Conclusion

This chapter presents an overview of changes and corresponding opportunities related to how philanthropy, social change organizations and leaders in the US are integrating market concepts into their work, value sets and organizational structures.

Social entrepreneurs have begun to use the tools and techniques of the for-profit sector relentlessly to create and sustain social value. Young philanthropists have demonstrated the potential of youth as fundraisers and grant makers. Women and people of colour have started to change how they are perceived: from being recipients, to being providers of philanthropy. New wealth creators have begun to turn their attention away from building wealth toward giving back. Corporate social innovators have launched new ideas for integrating investments in the common good into their business strategies and their corporate philanthropy.

These new ideas, new resources and new groups have the potential to transform philanthropy. Their potential, however, will not be fulfilled if the mechanisms of philanthropy and volunteerism remain a jumble of parts, each exciting in itself, but each disconnected from the others. While this cadre of innovators still operates mostly in solo fashion, the growing awareness of the value of collaborating is exciting and a major opportunity. What is needed is a vital centre, a market place where all can meet, exchange ideas and launch joint ventures. There is evidence that this is beginning to occur. Yet this momentum is only beginning, and the options for catalysing and nurturing it must stay in step with the pace of change and readiness, tracking learning and opportunities as they emerge.

The level of creativity and potential for new solutions to old societal problems is truly impressive. Philanthropy and volunteerism at the start of the 21st century are poised on the edge of tumultuous growth, in terms of both resources and creativity. Increasingly, philanthropic resources are controlled by populations who have not previously been much in evidence on the formal US philanthropic scene. The evolution of their generosity will have tremendous influence on the future landscape of US philanthropy.

9 A review of the literature

Documentation and reflection about entrepreneurial and market practices in philanthropy and nonprofits have been increasing as more organizations and funders venture further into experimentation.

This review of the literature attempts to summarize several insightful materials in circulation now within philanthropy and among social entrepreneurs and business leaders.

'Enterprising Nonprofits' by J. Gregory Dees (Harvard Business Review, January/February 1998)

This article describes four major pressures and influences that are pushing nonprofits into entrepreneurial models or commercialization. These include the following factors.

- A pro-business zeitgeist throughout the world.
- Nonprofit leaders are looking to deliver social goods and services in ways that do not create dependency in their constituencies.
- Nonprofit leaders are searching for financial sustainability and view earned-income-generating activities as more reliable funding sources than donations and grants. The sources of funds available to nonprofits are shifting to favour more commercial approaches, as few foundations want to provide ongoing funding and most want to invest for short periods in an effort to press grantees to become self-sufficient.
- Competitive forces from for-profits are leading nonprofit managers to consider commercial alternatives to traditional sources of funding. Dees offers a model called 'The Social Enterprise Spectrum' which describes the continuum from the purely philanthropic to the purely commercial. This model is described in the table below.

General methods	Purely philanthropic	Hybrids	Purely commercial
	Appeal to goodwill non-pecuniary rewards Mission driven	Mixed motives Some subsidy	Impersonal exchange Arm's-length bargaining Market-driven
Key stakeholder relationships Primary beneficiaries	Unclear or needy Not required to pay	Subsidized pricing Price discrimination Third-pay payers	Customer able to pay Priced for profit
Capital sources	Philanthropic donations/ grants	Mixed debt and donations or subsidized investments	Capital market rate Equity and debt
Work force	Volunteers with high commitment to social mission	Mixtures of representation and self-selection Balancing constituencies	Paid employees Focus on financial rewards
Suppliers	In-kind donations	Discounts, or mixture of in-kind and full price	Charge market prices
Governance	Mission-constrained, self-perpetuating board stewardship	Mixtures of representation and self-selection balancing	Board elected by owners Property rights Fiduciary responsibilities

'Virtuous Capital' by Christine Letts, William Ryan and Allen Grossman (Harvard Business Review, March/April 1997)

This article observes that a number of foundations are using the term 'venture philanthropy' to explain their strategies and to emphasize their interest in entrepreneurial action. Three major forces pressuring philanthropy are described to find new imagery and strategies.

- The retreat of the federal government from funding and delivering social services is increasing the demands on nonprofits and their funders and increasing the demands for effectiveness.
- New players in philanthropy are raising new questions, particularly those who believe that traditional charity is too focused on the satisfaction of the giver and insufficiently on social change and results.
- Large foundations are searching for new ideas and methods to create, bring into being and sustain effective social programmes.

The authors propose that foundations need to find new ways to make grants that not only fund programmes, but also build up the organizational capabilities that nonprofit groups need for delivering and sustaining quality. They highlight five relevant and adaptable venture capital practices: risk management, performance measures, closeness of the relationship, amount of funding and length of the relationship (usually about seven years). The authors are careful to point out that the venture capital model is not appropriate for all instances of grant making. Rather, funders should be able to opt – when appropriate – for a venture model. Some appropriate instances include helping to scale-up a proven young nonprofit, or to bring depth to a shallow organization that has effective programmes and potential.

The following chart presents a side-by-side comparison of venture capital and traditional foundation practice. The information in this chart is adapted from the 'Virtuous Capital' article and a subsequent presentation by Allen Grossman at the Northern California Grantmakers Association annual meeting.

Relevant practice	Venture capital	Foundations
Risk management	High degree of shared risk Funds are lost when projects fail	Low risk for foundation High risk for nonprofit organization (NPO) Funds themselves not at risk (must be spent)
Amount of funding	Substantial commitment to raise necessary capital	Partial commitment – management must continue fundraising
Duration/length of relationship	5–7 years Linked to success	1–3 years Arbitrary
Terms of engagement	Joined at the hip Small portfolios Partnership	Arm's length Large portfolios Supervision
Organizational capacity building	Funding to build capacity to successfully execute business plan	Funding primarily for programmes, not personnel, infrastructure, overheads
Performance measures	Clearly defined rewards and risks for all	Funder: reward is in grant making NPO: reward is in outcome
Exit strategy	Clear success, failure or projects left struggling	'Myth' of government take-out Burden on nonprofits
Results	1% of capital for all start-ups but 30% of companies that reach Initial Public Offering (IPO) stage	Harder to know. Not quantified. Same potential to support organizations to scale?

The U.S. Nonprofit Capital Market: An Introductory Overview of Developmental Stages, Investors and Funding Instruments by Jed Emerson

This paper characterizes the flow of resources into nonprofit organizations as 'capital investment' for educational and human services. Traditional fundraising devices of grants, annual campaigns, direct mail and endowment campaigns are all ways of raising 'capital' for essential services and social change activities. However, Emerson proposes, 'At a minimum … the Nonprofit Capital Market of the past will not be that of the future' (from J. Emersen and F. Twersky eds, *New Social Entrepreneurs: The Success, Challenge and Lessons of Nonprofit Enterprise Creation.* The Roberts Foundation, Homeless Economic Development Fund, San Francisco, September 1996).

The paper presents a basic framework for understanding the nonprofit 'capital market', discusses the types of organizational players active within it and outlines various capital instruments used to support the sector as a whole. Describing levels of funding from seed support through intermediate and then senior stages (e.g. self-capitalization and earned income) the paper also describes traditional as well as new sources of funding. Most intriguing among the new options are greater use of loans and lines of credit and opening up equity options such as market-based bonds and investments.

While advocating for a greater use of venture philanthropy practices, the paper acknowledges that financing the growth of nonprofits and/or their for-profit start-ups is difficult. Emerson claims that the nonprofit capital market is hindered by numerous issues including absence of market standards, lack of proven methods for demonstrating return on investment and lack of knowledge by both nonprofits and funders about capital options available.

This paper serves as a good introduction to the US nonprofit capital market, its players and investment instruments. Pressures and demands on the nonprofit sector require that leaders and funders work creatively to deliver the best service at the appropriate scale, while making use of the capitalization method that is appropriate to purpose and strategy. The paper enables both leaders and funders to begin thinking in these terms.

Bibliography

This chapter was informed by a variety of materials and publications. In addition to direct substantive sources on social entrepreneurship, philanthropy and business social responsibility, references were consulted on organizational design and theory, business development, economic trends, leadership development and ethics.

The following bibliography includes most of the books and articles consulted either for comprehensive study or for reference.

Philanthropy and social venture capital

'The Challenge for America's Rich', in: *The Economist*, May 30, 1998, pp.15–21.

Crutchfield, Leslie, 'Investors, Manna from Heaven', in: *Who Cares*, January/February 1998, pp.37–8.

Gray, Susan, 'A Former Insider's Crusade to Transform Thinking About Corporate Giving', in: *The Chronicle of Philanthropy*, June 4, 1998.

Letts, Christine, Ryan, William P. and Grossman, Allen, 'Performance Counts', in: *Foundation News & Commentary*, July/August 1998, pp.26–31.

Letts, Christine, Ryan, William P. and Grossman, Allen, 'Virtuous Capital: What Foundations Can Learn from Venture Capitalists', in: *Harvard Business Review*, March/April 1997, pp.2–7.

Hammonds, Keith H., Judge, Paul, Melcher, Richard A. and Wolverton, Brad, 'A New Breed of Philanthropist', in: *Business Week*, October 6, 1997, pp.40–4.

Maclean, Charles B. and. Greenberger, Jana B, *Philanthropy Now: Seeding the New Generation of Entrepreneurial Givers – Messages from Philanthropists and Could-Be-Philanthropists*, Portland, Oregon, 1998.

O'Toole, Patricia, "Reinventing 'The Gospel of Wealth'", in: *Leader to Leader*, Summer 1998, pp.44–9.

Rosenberg, Claude, *Wealthy and Wise – How You and America Can Get the Most Out of Your Giving*, Little, Brown & Co., Boston, 1994.

Rottenberg, Dan, 'The 100 Most Generous Americans', in: *The American Benefactor*, Fall 1998.

Sievers, Bruce, 'If Pigs Had Wings, It's Sexy to Compare Grantmaking to Venture Capitalism. It's Also Dead Wrong', in: *Foundation News & Commentary*, November/December 1997, pp.44–6.

Siska, Darlene, 'Future Grantmakers of America', in: *Foundation News & Commentary*, September/October 1998.

Van Slambrouck, Paul, 'Entering Golden Era of Giving', in: *The Christian Science Monitor*, September 15, 1998.

Business and social responsibility

Andreasen, Alan R., 'Profits for Nonprofits: Find a Corporate Partner', in: *Harvard Business Review*, November/December 1996.

Barrett, Amy K., Good, Regan and Howard, Manny, 'America's 25 Most Generous Companies', in: *The American Benefactor*, Summer 1998, pp.30–45.

Clohesy, William W., 'Untimely Thoughts on the Public Market', paper presented at the Twentieth World Congress of Philosophy, Boston, Massachusetts, August 1998.

Gray, Susan, 'Entering Another World, More People Are Leaving Charity Work to Start Socially Responsible Companies', in: *The Chronicle of Philanthropy*, April 9, 1998.

Hart, Stuart L., 'Beyond Greening: Strategies for a Sustainable World', in: *Harvard Business Review*, January/February 1997.

Hitachi Foundation, *The Road Less Traveled By: A Pioneering Approach to Global Corporate Citizenship*, November 1997.

Kaplan, Robert S. and Norton, David P. 'Using the Balanced Scorecard as a Strategic Management System', in: *Harvard Business Review*, January/February 1996, pp.75–85.

Logan, David, Roy, Delwin, and Regelbrugge, Laurie, *Global Corporate Citizenship – Rationale and Strategies*, Washington D.C., The Hitachi Foundation, 1997.

Nelson, Jane, *Business as Partners in Development, Creating Wealth for Countries, Companies and Communities*, England, The Prince of Wales Business Leaders Forum, 1996.

Social entrepreneurship

Dees, J. Gregory, 'Enterprising Nonprofits, What Do You Do When Traditional Sources of Funding Fall Short?', in: *Harvard Business Review*, January/February 1998, pp.55–67.

Dees, J. Gregory, *The Meaning of 'Social Entrepreneurship'*, October 31, 1998. Comments and suggestions contributed from the Social Entrepreneurship Funders Working Group.

Dees, J. Gregory, *The Social Enterprise Spectrum: Philanthropy to Commerce*, May 28, 1996. Note prepared as the basis for class discussion. This note benefited from materials originally developed in *Social Enterprise: Private Initiatives for the Public Good*, (HBS Case #9–395–116) by J. Gregory Dees and Elaine Backman.

Emerson, Jed and Twersky, Fay, eds, *New Social Entrepreneurs: The Success, Challenge and Lessons of Nonprofit Enterprise Creation*, San Francisco, The Roberts Foundation, Homeless Economic Development Fund, September 1996.

Leadbeater, Charles, *The Rise of the Social Entrepreneur*, London, Demos, 1997.

Rao, Srikumar, '100 Emperors of Peace, Turning Social Entrepreneurs Loose on our Nasty Problems', *Forbes*, September 7, 1998.

Skloot, Edward, ed., *The Nonprofit Entrepreneur: Creating Ventures to Earn Income*, New York, NY. Foundation Center, 1998.

Terry, Sara, 'Genius at Work, with his Potter's Hands, Bill Strickland is Reshaping the Business of Social Change. His Pittsburgh-based Program Offers a National Model for Education, Training – and Hope', in: *Fast Company*, September 1998.

Women, communities of colour and youth

Berry, Mindy L., *Native American Philanthropy: Expanding Social Participation and Self-Determination*, Battle Creek, Michigan, W.K. Kellogg Foundation, 1998.

Capek, Mary Ellen, *Women and Philanthropy: Old Stereotypes, New Challenges*, Battle Creek, Michigan, W.K. Kellogg Foundation, 1998.

Carson, Emmett D., 'Black Philanthropy: Shaping Tomorrow's Non Profit Sector', in: *The Journal: Contemporary Issues in Fundraising*, National Society of Fundraising Executives, Alexandria, Virginia, Summer, 1989.

Carson, Emmett D., 'On Race, Gender, Culture and Research on the Voluntary Sector', in: *NonProfit Management & Leadership*, Jossey Bass, Spring 1993.

Chao, Jessica, *Asian American Philanthropy: Expanding Circles of Participation*, October, 1998.

Cretsinger, Molly, *Youth Philanthropy: A Framework of Best Practice*, Battle Creek, Michigan, W.K. Kellogg Foundation, 1999.

Emerging Philanthropy in Communities of Color: A Report on Current Trends, Battle Creek, Michigan, W.K. Kellogg Foundation, 1999.

Latinos and Giving Survey, Hispanic Federation, 1999.

Organizational design, leadership and the new economy

Albion, Mark, *Making a Life, Making a Living: Reclaiming Your Purpose and Passion in Business and in Life*, Warner Books, New York, 2000.

Block, Peter, 'The End of Leadership', in: *Leader to Leader*, Winter 1997.

Block, Peter, *Stewardship, Choosing Service Over Self-Interest*, San Francisco, Berrett-Koehler Publishers, 1993.

Davenport, Thomas H. and Prusak, Laurence, *Working Knowledge, How Organizations Manage What They Know*, Boston, Harvard Business School Press, 1998.

Davis, Stan and Meyer, Christopher, *Blur, the Speed of Change in the Connected Economy*, Reading, Massachusetts, Addison-Wesley, 1998.

Drucker, Peter Ferdinand, *Post-Capitalist Society*, New York, Harperbusiness, 1994.

Handy, Charles, *The Hungry Spirit, Beyond Capitalism: A Quest for Purpose in the Modern World*, New York, Broadway Books, 1998.

Hawken, Paul, Lovins, Amory and Lovins, L. Hunter, *Natural Capitalism, Creating the Next Industrial Revolution*, Boston, Little, Brown and Company, 1999.

Heifetz, Ronald A. and Laurie, Donald L. 'The Work of Leadership', in: *Harvard Business Review*, January–February 1997.

Hesselbein, Frances, Goldsmith, Marshall and Richard Beckhard, eds, *The Organization of the Future*, San Francisco, Jossey-Bass Publishers, 1997.

Hesselbein, Frances, Goldsmith, Marshall, Beckhard, Richard and Schubert, Richard F., eds, *The Community of the Future*, San Francisco, Jossey-Bass Publishers, 1998.

Hock, Dee, *Birth of the Chaordic Age*, San Francisco, Berrett-Koehler Publishers, 1999.

Kelly, Kevin, 'The New Rules for the New Economy', in: *Wired*, September 1997.

Kelly, Kevin, *New Rules for the New Economy, 10 Radical Strategies for a Connected World*, New York, Viking Penguin, 1998.

Kleiner, Art, *The Age of Heretics: Heroes, Outlaws and the Forerunners of Corporate Change*, New York, Doubleday, May 1996.

Letts, Christine W., Ryan, William P. and Grossman, Allen, *High Performance Nonprofit Organizations, Managing Upstream for Greater Impact*, New York, John Wiley & Sons, Inc., 1999.

Malone, Thomas W. and Laubacher, Robert J., 'The Dawn of the E-Lance Economy', in: *Harvard Business Review*, September/October 1998, pp.145–52.

Rifkin, Jeremy, *The End of Work*, New York, Putnam's Sons, 1995.

Samuels, David, 'Philanthropic Correctness', in: *The New Republic*, September 18 & 25, 1995.

Schwartz, Peter and Leyden, Peter, 'The Long Boom', in: *Wired*, July 1997.

Seely Brown, John, ed. *Seeing Differently: Insights on Innovation*, Boston: Harvard Business Review Book, 1997.

Senge, Peter, Ross, Richard, Smith, Bryan, Roberts, Charlotte and Kleiner, Art, *The Fifth Discipline Fieldbook, Strategies and Tools for Building a Learning Organization*, New York, Doubleday, 1994.

Shapiro, Carl and Varian, Hal, eds, *Information Rules*, Boston, Harvard Business School Press, 1999.

Waldrop, M. Mitchell, 'The Trillion-Dollar Vision of Dee Hock', in: *Fast Company*, October/November 1996.

Wheatley, Margaret, 'Goodbye, Command and Control', in: *Leader to Leader*, Summer 1997.

Wilson, William Julius, *When Work Disappears, The World of the New Urban Poor*, New York, Alfred A. Knopf, 1996.

Web-based resources

American Benefactor	*www.americanbenefactor.com*
Ashoka: Innovators for the Public	*www.ashoka.org*
Business for Social Responsibility	*www.bsr.org*
Center for Venture Philanthropy –Peninsula Community Foundation	*www.pcf.org*
Cone Communications	*www.conenet.com*
Drucker Foundation for Nonprofit Management	*www.pfdf.org*

echoing green foundation	*www.echoinggreen.org*
Ewing Marion Kauffman Foundation	*www.emkf.org/entrepreneurship/index.html*
Fast Company Magazine	*www.fastcompany.com*
Global Business Network	*www.gbn.org*
Institute for Nonprofit Enterprise	*www.ine.org*
Joint Venture: Silicon Valley Network	*www.jointventure.org*
National Center for Social Entrepreneurs	*www.socialentrepreneurs.org*
National Foundation for Teaching Entrepreneurship	*www.nfte.com*
Net Impact	*www.srbnet.org*
Newtithing™ Group	*www.newtithing.org*
Philanthropy Journal Online	*www.pj.org*
Roberts Enterprise Development Fund	*www.redf.org*
Share Our Strength	*www.communitywealth.org*
The Entrepreneurs' Foundation	*www.the-ef.org*
The Philathropic Initiative	*www.tpi.org*
Women in Community Service	*www.WICS.org*
Women's Funding Network	*www.wfnet.org*

Current active Internet-based philanthropy, volunteerism and social change websites

(Note: this list is not exhaustive)

e-commerce profit sharing

www.Amazon.com
www.Borders.com
www.ebay.com
www.igive.com
www.4charity.com
www.charitymall.com
www.greatergood.com
www.shop2give.com

www.thehungersite.com
www.charityweb.net
www.mycause.com
www.shopgenerocity.com
www.shopforschool.com
www.shop4charity.com
www.shop2bless.com

Fundraising and donor services

www.donornet.com

www.givetocharity.com

www.donate.net

www.i-charity.net

www.virtualfoundation.org

www.charityvillage.org

www.e-grants.org

www.newtithing.org

www.redcross.org

www.hsus.org

www.litlamp.com

www.remit.net

www.kickstart.com

www.duo.org

www.charitiestoday.com

www.grantmatch.com

www.community.com

www.independantcharities.org

www.nextwaveworld.com

www.fund-online.com

Knowledge and capacity development

www.handsnet.org

www.impactproject.org

www.philanthropy.com

www.nonprofits.org

www.idealist.org

www.nonprofit.about.com

www.gilbert.org

www.oneworld.net

www.innonet.org

www.maguireinc.com

www.activecomputer.com

www.communitytechnology.org

Volunteering and service

www.volunteermatch.org

www.servenet.org

www.connectforkids.org

Events and auctions in communities

www.raffle-house.net

www.communitybids.com

www.celebrityauctions.com

www.2du.com

www.seeuthere.com

www.soldabsolute.com

www.yardsale-net.com

Full spectrum of services

www.helping.org

www.charitableway.com

www.benefice.com

www.guidestar.org

▼ Joseph C. K. Breiteneicher and Melinda G. Marble

Strategic Programme Management

1 Designing and developing a strategic philanthropic programme

1.1 Strategic philanthropy

When leaders of private philanthropic institutions are asked to identify sucessful elements in approaches to giving, they tend to identify a number of common themes: the use of giving to reflect the highest values of the donor, the need to create a focus for giving, the need to communicate funding criteria clearly to potential recipients and periodic reflection upon and assessment of the work.

They point out that giving away money is easy – many people give romantically and impressionistically. Giving it away effectively, however, is more difficult. It requires the donor to think strategically, using head as well as heart. Private philanthropy is perhaps best approached as an investment opportunity, requiring the same care, thoughtful approach and due diligence as other major business decisions. Effective philanthropy is strategic philanthropy.

What is strategic philanthropy? The development of a strategic philanthropic programme involves a commitment to:

- going beyond the process of reacting to the never-ending stream of requests for donations
- thinking through what social issues really interest the programme's founders
- learning more about those issues, through background readings, site visits and briefings by experts and other donors who have thought about the issue and have direct experience
- through research and analysis, identifying where philanthropic resources might make the most difference
- articulating the outcomes that should result from the philanthropy
- seeking out and forming partnerships with the best organizations and individuals to carry out this work.

It requires, therefore, developing one or more areas of focus for giving.

1.2 Why is focus important?

The Ford Foundation was once described as a 'large body of money surrounded by people who want some'. This irreverent but apt definition reflects the difficulties encountered by foundations that fail to articulate a mission or focus for their philanthropic efforts. These difficulties can include those listed below.

- The funding organization tries to be all things to all people, making small grants to many projects which are hard to track. Alternatively, it acts on impulse, making a seemingly random set of gifts that leaves the public bewildered about its intentions.
- The lack of context and goals to guide decision-makers make it difficult for them to evaluate funding requests, taxing their resources.
- Overwhelmed by large numbers of disparate requests, decision-makers can easily lose control of the process and simply give to organizations that are known to someone at the foundation.
- Foundation decision-makers become unsatisfied and wonder whether their giving is truly making a difference.

There are substantial benefits to developing a distinct focus for the foundation's programme efforts.

- A focus allows the foundation to concentrate resources in ways that can make a real difference.
- It provides a rationale for saying 'no' to requests that do not fit the foundation's interests.

- It assists grant seekers in determining whether or not they should approach the foundation.
- Decision-makers are provided with a context for reflecting upon and assessing the work of the foundation.

A funding focus can be articulated in one or a combination of the following ways.

- It can be **programmatic**, identifying a field such as the arts, education or community development in which to make grants. It can specialize within these areas, choosing areas such as modern dance or elementary education reform.
- It can focus on a **problem** or **issue**, such as homelessness or poverty and fund programmes that address it from a variety of fields.
- It can be **constituency-based**, choosing to support programmes that serve, for example, youth, immigrants or elders.
- It can be **geographic**, choosing a local, regional, national and/or international focus.
- It can identify preferred **methods or strategies** such as helping strengthen the management capacity of nongovernmental organizations or developing young leadership in several countries with a common knowledge base.

Some foundations choose a single focus area. Others choose two or more. In deciding upon a focus, it is important to consider what the resources of the programme will be. Can it stay abreast of developments in more than one field or issue area, for example?

Some foundations establish a permanent, broad focus in an area such as child welfare. Every few years they may reassess the field and choose to target their giving to specific issues within that broad arena. Others plan to shift focus periodically to address different interests of the foundation's leadership.

Effective foundations, however, tend to stay with a focus area for at least three to five years, deepening their own knowledge and expertise through their support of programmes in that area. If a foundation is interested in having an impact on social problems, it is important to recognize that significant change does not often happen quickly.

Some foundations cannot allocate all their resources to focused giving. For example, a family foundation may have certain traditions of giving to particular institutions that have come to depend upon them for support. A company may have charitable contributions it is expected to make to be a 'good citizen' in its home community. These foundations often start by setting aside a percentage of the grants budget for focused giving and reserve the rest for other gifts or programmes.

1.3 Developing a focus

The process of developing a philanthropic focus often begins with the identification of a working group of individuals who will shepherd that process. In the case of a family foundation, that might be the entire family, or a group of those most directly involved with giving. In a corporation, that group might consist of trustees or a selected group of employees from different levels of the organization. Some have found it useful to include outside expertise on a planning group, inviting individuals who are familiar with the workings of foundations or with charitable needs to join them. Some planning groups work on their own; others hire consultants or staff to facilitate their efforts.

If the planning group is a sub-set of the eventual foundation board, it is important that it be given a clear charge and that built into the process are opportunities to report back to, and obtain final decisions from, the full board.

The work of the planning group often proceeds through the following stages.

- **Reflection** on values and interests, leading to the identification of one ore more areas of focus.
- **Research**, including a discovery process to learn more about the potential for philanthropy in those areas of potential focus.
- **Refinement** of the focus, including articulation of a mission and operating principles for giving, as well as selecting tools and strategies the foundation will use to advance its giving mission.

Once the planning group has been identified, its first task is to identify and examine the motivating reasons to create a vehicle for giving. What has impelled the donor or donors to establish a giving programme? What are their interests and values? In cases where an individual has created a foundation after death through his or her will, that planning group may want to share their memories of the values, vision and gifts of the deceased, or do some research if these are not known.

The group can then seek consensus on the values and principles that should guide the new entity's giving, making sure they are in alignment with the interests of the donor or donors. Philanthropy is primarily an expression of values. Do the decision-makers for the new giving programme share common values that can be translated into giving?

For example, a family that is establishing a new foundation might begin its process by gathering together family members, asking them to reflect upon and discuss the following questions.

- What are your basic values? To what social issues or community institutions are you most passionately committed?
- What kinds of charitable gifts have you made in the past?
- Have those gifts reflected your basic values? Why or why not?
- What has been satisfying about your giving to date? Why?
- What has been unsatisfying or troubling and why?
- Do you know if your giving has made a difference? How?
- If the family's giving could stand for only one or two things, what would they be?
- Are there family dynamics or traditions you would like to sustain through this endeavour? Are there dynamics or traditions you would like to change?
- Are there areas of conflict within the family (whether inter-personal or different charitable interests) that must be acknowledged in developing a giving programme?
- Is there agreement among the family about what you should not do with your giving programme?
- What should the guiding principles of your family philanthropy be?
- Given the family's time, interest and resources, how many areas of interest or types of funding initiatives could be managed effectively?

A company seeking to establish a corporate giving programme could adapt these questions to examine its own culture. Instead of focusing on family values, the planning group might look at the company's values and history. It might also consider who its customers and employees are. What social needs and problems affect and concern them most?

The reflection process can be extremely simple or complex. It can be conducted via a written questionnaire, individual interviews, or informal discussion at a family meeting or company retreat. No matter how data is gathered, it is useful to have a meeting where all members of the planning group can discuss the questions and identify areas of consensus. This initial reflection process should lead to the identification of one or more areas of potential focus for the programme.

The next stage in the development of a strategic focus is research – an environmental study or community discovery process to learn more about the potential areas of focus and determine how a foundation might effectively work in those areas. This process begins with the planning group framing questions. What is it that we need to learn to refine our focus and operate effectively?

Perhaps for example, a foundation has agreed to focus geographically on a particular city. It might start with the following questions.

- What is the demographic make-up of the city? How is that changing?
- What are the city's most pressing needs and challenges as articulated by its government and by its citizens? Have those kind of soundings been taken?
- What are the city's strengths? What are its key institutions? Could funding support make them stronger?
- Who knows the city well and could best help the planning group learn about needs and opportunities for giving?
- How many nongovernment organizations are active in the city? Where does their funding support come from?

Or a foundation that was interested in homelessness as an area of focus might start by gathering data that answers the following questions.

- Who are the homeless? What data is available on numbers and causes? What are the gaps in data? What do the homeless themselves have to say about their situation?
- What are the primary causes of homelessness? Are there conflicting theories about cause? What information are the theories based on?
- What is the current government/policy response to homelessness? Are there gaps or problems private philanthropy could address?
- What organizations or programmes currently serve the homeless? Do they provide temporary shelter, permanent housing and/or address its causes?

No matter what the potential area of focus is, it is important to not only learn about the issue or community to be served, but also to pose some questions that address how a private foundation might make a difference.

- What other private foundations or other funders serve this area? What kinds of giving resources do they have? What lessons have they learned from work in this focus area?
- What is the role of government or public funding? Are there things it can or will not do?
- How will our foundation's giving compare in size to other donors? Are our resources modest or large in comparison?
- What do we know about what works in this field? Are there programme evaluations to draw upon? What remains to be learned?
- What – whether because of lack of money, lack of leadership, or other reasons – is not being done in this area? Can the foundation promote creative thinking that will generate new approaches, leadership and solutions? What roles should it play to be most helpful?

The research process can be an informal pooling of information or an elaborate research project. Some techniques that planning groups have found exceptionally useful include those listed below.

- **Interviews** (conducted by members of the planning group or an outside consultant) with a group of individuals who are broadly knowledgeable about community needs.
- **Focus groups** that gather together small groups of individuals and pose a set of pre-designed questions.
- **Gathering demographic and needs data** from local government agencies.
- **Identifying background reading and relevant research** (the Internet is becoming an invaluable tool for doing this) or commissioning surveys or other independent research.
- **Contacting local universities** to determine what academic research has been done on area needs.
- **Site visits** to selected communities or programmes that might be supported by the foundation.
- **Convening seminars or conferences** on the potential areas of focus.
- **Forming an expert advisory committee** or panel to provide feedback on needs and opportunities for funding.
- **Conversations with other donors**, local or national, in the field and with associations of donors.

These are all activities that planning group members can do themselves or obtain outside assistance to organize.

Once the research phase is completed, the planning group should revisit and refine its potential areas of focus, developing a mission statement for the programme. It may also want to articulate the operating principles it developed during its reflective phase.

It is important to consider the size and scale of the foundation in these deliberations. A fund with very modest resources is unlikely to have much impact with a focus as broad as 'promoting world peace' – unless it demonstrates great ingenuity in its strategies. The planners should consider whether, in the interest of consensus, too many areas of focus or one overly broad area have been developed.

Some planning groups find it useful to analyse potential areas of focus by ranking each according to the urgency of need in the area and the potential for impact given the size and scale of the foundation.

1.4 The 'how' of giving: choosing roles and vehicles

As a focus is being developed, foundation planners must consider not only the 'what' of the foundation's future giving, but the 'how'.

That process starts by posing a very broad question: what do we want to accomplish with our giving in X area?

There are many possible – and legitimate – answers to that question. Common responses might range from 'addressing immediate needs' to 'solving problems', 'offering opportunity', 'recognizing achievement', or 'generating creative thinking'. But the tenor of the answers will provide clues to the foundation's developing character as an institution.

In posing this question, it may help planners to consider how and whether the foundation seeks to be part of existing philanthropic traditions. Throughout history, there have been three major streams of philanthropy.

- **Charity** that seeks to provide resources directly to those who are needy through vehicles such as food, clothing or shelter programmes.
- **Patronage** that seeks to identify and nurture talent. The Nobel Foundation is a modern example of this tradition, which is also exemplified by Renaissance princes' support of artists.
- **Modern philanthropy** that seeks to identify and promote systemic solutions to the causes of social problems.

Strategic philanthropy can be practised in any of these areas. A programme that views itself as primarily charitable may want to focus on a particular area of need or to promote the more efficient distribution of resources to the needy. A foundation that takes a patronage approach may do so with a particular strategy in mind, for example finding and recognizing promising young leaders in a particular field. In addition, it might periodically convene those leaders to share their work with each other.

But modern philanthropy (the name is something of a misnomer, since this tradition began in the 16th century with the development of housing for the poor in Europe) is inherently strategic, since it attempts to define a problem, identify promising approaches and allocate resources to support solutions.

Foundations that practise modern philanthropy choose options from a range of roles. They may provide financial support to projects, programmes, organizations or individuals in the forms of grants, loans, or investments in social causes; or they may develop and operate programmes themselves.

They may be primarily responsive, identifying areas of focusing and selecting to fund the best ideas that are proffered, or they may develop proactive grant initiatives, identifying strong organizations and inviting them to apply for support to do particular things. Some foundations, as an extension of their strategic grant making, may choose to operate their own initiatives. They seek to play catalytic roles. They may restrict their activities to grant making, or they may go beyond grant making to active engagement in the social issues they care about or the organizations they support.

There is also a wide range of activities that foundations can choose to support or to sponsor themselves. Possibilities include:

- direct services to people in need
- prevention programmes or other efforts to address the root causes of social problems
- planning and development of new initiatives and ventures
- public education, advocacy and policy work
- community organizing
- media, film and communications activities
- research and evaluation
- awards
- training and scholarships.

A planning group should also consider what types of funding the foundation would provide. Possibilities include any or all of the following:

- unrestricted grants for general operating support
- funding targeted to a particular programme or service within an organization
- capital funds for facilities or equipment
- endowment funds for permanent programme support
- challenge grants to be matched by the organizations with funds from other sources.

As needs and requests increase, many donors have enhanced their philanthropic tools to include approaches that go beyond traditional grant making or programme operation. Donors now also use loans, loan guarantees and equity investments to pursue their mission. Some examples are given below.

- A foundation might make a low-interest loan instead of a grant to help a cultural institution purchase a new facility when it knows the organization has revenue streams that could repay the loan.
- A donor might guarantee a bank loan to ensure that a low-income housing project gets the permanent construction financing that it needs.
- When payments to community groups from governmental agencies for services provided are seriously in arrears, foundations can step in to provide low-interest cash flow loans that are guaranteed by the nonprofits' income.
- Other foundations have advanced loans against ticket revenues for cultural organizations that did not have sufficient working capital for their performance or exhibition.
- Foundations can place a portion of their assets in banks that then commit to providing more favourable credit terms for community organizations.
- In the area of the environment, foundations can combine grant support for a programme's operations with loans that enable land trusts to purchase environmentally sensitive property. The loans are repaid when permanent financing or other fundraising, which takes considerable time, is in place.

To foundations, these non-traditional funding decisions have the virtue of returning the investment funds so they can be used again for charitable purposes. To the recipient organization, they can encourage independence and build an organization's capacity to finance its activities. They also symbolize the more businesslike nature of much of strategic philanthropy.

The options selected from the range of tools and activities described above depend to a large extent on how the foundation characterizes itself as an institution. For example, some foundations use the analogy of a venture capitalist to describe their work. They believe that their mission is to seek out and provide start-up support to the most promising new ideas. A foundation that views itself as a venture capitalist thinks of its grants as investments, but measures success in social returns or outcomes, not in financial terms. It is often willing to support risky new enterprises because the potential for social return is so great. It expects some of its grants or programmes to fail and in fact may not feel that it is taking enough risks as an institution if all the projects it supports are successful. That foundation will often become very involved with the programmes it supports, providing technical assistance and helping them access other resources in order to make its investments successful.

Other foundations view themselves primarily as stewards of charitable resources whose primary function is to transfer funds from one sector to another. They might be compared to investors who maintain a portfolio of blue chip stocks, in that their primary concern is a sure social return. These foundations tend to feel more comfortable supporting established organizations or programmes that have proven themselves over time. They may provide operating support to these established programmes. They are less willing to take risks and they are particularly concerned with the cost-effectiveness of the programmes they support. A primary challenge for these foundations is continuous learning about what works and does not work in social programmes.

Other foundations again view their primary role as being a change agent that seeks to influence public policy or institutional changes through its work. In addition to providing programme or operating grants, these foundations tend to fund dissemination and communications efforts that advance the ideas of the programmes they support. They may use their resources to define and refine public policy issues through research, analyses, evaluation, conferences, seminars and other media. They may also seek to replicate promising approaches and programmes at new sites. Or they may seek to serve as a social conscience or 'gadfly' by becoming directly engaged in issues through sponsored studies, commissions, reports, statements and actions.

Many foundations, of course, choose to play a mix of the roles just described. Thinking what tools and strategies might be most effective in the particular areas of focus chosen by the foundation helps make the foundation's future course of action more concrete. After reviewing the tools and options available to it, the foundation may help the planning group to consider the following questions.

- What roles will the foundation play in its work within its area(s) of focus?
- How active will it be?
- What is its attitude towards risk and the possibility of failure?
- What philanthropic persona best suits the institution's vision, values, focus and resources?

This last question is perhaps the most fundamental of all. Another exercise that foundation planning groups have found helpful is to reflect upon and discuss the following scenario: imagine that it is the year 2010 and the X foundation is regarded as one of the most effective private charities in the country. What has it accomplished? What are people saying about it? What roles does it play to carry out its mission?

1.5 Periodic check-ups

Once a foundation has established a focus, it is important to develop a process for periodically revisiting its decision in the light of new realities. That may be as simple as an annual review of activities at a board meeting, or as elaborate as a full-scale independent evaluation of a giving programme after it has been established for several years. No matter how it is conducted, it is important to consider these questions.

- What were the underlying assumptions in our decision to adopt these focus areas? Are they still relevant? What have we learned from our funding experience thus far?
- How has the environment in which we are working changed since we developed our focus? What new developments are affecting the organizations or programmes we support? (These could range from funding trends to demographic changes.)
- Which grants or programmes that we have supported have been successful? Which have not succeeded? In either case, do we know why?
- Does the 'how' of our funding still make sense in terms of the 'what'?

2 The grant-making process: reviewing proposals and selecting projects for funding

2.1 Developing a grant review structure

Once a focus for giving has been established, a structure for soliciting, reviewing and deciding on grant requests must be developed. Reviewing proposals is the testing ground where a foundation enacts its visions and values, translating its focus and funding guidelines into practice. It also affords to staff and trustees the opportunity for ongoing learning and discovery.

Developing a structure for review involves making key decisions about:

- how often the foundation will make grants
- how much it has to spend and how the money will be allocated
- how the grant programme will be announced to prospective applicants
- who will make grant decisions
- what information they will need in order to make good decisions
- what criteria will be used to review proposals
- how they will gather information for decision-making
- how grant decisions will be made and communicated.

Existing foundation practice in each of these areas varies widely, as the examples below will attest.

2.2 How often will the foundation make grants?

This is determined by how frequently the foundation's trustees or grant-making group will meet to make funding decisions. Some foundations meet to review grant requests as infrequently as once a year, others as frequently as once a month. More common are quarterly or semi-annual decision-making meetings. Some family foundations schedule their grant-making meetings to coincide with family vacations or reunion times, while corporate foundations often include grant making as part of a company board meeting.

Another decision to address is whether to accept applications on a continual (rolling) basis or to establish grant-making deadlines. There are advantages and disadvantages to each. Accepting applications on a rolling basis provides a great deal of flexibility for the foundation; it can respond quickly to compelling requests or hold requests until it has received a certain number from a particular field for comparative purposes. It also allows the foundation to schedule decision-making meetings when it is convenient for board members. It sometimes, however, creates confusion among applicants who are not certain when a decision will be made about their proposal. If the decision is made to adopt a rolling application policy, it is useful to tell applicants approximately how long the review of their proposal should normally take (e.g. six weeks or six months).

Establishing grant-making deadlines provides applicants with a sense of clarity and certainty about when their proposal will be reviewed. It creates a fairly rigid structure for review that requires regularly scheduled grant-making meetings.

Setting deadlines involves determining how much time will be needed to review proposals prior to a decision-making meeting. At a small foundation with few staff and a highly targeted programme, that time may be very short. At a larger foundation that receives more proposals, more time might be required.

2.3 How much does it have to spend?

Most foundations attempt to estimate the income that will be available for grants during the year and establish a grant budget. In the US this budget is often dictated by the pay-out requirement, a regulation that requires private foundations to give away the equivalent of 5% of their assets each year.

How foundations allocate and manage their grant budget varies widely. Some set aside specific annual amounts for each of their focus areas, while others make all applicants compete for funds from the same pool. Some draw down the grant fund irregularly during the year, depending on the quality of funding opportunities with which they are presented. Others establish a grants budget for each decision-making meeting and approve grants totalling only the amount available for that meeting.

2.4 How will the grant programme be announced to prospective applicants?

How a grant programme is announced to a prospective pool of applicants has a tremendous impact on the quality of proposals received. It also determines to a large degree whether those served by the foundation perceive it as fair and accessible or remote and arbitrary. Deciding how to go about announcing a new giving programme involves first an assessment of the potential applicant pool. Is it very narrow, with relatively few qualifying organizations, or enormous? Is there the potential to be deluged by proposals?

Some foundations, in order to limit the number of proposals received, issue 'Requests for Proposals' (RFPs) to targeted groups and accept proposals only from those organizations. Others publish general guidelines and distribute them widely in the communities they serve.

Whether an RFP or a more general route is selected, the development of written guidelines is important. From the donor's perspective, they give a sense of direction and purpose for staff and trustees; they create an identity for the donor in the community. From the grant applicant's perspective, they ease the burden of fundraising by allowing organizations to focus their proposals more clearly. They also make funding decisions seem fairer and clearer.

Whether through an RFP or broad general distribution, giving guidelines should include the following:

- the foundation's mission and focus
- the type of support it provides (e.g. operating grants, fellowships, etc.)
- the things it does not fund (e.g. scholarships, research)
- term limits on grants (one or multi-year)
- its geographic range
- the preferred method of initial contact (telephone call, letter of inquiry or full proposal)
- guidelines for what is expected in a proposal or application form
- the process the foundation will use for responding to requests
- the schedule or time frame for decisions.

No matter how clear and detailed written guidelines are, many potential grant applicants will still have questions and will want to know whether the project they are proposing is consistent with the guidelines. It is best to have a strategy for handling those queries. Some foundations do it informally and respond to telephone questions, while others require something in writing first. A small number of donors offer periodic 'how to apply for a grant' workshops. These are typically hour-long sessions during which any potential applicant can pose questions about the guidelines and the application process. This allows donors who have a small staff or who receive a very large number of queries to handle them efficiently.

If the RFP route is selected, steps in soliciting grant proposals include:

- developing clear proposal submission guidelines, deadlines and decision-making criteria
- determining how open the RFP process will be and how it will be communicated to potential applicants

- developing a written packet of materials to guide applicants
- in some cases, holding a briefing to announce the RFP and answer questions about the application materials.

The advantage of this approach is that it targets the groups who are most likely to receive funding, saving other organizations the time and trouble of applying for funds. But the expectations of applicants that they will receive funding – and their disappointment if they are not selected – can be greater. Fairness and consistency of response by the foundation are crucial in a process as visible as an RFP.

2.5 Who will make grant decisions?

At many foundations, funding decisions are made by the full board of trustees. At some, however, this work is entrusted to a committee of the board, often called a distribution or grant-making committee. That committee may have full grant-making powers, or may make recommendations that are put to a full vote of the entire board. Some foundations have a distribution committee for each focus area which they fund.

At a few foundations, professional staff makes individual grant decisions, with the trustees setting broad policy and giving guidelines. Others allow staff the power to make small discretionary grants and reserve board involvement for major gifts.

2.6 What information will they need to make good decisions?

This involves determining what the board or other grant-making committee needs to know and offering some guidance to applicants on how it should be provided. In deciding what to ask for, a foundation should consider the fact that staff and board will have limited time in which to review requests. Except in extraordinary circumstances, most foundations will quickly begin receiving more good proposals in their focus area than they can afford to fund.

This means that a process for efficiently and fairly reviewing large numbers of requests must be developed. Proposal review is an imperfect process, more art than science, in which apples and oranges must constantly be compared. When decisions among good projects are difficult, there is a is a tendency to think 'If I only had one more piece of data'. The result is that many foundations collect more information about applicants than they will ever use. Reviewers often feel inundated with information.

This tendency can be mitigated to some extent in the design of the review process by asking those who will review proposals to reflect on three fundamental questions.

- What do I need to know about a grant applicant to do my job with *accountability*? This addresses the need for responsible stewardship to ensure that funds are not misused. The answers here might include a review of past financial statements, or the assurance that the organization's leadership is reputable.
- What do I need to know about an applicant to decide with *fairness*? This involves understanding the context of a proposal and the willingness to acknowledge one's own biases and assumptions. The answers here might include being able to compare the organization to others in its field, or to have data that places the work of the organization in context.
- What do I need to know about an applicant to perform with *excellence*, feeling assured that we have made the best possible funding decision? The answers here might involve looking at the impact of the organization's work, or gauging a particular constituency's satisfaction with its efforts.

Having reflected on these questions, reviewers are better able to design an application process that provides them with the information they need.

2.7 What criteria will be used to review proposals?

There are many factors that can be weighed in considering any programme. In designing a process for reviewing and discussing grant proposals, it is important to consider what criteria for funding matter most to the decision-making group. Possible factors to consider include those listed below.

Quality of volunteer leadership

- Is there an active board of trustees that understands the mission and purpose of the organization?
- Does the organization have membership, volunteers or other unpaid constituencies?
- Is the composition of the board appropriate?

Quality of management

- Are key staff competent and experienced?
- Are operating policies and procedures in good order?
- Does the organization have quality assurance mechanisms?

Track record

- Is there a solidly documented record of achievement?

Financial strength and stability

- Are accounting and financial record-keeping systems in place?
- Has there been financial stability over time?
- Is the funding base diverse and stable?
- Does the organization have strong fund development capacity?
- Is there a cash reserve?

Legitimacy in the community

- Does the organization have a high degree of community support and participation?
- Does it interact effectively with its various constituencies?
- Is there representation of the organization's constituencies or consumers at the board and staff level?
- Does it have a process in place for gauging community needs?

Quality of vision

- Is there a strategic plan for the organization or programme to be supported?
- Is there a sense of vision shared by staff and board?
- Is the timing right for this endeavour?

Urgency of need

- How urgent is the problem or issue addressed by the proposed grant?
- How did the organization identify this need?
- How does their assessment of the need compare with the analysis of others who know the field or community?

Who will be served?

- Is the programme targeted to a low-income population?
- Is it aimed at a particular minority or ethnic group?
- Will it serve a particular neighbourhood or community?
- Does it serve a special population in need, such as refugees or the disabled?

Efficiency/cost effectiveness

- What is the cost per unit of service?
- How does it compare to similar programmes?
- What would the social costs be of not offering this programme?

Potential impact

- Does the proposed programme represent a new model or approach?
- Will it affect large numbers of people?
- Does it have the potential to be a model that could be replicated elsewhere?
- Will it sustain or significantly strengthen a critical community resource?
- Does it have the potential to influence public policy?
- Does it have the potential to develop new concepts and contribute significantly to learning in this field?

Degree of risk

- Are the plans presented well-conceived and likely to work out as proposed?
- Is this a tested idea or approach?
- Do outside forces have the potential to hinder implementation of this programme?

Strategy/leverage

- Will our support encourage other donors to give?
- Will it build public support or credibility for this approach?

Potential for institutionalization and self-sufficiency

- Will our support significantly strengthen this programme/organization?
- If successful, is this programme likely to be replicated elsewhere?
- Is this programme likely to affect how other institutions provide services?
- Are there other potential future funding sources for this effort?

For most foundations, a few of these factors will be most critical in their decision-making process, others will be of lesser importance and still others will be of no concern at all.

2.8 How will we gather the information needed to make decisions?

2.8.1 Written proposals

For most foundations, a written proposal or application form is the first vehicle for gathering information on applicants. Here again, foundation practice varies widely, with some donors requiring grant seekers to complete detailed application forms and others accepting proposals in any format. It is useful to applicants and donors alike, however, to provide some guidance on what the foundation would like to see in a proposal. Often that takes the form of a brief outline of the components that should be included in a proposal. A typical outline might look like the one set out below.

Background of the organization

- mission
- history – how it started and why
- community or constituency it serves
- current programmes and key achievements
- staff and board structure
- size and scale of operations
- past funding history – who have been major supporters?

Programme or project for which support is requested

- statement of the opportunity or need addressed by the proposal
- broad goals of the project or programme
- methods or strategies to be used in carrying out the project or programme
- description of how the project or programme will be staffed and administered
- objectives and potential outcomes of the programme – what will happen as a result of this grant?

Evaluation and dissemination activities

- how will the project or programme be documented?
- what data will demonstrate that it achieved its goals and objectives?

Fit with the foundation's guidelines

- how does the proposed project or programme address the focus area and funding guidelines of the foundation?

Future

- if the programme is ongoing, how will it sustain itself after foundation funding is completed?

Budget

- projected budget for the organization or project for which funding is requested
- amount requested from the foundation
- list of other donors who have been or will be approached for support.

Attachments

- certification of the organization's nonprofit status (if required)
- list of board members
- financial statement for the most recent fiscal year.

This outline might be amended to address more directly the focus areas of the foundation. And, depending on what information is more critical to the foundation, different emphases and levels of detail might be required in different sections. One foundation, for example, might want extensive information on an organization's track record and past successes, while another would want more detail on the prospective programme.

In order to control the information flow, some foundations set a page limit, typically five to ten pages, on proposals. Still others ask for a brief letter of intent (one to three pages) providing background on the organization and request. They then review these letters and encourage the most promising applicants to submit full proposals.

Many foundations do a quick periodic review of proposals received to determine which ones fall within their guidelines and which do not. They then send an early denial letter to the applicants that are not on target. The swift 'no' is appreciated by grant seekers who can then use their energy pursuing other sources.

Some foundations base their entire review process on the written proposal or application. If possible, however, it is best to use the proposal as the starting point for a dialogue with and about the grant seeker that might include one or more of the following:

- a telephone call to the applicant, or personal meeting in the foundation's offices
- a site visit to experience the work of the organization directly
- contacts with others who know the organization and its work
- conversations with other current and potential donors of the project or programme
- a review of research or other data that provides a context for the request.

2.8.2 Direct contact

There are good reasons not to rely simply on the written materials. Face-to-face meetings with applicants allow foundation representatives to verify information contained in the proposal and assess the character of the people running the programme. In addition, the best proposal writers are not necessarily operating the best programmes.

Finally, programmes are always different – richer and more complex – than paper can convey. Talking to people who work in the foundation's field of focus and see the work directly provides a valuable context for making other grant decisions.

In preparing for direct contact with grant applicants, it can be helpful to remember the Yiddish proverb 'The man who has money is good looking, intelligent and he sings well too!' Foundation staff and board members are almost always treated like that 'man with money'. Few grant applicants want to question openly foundation policies or to argue with advice from a foundation executive. It is important for representatives of the foundation to acknowledge that fact and to encourage frank dialogue.

Courtesy and directness encourage a more open flow of information from applicants who may also be intimidated by the foundation. No matter how modest the funding source, applicants perceive it as having great power. They may be reluctant to share problems or obstacles they have encountered, preferring to paint a rosy picture of the organization. In order to obtain a realistic sense of what is going on, a foundation has explicitly to encourage open communication. One foundation executive tells grant applicants:

> I am not looking for perfect programmes to fund. Our job is to present our board with a balanced view of all the projects that have applied for funding. That includes a presentation of your strengths, but also the weaknesses and potential risks in making the grant. It's important that we do this because our trustees need to understand the real difficulties and obstacles that nonprofit organizations face. Also, if we decide to support you, we'll view that support as an investment. That means we'll want to know about any serious problems you encounter, so we can help you address them if possible.

The next, deeper level of information gathering on a programme is to make a site visit to see the work in action. There are many reasons foundations make site visits to at least some grant applicants. A donor may be unfamiliar with the applying organization and wants a first-hand look. Site visits also have the potential to educate donors about a new funding area or field. They provide a valuable context to how the organization operates in its community. They also provide the opportunity in some cases to hear first-hand from those who benefit through the organization's work.

The site visit also allows a foundation to get a sense of the physical location of the programme and the condition of the facility in which it is located. Is the location easily accessible to its constituents? Does the physical space appear adequate and to meet required standards? Are there obvious limitations that might impede the programme? Do proper office procedures seem to be in place? These are all questions that can best be answered through observation at the site.

Finally, some foundations do site visits because they want to be more visible donors, letting the community know that they are accessible and eager to support strong programmes. Some do them simply because the reality of programmes is always different from how they are presented on paper. And some do them as a kind of fairness test, a check on the biases and assumptions they might have when reading about the organization.

Some foundations do not conduct site visits because they have a small – or no – staff, and board members simply do not have the time. Others address that problem by doing a very small number of visits, or by taking board members on an annual tour of a few programmes. Some corporate or community foundations use employees or other volunteers to conduct site visits.

Foundation professionals who use site visits effectively generally agree on the following guidelines.

- Lay out ground rules for the visit in the beginning (or ideally, prior to the visit). For example, you should tell the organization how much time you will spend there, what you would like to see, whom you would like to meet and what general areas of information you are seeking.
- As far as time allows, however, let the organization tell its story in its own way. Allow time for the applicant to present information about its work before beginning to ask questions.
- Do not make surprise visits. It antagonizes organizations and makes them feel you do not trust them. The result is they are less willing to share honest information with you.
- If the organization you are visiting provides direct services, be sensitive to the need for client privacy and confidentiality of records. If you want to see files or observe a counselling session in progress, for example, let the applicant know beforehand and discuss confidentiality issues.
- Be careful about raising expectations. Some organizations think that if a foundation visits them, they are sure to get a grant. It is important to say explicitly that this is not necessarily the case.

What foundations look for or ask during meetings with applicants – whether on-site or in the foundation offices – varies greatly. Some donors develop a written checklist or standard interview format that they use for all site visits. But most conduct these meetings less formally. They use the written proposal as a framework for dialogue, going through section by section and asking questions about what was unclear or appeared weak.

In addition to asking for clarification or information, it is useful to pose questions during a meeting or site visit that require the applicant to reflect on the work of the organization. Some examples are given below.

- When you look back at the history of the organization, what makes you proud? What regrets do you have?
- What are three major things you have learned doing this work?
- What are the greatest opportunities you see in your work over the next five years?
- What are your greatest challenges?
- What skills or resources need to be developed within your organization for it to do its job better?
- How do you know your programme is effective? What doubts or questions do you have about it?
- What do you see as the greatest strengths or assets of the people or community in which you work?
- What happens to this organization after the current leadership leaves? What are you doing to prepare another tier of leadership?
- What, besides additional money, would make your work more productive and effective?

Meetings with applicants are also an opportunity to flesh out vague parts of the proposal, to make the programme more concrete to the foundation. In a service programme, for example, it can be useful to ask the applicant to trace what happens to a single client from the time they enter the programme until their departure, asking the following kinds of questions.

- How do staff interact with that person?
- What services are offered in what time span?
- What outcomes do staff look for in that person to tell them the work has been successful? How are those outcomes documented?
- Does the programme have a method for assessing client satisfaction?
- Does the programme keep track of former clients over time? What have they learned from that process?

In meetings with grant applicants, foundation representatives may find the need to help potential grantees clarify and articulate meaningful objectives for their work. An objective is a statement of the outcome or results that a programme expects to achieve in relation to the problem or issue it is attempting to address. It should be

- measurable – how can the foundation determine whether the objective was met?
- specific – who will be served and how will they benefit?
- realistic – what can be done about the problem/issue?
- time-limited – by when will the objective be accomplished?

Objectives often are weak or missing in many proposals. When they are there, they tend to be very broad and vague, or focused on processes rather than outcomes. For example, a group might list as an objective 'to offer four workshops on peer dispute resolution to high school students'. That is concrete and measurable, but it does not address what will happen as a result of the workshops. Will student skills be developed? Will they put those skills into practice? Resolve what kinds of disputes? Will the training affect other areas such as school attendance? Asking these kinds of outcome questions helps grant applicants to sharpen their focus and provides foundations with the information they need to assess whether an investment is likely to produce a good result.

2.8.3 Reference checks

In addition to meeting with applicants, foundations often conduct what amounts to a reference check on proposals by asking individuals who are familiar with the work of the organization for their comments. Sometimes they talk with someone, such as a board member or former client, who is directly involved with the organization. Or it might be useful to get the perspective of another organization that operates in the same geographic area or field. Contacting other donors who have supported the organization or researchers who know the field can be useful as well.

In doing this kind of information gathering, it is important to keep a few points in mind.

- It reduces anxiety if you let the applying organization know you will be doing this kind of check. It is important to stress that you will be asking for an assessment of weaknesses as well as strengths, that you expect that some criticisms may surface and that these do not necessarily mean that a grant will be denied. Neither do glowing reports necessarily mean a grant will be made.

- Be sensitive to the fact that many nonprofit organizations view themselves as in competition for funding. You may need to discount a peer organization's harsh criticisms if they are motivated by competitiveness.
- If you are going to show an applicant's written proposal to someone outside the organization, it is important to make this clear to the applicant organization.

2.8.4 Ethical issues

In all aspects of reviewing proposals, ethical issues emerge. One of the most troubling issues is that of how directive the foundation should be. From the vantage point of someone who sees a great many programmes, it is tempting for foundation officers to suggest changes, diagnose management problems and prescribe new programme areas to the organizations it is reviewing. This kind of assistance can be useful to and appreciated by applicants if it is offered in a skilful, non-coercive manner.

There is always the danger, however, that the applying organization will adopt advice it disagrees with in the hope of getting a grant. The result is a grantee who is not fully committed to the programme it is offering, which usually leads to weaknesses in management. There is the danger, too, that the grantee will acquiesce to the advice and then ignore it.

Also, it is all too easy for foundation officers to be prescriptive when they themselves are not directly engaged in managing programmes. For example, many foundations encourage organizations to collaborate with each other. In theory this is a wonderful concept, but in practice, there are many barriers to true collaboration, including competition for the same funding sources and crossing into each others' operating areas. Acknowledging and understanding these problems while still pressing for the goal of collaboration requires tact and skill.

2.8.5 Summarizing information

Once the review process for a particular request is complete, the information gathered must be summarized for the foundation's decision-makers. Some foundation boards are given copies of every full proposal received, along with staff notes on the review process. Others provide the board with the cover page from an application form, which contains summary data on the proposal.

But at many foundations, trustees do not review applications directly. Rather, they receive summaries of each application prepared by staff. The staff will prepare longer, more detailed summaries of projects they are recommending for funding and briefer descriptions of projects that are not recommended. The summaries are usually written up in a standard format.

The summary of a project recommended for funding would typically include some or all of the following sections.

- **Request** – usually a one-line summary of the amount requested and the purpose of the gift.
- **Background** – information on the requesting organization's purpose, major programmes and track record.
- **Proposed project** – a summary of the project or programme for which funds are requested.
- **Analysis or comment** – the staff's view of the proposed grant, which usually includes an assessment of the reputation of the requesting organization's board and staff and the stability of its finances, a description of the organization's strengths and weaknesses, the potential positive outcomes and the risks of making a grant.
- **Rationale for support** – a section that makes the connection between the project's purpose and the foundation's focus and funding criteria.
- **Recommendation** – what level of support the staff are recommending.

A summary of a project that is recommended for denial might include shorter versions of these sections and a rationale for denial.

2.9 How will grant decisions be made and communicated?

It is important for trustees or members of a grant-making committee to agree on the process for making decisions about funding. Most foundations either adopt a formal voting system with majority rule; smaller or family boards often work by consensus, discussing each grant until all trustees are comfortable with the decision. Some staff and boards use rating sheets that assign particular rankings to funding criteria; others rely on informal discussion of the merits of a project.

Whatever the ultimate decision on a funding request, it is important that it be conveyed promptly to the grant applicant. The donor must decide whether it is going to notify applicants by telephone or mail, or both. Many foundations develop a standard letter that is sent to all denied applicants. That letter is usually general in tone and refers to the competitiveness of the process and the need to make difficult decisions. Some include an invitation to telephone to obtain more feedback about the reasons for denial.

Many foundations also develop a standard grant award letter or agreement that applicants are asked to sign accepting the grant. That letter should include the following information:

- the amount of the grant
- the time period within which it should be expended
- the purpose of the grant, which may include a re-statement of the expected outcomes defined in the proposal
- any restrictions on how funds may be used
- the schedule for grant payment
- requirements for reporting on the use of grant funds.

Most foundations make their grant awards in one lump sum payment. Some enclose that payment in the award letter; others require the grantee to sign and return a copy of the letter agreeing to the terms of the grant before issuing a cheque. Still others pay grant amounts in quarterly instalments, with reports due prior to some instalments.

2.10 A final word

As noted above, grant review is more art than science. It is impossible to develop a perfect empirical process for the review of proposals; there are simply too many factors to consider, too much information to be reviewed. And not all giving decisions are rational ones; sometimes donors simply fall in love with a programme. The key is to look closely at the beloved one and be rational about its flaws.

It is impossible for a grant reviewer to be perfectly objective. We all have our biases, tastes and assumptions. But the best reviewers are willing to put those assumptions to the test, to acknowledge and question their own biases. While it is not possible to be objective, it is possible to be fair. Strong criteria and a clear process for review help in that quest.

The best grant making is informed not only by clear criteria and processes for review, but also by high ethical standards. This means:

- a commitment to a periodic review of the giving guidelines in the light of changing events and realities
- the recognition of mutual need between grant maker and grant seeker and the establishment of a relationship based on honesty and mutual respect

- awareness of the potential for conflict of interest or financial gain for foundation staff and board and avoidance of situations in which real or perceived conflict could occur
- grant makers must apply the same planning, evaluation and management standards expected of grantees to their own work.

The most effective foundations are truly learning organizations. They make a whole-hearted commitment to continuous questioning of the institution's vision, values and practices. They find, in the process, that the work becomes more engaging and deeply satisfying.

3 The grant-making process: controlling grants, managing grantee relationships and implementing funding initiatives

3.1 What are the basic principles of good grants management?

If, as the preceding sections have sought to emphasize, effective philanthropy models many of the best practices of investment behaviour, then the care and attention that go into managing grants or special funding initiatives are as important as the skill and due diligence applied to the initial decisions. Grant approval can be considered a starting point in a new relationship. In essence, the funder, by making a grant, has agreed to form a partnership with the recipient organization. That means a genuine commitment to a successful outcome for both parties. Those funders who see the relationship as a true partnership understand that they are investing in a process. This process entails trial and error. If managed effectively, the process will allow both partners to grow and learn from their work together.

From the foundation's perspective, the framework for successful management of the grantee relationship is established by its basic requirements. There are several fundamental components.

- **Treat grants as contracts**
  The foundation's programmematic expectations and requirements should be clearly delineated at the beginning. Many foundations now enter into a contract with the grantee that spells out the basic elements of the grant; others now ask the grantee to restate the goals it has for the project, expected outcomes and who within the organization will be the primary contact for the foundation.
- **Establish a reporting schedule**
  Within the grant contract, there must be explicit reporting requirements – regarding both what the foundation expects to receive and

when it should be reported. In response, the foundation should always acknowledge receipt of the information and provide an appropriate response to the data.

- **Respect confidentiality**
  Because the foundation may receive privileged data from the grantee (financial information or evidence of problems within the funded project), information provided by grantees must be treated with the strictest confidentiality. What the foundation learns is for its use only; if funders want their grantees regularly to provide relevant and useful data, that information must be handled with great respect.

Beyond the basic reporting requirements, there are a number of other key ingredients to creating and managing successful relationships between foundations and grantees. Among the more important are three that a number of proactive foundations have identified.

- **Recognize the funding partnership**
  Each sees the other as a valued resource; each recognizes the qualities and experiences that the other brings to the relationship which may help in its work. As a concomitant to this point, the foundation should endeavour to let grantees know that the foundation should be made aware of any significant changes in programme design or staffing. Equally, if unanticipated problems arise or if the public policy or regulatory context shifts measurably during the term of the grant, the grantee should inform the foundation and share its thinking regarding possible plans to make adjustments in the project.

- **Commit to a helpful hands-on presence**
  If at all possible, there should be periodic (e.g. quarterly or half-yearly, depending on the project and logistical matters) programme review meetings with grantees, including site visits when appropriate. These meetings are at the heart of a working relationship with grantees. Just as a venture capitalist would offer ongoing, hands-on support and guidance, the strategic foundation is engaged in its major funding initiatives.
  Regular site visits by the funder serve to remind the grantee of its commitment to the project and to refocus organizations on their original goals and objectives. Even with the best of intentions, organizations tend to lose momentum as they respond to myriad and competing pressures. Grantees have commented that in preparing for visitors they engage in much needed reflection and planning. These personal visits may be conducted by foundation

trustees, staff consultants and/or multiple grantees. Generally it is preferable to have a team of visitors who will bring multiple perspectives. The visits should be complemented by written reports that provide an additional vehicle for reflection.

- **Build capacity**

  As it works with grantees to help them fulfil programme priorities, a foundation may also provide guidance and technical assistance on recipients' organizational issues, especially those that may have surfaced during the foundation's due diligence proposal review. This is a more holistic approach to grant making that recognizes programme initiatives are often only as strong as the grantee's institutional infrastructure. Larger foundations may have staff or ongoing consultants who have valuable expertise in areas such as board development, strategic planning or fundraising, but even foundations with more modest resources should seek to help grantees' strengthen their organizational tools and skills.

  For example, one foundation recently underwrote a seminar on fundraising for all its grantees in a particular programme focus area. Another foundation helped connect grantees that had particular management or organizational experience to other grantees needing that assistance. The foundation paid the expenses of the consulting grantees in order to facilitate peer-to-peer training. Other funders will build a measure of funding into their grants for technical assistance, thus enabling grantees to purchase consultative services on an as-needed basis. Irrespective of the means, strategically inclined foundations are seeking to build the capacity of their grantee organizations. Not only is this wise management of grants, but it is also often a long-term investment in the ability of organizations to continue in their programme work, independent of further financial support from the initial funder.

  Obviously, the way in which technical assistance is structured will depend upon available resources as well as the nature of the grant. The larger and more complicated the grant, the more important the non-grant resources become. Similarly, it makes more sense to build in technical assistance when the grant is for a multi-year period. In such cases, the grantee can be given an opportunity to re-propose its project annually, based on learning to date, including barriers and strengths.

3.2 In the grants management process, what common organizational issues affecting grantees should foundations be aware of so that assistance may be offered?

While many funders merely write a cheque and request periodic progress reports, those funders with a more strategic approach invest non-grant resources in their partners' success. For while a grantee may have the best of intentions and a well-thought-out plan, they are likely to encounter unforeseen circumstances as they proceed to the implementation phase of the project. In fact, many projects fall apart because they cannot successfully make the transition from the written, planning stage to the active, implementation stage.

Almost every grantee will encounter unanticipated obstacles, as well as unknown strengths, as they implement their project. Common issues faced during the implementation stage include those listed below.

- **Leadership changes**

  Leaders are critical to organizations. When a staff director, school principal or board president leaves his or her position (for whatever reason), the direction of the entire project could be in jeopardy. Changes in leadership generally result in uncertainty until a new leader comes on board. His or her commitment to the project must be secured if the project is to get back on track.

- **Internal capacity**

  In order to carry out a project successfully, effective staff are critical. Often the key staff lack the necessary training to fulfil the specific requirements of the project. Often the key players might not all have the requisite commitment to the project's success. Especially in projects that call for changes within an organization, individuals might have the ability to stand in the way of progress deliberately if they find it threatening.

- **External forces**

  Constituencies outside the organization can often impede a project by overt opposition or a failure to provide needed support. For example, a community project may need approval from local government; a school project may need the support of parents. External forces can also affect a project by diverting needed resources and attention to other priorities. If an organization is faced with unanticipated problems it might not pay sufficient attention to the funded initiative. Many community organizations deal with crisis situations as a matter of course and, in the frenzy of day-to-day activities, they may lose sight of their original goals and plans.

- **Overambitious agenda**

  It is common for an organization to propose to do more than is realistic. Often this is proposed to satisfy the funder: grantees believe that only by being overly ambitious will they win approval. Just as common, however, is a failure to realize just how hard it is to make change. By failing to anticipate the common barriers to implementation, an organization will believe it can move forward at a much more rapid pace than is actually possible.

3.3 Common staffing approaches to managing grantee relationships

To ensure that a grant will follow through to success, a funder has a variety of options, which are not mutually exclusive, for effectively fulfilling its role in the partnership.

- **Hire programme staff**

  Ideally, internal staffing should be sufficient to work with grantees on an ongoing basis. The key role of staff is to develop an effective relationship with the grantee that allows for problem solving and capacity building. This type of relationship is not easy to establish since grantees tend to want to please a funder and worry that admission of mistakes will jeopardize the grant. Thus it is critical that expectations be discussed at the outset and that mutual trust is nurtured throughout the relationship. In order to accomplish this, staff should try to visit the grantee sites periodically to gain a first-hand perspective of the issues facing the organization, as well as to appreciate the community in which it resides.

- **Retain consultants**

  Those funders who view the implementation stage as an ongoing research and development phase invest heavily in outside consultants. Thus, in addition to receiving a direct grant, grantees also receive ongoing technical assistance. Consultants may help with generic issues such as long-range planning and management capacity or they may work on an *ad hoc* basis as particular problems are identified. Similarly, the funder may choose to hire one or more consultants with a variety of skills who can be called upon on an as-needed basis. The ability of a skilled consultant to make a difference is so important that some funders limit their assistance to this arena – rather than providing a programme grant, they pay qualified consultants to work on a long-term, intensive basis with their partners.

- **Convene grantees for peer-to-peer learning**

  A third means of providing ongoing guidance to grantees is to bring grantees together with one another on a regular basis. This type of convening allows grantees to share their experience and learn from one another. Structured effectively, such a forum also provides off-site opportunities for reflection and planning. It is another way of sending the message that 'we are in a mutual learning experience'. Furthermore, bringing grantees together with one another helps to show grantees that this is not just another grant, but rather they are part of an important endeavour.

3.4 In addition to its fundamental role of grant maker and monitor, are there other roles a foundation can play to aid the long-term success of its grantee projects?

There are several roles that more innovative foundations have utilized. First is that of convenor. Gathering together a foundation's grantees for peer-to-peer training has already been mentioned. Other approaches to convening include the following.

- Bringing together other funders oriented to similar issues or programme objectives to review overall grant-making experience, develop best practices information that could be shared with grantees and identify replicable programme models. Such convenings may also serve to allow funders to focus on important public policy issues or concerns that may affect their grant-making agenda or bring exemplary projects in need of additional support to the attention of other foundations.
- Inviting public officials, civic or community leaders, whose support may be crucial to the success of one or more of the foundation's projects, to a briefing on the background, motivations and objectives of a funding initiative or to share what had been learned from a project already underway.

Second is the role of developer of research or collateral materials that are related to the performance of grants or funding initiatives. A foundation may underwrite the development or distillation of academic research that broadly supports the work of its grantees. Some examples are given below.

- In a recent case, a foundation with a programme focus on helping to create affordable housing in more affluent communities, commissioned university-level research that investigated and supported grantees' claims that their new housing programmes did not result in diminished property values in the community – an issue that communities regularly raise in resistance to housing initiatives for lower-income families.

- In another case, a foundation with funding interests that concentrated resources on helping mentally ill adults live in the community underwrote research documenting successful approaches to re-integration of those who are de-institutionalized.
- In a related approach, a foundation with a major commitment to create a comprehensive service and housing model to serve disabled homeless individuals, underwrote the hiring of a communications consultant. The consultant designed public relations materials that each of its grantees could use and also created a media campaign around public awareness of the issue that supported the work of all the projects.

Third, there is the role of advocate. For some foundations, this is a logical outgrowth of their intense commitment to a particular cause or issue. In this role the foundation becomes a spokesperson or champion on behalf of its grantees and their priorities. It gives up its claim to objectivity (and perhaps its ability to provide common ground for convening others) in order to promote the work of its grantees or of other special initiatives the foundation may have.

3.5 What approaches are effective if a foundation desires to extend its strategic grant making to include the creation of special funding initiatives?

Part of any proactive foundation's grant-making tool kit should be a more entrepreneurial option that allows the foundation to design funding initiatives. These approaches go beyond responding to unsolicited requests, however much they are within the foundation's focus, to target specific projects that the foundation wishes to see implemented. They typically provide the foundation with greater control over the process and often help to focus greater attention and resources on key challenges.

These initiatives usually are a variation of a foundation's request for a response to a structured funding initiative. Two common approaches are described below.

3.5.1 Use of a Request for Proposal (RFP)

In this process the foundation defines in a written document what it wishes to accomplish and how organizations that decide to compete for funding should respond. A Request for Proposal (RFP) can be broadly descriptive or quite prescriptive. It can be broadcast to a wide audience or sent to a selected number. Elements include:

- the foundation's overall goals and motivations for the RFP
- what it specifically seeks to achieve in the initiative
- the programmatic approach it favours
- what the foundation expects to see in a proposal and the recommended form for a response
- the amount of funds available, *in toto* and per project
- a brief description of the selection process and a schedule.

3.5.2 *Use of a Request for Concepts or Qualifications*

These variations on the 'request' approach usually require less specific programmematic documentation from the respondent. They are often utilized as a screening mechanism to enable the funder to create a short list of possible grantees, with whom the foundation either negotiates a project proposal or who are then challenged to develop a response more like the RFP defined above. The advantage to the potential grantee of a Request for Concepts or Qualifications (RFC/Q) is that the process does not require excessive proposal design work from often hard-pressed community organizations, unless there is the distinct possibility of funding. The advantage to the foundation is that it does not have to review as many full proposals but, rather, commits to an iterative process for the project's development.

3.6 Is such an option available only to foundations with significant resources?

While there are common characteristics of such initiatives, size of funding is not one. As the brief examples listed below will illustrate, philanthropic funds committed can range from a few thousand to millions of dollars. What matters much more than the amount is that the programme's motivations, design and implementation are well thought out and fit with the foundation's mission, its human resources and its desire to be more proactive.

3.7 What characteristics of best practices are common to such initiatives?

The following common characteristics of best practices can be identified.

- The proposed initiative represents a logical next step for the foundation within its area of focus.

- The initiatives are often built upon or replicate models that have been 'field tested' by other credible foundations.
- The foundation sees the initiative as a funding vehicle that may achieve results which more conventional funding may not.
- There is a deep need for such an initiative and a responsive market of potential grantee organizations has been well researched and defined in advance.
- The initiative is custom-tailored to fit a foundation's objectives and resources.
- The design is 'user-friendly' for organizations that may wish to respond and compete for funds.
- The selection process is clearly defined.
- The initiative holds the potential to focus public attention on a pressing issue, to leverage private and public funds and/or to produce results that may provide significant change or major advances in an important field.

3.8 What measures are appropriate to structure and manage the implementation of special initiatives most effectively?

By definition, special funding initiatives are often more labour intensive than more conventional grant making. But if the initiative is a high priority for the foundation, then it should also recognize that it must invest resources in its own capacity to oversee and control the work.

If strategic philanthropy is, as referenced numerous times in these essays, social venture capital, then the investors need to take care that they have the ability to track, support and promote their investments.

The following elements are required:

- a commitment to hands-on management
- a sorting out among the foundation's existing personnel – trustees and staff – regarding an appropriate division of labour on key tasks
- a willingness to engage consultants or intermediary institutions to provide technical assistance to the foundation and recipient organizations at critical junctures in the project's life and, if necessary, to assume ongoing management supervision in situations where staff are not available
- a collegial approach that involves other funders as advisers to the initiative or, in the case of corporate programmes, seeks employee participation and assistance in the initiative's decision-making and implementation.

The following are several mini-case studies that exemplify how a foundation or donor translated its entrepreneurial spirit and focus on an issue into an extraordinary funding initiative. Each is drawn from TPI's recent work with clients. While they are uniquely different, they share core best practices characteristics: some are model approaches that have served other foundations equally well, while others offer a laboratory of research and design projects that could be replicated or expanded.

3.9 Examples of special funding initiatives

3.9.1 Youth Partners Initiative

In 1992, the Chief Executive Officer of an international financial services company decided to determine whether the company's foundation should alter its grant-making process to become more focused and more proactive. As a result, he set in motion a planning process that engaged a consultant to facilitate the planning and to survey all 2000 employees regarding their views about the most appropriate mission and focus for the company's charitable endeavours.

Process

A questionnaire was designed and distributed to all employees (80% responded). The consultant interviewed, in person, all senior management regarding the same questions. Focus groups of employees were also utilized to allow people to discuss what the company should stand for in its philanthropy. On the basis of the results of this early discovery, a preliminary focus on strengthening programmes serving youth from poorer neighbourhoods was established. Discussions with other foundations and community leaders yielded data on the need for a funding initiative that would help effective organizations build more comprehensive approaches to their work with young people.

Armed with data from inside the company and from its headquarters, the company initially established a three-year $800,000 funding initiative.

An RFP was developed with help from other foundations and distributed to all youth-serving programmes in the region (over 600 organizations). A volunteer panel of experts and funders assembled to provide an outside screening review of the responses – over 100 applications were received. A diverse group of employees was chosen from a list of volunteers to serve as the company's review team. They received training in proposal review from the company's consultant and began the task of winnowing the docket of proposals to a manageable list of those to receive greater scrutiny. Eventually, the team conducted site visits to ten finalists and then chose seven to recommend for funding.

The winning projects not only received grants but were also provided with ongoing technical assistance from the company's employees to strengthen the organizations' financial management and organizational development skills. In addition, the company established a work placement programme for young people who are participants in the projects.

Administration

Once the initial funding decisions were made and the consultant's principal work was completed, the company hired a part-time member of staff with strong programme skills and an extensive background in working with youth to serve as coordinator of the initiative and liaison link with the seven grantees in the community.

Summary

Response to the RFP affirmed the company foundation's focus and served to educate its leadership on the issue of youth at risk. The resultant grants leveraged additional financial resources and provided a vehicle for firm partnerships to be established between the company, its employees and the winning projects. Four years after the RFP was announced, those relationships continued. Because of the success of the first RFP process, the company, in 1996, committed to a second round of projects in 1996 and a third round in 1997.

3.9.2 Girls Action Initiative

In the summer of 1996, a new family foundation (with no staff but consulting help) developed and distributed an RFP that offered to provide grants to programmes which focus on helping pre-adolescent and adolescent girls be 'confident, competent and thrive in their lives'. The RFP was the culmination of a strategic planning process that the family had engaged in with the assistance of a consultant who facilitated the effort. The process drew on the family's values and a strong interest in 'girls and self-esteem'. The intersection of those values and passions was the germ of an idea for an initiative and provided a starting point for an investigation of what an RFP should seek to accomplish.

From extensive research and discussions with practitioners and experts, the family decided that there was a real need for an initiative that could support the creation of new models that, over time, have the potential to be adapted, expanded or replicated around the country.

In announcing the RFP, the foundation framed its interest:

> This initiative stems from the Foundation's concern that many adolescent girls fail to achieve their potential for a variety of reasons, including the following: some girls 'lose their voice' at the critical transition point between preadolescence and adolescence; many of our societal institutions place lower expectations on girls who may then internalize this lesser sense of worth; and many existing youth development programmes fail to understand and address the particular needs of girls. Moreover, while there is a growing body of research and a number of promising ideas for effectively reaching adolescent girls, there are few existing models that are comprehensive in their approach.

The Foundation's objectives for this initiative are to:

- Provide 'seed capital' to support creative, thoughtful approaches to working with girls, with a primary focus on those aged 8 to 14.
- Create effective models of comprehensive programmes for adolescent girls, which have the potential to be expanded and/or replicated by others over time.
- Promote shared learning about what works best, by offering an arena in which grant recipients can learn from one another and reflect upon and modify their programmes as needed over a three-year period.

Specific criteria articulated in the RFP were based on findings of the initial research on what types of programme elements are critical to the success of girls' programmes.

Process

The actual RFP process followed many of the key steps outlined in the previous case. In this situation, over 1000 organizations in the region received the RFP; 140 chose to respond and 22 received site visits. The consultant managed the RFP process. Family members shared review responsibilities, including site visits to the finalists. A panel of experts in the field assisted in winnowing the proposals and provided experienced guidance to the family in determining criteria for final choices.

Ultimately, the foundation chose 12 recipients who, in total, will receive $3 million over three years.

Administration

As part of the planning and RFP process, the family foundation identified a need to hire a part-time project coordinator who would monitor and oversee individual grants, provide guidance to grantees and become the human 'glue' that would bind grantees together in a collaborative relationship.

Evaluation

In addition to hiring a part-time project coordinator, the foundation has contracted with an independent research and evaluation firm to conduct an ongoing interactive evaluation over the three years of the grants initiative. This evaluation is designed to:

- provide support and feedback to individual projects' evaluations
- create a learning community among the grantees and promote the sharing of evaluation experiences and lessons
- assess progress and results of each of the projects and of the grants initiative as a whole.

Outcomes/summary

The first phase of the initiative was getting underway at the time of writing, but it had already met some of its initial aims. By disseminating the RFP to more community groups than those serving solely girls and young women, the foundation raised awareness of the RFP's focus and generated discussion about best practices in serving the healthy development of young women.

3.9.3 Innovations Grants Programme

In 1991, a corporate funder decided to create its own initiative to provide direct grants to public schools. Called the Innovations Grants Programme, the initial goals were:

1 to target funds directly to communities in which the company's headquarters were located
2 to create exemplary models of effective school change by building on existing knowledge concerning best practices.

After extensive research by TPI, the company decided to invest directly in individual schools and to offer multi-year cash grants as well as ongoing training and technical assistance. Rather than being prescriptive, the funder decided to invite schools to put forward their own vision, stipulating only that proposals focus on creating opportunities for all students to be successful.

Process

To launch this initiative, an RFP was crafted, asking applicants to describe their community and school, vision for the future, strengths and weaknesses and how they would build upon existing efforts to achieve fundamental school improvement.

The proposal review process involved employees of the company, who evaluated proposals and conducted site visits to semi-finalist schools.

For the first round of grants, an advisory committee consisting of the head of the company and education experts made final decisions. From a total of 161 proposals, 22 schools received site visits and nine schools were chosen to receive grants.

Initiatives funded by these grants included efforts to increase parental participation; provide opportunities for staff to learn about new methods of instruction and assessment; experiment with different ways of grouping students; and design new curriculums that were more responsive to diverse student needs.

Administration

In addition to three years of direct grant support to schools selected as grant recipients, the Programme provided a variety of professional development opportunities and technical assistance to the schools. The company sponsored semi-annual conferences, involving teams from each grantee site, which featured educators from exemplary schools and provided structured time for participants to plan and share with one another. In addition, periodic site visits by education consultants were made to each school throughout the year, along with hands-on technical assistance to help the schools implement their ideas effectively.

Evaluation

As part of the Innovations Grants Programme, schools that receive grants developed 'indicators of success' and refined these indicators over time, in order to develop internal capacity to evaluate what changes are working well within the school. The periodic site visits to schools were also used to evaluate how the schools were progressing.

In addition to these ongoing evaluation activities, the funder commissioned an independent evaluation of the Programme in 1995, which found that the Programme was an exemplary model for promoting school change. Most significantly, the evaluation found that the most important components of the Programme were the regular conferences and the hands-on technical assistance. Exposure to these programme components caused grantees to go much further in their reform efforts than they had originally intended.

Outcomes/summary

Based on the positive feedback from the independent evaluation, the funder decided to sponsor a second round of grants, launched in 1996. This round built upon lessons learned, while continuing to expand upon the original design. Continuation grants were awarded to the most successful of the original grantees and grants were awarded to new schools as well. Round II also emphasized the mentoring and coaching of the new schools by the 'veteran' schools. In this way, the corporation was continuing, in 2000, to experiment with and learn from new approaches to supporting school improvement.

Based on the changes being made as a result of this grants programme, several of the schools were receiving local and national attention as exemplary schools. For example, one of the schools received a 1996 Blue Ribbon Award from the US Department of Education. At another school site, the entire community came together to develop a common vision for education, as a direct result of a community summit sponsored through the Innovations Grants Programme.

3.9.4 National Environmental Education Initiative

In the summer of 1995, a multi-national industrial corporation sent an RFC to a selected list of 20 nonprofit organizations with an established record of accomplishment on the promotion and teaching of environmental stewardship. The RFC urged each environmental group to respond to the corporation's interest in supporting the creation or expansion of a model that would teach primary and middle school youth about the environment in a hands-on scientific manner.

Process

The company, which had recently incorporated the environment into its list of philanthropic priorities, worked with a consultant to:

- identify its goals in the environmental field

- outline what criteria it would want in an RFC initiative
- identify corporate personnel who would assume responsibility for participating in or managing the decision-making process
- determine the qualities needed in its grantees, including the capacity to manage a second round of challenge grants.

The consultant was then charged with:

- framing the issue
- developing a short list of environmental organizations that might be encouraged to respond to the RFC
- designing the RFC.

A committee of the company's senior management was then assembled to review recommendations from the consultant on possible finalists and determine a short list of projects to be visited. Six received site visits and three were invited in for a final interview. The organization chosen was then asked to work with the committee to design the actual scope, schedule and budget for the initiative. The winning organization received $3.6 million to expand its own efforts to teach young people and their school teachers about the environment (including the design of classroom material) and to design a model programme that could be replicated elsewhere.

Administration

The organization chosen received funding not only for its own programme and the design of a teaching model, but also to administer a second round of RFCs that would expand the effort to four or five other sites. The company decided that it did not have the personnel or experience to administer a national effort and that the administration of the second phase was best placed in an intermediary organization.

Outcomes/summary

The programme became a nationwide effort in less than two years. It received critical acclaim from educators and environmentalists. The company felt it had entered into a real, long-term partnership with the lead organization, which oversaw the overall programme's performance and reported regularly to the funder.

3.9.5 *Other examples*

In addition to these four cases, there are other examples of the innovative uses of targeted funding and of creative approaches to the administration of the resultant initiatives.

Housing for the disabled who are homeless

A family foundation with an interest in the housing problems of the disabled who are homeless underwrote a study to determine the extent of that need in the foundation's local area and to identify model approaches to the problem. When the study indicated considerable need and the severe lack of a comprehensive approach to the issue, the foundation underwrote the development of a model programme. Because the foundation did not have staff, it then created an intermediary organization to administer an RFP effort whose core funding the foundation provided.

In four years the foundation's initial $450,000 grant leveraged an additional $2.5 million in private philanthropy and $25 million in public funding. The intermediary, through an RFP process, chose ten projects that have produced over 300 units of 'supportive' housing. The intermediary continues to receive foundation support to enable it to provide ongoing supervision and technical assistance, especially in the financing of large-scale affordable housing projects, to the RFP's grantees. The foundation also calls on the intermediary to help it assess other requests it receives in related fields.

Self-sufficiency for shelter residents

A private foundation with a focus on the poor, especially women who are residents of emergency shelters for the homeless or victims of domestic violence, asked its most effective grantees who ran shelter programmes to identify measures that would help their clients become self-sufficient. The practitioners' responses focused on the need for flexible funds that would fill financial gaps in publicly financed training or educational programmes. Such financial shortfalls often kept shelter residents from taking full advantage of programmes that would help them learn a skill, complete high school or begin career-oriented education at a community college. As a result, the foundation developed a brief RFP that offered any shelter a replenishable grant of up to $7500 for use in filling the financial gaps in their clients' education or training.

The agencies that were chosen were expected to administer the flexible grants for individual clients' needs but were not allowed to subtract administrative fees. The foundation's RFP explained that the fund was intended to help grantees carry out their service mission. The foundation set a cap of $75,000 on the initiative in each of the first two years, over which time 15 organizations helped several hundred very poor people pursue their educational dreams. The funds that recipient shelters re-granted paid for such basics as books, tools, uniforms, transportation to classes and child care.

In addition to its provision of flexible funds, the foundation convenes the recipient organizations to discuss their work and to encourage them to work collaboratively on the public policy issues that affect their provision of services to clients.

Improving mathematics and science education

In 1994 the co-founder of a highly successful medical technology firm and founder of a family foundation launched a grants initiative designed to improve mathematics and science education at the middle school level (grades 6–8). The grants support teacher teams with ideas for innovative curriculum projects integrating mathematics, science and technology, as well as other disciplines. The initiative was developed through feedback from exemplary middle school teachers and administrators, obtained through a focus group discussion facilitated by a consultant. Based on this feedback, an RFP was designed, offering modest flexible funds to teams of teachers, along with a review process involving an advisory committee and site visits to applicant schools. As of September 1997, the donor had awarded a total of 30 grants and was launching its fourth round of grants through this initiative. In 1996, the donor funded an evaluation, which found that the initiative had acted as a catalyst in bringing teachers together to develop new teaching approaches focusing on hands-on learning projects. The donor's foundation has no permanent staff; the consultant firm and the public school's Office of Instructional Technology jointly administer the initiative.

In 1991 at the direction of a donor (an entrepreneur who wished to remain anonymous) TPI organized the first of what has become an annual event – a 'Neighbourhood Fellows' financial awards initiative for 'underpaid and unsung' community leaders. The donor, who abhors bureaucracy, did not want to provide support to institutions but did wish to recognize publicly the work of extraordinary citizens who are making a difference in people's lives.

The awards are designed not only to provide financial assistance but also to call attention to grassroots leadership in a city's neighbourhoods. Using a system of community spotters who are briefed on the donor's interests and basic criteria for selection, TPI culls through a pool of recommendees each winter to select six men and women who will receive a $20,000 gift over three years. The award initiative has become a community institution; it has also focused media attention on the remarkable work of ordinary people. The model has been replicated in at least one other community.

3.9.6 Conclusion

These are some of the hundreds of solid, documented examples of donors using innovative means to push the philanthropic envelope to make a difference. The approaches are often quite creative; they are always thoughtful and relevant. They also build in an appropriate capacity to monitor and guide the initiatives – and to learn from the experiences.

4 Post-grant monitoring and evaluation

4.1 An integral part of the overall foundation continuum

Every grant is a social experiment. In making a funding decision, a foundation is testing a hypothesis, or theory of action, about what works. Below are two examples of how a foundation executive might express these processes in the simplest terms:

> *If* we provide immigrants with literacy assistance, *then* they will move more quickly towards becoming productive members of our society.

> *If* we provide training in board development, conflict resolution and management skills to the heads of non-government organizations, *then* they will become more effective leaders.

Donors often do not think of their work in terms of these 'if/then' statements. Many foundations spend almost all their time on pre-grant review, with little energy devoted to the monitoring and evaluation that would tell them what happened as a result of the gift.

Why is this so? Most donors do not have the resources to fund the large-scale formal social science research that might definitely 'prove' whether social programmes are effective and so they are discouraged from any evaluation attempt. In addition, many foundations feel that the issues they care about elude objective measure. Many nonprofit organizations are wary of evaluation, fearing that any negative information it reveals will make the donor abandon them. This leads to an atmosphere of suspicion and mistrust that can make learning about what works difficult.

But part of strategic philanthropy is articulating the ideas about change that underlie the work of the foundation and testing and questioning those assumptions with rigour and fairness. Strategic philanthropy also involves the commitment to ongoing learning from foundation work. While that does not necessarily involve a formal full-scale research programme, it does involve looking into what happens once a grant is made, documenting successes and failures and capturing key lessons through monitoring, evaluation and dissemination efforts.

Post-grant monitoring and evaluation are part of a continuum of foundation activities that ensure that high quality decisions are made, that projects funded are performing to capacity and that the charitable dollars entrusted to the foundation are put to the highest and best use. Foundations that use post-grant monitoring and evaluation effectively view it as a learning tool. They see it not as a separate discipline or activity but as an integral part of their planning and management. In the words of American writer Mark Twain, they know that 'supposing is good, finding out is better'.

Planning for grant-making programmes should include agreeing on criteria for assessing their success or failure. The data generated by monitoring and evaluation helps in refining the focus and planning future programme improvement and direction. In effective organizations, planning and evaluation happen naturally and continuously and are always linked. Good evaluation work is an integrated part of an organization or programme life cycle, as illustrated by Figure 3.1 below:

Figure 3.1

Evaluation can perhaps best be thought of as one tool in a foundation's kit bag in its quest for quality. Some of the tools involve achieving quality through regulation, setting standards for performance and applying sanctions if these standards are not met. Others are enhancement strategies, which use positive reinforcements to reward quality and good work. Figure 3.2 shows various foundation quality activities and where they fit on the regulation/enhancement continuum:

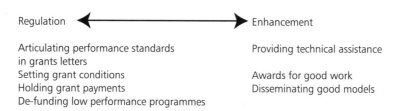

Regulation ←————————————→ Enhancement

Articulating performance standards   Providing technical assistance
in grants letters
Setting grant conditions   Awards for good work
Holding grant payments   Disseminating good models
De-funding low performance programmes

Figure 3.2

Obviously a mix of regulatory and enhancement strategies are needed to assure quality. Monitoring and evaluation can be used as either a regulatory or an enhancement strategy. They are probably most effective when they incorporate elements from both sides of the continuum.

Some foundations and government agencies use evaluation in a regulatory way. They have what might be termed an 'audit' mentality, seeking to ferret out and de-fund poorly performing programmes. Evaluations are often conducted after the fact, with little participation in the design and collection of data by programme managers. This kind of evaluation is effective at setting sanctions and establishing minimum standards for future performance, but it does not identify and encourage excellence. Another approach is a process that views evaluation as a learning tool, in which programme managers and the foundation mutually agree on evaluation criteria and methodology. Findings are shared throughout the process so that programme managers can make mid-course corrections. This approach tilts more towards enhancement, as its aim is to strengthen programmes.

4.2 How are monitoring and evaluation defined?

Monitoring is the process of reviewing grantee performance through reports, site visits or other methods. Evaluation is, most simply stated, an attempt to determine the worth or effectiveness of something based on a set of criteria. In foundation work, a periodic process measures how well a project met its objectives. Monitoring attempts to answer the question, 'Did the grantee do what was outlined in the proposal?' Evaluation, on the other hand, attempts to answer the 'So what?' question by looking at the programme's results or impact. While evaluation has associations with social science research, it is important to remember that as Michael Scriven, an evaluation theorist has said:

> It [evaluation] is not just a science [...] Disciplined evaluation occurs in scholarly book reviews, the Socratic Dialogs, social criticism and in the opinions handed down by appellate courts. Its characteristics are the drive for a determination of merit, worth or value, the control of bias, the emphasis on sound logic, factual foundations and comprehensive coverage.

Depending on which of the goals outlined above are most important, evaluation can be formative, looking at programmes while they are still in progress and generating information to help make mid-course corrections; and/or summative, a retrospective that sums up and assesses a programme after it has reached a particular benchmark.

Another way to define monitoring and evaluation is as a continuum of quality assurance activities at ever-deepening levels. In looking at a programme, we can assess the following.

- **The activity** – is the project to be assessed actually occurring?
- **The process** – is it occurring according to the original design? Is it being effectively managed?
- **Inputs** – what resources are available to the project and is it making effective use of them?
- **Outputs** – what is the project producing (how many clients served, etc.)?
- **Outcomes** – has the project produced the desired outcomes, results or change in the target population, etc.)?
- **Impact** – what is the project's impact on the problem it is addressing? On the larger community or institutions it seeks to influence?
- **Effectiveness/efficiency** – do the outcomes justify the resources allocated to the project?

The first four items on this list constitute ever-deepening levels of monitoring; the final three address evaluation.

4.3 What role should post-grant monitoring and evaluation play in the work of a foundation?

Donors who make effective use of monitoring and evaluation view them as tools to meet one or more of the following goals:

- to meet the good stewardship responsibilities of philanthropy by ensuring that funds are put to proper and effective use
- to learn more about the impact of their work on the field or community they serve and to determine what factors are responsible for impeding or enhancing the success of an initiative
- to make grantees more accountable
- to ensure that the foundation is accountable to grantees and the community served
- to serve as a check on the biases and assumptions of board and staff
- to gather information that will help make mid-course corrections in programme initiatives so they are more effective
- to identify and diagnose problems grantees are facing so they can be given assistance
- to build the capacity of grantees to assess and improve the impact of their efforts
- to document the case for a particular approach to social change or service delivery so it is credible to policy makers and other donors
- to assess their own performance as grant makers.

To determine what role monitoring and evaluation should play in its giving programme, a foundation can begin by asking a simple set of questions.

- Which of the goals above are most important to us? Do we have other goals for this work?
- Given that, what approaches will provide the information we need?
- What processes will credibly provide that information to us and/or to others who need to know (e.g. the grant recipients, other funders, policy makers, etc.).

Once a foundation has determined its goals, monitoring and evaluation can be as simple and informal as requesting and reviewing reports on grantee progress, or as complex as a multi-year research effort. The most successful efforts are tailored to the size, scale and complexity of the giving programme.

Foundations that use monitoring and evaluation effectively also signal their commitment to these activities before the grant is made:

- by ensuring that grantees have articulate, clear and documentable objectives in their funding proposal
- by asking questions during the review process about how the applicant organization measures its effectiveness and documents its work
- by modelling an attitude of openness and willingness to learn
- by soliciting feedback on the foundation's giving guidelines and performance.

4.4 Approaches to monitoring

The simplest approach to monitoring consists of requiring grantees to submit periodic progress reports. In deciding how to structure a reporting programme, it is important to assess what you want to know from your grantees and how often you would like to receive information. Many foundations simply ask for a report at the end of the grant year. Others require two reports annually, one mid-way through the year and a final report. If a grantee is experiencing difficulties, a donor may request more frequent reports.

To avoid being inundated with paper, it is useful to provide some guidance to grantees on reporting. Some foundations provide a one-page report form for completion. Others offer an outline of what should be covered. Grantee self-reporting is the sole monitoring activity most foundations undertake. Some, however, go further, either conducting site visits themselves to some of their funded programmes, or hiring others to do so. A foundation might want to make these kinds of site visits for varied reasons.

- It may have a grantee or group of grantees that is highly risky or struggling with internal problems and wishes to follow progress closely.
- It may want to learn more about the field or communities in which grantees are working by directly observing programmes.
- It may want to be engaged with grantees in ways that go beyond grant making, such as providing technical assistance, linking groups to other resources, or advocating for the groups' causes.
- It may want to get feedback about the work of the foundation.

A foundation may decide to conduct only an occasional site visit to a risky programme, or it may develop a full-scale effort that randomly samples and visits a group of its grantees each year. Conducting a post-grant site visit is similar to doing one before the grant is made.

If a foundation does not have the staff or board resources to do site visits, it is possible to use outside monitors. One large foundation administered a monitoring programme that used a team of part-time consultants, all with experience in the nonprofit sector, to visit grantees mid-way through the grant period. Their job was to assess progress, diagnose any problems and help the grantees obtain assistance for them. The monitors also asked grantees whether they had found the foundation's application process fair and clear. This both provided valuable feedback to staff and board about their performance and created a sense of trust and two-way dialogue between foundation and grantees.

Another community foundation uses volunteers to conduct monitoring site visits. It recruits individuals in the community who are interested in the work of the foundation, provides a training workshop and a format for interviews and asks each volunteer to conduct two to three site visits each year. The foundation has found that this approach has increased its visibility and credibility with business and community groups, who know more about the foundation and have increased respect for its work. Similarly, some companies use employee volunteers to conduct site visits.

4.5 Approaches to evaluation

While monitoring activities are fairly straightforward, thinking about effective evaluation becomes more complex. Crucial to the enterprise is deciding what needs to be learned in order to determine whether a programme has significant impact.

The way a foundation conceptualizes its role will affect the strategic choices it makes about evaluation. A foundation that views itself as a venture capitalist, for example, may want to focus on formative evaluation that helps identify and address grantee weaknesses. Evaluation could also help it decide when to 'invest' in a particular field and how long to stay in it. It can help identify the most promising new models and the elements of them that are essential to preserve in replicating the programme at other sites.

For a foundation that views itself as a change agent, evaluation is not just a tool for assessing the impact of programmes, but for attempting to influence policy as well. Unbiased, independent evaluation lends credibility to new services or approaches that can be used to 'sell' them to policy makers or to train others who wish to adopt them.

Foundations interested in evaluation can choose from many different kinds of activities ranging from informal assessment to major longitudinal research studies. They involve the elements listed below.

- **Assessing individual grants.** Options here include building the cost of independent evaluation into major grants or directly commissioning consultants to conduct an evaluation of a single grant, a cluster of grants or an entire portfolio.
- **Conducting cluster evaluations.** These aim to focus on progress in achieving the broad goals of a group of grantees or a grant programme. Cluster evaluations often involve grantees in a collaborative process designed to help them agree on reasonable evaluation criteria and documentation methods and collectively look at their combined progress and impact. This can be facilitated by an independent consultant and be a process of several stages, or it can simply involve foundation staff periodically convening groups of grantees. Another form of cluster evaluation might involve merely a collective review and aggregation of data from progress reports submitted by a group of grantees.
- **Providing training in assessment techniques and models to grantees.** This improves their documentation and quality assurance efforts.
- **Assessing the performance, practices and impact of the foundation's work as a whole.** This is sometimes done by surveying grantees, denied applicants, community leaders and others familiar with the work of the foundation. It can also include a self-analysis that breaks down grants made into categories such as constituency served, type of grant, budget size, focus area addressed, etc. This analysis is intended to reveal whether the foundation has been doing what it said it would in its grant guidelines.

Evaluations can also be conducted by a number of different actors:

- by foundation staff or board members themselves
- by grantee organizations, with or without outside assistance
- by independent consultants with expertise in the field
- by peer professionals or grantees.

Deciding who should conduct an evaluation is determined by a number of factors, including the time and resources of the foundation, the relative need for rigour or an expert outside review and the potential audiences for the evaluation and what they will find credible.

The professional discipline of evaluation originally emerged from the wish to use social science methodology as a tool for policy makers. It was founded on the rationalistic assumption that objective information will, on its own merits, influence the actions of decision-makers. The original concept of the evaluator was as a neutral, value-free scientist who observed and recorded data on programmes. Discussion of findings with programme managers was viewed as tainting the evidence, like talking to patients in a double-blind study of a prescription drug.

Over time, however, the field has changed to recognize that the scientific method is not always a practical approach to understanding and affecting social problems. The outcomes of many social programmes are difficult to measure and evaluation researchers and foundation managers alike recognize that few decisions are ever based solely on objective data. The fate of social programmes often rests more on political realities, the personal biases of decision-makers, expedience and economics than on their objective merits.

The result is that the field of evaluation has changed to accommodate more creative and practical approaches, borrowing techniques from anthropology, journalism and other fields to incorporate subjective and qualitative information into the gathering of hard data. While the central task is always to generate information with fairness and rigour, it can be gathered in many ways.

4.6 The challenges of evaluation design

Defining what needs to be learned from an evaluation is not always a simple matter, for what can be measured is not always what foundations most need to know. Evaluator Thomas Dewar describes the dilemma he faced evaluating delinquency prevention programmes in a monograph on evaluation:

> My own preoccupation with apprehension (arrests) and the field's experience were a barrier to understanding the human events, values and predicaments involved. Apprehension and treatment were finite, tangible, respectable and even fundable. The process of getting 'straightened out' was often disorderly, disturbing, informal and subtle. That is not to say that it can't be understood and supported. It is to say that one of the most important things to learn about a field or approach is what it takes for granted.

So while testing the hypothesis behind a grant may appear straightforward at first, when a foundation commits itself to finding out instead of supposing, the range of questions and approaches becomes as intricate and complicated as the patterns of light in a kaleidoscope. Behavioural change is a complex process that is influenced by many factors. Few programmes take place in anything comparable to a scientific laboratory where conditions can be controlled and outside influences minimized.

The approach to evaluation design, then, becomes like navigating near a submerged reef. The evaluator must look for indicators that provide some clue to the form of the mass underneath, marks to tell where the current is going. The foundation needs to decide what information will be enough to allow it to proceed with reasonable confidence, given that what is below can never absolutely be 'known'.

To illustrate this complexity of choices, suppose a foundation wants to assess the outcomes of a school literacy project that seeks to improve student writing. The outcomes could be:

- **Cognitive** – what information do the students now understand about writing?
- **Behavioural** – how do the students in the project now act? Do they write more? More easily? Better?
- **Attitudinal** – do they approach the task of writing with a different attitude and perceptions?
- **Organizational** – has the school site or district changed or improved its approach to teaching writing as a result of this project?

If the foundation decides it is most interested in what the students learned – the cognitive – it has another range of choices to measure:

- **Knowledge** – can the students pass a test on certain information or techniques?
- **Retention** – does the student retain some of the new writing skills learned over a period of time?
- **Application** – can the students apply their new writing skills to other tasks in other settings?
- **Analysis** – can the students use what they have learned to assess the work of others?
- **Synthesis** – can the students selectively distil pieces of what they have learned and apply them in other settings?

Some of these things can be easily measured; others cannot be measured at all. The foundation as decision-maker must balance the costs and difficulty of obtaining certain kinds of data with the added credibility it will provide. Is it enough to know, for example, that the students who participated in the literacy programme can pass a simple writing test immediately after the programme is over? Or to be persuaded of the project's usefulness, does the foundation need to know that they are using their new-found writing skills to improve performance in other courses?

And once some of these cognitive skills have been identified and documented, important questions still remain:

- **Did the programme cause these effects?** Can it be determined that the project influenced the observed results or could something entirely unrelated have created the same results? This concept is known as causality and a good evaluation always makes a thorough search for other possible explanations for the change or benefit that is attributed to the programme. This might be relatively easy in a literacy programme where it is easy to determine what other training in writing students might be receiving. It is particularly difficult in programmes that seek to address social problems such as crime, where many external factors may influence the reporting of crimes and arrest rates.
- **Are the measures used to conduct the evaluation valid?** Does the technique or instrument used in the evaluation adequately measure the results the foundation is looking for? A standard achievement test used by school departments may or may not be a valid measure of the results of a school literacy programme.
- **Does the evaluation provide comparison with alternatives?** Does it merely document programme results, or does it take the next step, comparing the programme's effectiveness with others in its field, or with results in a community that does not have the programme?
- **Can the results of the evaluation be applied more widely?** Is it reasonable to expect that the evaluation findings would hold true in other settings? How do we know? Sometimes what makes programmes successful is the 'how', not the 'what', which means that replicating them elsewhere is not a rote process. Have the factors that contributed to success in this programme been accurately identified?
- **Are the results of the evaluation credible to its primary audiences?** Regardless of the validity and reliability of the measures used, will people believe and accept evaluation results? A number of factors affect this subjective concept, including the credentials and world view of the evaluator, and the participation in the identification of evaluation criteria and design of those likely to be affected by the evaluation.

Faced with this baffling web of causality, a busy foundation person is tempted to revert to 'supposing' – or to select for evaluation those factors that are most quantifiable and easy to measure. It takes time and thought to decide just what it is that needs to be assessed about a programme and what information will satisfy key constituencies, but a thoughtful evaluation can help a donor organize hard data and more subjective impressions to bring its strengths and weaknesses to life.

It is important then, that foundations do not view evaluation as a source of definitive answers or a road map for decision-making. Rather, it is a limited tool and a useful process that can help bring rigour to the examination of programmes.

The best starting point in designing an evaluation for a particular programme is to articulate the theory of action or hypotheses behind the programme. It can be useful to try to state this in the simplest possible terms, as an 'if/then' statement.

The next step is to identify the foundation's motives for evaluating the programme.

- Why are we interested in conducting an evaluation of this programme?
- Will it provide data on whether this particular approach is effective?
- Are we concerned about the accountability and/or management of the grantee?
- Will it help us decide whether we ought to be placing our funds in this field or help us make a particular grant decision?
- Will it provide data that can contribute to knowledge in the field and the development of public policy or institutional change?
- Will it provide suggestions for strengthening the programme or improving services?
- Are there other reasons to evaluate the programme?

Then some questions about the 'how' should be addressed.

- When should the evaluation be conducted? Should it be formative or summative?
- Who will see the evaluation results? The foundation? The organization that is being evaluated? Other constituencies? Will the evaluation remain an internal document or will it be more widely disseminated?
- Who will develop the evaluation design and manage the process?
- What qualifications must the evaluator have to make this a credible study?

The next step is to identify, often with the help of an outside consultant, clear evaluation criteria by examining several questions.

- What is the target population or constituency(ies) of the programme? Does it include individuals, institutions and/or the community at large?
- What are the expected results of the programme? What short-term effects would tell us the programme is on its way to meeting those goals? What longer-term effects could be documented?
- How feasible is it to document these effects? What evidence would convince the audience for the evaluation that results have been achieved?
- What are possible negative consequences or unintended effects of the programme? How could an evaluator search for them?
- What would be the consequences of eliminating the programme (or of its never having existed)? Who would be affected? Who would complain? Who would be glad?

Addressing these issues should leave the foundation able to make a final 'go/no' decision on the evaluation based on answering the following questions.

- Can this programme be evaluated in any way that will provide meaningful information?
- Will this evaluation potentially change a foundation decision, policy or programme?
- Is our investment in our programme worth the potential cost of an evaluation?

It is also useful to examine honestly whether the foundation is itself open to receiving bad news about the programme or its own efforts. Sometimes funders become emotionally invested in the success of the programmes they support.

4.7 Reviewing an evaluation design

In reviewing an evaluation design developed either by an independent consultant or a grantee that is doing it own self-assessment, it is useful to consider several questions.

- Who is conducting this evaluation? The organization sponsoring the programme? An independent party with the foundation as client? An independent party with the programme as client?
- Is his/her background in this field and knowledge of evaluation sufficient to lend credibility to the evaluation?

- How is his/her professional training and experience likely to affect his/her view of the programme (e.g. an economist and a social worker might bring very different lenses to view a community development programme)?
- Is this a formative or summative evaluation? If formative, how will findings be shared and used to strengthen the programme? If summative, at what point will it be conducted? Is the timing right? Has the programme been operating long enough to produce results? What decisions, if any, ride on the outcome of this evaluation?
- Does the design include an appropriate mix of hard measures (data collection, tests, etc.) and qualitative data? How will qualitative data be gathered?
- Have programme managers or participants been included in designing the evaluation? Are they comfortable with the process? Open to hearing bad and good news?
- Has a theory of action for the programme been clearly articulated? Are the evaluation criteria acceptable both to the foundation and the programme's managers?
- Have the foundation and the programme managers agreed on the uses and dissemination of evaluation findings?
- Is the cost of the evaluation in scale with the foundation's investment in this programme?
- Does the evaluation design provide for comparison of the programme with other alternatives, or does it merely document programme results?
- If part of the evaluation includes looking for a change in attitudes, how will a baseline of attitudes be established? Will changes be measured through participants' own statements, by observed behaviour, or by other means? Will they be measured once, or on different occasions?
- Does the evaluation design address the issues of wider applicability and causality?
- Has the evaluator identified limitations and potential weaknesses in the methodology?
- Does the evaluation include a dissemination and/or implementation plan?

4.8 When monitoring and evaluation activities bring very bad news

If a foundation is committed to 'finding out' as opposed to 'supposing' about its own programmes and grantees and if it takes any risks at all in its grant making, sooner or later it will receive news of problems or failure. Whether this information comes via a formal evaluation or informal channels, it is important to assess whether the problems are due to malfeasance, incompetence, ignorance, conflict or external factors.

If the problems are due to malfeasance, the foundation's course of action is generally very clear and must be based on regulatory strategies. If funds have been misused, the foundation must cooperate in any investigation and use its influence to push the organization to change the leadership that allowed this to occur. Depending on the age and importance of the organization, the foundation may want to participate in efforts at re-organization that ensure that the problem will not occur again. If the problems are sufficiently severe or there is no core of the staff and board committed to change, the foundation may elect to de-fund the organization and walk away.

If the problems are due to incompetence, ignorance of proper procedures, or a lack of training, the foundation needs to determine whether the present leadership is both educable and open to change. If so, the foundation might want to protect its investment by providing funding for training or technical or management assistance. If educable leaders and the willingness to change are not present, however, the foundation will perhaps send the clearest message by saying 'no' to future funding until the problem areas have been addressed. It is difficult to force change on organizations that are not ready for it.

Often the problems encountered by programmes are caused by external factors, such as a political crisis in the community being served, or a resistance to new approaches by entrenched bureaucracies. In these cases, the foundation needs to understand such obstacles better and decide whether there is a role to be played in helping the grantee address them. It also needs to assess the grantee's flexibility and creativity in the face of obstacles.

In all cases, it is important to allow the grantee a chance to tell its story, to listen genuinely to its own analysis of the problems. Where will is good, the foundation should seek to be a partner in finding solutions. That is the best way to protect a philanthropic investment.

4.9 Final thoughts

In adopting post-grant monitoring and evaluation strategies, foundations should be guided by the following principles.

- For truly useful results, these activities should be driven by the values of the foundation and characterized by fairness, responsiveness and open communication.

- Monitoring and evaluation activities should be conducted in the context of a concern about quality and should be used to encourage and reward excellence, not to set minimum performance standards.
- Monitoring and evaluation activities should be linked within the foundation so that planning, research, grant making, post-grant work and dissemination become part of an ongoing cycle of organizational learning, assessment and renewal.
- When the foundation commissions evaluation of programmes, it should acknowledge that it is a partner in that effort and actively participate in developing the design and criteria.
- Whenever possible, the foundation should seek to build in monitoring and evaluation activities as projects begin, rather than conducting after-the-fact assessments.

5 Foundation persona: reputation, credibility and public presence

5.1 What are the special requirements of philanthropic stewardship?

The preceding segments of this section have focused on specific approaches to the development of programme design, implementation and evaluation initiatives that support a foundation's strategic funding goals. What follows is an attempt to place those activities in the critical context of the public and private realms in which foundations must function and to make a case for foundations to pay considerable attention to the special requirements of their philanthropic stewardship and to the needs and expectations of their stakeholders.

For a foundation seeking to make its mark in society, a positive persona (good reputation, credibility for its work) is its social currency. It allows a foundation to leverage its financial participation in projects and to engage and mobilize others in its work. It also gives the foundation legitimacy when it chooses to add its voice to the dialogue on important public policy questions. At its core, credibility for foundations rests on the two pillars of responsibility and relevance. How responsibly foundations deliberate and perform, and how relevant their work is to challenges that directly affect peoples' lives and the well being of their communities and societies will, in large measure, define their reputations.

Foundations must act in an accountable and responsible manner; this is not only a requirement of their special legal status in society, but it is also a central element of good business practice. Of equal import, foundations need to be viewed by their constituencies as showing evidence of commitment to such appropriate behaviour. A hallmark of many effective foundations is the great care with which they address this need. Increasingly, foundations realize that key determinants of the long-term success of their charitable aims are their credibility with stakeholders, including other funding institutions and their reputation within the communities they seek to serve. Perhaps, in the time of Rockefeller or Carnegie, gifts alone could produce the results their wealthy donors intended. Now, there may be some donors whose wealth makes them this generation's Carnegie, but for most foundations – whose resources require them to seek to leverage their work – their credibility is often what helps them extend their reach and increase their impact.

5.2 Why does a foundation's credibility or its reputation matter to its grant-making goals?

Philanthropy is about trust and relationships – among donors, between grantor and grantee or between the foundation and the communities it serves. Foundations do not function in a vacuum; to be successful they must work collaboratively with other private organizations, citizen associations and the public sector. Ultimately, to keep their full charitable charter, they must also enjoy the public's confidence. All of these issues require foundations to be seen as fair, open, ethical and committed to measuring and communicating their performance. To be less erodes the public and private support that allows foundations to develop their impact. To do less becomes a counterproductive act of omission that also damages the credibility of the philanthropic sector.

5.3 What is the historical context?

In a written presentation to trustees of family foundations, a community foundation executive stated:

> Foundations have an institutional aura and mystery about them that often communicates power, capacity and authority. This aura can easily eclipse the value and importance of community organizations and leadership. How can we as grant makers communicate an institutional image and attitude that conveys respect, invites accountability and nurtures opportunity? Pursuit of funding can

seem like an elaborate courtship to grantseekers because of the complexities of the process and the nuances involved in establishing an organization's credentials for support. How can a grant maker supply the human ingredients to dispel the mysteries and make the process for the grantseeker seem less like an obscure waltz to someone else's choice of music?

Philanthropy may be described simply as a private act for the public good. Traditionally, most philanthropists and their giving institutions have chosen to focus on the private nature of their work and to keep an extremely low profile with the public. While this may be admirable if motivated by a desire not to be seen as self-aggrandizing or not to taint the impact of the gift, this lack of information has contributed in the US to the public's perception of much organized philanthropy as a 'black box' from which funding mysteriously appears from time to time.

As confusing as this is for the general public, it can be particularly vexing for community leaders and grant-seeking organizations. The lack of openness or of ethical and appropriate behaviour on the part of the philanthropic establishment exacerbates concerns within the public sector about the lack of accountability of such large concentrations of wealth.

In addition to a need to demystify the philanthropic process, foundations must constantly be mindful of the 'Emperor's new clothes' syndrome as it applies to them: it is extremely difficult for foundations to be told the truth. J. K. Galbraith said, 'Nothing so great gives the illusion of intelligence as large sums of money'.

The power to bestow that is every foundation's prerogative carries with it the ability to deny. Because nonprofit and community organizations find it difficult to be critical of funding institutions, foundations often will not have access to information on unsuccessful activities or on inappropriate behaviour. Part of the effective foundation's persona is to provide clear, convincing evidence to its stakeholders that 'messengers of bad tidings will not be shot'. This is essential if foundations are regularly to reassess and renew their performance and objectives.

Further, there is always a risk that those affiliated with private foundations find the process of bestowing funds an opportunity for arrogant or inappropriate behaviour. It is not without justification that many fundraisers cite their own version of the 'golden rule' when identifying what frustrates them most in their dealings with foundations. 'He with the gold rules' may seem a witty aphorism; when applied to philanthropy, it is corrosive of the relationship a foundation must have with its primary stakeholders.

5.4 Are there accepted standards?

The canon of ethical behaviour for foundations includes specific guidance regarding measures aimed at establishing and maintaining credibility with philanthropy's various publics. There are a number of baseline standards that have been promulgated over several decades, including a set of principles developed by the US Council on Foundations. In 1983 the Council voted to require endorsement of its 'Principles and Practices for Effective Grantmaking' as a condition for acceptance in its membership. Former United States Ambassador to South Africa, James Joseph, then the Council's President, wrote in the preamble:

> In the end, the attempt to identify and affirm principles and practices constitutes a marriage of private and public values. This union preserves the social contract between private philanthropy and society and protects the legal charter, which makes each foundation a trustee of the public good.

Among the eleven 'Principles' are a number that speak directly to this issue of a foundation's credibility. This guidance is still relevant almost two decades after it was first drafted:

> Responsive grantmakers recognize that accountability extends beyond the narrow requirements of the law.[...] Grantmakers should establish and carry out policies that recognize these multiple obligations for accountability: to the charter provisions by which their founders defined certain basic expectations, to those charitable institutions they serve, to the general public and to certain state governmental agencies.

> Open communications with the public and with grantseekers about the policies and procedures that are followed in grantmaking is in the interest of all concerned and is important if the grantmaking process is to function well and if trust in the responsibility and accountability of grantmakers is to be maintained. A brief written statement about policies, program interests, grantmaking practices, geographic and policy restrictions and preferred ways of receiving applications is recommended. Prompt acknowledgement of the receipt of any serious applications is important. Grantseekers whose programs and proposals fall outside the interest of the grantmakers

should be told this immediately and those whose proposals are still under consideration should be informed, insofar as is possible, of the steps and timing that will be taken in reaching the final decision.

Beyond the filing of forms required by government, grantmakers should consider ways of informing the public concerning their stewardship through publication and distribution of periodic reports, preferably annual reports, possibly supplemented by newsletters, reports to the Foundation Center and the use of other communications channels.

The preservation and enhancement of an essential community of interest between the grantor and the grantee requires that their relationship be based on mutual respect, candor and understanding with each investing the necessary time and attention to define clearly the purposes of the grant, the expectations as to reports related to financial and other matters and the provisions for evaluating and publicizing projects.

Beyond the legal requirements that forbid staff, board members and their families from profiting financially from any philanthropic grant, it is important that grantmakers weigh carefully all circumstances in which there exists the possibility of accusations of self-interest. In particular, staff and board members should disclose to the governing body the nature of their personal or family affiliation or involvement with any organizations for which a grant is considered, even though such affiliation may not give rise to any pecuniary conflict of interest.

5.5 What are the key components of a foundation's public persona? What are the ingredients of a credible foundation?

A search of the literature, including the 'Principles' mentioned above and scores of interviews with practitioners, civic and nonprofit leaders and public officials yields considerable guidance on this subject. Although foundations are somewhat like snowflakes – no two are ever completely alike – they share common traits when the building blocks of their public credibility are analysed.

Key characteristics include:

- **Leadership** A foundation's willingness, perhaps a passion, to address important issues and to champion innovative approaches to those challenges are true marks of leadership in a philanthropic institution.

- **Courage** Dietrich Bonhoeffer observed that people (and institutions) become 'servile before fact'. Because foundations occupy such a privileged and advantageous place in society, being free of the profit-oriented pressures of business, they are presented with the opportunity to challenge conventional wisdom. Not accepting what 'is' but working toward what 'ought' to be in society may require real courage from a foundation's leadership.
- **Commitment to results** A demonstrated dedication to making a difference is a central quality of those foundations that wish to be seen as relevant to their society. To be driven by results is evidence that a foundation understands the precious and special nature of the resources at its command.
- **Accountability** A responsible, credible foundation is an accountable grant-making institution that measures and reports, internally and externally, on its overall and programme-specific performance set against its goals. The accountable foundation shares the lessons it has learned from its grant making with its stakeholders.
- **Involvement in public policy questions and promotion of vigorous public dialogue on important issues** Both as a participant and as a resource to those who must ultimately make decisions, a strategically inclined foundation is actively engaged in the policy debate and search for solutions to questions connected with foundation priorities.
- **Ethical behaviour** The integrity of the conduct of all those who represent a foundation – trustees, staff and advisers – is a direct extension of its mission and values, and a constantly visible reminder to its primary audiences or stakeholders of the respect the foundation attaches to its philanthropic stewardship responsibilities. Ethics also require that the foundation acts in a fair and honest manner when dealing with stakeholders, especially its grant applicants and grantees.
- **Evidence of a 'due diligence' approach to grant making** This needs to be demonstrated in the decision-making process regarding funding for projects and initiatives and in the analysis of programmatic outcomes. That philanthropic choices are made and followed up by the foundation with the same discipline and rigour as pursued by those involved with profit-making investments makes a powerful case for credibility.
- **Commitment to an open and frequent communications posture** As will be addressed in greater detail below, that a foundation commits itself to be in a dialogue with its various constituencies is an essential ingredient in its long-term reputation. The quality and

consistency of a foundation's communications are constant public reminders of the level of its dedication to its philanthropic purposes.

- **Care and collegiality with which a foundation works with other funders and with its grantee partners** That a foundation is respectful of its partners and interested in their thinking on issues of mutual concern is a basic component of a positive persona. In addition, that it concentrates attention and resources on building the capacities of the organizations which are recipients of its grants makes a further community statement about the foundation's desire to be in all respects a responsible philanthropic citizen and a wise investor in the community's organizational infrastructure.

Each of these qualities of a foundation's credibility is important. Three of these – public policy, communications and ethics – will receive special attention later in this section. To diverse foundations with different resources, needs and priorities, some may seem more important than others. Even in the best of philanthropic institutions, they are not always fully in evidence with the same level of strength. But taken together, they become a compelling philanthropic ensemble. With these basics in place, a foundation holds its work up to its public for scrutiny with the knowledge that it is truly a socially responsible institution.

Finally, there is one other basic quality that nurtures a foundation's reputation with its peers and stakeholders – humility. In the concluding words of a chapter on relationships with grant seekers in his seminal *Handbook on Private Foundations*, David F. Freeman writes, 'Humility is not a trait frequently associated with giving away money. It should be'.

5.6 Who are a foundation's stakeholders?

Each foundation must determine for itself who its principal constituencies are – those civic leaders, community groups, organizations and public agencies connected to its mission – and with whom it must maintain open and clear lines of communication. There are, in addition to the general public, specific audiences that a foundation needs to reach out to in its work and, most especially, in its communications.

In thinking about making an initial range of contacts (or in reviewing its present list) regarding its core constituencies, a foundation could ask the following questions.

- If the foundation has been making grants, who are its past and present recipients?
- Which nongovernmental organizations are directly involved in the foundation's areas of interest?
- Which governmental agencies have a mandate related to the foundation's?
- Are there any political leaders who have expressed a particular interest in the topics that are the foundation's focus?
- Are there academic institutions whose research involves subjects the same as or similar to the foundation's grant-making focus?
- Who are the exemplary civic, religious and community leaders who address the same range of issues as the foundation's?
- Who are the civic activists and advocates on issues of interest to the foundation?
- What other foundations are focused on the same issue as the foundation? Are there associations of funders with interests similar to the foundation's?
- Are there resource or research centres (e.g. public libraries) that collect information on foundations and which grant-seeking programmes consult when searching out potential sources of funds?
- Are there specific media that cover issues similar to the foundation's?
- Irrespective of affiliation, who are acknowledged to be the most insightful and creative observers of the issues and challenges that the foundation seeks to address?
- Which companies have a major stake in the communities in which the foundation may concentrate its work? Are there companies with a major product interest (and perhaps charitable interest) in the issues that are major foci for the foundation (e.g. building materials companies and the grant-making area of safe, affordable housing)?

Answers to the above queries provide a foundation with a beginning regarding a comprehensive list of audiences that it may seek to involve in its work and from which it may draw its basic stakeholders. The list also offers the foundation a contact or mailing list of people and institutions that should know about the foundation's mission, interests and – eventually – its grant-making efforts.

5.7 If an effective communications programme is a hallmark ingredient of a credible grant-making institution, what are the characteristics and approaches of 'best practices' foundations?

5.7.1 Key characteristics

Good foundation communications are:

- **Accessible or permeable** Stakeholders feel that the foundation is approachable and open to them, that it is user-friendly in its guidance regarding how to apply for funding support and in other communications materials.
- **Understandable** Stakeholders believe that they have a basic understanding of how the foundation goes about its business, including how decisions are made.
- **Frequent** Communications to the foundation's audiences are regular and consistent.
- **Informative** Over time, communications from a foundation – newsletters, reports and listings of funding decisions – not only deepen understanding about the foundation's workings but also begin to contribute to the public's understanding of important issues.

5.7.2 Best practices

There are several fundamental steps that are common among foundations. They begin with the development of materials on the foundation's mission and values, its current objectives and approach to grant making that will inform and guide those seeking the foundation's assistance or participation.

Two recent examples illustrate varying approaches that foundations are now employing to provide clear, concise information to their primary audiences. In one, a foundation in its start-up phase, the introduction to the foundation includes a description of its mission and a statement of values:

> The purpose of the foundation is to utilize its resources to benefit and enhance the health and well being of residents of the region. The foundation has two major goals in its commitment to healthy communities. It seeks to support efforts that promote wellness in the community and concentrate on preventive measures that address core challenges to the overall health of the community's families and individuals.

The foundation has a set of values that guide its work in the community. The foundation is committed to: exemplifying the highest ethics in the actions of its trustees and staff; providing for careful and prudent stewardship of its assets; functioning as a learning organization that listens, is open and inclusive, acts thoughtfully and fairly, evaluates its work regularly and shares its knowledge with others; focusing on a holistic approach to its mission, seeking to effect strategic systemic change and concentrating on long-term, sustainable improvements in the health and well-being of the people of the region.

In a second example from a foundation that is less than five years old, the trustees decided, after experiencing an initial round of grant making, to include a statement on their approach to grant making in all basic collateral materials and correspondence to those organizations seeking support:

The primary interest of the foundation is to promote approaches to homelessness that bring about long-term solutions. The foundation views its philanthropy as social venture capital and subjects its funding to the same rigorous analysis that would be applied to any serious investment decision.

The foundation is committed to support efforts that identify the significant public policy issues involved in addressing homelessness and to promote greater public dialogue and understanding regarding effective strategies to end homelessness.

In both of these examples the foundations have declared their overall vision, programme focus and grant-making intent. These words will introduce all general communications materials that the foundations employ and, in a relatively short time period, begin to frame the way the grant-seeking public thinks about the foundations. Clear, consistent information is more than a public relations necessity or a matter of an appropriate style for the foundation that wishes to act responsibly; done properly, the concatenation of communications materials establishes a persona that encourages leadership grant-seeking organizations to bring their best ideas forward to the foundation for consideration. In a very real sense, communications becomes the information basis for proactive or more entrepreneurial philanthropy.

In addition to the prefatory information described above, there are four other basic elements of a communications effort that directly support its grant-making work and underscore its credibility.

Develop application guidelines

The need to describe what information the foundation wants and how it wishes to receive the material has been outlined in an earlier part of this section.

Establish a process for handling enquiries and applications promptly and forthrightly

Foundations should not become 'black holes' where proposals or requests for information from grant seekers and enquiries from the public are concerned. Nothing will feed the public's view of foundations as arrogant institutions more effectively. Putting in place a simple system to log external communications, to determine the nature of each – e.g. proposal, concept paper, request for guidelines – and respond appropriately is an essential of good foundation management.

Develop a consistent method to report decisions on grants and other funding initiatives, especially declinations

A foundation needs to craft for itself, in a way appropriate to its style of grant-making work, a consistent manner of communicating with those applicants whose proposals were considered for funding. In terms of a foundation's reputation, how a foundation says 'no' is often as important as the specific decisions that are reached.

A best practices approach to declinations of serious requests would include the following points.

- A brief explanation of the primary reasons for the declination – e.g. limited funds, too many requests, not specifically targeted to the foundation's priorities.
- A schedule that indicates when the organization may reapply.
- Guidance to other funding sources, if possible, that may have an interest in the project.
- If appropriate, an invitation to discuss the project further – not to dissect the weaknesses of the proposal or to allow a reconsideration but to assert that the proposal was seriously considered and to offer guidance to the organization regarding how it goes forward with its work.

Publish and disseminate widely an annual report

This would include guidance on the foundation's current priorities and summary information on its annual list of grants. Many foundations also regularly publish a list of grants made each time the foundation convenes. This adds to the community's basic knowledge of the foundation and, if distributed to other funders, serves as an informal way to help grantees 'market' their programmes to a wider range of philanthropic resources.

There are several other examples of effective ways that foundations have 'thrown open their windows' to encourage public participation in and understanding of their grant-making work, including publishing reports on the lessons the foundation has learned from a number of grants within a field of focus and hosting meetings to share experiences with civic leaders active within similar areas.

5.8 Why is participation in public policy matters of direct importance to a foundation? Why is involvement in the public arena relevant to a foundation's credibility?

As stated previously, the hard work of grant making does not occur in a social or political vacuum. A key element of what makes a foundation's work strategic is its connection to and understanding of the public policies that shape, influence – and in some cases – directly determine the outcomes and long-term impact of a foundation's grant-making priorities.

Dennis Beatrice of the Henry Kaiser Family Foundation, in a paper to new healthcare foundations, wrote:

> Foundations are most effective when they enlist government to reinforce their grantmaking. This connection is necessary to go beyond demonstration projects and bring ideas to scale; provide resources to sustain foundation programmes; gain access to public programmes, where the foundation can reach broader populations that those directly benefiting from foundation activities; and assure that government programs are constructive or, at least, do no harm.

Brian O'Connell, founder and first president of Independent Sector, an international coalition of philanthropic and voluntary organizations, has said

> I spent a good deal of time consulting with foundations and corporations and the topic generally relates to the changing or future role of philanthropy. In most of these sessions, I attempt to lay out the major needs of our times including such urgent issues as governance of our cities, structural unemployment, strengthening public education, persistence of poverty, neighbourhood deterioration,

conservation of land and water, etc. The usual response I get is that each of these problems is utterly beyond the capacity of the foundation and that indeed almost all of them are so large in scope that costs of addressing them have to be left to government. This usually brings the discussion right back to the question, 'What can we do that is unique and important?' My answer in all such cases is, 'Use your power and influence to make our government more effective, including its capacity to deal with the big issues'. Making government work is almost always far more important than all the other worthwhile things we do.

This element of 'public engagement' for a foundation has a bearing on its credibility for the following reasons.

- Such work is evidence that the foundation recognizes that it must 'think upstream' when considering the context for its grant making decision.
- It sets an example of wealth that is not fearful of participation in the democratic process and of philanthropy that does not retreat from addressing the real issues in society.
- It provides an early warning system that may offset grant-making decisions.
- It forces a discipline on a foundation regarding contact with the public sector.
- It recognizes that a foundation's resources, even for the wealthiest, are modest when compared to government and that the leveraging of private/public funds is an essential element in addressing difficult or intractable issues successfully.

5.9 What types of major activities are appropriate for a foundation to consider undertaking in this realm?

In addition to having a 'seat at the table' and participating thoughtfully and vigorously in the public dialogue on issues of importance to the foundation, there are a number of key roles that a grant-making institution can play.

- Foundations can convene interested parties and provide 'elevated common ground' or acceptable neutral turf for debate and discussion.
- Foundations can inform the debate on public policy matters by sharing the relevant experiences and results of their grant-making activities.

- Foundations can underwrite the development of third-party research that may bring reliable data to issues that are controversial or not well understood.
- Foundations can, through support for public polling and other such opinion surveys, bring to policy makers a sense of the community's assessment and interest in an issue.
- Foundations can become the vehicles for the disenfranchised or the disaffiliated to have a voice on policy matters that affect them.
- Foundations can seek to inform the public about the parameters and particulars of issues.

5.10 What standards should guide the conduct of the foundation's personnel?

There has been increasing attention paid by leaders and observers in foundation work to the ethical issues presented by philanthropic wealth and grant making. As more foundations see that a significant measure of their effectiveness depends on the trust and confidence of stakeholders from the philanthropic, community, private and public sectors, there has been a drive to frame the ethical challenges confronting philanthropic institutions and to establish a base line for behaviour.

If philanthropy is a high calling, if stewardship of philanthropic funds is a sacred trust, then those affiliated with the work of foundations must see themselves as the philanthropic equivalent of 'Caesar's wife'. Michael Josephson of the Josephson Institute of Ethics, has written:

> The obligation to be worthy of trust for those who manage foundation resources pervades all phases of the philanthropic process. It requires a scrupulous sense of ethics – especially honesty, integrity, fairness, respect and accountability.

Josephson stated that generally those in philanthropic life observe the guiding principles of their special calling but that there are traps to be aware of. He said:

> Sometimes, however, participants in the philanthropic process allow their good motives and noble goals to create a moral complacency that can cause them to take for granted the propriety of their actions and the assumptions that underlie them.

Recently, trustees of a new private foundation decided that they needed to have a code of conduct in place before the institution began dealing with the community and before any grant making commenced. Their decision was based on the belief that a code would be an important symbol to their stakeholders of the seriousness of their undertaking and that such framework for their actions would keep them from 'complacency' or from treading on the values that were the moral motivation for the foundation's founding.

The trustees' thinking on this important matter is an instructive example. In addition to identifying the primary responsibilities and requirements of those who would serve, the trustees drafted a simple code:

> The trustees and staff of the foundation are held to the highest standards of conduct. Each person who serves the foundation is expected to adhere to the following criteria of ethical service:
>
> - Information gained from board deliberations, discussions with staff, or disclosures from applicant or grantee organizations will be treated with complete confidentiality.
> - Trustees will never compromise the foundation's integrity by making unilateral or unauthorized policy statements or pledges of support to potential recipients.
> - Trustees may not accept gifts or gratuities from applicants or grantees.
> - Trustees will file annually with the chief executive officer a listing of all their current non-profit memberships and board involvements.
> - The board and staff of the foundation are encouraged to play active roles in the community's life. This means that, from time to time, when potential conflicts-of-interest or the appearance of such conflicts inevitably arise, it is the foundation's policy to deal with such conflicts in as open and appropriate way as possible.
> - Conflicting involvements include:
>   - Trustees/staff serving as board members of applicant organizations;
>   - Trustees'/staff's immediate family members serving as board members of applicant organizations; and
>   - Trustees/staff or their immediate family being employed by or doing business with applicants or grantees.
>
> In cases of such conflicts or the appearance thereof, trustees or staff are expected to disclose the conflict prior to making any related grant decisions. Once such a disclosure has been made, the remaining trustees will determine whether there is a potential conflict-of-interest. Should it be so considered, the trustee involved shall abstain from voting and shall not participate in the discussion of the applicant organization.

All foundations should, as a best practice, craft such a code for themselves. It may be as simple as the one cited above or more elaborate, but the critical issue is that a code of conduct, spelled out and honoured in the foundation's daily work and deliberative processes, is an essential component of the credibility of a philanthropic institution.

5.11 Final words

Most foundations began their funding lives with good wishes and great expectations from their colleagues and stakeholders. The challenge is to build upon that preliminary level of respect. Once established (and vigorously maintained), a foundation's reputation serves as a simple statement of the seriousness of the funder's commitment to using wealth to benefit society. In the final analysis, a foundation's persona may be as critical to its enduring success as the size of its endowment or the amount of its grants.

Bibliography

Beatrice, D., *Grant makers in Health Conference Report*, 1994.

The Boston Foundation: *How to Apply for a Grant*, Boston, Massachusetts, 1995.

Broadbent, A., 'Dealco Meets the New Foundation', in: *Initiatives*, Vol. 4, No. 3, Winter 1996, Boston, Massachusetts, The Philanthropic Initiative, Inc.

Brody, D., 'Resolving Conflict', in: *Foundation News and Commentary*, September/October 1994.

Castle, A., *Evaluation Essentials for Small Private Foundations*, Washington, D.C., Council on Foundations, 1995.

Connell, J. P., *et al.*, *New Approaches to Evaluation Community Initiatives*, Washington, D.C., The Aspen Institute, 1991.

Council on Foundations, *Grantmaking Basics*, Washington, D.C., 1992.

Council on Foundations, *Operating Basics for Small Foundations*, Washington, D.C., 1983.

Council on Foundations, *Principles and Practices for Effective Grantmaking*, Washington, D.C., 1983.

Council on Foundations, 'Sample Values Statements for Private and Family Foundations', in: the *Family Advisor Packet Series: Values and Ethics in Philanthropy*, Washington, D.C., 1996.

Dewar, T. R., *Using Evaluation to Enhance the Foundation's Program Focus and Mission*, Hubert H. Humphrey Institute of Public Affairs, University of Minnesota, 1982.

Eisenberg, P., 'Philanthropic Ethics from a Donee Perspective', in: *Foundation News*, September/October 1983.

Freeman, D., *The Handbook on Private Foundations*, Washington, D.C., Council on Foundations, 1991.

Jacobs, F., 'The Five Tiered Approach to Evaluations: Context and Implementation', in: H. Weiss and F. Jacobs (eds), *Evaluating Family Programs*, 1988.

Johnson, R. R., *Developing an Evaluation Policy*, Exxon Education Foundation.

Josephson, M., *Ethics in Grantmaking and Grantseeking: Making Philanthropy Better*, Marina del Rey, California, Joseph & Elva Institute of Ethics, 1992.

Kendall, J. and Lilly, L., *Tips for Effective Grantmaking-Grantor Relations*, paper prepared for the Council on Foundations 1995 Family Foundation Conference. Washington, D.C., 1995.

Marble, M., *Social Investment and Private Foundations*, Washington, D.C., Council on Foundations, 1989.

Marble, M., 'Practical Approaches to Incorporating Evaluation into Grantmaking', in: *Initiatives*, Vol. 4, No. 2, Spring 1996.

Mayer, S. E., 'Building Community Capacity', in: *The Potential of Community Foundations*, 1989.

The Philanthropic Initiative, Inc., *Philanthropy for the Wise Investor: A Primer for Families on Strategic Giving*, Boston, Massachusetts, July 1996.

The Philanthropic Initiative, Inc., *Questionnaire on Philanthropy*, Boston, Massachusetts, 1996.

Scriven, M., *Evaluation Thesaurus*, Sage Publications, 4th edition, 1991.

Stone, D., 'Fostering Philanthropy', in: *Foundation News and Commentary*, January/February 1993.

Ylvisaker, P. N., *Small Can Be Effective*, Washington, D.C., Council on Foundations, 1989.

▼ Cathy Pharoah, Michael Brophy and Paddy Ross

Promoting International Philanthropy through Foundations

1 Traditional territory – new paths

International philanthropy is not new – from the early days of missionary work to the international aid programmes set up after World War II, governments, foundations, corporates, NGOs and individual donors have donated to people and causes in other countries.

Foundations, of course, have always played a key role in international philanthropy – in grant making, operating international programmes, providing a conduit for international funds from governments and individuals and in fundraising. The needs of modern global society, however, and the growth in international capital and labour markets pave the way for considerable development of international philanthropy. Unfortunately its potential will be difficult to achieve because huge stumbling blocks stand in its way. Cross-border donating is not always simple and generally does not attract the legal and fiscal concessions that national giving does. The legal and fiscal issues are different for each country, and it is likely to be a long time before they are harmonized. Within this situation foundations have come to play a key role in transacting cross-border philanthropic donations. The vast majority of current cross-border flows are transacted through major intermediaries, including philanthropic foundations. Building on their history of involvement with international causes, foundations are uniquely placed to raise awareness of the significance of international philanthropy, and to find new opportunities for facilitating, handling, supporting and developing it.

This chapter briefly reviews current levels of international cross-border giving and the main beneficiary areas, the current climate for international giving, the practical mechanisms for – and barriers to – making international donations by non-governmental donors such as foundations, individuals and companies, and how it can be developed. A specific focus is placed on how international giving can be made as tax-effective as possible, to ensure that donors can obtain similar tax-benefits (for themselves or for recipients), whether they are giving to recognized domestic philanthropic organizations or to needy causes in other countries.

2 Growth of international capital – a new donor pool

The growth of multinational companies, the deregulation of capital markets and the huge increases in investment gains of the 1990s have led to concentration of wealth amongst people with assets and interests in different countries. This group are a key pool of international donors, well-placed to be aware of needs in different countries and having a desire to help. As corporate and capital interests become increasingly international in nature, self-interest itself demands that the huge global imbalances of wealth and resources are addressed through increasing international philanthropy.

3 Why globalization means greater cross-border giving

While the needs of poorer countries have been recognized in the development of international aid programmes, why is international philanthropy assuming additional new significance today? Globalization is one key factor. It has many different implications for the development of civil society. Global markets bring individuals from different nation states into ever closer economic, social and political relationships with each other. A healthy global civil society is one way of expressing and consolidating these burgeoning, if as yet embryonic, new relationships. This means there is an increasing need to build civil society organizations with a broad international base.

This, however, is not the whole story. The development of global communication systems of all kinds means that people are much more exposed to needs in other countries – through travelling, reading, watching television and through the Internet. International news media means that there is much more immediate information about disasters and war zones. Many people want to respond to such needs directly through individual giving, as they do to needs at home.

Also as civil society organizations increasingly emerge to mediate between individuals, the state and the increasingly multinational private sector, many donors wish to help develop strong civil society organizations in countries where currently there are few.

Lastly, globalization brings a recognition that many issues such as poverty, peace and environmental sustainability can be tackled only at an international level by organizations with a genuinely international remit.

4 Why our multicultural society means greater cross-border giving

These 'macro-level' changes are occurring within important changes at the 'micro level' – it is indisputable that national populations are becoming increasingly multicultural. Waves of emigration throughout this century, the diasporas, the flight of refugees from civil wars and growing levels of economic migration mean that most countries now have populations consisting of many people whose nationality, culture, identity and family structures lie outside national boundaries.

Multiculturalism is integrally linked to international philanthropy. Some recent immigrant populations have very immediate relationships with people and needs in the countries they came from, and want to make a contribution to the problems they have left behind. Older immigrant populations, now including second, third and fourth generation members, want to support the cultures in other countries from they which they derive their own identity. Some who have prospered want to share a measure of their economic success with those in their home countries still in great need.

5 Out-of-date concept of philanthropy?

Why is philanthropy still regarded as lying mainly within national domains? Although historically philanthropy has often developed within national, ethnic or cultural boundaries, the culture of giving to whoever has needs, regardless of origins, is widely in place, albeit implicit rather than explicit. Sadly, organizations that explicitly support minority ethnic communities often find it hard to attract funding.

Individual donors generally give to needs, such as poverty, education, health and social care, without questioning that many of the ultimate beneficiaries may have come from other countries as refugees or recent immigrants and are particularly needy. Many major donors themselves come from non-indigenous (or mixed race) backgrounds. Recent research in the US, for example, is documenting the robust and generous tradition of giving amongst its Black communities. Although some of these gifts were specifically for the needs of Black women or poorer Black communities in the US, many were for Africa and many were for the benefit of all. Many governments and other funders now insist that funded organizations have equal opportunities policies for staff and beneficiaries.

It must be recognized, however, that foundations often inherit rather narrow criteria for giving from their founding endowments. While this is sometimes appropriate and acceptable, many countries have put fiscal and legal constraints in place to restrict benefit being applied too narrowly. Many foundations are conscious of need and interpret their benefit criteria as broadly as possible.

6 Current levels of cross-border philanthropic giving

How extensive is cross-border giving? While there is considerable data on international aid programmes, particularly government funding, there is very little information on private flows. Recent innovative research commissioned by CAF (Charities Aid Foundation) from the Johns Hopkins Institute provides some estimates on total philanthropic funds (government, corporate, foundation and individual) flowing from one country to another for four major donor countries: US, UK, Japan and Germany.

Table 3.1 Total outflows from major donor countries

Country	US$ billion
US	5.6
Germany	2.5
Japan	1.3
UK	1 (approx)*
Total	**10.4**

* British figures would be boosted if the £375 million grants from the British Council and university grants (fees and grants for British researchers and students in other countries) were included.

Within these broad figures, the private support element of cross-border flows is quite small. Figures available for Japan indicate that about 2.2% of all outflows came from private individuals and about 25% from foundations. In the US about 6% came from foundations and a further 10% from private individuals, but it should be noted that this private element was largely collected by philanthropic intermediary organizations, particularly of the 'Friends of' type.[1]

7 Individual support through international nonprofits

A slightly different picture emerges from a review of individual donor support for international organizations. Research conducted by CAF estimates that UK international fundraising charities get a substantial 33% of their income from private giving, about £380 million.

---

[1] 'Friends of' organizations are organizations set up specifically as intermediaries to collect funds from a variety of sources for a particular cause or interest, e.g. Jewish people living in Israel.

US nonprofit organizations classified as 'international' receive about 60% of their income from private contributions, nearly six times the average for all other nonprofits. The amount given is very substantial – estimated as $1.96 billion in 1997, representing 1.2% of total giving.

International organizations, many of which are in fact constituted by parent organizations in particular countries specifically for independent international fundraising and activity, raise large amounts from private contributions in the various countries in which they operate. UNICEF, for example, raises US$56 million in Germany, $23.4 million in Italy and in Luxembourg and $2.1 million in Spain. Greenpeace has a similar range, from $37.8 million in Germany to $9 million in the UK.

Evidence of country variations in levels of international activity comes from other sources. The international comparative research coordinated by the Johns Hopkins Institute, for example, shows international activity among nonprofit organizations ranging from 0.3% of all activities in the US to 2.6% in Spain. Domestic concerns tend to take precedence in people's minds and the public does not identify its own problems of, for example, unemployment, with those of nearby similarly placed neighbours. But a fundraising survey carried out by W. W. Rapp in five European countries found that at most 40% of people were willing to fund needs in other countries but this figure rises dramatically if 'other' was not seen as 'Europe' but as the Third World.

8 Foundations – a growing commitment to international giving

US foundations (such as the W. W. Kellogg Foundation, Ford Foundation, Charles Stewart Mott Foundation and Rockefeller Foundation) are major and growing supporters of international philanthropy and cross-border giving. Grants to international activities (including those to US-based bodies) were estimated as $970 million in 1994, an increase of 26% since 1990.

Grant making is widely spread, both geographically and in terms of fields of activity. Latin America, Eastern Europe/former Soviet Union, Sub-Saharan Africa and Asia/Pacific each received 15–20% of total grant dollars. In 1994 the largest amounts of money from US grant-making foundations went to (in descending order of amount): South Africa, England, Brazil, Mexico, China, India, Canada,

Hungary, Czech Republic and France. Poland and Romania also began to receive much greater funds.

International grant making by US foundations has grown steadily throughout the 1990s, with a shift of focus from international affairs and peace programmes, to the local needs and local organizations within developing regions and countries. This trend is likely to continue. Major grant makers such as Carnegie and Rockefeller have been reviewing their programmes, and are likely to increase the global dimension to their grant making. The William H. Gates Foundation is looking to fund world health issues and the Pacific North West. A broad range of activities received overseas grants from US foundations, the three most important being health and family planning (21% of total dollars), education (18%) and international development and relief (16%).

The bulk of international grant making is still accounted for by five major foundations (Ford, Soros, Kellogg, Rockefeller and MacArthur) whose giving accounted for over 60% of direct grants to overseas organizations. Many other foundations have small programmes of international giving.

New research from CAF shows that private UK trusts and foundations make about £98 million of grants to overseas causes, 6% of their overall grant making. This figure includes some grants to UK charities working overseas. International grants cover a wide range of activities but are somewhat skewed geographically. The main fields funded (by the larger trusts surveyed) were general international, tending to cover development (20% of grants), health (17%), social care (14%), education (12%) and religion (9%). The geographical breakdown is shown in Table 3.2 below.

Table 3.2

Region	% of total grants value
East and central Europe	16
Other Europe	17
Israel	15
Other Asia	15
South Africa	9
Other Africa	9
Pacific	1

As indicated, European foundations in many countries have also begun to play a role in international grant making. Western European (like US) foundation funding in the early 1990s tended to focus on central and eastern Europe. In the middle of the 1990s, however, there was some shift of interest and South Africa, Asia and western Europe emerged as key areas for funding. Over the last couple of years interest in the countries of the Mediterranean has grown, including the Arab countries, Turkey, Spain, Portugal and Italy. Countries which have received considerable funds from European foundations, including in-country foundations, include: Belgium, China, France, Germany, Ireland, Italy, Japan, Macau, the Netherlands, Poland, Portugal, Russia, Sweden and the UK.

9 US corporations and individuals – little international giving

Overseas giving by US companies was estimated as $137 million in 1990. This figure includes contributions by overseas subsidiaries, and other information suggests that the total may not have increased significantly. Most US corporations which make substantial donations internationally do so by supporting US charities working internationally or through subsidiaries outside the US.

Corporate interest in European community investment programmes is growing, particularly amongst American corporates, but not exclusively so. For example, the Dutch RABO bank is active in both the Netherlands and other countries. Marks & Spencer is also increasingly active in Europe and is seeking to expand its Children's Promise programme, currently working in Belgium, the Netherlands and France.

US companies increasingly active in Europe include Levi-Strauss, Chrysler, Nike, Kemberley-Clerk, Microsoft (particularly interested in education) and Johnson & Johnson (particularly interested in children). Corporate funders interested in Asia Pacific include Alcoa, American Express, AT&T, Coca-Cola, GE, Hewlett-Packard, Hitachi, Johnson & Johnson, Levi-Strauss, J.P. Morgan. Corporate funders interested in South Africa include Coca-Cola, IBM, Rio Tinto and in South Africa itself companies which fund local programmes include Anglo-American, DaimlerChrysler, Volkswagen, Deutsche Bank, BMW, Shell, BP and Woolworths.

10 UK companies – limited support of international activities

With some significant exceptions, UK companies do not give substantial support to overseas causes, at least from their UK budgets. A Directory of Social Change publication lists 530 companies making charitable donations, totalling just under £250 million, but less than 15% of these, with charitable budgets totalling approximately £50 million, are prepared to consider funding overseas projects – and the bulk of even these companies' expenditure goes to UK causes.

As in the US, many companies which give limited support to overseas causes from the UK are members of conglomerates with much larger international philanthropic budgets. Both BP and Rio Tinto, for example, have worldwide charitable budgets of around £20 million.

11 Barriers to international philanthropic giving

While there is enormous scope for international philanthropic giving, there are a number of barriers to achieving its full potential. In terms of attitudes, there are clearly wide variations between countries both in public attitudes towards international causes and in levels of support for international activities. There is also a range of considerable practical, legal and fiscal difficulties.

11.1 Tax and legal considerations

David Logan concluded in a pioneering study of transnational giving by European companies, that tax deductions are not a major motive for corporate giving. While tax incentives are not generally a major motivating factor in private giving, there is some evidence that they become increasingly important where very large gifts are involved and where they have a measurable – as opposed to marginal – effect in reducing the cost of giving. They also indicate government support for philanthropy, which in itself may be an influential factor in the package of motivations behind individual or corporate decisions to give. On balance, therefore, forms of giving which do not attract tax benefits may be seen as having a disadvantage.

11.2 Accountability and trust

Apart from technical difficulties, a different type of problem identified by corporations was the lack of any guidance in international giving, difficulties in identifying reliable organizations and poor evaluation processes for grants to organizations in other countries. The difficulty of assessing the competence of foreign charities is a major inhibiting factor, raised by the companies surveyed by the Conference Board and echoed in the sentiments expressed by the Grants Director of a major British trust, Charity Projects, 'We chose to channel all our funds through UK-registered charities [... so] that the grants we make can be properly accounted for'.

12 Developing mechanisms for facilitating cross-border philanthropic transactions

There are some current facilities for cross-border philanthropic transactions, and the first and most feasible step is for foundations to build on these, while also helping to address the additional issues of a lack of knowledge of the voluntary sector in other countries, and anxieties about systems of accountability and accreditation amongst some of the recipient countries.

12.1 Intermediaries for private donations

Turning first to current mechanisms, while direct donations to foreign charities by US donors are not normally tax deductible, there is a loophole. Tax-payers can make deductible donations to a US501(c)(3) charity submitting a 'non-binding recommendation' to the charity to pay the funds to a foreign charity. This provision is the basis for the creation of the many intermediary organizations developed to collect funds for international needs and which have been particularly successful in raising funds for Israeli causes.

In the UK, uniquely, tax deductions for charitable donations accrue largely to the recipient charity, in that charities can recover the basic rate of income tax paid by the donor on this element of his or her income. There are some small benefits to donors who pay higher rate income taxes under certain schemes, and new provisions which increase the scope for donor benefit were introduced in April 2000 which encouraged larger gifts by allowing gifts of stocks and shares to attract similar income tax reliefs as cash gifts. As in the US, no tax benefit is allowed for donations to foreign charities (and there are no treaty exceptions).

The procedure for passing on donations is however less discretionary, although like the US, the role of the intermediary organization is important. Tax-payers can make tax-efficient donations to CAF, which will hold the funds on their behalf, and they can subsequently require CAF to transfer money in their accounts to a UK charity or a foreign charity. There are various legal restrictions; in particular CAF, or any other UK charity, must not be seen to act as a conduit or agent which is receiving money only on the understanding that it is to be passed to a foreign charity.

In the US the intermediary organizations process a very large portion of individual donations for international philanthropy and provided a key model for CAF's development of CAF America. CAF America was established by the Charities Aid Foundation in the US as a 501(c)(3) tax-exempt organization, and also as a public charity, described in Sections 170(b)(1)(A)(vi) and 509(a)(1) of the Internal Revenue Service tax codes. This means that donors may claim the maximum tax benefits allowed by law for their contributions without the need for equivalency affidavits, letters of counsel or expenditure responsibility.

Its main aim is to provide information on international philanthropy, facilitate gifts and grants by corporations, individuals and foundations to charitable organizations worldwide, and to make international giving as easy as possible. CAF America provides the administrative services of writing cheques and foreign currency drafts, providing records of each organization supported and receipts which satisfy the IRS in relation to tax benefits. CAF America also fulfils all the administration needs and IRS requirements for foundations who do not wish to develop an international grant-making facility of their own, but would also like to make tax-deductible international grants. Through Donor Advised Funds (DAF) a gift of not less than $5000 may be made to CAF America out of which one-off international tax-effective gift donations can be made at the donor's will. The only requirement is that a minimum balance of $2500 is maintained at all times. Donors may make additional contributions to the fund at any time, and the tax deduction may be taken on the date of the initial contribution to CAF America. There are many other ways in which tax-effective funds for international giving can be donated and administered.

More recently CAF has established a special trust in London as an innovative means for US citizens resident and working in the UK to make tax-effective gifts to UK charities without losing their qualification for tax deductibility in the US. The Southampton Row Trust (SRT) is a dual registered charity, with a 501(c)3 US charitable trust registered in New York owning the share capital of a charitable company, limited by shares, and also with registration as a charity by the Charity Commission in the UK. A gift to the UK company using one of the UK income tax breaks secures tax efficiency in the UK, but the UK entity is disregarded by the US authorities who count the gift as if it had been made to the parent 501(c)3. These arrangements ensure that the UK resident American is not taxed in the US on the gross value of his UK gift.

SRT is essentially a grant-making charity and it operates under US tax rules as a donor advised fund. This means that it receives donations as unrestricted funds but invites donors to suggest which grantee organizations they would wish SRT to support. SRT's trustees would normally be able to accommodate donors' wishes, subject to verifying the eligibility of the intended beneficiaries.

12.2 Facilitating tax-effective US corporation giving

CAF America also offers companies a number of imaginative tax-effective programmes to support employees getting involved in international philanthropic giving to whatever cause, charity or country they wish. Initiatives include matching employees' gifts in disaster relief campaigns, facilitating matched employee international giving and the administration of 'employee-directed' gifts programmes.

12.3 Using global networks

In offering international giving services, CAF needs to be able to draw upon the expertise and knowledge of foundations and others in different countries. With this in mind, CAF has established its own network of offices in Moscow, Bulgaria, India, South Africa and Australia. CAF has also developed a considerable database of potential recipient organizations in other countries. CAF also works with other European foundations to facilitate and ease the somewhat cumbersome mechanisms available for making international gifts.

12.4 The Transnational Giving Agreement

To cut down administrative costs and heavy bureaucracy, three European foundations – the *Roi Baudouin*, the *Fondation de France* and CAF – developed a transnational giving agreement. This consists of a formal contract to cooperate over tax-effective cross-border donations between the three countries; it effectively operates as a compensation scheme within which donations for any of the partner countries are made tax-effectively to the partner foundation in the donor's own country. The foundations keep a record of donations to other partners, and the total amounts accumulated in each foundation are used either to offset each other or to make compensatory payments where unequal amounts have been accumulated.

12.5 The role of community foundations in international philanthropy

It is clear that one-off tax-effective cross-border gifts may be cumbersome and costly to transact, particularly where smaller amounts are involved. Difficulties are compounded by lack of knowledge and understanding of recipient countries and organizations. One approach which offers a way of circumnavigating some of these difficulties, and one which European and US foundations (such as the Charles Stewart Mott Foundation), have become increasingly interested in developing, is the establishment of local community foundations. Local community foundations provide 'safe' havens for gifts to a particular country, which can then be distributed in accordance with locally determined needs and in accordance with local procedures. A number of one-off gifts can be made from a single donation to a community foundation, cutting down the transaction costs of the international gift. International networks of foundations can help each other transact cross-border donations through sharing knowledge, expertise and facilities.

12.6 Global communications

Global communications already, and will increasingly, play a huge role in stimulating international philanthropy. Use of new technology, in particular the worldwide web, enables philanthropic organizations in any part of the world to provide information about themselves, and to communicate with potential donors. Foundations can play a key role in both helping smaller charities to access the Internet, and to transact their donations cost-effectively and speedily. Through developing online donations facilities, intermediary foundations encourage international giving and streamline the bureaucracy, enabling donors to receive acknowledgements of their gifts within ever shorter periods of time.

13 Holistic approaches

There is no one single answer to the challenge of promoting international philanthropy and cross-border gifts with maximum tax benefits from donors in one country to those in another. A whole basket of issues needs to be tackled – information, accountability and trust, good practice, imaginative schemes for raising funds for international giving and reliable, streamlined mechanisms for transaction which enable gifts to be made tax-effectively. Through its offices in a number of emerging economies including Russia, Bulgaria, India, South Africa, West and East Africa CAF is developing a range of services to help donors of all kinds make their gifts easily and safely, including grant-making, information, banking, trust and loans facilities. Foundations are particularly well placed to support such infrastructures, including the important task of backing the growth of indigenous self-sustaining funding mechanisms for the NGO sector in the Third World. In India, for example, CAF has begun to establish payroll giving, in Bulgaria CAF is supporting the development of a pooled deposit scheme to help organizations protect their small and vulnerable funds from erosion through inflation, and in South Africa CAF has helped negotiate preferential banking services for NGOs.

These are put forward as examples of the ways in which foundations can facilitate cross-border giving, particularly from donor countries where preferential legal and fiscal treatment of philanthropic donations exists. Another key way in which foundations in donor countries can help to develop the financial sustainability of NGOs is by lobbying for legal and fiscal concessions in countries where there are none.

13.1 Laborious procedures

Foundations can also lobby for the legal and fiscal frameworks in the wealthier donor countries to be eased. The two-stage procedures for making tax-favoured donations to overseas charities described earlier are somewhat cumbersome, and not easy to explain to all potential donors. They are also not totally efficient – for example, the US 'Friends of' organizations cannot in practice transfer all the funds they receive to foreign charities. Such restrictions make tax-effective donations to organizations in other countries considerably more difficult and restricted than domestic giving. Apart from anything else, it means that the donor must know about intermediary organizations and their role as well as the foreign charities or causes they wish to support. Technical and tax problems were identified by corporations as a key barrier to giving to other countries. One immediate target for the UK and other European countries might be to follow the example of the US tax administration which, while resisting major concessions, has been prepared to accept provisions in tax treaties with Canada, Mexico and Israel allowing US citizens to offset donations to charities in these countries against income derived in the country concerned; while tax harmonization in Europe may be decades away, European tax authorities might be persuaded to allow tax benefits for donations to charities in poorer Commonwealth countries (for the UK) or former colonies with whom they have long-standing links.

Bibliography

AAFRC Trust for Philanthropy, *Giving USA*, 1998.

Action Aid, *Trusts in a Closer World*, 1997. Quote from Maggie Baxter.

Anheier, H. K. and List, R., *Cross-border philanthropy*. CAF and CCS LSE, Kent, Charities Aid Foundation Publications, 2000.

Casson, D. and Smyth, J., *Guide to UK Company Giving*, 1999, London, Directory of Social Change. 1999.

Conference Board, *Benchmarking International Corporations*, New York 1996.

Garonzik, E. *et al.*, *The European Grants Index*, Brussels, European Foundation Centre, 1998.

Hems, L. and Passey, A., *Individual Giving Consumer Research*, London, National Council for Voluntary Organisations, 1999.

Logan, D., ed. *Transnational Giving*, London, Directory of Social Change, 1993.

Peebles, J., *The Handbook of International Philanthropy*, Chicago, Bonus Books, 1998.

Pharoah, C. *et al.*, *Dimensions of the Voluntary Sector 1998*, Kent, Charities Aid Foundation, 1998.

Renz, L. *et al.*, *International Grantmaking*, USA, The Foundation Center with the Council on Foundations, 1997.

Salamon, L. *et al.*, *The Emerging Sector – a Statistical Supplement*, Baltimore, Johns Hopkins University, 1997.

Salamon, L. *et al.*, *The Emerging Sector Revisited*, Baltimore, Johns Hopkins University, 1998.

Salamon, L. *et al.*, *The International Guide to Non Profit Law*, New York, John Wiley and Sons, 1997.

Taft Group, *Directory of International Corporate Giving*, Michigan, 1998.

UNICEF, Annual Report, 1998.

▼ Section **IV** ▼

Legal and Fiscal Framework and State Supervision

▼ Ulrich Drobnig

Foundations as Institutionalized Charitable Activity

1 Introduction

1.1 The foundation as an institution

Most individuals and corporate entities exercise charitable activity on a more or less discretionary and *ad hoc* basis. These persons and entities give money or render other assistance on a voluntary basis, as and when they receive appeals for help and are willing and able to act upon them. Individuals and corporate entities also often determine the beneficiaries of their action on a case-to-case basis. The amounts of money given or the value of services or goods transferred vary, as a rule, and are usually modest.

A benevolent person, enterprise or other entity may, however, be willing to go one step further and enter into a binding commitment to make regular payments or to render services or goods to one or more beneficiaries. While this commitment is an obligation that the benefactor must honour, the result is that the beneficiary may safely rely upon a contractual promise.

A still stronger commitment can be undertaken by a benefactor who is willing to devote certain assets from his or her property to the promotion of specific purposes. The benefactor's motives and the purposes to be promoted may be of the most varied kinds, such as religious, social, scientific, cultural or charitable. In order to separate the devoted assets from the benefactor's general estate and to protect them from his or her creditors, those assets may be transferred to a separate legal entity. In order for the legal entity to be made independent from the founder's subsequent will and whims, especially after his or her death, the entity must be equipped with a legally binding document as well as an independent and responsible management. Such an 'institutionalized' donation also gives greater security to the beneficiaries.

The legal entity's legal personality allows it to:

- hold property
- to take part in legal transactions
- have standing in court.

Certain unincorporated legal forms of institutionalized charitable activity, such as a trust, do not enjoy legal personality (see 7.1.2). The careful drawing up of the governing document and the creation of a legal entity will therefore require appropriate advice and the services of a responsible manager will involve an ongoing expense. The incorporation of a legal entity will therefore regularly be chosen where a larger amount of assets is to be dedicated.

This chapter will focus primarily on the choice of a foundation as the legal form adopted by individuals or corporate legal entities for institutionalizing their charitable activity. Section 6 of this chapter will identify alternative legal forms and present their comparative advantages and disadvantages as against a foundation.

1.2 Legal sources

Carefully drawn up legislation can help to ensure that a foundation's purposes, as defined in its governing documents, continue to be pursued in the manner intended by the founder, even after he or she is no longer involved in the management of the foundation. All legal systems in Europe include explicit legal regulations specifically devoted to foundations and equivalent institutions, such as charitable trusts and companies. A list of relevant legislation by country is set out in Appendix II. A few general pertinent observations are made here.

1.2.1 Regulations in or outside a civil code

The first general issue is whether the relevant provisions are contained in a country's civil code or in one or more separate legal instruments. This issue arises, of course, only for countries that have a civil code, which is not the case in Cyprus, Denmark, England and Wales, Finland, Ireland, Scotland, and Sweden. Instead, foundations in these countries and jurisdictions are regulated by specific statutes.

The remaining countries on the Continent are sharply divided on this issue, one that goes far beyond mere legislative choice. The currently valid civil codes that were enacted in the 19th century (starting with France, Belgium and Luxembourg, followed by Austria and Spain) do not contain provisions on foundations (and associations). The reason for this omission is ideological: after the French Revolution, the state was hostile toward any intermediary powers that might interfere with the direct relationship between state and society. The same was true for the civil codes in the Communist/Socialist states of eastern Europe. In both groups of countries (except now Hungary), foundations are regulated by special legislation outside the civil codes.

By contrast, the civil codes enacted in the 20th century recognized the need for civil society by inserting rules on foundations (and associations) into the codes. They were even granted prominent places near the beginning of the codes, following the provisions on natural persons. The lead was taken by the German Civil Code of 1900, followed by the Swiss Code of 1907, the Italian, the Greek and the Portuguese codes of 1942, 1946 and 1967, respectively, and, most recently, the Dutch Code (Book Two on legal entities of 1976).

1.2.2 Unified and split national legal regimes

A second general issue is whether a country's provisions and rules on foundations govern only a single type of foundation or several types. While most countries have a unified system, there are a few exceptions deserving a brief explanation.

Cyprus

A very special example is offered by Cyprus, where two institutions that are usually thought to be incompatible co-exist. A short statute deals with a few specified problems encountered by English-type charities and for all other issues generally refers to the 'law relating to charitable trusts for the time being in force in England' (Cap. 41 s. 15). In addition, a statute adopted in 1972 deals with associations and 'institutions' (i.e. foundations) and follows the Continental approach.

Germany, Spain and Austria

In Germany, the split of regimes is made horizontally: while the private law aspects of foundations are regulated by the Civil Code uniformly for the whole country, the public law aspects (such as approval and supervision) are governed by differing laws of the 16 Länder, respectively, the criterion for application being the seat of the foundation. By contrast, in Spain and Austria the division is made vertically. While the Spanish statute of 1994 establishes a uniform legal regime for foundations in the whole country, five of the 17 autonomous regions have enacted regional statutes for foundations whose centre of activity is in the respective region (Basque country, Canary Islands, Catalonia, Galicia and Navarra). A similar approach has been adopted in Austria.

Austria, Cyprus and Greece

A third kind of split exists in Austria, Cyprus and Greece. Each of these three countries has two sets of basic laws on foundations which regulate two fundamentally different types, namely foundations pursuing a public benefit purpose, on the one hand, and foundations pursuing a private benefit purpose, on the other hand. For details of this see 4.

2 Foundation as a specific institution

A comparative survey reveals that in most European countries a specialized institutional form for conducting charitable activity exists which is called a 'foundation' in the various languages. In the Germanic countries, the name '*Stiftung*' (*stiftelse, stichting*) even indicates how a foundation comes into being – by devoting property to it. By contrast, in Belgium the relevant institution is not called *fondation*, but officially bears the name *établissement d'utilité publique*, that is institution of public utility.[1] This name is indicative of the formal coming into existence of the institution, namely by administrative fiat, and especially its purposes. Formerly, the same was true in France and in Luxembourg, but both countries changed the name and adopted the 'common' term *'fondation'*, without changing the relevant substantive provisions. This confirms that in essence the same institution is involved. The Greek term used in Greece and Cyprus differs slightly and means 'institution'.

In sharp contrast to the situation in the continental European countries, England and Wales, Ireland and Scotland have not institutionalized the foundation as a separate legal form. In these three jurisdictions, charitable activities are conducted by relying on appropriate general devices and institutions of private law, especially the trust and the company limited by guarantee, which offer many of the same characteristics as a foundation on the Continent.[2] While the lack of an identical charitable institution has not prevented a thriving charitable sector from arising in these jurisdictions, comparison on the institutional level is made more difficult by this absence of equivalent forms.

In spite of this lack of equivalent forms, the term foundation is generally used in this book in a broad, untechnical sense thus also covering the functionally equivalent institution in jurisdictions with a common-law tradition. Only where special legal aspects of the law in these countries are involved will reference to the precise legal terms be made.

3 Definitions of a foundation

3.1 Statutory definitions

Some continental European countries offer statutory definitions of a foundation. While varying in detail, a basic pattern can be identified. The broadest and therefore most general definition is to be found in nine countries (Austria, Cyprus, Czech Republic, Estonia, Greece, the Netherlands, Slovenia, Sweden and Switzerland). In these countries, a foundation is defined by three basic elements:

---

[1] Current proposals to amend the Belgian statute would change the name of the *établissement d'utilité publique* to *fondation*.

[2] Refer to Garcia-Andrade: Establishment, Amendment and Liquidation of Foundations and Gallop: Cross-border Issues facing Foundations and their Donors.

- its assets
- must be devoted
- to serve a specific purpose.[3]

Estonia and the Netherlands add that the foundation is a legal entity, but one without members.

The French, Spanish and Luxembourg definitions also contain the above three basic elements, with one significant variation: the purpose to be served is expressly required to be of general interest.[4] Austria, Cyprus and Greece also require of certain foundations that their purpose be of a charitable or public beneficial nature. Belgium likewise uses for its institution of public utility (see 2 above) in essence the same three basic elements, but in keeping with the official name of the institution, requires it to be only for the pursuit of public purposes.[5]

France, the Netherlands, Spain and Sweden allow a deviation from the first of the three elements: instead of a devotion of present assets it is possible in France and Spain to spread the founder's contribution over a maximum of five years.[6] The Netherlands does not require any initial capital. And Sweden allows the creation of so-called collection foundations where the future financial results of collections are devoted to a specific purpose.[7]

It is amazing that the one element usually associated with a charitable or public benefit foundation, namely its nonprofit-distributing character, is mentioned only in the Belgian, French, Luxembourg and Spanish statutes.[8]

---

[3] Austria: § 2 (1) Federal Law on foundations and funds and § 1 (1) Federal Law on private foundations; Cyprus: s. 2 of Law 57/72; Czech Republic: Article 1 (1) Foundation Act; Estonia: § 1 (1) Foundation Act; Greece: Article 61 and 108 CC; Liechtenstein: Article 552 (1) sent. 1 Law on persons and companies; Netherlands: Article 2:285 (1) CC; Slovenia: Article 1 (1) Foundation Act; Sweden: part 1 § 2 (1) Foundation Law; Switzerland: Article 80 CC.

[4] France: Article 4 Law on corporate foundations (*foundations d'enterprise*), revising Article 19 Law on the *mécénat*; Spain: Article 1 (1) Foundation Law; Luxembourg: Article 27 (2) Law on nonprofit associations and foundations; Austria: § 2 (1) Federal foundations and funds Act.

[5] Belgium: Article 27 (2) Law on nonprofit associations and institutions of public utility.

[6] France: Article 4 Law of corporate foundations inserting Article 19–7 of the Law on the *mécénat*; Spain: Article 10 (2) Foundation Law, provided that the initial instalment amounts to 25% of the total contribution.

[7] Sweden: part 11 § 1 and 2 Foundation Act.

[8] For Belgium, cf. footnote 5, for France, Luxembourg and Spain, cf. footnote 4.

3.2 Extra-statutory definitions

In other countries of continental Europe, in spite of the absence of a statutory definition, courts and legal scholars essentially agree on the basic three elements set out in 3.1. This is true for Bulgaria, Finland, Hungary, Italy and Luxembourg. The first three countries add as an additional element that the foundation must be a legal entity. Possibly the same effect is also achieved in Italy and Luxembourg since in these countries it is said, respectively, that the assets must be 'institutionally' devoted to the pursuit of a defined purpose or that the fund of assets must be 'personalized'.

3.3 Lack of definition

In view of what has been said before (see 2), it is not possible to expect legal definitions of a foundation in England and Wales, Ireland or Scotland.

3.4 Exclusive use of the name 'foundation'

The recent statutes of the Czech Republic, France, Slovenia, Spain and Sweden reserve the designation of 'foundation' exclusively for foundations created according to the applicable provisions on foundations.[9] Other legal entities may not therefore use the term foundation in their name. A similar prohibition against the use of the name 'charity' by a non-charity exists in Scotland.[10] In England and Wales, a registered charity must state that it is a registered charity in all notices, advertisements and other documents specified in Section 5 of the Charities Act 1993. This requirement might imply that non-registered charities may not make a similar statement as this would mislead the public and undermine their confidence in registered charities.

There is no comparable protection in other countries. In Germany, where the term 'foundation' is not so reserved, the term may only be used if it does not deceive third parties about the true character of the 'enterprise'; in other words, the company or association must pursue charitable purposes and otherwise conform to the basic elements of a true foundation.[11] Slovenia has even taken one step more by allowing

---

[9] Czech Republic: Article 1 (3) Foundation Act; France: Article 20 of Law no. 87–571 of 23 July 1987; Slovenia: cf. Article 36 Foundation Act; Spain: Article 3 (2) Foundation Act; Sweden: part 1 § 6 (2) Foundation Act.

[10] Law Reform (Miscellaneous Provisions) (Scotland) Act 1990 s. 2.

[11] Cf. various authors in *v. Campenhausen* (ed.), especially *v. Campenhausen*, Erscheinungsformen (§ 2) no. 19–21; *Hof*, Die Entstehung der Stiftung (§ 7) no. 25 and 125; cf. also *Pöllath*, Unternehmensstiftung (§ 13) no. 121–32.

non-foundation legal entities to add the term 'foundation' to their name, provided these legal entities were created for public or charitable purposes.[12]

4 Nature of the purpose(s) to be pursued

It is one of the three basic elements (see 3.1) of a foundation of the continental European type that assets must be devoted to a specific purpose. This particular aspect is also shared by the English, Welsh, Irish and Scottish laws of charities: funds must be devoted to a specific purpose (or purposes). However, continental Europe is divided with respect to the nature of the purposes that may be pursued with the devoted assets.

In about half the countries of Europe, the purposes of a foundation or a charity must be of a general (i.e. a public) nature. This is true in Belgium, France, Luxembourg, Portugal, Spain[13], England and Wales, Ireland, Scotland[14] as well as in most eastern European countries.[15] The detailed definitions of 'public purpose' vary from country to country and need not concern us here. The essence of the public purpose can best be demonstrated by contrasting it with the wider concept of permitted purposes that prevails in the remaining group of countries.

In this group, the permitted purposes of a foundation are not limited to those of a public nature. In some countries it follows by negative implication from the fact that the purposes to which a foundation's property must be devoted are not qualified or restricted in any way, for example in Estonia, Greece, the Netherlands and Sweden.[16]

---

[12] Article 34 (1) Foundation Act.

[13] In Belgium already the official name 'institution of public utility' clearly indicates the required public purpose(s); these are enumerated in Article 27(2) of the Belgian Law; Luxembourg: Article 27(2) Law on nonprofit associations and foundations. In France, a foundation only acquires legal personality if it is recognized to be of 'public utility' (*utilité publique*), cf. Law on corporate foundations Article 1, 3 (2) and 4. Portugal: Article 188(1) CC; Spain Article 1(1) and 2 Foundation Law; Article 2(3) expressly excludes foundations whose purpose it is to benefit the spouse of the founder or relatives up to the fourth degree.

[14] Cf. the definition of 'charity' in *Income Tax Special Purposes Commissioners v. Pemsel*, [1891] A.C. 531 (H.L.) per *Lord Macnaghten*; this definition is also still regarded as binding in Ireland. For Cyprus s. 2 Law on Charities (Chap. 41 of the Laws of Cyprus, 1959 ed.); s. 15 refers generally to the 'law relating to charitable trusts for the time being in force in England'.

[15] Czech Republic: Article 1(1) Foundation Act; Hungary § 74A(1) CC; Slovenia: Article 2(1) Foundation Act; Article 2(4) expressly excludes foundations for the benefit of named persons or family members.

[16] For references cf. footnote 3.

Finland requires that the purpose be 'useful'[17] – but this term is much broader than 'public'. Liechtenstein expressly mentions church, family and public purposes.[18] Switzerland, Denmark and Italy as well as some of the German states, on the other hand, have separate provisions for family foundations.[19] Austria, Cyprus and Greece have even two separate statutes, one for public benefit foundations and one for private benefit foundations.[20]

5 Duration

5.1 Unlimited duration as a rule

Most foundations are created without time limit. In fact, some foundations have existed for several centuries, especially certain organizations devoted to the never-ending task of providing charitable assistance to poor and sick people. Generally, foundation law also assumes that the duration of foundations is not limited in time, although this is only rarely spelt out.[21] But the 'eternal' character of foundations is implied by the specific provisions on the preservation of a foundation's assets and also by the rules on the amendment of a foundation's purpose when the purpose originally fixed by the founder can no longer be realized.

5.2 Voluntary limitation of duration

It would, however, be unrealistic and even constitute an undesirable restraint on voluntary giving if legislators or authorities were to require foundations to be created only for an unlimited duration. In Austria, Denmark, Estonia, Finland, France, Greece, Hungary, Liechtenstein and Portugal, the legislators expressly allow foundations to be created for a limited period of time; in France, however, a

---

[17] Section 5 (2) Foundation Act.

[18] Article 552 (1), 553 Law on persons and companies.

[19] Switzerland: Article 87 and 335 (1) CC; Denmark: § 7 Foundation Act; Italy: Article 28 (3) and 699 CC. Germany: several states have special preferential provisions on family foundations, cf. footnote 29. The state of Brandenburg does not allow family foundations (§ 6 (2)(d), (3)(b)).

[20] Austria: footnotes 3 and 4; Greece: cf. Article 108–121 CC as the general regulation and Law 2039/1939 for charitable foundations.

[21] Austria: § 2 (1) Law on foundations and funds: assets must be devoted 'permanently'; similarly Hungary: § 74A (1) CC (but see footnote 22); Spain: Article 1 (1) Foundation Law. Slovenia uses a slightly more flexible formula: 'as a rule permanently', cf. Article 2 (1) Foundation Act.

minimum period of five years has been fixed for corporate, not public utility, foundations.[22] German legal scholars regard time limitations as an expression of the founder's autonomy, yet object to foundations being created for too short a period; five years is suggested as a minimum period.[23]

Austria (only for public benefit foundations) and the neighbouring Czech Republic have even created a special type of time-limited foundation, a so-called fund. The Czech regulation is very clear and simple – almost all the legislative provisions expressly cover both foundations and funds; the only major exceptions are that – contrary to a foundation – a fund does not require a minimum capital and that it may use 'all its assets' in order to achieve its purposes.[24] By contrast, the Austrian rules are rather complicated. First, they are part of the regulation of public benefit purpose foundations only since these must be of a permanent nature (see footnote 20). Secondly, there are 17 provisions dealing with funds which in most respects are very similar to corresponding provisions on public benefit purpose foundations. And third, a foundation whose income no longer suffices for the permanent fulfilment of its (public benefit) purposes may be converted to a 'foundation-fund', provided the assets are likely to be sufficient to fulfil the purposes of the foundation for (another) 20 years.[25]

England and Wales, Scotland and Ireland proceed from quite a different starting point. Given that the foundation does not exist as a special legal form, general devices and institutions of private law are utilized for charitable purposes, especially the charitable trust and the company limited by guarantee. These forms grant substantial freedom and allow the 'founders' to limit their duration or to set their duration for an unlimited period.

---

[22] France: Article 4 Law on corporate foundations, inserting Article 19–2 into the Law on the *mécénat*; Austria: § 9 (1) no. 6 Law on private foundations; Denmark: cf. § 9 (5) Foundation Act; Estonia: cf. § 43 no. 4 Foundation Act; Finland: § 18 (1) Foundation Act; Greece: Article 95 Law no. 2039/1939; Hungary: cf. § 74 E (1) (b) CC; Liechtenstein: cf. Article 568 Law on persons and companies; Portugal: Article 192 (1) (a) CC.

[23] *Hof*, H., § 4 no. 64 and § 7 no. 32.

[24] Article 2 (3) and 3 (4) Foundation Act; cf. also Article 7 (4) on winding-up of a fund after it has spent its assets and it is therefore unable to fulfil its purpose.

[25] § 19 (1) Foundations and Funds Law; the founder may however exclude such conversion.

6 Distinctive characteristics of a foundation

When should a donor interested in 'institutionalizing' his or her charitable activity choose to establish a foundation rather than another form of organization? The distinctive characteristics of a foundation are discussed below and compared with those of other forms of organization.

6.1 Foundation versus association

Foundations and associations have in most countries one common denominator: both are subject to the non-distribution constraint (prohibition against distributing the profits or earnings of the entity to 'owners', managers, staff, or other persons closely associated with the organization) – provided that the organizations pursue a non-profit purpose. Most civil codes and some special statutes therefore regulate both types of nonprofit organizations in close proximity or even in a partly integrated manner.

On the other hand, there is one feature that clearly distinguishes foundations from associations – the absence of members in a foundation. This absence of members (and therefore the absence of the controls that might otherwise be exercised by them) is generally regarded as a major reason for the considerably greater degree of state control to which the creation and functioning of foundations are subjected in most countries as compared to membership organizations.

6.2 Foundation versus company

In countries where the law does not require certain legal forms to be selected for the pursuit of charitable activities, donors may choose between the form of a foundation and that of a company (Germany, Liechtenstein, the Netherlands, and Switzerland). In these countries, the foundation's governing statutes must ensure that:

- the charitable entity will pursue a charitable purpose
- any profits earned by the entity will not be distributed to the 'founders' (the 'non-distribution constraint').

These two factors, the statutory purpose and the non-distribution constraint, are thus usually the decisive criteria in determining whether the entity qualifies as a charitable organization. In Denmark there is even a special statute governing foundations exercising a commercial activity.

On the other hand, in many countries commercial companies are not obliged to pursue their activities for profit.[26] Belgium has recently even introduced a special variation of company, the company 'with a social purpose' (*société à finalité sociale*), which is designed for companies wishing to pursue a social purpose and wishing to distribute their profit to the 'partners' only to a limited extent.[27]

In England and Wales, Ireland and Scotland, due to the absence of the foundation as a separate legal institution, one of the major vehicles of charitable activity are companies, and more precisely companies limited by guarantee (see 2). By limiting the shareholders' guarantee to a merely nominal amount (such as £1), this form of company can be brought, in reality, very close to a company without a capital – except for the funds devoted to the charitable purpose(s). The charitable company limited by guarantee is the preferred legal form for any charity that engages in any form of activity that carries significant financial risks since it offers the protection of limited liability to its directors. When using a company limited by guarantee for charitable purposes, it is necessary for the founders to adapt the purpose clause of the memorandum of association so as to express in it the charitable purposes and to exclude any distribution of profits or assets to the members.

An important difference between foundations and companies lies in the level of supervision of the legal entity. In most countries, foundations must obtain an administrative approval to be incorporated and are subject to ongoing administrative supervision after incorporation (see van Veen: Supervision of Foundations in Europe). In Germany, for instance, the absence of supervision of a company (GmbH) has significant consequences since the company, unlike a foundation, will not have to ensure that its capital is adequate for the pursuit of its purpose, and may decide in accordance with its own internal governance rules whether or not to dissolve the company at a later time – a foundation on the other hand is usually established in perpetuity. The supervision exercised by the tax authorities will be the same for a foundation and a company in Germany since in both cases the authorities will be concerned to ensure that the entity continues to pursue a purpose qualifying for the special tax privileges.

---

[26] Bulgaria, Germany, Greece according to general rules. Express provisions in Liechtenstein: Article 107 (2) Law on persons and companies, and Slovenia: Article 1 (4) Law on commercial companies.

[27] Company Law of 1935 part 7*bis*, as inserted by Law of 13 April 1995. Article 164*bis* § 1 enumerates nine requirements that must be fulfilled by the company's charter in order to qualify as a company with a social purpose.

As discussed at greater length in van Veen: Supervision of Foundations in Europe, supervision can be justified by the fact that the pursuit of the fixed purposes and the administration of a foundation are not subject to the controls of membership found in associations and companies. The absence of members (see 6.1) is again an important distinguishing characteristic of foundations, which are crystallized around a fund of assets – an *universitas bonorum*. For England and Wales, Ireland and Scotland this characteristic is probably also present where a charity is conducted not as a company but as a trust. The trust has a trust *res* but no members, the trustees being the equivalent of the directors and officers of a continental foundation – with the difference, though, that the trustees have legal (not beneficial) title to the trust *res*.

6.3 Public purpose and private purpose foundations

The three basic elements of the statutory and non-statutory definitions of a foundation refer to a purpose to which assets must be devoted but do not, in general, specify the nature of that purpose (see 3.1). In about half the countries of Europe only a public benefit purpose may be pursued by a foundation.

However, the remaining European countries do not impose such a restriction and therefore also allow foundations to pursue a private benefit purpose. The most important private benefit purpose pursued is the financial support of a family, usually that of the founder. For instance, the founder may specify as the purpose of the foundation the giving of financial support to all members of a family or, more frequently, to special groups of them (such as the young or the old or destitute family members).

In Liechtenstein and Switzerland, family foundations are not subject to registration.[28] More importantly, in these two countries as well as in some German states, family foundations are exempted from state supervision.[29] This is justified by the fact that in family foundations most potential beneficiaries know each other and will therefore exercise control over their family foundation's administration – a control otherwise absent in memberless foundations.

---

[28] Liechtenstein: Article 106 (2), 557 (2) Law on persons and companies; Switzerland: Article 52 (2) CC.

[29] Liechtenstein: Article 564 (1) Law on persons and companies; Switzerland: Article 87 (1) CC; German states: Berlin § 10 (4), Bremen § 17, Hessen § 21, Mecklenburg-Vorpommern § 27, Niedersachsen § 10 (2), Rheinland-Pfalz § 27; cf. also Bavaria Article 18 (1)). Special rules for family foundations have been enacted in Berlin § 10 (2) and (3) and Hamburg § 14 (2).

It is important to note that private benefit foundations do not enjoy the same tax privileges as public benefit or charitable foundations.

6.4 'Accessory' (or 'dependent') foundations

A 'minor', although in practice very important, form of a 'foundation', is the so-called accessory or dependent foundation (in some countries, these are also referred to as nominal or donor-advised funds). In contrast to the independent foundation with which this book deals, the accessory or dependent foundation has no organizational framework of its own and lacks legal personality. It is used when a donor intends to devote assets to a more or less specific purpose but due to the limited value of those assets, the short time limit for the fulfilment of the purpose, or for other reasons does not want to create an independent body for the administration of those funds. Obviously, an accessory or dependent foundation does not need to establish an independent body, which entails certain costs to cover administrative and professional services exclusively related to the body's incorporation and subsequent supervision. It is estimated that the number of such accessory or dependent foundations surpasses that of independent foundations.

The so-called accessory or dependent foundations are funds which are transferred by the donor to another person or legal entity (possibly a genuine, i.e. independent, foundation) in order to be utilized for the purposes specified by the donor. Accessory or dependent foundations are not themselves subject to the legislation on foundations and are not separately subject to state approval or control. An exception is to be found in two German states[30] and to a limited degree in a third.[31] The organization on which they depend for management and administration, however, may be subject to state approval and control. The state therefore might ultimately exercise indirect control and supervision over accessory or dependent foundations.

Relevant legislative provisions applying specifically to accessory or dependent foundations are very rare. Some provisions that do exist specify that the lack of legal personality is the distinctive criterion of the accessory foundation. All provisions qualify the function of the

---

[30] Saxony and Saxony-Anhalt: § 28 (2) of the Foundation Law of the former German Democratic Republic (GDR) 1990 declares applicable by analogy the rules for independent foundations; this provision was abrogated by Thuringia.

[31] According to § 32 Law Nordrhein-Westfalen if a legal entity of public law has been entrusted with the administration, the authority in charge of controlling this entity shall also control whether the donor's intention is properly performed by that entity.

recipient of the assets as that of an administrator in trust.[32] Liechtenstein refers to the underlying transaction as a donation or a testamentary disposition.

In England and Wales, Ireland and Scotland, the transfer of funds by the settlor of a trust to the trustee(s) is based upon the similar legal structure as the accessory foundation of the continental European countries. A trust, however, differs from an accessory foundation to the extent that the legal and beneficial ownership is split between the trustees and the beneficiaries of the trust, respectively. In England and Wales, Ireland and Scotland moreover, charitable trusts, unlike accessory foundations, must receive the confirmation of the Charity Commission, the Financial Intermediaries and Claims Office (FICO), or of the Commissioners of Charitable Donations and Bequests, respectively, of their charitable status. Once their charitable status is confirmed by the respective authority, the trust will be subject to supervision exercised by these or other authorities (see van Veen: Supervision of Foundations in Europe). Moreover, in England and Wales, Ireland, Scotland and Cyprus, trustees themselves may be incorporated in order to limit their own liability (see 7.1.2.).

Funds received by an independent foundation in the form of a dependent or accessory foundation are usually treated as a 'restricted fund'. The fund therefore has to be accounted for and invested separately from the other assets of the independent foundation.

---

[32] Liechtenstein, Article 552(1) Law on persons and companies; German states Saxony, Saxony-Anhalt and Thuringia: § 28(1) of the Law mentioned in footnote 30, in addition, the German state Nordrhein-Westfalen § 2(2).

[33] Czech Republic: Article 1 (2) Foundation Law; Slovenia: Article 1 (2) Foundation Law; cf. also Sweden: part 1 § 4 Foundation Act.

[34] Austria: § 6 (4) and 26 (4) Law on foundations and funds; Belgium: Article 30 (1) Law on nonprofit associations and institutions of public utility; Germany: § 80 CC; Greece: Article 108 CC; Italy: Article 12 (1) CC; Luxembourg: Article 30 (1) Law on nonprofit associations and foundations; Slovenia: Article 5 (2) Foundation Law; Spain: Article 3 (1) Foundation Law.

[35] France: Article 4 Law on corporate foundations, inserting Article 19–1 (1) Law on the *mécénat*.

[36] Finland: § 8 (1) Foundation Act.

[37] Austria: § 7 (1) Law on private foundations; Bulgaria: Article 147 Law on persons and the family; Czech Republic: Article 5 (1) Foundation Act; Finland: § 8 Foundation Act; Hungary: § 74A (2)–(5) CC; Liechtenstein: Article 106 (1), 557 Law on persons and companies.

7 Legal entity and capacity

7.1 Foundation as a legal entity

7.1.1 Continental Europe

In Austria, Estonia, Finland, France, the Netherlands and Sweden, the statutory definition of a foundation comprises its qualification as a legal entity (see 3.1); other countries add it to the definition.[33] Most countries mention it only as a consequence of the creation of the foundation.

Legal personality is usually acquired by virtue of administrative approval[34] or of publication of that decision[35] or registration after approval.[36] Where administrative approval is not necessary, registration alone usually confers legal personality;[37] in the Netherlands generally and in those countries where even registration is dispensed with for certain types of foundations, such as family foundations, legal personality is acquired by the formal act of creating the foundation. However, in Belgium and Luxembourg, a foundation which has not published its statutes or the names of its administrators cannot avail itself of its legal personality *vis-à-vis* third persons whereas the latter can invoke it.[38]

7.1.2 European countries with a common-law tradition

In England and Wales, Ireland, Scotland and Cyprus, only if the founders choose the form of a company limited by guarantee for their charitable activity will it acquire legal personality upon registration in the respective Companies Register.[39] As discussed earlier (see 6.2), in order for the company to obtain charitable status, the memorandum and the articles of association have to be adapted so that the purpose clause of the memorandum specifies the charitable purposes to be pursued, and prohibits any distribution of profits to the members. In England and Wales, any amendment of such clauses is subject to the approval of the Charity Commission. The company's name must include the terms 'charity' or 'charitable' and the full name must appear in all correspondence, publications, invoices, legal documents and negotiable instruments.[40]

---

[38] Belgium: Article 43 Law on nonprofit associations and institutions of public utility; Luxembourg: Article 43 Law on nonprofit associations and foundations.

[39] England, Wales and Scotland: Companies Act 1985 s. 13; Ireland: Companies Act 1963 s. 18 (2).

[40] Sections 64 (2), 68 Charities Act 1993; cf. also s. 14 (2) Law Reform (Miscellaneous Provisions) (Scotland) Act 1990.

By contrast, the trust as such does not enjoy legal personality since it consists merely of a transfer or setting aside of a fund of assets to the trustee for the benefit of a specified class of beneficiary. In order for trustees to protect themselves from being personally liable for debts or obligations of the trust or for settlors to avoid having to change trustees due to death, incapacity or resignation of individuals and the consequential need to transfer the trust property, legislation allows trustees of charitable trusts to be incorporated. Such legislation exists in England and Wales, Ireland and Cyprus.[41] The English and Welsh legislation, being the most elaborate, is briefly described as follows. When individual trustees wish to be incorporated after the creation of the trust, they must seek authorization from the Charity Commission. The Charity Commission may also grant such authorization on its own initiative. If the Charity Commission grants the request and issues a certificate, the trustees can become a legal entity; their rights and obligations as well as any property or asset held by any other person in trust for the charity will pass to the new entity. The trustees, however, remain 'answerable and accountable' for any property of the trust and any acts, omissions and defaults as if no incorporation had been effected. The Charity Commission may at any time amend the certificate of incorporation or dissolve the legal entity.

7.2 Effects of legal personality

The effects of a foundation's acquisition of legal personality are sometimes laid down expressly in law, especially in some Scandinavian countries and in England and Wales.[42] Discussion of these effects for foundations is hardly necessary since the specified consequences of incorporation (i.e. acquisition of legal personality) do not differ from the general effects of other forms of legal entities acquiring legal personality, namely to have legal capacity to hold property and to incur obligations as well as the ability to sue and be sued. In other words, the general rules on the powers of a legal entity apply and, generally speaking, these are almost the same as those of a natural person. Greece and Liechtenstein try to define the limit by excluding those legal relationships that presuppose the qualities of a human being.[43]

---

[41] England and Wales: part VII Charities Act 1993; Ireland: ss. 2–4 Charities Act, 1973; Cyprus: ss. 2–9 Charities Law.

[42] Cf. Finland: § 8 (1) Foundation Act; Sweden: part 1 § 4 Foundation Act; England: s. 50 (4) Charities Act 1993.

[43] Greece: Article 62 CC offers this general formula, whereas in Liechtenstein in Article 109 (1) and (2) Law on persons and companies the relevant natural qualities of a human being are enumerated.

The principle of full legal personality of foundations implies in most countries that foundations have full powers to:

- hold and acquire assets
- make grants and other dispositions
- create nonprofit institutions or even commercial companies
- sue and be sued in their own name.

Such freedom of action, although only within any restrictions that may be spelt out by the governing document of a specific foundation, exists in Bulgaria, Cyprus, most German states, Hungary, Ireland, Italy, Liechtenstein, the Netherlands, Scotland, Sweden and Switzerland.

By contrast, other countries, especially the jurisdictions with a common-law tradition, limit the extent of legal personality to the purposes for which a foundation has been created. Additional powers, such as the creation of and investment in a commercial company, have to be authorized by an express clause.

7.3 Restrictions on a foundation's powers

A few countries expressly impose certain limitations upon the powers of foundations. These restrictions appear to be motivated by various considerations of public policy. Some restrictions are obviously inspired by the fear of foundations amassing too much property (see 7.3.1 and 7.3.2). Others are directed at restricting the activity of foundations (see 7.3.3 and 7.3.4).

7.3.1 Immovables

France, Belgium and Luxembourg are the only countries that generally restrict the holding of immovables. Their acquisition or possession is allowed only insofar as this is necessary for the fulfilment of the foundation's purposes.[44] In many countries, all transactions concerning a foundation's immovables, because of the values involved, must be expressly authorized by the governing document.

---

[44] France: Article 4 Law on corporate foundations, inserting Article 19–3 Law on the *mécénat*; Belgium: Article 35 Law on nonprofit associations and institutions of public utility; Luxembourg: Article 35 Law on nonprofit associations and foundations.

Several other countries restrict dispositions of a foundation's immovable property. England and Wales, some of the German states and Greece allow dispositions only upon approval by the supervisory authority.[45] In Spain, this authority must be informed and in certain cases must approve of the disposition.[46]

7.3.2 Donations to a foundation

Several Romanic countries restrict in various ways the acceptance of donations made to a foundation. French corporate foundations are absolutely prohibited from receiving gifts or legacies.[47] In Belgium and Luxembourg such donations may not, as a rule, be accepted without the approval of the supervisory authority; an exception is only made for the donation of movable assets up to the value of Bfrs440,000 (€10,907) or Lfrs500,000 (€12,395), respectively.[48] Luxembourg qualifies the permission requirement in two respects: on the one hand, a provisional approval may be granted; on the other hand, an approval will be refused if a foundation has not performed its obligations to have all required registrations made and to have annual accounts submitted.[49]

By contrast, in Spain the approval of the supervisory authority is required if a foundation intends to refuse the acceptance of an inheritance or a legacy.[50] On the other hand, an inheritance or legacy to a foundation is always deemed as accepted subject to the *beneficium inventaris*, that is liability is limited to the funds of the succession. And the acceptance of gifts or legacies which are subject to conditions that may conflict with the foundation's purposes is subject to approval by the supervisory authority (see footnote 50).

---

[45] England and Wales: ss. 36–40 Charities Act 1993; German states: Baden-Württemberg § 13 (1) no. 1, Bavaria Article 27 (1) no. 3, Nordrhein-Westfalen § 21 (1); Greece for charitable foundations: Article 71–72 Law 2039/1939.

[46] Spain: Article 19 (2) Foundation Act.

[47] Article 4 Law on corporate foundations, inserting Article 19–8 (2) Law on the *mécénat*.

[48] Belgium: Article 36 Law on nonprofit associations and institutions of public utility; Luxembourg: Article 36 (2), 16 (1) Law on nonprofit associations and foundations. These values are subject to annual adjustments.

[49] Article 36 (2), 16 (2) and (3).

[50] Article 20 Foundation Law.

7.3.3 Economic activity

General considerations

Economic activity conducted by charitable foundations might at first sight seem to run counter to one of the very basic characteristics of foundations, namely their pursuit of a public benefit or nonprofit purpose. Yet, in practice, many states merely require that the principal purpose of the foundation should not be to engage in economic activities in order to earn a profit and distribute this profit to the founder(s) and the staff of the foundation. In short, the economic activities should not distract a charitable foundation from its pursuit of the greater purpose of benefiting the public and should not confer a private benefit on persons involved in the foundation. These two factors distinguish a charitable foundation from a commercial company (see 6.2) or from a private benefit foundation (see 6.3). In other words, engaging in economic activity may be compatible with the characteristics of a foundation, if and insofar as the profits gained are used exclusively for the purposes of the foundation.

In addition, there may even be a positive relationship between economic activity and foundations when the income produced helps to ensure a more or less permanent flow of revenues to be used for the future financing of those activities of the foundation for which it has been created. In eastern Europe, in particular, where private wealth could not be accumulated in the past decades, foundations depend even more than elsewhere on present and future economic activity in order to acquire the financial means to pursue their beneficial purpose(s).

A further consideration becomes relevant, if and insofar as foundations which pursue public benefit purposes and therefore benefit from tax privileges, exploit an enterprise. In these cases, there is a certain risk that competition will be distorted since a tax-privileged foundation's enterprise may be able to produce or trade at a lower cost and therefore lower prices, than other non-privileged enterprises.

General rules

Deriving income from assets which bear civil 'fruits', such as interest on monetary funds or bonds, dividends on shares of public limited companies, etc., does not constitute 'economic activity' since it does not involve active participation in economic affairs but merely deriving benefits from holding property.

There is broad agreement that economic activity undertaken by a foundation which is based upon the exploitation of its assets, such as renting of its immovables,[51] or collecting fees for visits of its institutions or collections, is permitted. The same is true for 'small' and occasional business, such as organizing a lottery, social or sport events, or public collections.[52] A foundation established for disabled people may also perhaps sell in a shop goods made by disabled persons who are employed for the making of such goods.

Genuine (i.e. constant) economic activity by a foundation must be permitted in its governing document.

Most countries prohibit economic activity by the foundation itself if this predominates in the foundation's activities[53] or is even its only activity.

The income from any economic activity, whether small or large, must exclusively be used for fulfilling and promoting the foundation's purposes.

Indirect economic activities

There is a much more moderate attitude towards economic activities which are carried on by a commercial company in which the foundation has merely a more or less comprehensive participation. According to the policy of the Charity Commission of England and Wales, any economic activity of any size which does not relate directly to the charity's purposes should be carried on by a separate commercial company. Such clear separation of entities and properties serves to protect the foundation since it is insulated from the economic risks to which any commercial enterprise is exposed, especially insolvency. Another advantage is the clear separation between the administration of the foundation and the management of the associated company. In Germany, it is not uncommon for the voting rights of the shares belonging to the foundation to be held not by the foundation but by a separate entity in order to preserve the foundation's charitable status.

---

[51] Expressly Czech Republic: Article 23 (1) Foundation Act.

[52] An enumeration of permitted activities is to be found in the Czech Republic: Article 23 (1) Foundation Act. Exceptionally, public collections are prohibited for corporate foundations in France: Article 4 Law on corporate foundations, inserting Article 19–8 (2) Law on the *mécénat*.

[53] Czech Republic: Article 23 (1) Foundation Act; Finland: § 5 (2) Foundation Act; Hungary: § 74 A (1) CC; cf. Estonia: § 46 (1) no. 2 Foundation Act.

In line with these considerations, the Czech Republic and Spain expressly allow shareholdings in companies in which the shareholders' liability is limited. However, the two countries set limits on such holdings: while Spain requires a majority of the shares, Czech law limits holdings in any one company to a maximum of 20%.[54] Participations in partnerships are not permitted in the Czech Republic; in Estonia and Spain, a foundation is merely enjoined from becoming a partner with unlimited liability.[55]

7.3.4 *Political activities*

The attitude of legislators with respect to support of political activities by foundations is split. An abstract definition of the term 'political activity' is impossible; it can usefully be discussed only in the context of specific restrictions.

To some degree, the existence and extent of restrictions upon political activities are connected with the nature of a foundation's permitted purposes. Where these are not limited, the pursuit of political activities is often unobjectionable. Thus, in Germany and the Netherlands, freedom of political activity is obviously derived from the absence of any legislative limitation of the purposes that may be pursued by a foundation. In the Netherlands, the scientific institutions of political parties were explicitly recognized as being of public benefit in 1954. In Spain, the very wide and open-ended definition of the general interests which must be pursued by a foundation[56] is the basis for the conclusion that political purposes may also be pursued. In Bulgaria, the same result is derived from an argument *e contrario* the constitutional prohibition (Article 12) of political activities for associations.

In other countries, where foundations are only allowed for the pursuit of public purposes, this term is often understood in a narrow sense as far as the pursuit of political goals is concerned. Since political goals are usually formulated by political parties and therefore often differ, it is difficult if not impossible to determine which of several parties pursues 'the' public benefit. Consequently, in several countries, support of political activities by foundations is expressly prohibited. Such prohibitions exist in the Czech Republic[57] and in the administrative

---

[54] Spain: Article 22 (3); Czech Republic: Article 23 (4).

[55] Czech Republic: Article 23 (5) Foundation Act; Estonia: § 2 (4) Foundation Act; Spain: Article 22 (1)–(2) Foundation Law.

[56] Article 2 (1) Foundation Act.

[57] Czech Republic: Article 21 (6) Foundation Act.

practice of the Charity Commission of England and Wales. In practice this is understood to exclude any support for, or fight against, any political party or politician as well as any activity directed at changing the existing law, except where it is ancillary to a charitable purpose.[58] Apparently a similar line is drawn in Switzerland. By contrast, Belgium and Luxembourg exclude any political activity since politics are not mentioned in the small catalogue of admitted public purposes.[59]

8 Conclusion

In concluding this chapter, it is of primary interest to juxtapose and evaluate the 'continental' and the common-law approaches to the institutionalization of sustained charitable activity. Whereas on the Continent (including Scandinavia) the foundation as a specific institution has been developed for this purpose, the jurisdictions with a common-law tradition have mainly made use of the charitable trust and the company limited by guarantee. Apart from this institutional aspect, most of the practical legal issues that call for solutions are identical on both sides of the Channel. Mutual comparisons, therefore, are both possible and fruitful and a broad range of choices is open to would-be benefactors.

---

[58] Cf. the guidelines of the Charity Commission on Political Activities (reprinted in Picarda, *The Law and Practice Relating to Charities* [edn 2, 1995, 1087 *et seq.*]); cf. also Sprince, *Political Activity* 35–7.

[59] Cf. Article 27 (2) of the Belgian and Luxembourg Laws (footnote 48).

▼ Jorge García-Andrade

Establishment, Amendment and Liquidation of Foundations

1 Introduction

This chapter deals with the procedures, requirements and formalities of setting up a foundation in 24 European jurisdictions.[1] Other aspects, such as the amendment of the statutes and the dissolution of a foundation, are also considered. Although there are no common rules for establishing a foundation in Europe, or even a common type of foundation, some general requirements and main characteristics can be identified in all jurisdictions and are briefly described in this chapter.

A survey of the laws governing foundations in Europe reveals that all the different jurisdictions considered have a functional notion of what a foundation does, even though the legal definition of a 'foundation' may vary considerably from jurisdiction to jurisdiction, or may not even exist in some jurisdictions. In order to compare the laws governing foundations all over Europe, a set of defining characteristics has been identified for the purposes of this book and will be outlined later (see 3.1).

This chapter will extract the general rules applying in Europe by examining groups of jurisdictions that are similar. A comparative analysis of these rules will help identify the main legal and administrative characteristics of the various jurisdictions. Practices that may be considered useful, and therefore recommended as standards for the future, are specifically outlined.

The following paragraphs summarize the principal issues to be addressed in this chapter.

- First, the **legal guarantees** provided by the various jurisdictions to protect the right to establish a foundation will be examined.
- The different types of foundations existing in Europe will then be classified according to common characteristics. Three basic legal forms for conducting typical 'foundation' activities can be identified: foundations in a narrow sense, membership organizations and trusts and trust-like devices.
- For the discussion of the **acquisition of legal personality**, the three main legal forms of foundations identifiable in Europe will be analysed separately: foundations in a narrow sense, membership organizations and trusts.

---

[1] The terms 'Europe' and 'European' in all the chapters of the legal and fiscal section of this book refer only to the 24 jurisdictions included in the survey on which the authors of these chapters concentrated for reference. See Appendix I for a summary of the information gathered in this survey.

- **Registration requirements** will be described to the extent that they differ from the incorporation procedures.
- An analysis of the **qualifying purposes** merit more detailed attention: whereas in some countries foundations may only exist for the pursuit of certain qualified goals, other jurisdictions consider those purposes merely a requirement under tax law for entities to be awarded charitable status, (i.e. tax privileges).
- With regard to **amendments and conversions**, the legal systems are divided into two main groups: the first seems to be more respectful of the founder's will; the second gives priority to general interests as opposed to the donor's will in cases of conflict between them.
- Finally, the legal provisions applying in various systems with regard to the **dissolution** of a foundation and the treatment of its assets upon liquidation will be described: some countries accept any stipulation stated by the donor, but a majority of jurisdictions require that assets of the foundation upon liquidation be destined for public agencies or charitable entities.

2 Right to establish a foundation guaranteed by law

2.1 Protection on a national level

Three main systems exist in Europe concerning the legal guarantee protecting the right to establish a foundation. The jurisdictions included in this survey may be classified according to the legal source of the guarantee offering the protection. In a number of countries, the constitution expressly guarantees the right to establish a foundation. Other legal systems do not guarantee this right, but provide for a more encompassing right of association that implicitly covers the right to establish a foundation. Nevertheless, most constitutions do not include either an express right to establish a foundation or a more encompassing right of association. In some jurisdictions, the right to establish a foundation is guaranteed by an act of parliament or by case law.

2.1.1 *Express constitutional protection*

Only three of the 24 countries considered have included the right to establish a foundation in their constitutions.[2] The Danish constitution of 1953 mentions this right in Article 78. The constitution of the

---

[2] It could be considered that the right to establish a foundation, called 'institution' under the Law of 1972, is also guaranteed by the Constitution in Cyprus.

Republic of Estonia guarantees not only the right to establish a foundation, but also a broader freedom to form nonprofit organizations (Article 48). An additional Act of Parliament expands this constitutional freedom and specifies a guarantee for foundations.

The Spanish constitution of 1978 guarantees the right to establish a foundation for general interest purposes. This constitutional safeguard even requires that the law governing foundations be of a special nature: it has to be an act of parliament, so that no other authorities may govern these issues through statutory law. In addition, Parliament may regulate foundations, through acts of parliament, but may not prohibit or restrict them in such a way that the legal form would in practice become obsolete.

Why was this provision included in the Spanish Constitution? Its existence stems from the events of the 19th century when the prohibition against foundations contributed to the ruin of many hospitals, convents and houses of charity. The rationale underlying this prohibitive policy was to avoid property being controlled by the 'dead hand' of the testator, hence the French term *mortmain* for the legislation prohibiting gifts to charities for use in perpetuity. By contrast, the 1978 Constitution tries to prevent such a policy from being re-adopted by restricting the power of the legislators.

2.1.2 Implied constitutional protection

Most constitutions do not mention the right to establish foundations expressly, but contain an indirect or implied legal guarantee. The main provision for an indirect guarantee is to be seen in the freedom of association. Three out of the 24 European countries surveyed recognize such a guarantee and link it to the freedom to establish a foundation (Italy, Portugal and Slovenia). For example, Article 25 of the Italian Constitution grants people the freedom to organize themselves for purposes that are not against the law. Although differences between both rights exist, they share some characteristics when the freedom of association is interpreted as including the right of people to get together for some general interest under a certain legal form. One possible legal form is the foundation.

In jurisdictions where the guarantee of the right to establish a foundation may be inferred from the freedom of association, the guarantee is not as strong as in those jurisdictions where the right to establish a foundation is expressly recognized in the constitution. Since a narrow interpretation of the freedom of association would not necessarily include 'genuine' foundations a state could fulfil the legal requirements of the constitution while not giving full protection to foundations. The position of foundations, as a result, is more delicate and uncertain than in jurisdictions in which there is express constitutional protection of the right to establish a foundation.

If one considers the right to establish a foundation and related civil rights and freedoms, it is interesting to note the cases of Liechtenstein and Slovenia, where the right to set up a foundation is considered as flowing from the individual's right to own and dispose of property. According to Spanish and German law the right to establish a foundation may also be viewed under a similar interpretation because foundations can be described as a legal extension of an individual's personality or wealth during lifetime and after death. To the extent that private property enjoys constitutional guarantees, the right to establish a foundation could be regarded as being encompassed in such a right.

2.1.3 *Protection granted by an act of parliament or by case law*

Most countries included in the survey guarantee the right to establish a foundation only or primarily by an act of parliament or by case law. This is the case in Austria, Belgium, Bulgaria, the Czech Republic, England and Wales, Finland, France, Germany, Greece, Hungary, Ireland, the Netherlands, Luxembourg, Scotland, Sweden and Switzerland.[3]

2.2 General remarks

The classification provides some insight on how society's perception of a foundation varies from one country to another. As mentioned above, in a few countries foundations are deemed to be assets serving a purpose and, therefore, an extension of the right of property. However, in many other legal systems foundations are not merely bound to the right of property, but also to the freedom of association or in some broader terms to a personal freedom to pursue charitable aims by private means. These 'philosophical' distinctions should be taken into account when analysing the more detailed rules of the various European legal systems.

---

[3] In Hungary section cf. 74/A of the CC; in Bulgaria cf. The Persons and Family Act 1949; in Finland cf. Foundation Act 1995; in Sweden cf. Foundation Act 1994; in Greece cf. articles 108-121, CC; in the Czech Republic cf. Foundation and Endowment Trusts Act 1998; in Portugal cf. CC; in Austria cf. Federal Foundations and Funds Act; in Germany cf. articles 80-88, CC; in Scotland, cf. Law Reform Act 1990; in England and Wales, cf. Charities Act 1993; in Ireland, cf. the regulation of Revenue Commissioners concerning charities; in Switzerland cf. CC; in the Netherlands cf. CC.

2.3 The need for protection on the European level

An analysis of the European rules governing the way public agencies contract with private entities ('public procurement') may serve as an example of the difficulties to be expected in the years to come, as for-profit and nonprofit entities compete increasingly for public contracts.

Under European law, public agencies interested in entering into a contract for the supply of services over a certain minimum threshold must open the bid to competition and make their decision on the basis of objective criteria in a relatively transparent procedure. These agencies should not therefore prefer bids tendered by a particular type of legal entity, for example, a foundation. In Spain, however, the constitution's recognition of the right to establish a foundation not only implies a guarantee for creating foundations, but might also be construed as justifying measures that favour the activities of foundations. Thanks to this constitutional protection, a rule favouring foundations over for-profit companies in a public procurement bid might be considered lawful in Spain. This is particularly likely to be the case when the public contract calls on the foundation (i.e. the contractor) to perform services that are directly related to its inherent or stated charitable purpose. Consequently, in the light of the apparent conflict between European procurement rules and the Spanish constitution, the question of how far public agencies can prefer a charitable foundation when it competes against a for-profit company in a public procurement bid remains unanswered.

As public local agencies contract out more and more of their services, in an attempt to reduce the role of the state, there is bound to be increasing tension between for-profit and charitable entities as they compete for contracts. For-profit entities might even claim that European State Aid rules are being violated because of the privileges enjoyed by these charitable organizations and their conferral of a competitive advantage in the bidding process. Member states and the European institutions should begin addressing these issues and enact rules that promote the role of charitable organizations, such as foundations, in society, while ensuring adequate fairness and competition.

3 Different legal types of foundations existing in each jurisdiction

Jurisdictions in Europe offer a wide range of foundation types. The variations depend on the criteria used to define types of foundations.

In most cases a variety of institutional forms can even be identified within each legal system. It is of particular interest to try to distinguish between the common types of foundations existing in various European countries and then analyse the legal forms offered by private law for the pursuit of public interest activities in a wider sense. Different criteria used to classify the different types of foundation could be:

- legal personality and membership (used to help examine foundation-like devices under private law)
- the distinction between public and private law foundations
- the distinction between foundations governed under ecclesiastical and civil laws.

3.1 Devices under private law for setting up a foundation

According to the definition of a foundation developed in Drobnig: Foundations as Insitutionalized Charitable Activity, an entity should have the following three elements to be considered a foundation:

- its assets
- must be devoted
- to serve a specific purpose.

However, different types of legal form of entity meet these characteristics, as discussed below.

3.1.1 Foundations in a narrow sense

The legal form found in most jurisdictions is the foundation itself, here referred to as a 'genuine' foundation, as a prototype possessing the three features above. Foundations are usually defined as legal bodies created by an endowment for the pursuit of a specific aim. The two distinctive features of foundations *vis-à-vis* other forms is that they enjoy personality *and* have no members. The legal form of foundations is expressly recognized in all countries surveyed, except a few: England and Wales, Ireland, Scotland and Cyprus. In these countries, the law provides for other forms such as charitable trusts and membership organizations, which can be designed to be functionally equivalent to a foundation.

3.1.2 Membership organizations

In some countries the legal forms involving membership, such as associations and companies, can be used as vehicles to accomplish the same purposes and have almost the same characteristics as foundations.[4] Companies used as a foundation vehicle may seek and earn a profit, but may not distribute it among their shareholders or members, in other words, they must be nonprofit-distributing organizations. As described in Drobnig: Foundations as Insitutionalized Charitable Activity, the non-distribution constraint is a principal characteristic of any qualifying nonprofit organization, including a foundation. Hence, provisions in a charitable company's memorandum and articles of association are needed to ensure that profits and income will not be distributed and will be used exclusively for the pursuit of its qualifying purposes. The main adjustments can be summed up as follows.

- In order to acquire recognition as a nonprofit entity, the company's memorandum and articles of association must contain a prohibition on the distribution of profits or assets to its members and directors.
- Its memorandum and articles of association need to state some non-commercial purposes for which the company exists (i.e. charitable objectives).
- Some provisions of the memorandum and statutes should ensure that the above conditions can not be altered freely, that is without proceedings carried out in public or before authorities, registrars or courts.

Besides these qualifications, some characteristics can be identified in different laws regarding companies that act as a foundation vehicle:

- They may have members.
- They are usually limited by guarantee, not by shares (this is the case in the laws of Ireland, Scotland, England and Wales).
- These kinds of companies often enjoy limited liability.
- Companies do not necessarily need to be endowed.

In Germany, organizations, such as associations or companies, that pursue charitable purposes other than in the form of an independent foundation are not subject to supervision by state authorities – fiscal supervision not being considered here.[5]

Under the Bulgarian Commerce Act 1991, companies may also be established for nonprofit purposes. In the Netherlands a company

---

[4] For further information see Drobnig: Foundations as Institutionalized Charitable Activity, sections 6.1 and 6.2.

[5] In Germany associations or companies might have the same purposes as a charitable foundation, and denominate themselves, for example, as '*Stiftung-GmbH*', although some differences arise when considering the tax deductibility of initial donations and also in case of liquidation.

limited by shares may also be a suitable legal instrument to act as a 'foundation', provided that the company qualifies as such (from the fiscal point of view) because of its public benefit activities.

3.1.3 Trusts and trust-like devices

In some jurisdictions many charities whose governing documents identify them as 'foundations' are in fact established as a charitable trust. A charitable trust is the predominant form of charity in jurisdictions with a common-law tradition, as in England and Wales, Ireland, Scotland, and even Cyprus. However, trust-like devices can also be found in Continental legal systems, for instance, in the Czech Republic, Germany, the Netherlands, Spain and Liechtenstein. It may be interesting to note that in the Czech Republic foundations and endowment trusts are considered 'associations of property' as compared to 'associations of persons'. The fiduciary body of assets available under German law (*unselbständige Stiftung* or *Treuhand*)[6] is based on the transfer of assets to a legal person already in existence, in practice mainly local governments, universities and religious communities. As German property law does not know a concept of splitting ownership between legal and beneficial ownership, the receiving organization holds full legal ownership but is contractually bound to administer the fund according to the stipulations of the donor. A similar legal instrument is also known in the Netherlands (*fonds op naam*), and in Spanish ecclesiastical law (*fundación pía no autónoma*). In Liechtenstein, trusts rarely conduct a charitable activity, as their use is typically more concerned with conferring a private benefit.

As defined in English and Welsh law, in general, a trust is a fiduciary relationship whereby the trustees hold property in trust for the benefit of the beneficiaries. Therefore, it is necessary to create an endowed capital to constitute a trust. Trusts do not enjoy legal personality, and thus do not have limited liability, as do other legal forms such as companies, associations or foundations. However, they can sue, be sued, and hold property and obligations in the names of their individual trustees. Another qualifying characteristic of a trust is that it may be established for either private or charitable purposes, depending more on the will of the settlor than on the law. As trusts as a legal device are unknown in most legal systems on the European Continent, trusts set

---

[6] In practice, the '*unselbständige Stiftung*' and the '*Treuhand*' are very often used as alternatives to a foundation when the amount of the initial donation is not sufficient to constitute an independent foundation.

up under common law may meet with some problems regarding recognition when acting abroad.[7]

3.2 The place of foundations in the dichotomy of public and private law

3.2.1 Introduction

Governments and public agencies have specific legal instruments at their disposal with which they can achieve public objectives. These legal instruments under public law are different from those intended for use by private persons to pursue private interests. Consequently, public and private bodies usually have different legal instruments at their disposal and may be governed under different laws: private bodies under private law and public bodies under public law. Foundations and charities may nevertheless be considered an exception, to the extent that they are private persons engaging in activities of general or public interest.

3.2.2 The freedom of choice of the state as a founder

When the state acts as a founder, it may set up either a public law foundation or a private law foundation. If the new body is a foundation established under public law, it will be considered as being part of the state's administration. In Germany, public law foundations may employ civil servants and may not fall into bankruptcy. Yet, due to the publicly beneficial nature of foundations, even foundations established under private law are well suited to pursue public tasks. Of course, this choice only exists in those jurisdictions where a distinction is made between public and private law in the field of charity law. In England and Wales, Ireland and Scotland, little distinction is made between public and private law in the field of charity law.

For various reasons the state might prefer to set up a foundation that is formally classified as being a foundation according to private law. What are these reasons? Private entities are usually more flexible in their governance. From a budgetary point of view it is often advantageous not to employ people governed by the rules of the civil service. Moreover, any surplus at the end of the year may remain with a private law foundation, whereas a public body would usually have to return such a surplus to the general budget. Finally, tenders for contracts made by a private law foundation might not be subject to

---

[7] See Gallop: Cross-border Issues facing Foundations and their Donors, 2.1, for formalities required in host jurisdictions for foreign foundations to conduct activities.

mandatory rules of public procurement, as would those made by a public law foundation.

3.2.3 Public foundations: the tension between the formal classification and the control exercised by the state

If the state decides to set up a foundation according to private law, special problems can arise, because the state will directly or indirectly control a foundation which formally has to be classified as private and thus *prima facie* independent from the state. These private law foundations dominated by the state can be referred to as public foundations, (not to be confused with public law foundations). Included in the definition of public foundations would be foundations incorporated by public agencies, foundations in which a majority of the board members is elected by public agencies, foundations whose main source of funds is public[8] and more generally perhaps, foundations that act more as an appendage of the public sector than as a manifestation of civil society. In practice, tension can arise between the alleged private nature of these foundations and the control in fact exercised by public agencies.

3.2.4 Unresolved questions concerning the legal environment of 'public foundations'

The legal regulation of these 'public foundations' is far from uniform throughout Europe. Legal certainty is often lacking since these entities – in spite of their private character – are not set up in a typical foundation form, but rather are entities individually created by an act of parliament and therefore are created upon the discretion of parliament. A foundation that does not meet all the conditions required under the Foundation Act may be nevertheless set up by an act of parliament in Austria, Cyprus, Estonia, Finland, and Liechtenstein, where public foundations are not governed by general private law, but by acts of parliament.[9] In Austria, public foundations are permitted and provided for by law, yet to date none exists. In Bulgaria, a Council of Minister's decree is required for a foundation to be considered public – to date only one public foundation has been created in Bulgaria. In Estonia, there are foundations regulated under public law, although there is no legal distinction. In Spain, some public foundations play an important role in the conservation of monu-

---

[8] When considering the source of funds to determine whether a foundation is 'public' or not, those funds should be analysed from a budgetary point of view and not as gifts without continuity.

[9] In Cyprus public foundations may also be established by the competent local court.

ments linked to the royal crown and lately in managing some public health hospitals.

The following aspects of public foundations should also be taken into account.

- Since the authority that establishes or controls the funds or the foundation's board may exercise the supervision over the entity, the 'self-governance' criteria used in the definition of a foundation adopted for this book will be met.
- In countries with a federal structure, like Spain, the supervisory authority (for instance a *Comunidad Autónoma*) may differ from the founding authority (for instance, local authorities or public universities). If these two authorities are constitutionally recognized as being autonomous, there might be conflicts of authority, to the extent that the founding authority would be subject to the jurisdiction of the supervisory authority when acting through the foundation, and that would be inconsistent with the Constitution.
- Among the many issues not completely solved when public agencies act through foundations are some legal ones: for instance, the scope of contracts, the status of the employees, applicability of budgetary rules, and liability of the board of the foundation.

3.3 The distinction between ecclesiastical and civil law foundations

In countries like Bulgaria, Germany or Spain foundations may be ruled by either civil law or by ecclesiastical law (the Church has its own law).[10] In Bulgaria, for example, only religious foundations require prior approval of the government to come into existence. A fundamental difference between foundations under ecclesiastical and civil law in Germany is that ecclesiastical foundations are established before and supervised by church authorities rather than civil institutions. Nevertheless, ecclesiastical foundations are subject to the same scrutiny by the tax authorities regarding their charitable status.

Problems can arise when trying to classify a foundation as an ecclesiastical or a civil foundation. Both enjoy the same tax treatment. In Spain, classification becomes relevant because Spanish ecclesiastical foundations have to be registered in a civil register, notwithstanding that the supervisory body is a religious authority. The civil authorities tend to classify all foundations that pursue religious aims as ecclesiastical, whereas religious authorities posit that ecclesiastical

---

[10] Organs of the Church are not considered under the concept of ecclesiastical foundations. Only foundations within the structure of the Church are considered here.

foundations are only those erected under ecclesiastical law. The fact that the criteria for determining whether a foundation is ecclesiastical or civil are somewhat imprecise could potentially lead to litigation over a foundation's ultimate classification, where such classification has legal or practical consequences.

4 Acquisition of legal personality

Most countries recognize the legal personality of foundations, whereas trusts are an exception to this rule (see Gallop: Cross-border Issues facing Foundations and their Donors, 2.1, for a more detailed description). Such recognition eases the day-to-day activity of foundations, as it enables foundations (with some restrictions mentioned in Drobnig: Institutionalized Charitable Activity, 7.3) to hold rights and incur obligations, and therefore to sign contracts, employ staff, or sue and be sued. The procedure for acquiring legal personality varies depending on the legal form of a given foundation. For this reason, the three main legal forms of 'charitable foundations' will be analysed separately.

4.1 Foundations in a narrow sense

4.1.1 The deed and statutes

In all jurisdictions, setting up a foundation requires the drafting of a deed and governing documents (hereafter 'statutes'). According to the laws of some jurisdictions, such as the Netherlands and Spain, the will to establish a foundation must also be specifically expressed. Either the deed, the will, or the statutes must contain the rules under which the foundation will be governed. These rules are fundamental to a foundation, as they will determine how the entity operates and potentially even its future status.

Either the deed or the statutes must set out the distinctive characteristics of the entity:

- the name of the foundation
- its legal address
- its purpose
- the activities it will develop in pursuit of such purposes.

The deed and statutes must contain sufficient information to determine the future beneficiaries of the foundation's activities. They usually also define the foundation's internal organizational arrangements:

- identifying and appointing the directors (or trustees) of the foundation
- defining the powers to be enjoyed by directors
- the number of directors
- establishing whether and how directors hold offices in the foundation
- the manner in which the directors will hold meetings and adopt decisions
- who will sign documents in the name of the foundation (a mandatory representative power is usually needed)
- how the foundation will be managed
- whether the directors may delegate some of their functions to one or more persons or entities
- the foundation's policy concerning investments, accounting and distribution of funds.

These rules are some of the most common ones included in the deed and statutes of a foundation in many countries.

The amount of the endowment is usually established in the deed or it will be specified when the deed is drafted.

Most countries provide that a foundation may also be established by a last will document, which must contain sufficient information similar to that mentioned above for foundations established during the life of the founder, or it must appoint an executor or an authority that will take care of the related formalities. In the last will document, the founder must express his or her intent to establish a foundation and the sum of funds with which it shall be endowed. In addition, he or she may leave special instructions to be followed by the executor or the authority. The foundation will usually acquire legal personality upon receipt of the governmental approval or registration, as the case may be.

4.1.2 Governmental approval

The first and primary question that arises when discussing the governmental approval needed for the establishment of foundations is why foundations in most countries need approval and post-incorporation supervision at all, since other private entities are not usually subject to similar requirements. Since all countries require that legal entities, whether charitable or not, fall under the supervision of the tax authorities, it is not very controversial to require that foundations be subject to tax-authority supervision.

Given the characteristics of foundations, governmental approval for a foundation's establishment, or, at least, some governmental supervision during the establishment of a foundation, may be justified.[11]

One justification for requiring pre-incorporation approval or post-incorporation supervision of a foundation pursuing general interest aims might be to protect the interests of beneficiaries as well as of third parties that might rely on the charitable status of the foundation when making a donation or volunteering some help. This seems to be the grounds for heightened supervision in countries like England, Scotland, Ireland and Wales, where all charitable entities are under the supervision of a public authority. Since pursuing public interest goals is usually considered a matter of public law (see 3.2), the activities of a private entity undertaken in the pursuit of such public interest goals might arguably justify public authority supervision.

The second justification for state supervision is the need to protect the donor's will. A foundation's particular characteristic of being a set of assets with no personal owner to supervise them provides further justification for governmental approval and supervision. Compliance with the donor's will cannot always be supervised by the founder himself or herself, either because of his or her death or because he or she has chosen not to participate actively in the governing board of the foundation.

Furthermore, foundations are only governed by a single governing body obliged to perform all the functions without any higher controlling authority (see also 4.1.7). Other organizations, such as companies or associations, have shareholders or members to oversee the management of the organization's board. Members and shareholders in these organizations take the most significant decisions relating to the organization's accounts, strategy, amendments of statutes and dissolution, to mention but the most crucial matters. Foundations, by contrast, have only a single board or body that is responsible for taking all decisions without any control by other interested persons. This absence of outside control over the management of a foundation is usually another justification for public authorities exercising a degree of supervisory power.

In some countries like Belgium, France and Spain the objections to *mortmain* have also justified legal provisions requiring state approval of the establishment of a foundation. In France, the procedures for a

---

[11] See van Veen: Supervision of Foundations in Europe.

foundation's approval are so complex that obtaining public approval may take between six months and two years.

With respect to the absence or presence of governmental approval in the establishment of foundations, two main groups of jurisdictions may be distinguished among the European countries surveyed:

- those where governmental approval is not required, like the Czech Republic, Estonia, Hungary, Liechtenstein, the Netherlands and Switzerland
- those where such an approval is indispensable for establishing a foundation, like Austria, Belgium, Finland, France, Germany (Article 80 of Civil Code), Luxembourg, Italy (Article 12 of Civil Code), Slovenia, or Spain (Articles 3 and 36 of Foundations Act).

In Switzerland and Liechtenstein, although approval is not required for establishing a foundation, the entity will not have its legal personality recognized until it is registered in the Registry of Commerce. In the countries where no approval is required, a single executed deed, provided that certain formalities are observed, is sufficient for the foundation to acquire legal personality. Nevertheless, the absence of requirement for governmental approval in the setting up of a foundation does not mean an absence of public intervention, as foundations usually remain subject to public supervision – Dutch law is an exception.

Where government approval is required the criteria used and the margin of discretion left to authorities in deciding on whether or not to grant permission to a new foundation varies from one country to another. However, the two main criteria guiding public authorities in granting permission – besides fulfilling the legal requirements – are:

- the necessary amount for the endowment (see 4.1.8)
- the qualifying purposes of the entity (see 6).

Where a minimum fixed amount is required (as in France and Italy), or the qualifying purposes are included in a more or less definite list (as in Belgium, Luxembourg or Spain), the discretion of the authorities is more limited than elsewhere. Authorities have more discretion in jurisdictions without a fixed list of qualifying purposes or where the purposes listed are only broadly specified. In conclusion, the most desirable system for establishing foundations would require a low (or no) endowment amount, and would consider purposes deemed to be of general interest, provided the list of such purposes included a catch-all provision allowing other similar purposes to qualify.

It should be emphasized that the governmental approval discussed in this paragraph differs from fiscal approval or fiscal supervision, the aims of which are more oriented at fiscal considerations than at the recognition of foundations.

4.1.3 Professional advice involved

Around half of the European laws surveyed require a notary or other kind of professional to be involved in the establishment of a foundation. In the other cases, although a professional may not be required, it is advisable to consult one since the laws and procedures for establishing a foundation can be complex.

4.1.4 Acquisition of legal personality

The timing of a foundation's establishment does not necessarily coincide in all legal systems with the foundation's acquisition of legal personality. Regarding the acquisition of legal personality, three different systems may be distinguished in Europe.

- In some countries, like the Netherlands, foundations obtain their legal capacity at the same time as they are established. Therefore, the deed has the effect of both establishing the foundation and attributing legal capacity to it.
- In most countries, where governmental approval is required for the establishment of a foundation, that approval itself attributes legal capacity to the foundation (as distinct from the deed which precedes approval).
- Finally, other countries (Estonia, Hungary, Liechtenstein or Switzerland) do not require governmental approval for the establishment of foundations. In these jurisdictions, a foundation will not acquire legal personality unless it is registered with a registrar. In Finland and Spain, foundations are required to register (in addition to obtaining government approval) in order to acquire legal capacity.

4.1.5 Requirement of statutes

A distinction needs to be made between the deed of constitution and the statutes. The deed usually expresses the donor's will to establish a foundation. In providing for the endowment and the appointment of directors, the statutes are a more detailed document setting out the internal organization and governance of the foundation.

All the countries surveyed require a foundation to be governed according to some organizational documents or statutes. When drafting the statutes, the founders must keep in mind that some jurisdictions do not allow them to be altered easily; the statutes should therefore be a comprehensive document providing for a foundation's governance for eternity.

4.1.6 Number of founders

The experts of most of the countries surveyed emphasize that one of the distinctive characteristics of a foundation compared to other legal entities is the number of persons required to constitute them. While at least two persons are required to constitute an association under most European laws, a single person may establish a foundation, while there is no maximum number of founders permitted.

4.1.7 Internal organization

Most jurisdictions grant the founder a significant degree of discretion when determining the internal organization of the foundation. The relevant laws in these countries contain very few requirements with respect to a foundation's internal governance. In Switzerland, foundations are managed by a governing council or board consisting of at least one person, either legal or natural; in Austria, the minimum size of the board is also one person; in Liechtenstein, foundations are also governed by an administrative council; in the Netherlands, the law provides that the foundation will be represented by a board of directors, unless the statutes provide otherwise; in Germany, the board's function can theoretically be performed by a single person, although in practice the authorities show themselves quite reluctant to accept a single director (unless he or she is the donor). Finally, in Italy, at least two members must serve on the governing board (i.e. the president and someone else); Spanish law requires a minimum of three board members. French law is an exception to the recognition of the founder's will since a maximum of 12 members is permitted for the board. While only a few of the board members may be appointed by the founder (usually one-third), another third will be appointed by the authorities and the remaining third will be co-opted by the other members.

In short, the donor enjoys a large degree of freedom when determining the rules to govern the foundation's internal organization. A single board or council usually governs foundations, and most jurisdictions allow the board to be composed of a single member.

Estonian law differs from other jurisdictions in so far as it requires foundations to have a multitiered structure consisting of a management board, a supervisory board and an auditor. In Finland, the presence of two auditors and two deputy auditors is also required.

In Hungary, the management of a foundation may be transferred to an existing legal entity to perform the supervisory duties instead of a governing board.

4.1.8 *Minimum endowment*

European jurisdictions know two concepts of dealing with endowment specifications. Some countries do not require a minimum capital for the establishment of a foundation, but rather require that the foundation's capital must be reasonably proportionate to the purposes to be pursued. This is the case in countries like Estonia, where a court can dissolve a foundation if its assets have become insufficient; Sweden, where the capital must be adequate for the purposes; Germany, where the required amount may vary from one state to another but is typically around DEM100,000 (€51,129) and must be adequate for the purposes; and Austria, where the endowment should be sufficient to pursue the goals for eternity. Other countries specify an exact minimum requirement for endowing a foundation on its establishment, like the Czech Republic, where CZK500,000 (€13,730) are required for a foundation (not for endowment trusts); Italy, where Lit.200,000,000 (€103,291) are required unless the foundation holds real property, or Liechtenstein, where CHF30,000 (€19,173) are needed.

In Sweden, collection foundations do not require any initial capital. But in this kind of foundation one or more persons must provide in a charter that money paid to the foundation after an appeal to the public will be independent property and will remain earmarked for the pursuit of certain purposes.

French law follows a hybrid system, as it requires FrF5 million (€762,245) as a minimum endowment, but the amount may be even higher depending on the aims that the foundation pursues – between 5 or 7 million French francs. The endowment can be lower for foundations established by companies pursuant to Act number 90.559 of July 4 1990.

In England, no minimum endowment is specified, although the lack of sufficient financial means could lead to a considerable delay in being registered with the Charity Commission.

Many foundations in Europe are endowed with large inheritances. However, the minimum amount required to constitute a foundation usually does not support a foundation's activities for a long time, except at a very limited level. French law may be an exception to this rule. The legislative rationale for not requiring a large amount of money or assets when establishing a foundation is that foundations should not be static inheritances incurring expenses, but rather active organizations that should generate or collect extra funds to survive and pursue their aims. Here the relevance of allowing foundations to pursue commercial activities may be noted. In such jurisdictions not stipulating a high threshold, the amount required to establish a foundation is perceived more as a seed to be sown and grown than as a harvest to feed a foundation's whole existence.

It should be noted that in some jurisdictions certain heirs ('forced heirs') of private estates are protected. Where a compulsory percentage of someone's inheritance may be reserved by law to certain defined descendants, endowing a foundation with assets that exceed such a percentage might lead to a challenge of the endowment by the heirs in court. (See Gallop: Cross-border Issues facing Foundations and their Donors, 4.2, for a discussion of the implications of forced heirship rules in Europe).

4.2 Membership organizations

The laws of England and Wales, Ireland and Scotland enable companies limited by guarantee to act as charities, that is to act in a way equivalent to foundations.[12] These charitable companies do not usually have any share capital,[13] but have members, at least one of whom who must guarantee the debts and obligations of the company up to a stated amount in the event of dissolution.[14] Companies limited by guarantee are separate legal entities incorporated under general law. In Germany, companies acting as foundations may have a share capital and their shareholders may recover their capital in the event of dissolution, although all other assets in the company must be earmarked for nonprofit purposes.

The incorporation of a charitable company limited by guarantee requires the drafting of a memorandum and articles of association and then filing them with the registrar or house of companies. In Ireland, at least seven subscribers are required for the incorporation of a company limited by guarantee.

---

[12] See Drobnig: Foundations as Institutionalized Charitable Activity, 6.2.

[13] It is rare, although possible to establish an English charitable company with share capital. In that case, the shareholders may not be entitled to the distribution of profits or a surplus dissolution.

[14] The amount stated for guarantee is usually: £100 in Scotland; in England and Wales there is no minimum capital requirement; £1 per member in Ireland.

The incorporation of a company limited by guarantee and the acquisition of legal personality do not automatically signify the acquisition of charitable status. A company must seek confirmation of its charitable status from the Charity Commission in England and Wales, the Scottish Charities Office in Scotland or the Inland Revenue Commissioners in Ireland. In order to turn an ordinary company into a nonprofit body, its statutes must include a clause prohibiting the distribution of profits or assets to its members. As a result of that clause, the company's assets must be earmarked to go to other charitable entities or similar charitable purposes in the event of dissolution.

With regard to the internal organization, no general rules may be stated, because they can vary considerably from one jurisdiction to another. In England and Wales no minimum or maximum number of members of the board of directors is required; in Scotland, companies must appoint a company secretary, and in Ireland at least two directors are required to govern the company.

Companies may acquire charitable status, whereas, in general, charities are prohibited from converting to non-charitable companies and thereby losing their charitable status.

4.3 Charitable trusts

As mentioned before, a trust does not itself enjoy legal personality, although it has some legal capacity once it comes into existence. The procedure for creating a trust is again separate from the one needed for the trust to have its charitable status recognized. Trust-like devices that exist in some continental European jurisdictions will not be considered here.[15]

Under the laws of England and Wales, Ireland and Scotland, the first step consists of the settlor signing a deed of trust identifying certain items: the identity of the trustees, the endowment, and the object of the trust. At least in Scotland, the deed must invariably be in writing and formally signed. The trustees must be appointed in the deed, and be committed with an endowment in order to establish the trust and attain its purposes. It should be noted that there is no minimum capital required and that the purposes of the trust must also be defined in the deed.

---

[15] See Drobnig: Foundations as Institutionalized Charitable Activity, 6.4 and Gallop: Cross-border Issues facing Foundations and their Donors, 2.1.2.

Once the trust deed is duly signed by the settlor of the trust, the deed must be delivered to the trustees with the committed property. Then the trust comes into existence under general law, although it cannot yet be considered a charitable trust until recognition, as mentioned above.

The procedure is quite flexible, as incorporation, governmental approval and professional participation are not required, although it is advisable to have the trust deed drafted by a professional.

A single settlor may create a trust, without specifying anything in particular about the trust's internal organizational structure. Nevertheless, the following restrictions may be observed.[16] Although theoretically a single trustee may act as the sole trustee, the Charity Commission of England and Wales would object to the registration of a trust with a single trustee, unless it was a legal entity. If the trust holds land, at least two trustees must be appointed for the trustees to be able to give a purchaser a good receipt on sale. In the case of Scottish trusts, the Lord Advocate may appoint additional trustees to a charitable trust to bring the number of trustees up to three. Beyond this, the organizational arrangements will very much depend on the contents of the deed and on how the trustee or the body of trustees decide to manage the trust.

In Cyprus, the trustees of any charity may apply to the Council of Ministers for a certificate of registration of any such charity as a corporate body. Thereupon the trustees will become a body corporate (Section 2 of the Charities Law).

5 Registration requirements

Most laws in Europe, except a few like Belgium's or Sweden's,[17] require foundations to be inscribed in a public register. There are different systems regarding the type of registrar institution where foundations must be inscribed: some laws specify special registers for foundations and other charitable entities, while other jurisdictions provide for foundations to be inscribed in the general commercial registers. Among the jurisdictions specifying such special registers are Spain and Austria. In Germany, such a system was a topic of discussion in a reform debate. In many other countries foundations do not have their own register, but they share the register with commercial

---

[16] The trustees of a charitable trust may be incorporated; see Drobnig: Foundations as Institutionalized Charitable Activity, 6.4.

[17] Registration is necessary for foundations in trade or business and foundations whose assets are very worthy.

entities (the Czech Republic, Luxembourg, the Netherlands, and Switzerland). In Italy, foundations are inscribed in the general register for legal persons.

Although in some systems the acquisition of legal capacity of the foundation coincides with the inscription in the public register, registration requirements are usually intended more for publicity than for recognition of an organization's legal capacity. The underlying rationale in favour of publicity through the registration of a foundation is the same as for companies and other entities: third parties may need to know whether an institution really exists, who is entitled to sign in its name, and whether there are restrictions on its ability to enter into contracts. Public registers serve the purpose of securing legal transactions against lack of information and lack of transparency.

6 Qualifying purposes[18]

All countries define certain criteria that have to be met for an institution to qualify as a charitable foundation ('charitable' and 'foundation' being two separate concepts that give rise to either legal or fiscal consequences). In some countries, the 'charitable' criteria are legal requirements that an institution must satisfy in order to qualify for incorporation as a 'foundation', while in other countries the criteria, if met, enable the foundation, which is established by meeting a different set of legal criteria, to qualify as 'charitable', and thus to be eligible for tax privileges. For instance, in Belgium, a foundation may only be created for the pursuit of a public utility purpose, defined by law as being religious, philanthropic, scientific, educational or artistic. If an institution does not pursue one of these stated purposes it may not be established as a foundation. Therefore, pursuing one of these qualifying purposes is a legal precondition to incorporation. In Belgium, if an institution qualifies for incorporation, the tax privileges, at least the tax exemption for the foundation, will automatically follow. In several other countries, however, a foundation may by law pursue both a private benefit and public benefit. The actual purpose pursued by the foundation will, however, be examined to determine whether the foundation qualifies for charitable status, entitling it to tax privileges. In these jurisdictions, the qualifying purposes give rise to tax, not legal, consequences.

---

[18] A distinction may also arise between fiscal and civil law requirements considering the purposes of a foundation.

Although in some jurisdictions the legal form of a 'foundation' may be used to serve either public interest or private benefit purposes, according to most European laws, foundations that pursue private benefit purposes are not considered to be charitable, as such status usually requires a foundation or other nonprofit entity to pursue some 'public utility' or 'public interest' purposes.

An analysis of the laws of the various jurisdictions shows that charitable status is only awarded to those entities that pursue goals that benefit the whole of society or at least a large, unspecified part of it. A similar principle is expressed in many different ways: the pursuit of 'socially useful activities' (Italy), 'generally useful or charitable aims' (Slovenia), serving 'public purpose' (Hungary), the 'public interest' (Luxembourg), a 'useful purpose' (Finland) or 'public purposes' (Germany). Goals should, amongst others, be 'beneficial to the community' (England, Wales and Scotland), conducive to the 'advancement of the community' (Austria), for the 'public benefit' (Estonia), or institutions should pursue 'general interest aims' (Spain). In other words, although the terms defining the purposes that are eligible for charitable status may vary from one jurisdiction to another, the general principle underlying these definitions is almost identical in all the countries surveyed. A few common elements may be found in the definitions of purposes that entitle an entity to be recognized as a charity and these are listed below.

- Purposes should provide a benefit to the public at large, advance the community at large, or provide benefits to a large segment of society or act for the common good.
- Beneficiaries should be indefinite or be such a large number that private, individual benefits are excluded. In Scotland, including both private and public interests in the definition of a foundation's purposes will exclude the entity from being charitable (for instance, foundations created to preserve historical buildings benefit the whole society but also benefit, more directly, members or owners). Federal law in Austria considers an entity to be charitable even though it may benefit a particular group of persons, and Spanish law provides for foundations pursuing the preservation of historical monuments to be acknowledged, even though their owners may also receive a benefit, as long as the community benefits as well. German law allows for up to one-third of the income of an otherwise charitable foundation to be paid out to its donor or the family for the purpose of their maintenance without endangering the foundation's charitable status.

- Foundations are considered charitable in countries such as Spain and Switzerland if their purposes do not benefit specific persons or members of a family. Although the existence of family foundations is permitted in Germany (they were historically considered as serving the common good because they freed the government from caring for needy family members) family foundations are currently viewed as producing private benefits and thus not entitled to charitable status.

- One exception to the private benefit restriction mentioned in the preceding paragraph is when the purpose is to help employees of a company. Although the employees of a company are not indefinite or inspecific, some laws, such as the Spanish one, attribute charitable status to foundations aiming to help employees. In Germany, however, these purposes are considered to be of 'private benefit' and foundations pursuing such purposes fail to be eligible as charities. Meanwhile, in Sweden a special type of foundation, called a 'profit sharing foundation', can be created for the purpose of granting a right to the employees to participate in a company's profits. This type of foundation is not, however, considered charitable.

- Besides the well-known four heads of charity in Ireland, Scotland, England and Wales (the advancement of religion, the advancement of education, the relief of poverty and other purposes beneficial to the community), many other aims can be pursued by foundations according to the law in other jurisdictions: the promotion of philanthropic, religious, scientific, artistic or educational purposes in Belgium; or aid for the development and support of members of the army and their families in case of economic hardship in Italy.

- Jurisdictions such as England and Wales, Ireland and Scotland prohibit a charitable foundation from carrying on political activities, unless such activities are ancillary to the charity's purposes.

- **One fundamental criterion for recognition of charitable status prevails over any of the above-mentioned considerations: the entity must be nonprofit-distributing in nature** (i.e. it may not distribute any profits or earnings to 'owners', managers, staff or other persons closely associated with the foundation).

In several jurisdictions (Germany, Liechtenstein, the Netherlands and Switzerland), the distinction between a charitable and a non-charitable entity is more concerned with its fiscal status than with the nature of the legal body.

7 Amendments and conversions

Two different concepts may be observed concerning the regulation of amendments, mergers, split-offs or conversions in Europe. Although jurisdictions generally acknowledge the generosity of the founder endowing a foundation, his or her will is neither the only nor necessarily the most relevant factor to consider when the rules governing an existing foundation are to be amended. Since a foundation is supposed to act in the pursuit of the common good, the public's interest can be seen to justify some legal limitations on the donor's will. Circumstances may arise in which the authorities have to give priority to the general interest or the public interest over the donor's will. When these two considerations are in conflict, foundation law has to reconcile them by finding a balance between the respect due to the donor's will and to the public interest. The more time that has passed since the establishment of the foundation, the greater the tension between these two factors will probably be, because the circumstances under which the foundation was established are likely to have changed significantly.

The founder can reduce the risk of conflicts arising by attempting to foresee changes of circumstance under which the foundation may operate in the future and by providing sufficient powers (in the creation deed or the statutes) to the directors to take the necessary steps to make the required changes. If such changes are foreseen and accounted for, no problem will usually arise when amending the statutes because of mergers, split-offs or any other alteration of the founder's will, such as conversion.[19]

7.1 Amendments

Where the donor has prohibited or not foreseen any such alterations, and circumstances require them, the tension between the donor's will and the public interest will increase. In these cases a decision must be taken and will vary in the degree of respect given to the donor's original will. Some jurisdictions, such as Bulgaria, Estonia, Greece, Liechtenstein, the Netherlands, and Spain tend to give preference to the fulfilment of the general interest, while other countries, such as Germany and Switzerland tend to give greater preference to the

---

[19] In France, founders have less freedom in drafting the foundation's statutes as they must use a model adopted by the *Conseil d'Etat*. The approval of the public authorities, whether governmental or judicial, may still be required for an amendment, merger, split-off or conversion.

respect of the founder's will. A special case may be found under English and Welsh law (and very similar under Finnish law), where the Charity Commission may allow changes in the purposes pursued if:

- the charitable goals demonstrate a general rather than a specific charitable intention
- the purposes of the charity have become impossible to fulfil
- only a part of the gift can be utilized for the originally intended purposes
- the property of the charity could better be amalgamated with other charities' property to the same end
- the original purposes are no longer suitable, being outdated or already fulfilled.

Whether preference is given to the donor's will or to the general interest, any adjustment of the foundation's organization to cope with altered circumstances is made by amending the foundation's statutes. The laws in all countries surveyed allow the founder's will to be altered.

- In England and Wales, the procedure for amending the statutes varies depending on the aspects needing alteration. The objectives of the charity may only be amended if the trustees have a specific power to do so.
- In Switzerland, only the supervisory authority, in consultation with the governing board may alter the statutes, although in general, a foundation's purposes cannot be altered by choice.
- In Germany, the board may alter the statutes by obtaining the approval of the authorities. The authorities may even take the initiative to amend a foundation's purposes when they have become obsolete or contrary to the common welfare (in Spain the system is quite similar to the one in Germany).
- In Liechtenstein, statutes may be amended when they themselves provide for it, otherwise third parties or any participant in the foundation may request an amendment, but in these two cases the approval of the public register is required.
- In the Netherlands, the board may amend the statutes only if the statutes provide for such a possibility; otherwise, the district court has the authority to amend them.
- In Belgium, the statutes may be amended only by law or pursuant to an agreement between the government and a majority of the foundation's directors.

- If the statutes of a Luxembourg foundation do not provide for the power to make an amendment, the approval of the authorities and the consent of the majority of directors are required.
- If the aim of an Italian foundation has been achieved or barely results in a public benefit, the government can approve or can on its own initiative amend the foundation's purposes according to the will of the founder.
- Austrian law only allows for changes if it is impossible to carry out the foundation's purpose without changing the statutes and then permits only the absolutely necessary changes to be made.
- In Sweden, the amendment of the donor's will requires the permission of the Swedish Judicial Board for Public Lands and Funds.
- In Greece, a presidential decree may amend a foundation's statutes.
- In Hungary, a court order may initiate the merger of two foundations.
- In Estonia, the supervisory board (authority) may amend the articles of a foundation if the founders do not do so or if it has been so empowered in the statutes.
- In Finland, the approval of authorities is necessary to amend a foundation's statutes.

When assessing the various systems with regard to future changes in the rules governing a foundation, it is interesting to consider whether all provisions stated by the founder should enjoy the same protection from amendment. There are some issues addressed in a foundation's statutes, such as its goals, the definition of beneficiaries, the rules for appointing the members of the board, or the final destination of the funds in case of liquidation that seem to deserve a stronger guarantee against amendments than other organizational provisions, such as the address of the foundation, the way the directors meet or how they adopt decisions. The differentiation between the deed and the statutes could serve a useful purpose in distinguishing between 'unalterable' stipulations and less significant provisions that need to be included merely as part of the procedure of creating a foundation. In Finland and Sweden protection from amendment differs according to the provisions to be amended.

A last thought concerning modern foundations must be kept in mind when dealing with the amendment of the founder's will. As stated before, the respect for the founder's will originates from the acknowledgement of the original transfer of private assets in the form of an endowment to the foundation. However, provided that in some countries the amount required to set up a foundation is not large (in

Spain the minimum required is around €6000) and the public interest may deserve consideration, the prevailing weight to be given to the founder's will could be questioned.

7.2 Conversions

Procedures for mergers, split-offs or conversions involving charitable foundations are not often addressed in the laws of the countries surveyed. Some jurisdictions, such as Estonia, Luxembourg, and the Netherlands, do not provide for special procedures or formalities in the case of mergers, split-offs or conversions (see, for example, section 18, Part 1, Book 2 of Dutch Civil Code for conversions). In Germany conversions have been discouraged.

This chapter will focus on the issue of conversions as a deeper examination is required of the balance between diverse interests: of the public, the donors and the other stakeholders in the foundation. (See also van Veen: Supervision of Foundations in Europe, 4.3.) To talk about converting other legal entities into charitable foundations may sound rather odd in many countries where the influence of Roman law is especially strong. However, in many other jurisdictions it is a relatively common practice to consider converting legal entities into charitable foundations.

Actually, in the light of the interests involved, it would be more reasonable and much more practical for the law to allow and provide for the conversion of other legal bodies into charitable foundations. There are at least three main reasons for providing legal procedures for such conversions. Before enumerating these reasons, however, it should be recalled that modern societies are under pressure to maintain flexibility and provide for a variety of legal instruments for achieving their general interest aims. For instance, in Spain and other countries where conversion is not provided for by law, interested parties can circumvent the restrictions by following complicated and expensive procedures, such as dissolving the former entity, then taking all assets and transferring them to the new foundation, or by a foundation establishing an affiliated new institution and keeping both entities alive, which entails inefficiencies.

- The first reason is related to the security of creditors, employees and holders of rights against the existing entity. There is more security and guarantees for these interested parties in those jurisdictions where the company or the association involved may be converted into a foundation since there is continuity in the legal personality, contracts and legal relations. Where the law does not provide for conversion, the dissolution of the existing entity in order to convert it into a foundation entails the termination of all relationships in which the entity was a party and hence gives less guarantee for third parties.

- The second reason is the cost of the non-conversion: both dissolving the original entity and maintaining two entities – the new foundation and the original institution – in existence involves high costs.
- And finally, general interests are better served when an entity, initially conceived to make a profit or to achieve a private interest, may be converted into a charitable foundation than when such possibility is not provided or allowed by law. The more resources that are earmarked for the general interests the better the general society should be served.

In Austria, Estonia, Finland, Hungary, Spain, Sweden, and Switzerland, the law does not provide any legal instruments for converting a company or an association into a foundation. Since every form of entity seems so essentially different from other forms – different in their legal nature – the law does not deal with conversions that alter the very nature of an entity. In a couple of other countries, like Germany or Luxembourg, no special procedure for conversion exists.

By contrast, in a few other jurisdictions conversions are a common procedure for legal persons. In the Netherlands, where the decision to convert an entity into a foundation must be made by at least 90% of the votes cast in favour, the statutes must be amended to bring them into compliance with the requirements of the new legal form, and the permission of the district court is needed (section 18, Part 1 Book 2 of Civil Code). In Denmark, however, the conversion of other legal forms into a foundation involves fewer requirements.

In Ireland, Scotland, England and Wales no other legal bodies can convert themselves into a trust, although it is possible for a non-charitable trust to convert into a charitable one. This conversion may be carried out when the deed gives sufficient powers to the trustees to do so. If there are good reasons, a charitable trust may seek authority from the Charity Commission of England and Wales to transfer its assets to a new one.

In this respect, conversions of any other legal bodies to foundations may be distinguished from conversions of foundations to other legal forms. It should be underlined that a conversion of a foundation into a legal form that does not guarantee the pursuit of public interest objectives or the nonprofit nature of the organization, may betray the confidence and efforts that donors and volunteers put into the foundation. Therefore, although in England, Wales and Scotland conversions of entities are allowed as a general rule, when they take place from a foundation into another entity that does not have charitable status, they are forbidden unless special authorization is obtained. In England, Wales and Scotland, even though a specific power to convert is attributed to trustees, a charitable trust is prohibited from abandoning its charitable status. A similar rule seems to apply under Austrian law (although conversions of public benefit foundations to private foundations are allowed under Article 38 of the Private Foundations Act) when converting a general interest foundation into a private benefit foundation for the purpose of accumulating the settlor's private wealth. In the Netherlands, court permission is required to convert a charitable foundation to another form, and after the conversion of a foundation, judicial approval is again required for the new legal entity to use the assets of the former foundation for a purpose other than that of the original foundation.

8 Dissolution

A comprehensive analysis of a legal person, such as a foundation, should cover all the stages in its legal existence: its establishment, amendments during its existence and its dissolution. When discussing a foundation's dissolution, the core issues relate to bankruptcy and the disposal of assets on liquidation.

8.1 Bankruptcy

Creditors confronted with the bankruptcy of a charity should keep in mind that in some countries charitable status may give special protection to the charity's assets, as was the case under Spanish law until the law of 1994. Nowadays legal scholars in Spain do not agree on whether or not a judge wishing to enforce a creditor's right should first address the supervisory authorities. In most countries the laws do not provide any special stipulations for this case (see Italian, Swiss or Portuguese Civil Codes). However, article 86 of the German Civil Code contains a reference granting a privilege to foundations against creditors that may extend far beyond the problems of a creditor trying to recover from a foundation. Companies or individuals wishing to sign contracts with foundations may ask for extra guarantees, such as insurance or third parties' guarantees, in case the foundation breaches the contract. Such additional measures, however, cause transactions to be more expensive for foundations.

8.2 Distribution of assets

Two main legal systems exist for the disposal of assets on liquidation.

- According to the first system, the law does not expressly refer to the question or it recognizes the discretion of the founder or of the board of directors to designate the assets.
- In the second system, the law restricts the destination of assets, for instance, by requiring that the assets be distributed to other charitable entities, or by requiring spending on similar purposes or amongst the beneficiaries stated in the statutes.

Some jurisdictions, such as Finland, Hungary, Italy, Luxembourg, the Netherlands, and Switzerland, require only that the funds be distributed upon liquidation according to the provisions in the statutes. The laws in these jurisdictions do not impose specific requirements for the distribution of the assets.

Charitable companies limited by guarantee in Ireland, Scotland, England and Wales must expressly prohibit in their articles of association the distribution of any property or assets of the companies to their members. The articles of association must thus provide that in case of dissolution, all company property will be contributed or transferred to some other charitable body. Laws in Austria, the Czech Republic, Denmark, Spain and Sweden provide similar clauses. The destination must be for charitable purposes or be to charitable entities. Such a destination must also be fulfilled in Liechtenstein if a foundation wishes to obtain and maintain tax benefits. In Cyprus and Estonia, tax laws prevent foundations from distributing the assets among its members. In Germany and Slovenia the surplus after liquidation must be distributed for the purposes stated in the foundation's statutes. In Belgium, assets are transferred to the government in order to allocate them to purposes as close as possible to those originally intended. In Bulgaria and Greece, assets are also given to the government and seem to remain within public agencies.

The reader may notice that in those legal systems where the assets on liquidation are distributed for the pursuit of similar goals or to other charitable organizations, as required by law, the assets have a stronger link to the purposes for which they were earmarked rather than to legal bodies that held them. Although a foundation may be dissolved, merged or converted, the earmarking for some specific purposes does not accompany the legal entity but the assets. Whatever the assets may be destined for, the earmarked end accompanies them. Even if the entity holding the assets is dissolved, these assets remain earmarked for the charitable interest.

Bibliography

Badenes Gasset, R., *Las fundaciones de Derecho privado*, Vols. I and II, Bosch, ed., Barcelona, 1986.

Beneyto, R., *Fundaciones sociales de la Iglesia católica. Conflicto Iglesia-Estado*, Edicep, ed., Valencia, 1996.

De Castro, F., *La persona jurídica*, Madrid, Civitas, 1981.

De Lorenzo R. *et al.*, *Comentarios a la ley de fundaciones y de incentivos fiscales*, Vol. I, Escuela Libre Editorial and Marcial Pons, ed., Madrid, 1995.

De Lorenzo R., *El nuevo Derecho de fundaciones*, Marcial Pons and Fundación ONCE, ed., Madrid, 1993.

García-Andrade J., *La fundación: un estudio jurídico*, Madrid, Escuela Libre Editorial, 1997.

Pomey, M., *Traité de fondations d'utilité publique*, Paris, Presses Universitaires de France, 1980.

▼ Paul Bater and Oliver Habighorst

Tax Treatment of Foundations and their Donors

1 Introduction

This chapter examines from a comparative perspective the tax treatment in Europe of nonprofit foundations established for purposes of public benefit. From a fiscal perspective such foundations should be distinguished from family foundations, which in some states may be eligible for tax relief but generally fall outside the scope of tax privileges that are granted to public benefit organizations as a matter of public policy.

In this chapter the authors are concerned primarily with the tax treatment in domestic law of the foundation itself, its founders and other donors to the foundation. Certain tax and tax-related issues (such as the definition of public benefit purposes, fiscal sanctions, and cross-border taxation) are addressed only incidentally in this chapter and, where appropriate, the reader is referred to other chapters of this book for a fuller discussion of the issues.

In contrast to the legal aspects of foundations discussed in the other chapters, the tax law applicable to foundations in the UK is the same throughout the three legal jurisdictions (England and Wales, Scotland, and Northern Ireland). Consequently, the observations in this chapter concerning the tax treatment of foundations in the UK can, unless otherwise stated, be assumed to apply to all foundations, whether established in England and Wales, Scotland or Northern Ireland.

The discussion is structured as follows.

- In the first part, the structure of the various tax systems in Europe is described. The tax privileges that are available to facilitate the work of the foundation are then compared, including the foundation's ability to earn income from commercial activities.
- In the second part, the tax reliefs applicable to donors are considered, as regards both the initial endowment of a foundation and subsequent gifts to the foundation.
- Finally, the authors draw conclusions on the present state of the tax laws on foundations in Europe and their future development.

2 Tax treatment of a foundation

The tax systems in the 24 jurisdictions included in this survey are substantially similar in structure, although significant differences in the detailed interpretation of the relevant laws and their application to foundations remain.

As a matter of tax policy, all states grant some tax privileges to non-profit foundations. In this respect foundations do not generally receive either more or less generous treatment than other forms of nonprofit public benefit organizations.

2.1 Indirect tax privileges

The main sources of revenue from indirect taxes are customs duties and value added tax (VAT). All the countries surveyed are members of the World Trade Organization, including Estonia, which has recently been admitted to membership now that it has amended its domestic laws to comply with its commitments as a member. These commitments require member countries to apply import taxes on the basis of a common tariff standard and to reduce those taxes over time.

All countries have also introduced VAT. While different tax rates apply in different states, the tax base has been substantially harmonized in the EU member states by the EC 6th VAT Directive[1] and those states seeking admission to the EU will be required to adapt their VAT law as necessary to comply with the 6th Directive. Outside the EU, two of the states in the European Economic Area (EEA), Liechtenstein and Switzerland, form a separate customs union that operates a common system of VAT modelled on the EC law.

In the field of indirect taxes the extent to which the tax base has already been harmonized within Europe limits the freedom of individual states to grant tax privileges to foundations. As regards customs duties, their impact on foundations is in any event generally limited, by the nature of their activities, to the import or export of goods for public benefit purposes by those foundations that are permitted or choose to conduct their activities directly rather than indirectly by making grants to fund the operations of other NGOs.

The European customs and VAT exemptions for cross-border transactions are addressed in detail in Gallop: Cross-border Issues Facing Foundations and their Donors, 2.5.1 and 2.5.2.

2.1.1 VAT exemptions for domestic transactions

Exemption from VAT is granted for specific supplies of goods and services rather than as a general relief for the tax-payer making the supply. The scope of the exemptions available under EC law for public interest activities, as prescribed in the 6th VAT Directive, includes the following services which foundations may be undertaking: hospital and medical care; welfare and social security; protection of children; education; sport; culture; fundraising; and transport services for sick or injured persons.[2]

VAT costs for foundations

The effect of VAT on foundations requires a more detailed explanation. In contrast to the way in which other taxes work, the fact that a foundation is not subject to VAT or that the goods and services that it supplies to its beneficiaries are exempt from VAT does not mean that the foundation bears no VAT costs. VAT was conceived as a tax on the final consumer of goods and services: in most cases this will be an individual member of the public buying from a retail outlet for his or her private use. Business consumers can usually pass on the VAT that they pay on their purchases of similar goods and services to their own

---

[1] Sixth Council Directive of 17 May 1977 on the harmonization of legislation of member states concerning turnover taxes (77/388/EEC), O.J. No. L 145 of 13 June 1977.

[2] Article 13, 6th VAT Directive.

customers so that the only costs they incur as tax-payers are the costs of recording, administering and collecting the tax from their customers for the benefit of the government.

Most foundations, and indeed other forms of nonprofit organization, are in a different position as the design of VAT requires that it is imposed on all forms of economic activity, whether or not for profit. Yet the nonprofit character of a foundation's purposes limits its ability to pass on to its beneficiaries, and their ability to pay, the VAT that is charged to the foundation on its own purchases of goods and services. Any VAT that a foundation does not pass on to its beneficiaries, whether by reason of law (because the foundation does not carry on an economic activity or because the economic activity concerned is exempt from VAT) or by choice (because its beneficiaries cannot afford to pay the extra cost) becomes a permanent cost to the foundation. Thus, a foundation that is not subject to or 'exempt' from VAT will generally pay more VAT than one that is 'fully taxable'.

As with customs duties, the harmonization of the tax base by the EC 6th VAT Directive allows individual states limited discretion to grant relief from VAT to foundations. It would be possible for states to grant relief indirectly (e.g. through public expenditure by making compensatory grants or increasing existing grants to foundations) without breaching EC law, but there is no general provision in the EC VAT laws that would allow a member state to grant broad-based relief in the form of a direct reduction of the tax rate or the tax base other than as part of the existing framework of reliefs in the 6th Directive. The UK nonprofit sector has lobbied the UK government for the introduction of a specific grant scheme to compensate the sector for part of its VAT costs but without success to date. In some EU member states it appears that some or all of the VAT costs incurred by certain nonprofit organizations (e.g. those engaged in the provision of services that are priority areas for the allocation of government expenditure, such as health and education) are effectively reimbursed by means of their inclusion in the amount of government grants disbursed by the government departments with responsibility for funding the delivery of the services concerned.

It has been noted above that for VAT purposes it is not usually beneficial to a foundation to have no economic activity. Yet there are two common functions of a foundation that in most circumstances will not give rise to an economic activity in VAT law: grant making and investment. The VAT principle that subjects to tax only supplies of goods and services for a consideration that is linked to the supply generally operates to exclude from liability philanthropic grants to fund the conduct of economic activities by other organizations. In the case of investment operations that are independent of an economic activity, the European Court of Justice has ruled that the investment operations of the largest foundation in the UK (which is reported to be the largest foundation in the world) cannot be regarded as an economic activity in its own right, regardless of the size of the investment portfolio and the organization of its management.[3]

The burden of irrecoverable VAT costs on foundations should not, however, be overstated. Taking the nonprofit sector as a whole, it is estimated that about 60% to 80% of most NGOs' costs are staff costs, which are not subject to VAT. Thus, large amounts of irrecoverable VAT tend to arise only in large NGOs or where a NGO incurs large capital costs, for example on a new building or a computer system. That said, even assuming that there is no further extension of the current limited application of VAT to supplies of real-estate, the burden is likely to increase merely by reason of the growth in size of the nonprofit sector and increases in the price of real-estate.

Existing and potential relief measures for foundations

Within the current structure of the tax, there are two main opportunities for states to reduce the burden:

- to reduce the rate of VAT applicable to goods and services purchased by a foundation
- to tax goods and services supplied by a foundation to its beneficiaries but at a rate that is substantially below the standard VAT rate in force.

The first option benefits all foundations, whether or not they are engaged in economic activity. The second can apply only to those foundations engaged in economic activity; it benefits foundations to the extent that the tax rate is sufficiently low to make it acceptable to pass on the cost to their beneficiaries and that the purchases on which the foundation has incurred most of its VAT costs are used for, or otherwise related to, the provision of the goods and services to the beneficiaries.

In theory, it is possible to minimize the burden by reducing the tax rate to zero. A zero rate means that the foundation does not have to charge VAT on the delivery of its services but, in contrast to an exemption from VAT, it is allowed to reclaim VAT paid on its purchases.

---

[3] *Wellcome Trust Ltd. v. Commissioners of Customs & Excise*, Case C-155/94, ECR [1996] I-3013.

However, the EC has decided as a matter of policy that, in the interests of completing an internal common market, member states should no longer be allowed to apply zero rates except to the extent currently permitted under the terms of a specific derogation granted to a particular state.

In the countries surveyed, only Ireland, Portugal and the UK among the EU member states have reduced to zero the rate of VAT charged on certain goods and services when supplied to foundations (in Greece the relief is limited to imports by specified foundations). Similar reliefs exist in some of the applicants to join the EU (Bulgaria, Cyprus, Hungary) but it remains to be seen whether they will be phased out during the accession process.

None of the EU member states operates a reduced VAT rate for all supplies by foundations to their beneficiaries. Where such reliefs exist, the reduced rate applies only to limited categories of supplies. The broadest relief is found in Belgium, Germany, Greece and Luxembourg where the standard VAT rate is reduced to between 3% and 8% on supplies of social services by foundations in furtherance of their public benefit purposes (in Germany this relief is not available to educational and cultural institutions or to homes for old and disabled people).

Reduced tax rates also apply in some non-member states, for example to supplies of new buildings, repairs of existing buildings, and aid for disabled people (Czech Republic), admission fees to cultural events (Estonia), and to supplies of social housing (Hungary).

Most states (including the EU applicant states) also operate 'small business' exemptions which enable organizations with a low level of economic activity (defined by reference to annual sales) to avoid the requirement to register as a tax-payer and account for VAT on supplies to their customers or beneficiaries. The limit above which registration is required is generally not more than €13,000 except in Austria (€22,400), Ireland (€50,000), and the UK (€65,500).

2.2 Direct tax privileges

With regard to direct taxation, all states impose income taxation on the profits of legal entities and on the income of individuals. For these purposes and subject to special rules in some states to exempt or provide relief for gains arising on the disposal of certain categories of favoured assets (most commonly, shares and securities), most states include capital gains in income and tax such gains or relieve them from taxation accordingly.

All the states surveyed (with the exception of Cyprus and Estonia) levy taxes on the transfer of wealth in the form of a gift and/or inheritance tax; most states require the donee or heir to pay the tax. A minority of states (Finland, Germany, Liechtenstein, Luxembourg, Sweden, Switzerland) also tax the accumulation of wealth by legal entities by imposing a net wealth tax on the annual value of their assets net of any related liabilities.

In contrast to the indirect tax systems in Europe, no attempt has yet been made at a regional or multilateral level to harmonize direct taxation. The EC has shown some interest in proposals to harmonize direct taxation of businesses, notably following its decision to set up the Ruding Committee of Independent Experts on Company Taxation in 1990. However, when the Committee reported in 1992 its main recommendations were not received with great enthusiasm, with the result that limited real progress has been made to date. Consequently, the direct taxes in force in the states surveyed show considerable variations both in the measurement of the tax base and the rates of tax imposed.

A similar divergence is apparent in the field of direct tax policy concerning nonprofit organizations. It is unlikely that this situation will change in the near future, since the EC has indicated that it is inclined to leave the development of tax policy towards the nonprofit sector in the hands of member states on the basis that this approach is in accordance with the principle of subsidiarity.[4]

2.2.1 Definition of public benefit purposes in direct tax policy

In particular, there is no common approach to defining the public benefit criteria that each state uses to determine which categories of nonprofit organizations will be granted tax privileges. Typically, one of the following three approaches is used in the legislation:

- a closed list of public benefit purposes
- an open list of purposes where the wording of the legislation provides for 'other' or 'similar' public benefit purposes to be recognized to those specifically listed
- lack of any definition of public benefit purposes, in which case the recognition of the status of individual nonprofit organizations is determined on a case-by-case basis by the court or the relevant body.

---

[4] See the European Commission communication on 'Promoting the role of voluntary organizations and foundations in Europe', COM (97) 241 final, 6 June 1997.

It should also be noted that some states use a different definition of public benefit purposes for non-tax purposes (see Garcia-Andrade: Establishment, Amendment and Liquidation of Foundations) and for determining which nonprofit organizations can receive gifts that qualify for tax privileges (see 2.2.2).

The closed list approach is found in some civil law states, whereas there are examples of both common-law and civil law countries that have adopted the more flexible approach of the open list. However, there are considerable variations between the number of categories of public benefit purposes that qualify for tax privileges in different civil law states; these range from relatively few listed categories (Belgium, Luxembourg, Sweden) to longer lists (Italy) that may in practice be as broad based as the open list approach. It should also be noted that a state that has specified an apparently closed list in its law might in the practice of the relevant authorities adopt a more open approach: this is the case in Germany.

A minority of states (Finland, Greece) appear to follow the third approach: whether this leads to a relatively open or closed mechanism will depend on the policy of the decision-making body in each state.

The different tax treatment accorded to some categories of foundation straddles the different legal systems in Europe. Organizations that promote amateur sport receive tax privileges in most countries, but not in Belgium or the UK. Support for the environment receives explicit approval in some states (Austria, Bulgaria, Estonia, Slovenia). Some states (e.g. Austria) restrict the geographical area of operation to the territory of the state concerned when granting tax privileges, although most states recognize organizations engaged in international aid activities for the benefit of people in need in developing countries.

These variations can be explained partly by the different legal concepts of public benefit in the various legal jurisdictions. The legal meaning of 'charity' in the three states with a common-law background (Cyprus, Ireland, UK) originated outside tax law and was largely developed by the courts in these countries in the course of determining the validity of gifts intended to support a purpose; it was adopted, essentially unchanged, by the legislature for the purpose of determining which organizations should qualify for tax privileges. The civil law states show a more diversified approach, ranging from the relatively liberal attitude in the Netherlands to the more restrictive regimes in France, Belgium and Luxembourg. Such restrictions tend to reflect historical tensions between the state and foundations.[5]

Differences in the procedure required to obtain direct tax privileges (see 2.2) may also influence the approach to defining public benefit purposes. It can be predicted that, if the definition of such purposes or its application lies in the hands of the tax authorities, they are more likely to adopt a restrictive approach to the interpretation of the law (in order to protect revenue) than, for example, a government department with a specific responsibility for public expenditure in furtherance of one or more areas of public benefit. These considerations also have a bearing on the flexibility of the law in each state to adapt the meaning of public benefit purposes to reflect changing conditions in society.

2.2.2 Prohibited activities

The restrictions most commonly found on the activities of foundations are restrictions on political and commercial activities. The taxation of commercial activities is discussed in 2.2.5 below.

Most states restrict political activities to some extent, either by a specific prohibition in the law on foundations or the tax law, or by excluding political activities from the definition or interpretation of which activities satisfy the public benefit test (see Drobnig, Garcia-Andrade and van Veen). The most liberal states in this regard are the Netherlands (which assumes political activities to be in the public interest), Spain and Switzerland (which permit political activities if in the public interest). Specific prohibition of political activities is found in Germany, Hungary and Liechtenstein. The UK can be said to follow a middle course, distinguishing between political purposes (which are prohibited, e.g. support for political parties) and most forms of political activity (e.g. lobbying and campaigning) which are generally permitted, provided that they are undertaken in pursuit of the organization's stated public benefit purposes).

Other limitations on the activities of foundations include restrictions on permitted investments and minimum distribution requirements (van Veen: Supervision of Foundations in Europe). These restrictions can have fiscal consequences to the extent that failure to comply with the law leads to total or partial loss of tax privileges. Some countries specify that a minimum percentage of income must be applied to the

---

[5] See 'Das internationale rechtliche Umfeld' by Dr. Frits W. Hondius in *Handbuch Stiftungen*, ed. Bertelsmann Stiftung, Gabler Verlag, Wiesbaden, 1998.

stated public benefit purposes (e.g. 80% over a five-year period in Sweden; 70% over three years in Spain). Others provide simply that exemption from income tax is conditional on the income being applied to public benefit purposes (e.g. Ireland, UK). A minority of states also restrict tax privileges if the foundation makes investments that are not authorized by law (e.g. in the UK, investment in unlisted shares, including shares in a subsidiary company, requires prior approval by the tax authorities).

Other anti-abuse measures may be found in the tax laws instead of or in addition to the specific laws regulating the formation and governance of foundations, for example activities that confer a material benefit on an individual connected with the foundation are specifically prohibited by the tax law in some countries (Estonia, Slovenia).

Aside from specific anti-abuse measures, there is a more general rule of law in several states (e.g. France, Netherlands) that can operate to deny the validity of a foundation, even if the purposes stated in the governing document are admitted to be of public benefit, on the grounds that the establishment of the foundation is an abuse of law (*fraus legis*). The concept of abuse of law is found in both tax law and general law. Its application to the creation of a foundation implies that the governing document does not reveal the real intentions of the founder, usually where an act of essentially private benefit is masquerading as a gift for the benefit of the public.

2.2.3 *Procedure for obtaining tax privileges*

The procedure for a foundation to obtain tax privileges also varies considerably, regardless of the legal system concerned. The principal forms of procedure found in Europe are:

- application to the tax authority
- decision by Ministry of Finance (Cyprus, Luxembourg)
- decision by non-departmental (semi-independent) government body (the Charity Commission in England and Wales);
- decision by court (Hungary).

In a minority of jurisdictions (Austria, England and Wales, Finland, Hungary, Italy, Slovenia) the decision on the public benefit status of the foundation will automatically determine its entitlement to tax privileges. In the other states access to tax privileges is decided separately.

In several states (Austria, Bulgaria, Greece, Netherlands, Sweden) there is no formal procedure; tax privileges must be claimed when appropriate and are granted or refused on an *ad hoc* basis. This lack of a formal procedure is mitigated in some cases (Austria, Netherlands, Sweden) by the availability of advance rulings on public benefit status, although such rulings are not always binding on the tax authority (Austria). Advance rulings are also found in states with a formal procedure (Germany).

2.2.4 Income tax privileges

The sources of income of nonprofit organizations can generally be divided into three classes:

- grants and other forms of support from central and local government
- private giving (donations and other forms of raising funds from the public)
- self-generated income (income from investments and income from the provision of goods and services).

Most income tax systems do not include public sector grants and subsidies in taxable income unless the grant is funding a form of commercial activity. Even so, most states distinguish between those commercial activities that are related to the nonprofit purposes of the organization ('related business income') and those that are not ('unrelated business income'). This distinction is discussed further below in 2.2.5.

Similarly, donations are not generally regarded as taxable income unless the recipient is providing the donor with a valuable benefit in connection with the gift or where there is some other personal connection with the donor. The tax treatment of other forms of fundraising, such as fundraising events and sponsorship, typically depends on whether the nature of the fundraising activity can be assimilated to a donation or whether it resembles more closely a commercial activity.

The taxation of investment income is particularly important to foundations because of their reliance on endowments. The most common approaches found in the survey were:

- to exempt all investment income
- to exempt certain categories of income and tax others at normal or special rates
- to tax investment income only at the lower withholding tax rates applicable to certain categories of income.

Full exemption was found in Estonia, Finland, Ireland, Liechtenstein, Luxembourg, Switzerland, and the UK. Tax is withheld in Cyprus, Germany and the Netherlands but it can be reclaimed by the foundation; withholding tax is also imposed in Austria and Belgium but these states do not allow the tax to be refunded. The mixed approach operates in Spain (where some foundations that are granted 'special' tax treatment are exempted from tax on real-estate income) and Sweden (where real-estate income is fully taxed but other investment income is exempt).

Greece taxes income from securities at a full rate and real-estate income at a reduced rate. Hungary applies a unique rule, whereby investment income is allocated to unrelated or related business income and taxed or exempted accordingly.

Capital gains on investments are normally accorded the same treatment (taxation or exemption) as income from those investments. The treatment of capital gains on other assets tends to vary according to the nature of the assets. Some states exempt all capital gains (e.g. Greece, Ireland and UK). Others tax certain gains, for example on assets used for commercial activities (Denmark, Finland, Slovenia) or on real-estate assets (Belgium, if owned for less than five years; Switzerland).

2.2.5 Taxation of income from commercial activities

Some states allow foundations to engage in commercial activities provided that they do not become the dominant activity (Estonia, Finland, Hungary, Spain, Switzerland, UK). Others permit unlimited commercial activity but deny the activity any tax privileges if it competes with a similar activity carried on by a Dutch private sector business (the Netherlands). A few states (Austria, Cyprus) restrict the conduct of commercial activities to those, which are specifically related to the pursuit of the stated public benefit purposes.

The danger that commercial activities may lead to the loss of tax privileges probably exists in most countries, simply because it is not easy to keep commercial activities within the boundaries of what is acceptable to the authorities. France has recently found this to be an issue that required the production of detailed guidance from the tax authorities.[6] Reports from Belgium, Germany and Switzerland suggest that this issue is perceived to be a significant risk in these countries. It is difficult to measure the relative risks in individual

---

[6] See Instruction of 15 September 1998, BOI 4H-5-98.

states without more specific research; however, differences between states could be attributed to the degree of supervision exercised by the tax authorities and/or the extent of complaints of unfair competition received from private sector businesses.

The tax treatment of income from commercial activities commonly varies according to whether the income can be classed as related or unrelated business income. This distinction is justified primarily by reasons of economic policy. The exemption of income derived from activities that directly fulfil the stated public benefit purposes of the organization can be seen to further commonly accepted social goals. The extension of this exemption to commercial activities that only indirectly assist such goals – to the extent that the profits are used to fund the pursuit of the public benefit purposes – can, however, be viewed as facilitating unfair competition with similar private sector enterprises.

Most states in the survey observe this policy in exempting related business income and taxing unrelated business income at standard corporate income tax rates. Some states (Austria, Belgium, Bulgaria, Estonia, Luxembourg, Sweden) tax all business income whether or not related to the organization's public benefit purposes. The only states that exempt unrelated business income are Cyprus (provided that the profits are applied to the organization's purposes) and Finland and Sweden (only in the case of certain 'special' nonprofits). Other states allow a 'small business' exemption for unrelated business income below a specified amount (Germany, Hungary, the Netherlands). A similar exemption entered into force in the UK from April 2000. The Netherlands also has a special exemption for business income obtained through the use of volunteers.

Where a foundation engages directly in commercial activities, it will be necessary to allocate its expense between taxable and exempt activities in order to measure the true profit arising from the taxable activities. This requires careful consideration of how to account for and report general overheads and other costs that are not directly attributable to particular activities.

In addition to income tax, a separate business tax is imposed on income from commercial activities in a few states (France, Germany). In Germany this tax (*Gewerbesteuer*) operates effectively as a surcharge on taxable income at rates determined by local government; however, in the case of foundations it is levied only on unrelated business income excluding any donations received.

Even when it is not required by law, many foundations choose to conduct commercial activities indirectly, usually via the medium of a wholly-owned subsidiary company established for this purpose. This is not achieved easily in all states: in Austria, for example, the establishment of a commercial company by a foundation could call into question the nonprofit character of the foundation and prejudice its entitlement to tax exemption. The subsidiary company is generally liable to corporate income tax on its profits without the benefit of any tax privileges attaching to the foundation, but in practice it is often possible to reduce the tax burden by charging the subsidiary, within reasonable limits, for the benefit of financial support or other services provided by the foundation.

In theory, no state grants tax exemption to a group comprising a foundation and its subsidiaries but in practice it is sometimes possible to achieve a similar result in some countries. In the Netherlands there is an informal practice whereby the subsidiary is not taxed if the profit is distributed to the parent foundation. The situation in the UK should also be noted: if a subsidiary company donates all its profits to the parent foundation it is possible to convert otherwise taxable income in the subsidiary into exempt income in the foundation because such donations are fully deductible from the profits of the subsidiary.

2.2.6 Gift and inheritance tax privileges

The establishment of a foundation by way of an initial gift of an endowment typically requires consideration of the laws imposing taxes on the transfer of wealth. All the states surveyed (with the exception of Cyprus and Estonia) levy taxes on the transfer of wealth in the form of a gift and/or inheritance tax. Most European states impose the tax on the person receiving the benefit, whether the gift is made during the donor's lifetime or after death. Some countries (Slovenia, Ireland and the UK) levy the tax on the donor.

Most European states exempt from such taxes an initial endowment of a foundation that satisfies the state's public benefit criteria. In those states that do not grant such a broad-based exemption either to donor or donee (Austria, Belgium, France, Netherlands), the tax rates on gifts to foundations range from 2.5% (Austria) to 11% (Netherlands). However, the regime in the Netherlands incorporates some features that assist in the establishment of a foundation. These include an exemption for gifts by one foundation to another, and a *de minimis* limit (for 1999, NLG8254 (€3746) for lifetime gifts and

NLG16,167 (€7336) for inheritances) for tax-free gifts by a donor. The latter relief may assist a foundation to be established with an endowment if several donors are involved rather than a single founder, although this is likely to be practicable only in the case of lifetime gifts.

It should also be noted that some states that have a broad-based exemption for gifts to foundations use a definition of public benefit purposes that is more limited than is generally found elsewhere, and the standard tax rate on non-qualifying gifts (30% in Sweden) could therefore apply to gifts that would be exempt in other jurisdictions.

In these respects, the states surveyed do not grant any special tax treatment to the initial endowment of a foundation when compared to the tax privileges available for similar gifts to a foundation subsequent to its establishment. From the perspective of the foundation, the tax treatment of such gifts, whether in cash or in kind, does not differ materially from the treatment of the initial gift on establishment (for the treatment of the donor see 3). The exception to this rule is a new element of German law just introduced in June 2000 which includes a special allowance to the donor for initial endowment gifts at a rate of DEM600,000 (€306,775) (to be carried forward over ten years, i.e. resulting in an actual annual allowance of DEM60,000, or €30,677).[7]

It is also possible in fiscal theory to regard the initial endowment of a foundation as a receipt that has the characteristics of income in the hands of the foundation rather than representing a transfer of capital. However, the reports received suggest that an initial endowment would not be regarded as taxable income in any of the states surveyed.

As regards taxes other than income tax and gift and inheritance taxes, the regime in Liechtenstein deserves attention. Although foundations enjoy a wide range of tax exemptions in Liechtenstein, the state levies a duty at the rate of 1% of the initial endowment on all ecclesiastical, charitable and family foundations.

2.2.7 *Other taxes on foundations*

Other taxes on legal entities that are found in several states include:

- taxes on the ownership and/or occupation of real-estate (Belgium, Bulgaria, Cyprus, Estonia, Finland, Germany, Greece, Italy, Luxembourg, Netherlands, Spain, Sweden, UK)

---

[7] 'Gesetz zur besonderen steuerlichen Förderung von Stiftungen' vom 14.7.2000, *Bundesgesetzblatt* Teil I, Nr. 33, G 5702, ausgegeben zu Bonn am 25. Juli 2000.

- taxes on the transfer or registration of ownership of certain forms of property such as shares and securities or real-estate (Belgium, Cyprus, France, Ireland, Netherlands, UK)
- federal or local business tax (France, Germany, Hungary, Luxembourg, Portugal, Spain).

The form of the business tax varies in each country. It may constitute an additional tax on the profits or net income of a legal entity (e.g. in Germany), a tax on gross revenue (e.g. Hungary), or a tax based on specific factors such as the activity or the location of the activity (e.g. Spain).

None of the states surveyed levies any taxes that apply to foundations alone. However, several states levy taxes on real-estate, net worth, and transfer of ownership of property that can be imposed on foundations as well as other tax-payers.

- **Real-estate taxes**
  Found in Belgium, Bulgaria, Cyprus, Estonia, Finland, Germany, Greece, Italy, Luxembourg, Netherlands, Spain, Sweden and the UK. Full exemption is available in Cyprus and Italy, and foundations are substantially exempt in the UK. In other states the tax rates range from 0.2% in Bulgaria to 35% in Greece (some limited exemptions are available).

- **Net worth taxes**
  Levied by Liechtenstein, Luxembourg and Sweden. Luxembourg exempts foundations without any commercial activities, and Sweden grants exemption if the organization qualifies for exemption from income tax. Liechtenstein exempts foundations with charitable purposes, and imposes a capital tax at a rate ranging from 0.05% to 0.2% (the lower rate applies to larger foundations) for other foundations without business activites in Liechtenstein.

- **Transfer taxes**
  Imposed in Ireland, Spain and the UK but foundations generally enjoy full exemption.

- **Social security contributions**
  Foundations are also liable to taxes and social security contributions in their capacity as employers. It is standard policy in Europe and in most countries worldwide not to grant relief from these taxes to nonprofit organizations.

Foundations may also incur liability to tax (generally, income tax) in respect of payments that they make to their suppliers or lenders –

or even their beneficiaries (e.g. in Estonia). A requirement to deduct tax from the payment concerned is usually imposed as a method of ensuring that the state receives a minimum amount of tax revenue in circumstances where it may be difficult or expensive to collect tax from the recipient. Typically, the legislation allows the state to collect the tax from the payer whether or not it actually deducts the tax from the payment concerned. Generally, foundations in Europe are not relieved from such obligations.

2.2.8 Specific funds

Mention should also be made of those countries where certain tax revenues are allocated to a specific fund. These are not, as such, taxes on foundations but taxes that raise funds that are dedicated to public benefit activities in which foundations may engage.

A prime example of this is the church tax that is levied in several countries (e.g. Austria, Finland, Germany, Sweden, Switzerland). Typically, the church tax is a tax on the income of individual members of the relevant church. The revenue may be collected directly by the church or by the state on its behalf; in either case the revenue is used to fund the religious, social welfare and other activities of the church.

A similar concept allows individual tax-payers an option to designate that a percentage of their annual income tax payments should be transferred by the government to the Church or to a specific non-profit public benefit organization. In Italy and Spain tax-payers can designate a fraction, currently 0.5%, of their taxes to go to the Church or to government programmes to help those in need. In Hungary, tax-payers can designate 1% of their income tax to be transferred to a registered church, and a further 1% to a public benefit organization, including a foundation, that has been established for at least 3 years.[8]

Several countries also allow tax-payers to give property to the state or state-approved bodies in lieu of payment of certain taxes, usually gift and inheritance taxes, (e.g. Ireland, Netherlands, UK). Typically, the property concerned must be of value to the national cultural heritage and the donee must be a major museum or similar cultural institution. Some countries offer the donor an incentive, for instance in the form of a discount on the tax liability discharged by such gifts. Approved cultural foundations can benefit from such schemes in those states that allow non-state bodies to participate.

---

[8] Act CXXVI of 1996 'On the use of a specified amount of personal income tax in accordance with the tax-payer's instruction'.

3 Tax treatment of the donor

A donor considering establishing a foundation will probably be concerned about the tax treatment of their initial endowment and subsequent donations as well as the tax treatment of gifts received by the foundation from third parties. However, a donor's choice of a foundation as the legal form for institutionalizing their charitable activities is not only motivated by the tax treatment of the foundation-in-formation and its contemplated activities, but also by other factors, including the following:

- An individual must possess a high degree of idealism to decide first that private property is to be used for public benefit purposes, thus rendering it unavailable for private consumption, and second to be prepared to donate substantial property to create a foundation to serve this public benefit.
- The recognition that a donor receives from the public and the government may also influence his or her decision to establish a foundation. The government's recognition will find its expression, not entirely but primarily, in the privileged tax treatment of the founder and subsequent donors. This may be in recognition of their generosity in easing the state's financial burden where their core activities promote the 'general welfare' (generally understood by a modern state as the duty it owes its citizens). For example, a founder whose foundation enables the establishment and operation of a museum will ease the financial burden of the state to the extent that it is the state's duty to encourage the establishment of such museums for the benefit of its citizens.

The following principle appears to be generally recognized throughout Europe:

- the burden on public budgets is eased to the extent that a citizen finances activities that might normally be considered a state's duty to conduct.

Usually, the state reciprocates only by reducing the donor's taxable income by the amount of the donation, which in turn leads to a 'relief' in an amount corresponding to the founder's or donor's personal tax rate. Consequently, the public sector will always benefit in terms of a net amount.

It is noteworthy that the tax benefits available to founders and donors vary considerably under the laws of the various European countries surveyed. The range of issues on which the national laws differ span from the qualifying purposes that a foundation must pursue for donors to the foundation to be eligible for tax relief and the amount and scope of such tax relief to procedural issues, such as the valuation of in-kind donations. In determining the degree of tax relief available to donors, a distinction is often made between individual and corporate donors.

3.1 Tax deductibility of donations

The tax treatment of founders and donors (i.e. the tax privileges received upon their making a donation) in the various European jurisdictions surveyed will depend largely on whether the foundation qualifies as a tax-privileged body. Without exception, tax benefits are available to donors only if the beneficiary, (i.e. a tax-privileged foundation) qualifies for such privileges. As will be seen below in 3.2, there may also, however, be some additional requirements to satisfy before donations are tax deductible to the donor.

The requirements that a foundation must fulfil in order for it to be eligible for tax privileges have been outlined in Garcia-Andrade: Establishment, Amendment and Liquidation of Foundations as well as in 2.2.1. These requirements, especially the definition of qualifying purposes (public benefit purposes), differ widely from one country to another, and of course are of particular interest to potential donors.

Through their donation, donors often seek to support an organization that pursues purposes which aid the public benefit and fill a need, perhaps because of a lack of engagement by the state, the public or even the nonprofit sector.

It is not always easy, however, for a donor to find out if the purpose contemplated would enable the foundation to qualify for tax-privileged status, a prerequisite for the donation to be tax deductible for the donor. A donor, of course, would prefer to be certain in advance that a purpose qualifies as being for the public benefit.

A closed-list approach, as discussed above in 2.2.1, would appear to provide the certainty sought by the donor, especially if the legal definition is interpreted reliably by courts and administrative authorities (e.g. tax authorities).

A similar level of certainty could also be attained with an open list of purposes, if the open list is substantiated by a list of specific purposes. This is the case in Germany where a long list of purposes also describes other areas of public benefit that are not mentioned in the open list contained in the tax code.

To conclude, according to the information received from the countries surveyed, potential donors in all countries can find a reliable basis for their contribution and for the tax deductibility of their donations.

3.2 Procedural requirements for the donor's tax relief

3.2.1 The timing of the donation

Almost all European jurisdictions grant founders and donors certain tax privileges for donations made to qualifying foundations. With the exception of a few countries (France and Slovenia), countries do not distinguish between the initial donation made to help establish a foundation and donations made afterwards. Initial donations are tax deductible to the same extent as donations made after a foundation's establishment.

3.2.2 Procedural issues

It is usually not sufficient for founders and donors to contribute funds to a foundation pursuing one or more qualifying purposes, as defined by law. If a donor wishes to claim tax relief, evidence is often required that the foundation receiving the donation has been approved as a tax-privileged foundation. In addition, proof that the donation has been made is frequently requested. The applicable provisions vary greatly in this respect; the general concern is, however, to ensure legal certainty by providing a reliable method of proof for payment transactions between the parties concerned (foundation, donor, tax authorities).

In Germany, for instance, this is achieved by entitling tax-privileged foundations to issue a certificate of deductibility that the donor needs in order to claim tax relief on his, her or its income tax/corporate tax return. Up until the end of 1999, however, in most cases donations to a nonprofit organization in Germany had to be transferred to a state institution which transferred the donation to the recipient and issued the certificate to the donor. In Germany, a foundation's eligibility for tax privileges is first determined on the basis of a foundation's governing documents. A final decision on the tax-privileged status will be made later, on the basis of the actual work of a foundation.

In other legal systems tax-effective donations can be granted only to foundations that have acquired an official approval or are included on an official list after having been approved. The procedure for obtaining this approval varies greatly from country to country. Official approval is required in Austria, Belgium, Cyprus, Estonia, France (for collecting intermediary organizations), Hungary, Italy, the Netherlands, and Spain. In Denmark a list of institutions whose donors are entitled to tax deductions is available. In Liechtenstein, Switzerland and Luxembourg the official approval leads to an official list of tax privileged foundations. In Austria the state revenue directorate publishes a list of approved organizations annually in the federal gazette of the fiscal authorities. In Greece the legal entities enjoying tax privileges are listed in a joint ministerial decision of the Ministers of Finance and Culture.

The requirement of official approval might influence the motivation of potential donors to give, and thus the ability of foundations to attract donations. A foundation that can refer to an official approval might have a better chance of attracting donations. Notwithstanding, there is no survey available showing that countries demanding official approvals before granting a tax-privileged status have a more dynamic nonprofit sector than countries that do not require such approval.

3.3 Extent of the tax relief: distinction between individual and corporate donors

Almost all European tax systems provide that the initial or further endowment of a foundation, as well as any subsequent donations to a foundation, can be considered for the purpose of assessing the donor's income or corporate tax. Founders and donors may thus deduct donations made to tax-privileged foundations from their taxable income. Only a couple of European states do not grant this tax privilege to all founders or donors. In Sweden and Finland, for instance, only donations by corporate founders and donors can be considered for tax purposes, while individual founders and donors do not enjoy such privileges. Corporations in Ireland may only deduct donations made to an approved charitable body that has had charitable tax status for at least three years. Once again, this condition only applies to corporate tax deductions, not individual tax deductions.

In the majority of the European states both individual and corporate donors, natural persons and legal persons are entitled to claim tax relief for their donations to tax-privileged foundations. For the purpose of determining the extent of the tax relief that can be claimed, a distinction is often made as to whether the donation comes from a corporation or an individual. The distinction regularly relates to the absolute amount, or the relative amount (mostly based on total earnings or turnover), up to which donations can be considered for the purpose of deduction. The technicalities of the different legal systems will not be discussed here. A country-by-country list of relevant legislation is provided in Appendix II. As an example, the applicable provisions in Estonia, Germany, and the UK will be discussed below, because they illustrate the spectrum of possible regulations among the European states.

Estonia

According to Estonian tax law a physical or legal person making a donation to a listed foundation may deduct the amount from the taxable income. The law requires donors to report such deductions in their annual income declaration and permits legal persons to deduct up to 10% of their total taxable income while physical persons may deduct up to 5% of their taxable income for gifts to listed foundations. Thus, according to this clear rule, legal persons can claim double the amount available to physical persons for donations to listed foundations.

Germany

While there are many ways to deduct donations made to nonprofit foundations as a special expense, there are certain limits. The limit is usually 5% of the gross income or 2% of the sum of the total turnover, plus wages and salaries paid in the respective calendar year. By including wages and salaries companies may make donations even in years when they make losses. Turnover, wages and salaries of a partnership are allocated to the individual partners in proportion to their respective profit shares for tax purposes. Individual partners may then choose between the 5% limit of gross income and 2% of the sum resulting from turnover, wages and salaries. For donations made to organizations pursuing scientific, charitable and cultural purposes recognized to be particularly deserving of promotion, the percentage rate increases from 5% to 10%, whereas the rate of 2% applicable to turnover, wages and salaries does not increase; the most favourable method of computation may always be used.

As a result of the upper limit of 10% of the gross income the deduction of donations frequently proves to be insufficient, in particular for a foundation-in-formation. If a cultural foundation is endowed with the modest amount of DEM500,000 (€255,646), this would require a taxable income of DEM5 million (€2,556,459) based on the 10% limit. In order to provide some compensation, income tax law permits the donor to allocate the tax deduction for large donations over several tax periods. If a donation to a foundation promoting scientific, charitable or cultural purposes exceeds DEM50,000 (€25,565), the donation can be allocated to seven tax periods, that is the one preceding and the following five tax periods, and may then be deducted as a special expense. Section 9 (1) No. 2 Corporate Income Tax Act contains a corresponding provision for corporate income tax-payers, but reduces the allocation to six years. As from the year 2000 additional relief has been available to tax-privileged foundations. Initial endowments of up to DEM600,000 (€306,775) and further donations up to DEM40,000 (€20,452) a year are deductible in the year of the donation. This new law, which applies in addition to the other general fiscal deductions for donations to nonprofit organizations, thus provides an improved tax relief for donations of up to DEM400,000 (€204,517). Otherwise, the general legislation will be more favourable.

The option of spreading large donations over a period of seven (six) years applies only for scientific, charitable or cultural purposes that are recognized as particularly deserving of promotion. The endowment of foundations established for other nonprofit purposes cannot be allocated over seven (six) years for tax purposes. The ongoing reform efforts occurring in Germany in recent years might result in a further improvement of the tax framework conditions. The catalogue of tax-privileged purposes as well as the procedure to claim tax relief might also be reviewed.

United Kingdom

For a different reason the tax situation in the UK should be mentioned. The UK is the only country in Europe where there is no limit on the amount of tax-deductible donations. Donors in the UK enjoy this tax deductibility without any kind of ceiling, unlike that faced by donors all over Europe. It would be interesting to establish whether this is the reason for the significant charitable tradition in the UK. From April 2000 further improvements of these conditions have come into effect. The £250 minimum limit for donations under the Gift Aid scheme as well as the £1200 maximum limit for payroll giving have been abolished.

3.4 Permissibility and tax treatment of in-kind gifts

Frequently, in addition to or in lieu of cash donations, the founder wishes to transfer an in-kind gift to the foundation at the time of its establishment or thereafter. Can a founder also derive tax benefits from making an in-kind gift to a foundation? The nature of an in-kind gift can vary. The founder may for instance transfer real-estate, shares in companies, or even art collections to the foundation. It is also conceivable that a donor would like to donate the use of goods or services, for instance the labour of a donor's employees to a foundation. If this is the case and the donation leads to a donor's tax relief, a further question arises: what is the value of the in-kind gift for purposes of assessing the relief to the donor?

The answer varies greatly from one European jurisdiction to another. In many cases the deductibility of gifts is limited to donations in cash. States where no tax relief is available for in-kind gifts include for instance Belgium, Cyprus and Ireland. Also to be mentioned in this context are Sweden and Finland, where gifts to foundations may not, as a rule, be deducted from an individual donor's tax (see below).

By contrast, there are quite a few European states where the treatment of in-kind gifts varies only slightly from the treatment of cash donations. The differences are as a rule limited to the mechanism of value assessment. In Bulgaria, for instance, the value of in-kind donations is assessed on the basis of the book value of the objects in the balance sheets. In Portugal, in-kind gifts are as such permissible and treated in accordance with the general rules so that only their value has to be approved. Likewise, the codified tax law in France does not provide for special provisions in this respect, nor is a fundamental distinction made in Slovenia.

Germany

In Germany, in-kind gifts are as such permissible and capable of being considered for tax purposes. A transfer of use and services will not permit the founder or donor to deduct the amount of their value. To the extent that in-kind gifts are recognized for tax purposes, their value will have to be determined, especially for purposes of the certificate of deductibility. Methods of assessments might be different for works of art, real-estate, shares in a company, services and staff secondment. In order to determine the value of a work of art, an expert opinion is usually obtained. This is also the procedure for a transfer of real property, at least if it is owned by a private person.

If business assets are transferred by the donor to a nonprofit foundation, the result will automatically be a realization of the hidden reserves of the donor, since the assets concerned must first be separated from the other business assets.[9] For income tax purposes the

---

[9] Seifart, Section 40 ann. 44 *et seq*.

separated business assets, including shares, are considered on the basis of their value as part of an enterprise. In order to minimize the effects of a separation of business assets without consideration, Section 6 (1) No. 4, sentence 4, of the Income Tax Act provides for a so-called book value privilege (*Buchwertprivileg*). Accordingly, business assets may be separated at book value if the assets concerned are then transferred directly and free of charge to a tax-exempt foundation for use in accordance with its tax-exempt purposes. Up to 1999 this privilege has applied to all tax-exempt foundations pursuing scientific, charitable, cultural or educational purposes[10] and has been extended to all tax-privileged purposes beginning in 2000.

England and Wales

In England and Wales in specific (as opposed to individual) instances donors can obtain tax relief on certain types of support given to charities. There is limited relief for certain gifts in-kind by businesses to educational establishments.[11] This relief is available not just to companies, but also to persons carrying on a trade. The gift must be of an article manufactured by, or of a class or description sold by, the donor in the course of his trade, which qualifies as machinery or plant in the hands of the educational establishment. The gift can also be an article used by the donor in the course of his trade or profession and in respect of which capital allowances have been claimed under the Capital Allowances Act 1990. Under the first category the gift is not treated as a disposal from trading stock and no amount is required to be brought into account as a trading receipt in relation to the gift. Under the second, there is no requirement to bring into account any disposal value for the purposes of Section 24 No. 6 of the Capital Allowances Act 1990, thereby providing relief from any balancing charge which might otherwise have occurred on the disposal. Relief in similar terms is available for in-kind donations to poor countries.[12] This relief is currently only available on gifts to 31 December 2000, but by Section 55 of the Finance Act 1999 the scope of the tax relief is extended to cover any charitable cause. Expenditure incurred in the provision of services is not generally allowed as a trading expense on the grounds that it is not incurred for the purposes of the trade.

---

[10] The legal basis was the *Standortsicherungsgesetz* dated 13 September 1993, *Federal Tax Gazette I* 1993, 774, extending the book value privilege to all purposes which are tax-privileged according to Section 10 b sub-sec. 1 sentence 1 Income Tax Act, see Glanegger, in: Schmidt, ESAG, Section 6 ann. 427.

[11] Section 68 of the Finance Act 1991, now contained in Section 84 ICTA 1988.

[12] Section 74 of the Finance Act 1998.

The cost of the secondment of staff may be deducted from business profits[13] where a trader makes available to a charity the services of an employee on a temporary basis. The effect is that the employee's salary is deducted although it should be noted that a trader may not employ a person specifically for a charitable secondment. Donations of real property are not tax deductible. As far as a valuation of an in-kind gift is needed, an agreement with the Inland Revenue will be sought in practice on the basis of a professional open-market valuation.

Estonia

Under Estonian tax law monetary gifts and in-kind gifts are treated in the same way as other gifts. Usually, the tax-payer must make the deduction claim and assume responsibility for procuring it. In-kind donations are deducted at fair market value of the item donated.[14] The book-keeping process indirectly involves auditors because they must verify annual accounts. If tax authorities do not agree with this valuation, then they may require their own audit, which the organization can dispute in the administrative court.

Italy

Under Italian legislation, generally all donations to a foundation will be tax deductible. For in-kind gifts, some tax deductions will be allowed. For instance, if a donor seconds its workers to an ONLUS, it can deduct the expenses relating to the worker's remuneration up to the amount of 0.5% of the donor's total expenses for staff. Italian law mentions nothing concerning artwork, shares in a for-profit company or services rendered for no or less remuneration. Food and pharmaceutical products, as well as goods produced by the donor company that are donated and related to the foundation's activity, will be tax deductible for the donor. These exemptions are valid for gifts made by individuals, non-commercial organizations, companies and commercial entities whether or not they are resident in Italy.

Luxembourg

In Luxembourg no distinction is made between the treatment of monetary gifts and in-kind gifts. According to the Luxembourg law, donations are valid only if made by authentic deed. This provision excepts manual donations (e.g. the payment of a sum of money on an

---

[13] Section 86 Taxes Act 1988.

[14] Article 29 Property Act.

account) or the informal transmission of movable property or bearer shares to the recipient.

But, if the donation is made by an authentic deed, registration tax is due on the actual value of the asset. The donor must declare this value, and the tax authorities are entitled to rectify this value if they do not consider it to conform to the actual market price of the asset.

The Netherlands

The Dutch tax laws permit the donor to make tax-privileged in-kind gifts. For the calculation of the deduction by the donor for private income tax and for corporate income tax purposes the gift has to be valued at fair market value. However, when the gift consists of shares quoted on a public stock exchange, the list price is the applicable value. There are no official procedures for assessing the value of the object. It is possible to agree in advance on the fair market value with the tax authorities on request.

Sweden and Finland

In general, donations do not produce a tax deduction for individual donors according to Swedish and Finnish tax law. However, in these countries if the donor carries on a trade or business that enjoys a direct benefit from the donation for its business activities, the donation may be tax deductible as a business expenditure.

Spain

According to Spanish tax law, donations do not produce tax deductions to legal entity donors. However, there are certain exceptions where the foundation rather than the donor enjoys the more favourable tax regime. Only private donors generally enjoy tax deductibility.

In Spain in-kind gifts have been subject to complex provisions; up to the end of 1999 only in-kind gifts which were part of the tangible assets and helped to pursue the general interest aims were deductible. Therefore, services rendered for no or less remuneration, staff secondments, discounted facilities or discounted products were not deductible. This tangible-assets requirement has now been waived. So, beginning in 2000, in-kind gifts lead to tax deductibility for the donor. Artworks are deductible on the basis of fair market value. In-kind gifts enjoy the same deductibility as explained above for monetary gifts. The limit of deductibility is increased for artworks to 30% of taxable income or 3% of the entity's turnover. The assessment of in-kind gifts of artworks is managed by a special public agency called *Junta de Calificación, Valoración y Exportación*. This agency also carries out other relevant functions connected with artworks.

3.5 Establishing a foundation as part of a founder's estate plan

As far as tax advice is concerned, considerations as to whether a foundation should be established play an important role in connection with the structuring of last wills, independently of the legal system concerned. Foundations which according to their statutes pursue charitable objects are in several states exempt from inheritance tax with respect to the assets donated under a will. This tax exemption applies to all transfers in connection with the establishment of the foundation and during its entire existence. It is necessary to determine the period over which the requirements for a tax exemption have to be fulfilled after the donation has been made, to avoid possible loss of tax exemption status with retrospective effect. Under German tax law the recognition as a tax-exempt body must be maintained for at least ten years. Otherwise, the tax-exempt status will cease to apply and taxes must be paid on the donation retroactively (Section 13 (1) No. 16 b sentence 2 Inheritance Tax Act).

With respect to the tax benefits available in all European legal systems, a tax-exemption will typically only be granted if the donor or testator has ordered a direct transfer to a tax-privileged foundation. The tax treatment of heirs who have received a legacy, and are then willing to donate the legacy in whole or in part to a tax-privileged foundation, therefore needs to be taken into consideration. The heirs are subject to unlimited inheritance tax and can claim tax relief only in accordance with general rules.

Germany

German inheritance tax law provides for limited possibilities permitting the heirs actively to influence and 'correct' the last will. Foundations which are established by the heirs and not the testators may be exempt under Section 29 (1) 4 of the Inheritance Tax Act, which permits the heir to establish a German foundation or to donate inherited assets to an existing German foundation within 24 months of the death of the testator. In the case above the inheritance tax will not be payable by the heirs with retroactive effect. The aim of the legislation is to encourage heirs who have received a legacy or a gift *inter vivos* to support purposes of public benefit by way of donations. Thus, heirs are not only to be exempt from the burden of inheritance tax with respect to their own donations to these institutions, but to the same extent with respect to donations made from the assets of the estate. A person who endows a foundation with assets from an estate or donates such assets to an existing foundation is for tax inheritance purposes thus treated as a pass-through agent between the testator and the tax-privileged foundation.

United Kingdom

In the UK it is also possible to amend a will with retroactive effect if all the heirs agree by executing a 'deed of variation' within two years after the death of the testator. This can be used to substitute a gift to a charity for a legacy – and thus reduce inheritance tax liability – but only in the case of property owned on death. An equivalent procedure for varying lifetime gifts does not exist.

Spain

In Spain, heirs are not motivated to correct the last will, because if they wish to incorporate a foundation with the assets received from a last will this will be considered as a simple donation by the heirs. They will, of course, have to pay the inheritance tax and then enjoy the tax deductibility of gifts donated to a foundation. So the last will cannot be altered – but the tax burden of the heirs might be neutralized by the tax deductibility of the endowments.

Other countries

Similar provisions permitting a 'correction' of the testator's will are not incorporated, as far as apparent, in the codified tax laws of many other European countries, although the general practice of the fiscal authorities may lead to similar results. In any case it is instrumental in relieving the state of the performance of its public duties to the extent that the heir uses the estate for tax-privileged purposes in the same way as a foundation established by the testator.

3.6 Lack of tax privilege – protection of confidence and liability

A tax-payer who wishes to make a donation to a foundation which is known to him as a tax-privileged foundation as a rule relies on the availability of tax relief (i.e. that the conditions under which a donor is entitled to deduct the donation according to the applicable national tax provisions are in fact fulfilled). The donor will expect this to be the case if the foundation is entered in a register listing tax-privileged organizations where provided for under applicable national law. This approved basis for tax-privileged donations is found in several countries. The confidence of the donor can also be based on the work of the foundation; with charitable causes which are in some cases pursued with great publicity it will help to build the donor's confidence if the foundation has also been approved as far as tax benefits are concerned. Furthermore, a protection of confidence follows from the certificates issued to the founder/donor.

Nevertheless, the donor can be disappointed in his or her expectations. The recipient can, contrary to the donor's expectations, fail to qualify as a tax-privileged foundation and, consequently, the tax deductibility of the donation would no longer be safeguarded for the donor. Furthermore, the donor is unable to ensure that the recipient will in fact use the donation for privileged purposes.

Germany

A reliable example of a clear risk distribution between the interests of the donor and the interests of the tax authorities (who will only grant the tax deduction if the donation is in fact used for tax-privileged purposes) can be shown in German legislation. Here the tax-payer may in good faith rely on the accuracy of the certificate of deductibility. The tax authorities may not refuse tax relief on the grounds that the certificate is inaccurate. The protection of confidence is only denied if the tax-payer has acted in bad faith and obtained the certificate of deductibility by unfair means or by making wrong statements. The same applies if the inaccuracy of the certificate of deductibility was known to the tax-payer or the tax-payer's lack of knowledge is due to gross negligence. The protection of the donor's confidence is further supported by a liability of those persons who are responsible for the resulting loss of taxes. Accordingly, anyone who wilfully or by gross negligence issues a certificate of deductibility or causes the donation to be used for purposes other than those indicated on the certificate is liable for a loss of taxes.

United Kingdom

If a UK charity does not use a donation for public benefit purposes the tax authorities can normally penalize only the charity, but not the donor. Even if the foundation were to lose its charitable status, in most cases this would not have a retroactive effect. In practice, even where there is a procedural error by the donor which results in his or her gift being deemed invalid – which has happened quite often with donations under a deed of covenant – most UK charities would prefer to pay back the tax reclaimed themselves, rather than ask the donor to pay, in order to limit any loss of public confidence.

Spain

In Spain a donor can rely on the foundation's certificate to assure the deductibility of gifts. Furthermore, foundations have to inform the tax authorities in general of any gift received as suitable for tax deductibility. Under these provisions two cases might happen. Tax authorities might compare the certificate shown by a donor with the information received from the foundation and where they are not consistent the tax deductibility of the donation will be refused by the authorities. If the tax authorities accept the deductibility of the donation but a few years later discover that this was inappropriate, e.g. because the foundation did not use the donation for its tax privileged purposes, the tax authorities usually consider that they cannot blame the donor. The foundation alone will be responsible.

Other countries

Other countries (e.g. the Netherlands) cover questions of risk distribution mainly by providing a ruling on a questionable donation by the tax authorities before it is made.

Such a clear rule of law establishing the protection of confidence and liability with respect to donations cannot be found in all the legal systems of the other European states. The income tax conditions permitting public benefit foundations to receive tax-free donations from donors in exchange for certificates of deductibility do not yet provide a rule establishing protection of confidence and liability. Nevertheless, an appropriate risk distribution between the parties concerned and the tax authorities might be achieved on the basis of the general principles of the respective national tax laws.

4 Conclusion

Whenever the design of a country's tax system is under review, consideration should be given to the formulation of a policy on the grant of tax privileges to nonprofit organizations. During the early years of the 20th century, when most income tax systems were taking shape, this was not seen as a priority with the result that the grant of such privileges in several states evolved on an *ad hoc* basis. More recently, and with particular reference to an increase in the number of independent states since World War II, international fiscal policy-makers have attempted to design model tax codes[15] incorporating basic principles that can be recommended for adoption by governments seeking to improve the quality of their tax legislation. More specifically, a recent initiative by the World Bank[16] focuses on the contribution of the legal and fiscal environment in different countries to the development of civil society.

Collectively, these models feature the following recommendations on taxation of nonprofit public benefit organizations.

- Preferential treatment or exemption from customs duties on imported goods or services used to further the stated public benefit purposes.
- Exemption from VAT on certain classes of supplies of goods and services, generally with a corresponding restriction on deduction of VAT incurred on purchases.
- Exemption from income tax on donations and grants, investment income and capital gains.
- The permitting of commercial activities provided that they do not constitute the main purpose or activity of the organization.
- Income tax deductions for individual and business donations to public benefit organizations subject to a maximum (annual) limit.

As regards the taxation of income from commercial activities and other taxes, there is no general consensus among policy-makers. The revised discussion draft of the World Bank report suggested that the extent to which tax privileges should be granted to public benefit organizations could be decided by each government with reference to how far each wished to use the tax system to encourage the development of such organizations, having regard to the issue of possible unfair competition with the private sector and considerations of tax administration.

Considering these recommendations with reference to the specific case of foundations, it is apparent that additional features, listed below, are needed to provide an adequate framework for the establishment and operation of foundations.

- Relief from gift, inheritance or other taxes on the transfer of capital are a prerequisite for the creation of a foundation with a substantial endowment.

---

[15] E.g. 'Basic World Tax Code', Harvard University International Tax Program, 1992 (published in *Tax Notes International*, Vol. 5 Issue 23, 5 December 1992).

[16] 'Handbook on good practices for laws relating to non-governmental organizations' (revised discussion draft), World Bank, Washington DC, September 2000.

- Tax laws should enable a foundation to maintain, and hopefully increase, the value of its endowment over time by permitting investment in a broad range of public and private sector assets, subject to appropriate safeguards to protect against imprudent investment and to ensure that the income is regularly applied to the stated public benefit purposes.
- The rules for donors should provide for tax relief on gifts of shares and securities, as well as for cash donations.
- Finally, it should be noted that, whereas income tax credits for donations can provide more tax neutrality between different donors, under a progressive income tax system income tax deductions tend to be more valuable to wealthy donors.

How do the tax systems in Europe measure up to these standards ? By and large, taxes on the transfer of capital are not a barrier to the creation of foundations in Europe. And in Liechtenstein, where there is a specific tax on the establishment of a foundation, the tax can be likened to a fee for access to the comparatively generous approach to exempting non-commercial income of foundations from income tax; however, there is no corresponding incentive for the founder or donor.

Even if tax is not often a barrier to establishing a foundation, it is certainly more difficult for a foundation to avoid paying taxes in respect of its activities. Foundations that carry out their public benefit activities directly, rather than by making grants to other organizations, will generally be exposed to irrecoverable VAT; at present the UK appears to have the most favourable regime by virtue of its use of certain zero rated supplies to or by charities, but it is uncertain for how long they will be allowed to remain. Foundations that receive government grants may find that other countries are more generous in adjusting the amount of their grants to allow for irrecoverable VAT.

For complete exemption from tax on income from investments and commercial activities, the most favourable locations are Cyprus, Denmark, Switzerland and the UK. In Denmark this is conditional on full distribution of income and in the UK it is necessary to set up a wholly-owned subsidiary company to obtain effective tax exemption on income from commercial activities. In Switzerland capital gains on Swiss real-estate remain liable to tax.

As regards tax relief for the donor, the UK is the only country where there is no limit (other than the donor's income) on the amount of the deduction that can be claimed in one year for a cash donation to a foundation. Some other countries with annual limits on deductions allow relief for excess gifts to be spread over a number of years (e.g. Germany, Greece).

Where gifts in-kind are concerned, generally the donor will be more interested in the regimes in Germany, Italy and the Netherlands. Spain is also attractive, particularly where gifts of works of art are involved. To date the situation in the UK has been less satisfactory; relief is only offered from tax on capital gains and transfer taxes. The position has improved since April 2000 when the government introduced income tax relief for gifts of listed shares and securities.

Finally, it should be noted that the relative attractions of each jurisdiction are considered here only from a purely domestic viewpoint. Today it is increasingly common for the wealth that endows foundations to be earned and managed internationally. Founders with these characteristics will look beyond their national borders to determine an ideal location for their philanthropy. In these circumstances the issues considered in Gallop: Cross-border Issues Facing Foundations and their Donors, will be of equal, if not greater, importance.

Bibliography

Alfandari, E. and Nardone, A. eds, *Associations et Fondations en Europe*, Lyon, Editions Juris-Service, 1984.

Bater, P. ed., *The Tax Treatment of Cross-border Donations – Including the Tax Status of Charities and Foundations*, Amsterdam, International Bureau of Fiscal Documentation, looseleaf, 1994-99.

Cahiers de droit fiscal international, Vol. LXXXIVa, Subject I, 53rd Congress of the International Fiscal Association, Eilat 1999, The Hague, Kluwer Law International, 1999.

George, C. ed., *International Charitable Giving: Laws and Taxation*, London, Kluwer Law International, looseleaf,1994–8.

International Center for Not-for-profit Law *Handbook on good practices for laws relating to nonprofit organizations*, (revised discussion draft) Washington DC, World Bank, 2000.

Kiessling, H. and Buchna, J., *Gemeinnutzigkeit im Steuerrecht*, 6th edn, Achim, 1997.

Neuhoff, K. and Pavel, U. eds, *Trusts and foundations in Europe*, London, Bedford Square Press, 1971.

Salamon, L. M. ed., *The International Guide to Nonprofit Law*, New York, John Wiley, 1997.

Seifart, W. and von Campenhausen, A. eds, *Handbuch des Stiftungsrechts*, 2nd edn, Munchen, 1999.

▼ Wino J.M. van Veen

Supervision of Foundations in Europe: Post-incorporation Restrictions and Requirements

1 Introduction

This chapter deals with two closely related aspects of the regulation of foundations:

- the obligations, requirements and restrictions that apply to foundations and their managing directors/trustees
- the manner in which compliance therewith is monitored, enforced and ultimately sanctioned.

For reasons of convenience, the former aspect will be referred to as post-incorporation regulation, whereas the latter will be referred to as 'supervision'. The term supervision thus is not used in the narrower sense of monitoring the performance of the board of directors/trustees. It is used in the broader sense, encompassing also the competencies to intervene if a foundation or its managing directors/trustees fail to act in accordance with the applicable requirements and obligations.

Post-incorporation regulation and supervision of foundations is provided for in all countries included in this survey. As a rule the state plays an important role in this respect, although in a substantial number of jurisdictions local governments and other parties can also be instrumental in the supervision of foundations, more particularly the board of directors/trustees of a foundation (see 2). With regard to countries where the state is involved in the process of founding foundations (see Garcia-Andrade: Establishment, Amendment and Liquidation of Foundations), post-incorporation regulation and supervision is a logical sequel of the state's involvement in the founding process. The interests a state may have in regulating and controlling the establishment of foundations are also relevant after a foundation has come into existence. However, even countries where the state has no role to play in establishing foundations provide for some form of post-incorporation regulation and state supervision.

Interestingly, some states take an active approach to their role in supervising foundations. In countries with a common-law tradition the approach is predominantly that the state acts as *parens patriae* on behalf of the as yet undefined beneficiaries that are unable to enforce the charity themselves.[1] In other countries, such as Germany[2] and Greece (e.g. Article 2 of Compulsory Law 2039/1939) the approach taken is that the state's task is to ensure the will of the founder is respected and executed.

---

[1] Picarda, p. 513-8.

[2] See Schiller, p. 53.

The approach taken by government with regard to its supervisory role is a significant consideration. When for example authorization is requested to alter the purpose of the foundation, or to execute a certain transaction, a test strictly following the will of the founder is likely to result in a more conservative decision than one taking the interests of the beneficiaries or the public into account. Taking the founder's will at the moment of establishment of the foundation as the focal point might also lead to the prohibition of any change of purpose.[3] Although in law a change of purpose when subject to state approval (see 4), is generally speaking allowed under similar conditions, the final result may vary depending upon the point of reference taken. Thus it is not just the way the law is written that determines its impact on foundations. The manner in which it is interpreted and applied is similarly important.

The issue of post-incorporation regulation and state supervision over foundations and foundation-like institutions is a long-running one.[4] Governments have taken a traditionally reserved position regarding independent institutions like foundations. Depending on particular periods and political situations, several related reasons can be cited. One of them is that foundations provide for the possibility of the accumulation of wealth that, by the nature of their structure, can be applied efficiently and deliberately to promote changes in society. As a consequence, the more a state claims a monopoly in deciding the public good, the more foundations will be regarded as suspicious institutions threatening the monopoly of the state. The philosophy of the state and its government, is thus an important factor in the law governing voluntary organizations, and independent foundations in particular.[5]

Related to this, the political rulers have traditionally objected to the accumulation of property in independent institutions as such. Property accumulated by such institutions, initially primarily church-related institutions, fell outside the jurisdiction of worldly rulers and, as a consequence, was also excluded from taxation, directly affecting the financial position of those rulers. The indefinite duration (at least in principle) of independent institutions compounded rulers' concerns. A further objection to the accumulation of property is that it is taken out of circulation, with potentially a paralysing social and economic effect.

---

[3] See e.g. Article 74/B subsection 5 Hungarian CC, Book IV.

[4] For a treatise on motives for state supervision of foundations see, Schiller, pp 27–42 and 51–56.

[5] Not just with regard to foundations, but with regard to corporations in general, see Rajak; see also Van der Ploeg, p. 73.

As a result, an individual's right to determine the destiny of his or her property for an indefinite period of time after his or her death by establishing a foundation and transferring assets to it, was contested. The state would have to allow the founding of foundations, but it would (initially) usually restrict foundations to serving a purpose that helped relieve the state from its tasks, or a purpose that the state deemed beneficial to the public in general. Establishing a foundation was subject to a concession by the state, which possessed discretionary power either to grant or refuse this concession. The concession system implied that the state could impose conditions upon the foundation, subjecting it to requirements and restrictions as well as imposing supervision or some level of control over its the management. The concession system and traces of it are still present in a number of countries in Europe, for instance, where foundations can be set up for public benefit purposes only.

1.1 The term 'public benefit'

The term 'public benefit' needs some clarification. In most legal systems, charitable purposes are merely a sub-category of public benefit purposes that also includes, for instance, religious, scientific, cultural and educational purposes. In the UK-based common-law tradition, however, the situation is exactly the opposite, 'charitable' being the comprehensive term, encompassing what would in most Continental legal systems be considered a purpose of public benefit rather than specifically charitable. In this chapter the term 'public benefit' will be used as the comprehensive term for reasons of convenience. Admittedly the term 'public benefit' is in a way arbitrarily chosen. In fact, the most direct translation from many countries included in the survey would be 'public utility' rather than public benefit (e.g. *gemeinnützig, algemeen nut, utilité publique*). The conditions that apply to the purpose and activities to qualify as a public benefit foundation differ among the jurisdictions. (See Garcia-Andrade: Establishment, Amendment and Liquidation of Foundations, for more detail regarding such qualification).

The call for citizens to participate in the building of a 'civil society' is today widely supported by governments. Foundations as well as associations are important vehicles for such participation, allowing citizens to take responsibility, in a structured manner with an adequate legal status, for those issues that they feel are important. In addition, there have been a number of developments in the field of civil rights that under the European Convention on Human Rights also apply to legal persons, one of the vehicles allowing citizens to enjoy their fundamental freedoms and rights. Obviously, the present-day situation in Europe is different from the situation a century, or even half a century, ago, affecting the rationale and justification of requirements, restrictions and (state) supervision applicable to civic organizations such as foundations. This chapter is therefore concluded with comparative observations and reflections specifically on this subject (see 6 and 7).

2 The organization and modalities of supervision

2.1 Introduction

State supervision of foundations can be organized in many different forms, and be charged to a variety of public supervisory authorities. The instruments, tasks and competencies of those authorities also vary greatly, as will be discussed later. With regard to the organizational aspect of governmental supervision, a distinction is commonly made between supervision from a fiscal point of view and supervision of a general nature regarding compliance with the law and the governing document of the foundation. The legal instrument determining the name, purpose and other fundamental characteristics of the foundation is known by different terms in the various countries and can be translated into English in various ways (charter, statutes, by-laws, articles of incorporation, deed of trust etc.). For reasons of convenience and to avoid misunderstanding, the neutral term 'governing document' will be used in this chapter to indicate exactly this legal instrument.

- **The fiscal supervision** regards eligibility of the foundation and/or (part of) its activities for fiscal privileges. This supervision is performed by fiscal authorities. Some countries have a specific department within the revenue service for dealing with charitable and public benefit organizations, such as the Financial Intermediaries and Claims Office in the UK. In other countries such a specialized department may not be present although there may be a *de facto* specialized department charged with the implementation of the most important fiscal law. An example of this is the Inspection of Registration and Succession in the Netherlands. Section 2 deals primarily with non-fiscal supervision.
- With regard to the **supervision regarding compliance with the law and the governing document** of the foundation, the variety

of supervisory schemes is much wider as compared to the fiscal supervision. Most commonly supervision is charged to an organ of public administration at a national and/or regional or local level, a special supervisory authority, the public prosecutor or attorney general, or the court. These bodies have in common that they are not connected to a specific foundation and in this respect are external supervisors (see 2.2).

The law may provide for the striking of empty shell foundations from the public registers and subsequently dissolving them. In the Netherlands for example, this power is given to the Chamber of Commerce and Industry that keeps the relevant public register (Article 2:19a CC). This is primarily an administrative instrument and not so much a form of supervision as discussed in this chapter. For reasons of comprehensiveness, however, it should be mentioned.

In a few countries, there are also mechanisms that provide for supervisory relations that are related to specific individual foundations. This is done by a supervisory body within the foundation or through the participation of people appointed by the supervisory authority in the managing board of the foundation. This type of supervision will be referred to as 'internal' supervision (see 2.3).

To conclude, the law may provide for specific obligations to the public, promoting transparency, and thus a form of social supervision, which is accompanied by a right of third parties to take, or request, legal action (see 2.4).

2.2 External supervision

In a small majority of the countries included in this research, supervision of foundations is conducted by a public administration body, in some cases including the office of the prime minister or the council of ministers. In most cases however, the supervision is charged either to the ministry of interior, the ministry of finance, the ministry of justice, or the ministry whose field of responsibility is most closely related to the purpose of the foundation (see Appendix I, Question 20). In the latter case the ministry of education would supervise foundations with an educational purpose, the ministry of culture those with a cultural purpose, etc.

The supervisory tasks may be charged to decentralized units of a ministry, or may be the autonomous competence of a local authority. An example of the former is found in Slovenia, an example of the latter is found in Sweden where in accordance with 9 kap. 1 § Foundation Act, the county administrative board (*länsstyrelse*) is the competent authority unless the government appoints another authority.

In other countries, the situation is more complex. Supervision at a national level might be combined with supervision at a local level or regional level, or the geographical scope of activities of the foundation might determine which body has supervisory authority regarding its activities. In the latter case, the authority of supervision is determined on the basis of the concept of subsidiarity. As a result supervision over foundations can lack uniformity within one country. Each of the jurisdictions should be dealt with separately in order to describe the manner of supervision in such a country adequately.[6]

The alternative to supervision by a body of public administration is supervision by a body with a more or less politically independent position. In that case, the supervising authority may act on a national level, yet not be exclusively responsible for the supervision of foundations. In a number of countries, this type of supervision is chosen. The element of relative independence is, however, about as much as these bodies have in common. The degree of specialization and the instruments and sanctions available to the supervisors vary substantially. The relevant body may, as is indicated by its name, be charged with a variety of tasks, among which is the supervision of foundations, for instance the National Board of Patents and Registration in Finland. Or it may be charged with supervision of nonprofit organizations in general, such as the Register of Non Profit Organizations in Estonia, or as is the case is some countries be charged with the supervision of public benefit organizations in particular. Examples of the latter category are the Scottish Charities Office and the *Protectorados* in Spain as well as the Charity Commission for England and Wales.

In relatively few countries supervision is left to the court or the office of the public prosecutor or attorney general. The law does not always charge these offices with supervision, but occasionally merely gives them certain powers they can use at their discretion. This is for example the case in the Netherlands, where public prosecutors may use their powers, but are not compelled to do so.

In practical terms the nature of the supervisory body is relevant for the nature of the supervision. A body of public administration is more likely to include public policy considerations in the performance of its supervisory tasks than a body with a more independent

---

[6] For Germany see for instance Büermann, p.1009–38.

position. However, the Charity Commissioners of England and Wales, despite their relatively independent position, demonstrate some concern with public policy issues.[7] In this respect, supervision by the courts or the public prosecutor or attorney general is most likely to be uninfluenced by public policy concerns and be focused on legitimacy rather than efficiency or what is considered desirable from a public policy point of view.

2.3 Internal supervision

2.3.1 Internal state supervision

In a few countries one or more representatives of the state may be appointed to the board of directors. In Greece, the Council of National Bequests[8] may propose to the foundation's administration to have a council representative on the foundation board for achieving better supervision (Article 21 Law 4154/1961). Unless provided for otherwise in the governing document this member has the right to vote in foundation board meetings.

In France the direct influence of the government on the management of a foundation is the most far-reaching of the countries included in this survey. The requirements in French law are that civil servants (representatives of the *pouvoir publics*) should be appointed to the board (*conseil d'administration*) of a foundation although their number should not constitute the majority. In practice, the *Conseil d'État* recommends as a rule that one third of the board members should be public servants, another third of the initial board should be appointed by the founder, while the remaining third is appointed by the other board members. With regard to foundations with a specific purpose or character, other similar conditions may be prescribed, the rationale for which is apparently to achieve independence from the founder.

These provisions provide direct influence in terms of participation in decision-making by the foundation's 'supervisor'. The explanation for these government–foundation relations must be sought in the history of a country. However, it is clear that the more influence the state has on the composition of the board and the participation of

---

[7] For a recent critique on this issue, see Chesterman, p. 333, *et seq*.

[8] Composed of a) a judge of the Supreme Court, b) a legal counsel of the state, c) a director of the Ministry of Finance, d) an employee of the Ministry of Health and Social Welfare or the Ministry of Education and Religion, e) a vice-director or manager of the National Bank of Greece, f) two independent individuals (Article 3 Compulsory Law 2039/1939).

civil servants on the board, the more the foundation will resemble an institution of public law and thus lose its independent character.

2.3.2 Internal 'civil' supervision

The traditional form of supervision encompasses an external supervisory body that is not specifically connected with an individual foundation. An alternative or complement to this form of supervision might be the creation of a supervisory board that supervises the board of directors/trustees. This form of supervision is reminiscent of the concept of the supervisory board in commercial companies, as is known in some continental European countries.

This form of supervision is not commonly prescribed by law. It is done, however, in a few countries, underscoring the organizational character of the foundation as an independent legal entity. Examples of countries where a supervisory board is prescribed by law are Estonia and in Hungary. The concept of the supervisory board also exists in for instance Macedonia, a country not included in this survey (Law on Citizens Associations and Foundations (1998), Article 63).

In Estonia, a supervisory body is mandatory for foundations in general (Article 16 Foundations Act). In Hungary, on the other hand, a supervisory body is mandatory only for foundations recognized as a public benefit organization under Law CLVI of 1997 if its annual income exceeds five million HUF. The governing document of the foundation must provide for the establishment and presumably the manner of appointment and dismissal of the members of the supervisory body. The members have, apart from any powers granted in the governing document, extensive rights to information and access to meetings of the board of directors.

If the supervisory board learns of a violation of the law or any other events, acts or omissions seriously violating the interests of the organization or a fact giving rise to liability of the directors, it shall convene a meeting of the board of directors, provided that the board is in a position to correct the situation. If the board of directors does not take appropriate action to restore the legality of the operation of the foundation, the supervisory body shall immediately inform the public prosecutor (Article 11, Law CLVI 1997). This mandatory supervisory board thus performs a dual function. On the one hand it is established and formed in accordance with the governing document of the foundation to guard over the interests of the foundation, but on the other hand it must by law inform the public prosecutor of certain findings. In this respect it has the position of a civil servant.

This form of supervision may be applied voluntarily. To my knowledge, a supervisory board is quite often used by foundations in the Netherlands, a country in which state supervision of foundations in general is quite limited and not very effective. Providing for a supervisory board in the Netherlands is often deemed desirable for promoting good governance and strategically-wise decisions or is sometimes required to receive financial or other support from private or public sources. In case of a breach of duty, the supervisory directors are personally liable in a similar way to managing directors. In general, the laws of countries included in this research do not prohibit an internal form of supervision, although when extensive state supervision is provided for, the need to establish voluntary internal control is obviously less pressing and, perhaps, less desired by all parties.

Normally, the members of the supervisory body would have to guard over the interests of the foundation, and are equipped with the necessary powers to enable them to perform this function. These powers would in the Netherlands typically provide for a right to information, to approve the annual accounts and reports, to appoint, suspend and dismiss members of the governing board as well as the power to represent the foundation in cases of conflicting interests between the foundation and one or more of its members of the governing board. It might also include the approval of certain sensitive decisions, including the budget, major investments and amendments to the governing document.

2.4 Social supervision, transparency and the role of third parties

Third parties are persons that have no direct legal relationship with the foundation. The concept of third parties thus excludes persons who occupy a position on any of the foundation's organs or otherwise have powers under its governing document or who have a contractual relationship with the foundation. Third parties may, however, have a legitimate interest in the proper conduct of affairs of the foundation. Without any specific provisions in the law, they would not be in a position to take any legal action against a foundation on the grounds that it is not acting in accordance with its governing document.

The persons who might have such a legitimate interest include for example the founder, the (potential) beneficiaries or volunteers for the foundation. With regard to the legal position of the founder, most jurisdictions have provisions in the law granting the founder certain rights *vis-à-vis* the foundation. This may include altering the foundation's governing document[9] or supervising the board of directors/trustees.[10] The founder as a rule also has the right to file a motion for dissolution of the foundation on the grounds of the foundation operating in violation of its governing document or lacking sufficient assets to achieve its purpose. The rationale for granting any such rights to the founder is obvious; the founder is after all the founder. A dissolution will not, as a rule, have the effect of returning the remaining assets to the founder (see 5.7).

For (potential) beneficiaries (and even less so for other persons), the legal rationale is not so clear. With regard to beneficiaries, a distinction must be made between the situation where the beneficiaries are described in general terms, and the situation where they are sufficiently clearly described in the foundation's governing document that their identity can be established. In the latter situation the relationship between the foundation and the beneficiaries is considered legally relevant. The beneficiaries as such may then have been granted certain rights. For instance, in Luxembourg the beneficiaries have to consent to an amendment of the governing document (see 4), and in Germany the original beneficiaries cannot be removed by amending the governing document (Article 87 sub 2 BGB, with regard to dissolution see Article 88 BGB).

A substantial number of countries grant certain rights to third parties in addition to the founder and the 'recognized' beneficiary, provided that they have a legitimate interest. These rights may include all or some of the following (see Table 4.1):

- a right to information
- a right to seek enforcement of the law and internal rules of the foundation
- a right to file a complaint
- a right to file a motion for dissolution (see also 5.7)
- a right to file a motion for dismissal of board members/trustees.

As implied above, not all laws grant rights to third parties (see Table 4.1), or the right to start legal proceedings may be subject to approval.[11] Apparently in some countries the state is seen as the only

---

[9] E.G. Hungary, Article 74/b sub 5, though not the name or purpose.

[10] E.g. Macedonia, Law on Citizen Associations and Foundation, Article 42; Finland, Article 15 Foundations Act, a founder may submit a request for rectification for breaches of duty.

[11] E.g. in England and Wales, permission from the court or Charity Commissioners is required, Article 33 Charities Act 1993.

Table 4.1 Rights of Third Parties

	Receive information	Enforcement of law and internal rules	File a complaint	Other
Austria	–	–	–	–
Belgium	–	–	–	*
Bulgaria	Yes†	–	–	–
Cyprus	–	–	Yes	–
Czech Rep.	Annual accounts	–	–	–
Denmark	–	–	–	–
Eng & Wales	–	–	Yes	–
Estonia	Yes	Yes	–	–
Finland	Yes	–	–	–
France	–	–	–	–
Germany	+/–	–	–	–
Greece	Annual accounts published	Yes	–	–
Hungary	Yes + information is public	–	Yes	–
Ireland	Annual accounts public	–	–	–
Italy	–	Yes	–	–
Liechtenstein	Yes	Yes	–	–
Luxemburg	Annual accounts published	Yes	–	–
Netherlands	–	–	–	****(***)**
Scotland	Yes	–	Yes	–
Slovenia	–	–	–	–
Spain	Yes	–	Yes	–
Sweden	Information is public	–	Yes	–
Switzerland	–	–	–	–

†   For public benefit only
*   Annulment of resolutions
**   Request dissolution
***   Request dismissal of board members/trustees
**** Enforcement of legal and internal rules governing the foundation through the court, reversal of changes to governing document in specific cases. With regard to foundations that have established a works council, trade union which has members among the employees of the foundation (as well persons granted this right in the governing documents or contract) may request a formal enquiry procedure, art. 2:236, 347 CC.

or at least the principal party with an interest in the proper functioning of foundations. In contrast, in several other countries more room for third party action is created, thus acknowledging the public's interest.

In this respect two aspects are particularly relevant. The first is the access of third parties to the information required to decide whether or not grounds for action exist. Effective enforcement of rights by third parties can only be achieved if the foundation is sufficiently transparent. The availability of the annual reports to the public either through publication, public filing or providing a copy on request, is a key aspect in this respect (see 3.1 and Table 4.3). Interestingly, quite wide transparency requirements apply for example to public benefit foundations under the Hungarian CLVI Act, Articles 5 and 7, including publishing the most relevant data, communicating their decisions to the persons involved and the public, and providing access to the documents related to its activities to anyone interested. In addition, its operations are open to the public in a general sense. Provisions of a similar nature are also found in other countries in central and eastern Europe, for instance, in Croatia and Macedonia. The exact scope of these provisions remains unknown to the author and will probably be developed in case law over time. It would seem however that too extensive an application could violate a foundation's right to privacy as guaranteed under Article 8 of the European Convention on Human Rights.[12]

The other, and more challenging, aspect with regard to the potential of third party action is determining under which conditions a third party has such an interest in the conduct of affairs of the foundation that it justifies an action against the foundation. It appears that in the various jurisdictions, a different approach is taken with regard to this issue. In some countries the concept of a third party is quite wide, in others it is restricted to persons whose rights are affected, or to persons who are under threat of suffering specific harm in relation to the foundation.[13] Interestingly, under some laws the category of third parties with a justified interest is widened where beneficiaries are not accurately described in the governing document; in this case all persons that meet the general description are considered beneficiaries.[14]

---

[12] See European Court of Human Rights, Judgment of 16 December 1992, Series A, nr. 251-B EHRR (1993, para. 31 (Niemetz v. Germany), and Denters and van Veen section, 5.2.

[13] The Netherlands, Supreme Court 25 October 1991, NJ 1992, 149.

[14] E.g. Estonia, Article 39 sub 2 Foundations Act; Macedonia, Article 65 sub 2 Law on Citizens Associations and Foundations 1998.

Ultimately, the judiciary will decide if an applicant sufficiently meets the criteria of a third party with a legitimate or justified interest.

To conclude, the issue of supervision reflects the issue of the transparency of foundations in a broader sense. Are foundations, especially those that claim to serve the public benefit, accountable in some way to the public or toward the state? Under what conditions can interested members of the public take action to promote compliance with the law and internal regulations of a foundation? The answer begins with the availability of relevant information to the public. Furthermore, legislators and courts may choose to widen or narrow the category of such interested parties. Interestingly, young democracies in Europe take the lead in experimenting with a high degree of transparency and creating more room for third party actions through the combination of transparency requirements and widening the circle of persons that qualify as a third party with a justified interest.

3 Post-incorporation obligations, requirements and restrictions

3.1 Book-keeping, annual accounts and reports

As a rule, a relevant state authority has certain powers to enforce the proper application of the foundation's property, that is application of the foundation's property in accordance with the law and the governing document of the foundation. In this respect, one can distinguish between powers regarding the effectiveness of the board of directors/trustees and those safeguarding legitimacy of their acting on behalf of the foundation.

- The aspect of legitimacy concerns the acting in accordance with the law and the purpose of the foundation as laid down in its governing document.
- The aspect of effectiveness regards whether the board of directors/trustees has made the right decisions, or taken the appropriate action to realise the best results for the foundation.

The relevant state authority is generally given the power to audit, at random or upon special authorization by the court, the books of the foundation or to investigate its actions. The power to investigate foundations will be dealt with in more detail in 5.2.

The effectiveness of supervision depends to a large extent on the availability of the relevant information to the supervisory authority and other potential 'supervisors' (see 2) and the quality of such information. Elementary in this respect are:

- the obligation to conduct proper book-keeping
- the preparing of annual accounts and reports, as well as subsequently the filing, submitting or publication of the annual accounts and reports.

The laws in the countries included in this survey require that the foundation, or rather the board of directors/trustees, shall properly keep books and other relevant documents, and prepare an annual account and annual report. Generally, these documents have to be retained for a certain number of years.

With regard to the keeping of books and other relevant documents, the primary requirement is that the manner in which this is done should allow for the determination of the rights and obligations of the foundation. In this respect it is not just relevant with regard to the accountability of members of the governing board/trustees, but is also a prerequisite for proper management of the foundation. In general the law prescribes no specific methods for the keeping of books and administration, although it might require that the relevant documents or some of them, for instance the annual accounts, be kept in paper or it might allow all or certain documents to be furnished to other information carriers.

The requirements regarding the content and form of the annual account and report show more variation among the countries included in this survey, and occasionally also within one country. In the latter case, the requirements are usually related to the size of the foundation, more specifically its annual income, expenditure or annual turnover. The variation mainly regards the components of the annual accounts (e.g. whether they consist of a balance sheet and/or account of profit and loss) and whether or not an independent (in some cases also certified) accountant shall audit the accounts. Also specific book-keeping and accounting requirements may apply to foundations running a commercial enterprise. Commonly this entails an audit by a (certified) accountant and the publication of the accounts.[15]

---

[15] For instance Hungary, Article 12, Governmental Decree 8/1996, Sweden Foundation law, 3 kap. 1 §, or the Netherlands with regard to foundations running a large enterprise generating 6 million guilders (approximately €2.7) turnover during a certain number of consecutive years, Article 2:360 CC.

To make the annual accounts and reports available, these documents may have to be filed in a publicly accessible register, may have to be submitted to the relevant supervisory authority(ies) or may have to be published in a national or sometimes local newspaper.[16] In some countries a combination of these requirements applies to foundations, especially foundations serving a public interest purpose. In addition, in for instance England, Scotland and Hungary,[17] these foundations must make a copy of the annual document available to the public. The latter provisions are aimed at promoting transparency and 'social' supervision (see also 2.4).

Publicly accessible registers for filing annual documents may be held by the chambers of commerce and industry, the courts, a ministry or some other special agency. The authorities to which the reports must be submitted include ministries, local governments, tax authorities or another supervising authority. It should be noted that information submitted to a supervisory authority may not be made available to the public. The supervisory authorities often do not function as publicly accessible registers. For transparency purposes, therefore, the obligation to file annual documents at such a register, or other publication requirements, should be in addition to an obligation to submit annual documents and other information to the supervisory authority.

In only a few countries, is there no general obligation to submit, file or publish the annual reports and accounts. This is, for instance, the case in France and the Netherlands.

However, if an organization seeks recognition by the tax authorities as serving the public benefit (such recognition is under Netherlands law not required to enjoy the fiscal privileges when in fact serving a public benefit purpose), the fiscal authorities require the annual documents to be submitted to them.

The tax authorities may in general, nevertheless, request a copy of the annual accounts and records to monitor compliance with fiscal provisions. Especially when there is no obligation to file, publish or submit annual documents, the relevant authority is dependent on complaints or other information from the public respectively, or has to be otherwise alerted such as through a court decision that a foundation is declared bankrupt. Supervision is in these cases prone to be ineffective, or at best, retaliatory rather than preventive in character.

---

[16] E.g. Greece, Article 101 Compulsory Law 2039/1939.

[17] Article 5 Law Reform Act 1990, Article 19 Act CLVI 1997 respectively.

3.2 Pay-out, application to activities and reserves

3.2.1 Restrictions: application, management costs and conflicting interests

The most general of restrictions and requirements regarding expenditure of the means of the foundation is that the expenses made should be compatible with and serve the purpose of the foundation as laid down in its governing document. A violation of this rule leads to a breach of duty and may lead for instance to personal liability of the managing directors (for sanctions see 5). Occasionally, the approved budget also has a binding character. This is for instance the case in Greece where board members are liable for expenses made acting outside the approved budget of the foundation. A similar sanction applies to transferring credits from one item of the budget to another without prior approval. Thus the budget which pursuant to Article 102 of the Compulsory Act 2039/1939 is subject to approval by the Ministry of Finance, is in fact a binding document for the managing board (see 5.5).

In addition, foundations are as a rule prohibited from distributing their revenue or assets to their founders, board members/trustees or other officials. This may include the spouse and relatives of the founder up to the fourth degree of kinship.[18] Moreover, in the Netherlands, for instance, a foundation may not pay out any benefits unless these pay-outs are of an 'ideal or social' character (Article 2:285 sub 3 CC).

Reimbursement of reasonable costs incurred by those serving on the board of directors/trustees is not generally prohibited. Also most countries allow board members/trustees to be paid for their services, provided that the salary is not excessive and conforms to market standards. There are however exceptions to this rule. In some countries, members of the board of directors/trustees are expected to fulfil their duty voluntarily and without remuneration.[19]

As a rule there are no specific limitations on the costs of management, including administrative costs, of foundations in general. In some countries, however, such restrictions are present. These restrictions may be set in the law in an unambiguous manner, or in general terms. In Estonia, for example, the administrative costs of public benefit organizations must be connected directly to the objectives of the

---

[18] See for instance in Spain, Article 2 of the Law 30/1994.

[19] For instance in Spain, Article 13.4 of Foundations (Law 30/1994). Similarly for the United Kingdom, see Salamon, p. 332; this rule may be overridden in the relevant document of the foundation, see Picarda, p. 465.

foundation, and the amount must be justified by the nature of the organization's activities and objectives. Alternatively, the law may require the governing document of the foundation to provide restrictions on administrative costs. An example of the latter is found in the Czech Republic, where the governing document must limit the annual expenses related to management to a certain percentage of a) total annual income, b) total contributions received, or c) the value of the foundation's property. Here it should be noted, however, that in some countries, the supervisory authority is involved in setting the budget or can take action if it finds that the foundation is not operated efficiently (see 3.2.2). In these cases a foundation consequently is *de facto* restricted in its expenses on administrative costs to the extent that the supervisory authority allows or may question the amount of such expenses.

Although in some countries there is an idealistic rationale for these restrictions they are unmistakably, though not exclusively, related to the fact that the foundation needs to be protected against its board members/trustees. Similarly, transactions in which the foundation and – directly or indirectly – any of its officials are involved, pose the threat that an official will allow his or her personal interest to prevail over that of the foundation. Most countries have a rule prohibiting directors/trustees from acting on behalf of the foundation when there is a conflict of interests with regard to the persons involved. However, these rules are not always codified, nor are the prohibited transactions described in detail.

In fact, only a few countries specify certain transactions that are prohibited altogether. For instance in the Czech Republic, transactions regarding endowed assets with members of the board or persons related to them are not allowed. In Sweden directors are generally prohibited from dealing with cases where conflicting interests are involved including representing the foundation (2 kap. 21 § Foundation Law). In addition, it is prohibited for foundations to give loans to founders, members of the board of directors, their relatives or legal persons of which they are a member of the board of directors (2 kap. 6 § Foundation Law). Furthermore, in the case of conflicting interests, the foundation shall be represented by the County Administrative Board.

3.2.2 Application requirements versus reserves

Pay-out and application requirements relate directly to the issue of the realization of the purpose of the foundation. The realization of the purpose of a foundation cannot be achieved if it does little else than accumulate assets. Furthermore, from a socio-economic point of view, it is undesirable to allow such funds simply to exist without actually serving a specific purpose. Requirements regarding the application of the foundation's assets are therefore not without meaning in this respect. In the majority of the legal systems included in this survey the law requires that assets of the foundation must be used for the realization of the foundation's purposes, without any further specifications or conditions. The supervisory authorities that are charged with ensuring that the board of directors/trustees follow the instructions laid down in the governing document may take action in case of a breach of duty committed by them.

Typically, lack of sufficient activity aimed at realizing the purposes of a foundation may under certain conditions allow legal action by the supervisory authorities (see also 5). If a foundation performs no activities or none that are significant, including pay-outs in accordance with its purposes, it is initially likely that a foundation's tax-exempt or public benefit status will be at risk. The point at which a foundation can be deemed sufficiently inactive to give rise to legal action is not, however, by its nature crystal clear.

For this purpose pay-out requirements are deployed by some countries to create such clarity in the law. These requirements are as a rule defined as a percentage of revenue to be expended on the foundation's purpose. The percentages range from 50% to 80% of revenues to be spent, or earmarked, within a one to five year period.[20] These requirements are usually relevant from a fiscal point of view, but may be an obligation related to the legal form of a foundation in general as well.[21] Non-compliance with the requirements will then result in a breach of duty of the board of directors/trustees, rather than having merely fiscal repercussions.

Although pay-out requirements are a helpful instrument in this respect, they do not allow for the flexibility to make adjustments in reaction to incidents that are not brought on by the foundation itself.

Countries having a common-law tradition in particular adopt a different approach with regard to charitable trusts. Typically, no specific legal requirements regarding pay-out or application to activities exist,

---

[20] E.g. Sweden 80% of income; Germany 75% of net income on capital investments; Spain 70% of income; Finland 50% of revenues.

[21] For instance, in Spain, Article 25 Law on Foundations.

yet trustees have to account for, and be able to explain why, any revenues are not paid out or spent on charitable activities. In general, trustees have to justify retaining income rather than applying it for its charitable purposes. If the relevant authority finds the justification insufficient, the foundation may face enquiries and in addition a reduction in its tax relief.

Moreover, a charity is required to apply income other than in the form of donations and some government grants to its charitable purpose, or else this income will be taxable.[22] In addition, in the UK a charity risks a proportional reduction of tax reliefs when incurring non-qualifying expenditures, including investments and loans that are not approved for tax purposes, to the extent that it has income and gains other than in the form of donations exceeding £10,000 and it has a surplus of such income over its expenditure on its stated charitable purpose in that year.

Thus, in common-law jurisdictions, despite the fact that the law regarding reservations is described in generic terms, the supervisory authorities in fact appear closely involved in the reservation/application policy conducted by the trustees.

3.3 Investment and portfolio requirements and restrictions

Not very many countries report the existence of specific investment and portfolio requirements. In fact in many of the countries included in this survey, there are no specific provisions prescribing which investments are allowed and which are not. The matter of investment policy is usually dealt with in general rules. The first of these rules is that the governing document should allow implicitly or explicitly for the board of directors/trustees to make certain investments. With regard to the latter, investments are commonly allowed, unless this is in conflict with the purpose of the foundation.

Similarly, the duties of the board of directors/trustees with regard to investments and investment policy are often not laid down explicitly in statutory law. An exception to this rule is found in Finland where the Foundations Act (Article 10) states that the board of directors shall secure profitable investment of assets. The essence of the applicable rule is that the governing board/trustees should act as ordinarily prudent persons when making investments. This relates to the standard of performance required in general of the board of

---

[22] Article 505, Income and Corporation Taxes Act 1988.

directors/trustees (see 5.5). Generally this implies that the members of the board of directors/trustees should take care to make investments that are beneficial to the foundation, and not to make speculative investments. An interesting duty in respect of investment policies is found in Hungary, where a public benefit foundation under the Act CLVI of 1997, or rather its board of directors, is required to set its own investment regulations. The content and form of these regulations are not prescribed in detail by the law.

In a number of countries more detailed and specific provisions apply with regard to investments. These requirements may include restrictions on the kind of assets in which a foundation can invest and may require government approval before a foundation performs a specific transaction. A good example of these requirements is found in Greece. First of all, the law requires that revenues from the transfer of (charitable) assets have to be deposited on an interest bearing account. Otherwise, investments are allowed only in specifically mentioned assets, or in assets (including foreign ones) where the investment is profitable and safe and does not conflict with the realization of the foundation's purpose. In addition, any investments made by the foundation are subject to prior approval of the supervisory authority, and any lending of money is, apart from being subject to approval, allowed only at an interest rate of 5% and guaranteed by sufficient securities. The supervisory authority (the minister of finance) also determines the terms of the loan agreement and the guarantees provided.[23]

Government authorization of investment decisions exists outside Greece, in some *Länder* in Germany and in Austria. In Austria for instance, a major sale of assets is subject to approval and will be granted where the sale does not jeopardize the realization of the purpose of the foundation. In the Czech Republic, the foundation's registered assets cannot be alienated during its existence. In addition, funds must be deposited at a special bank account or be used to buy government securities. Participation in a joint stock company may not exceed a certain percentage of the foundation's assets and 20% of the issued stock of the company. In England and Wales and in Scotland under the Trustee Investment Act 1961, authorization by the supervisory authorities is required only when the trust deed does not provide sufficient authorization to the trustees. Statutory law based on the 1961 Act prescribes the manner in which the assets of

---

[23] Articles 37, 73 and 100 Compulsory Law 2039/1939.

the trust can be applied in a narrower and wider range of investments. The supervisory authority can also order a division of trust assets over such investments.

The type of regulation described above indicates direct state involvement in the application and investment of the means of a foundation. This does not necessarily prohibit foundations from making ethical investment policies, leading to less profitable investments. Only Scottish law is more rigid on this point, demanding that the best result for the charity shall be sought. To a lesser extent this is the case in England and Wales, where the trustees must look for the best overall return possible for the charity leaving less room for their personal views than in jurisdictions where trust law is not applied.

3.4 Donations

A somewhat peculiar issue is the competence of foundations to accept donations. In a way, supervision of this competence is related to the issue of reserves building, in the sense that the state might want to be able to control any growth in a foundation's property. Other possible explanations for state authorization of donations could be to check whether the donation and the possible obligations attached to it are compatible with the purpose of the foundation, or that the donation will not cause any damage to the foundation. The establishment of the identity of major donors to foundations could also be of interest to the state. However, neither of these reasons seems sufficiently convincing to establish the necessity of such provisions.

In fact, not many countries restrict the competence of foundations to accept donations (*inter vivos* or testamentary) but there are countries that subject certain donations to governmental approval or a notification duty.[24] For instance, in Luxembourg, Grand Ducal approval is required for donations exceeding LUF500,000 (€12,395) (Article 16 and 36 Law of 21 April 1928 on Nonprofit Associations and Foundations). The case is similar in Belgium with regard to donations (other than *dons manuels*) exceeding BEF400,000 (€9916), as adjusted. French rules are too complicated to describe here, but in general accepting donations and legacies is subject to authorization

---

[24] For example, in Slovakia, Article 38 Law on Foundations with regard to donations exceeding SK5000. The notification should include the amount of the gift as well as the full name and address of the donor.

from the prefect. Corporate foundations however may not receive donations.[25]

As a rule, accepting donations is not subject to restrictions other than that the gift or the obligations attached to it shall be compatible with the foundation's legal capacity (in particular with regard to real-estate) or its purpose. Interestingly, what is considered compatible is not uniform. For instance, in Austria, a gift comprised of shares in a for-profit company is considered to be incompatible with the purpose of a public benefit foundation, whereas in many countries the possession of shares would not as such be in conflict with a public benefit purpose, although a maximum may apply to the possession of shares (see 3.3). The responsibility for accepting gifts and ensuring that they are compatible with the purpose of the foundation lies with the board of directors/trustees.

3.5 Fundraising

In the majority of the countries included in the survey the regulation of fundraising is restricted to the issuance of a permit by the local government. This applies to fundraising activities in public places, more particularly to door-to-door or on-the-street solicitation of donations, and the organization of lotteries or other games of chance among the public. Other forms of fundraising are virtually unregulated other than by general provisions of criminal law. Occasionally specific forms of solicitation are prohibited altogether. For instance, in the Netherlands an organization is prohibited from selling goods by telephone when it is suggested or implied that (part of) the proceeds will benefit some public benefit organization (Article 435e Penal Code). In a number of countries no regulation applicable to fundraising was reported at all. Among these countries, we can count Belgium, Bulgaria, the Czech Republic, Denmark, Estonia, Hungary, Italy, Liechtenstein, Slovenia and Spain.

The rationale for governmental regulation of fundraising is obviously to protect its citizens from harm caused by crime, fraud, misrepresentation and undue annoyance. Requiring a permit allows the government at least to establish the identity of those raising funds and their authority to act on behalf the foundation, as well as the time, and to a certain extent the manner, of solicitation. Ideally it should enhance trust and confidence among the donating public in fundraising organizations.

---

[25] See Alfandri and Nardone, p. 157-8 and 165-6 and Frotiée and De Monseignat, France 6-7.

A permit for fundraising activities in public may be required by national law or on the basis of a local ordinance, depending on the type of fundraising and the country involved. As a rule the issuance is made conditional upon the submission of a financial report showing the costs and revenues of such a fundraising activity, and is valid for a limited time.

In France, Law no. 91/772 *relative [...] au contrôle des comptes des organismes faisant appel à la générosité publique*, requires fundraising appeals to be announced beforehand, and the accounts and utilization of the funds raised are subject to control by the *Cour des Comptes*. In addition, in France corporate foundations cannot raise funds.[26]

More comprehensive regulation exists in the UK, which has the most detailed laws regulating fundraising. This regulation is found in the Charities Act and a number of other acts including the Lotteries and Amusements Act 1976 (amended 1993). In addition to the regulation applicable to the fundraising foundation, those involved with fundraising for personal benefit (the professional fundraisers and commercial participants) are also subject to regulation. The former parties are forbidden to be involved in charitable fundraising unless it is done in accordance with an agreement with the charity they (claim to) represent. The form of the agreement is prescribed by the Charitable Institutions (Fundraising) Regulations 1994. Fundraising by telephone, television and radio are not regulated.

Next to governmental regulation, in a number of countries a form of self-regulation has developed over time. Self-regulatory organizations exist in Austria, England and Wales, France, Germany, the Netherlands, Norway, Sweden, and Switzerland and initiatives to establish rating systems are taken in other countries such as Denmark and Belgium. The self-regulatory organizations are members of the International Committee on Fundraising Organizations (ICFO), which also has members from the USA and Canada.

In general self-regulatory organizations operate a set of standards with which the affiliated organization, or those that seek affiliation, must comply. Organizations that comply with the applicable standards are accredited, which gives the right to use a logo or other easily recognisable device ('seal of approval') to enable the public to identify the organization readily as being accredited. In Sweden such organizations receive a special account number starting with '90' ('90-account'). These standards generally contain requirements

---

[26] Salamon, p. 114.

regarding the functioning and composition of the governing board, application of funds to the realization of the purpose, fundraising practices, financial management, accountability, and transparency. Apart from issuing a seal of approval, as a rule the self-regulatory organizations coordinate or are involved in coordinating fundraising appeals on a national level to avoid confusion among the public.[27]

4 Alteration of purpose and other structural changes

4.1 Rationale for provisions regarding the alteration of the foundation purpose

Provisions in the law regarding the altering of articles of the governing document are particularly relevant for foundations. Foundations are set up for an indefinite period of time; it may later become clear that the realization of the purposes set out in the governing document is no longer possible or relevant in the manner described. To avoid redundancy of the foundation, an alteration of the foundation's purposes may be necessary. The founder(s) may not have authorized an amendment to the purpose of the foundation or to its governing document in general. A change of the purpose of the foundation however directly affects the application of the foundation's property to the purpose it was initially destined to serve. The governing board/trustees therefore cannot as a matter of law be granted the power to amend the governing document, unless adequately authorized by the founder(s). The same applies to other structural changes such as a conversion to another legal form, a merger, split-off or the dissolution of a foundation. The involvement of the state with an amendment to the purpose of the foundation or another structural change is usually justified to promote both longevity of the foundation and the protection of the property for the initial purpose or a purpose closely related to it.

Also relevant with respect to such changes are whether or not the authority to supervise a foundation is generally connected to its legal form, and/or related to its purpose being for a public benefit. As seen in 2, the specific purpose or scope of activities may determine the supervisory authority, depending on the legal system involved. A change of purpose from a public benefit to a private benefit purpose

---

[27] For more details about self regulation of fundraising in the Netherlands see van Veen's contribution to Salamon, p. 242–3.

would in addition most probably remove the foundation's property from public scrutiny, this property having been built up with public support and indirect public funds by means of fiscal privileges. Similar issues arising in the case of a voluntary or involuntary dissolution will be discussed in more detail in 5.

4.2 Restrictions regarding alterations: substance and competence

With regard to provisions relating to the issue of altering the articles of the governing document, a substantial variation in schemes is deployed. These schemes focus overall on two relevant aspects:

- the nature of the changes
- the power to change the articles of the governing document.

With regard to the nature of the change, the restrictions regarding amendments to the purpose of the foundation are often stricter than those regarding other provisions. For example, the law may allow for an unauthorized change of the articles of the governing document if thus provided for in the governing document, but a change to a foundation's purpose will usually need the authorization of a state body.[28] The power of the founder is thus restricted in the sense that he or she cannot authorize the directors/trustees to alter the purpose of the foundation. An alteration of the purpose may also be prohibited altogether, as opposed to other articles of the governing document. For example, in Hungary, the name and purpose of a foundation are inalterable (Article 74/B subsec. 5 Book 4 CC). Similarly under Swiss law, a foundation's purpose in principle cannot be altered (Article 85/86 CC).

As a rule, however, a change of purpose is allowed only under certain conditions, in particular that it is necessary to change the purpose because it can no longer be achieved as it is prescribed, or that for other reasons a change is necessary to allow the foundation to function in accordance with the founder's will. In Greece, however, the articles may be amended by presidential decree, against the will of the founder, if necessary, for the preservation of the foundation's assets or accomplishment of its purpose (Article 119 CC). The relevant laws typically prescribe that the changes shall be restricted to the minimum so that the new description shall resemble the original as closely as possible. If a foundation is found to be 'beyond repair' it must be dissolved. See 5.7.

---

[28] E.g. in Sweden, 6 kap. 3 § Foundations Act and England and Wales, with regard to charitable companies, Article 64 Charities Act 1993.

With regard to the power to change the governing document, approval by a public supervisory body or court is commonly required. In a number of jurisdictions, the governing document may grant the power to change the governing document to an organ of the foundation without such approval. This power may go as far as including altering the purpose of the foundation without any restrictions, other than those that apply to foundations in general, for example in the Netherlands (Article 2:293 CC). As a rule the organ that is competent to make amendments is the board of directors/trustees.

The only country that as a rule allows a change of articles without approval is Estonia. The law in Estonia allows the supervisory board of a foundation to alter the statutes; this power is however restricted to changes that are necessary because the foundation cannot act in accordance with its purpose as prescribed in its governing document (due to changing circumstances) and the founders cannot (or fail to) make the necessary amendments (Article 41 Foundations Act).

The character of the involvement of the state, if required, to alter the governing document is quite diverse. One approach is that the initiative, or at least the acceptance, of the founder(s) or relevant foundation organ(s) is required.

Usually the relevant organ is the board of directors/trustees. In Liechtenstein however, unless otherwise provided, the founders and the foundation's board, as well as the designated beneficiaries, have to come to an agreement, which is subsequently subject to the approval of the Public Register (Article 552 PGR jo. § 39 and 165 TrUG).

The role of the state in this scenario is restricted to giving approval to any changes in the governing document, including the purpose of the foundation. The supervisory authority or the court could perform this function. Court approval exists for instance in the Netherlands if the governing document does not provide for the power to amend the articles and its unaltered preservation leads to consequences that are deemed reasonably undesirable at the time of establishment (Article 2:294 CC).

A fundamentally different approach is that the supervisory authority has the power to alter the articles, and may even do so on its own initiative without the consent of any of the foundation's organs. The relevant foundation organ may only file a request for alteration but it cannot make any amendments itself, nor is its consent required to make an amendment.

Asking the opinion of the board of directors may be required, as is the case for instance in Germany and Bulgaria. In Greece, amendments to the governing document can be made by Presidential Decree only (Article 110, 119, 120 CC).

It would seem that in this latter scheme the underlying thought is that ultimately the foundation, or at least the property of the foundation, is part of the public domain rather than being an independent entity within society.

4.3 Merger, split-off and conversion

A merger, split-off or conversion constitutes a fundamental organizational and structural change in the life of a foundation. Evidently, similar questions to those related to alteration of the purpose arise. In addition, the justified interests of any creditors of the foundation in question have to be taken into consideration. Any of these changes can follow different routes. The most traditional one is the dissolution of the foundation followed by the establishment of another legal person and the transfer of the assets to it. In this scenario, the rules regarding dissolution and destination of remaining assets apply.

A number of countries (e.g. Bulgaria, the Netherlands, England and Finland), however, also have special provisions for one or more of the above-mentioned transformations, providing for continuation of the legal identity of (at least one of) the foundations involved, or a transition of property without winding up the disappearing foundation or charitable trust involved. In this manner a foundation can be converted into another legal form, such as a company or an association, or could merge with another foundation and thus cease to exist without being dissolved.

In those jurisdictions that have the concept of a fundamental structural change without dissolution of the foundation, similar protective provisions to those that apply to an alteration of the foundation's purpose are enforced. For example, in the Netherlands, court approval is required for any conversion, merger or split-off if the governing document prohibits change of one or more of its provisions. The court can impose the conditions it sees fit to protect the will of the founder, the interests of the beneficiaries or other interests involved. In cases where a change in the governing document is allowed without court approval, the same applies to a conversion, merger and split-off.

Another approach is found in Finland, where a merger is allowed only where it will be beneficial to the realization of the foundation's purpose, and only with a foundation that has the same (although not necessarily identical) purpose (Article 17a Foundations Act).

5 Instruments and sanctions

5.1 General remarks

In the sections above some prerequisites of adequate (state) supervision have been mentioned. The most important of these are in the author's view the obligation of proper book-keeping, to draw up the annual accounts and reports and subsequently submit, file and/or publish these annual accounts and annual reports (see 3.1). In this manner, the supervisory authorities at least have or can obtain the most basic information regarding foundations. It also allows for monitoring or eventual investigation of a foundation's actions over a period of years. When there is no requirement to submit, file or publish annual accounts, supervision is virtually restricted to reacting to complaints from the public, more particularly 'insiders', insolvency proceedings, or publicized scandals. The authorization of certain resolutions or transactions has been dealt with (see 3.2 and 3.3). The relevance of regulatory schemes regarding alteration of a governing document, and in particular changes to the purpose of the foundation, were discussed in 4, with reference to other structural changes.

The above-mentioned elements of the regulation of supervision are basically preventive by nature. They are designed to avoid certain situations or at least to provide documentation to enable monitoring and investigation of policies, activities and the financial state of affairs of foundations. This section will elaborate further on the issue of preventive measures, but will subsequently focus on the other aspect of supervision, which is the disciplinary side. What are the instruments and sanctions that supervisory authorities have at their disposal when they suspect or have concluded that a foundation acts in breach of the law or its governing document?

As a rule the legal systems provide for some or all of the following instruments and sanctions, namely:

- loss or reduction of tax privileges
- investigation of the foundation's bank accounts, books and administration (5.2)

- instructions and injunctions regarding resolutions and activities of the governing board/trustees (5.3)
- dismissal and replacement of members of the board of directors/trustees (5.4)
- civil liability of members of the board of directors/trustees (5.5)
- disciplinary measures or criminal proceedings against the foundation and/or its members of the board of directors/trustees (5.6)
- dissolution of the foundation (5.7).

The first on the list, fiscal sanctions, is in practice an important one. As fiscal issues are discussed in Bater and Habighorst: Tax Treatment of Foundations and their Donors, they are not dealt with here.

5.2 Inspections

Most jurisdictions allow either the supervisory authority or the tax authorities, or both, to ask for information and investigate the books and administration of the foundation. Tax authorities are in general given the right to check on potential taxable subjects. The right to inspect the books and activities by tax authorities is all the more justified taking into account that as a rule foundations claim certain fiscal privileges. With regard to other types of inspection, the legal issues are more complex. In this section, therefore, the non-fiscal inspection is dealt with.

At this point it should be noted that in some legal systems a formal enquiry procedure exists, similar to that operating in a court of law. This procedure is distinct from a supervisory authority's general powers to investigate, in that it allows, for example, for evidence taken on oath, etc., and it can be conducted under supervision of the court.[29] These formal enquiry proceedings go beyond the regular inspection of bank accounts, books and administration. A formal enquiry procedure may be available to third parties (see 2.4).

With regard to the power to inspect bank accounts, books and administration of foundations the laws of the countries included in this survey are uniform in that as a rule they allow such inspection. The main differences exist when looking at the conditions under which such inspections are allowed. Occasionally an inspection can be conducted at any time by the supervisory authority; most commonly, however, an inspection can be conducted by the supervisory

---

[29] E.g. under Article 8 and 9 Charities Act 1993, or in the Netherlands pursuant to Article 2:344-359 CC, with regard to foundations that have, in compliance with the obligations under the Law on Works Councils, established a works council.

authority only when irregularities have come to light.[30] More restrictive is the position taken in some countries that a court order is required for obtaining access to the bank accounts, books and administration to conduct an inspection.[31] Although the power to perform investigations is an important instrument for the supervisory authority, a power to enter at random or without proper justification and adequate procedures, the office of a foundation and office or house of its managing directors is suspicious under Article 8 of the European Convention on Human Rights.[32]

A refusal to cooperate with the authorities may constitute an offence and thus give rise to administrative, fiscal or criminal proceedings.[33] In some countries, it may result in civil sanctions only, ultimately the dismissal of relevant board members/trustees. With regard to penal and civil sanctions also see 5.6.

5.3 Instructions and injunctions

With regard to instructions, a difference should be made between:

- the obligation to submit, file or publish the annual accounts as well as to comply with other formal requirements
- instructions regarding the performance of duties in general.

With regard to the first, these requirements could be seen as being of an administrative nature, where the independence of a foundation or its governing board/trustees in matters of achieving the foundation's purpose is not involved. Non-compliance with these obligations is often sanctioned by means of disciplinary fines (see 5.6).

With regard to the performance of duties *vis-à-vis* the foundation in general, however, a number of jurisdictions allow the supervisory authority to give instructions to the governing board/trustees, ordering them to perform their duties in a proper manner. The supervisory

---

[30] E.g. the Charity Commissioners of England and Wales, Article 8 and 9 Charities Act 1993, and the (Finland) National Board of Patents and Registration, Article 13 Foundation Act.

[31] E.g. in Czech Republic and in the Netherlands, the public prosecutor to request court order against the board of directors of foundation to present the books, only if there are serious grounds to suspect that they have acted in breach of the law or statutes of the foundation, and after such a request has unsuccessfully been directed towards the board of directors (Articles 2:297 and 2:298 CC).

[32] Article 8 ECHR also applies to legal persons, European Court on Human Rights Judgment 16 December 1992, Series A, nr. 251/B *European Human Rights Report* (1993), para. 31. See Denters and van Veen, section 5.

[33] E.g. Greece, Article 140 Compulsory Law 2039/1939.

authority may in certain situations issue an injunction prohibiting the execution of a resolution.[34] In these cases, the competencies of the supervisory authority reach beyond accomplishing compliance with formal requirements and inspecting whether or not a foundation acts in accordance with its purpose and the law in general. The supervisory authority is given the competence to take correctional measures.

It is worth noting with respect to instructions and injunctions that the situation in the countries involved in this survey is not uniform. Many countries require a court order to issue correctional measures rather than allowing the supervisory authority to take them. One could argue that in practice this difference would not be very significant, since the measures to be imposed by the supervisory authority are also subject to challenge in a court of law. However, the fact that the supervisory authority is authorized to issue correctional measures itself implies that it has a stronger supervisory position over the foundations than where a prior court order is required. There are a number of factors contributing to the fact that it is unattractive to challenge a decision by the supervisory authority. First of all financial considerations play a significant role. Second, the personal interests of the directors/trustees are not weighty enough to enter into time-consuming proceedings. Finally, the prospect of entering into proceedings against a supervisory authority that could take correctional measures again in the future can be daunting.

5.4 Appointment and dismissal of board members/trustees

The power to appoint members of the board of directors/trustees is distinct from the power to dismiss. Given that the foundation has no members, it is necessary to provide for an instrument to appoint board members to avoid foundations being inactive and having property tied up indefinitely without being used. Usually, the court or supervisory authority is given the power to appoint members of the board of directors/trustees in cases where, for some reason, an appointment in accordance with the governing document is not possible.[35] Thus, it is not necessarily the case that upon dismissal of a board member/trustee, the court or relevant supervisory authority

---

[34] In e.g. Sweden the County Administrative Board may prohibit the execution of a resolution, and in addition may combine an instruction with a fine. A dismissal of board members on grounds of breach of duty, however, requires a (district) court order, 9 kap. 5 and 6 §.

[35] In the Netherlands the court (Article 2:299 CC), and in England and Wales, Charity Commissioners (Article 18 Charities Act 1993). Interestingly, the Charity Commissioners may also appoint a receiver, under the same provision.

can appoint another person to a resulting vacancy. Usually an appointment would be done in accordance with the governing document, where possible.

A dismissal of board members/trustees is a measure applied primarily to remove those found acting in serious breach of duty toward the foundation. It may in addition lead to a disqualification to act as board member/trustee in other organizations for a certain number of years following the dismissal. For instance, in the Netherlands a dismissal disqualifies the board member involved from holding a directorship of a foundation for a period of five years following his or her dismissal by the court (Article 2:298 CC).

Occasionally, however, dismissal by court order is not a disciplinary measure but used to remove, for example, board members that are in a state of bankruptcy.[36]

5.5 Civil liability of members of the board of directors/trustees

With regard to civil liability of members of the board of directors/trustees, the variation in positions taken in the relevant countries shows less diversity in comparison to the other subjects discussed in this section. Most countries recognize the concept of limited liability of the foundation, meaning that board members/trustees are not personally liable for any of its obligations. Interestingly, this limited liability can be lifted as a method of sanction in some countries. For example, in the Netherlands the board members will be, in addition to the foundation, jointly and severally liable for all obligations of the foundation resulting from acts that they performed legally binding the foundation before it was registered (Article 2:289 CC). The failure to comply with the obligation to register a foundation is thus sanctioned by withholding the privileges otherwise provided by the corporate veil, or limited liability only arises upon registration of the foundation. In Estonia a similar provision lifting the limited liability exists.[37] Only rarely does it seem that the concept of limited liability will be entirely denied.[38]

The general understanding is, also, that board members/trustees shall be liable for damages to the foundation caused by a breach of duty towards it. The principal normative framework for establishing a breach of duty in most countries included in the survey appears

---

[36] For instance in Sweden 9 kap. 5 § Foundations Act.

[37] See Article 13, 23 and 32 Foundation Act, for directors' liability.

[38] See however Cyprus, Article 37 Associations and Institutions Law, Part III.

derived from the principles of agency. There is some diversity in this respect to the extent that in some countries liability is restricted to board members that serve as employees of the foundation (e.g. in the Czech Republic). In other countries, for instance, Bulgaria, the extent to which unpaid officials can be held liable for breach of duty remains under debate.

Interestingly, in Greece board members are liable for expenses incurred when acting outside the approved budget of the foundation (see 3.2.1).

As a rule the foundation itself or the supervisory authority can instigate actions against the relevant board member. In Finland, acting in breach of the governing document or the Foundations Act may lead to civil liability toward third parties for damages incurred by such acts (Article 12a Foundations Act). In Austria, board members can also be held liable when the debts of the foundation exceed the assets, in accordance with company law rules. Similarly in the Netherlands with regard to foundations that are subject to company law taxation, board members are jointly and severally liable for a deficit in bankruptcy in cases of obvious mismanagement that can be assumed to have been an important cause of the bankruptcy. Such mismanagement is assumed in case of failure to comply with book-keeping and publication requirements (if applicable) (Article 2:300a CC).

To conclude, personal liability toward third parties may occur in some countries when in the capacity of managing director, a director personally performs a wrongful act (tort) against a third party. This liability is however a matter of general tort law and not so much of foundation law. It will not therefore be elaborated upon here.

5.6 Criminal and (administrative) punitive liability

With regard to criminal liability, a distinction should be made between:

- a crime committed by or under the cover of a foundation
- criminal proceedings against board members/trustees for breach of duty.

With regard to the first type of criminal liability, not all countries included in this survey are familiar with the concept of corporate criminal liability, for instance Bulgaria and Hungary. Under this concept, any criminal act performed by or in the name of the foundation may lead to criminal proceedings against the leading officials of the foundation at the time the crime was committed. A similar situation may very well exist in countries that are familiar with the concept of corporate criminal liability, allowing for criminal liability of both the foundation and the persons acting as board members at the time the crime was committed.[39]

Of more interest is that in some countries a breach of duty *vis-à-vis* the foundation potentially constitutes a criminal act. For example, in Greece, under Article 143 Compulsory Law 2039/1939, any offence in the pursuit of the foundation's purpose, in the management or use of assets of the foundation, may be punished in accordance with provisions in the Penal Code. Similarly, in Estonia, board members risk criminal liability not only when they cause serious damage by abusing their official position but also when they fail to perform their duties in the manner required.[40] In the Netherlands, the cooperation or authorization of an act that constitutes a serious breach of the law or governing document or book-keeping requirements, may lead to criminal sanctions against directors or supervisory directors where the resulting losses have caused bankruptcy to the foundation (Article 342-343 Penal Code).

Such specific penal provisions are not apparently provided for in all jurisdictions; obviously this does not exclude the possibility that a director acting in breach of duty can commit a crime in general terms, for example, embezzlement. Such jurisdictions may, however, impose the sanction of fining. A fine is often imposed upon a foundation for failure to comply with reporting or filing requirements. Among the countries that are included in this survey, no provisions have been discovered which allow a fine to be imposed personally on a foundation's directors/trustees for acting in breach of duty *vis-à-vis* the foundation. In the case of charitable trusts, the fine will be imposed upon the trustee personally.

5.7 Dissolution and destination of remaining assets

In most jurisdictions included in the survey a foundation can autonomously be dissolved by the decision of a foundation organ, if thus provided for in the governing document. If however the law allows no alteration of the governing document by a foundation organ (see 4), it would not as a rule allow a dissolution resolution by a foundation organ either. Foundations may nevertheless be established for a limited period of time, at the lapse of which they dissolve

---

[39] E.g. in the Netherlands, Article 51 Penal Code.

[40] Articles 161 and 162 Penal Code. Similarly pursuant to Article 259 Bulgarian Penal Code, persons involved in the management commit a crime when e.g. the foundation does not perform activities in pursuit if its purpose, or carries out prohibited activities.

automatically. Dissolution can also be ordered by the court or the supervisory authority. Such an order is not necessarily a correctional measure. A dissolution may be ordered in general in one or more of the following situations (with variations in formulation and detail) namely:

- the foundation lacks sufficient assets to achieve its purpose, and there is no prospect that these assets will be acquired
- the purpose of the foundation can no longer be achieved or has become obsolete
- the foundation continuously acts in violation of the law, the public order or its governing document.

With regard to the competence to decide or order a dissolution, basically the same procedure applies as to altering the purpose of the foundation (see 4), except that in case of dissolution on the last ground mentioned above, a court order may be required where this would not be required for dissolution on one of the other grounds.[41]

The first two grounds will be met where the foundation cannot meaningfully fulfil the purposes for which it was established. As discussed above, a slight change of purpose can sometimes solve the problem; in other cases, only changing the essential elements of the original purpose would cure the problem. In such a scenario, the foundation must be dissolved to prevent the remaining property from lying in dead hands. The last of the three grounds has a punitive or protective element.

Typically the law describes what should happen to the remaining assets, if any, after liquidation of the foundation. In the majority of the countries included in this survey, the destination of such assets may be determined by or in accordance with the governing document. In some jurisdictions the law requires that the governing document shall describe the destination or the manner in which the destination shall be determined (e.g. in the Netherlands pursuant to Article 2:286 CC). If it is impossible to execute provisions laid down in the governing document or if they do not provide for the destination of the assets, then the most common procedure is for the assets to be offered to another foundation with a similar purpose, and subsequently, if this is not successful, to be transferred to the state. Occasionally the purpose or location of the seat, for instance in the Czech Republic, determines which constitutional entity will be the designated recipient. In some cases, if there are no provisions laid

---

[41] E.g. Finland, Article 18 Foundations Act.

down in the governing document, or if these are not effective, the assets are transferred to the state directly.[42]

The state, when acting as the recipient, shall either apply the assets for beneficial purposes in general, for purposes similar to those of the foundation,[43] or be obliged to transfer the assets to a foundation with a similar purpose.[44] The same applies in Italy, but only if the governing document does not provide for the destination (Article 31 CC). Interestingly in Switzerland a punitive dissolution order causes the relevant clauses in the governing document to be put aside and the remaining assets to be transferred to the federation, canton or municipality with which the purpose of the foundation was connected (Article 57 CC).

5.8 Miscellaneous remarks

In general the measures and sanctions are imposed only after the foundation and the board members/trustees have been given the opportunity to correct the (alleged) irregularities. This may take different shapes. In some jurisdictions the supervisory authorities may have the competence to give specific instructions to the board members/trustees. In others the foundation or board members/trustees are merely given a *terme de grace* to allow for correction. In this process of correcting the irregularities, the supervisory authority is in a position to advise and assist the foundation and its board members/trustees, which in some cases is explicitly part of their task but is otherwise often is a matter of practice.

A subtle difference of a procedural but practical nature regards which state body can determine that there is an irregularity and consequently impose measures against the foundation and or its board members/trustees. In some jurisdictions, the supervisory authority itself can determine the relevant body and subsequently impose measures (see also 5.3). If the body is part of the public administration, and not independent from government, this from a legal point of view is an inelegant approach to imposing measures when foundations are viewed as institutions of private law, rather than as institutions belonging (partly) to the public administration.

---

[42] Cyprus, Article 45 Associations and Institutions Law, Part III (with regard to institutions incorporated under the Cypriot Charities Law, Chap. 41 section 15, English Charity Law applies; Estonia, Article 56 Foundations Act (for tax-exempt foundations it is not allowed to pay-out remaining assets to the founders); Greece, Article 77 CC).

[43] E.g. Finland, Article 19 Foundations Act.

[44] E.g. Hungary, section 74/E (5) CC.

As pointed out in 5.3 the fact that a measure imposed by a supervisory authority can be challenged in a court of law does little in practice to improve the legal position and independence of the foundation *vis-à-vis* the supervisory authority. Incidentally, a procedure to challenge decisions by the supervisory authority in a court of law is not always provided for, but may be restricted to review, for instance by the ministry of justice or finance. The absence of a procedure for bringing the case to an impartial and independent court constitutes a breach of Article 6 of the European Convention on Human Rights.[45]

When the approach is taken that foundations are a form of private initiative, not belonging to the public domain, it would seem more appropriate for the supervisory authority to take provisional measures if necessary, but that a court order be required to effect any definite sanctions, including removal of board members/trustees and the overturning of resolutions of the board of directors/trustees.

6 Comparative observations

The nature and elaboration of post-incorporation regulation and supervision of foundations differs substantially among the countries included in the survey. Not only does the level of detail of requirements and restrictions vary, but also the character of the supervisory authorities and the powers assigned to them show extreme differences. A comparative analysis can therefore only be attempted on a certain level of abstraction, referring to the differences rather than the nuances of the approach towards foundations in the various jurisdictions.

6.1 Purpose and activities, general remarks

Public benefit foundations are subject to more supervision than other types of foundations. This is most clearly demonstrated in those countries that allow foundations to be set up for purposes other than public benefit but have a special law governing the supervision and structure of foundations with a public utility purpose (see Table 4.2). Foundations that are not under the regime of this specific public benefit or utility legislation are not subject to rigorous government supervision. In a number of countries such as Liechtenstein, Switzerland and some German *Länder*, family foundations are similarly exempted from

---

[45] See Denters and van Veen, section 5.4.

Table 4.2 Restricted to purpose of public benefit

Austria	No *
Belgium	Yes **
Bulgaria	No
Cyprus	No*
Czech Republic	Yes
Denmark	No
Eng & Wales	Yes
Estonia	No
Finland	No (useful)
France	Yes
Germany	No ***
Greece	No *
Hungary	No *
Ireland	Yes
Italy	No *
Liechtenstein	No
Luxembourg	Yes
Netherlands	No
Scotland	Yes
Slovenia	Yes
Spain	Yes
Sweden	No
Switzerland	No

*   A special law applies, regulating foundations with a purpose of benefit.

**   A recent law proposal would allow foundations to be set up for other than public benefit purposes.

*** This survey did not include the laws of all *Länder*.

state supervision; to strike the balance, these non-public benefit foundations also enjoy, as a rule, less favourable tax-treatment and other privileges. The same logic applies, more or less explicitly, to other countries as well.

6.1.2 Foundations restricted to public benefit purposes

It is interesting to note that in jurisdictions where foundations can be set up for public benefit purposes only, which is in about half of the countries included in the survey (see Table 4.2), public benefit foundations are generally subject to stricter regulations and more governmental involvement than public benefit foundations in juris-dictions where foundations can be set up for non-public benefit purposes as well (see 3 to 5 and Table 4.3).

Restricting foundations to public benefit purposes implies that, in legal terms, a foundation can exist only if it operates for this purpose. As a consequence, when there is a change in what is considered to be of public benefit, a foundation pursuing a disqualified public benefit purpose may ultimately have to be dissolved. Similarly, if it is deter-mined that a foundation is in fact not operated for the public benefit this implies a violation of the legal requirements that apply to the foundation as such, which constitutes a more serious breach of the law than for instance not complying with fiscal requirements. The same may apply to countries that have a separate law for public bene-fit foundations which allows no 'conversion' to a non-public benefit foundation.

The fact that foundations can be set up for all kinds of purposes pro-vides for more independence from the state. A foundation that has enjoyed public benefit status but no longer qualifies as such may lose its tax-exempt status, certainly a severe penalty, but of a different nature than sanctions imposed personally on the members of the board of directors/trustees or the threat of dissolution of the founda-tion.

6.1.3 The role of foundations in society versus that of the state

It is important to note that although sometimes the law prescribes that a foundation should serve some public benefit purpose, in fact this cri-terion is applied in such a manner that allows foundations to be used for what would ordinarily be considered a private benefit purpose – at least for taxation purposes and supervision – such as a family founda-tion. This is for example the case in Hungary and in Italy (also see Drobnig: Foundations as Institutionalized Charitable Activity).

With regard to this requirement, the Hungarian Supreme Court has declared that

> a purpose is in the public interest [...] even if it serves a small group of people or one person as long as it is not primarily a business activity and is generally accepted as being beneficial to the public.[46]

---

[46] Second Statement of the Public Administrative Department of the Supreme Court, source: Gabor Gyorffy, 'Hungary', note 11, in: D.B. Rutzen, *Select legislative texts*, Washington DC, ICNL, 1995. The requirement is laid down in Article 74/A Civil Code, Book 4.

Table 4.3 Post-incorporation Restrictions and Requirements

	Annual reports submitted/filed or published	Pay-out requirements	Investment restrictions/ requirements	Investment policy transactions	Approval required
Austria	Yes	–	Yes, Civil Code requirements	Changes must be approved	Major sales affecting purpose
Belgium	Yes	–	–	–	Certain donations
Bulgaria	Yes	–	–	–	–
Cyprus	Yes	–	–	–	Sale of charitable assets/ real-estate
Czech Republic	Yes	**	Yes, regarding possesion of securities	–	–
Denmark	Yes	–	–	–	–
Eng & Wales	Yes°	***	Yes°°	Changes can be ordered	Yes°°
Estonia	Yes°	–	–	–	–
Finland	Yes	Yes (fiscal)	Must secure profitable investment	–	–
France	Yes	–	–	–	Certain donations
Germany	Yes	**** (fiscal)	***	Yes	–
Greece	Yes	–	Yes	–	Loans to municipalities
Hungary	Yes*	–	–	Internal regulations required°	–
Ireland	Yes	***	Yes	–	Yes

Italy	Yes	–	–	Yes°	–
Liechtenstein	Yes*	–	Maintaining minumum capital, activa should cover debts	–	–
Luxembourg	Yes	–	–	–	Certain donations
Netherlands	No	–	–	–	–
Scotland	Yes°	***	Yes°°	Changes can be ordered	Yes°°
Slovenia	Yes	–	–	–	Reduction of capital/real-estate
Spain	Yes	70% of income within 3 yrs	–	–	Declining of inher./legacies when more then 20% of assets are involved or important goods
Sweden	Yes	Yes (fiscal)	Acceptable way	Resolutions may be reversed	–
Switzerland	Yes*	Reasonable ratio assets/income/spending	–	Sale may be ordered	–

*   Only for public benefit foundations.
°   Reports must be provided to any member of the public on request.
°°   Relevant are governing document and Trustee Investment Act 1961. Authorization may be given when missing. Regards charitable trusts only.
**   Clear restrictions regarding total expenditure on management.
***   Restrictions regarding reservations apply.
****   Foundations are expected to accumulate income to a certain extent.

As a result, there are virtually no specific restrictions to the purposes for which foundations can be established in Hungary, other than primary purpose business activities and, of course, activities that are contrary to the law and public order.

In Italy, foundations are also required to serve a public benefit purpose, but in practice family or similar private benefit serving foundations are allowed, providing that they have as their aim the support of education or needy members of any or group. In most other jurisdictions included in this survey, this aim would not qualify a foundation as a public benefit organization.[47] To underscore this fact, to be recognized as public benefit foundation with the tax benefits and privileges attached to it, foundations in Hungary and Italy would have to comply with the additional requirements laid down in the laws on public benefit organizations in the respective countries.[48]

Despite this point of similarity, Hungary and Italy are a world apart with regard to government involvement in the establishment and supervision of foundations in general. For instance in Hungary no governmental recognition or approval to establish a foundation is required, whereas in Italy such recognition is required to obtain legal personality. Also in Hungary, the supervisory authority is the public prosecutor. In Italy on the other hand the relevant ministry is the supervisory authority over foundations. Thus foundations in Hungary are subject to supervision by the public prosecutor, whereas in Italy supervision is in the hands of the public administration. The relevance of this difference was discussed in 2.2. It is interesting to note that the dominant political philosophy regarding the role of foundations in society in both countries is different. In Hungary it is accepted that foundations can and should play an important role in the democratization of society and the denationalization and deregulation of the Hungarian economy, whereas in Italy the line of thinking is clearly more state centered, especially with regard to fields such as welfare, education and scientific research.[49]

---

[47] That is not for taxation purposes (see Bater and Habighorst: Tax Treatment of Foundations and their Donors), but also not for eligibility purposes where a public benefit purpose is required, e.g. in Spain, Article 2.2, 2.3 Law on Foundations, foundations must have a socially important purpose and the group of beneficiaries shall be open and is not allowed to be limited to predetermined individuals.

[48] For Hungary, Act CLVI of 1997 on Public Benefit Organizations, and for Italy, ONLUS law (Legislative Decree of 4 December 1997, no. 460, Reform of the Tax Laws Governing Non-Commercial Bodies and Socially-Useful Non profit Organizations).

[49] See Predieri, p. 232, in contrast with Kuti's contribution to Salamon, p. 130.

In general, countries that advocate a strong government influence on society put more emphasis on the supervision of foundations than countries where private initiative is viewed as an important social driving force. As a rule, countries in the former category charge this supervision to a body of the public administration. An extreme example of such a country is France, where concern to secure independence of the foundation from its founder has resulted in what appears to be *de facto* control by the state (see 2.3.1). An example of a country belonging to the latter category is the Netherlands,[50] where supervision is left to the public prosecutor (see 2.2). Partly because of the absence of an obligation to file or publish the annual accounts and partly because a prior court order is required for any legal action by the public prosecutor, state supervision is reduced to a minimum. In contrast, more rights are granted to third parties than is the case in France where third parties have no rights at all. Similar observations apply to Hungary and Italy (see 2.4 and Table 4.1).

6.2 The conceptual view regarding foundations

Traditionally, foundations are associated with property dedicated to the realization of a specific, well-defined purpose. The attribute of legal personality allows for perpetuity and independence from the founder(s) or the members of its organs that manage the foundation at any given time. The concept of the charitable trust results in a very similar legal concept without legal personality. The survey shows that the concept of a foundation in the majority of the countries included is based on this model. The foundation is, in these countries, either characterized in terms of property dedicated to a specific purpose, or in terms of the act that results in the establishment of such a foundation: the transfer or dedication of property to a specific purpose. A foundation is thus required to have an endowment from its inception (see Drobnig: Foundations as Institutionalized Charitable Activity).

In some countries, however (e.g. Estonia[51] and the Netherlands) the foundation is primarily considered to be just one of the types of legal forms available for private initiative, and not simply a legal form for dedicating property to a specific purpose. In these countries, a foundation is not required by law or administrative practice to have an endowment or to maintain a minimum capital. What distinguishes

---

[50] For the role of non profit organizations in Dutch society and their impact on economy, see Burger, *et al.*

[51] In Estonia the freedom to form foundations, as a sub-category of nonprofit organizations, is guaranteed under the Constitution, Article 48.

the foundation in these legal systems is that it has no members as defined by law.[52] Consequently, the law requires no other body than the board of directors. This, however, does not imply that apart from the board of directors/trustees, no others can be involved in the governance of the foundation, if this is provided for in the governing document of the foundation (see 2.3) or by law.[53] Such legal systems, to a large extent, deal with foundations in the same manner as they do with other legal persons.

This concept of the foundation as a legal form for organizations next to that of the associations with its particular characteristics, is in the author's opinion found (not exclusively, but rather less explicitly) in some other countries. In Hungary, for example, the law provides for the possibility of creating an 'open' foundation, a foundation that anyone may join under the conditions prescribed in the governing instrument (Article 74/B sub 4 Book IV CC). In addition there are no minimum or maximum capital requirements in Hungary. In several other countries legal reforms are being considered or have been recently implemented. In Belgium, for example, legal reforms are underway, introducing a foundation concept that has similarities to that in the Netherlands. In Italy, in the recent ONLUS legislation,[54] the public benefit foundation was brought under the umbrella of nonprofit organizations.

At the one extreme, therefore, the foundation is primarily considered to be 'property' dedicated to a specific purpose. This particular view exists in its most pure form, in my opinion, particularly in countries with a common-law tradition, where the charitable trust is concerned. At the other extreme are the legal systems mentioned earlier that recognize the foundation as a legal person, not necessarily having an endowment, and allow much flexibility in its organizational structure without members. The different concepts of a foundation may also reflect for instance the qualification of those charged with the realization of the purpose of the foundation. Where the foundation is strongly viewed as property dedicated to a specific purpose, the officials of a foundation are referred to as trustee, *administrateur* or

---

[52] The concept of which is dependent on the laws of the relevant country, and falls outside the scope of this chapter.

[53] For instance in the Netherlands with regard to employees in the Law on the Works Councils, to employees, pupils and their parents in the field of education and to clients or their representatives with regard to youth care, and health and nursing care institutions that receive government subsidies.

[54] Legislative Decree of 4 December 1997, no. 460, Reform of the Tax Laws Governing Non-Commercial Bodies and Socially-Useful Non profit Organizations.

equivalents thereof, rather than managing director, *bestuurder*, etc. The former qualifications are reminiscent of those applied when someone is charged with taking proper care of property that belongs to someone else who is not capable of doing so him- or herself. The latter qualifications refer to a more autonomous position with regard to applying the foundation's means to achieve its purpose.

Interestingly, the involvement of the state in the management and supervision of foundations, as well as in the level of detail of the applicable requirements and restrictions, is as a rule considerably higher in countries where the property concept is predominant as compared to countries where such is not the case.

7 Reflections and concluding remarks

Comparing different European legal systems with regard to the post-incorporation regulation and supervision of foundations is not an easy undertaking, neither is reflecting and commenting on the various differences that exist among the legal systems in Europe. Obviously the various systems of regulation and supervision described in this chapter all have their advantages and disadvantages. As a starting point the author takes two elementary issues affecting the relationship between the state and its citizens:

- the fundamental rights and freedoms as guaranteed by the national constitutions, as well as on a European level by the European Convention on Human Rights (ECHR)
- the widely shared view of a civil society in which citizens are welcomed and to some extent expected to take responsibility in shaping and developing it.

Some examples of the relevance of the ECHR with regard to supervision have been mentioned above (see 2.4, 5.2 and 5.8). More fundamental is the issue of the right to establish foundations. As is dealt with in Garcia-Andrade: Establishment, Amendment and Liquidation of Foundations, both the freedom of association and the freedom of property are relevant in this respect.

Depending on the concept of foundations in a particular jurisdiction one reference might be more convincing than the other. With regard to charitable trusts, for instance, an appeal to the freedom of association is not likely to be very convincing, whereas in countries where foundations are recognized as a nonprofit organizational form, the freedom of association is more easily understood to extend to foundations as well as associations.[55]

The ECHR allows restrictions to the rights and freedoms described only to the extent that such restrictions are **necessary in a democratic society** to protect a limited number of interests including national security, public order, the prevention of criminal acts and the rights of others. Supervision of foundations could thus be justified, for instance to protect the interests of the founder, creditors or beneficiaries, as well as to prevent criminal acts. In this respect it is relevant that foundations are typically non-membership organizations.

This is not necessarily true for countries with a common-law tradition, in which the foundation is not a legal form but is used to refer to an entity that relies on the income from its endowment rather than by subscriptions or collections, the endowment being obtained from one or a limited number of founders. Under common-law jurisdictions a foundation could either be a trust or a membership organization such as an incorporated association or charitable corporation, more specifically a charitable company limited by guarantee.[56]

As a result, there is no intrinsic system of supervision as is the case with membership organizations, where the membership checks on the board of directors and its policies, at least annually. In addition the potential beneficiaries as a rule, have no legally relevant relationship with a foundation (see 2.4). As a consequence, foundations are relatively impervious to external influences. In particular when foundations claim to serve a public benefit purpose a state can for the reasons mentioned above justify its need to be informed about the conduct of affairs of a foundation and to have at its disposal mechanisms to intervene when necessary. Where foundations with a public benefit purpose receive tax reliefs, as is the case in most countries (see Bater and Habighorst: Tax Treatment of Foundations and their Donors), the state has an additional interest that can be used to justify supervision of foundations.

This being said, the fundamental question is: to what extent is state involvement with foundations and their management justified? From a social and legal point of view the fact that a rationale exists for state supervision is not enough to justify any form of state involvement with foundations in general. State involvement, where it constitutes a

---

[55] Compare Alkema, p.59 and Van der Ploeg, p. 55.

[56] Hill, p. 197. See also Drobnig: Foundations as Institutionalized Charitable Activity.

restriction of fundamental rights and freedoms in general, is justified only to the extent that it is necessary as described earlier. Similarly the concept of a civil society presupposes that civic organizations can be established and operated free from undue state influence.

Following this line of thinking it can be argued that in a civil society which respects the fundamental rights and freedoms of its subjects, state involvement with the management of foundations should be restricted to what is necessary to protect the interests involved. The restrictions should be proportional to the legitimate interests the state seeks to protect. Monitoring the manner in which the board of directors/trustees perform their duty through requiring the annual reports to be submitted, filed or published and requesting additional information when irregularities occur in this respect seems proportional. However, the question then arises of whether or not it is necessary to require prior government approval for certain transactions, such as accepting donations or making certain investment decision. The same is true when judging the efficiency of management decisions.

From a legal point of view there are no convincing arguments in favour of a supervisory authority being in a position to take over the management of a foundation, *de facto* or *de jure*. This supports the view held in many – but not all – countries in Europe that supervision of foundations should be normative and restricted to legitimacy control (see also 3).

It is remarkable that to date a number of countries within Europe have apparently maintained a concession system or elements of such a system in their post-incorporation regulation and supervision of foundations.[57] This includes the need for government approval for the establishment of foundations, where such approval is discretionary, rather than normative. Also restrictions imposed on public benefit purposes are reminiscent of a concession system, in particular if they are applied in such a manner that a foundation can be established only in support of the government, or only permitted to hold and express views that are in compliance with public policy. The state also has more discretionary power when determining to which type of foundation it wishes to grant tax reliefs or other support, since this does not affect the freedom to establish and operate a foundation.

With regard to post-incorporation regulation and supervision, traces of a concession system are revealed, for instance, in:

---

[57] With regard to Germany, see Schmidt, p. 229.

- the fact that a body of the public administration has the power to amend the governing document of a foundation
- the power of the state to overrule certain decisions of the governing board without a prior court order (see 5.3)
- the power of the state to appoint members of the board of directors/trustees (see 2.3.1).

Provisions of this nature suggest to my opinion that the foundation is to a certain degree considered to be an institution belonging to the public domain, rather than an institution of civil law belonging to the private domain.[58]

In the light of the apparent harmonization of the European view of society and the meaning of civil rights, a more uniform approach towards foundations on the Continent might be expected. However, if there is one thing the survey reflects it is that with regard to the regulation of foundations and the view of the role of foundations in society Europe is still, and probably will continue to be, fundamentally diverse.

Bibliography

Alfandari, E. and Nardone, A., *Associations et Fondations en Europe, regime juridique et fiscal*, Lyon/Paris, Éditions Juris-Service/AGEC, 1994.

Alkema, E., 'Freedom of association and civil society', in: *Freedom of Association*, Strasbourg, Council of Europe Press, 1994.

Büermann, W., 'Stiftungsautonomie und Staatsaufsicht', in: *Handbuch Stiftungen*, Gabler, Wiesbaden, Bertelsmann Stiftung (ed.), 1998.

Burger, A., Dekker, P., Van der Ploeg, T. J. and van Veen, W. J. M., 'Defining the Nonprofit Sector: The Netherlands', in L. M Salamon and H. K. Anheier (eds), Baltimore MD, The Johns Hopkins Comparative Nonprofit Sector Project, Working paper number 23, 1997.

Chesterman, M., 'Foundations of charity law in the New Welfare state', in: *Modern Law Review*, 1999.

Denters, E. and van Veen, W. J. M., 'Voluntary Organizations and the European Convention on Human Rights', in: *International Journal for Nonprofit Law*, Issue 2, Washington, December 1998.

Frotiée, P. and De Monseignat, R., 'France Country Report', in C. George (ed.): *International Charitable Giving: Laws and Taxation*, Kluwer International Law publishers, Supp. 1995, p.9.

---

[58] See with regard to this issue the interesting treatise by Richter, esp. p. 456 *et seq.*

Hill, C. P., 'England and Wales', in: K. Neuhoff and U. Pavel (eds), *Trusts and Foundations in Europe*, London, Stifterverband für die Deutsche Wissenschaft, Bedford Square Press, 1971.

Picarda, H., *The Law and Practice Relating to Charities*, 2nd edn, London, Dublin & Edinburgh, Butterworths, 1995.

Predieri, A., 'Italy', in: K. Neuhoff and U. Pavel (eds), *Trusts and Foundations in Europe*, London, Stifterverband fur die Deutsche Wissenschaft, Bedford Square Press, 1971.

Rajak, H., 'The legal personality of associations', in: F. Macmillan Patfield, (ed.), *Perspectives on Company Law I*, London etc., Kluwer Law International, 1995.

Richter, A., 'German and American Law of Charity in the Early 19th Century', in: R. Helmholz and R. Zimmerman, *Itinera Fiduciae, Trust and Treuhand in Historical Perspective*, Berlin, Duncker & Humbolt, 1998.

Salamon, L. M., *The International Guide to Nonprofit Law*, New York etc., John Wiley & Sons, 1997.

Schiller, T., *Stiftungen im gesellschaftlichen Prozess*, Baden-Baden, Nomos Verlagsgesellschaft, 1969.

Schmidt, K., 'Konzessionssystem und Stiftungsrecht', in: A. Frhr. von Campenhausen, H. Kronke and O. Werner (eds), *Stiftungen in Deutschland und Europa*, Düsseldorf, IDW-Verlag, 1998.

Van der Ploeg, T. J., 'A comparative legal analysis of foundations', in: H. K. Anheier and S. Toepler (eds), *Private Funds, Public Purpose*, New York etc., Kluwer Academic/Plenum Publishers, 1999.

▼ Bradley Gallop

Cross-border Issues facing Foundations and their Donors

1 Introduction

In this era of globalization, with new means of communications bringing the four corners of the globe closer together, and with trade liberalization measures eliminating national barriers to products imported from other lands, it is no longer justifiable for national barriers to be erected and maintained against charitable foundations and other nonprofit organizations operating across their borders. Yet, despite these changing times, the legal and fiscal framework applying to charitable foundations remains national and continues to reflect the cultural, historical, and religious values of the national community, rather than of a larger community.

These national barriers are even more significant for grant-seeking organizations than for grant-making organizations, because of the additional difficulty in obtaining funds from individual and corporate donors in foreign lands and engaging in activities in the field abroad. Grant-making orgainzations, such as many foundations, are less dependent on funds from individual and corporate donors[1] and their activities abroad are of such a nature that they are less affected by national barriers. For these reasons, among others, grant-making foundations are generally not as limited as associations in their activities across borders.

Foundations that are active in cross-border activities, however, will face different challenges at the national level. These foundations are more likely to have to deal with supervisory authorities worried about the foundations' activities abroad being either inconsistent with their governing statutes or diminishing the public benefit to the home community, points on which foundations are required to satisfy the authorities to obtain charitable or tax-exempt status.

In view of the dramatic changes in human society and welfare that foundations have enabled through financial support (e.g. polio vaccine, AIDS research, and academic scholarships, to name a few), it would be a great loss if foundations were not able to play their full catalyst role beyond the national borders of their homeland. It is

---

[1] As will be described in this chapter, individual and corporate donors are more likely to be discouraged from making a donation to a foreign nonprofit organization because they will generally not receive any tax benefits, such as a tax deduction, relating to their donation. To the extent that individual or corporate donors may treat a donation as a business expense, rather than as a charitable donation, they might be more inclined to contribute funds to a foreign nonprofit organization. Government and intergovernmental bodies (e.g. European Union, World Bank, or UNESCO) are not influenced by tax considerations when granting funds to nonprofit organizations, including foundations, for projects, as they are not themselves tax-payers.

important to remember that foundations do not act alone, but often provide only part of the funds or other resources required for a project. Foundations generally expect the organization running a project to obtain funds from other sources: governments, partner organizations, other foundations, corporations, and even an organization's own resources. A foundation's funds thus usually have a multiplier effect, which it would be a shame to lose because of anachronistic national barriers to cross-border giving.

The first part of this chapter will examine and analyse the legal and fiscal treatment of charitable foundations engaged, or wishing to engage, in cross-border activities, as a donor or as a beneficiary of funds, or even as an actor operating its own programmes. In this section, the reader will come to understand how much national barriers, whether explicit or implicit, prevent foundations from fully playing their catalyst role throughout Europe. These barriers are especially unfortunate at a time when there is a pressing need to strengthen the role and contribution of civil society organizations as a means of increasing solidarity between the peoples of Europe and of reducing the democratic deficit and public mistrust in state and European institutions.

The second part of this chapter will identify and explore some public and private initiatives that can help foundations and their donors to overcome the current legal and fiscal barriers to cross-border activities. Through these initiatives, foundations will be enabled to play a role outside their national borders.

Since this book will be used by persons interested in establishing *inter vivos* and testamentary foundations, a third section will examine the particular considerations of someone establishing a foundation in another country as part of her or his estate planning exercise. Forum shopping (i.e. searching for the jurisdiction with the most favourable legal and fiscal framework) can in this respect be extremely interesting, not only to find the jurisdiction that is most favourable for the activity envisaged, but also the most favourable from a tax planning perspective.

2 National barriers to cross-border giving

2.1 Recognition of a foundation's legal personality abroad (host country)

In almost all countries surveyed, with the exception perhaps of the UK and Ireland (where a charitable trust[2] is used as a vehicle rather than a company limited by guarantee) a foundation is deemed by law to be a legal person.[3] As a legal person, a foundation is able to enter into a contract, hold property, engage in legal proceedings, and otherwise act in accordance with the law in its own name.

Under the rules applicable in most jurisdictions, if a foundation is legally established in its home jurisdiction and has legal personality there, its legal personality will also be recognized by the host jurisdiction. National rules governing conflicts of law help public and private authorities determine the recognition due to a foreign foundation.

Recognition of legal personality does not, however, mean recognition of public benefit or tax-exempt status, but merely that the foundation may enter into contracts, engage in legal proceedings,[4] and otherwise enjoy the benefits and be subject to the obligations of a legal person in the host jurisdiction. Nor does recognition of legal personality as a matter of law eliminate all problems that a foundation may encounter when acting in foreign lands and required to provide proof of its legal personality. Foreign administrative bodies, landlords, and banks accustomed to seeing documents in a certain format may request an official translation of documents and even require that they be legalized or authenticated.[5] Meeting these apparently simple requirements will add to the expense and burden of operating abroad.

---

[2] Although trusts in the UK and Ireland do not have legal personality, their trustees may be incorporated, thus obtaining some of the advantages of legal personality, e.g. limited liability for those individuals managing or administering the trust.

[3] See Drobnig: Foundations as Institutionalized Charitable Activity (6.4 and 7.1.2) and Garcia-Andrade: Establishment, Amendment and Liquidation of Foundations (3.1.3) for a full description of legal personality and the consequences for a foundation of acquiring legal personality.

[4] There may be other factors needing to be considered to determine whether or not a foundation may be sued in another jurisdiction. Rules of private international law will help determine whether there is a sufficient basis for a foundation to be brought before a foreign jurisdiction.

[5] See The Hague Convention Abolishing the Requirements of Legalization for Foreign Public Documents, concluded on 5 October 1961, in force in all countries surveyed. This Convention reduces all of the formalities of legalization to the simple delivery of a certificate in a uniform prescribed form, entitled 'Apostille' by the authorities of the state where the document originates. The Apostille certifies the authenticity of the signature, the capacity in which the person signing the document has acted and where appropriate, the identity of the seal or stamp which it bears. Although the Apostille simplifies the authentification procedure, it does not prevent public authorities or private organizations, such as banks, from requiring the document to be accompanied by an official translation made by a certified translator. Despite the use of the term 'public documents' to define the scope of application, this Convention also applies to commercial documents, such as contracts and powers of attorney.

See also the 1968 Brussels Convention on jurisdiction and the enforcement of judgments in civil and commercial matters (consolidated version), OJ C 27/1 of 26 January 1998. This Convention is applicable in all member states of the European Union and simplifies the procedure for recognizing judgments and authenticated documents from other member states of the European Union. Translation of documents may still be required.

Foundations and other nonprofit organizations can encounter problems when asserting their legal personality in foreign lands due to the close relationship between a foundation's legal status and its stated purposes. For example, in several countries a foundation may only be established for certain publicly beneficial purposes specified in a law or in the civil code.[6] A foundation in these jurisdictions must pursue these purposes only, otherwise its legal status may be challenged by the supervisory authorities, or even other parties.[7] The purposes allowed under one country's laws are unlikely to be exactly the same as those allowed under another country's law. Other countries are not, therefore, always prepared to recognize the legal personality of foundations or other nonprofit organizations that are established elsewhere for purposes which are not allowed under their own laws. When the authorities of the host jurisdiction try to assimilate the foreign foundation into their own system they will fail, and may hence be inclined to erect barriers to a foreign foundation's ability to act in the host jurisdiction.

In addition, since foundations are usually subject to heightened supervision,[8] as opposed to other nonprofit organizations, jurisdictions may wish to stipulate that a foreign foundation proposing to engage in activity should comply with some registration process or other formality in the host jurisdiction to ensure that it meets local requirements. In this way, the host jurisdiction can protect local donors and ensure that the public order is being upheld (see 2.2).

2.1.1 The European Convention on the Recognition of the Legal Personality of International Non-Governmental Organizations 1986

This Convention, which entered into force on 1 January 1991, also provides a legal basis requiring the party states[9] to recognize international NGOs that are active within their borders. Article 2 of the Convention specifically provides that the legal personality and capacity, as acquired by an NGO in a party state, must be recognized as of right in the other party states. Four remarks concerning this Convention must nevertheless be noted.

---

[6] See Garcia-Andrade: Establishment, Amendment and Liquidation of Foundations (6).

[7] See van Veen: Supervision of Foundations in Europe (6.1.2 Foundations restricted to public benefit purposes).

[8] See van Veen as above (6.1 Purpose and activities, general remarks).

[9] Of countries surveyed, only Austria, Belgium, France, Greece, Portugal, Slovenia, Switzerland, and UK have signed and ratified the Convention. Cyprus has signed it, but has not yet ratified it.

1 According to Article 1, the Convention applies only to 'foundations, associations and other private institutions' (NGOs) having a nonprofit-making aim of international utility. The Convention does not expressly mention 'trusts', thus leaving some doubts as to their inclusion, although they might have been feasibly envisaged under the terms 'foundations' or 'other private institutions'. However, given that the Convention aims to have party states recognize the legal personality of international NGOs and that trusts do not have legal personality, it is probably fairly safe to assume that they are not covered or affected by the Convention. Perhaps the drafters of this Convention hoped that the problem of trusts and their recognition would be resolved by the Hague Convention on the Law Applicable to Trusts and their Recognition of 1 July 1985 which was being drafted at roughly the same time as the European Convention (see 2.1.2 for a discussion of these problems and the Hague Convention). The result, however, is still to be seen.

2 In order for the Convention to apply to an NGO, four conditions laid down by the Convention must be met:

- the organization must have a 'nonprofit-making aim of international utility'
- the organization must be established by an instrument governed by the law of a party state
- the organization must 'carry on its activities *with effect* in at least two States'; and
- the statutory office of the organizations must be in one party state, while the central management and control are in either that same party state or another party state.

Nowhere in the Convention do the drafters define which aims are to be considered as having an 'international utility'. This obvious omission is likely to be intentional in order to avoid a debate between the party states as to which aims qualify as being both 'nonprofit-making' and of 'international utility' – a debate which might sabotage their efforts to reach an agreement. Agreeing to a common definition would unfortunately be a lengthy and probably fruitless endeavour. According to the Commentary on the Convention, the aim of an NGO must be of benefit to the international community, thereby excluding NGOs of purely domestic utility and 'other political organizations whose aims and activities are centred on the domestic problems of a given country'. This interpretation would appear to exclude NGOs acting abroad in a single country, for example to rebuild post-war Kosovo. The Commentary also refers to the examples mentioned in the third paragraph of the Convention's preamble – work in the scientific, cultural, charitable, philanthropic, health and education fields – as an aid to interpret activities that have a value to the international community.

The Convention also provides no guidance in defining the phrase 'with effect' mentioned in the third condition listed in number 2 above. If a foundation grants money to NGOs in other countries, for example, does this constitute carrying on an activity 'with effect' in at least two states?

Likewise, for the fourth condition listed in number 2 above to be fulfilled, an NGO's statutory office and central management and control must both be in a party state. With only eight countries having presently signed and ratified the Convention, this condition severely limits its applicability. When either the statutory office or the central management and control are located in a non-party state, the Convention will not apply. In a recent unpublished case, the Belgian authorities refused to recognize a Dutch foundation, which contested by stating that Belgium was a party state to the European Convention and therefore should recognize the legal personality of the Dutch foundation. The Belgian authorities, however, replied, 'yes, but the Netherlands is not'.

3 Although under Article 2 of the Convention the legal personality of an NGO from a party state is recognized as of right, the exercise of the rights arising out of a foreign NGO's legal capacity may still be subject to special procedures or certain restrictions where these are required by essential public interest. If all NGOs are required to register or seek approval, for instance, before conducting fundraising activities, foreign NGOs would also have to register or seek the same approval. They would thus be subject to the same obligations, even though these might not be required in their home jurisdiction.

4 The Convention only requires party states to recognize the legal personality of NGOs established in another party state. It does not require the party states to confer on the foreign NGO any tax privileges enjoyed by like organizations established domestically, nor does it require party states to recognize the tax privileges enjoyed by the foreign NGO in its home jurisdiction. In this respect, a foreign NGO wishing to benefit from the tax privileges enjoyed in the host country would most likely have to comply with all requirements applicable in the host country for an NGO in order to qualify for such tax privileges.

Until more states become party to this Convention, it will have limited practical effect, especially in light of its restricted scope – applying only to 'international' NGOs and dealing only with the issue of recognition of legal personality. The limited scope probably reflects the enormous challenges that the drafters tried to meet. Hopefully, this Convention will be the first block on which a more enabling legal framework for organizations and donors involved in cross-border activities will be built.

2.1.2. Charitable trusts

An important exception to the general rule of recognition of a foundation's legal personality lies with charitable trusts established in common-law jurisdictions. Since trusts do not have legal personality, they may encounter administrative and everyday problems when operating in other European countries on the Continent, for instance opening bank accounts, holding property, signing contracts, or being a party to court litigation.

The treatment of trusts on the European Continent is not easy to summarize in a few lines. Numerous treatises and articles have been written on the subject without really clarifying the subject for the layperson.[10] Being a distinct legal form, trusts have baffled businesspeople and authorities alike on the Continent, as they simply do not know how to treat them or fit them into their own systems. Yet their importance in common-law jurisdictions has obliged other countries to seek a solution that fits their customs.

A very few non-common law countries have tried to clear the confusion by recognizing trusts in law. Of the countries surveyed, Cyprus,[11] Liechtenstein, and the Netherlands are the only ones to do so formally.

A handful more countries do not recognize trusts in their law, but do recognize foreign trusts, that is trusts that are duly established in countries where they are permitted (Austria, Belgium, Germany, Italy, Luxembourg and Switzerland).

Of the countries surveyed, only Italy, the Netherlands and the UK though have signed and ratified the Hague Convention on the Law Applicable to Trusts and their Recognition of 1 July 1985, while Cyprus, France, and Luxembourg have signed, but not ratified the

---

[10] See Bierlaagh et al., *The International Guide to the Taxation of Trusts.*

[11] As a result of the British administration of the island between 1878 and 1960, the Cypriot legal system contains many holdovers from the common-law system.

Convention. The Hague Convention, similar to the European Convention for international non-governmental organizations, described above in 2.1.1, provides recognition of trusts as of right in the other signatory countries, as long as certain conditions have been met in the home state.

The following countries do not recognize any trusts in law, even foreign trusts: Bulgaria,[12] Denmark, Estonia,[13] Greece, Hungary, Slovenia, Spain, and Sweden.

In Finland, the treatment of trusts remains unclear. Although trusts are not recognized in law, they are recognized by the tax authorities as a corporation or nonprofit organization. This ambiguous practice would make an advance ruling very worthwhile for any charitable trust wishing to engage in activities in Finland.

2.2 Formalities required of foreign foundations conducting activities in host jurisdictions

A foundation wishing to conduct activities in a foreign jurisdiction might have to carry out certain formalities in the host jurisdiction. In this respect, it should be noted that a foundation's activities abroad can take several forms. For instance, a foundation overseeing many projects in a region or country may wish to establish a representative or branch office there to facilitate communications with local partners and authorities. Likewise, a foundation may desire to establish an office in a city where there are several other foundations or intergovernmental organizations in order to enable regular contact with them. Alternatively a foundation may simply intend to seek funds from potential individual and corporate donors in another country and for this purpose will need to increase its presence there.

Unfortunately, foundations and other nonprofit organizations do not, however, enjoy the same privileges as citizens and economic entities in the EU to be able to move freely from one jurisdiction to another.[14] The Treaty of Rome itself provides specific guarantees to persons and economic entities to circulate within the EU and seek economic opportunity.[15] Numerous legislations have been adopted to implement these guarantees and to harmonize the rules governing

---

[12] Bulgaria is expected to join the Hague Convention and other like conventions soon.

[13] New legislation is expected in Estonia.

[14] See below 3.1.4 (Multilateral measures: European Union).

[15] Articles 39 to 55 (ex Articles 48 to 66) of the Treaty Establishing the European Community.

companies and other types of legal entities. Although companies do face some administrative problems when planning to operate outside the borders of their homeland, the barriers have been considerably reduced and the companies themselves have the Community legislative framework to support them if the barriers appear to infringe their 'constitutional' rights. Foundations and other nonprofit organizations, however, do not have any express provisions in the Community treaties that enable them to rely on the support of European institutions to apply pressure on member states to eliminate their barriers. Unless a foundation carries out the required formalities, its legal forms may not be recognized (this is even more likely in the case of a charitable trust[16]) and its tax-exempt status may simply be ignored.

2.2.1 Authorization to conduct activities

Foreign foundations wishing to carry out activities in Austria, Cyprus, Estonia and Italy must obtain official recognition not only of their legal personality, but also of their right to conduct such activities in these jurisdictions. Obtaining this recognition entails following a procedure and taking other administrative steps.

Austria's requirement that foundations obtain recognition may be in violation of the European Convention on the Recognition of the Legal Personality of International Non-Governmental Organizations (see 2.1.1) if the foundations originate from another party state. Article 2.2 of this Convention allows a party state to impose restrictions, limitations or special procedures governing the exercise of the rights arising out of an NGO's legal capacity only when they are required by essential public interest. In determining whether these restrictions, limitations or procedures are consistent with the provisions of the Convention, it would probably make a difference if they were also imposed on national NGOs.

In France, foreign foundations carrying out nonprofit activities on a permanent basis or wishing to acquire the same legal capacity as French foundations, for instance, in order to be able to receive donations, must obtain official recognition as having a public utility. Foreign foundations otherwise wishing to carry out activities in France on an occasional basis need not obtain such recognition.[17]

---

[16] See above 2.1.2 for a discussion on recognition of trusts.

[17] Huc, S. and Bouzoraa, D., 'France Country Report' in: Bater, P. ed., *The Tax Treatment of Cross-Border Donations*, IBFD Publications BV, Supp. 9/1997, p. 1; Alfandari, E. and Nardone, A., *Associations et Fondations en Europe*, Lyon, Editions Juris Service, 1994, p. 165.

2.2.2 Eligibility for tax privileges

In most other jurisdictions, official recognition is required only if the foundation wishes to enjoy the tax privileges available to other charitable foundations in the host jurisdiction.[18] A foundation can hence examine whether the benefits of recognition outweigh the costs and burdens of obtaining recognition. Nevertheless, in these jurisdictions a foundation will not be obliged to have such recognition in order to operate in the host jurisdiction.

Only the Netherlands has a special simplified procedure that allows foreign charitable organizations to apply for recognition. Any foreign charitable organization can apply to the Ministry of Finance for the approval that authorizes donations made to the organization by Dutch tax-payers to be tax deductible.[19] In order to qualify in the Netherlands, an organization must show that its sphere of influence or of work includes the Netherlands, or that it does not include the Netherlands but that its activities are conducted on a global level, for example, for the protection of the environment.

Needless to say, a foundation will not need to satisfy any additional legal requirements if it is dually registered in the host country.[20]

2.3 Home jurisdiction restrictions on foreign activities or transfers of funds

There are few express restrictions in the home country on a foundation conducting activities or transferring assets abroad. To the extent that the international activity is permitted in the foundation's statutes, the foundation will generally be seen as merely pursuing its stated purpose by conducting cross-border activities.

Nevertheless, in some countries founders wishing to establish a foundation that intends to engage in cross-border activities may face difficulties when incorporating the foundation in the first place. In these countries, the supervisory authorities may feel that there is insufficient benefit to the national community. Likewise cross-border activities may have difficulty falling within one of the categories mentioned in the country's laws governing charitable foundations.

---

[18] Belgium, Bulgaria, Czech Republic, Denmark, Greece, Ireland, Liechtenstein, Luxembourg, the Netherlands, Portugal, Slovenia, Spain, Sweden, Switzerland and the United Kingdom.

[19] Article 47, paragraph 5, Income Tax Act and Article 16, paragraph 3, Corporate Income Tax Act. As of January 1999, only 13 foreign foundations had received official approval.

[20] This is the case for Austria, Bulgaria, Cyprus and Italy. See below 2.6.1 for a discussion on dual registration.

For example, in Germany, the law does not provide general restrictions on foreign activities or financial engagements abroad, yet foundations wishing to conduct activities or to grant funds abroad might be obliged to explain to the tax authorities how these activities will benefit German tax-payers. In Germany, as in many other countries, tax authorities might require demonstration of some benefit to the national community as the price for the tax privileges accompanying a foundation's nonprofit status since these privileges reduce the tax income collected by the state. Cross-border activities can thus threaten a foundation's ability to qualify for tax benefits as a nonprofit organization.

Foundations established in these countries might also face later challenges to their legal status by the supervisory authorities if their cross-border activities appear to infringe the spirit of the law.

2.3.1 Express restrictions on cross-border activities

The few countries that do expressly restrict cross-border activities include Austria, Bulgaria, Cyprus, and Hungary. Austria requires that a charitable foundation's activities be carried out in Austria, unless the foundation is a development organization transferring funds to Third World countries[21] or the foundation has obtained a specific tax ruling on the basis of reciprocity.[22] Bulgaria, Cyprus and Hungary allow foundations to carry out activities abroad, but require approval for transfers of funds abroad.

2.3.2 Restrictions on tax privileges

The extent of activities abroad, however, may also jeopardize a foundation's qualification as an organization eligible to receive tax deductible donations since some states require that a foundation provides a public benefit, which is interpreted in a national context as applying to the national community.

For instance, France allows a foundation to carry out its activity throughout the globe, but places certain limits on the foundation's activities if it wants donations made to it to be tax deductible. In order for a donor to deduct a donation made to a foundation, the foundation's activities must be carried out in France, except where they are in the interest of international humanitarian missions in

---

[21] Austrian Development Aid Act, Article 1; Austrian Federal Tax Code, Article 34(1).

[22] Decree of 18 February 1994 by the Austrian Federal Ministry of Finance, published in EAS 392.

which France participates,[23] or aimed at promoting French culture, language and scientific knowledge, provided the foundation carries out at least part of its activities in France.[24]

Likewise, in Belgium, the administrative regulations for implementing Article 104 of the Income Tax Code, which sets out the requirements for eligibility to receive tax-deductible donations, contain numerous provisions requiring the non-profit activity to be carried out exclusively or almost exclusively in Belgium.

Foundations in France and Belgium that engage in cross-border activities would risk not being eligible to receive tax-deductible donations or losing their eligibility at the time of renewing this privilege. In Belgium, for instance, eligibility to receive tax-deductible status is reviewed by the Ministry of Finance every three years. The review process includes an examination of the organization's activities to verify compliance with the conditions.

2.4 Lack of tax deductibility of donations to foreign foundations

The refusal of almost all European countries to extend to donors the privilege of tax deductibility for donations made to foreign charitable foundations and other nonprofit organizations is one of the greatest national barriers to cross-border philanthropy. If national and European politicians truly wish to encourage civil society organizations to contribute more in other regions in Europe, and wish to promote greater solidarity among the peoples of the EU, they should take steps to eliminate this barrier. If the people of Europe are to begin to consider themselves as 'European citizens', they should be encouraged to donate to causes and organizations across their borders. In a Europe with a single currency, it becomes even more anomalous that a citizen cannot simply write a cheque and send it to a nonprofit organization in another European state without losing the privilege of deducting the donation from his or her income. With income tax rates approaching 50% in some states, this barrier is all the more significant. As anomalous is the case of citizens residing and working in border regions. For example, a citizen who is residing in Belgium and working in France may not deduct from their Belgian income taxes donations made to a French nonprofit organization active in their workplace community.

---

[23] Frotiée, P. and de Monseignat, R, 'France Country Report' in: George, C. ed., *International Charitable Giving: Laws and Taxation*, Kluwer International Law publishers, Supp. 1995, p. 9.

[24] Huc, S. and Bouzoraa, D., 'France Country Report' in Bater, P. ed., p. 8.

The five countries which do not impose this loss of privileges on cross-border donations are:

- Denmark and Italy which allow such deductibility
- Bulgaria and the Netherlands which allow it upon government approval (Ministry of Finance)
- France which allows it if the charitable foundation conducts non-profit activities in France.[25]

2.4.1 *The role of domestic qualifying intermediaries*

In general, European states allow donations made to foreign foundations to be deducted if made through a domestic qualifying intermediary, provided donations abroad are permitted under the intermediary foundation's statutes. The use of a qualifying intermediary is one of the primary ways used to circumvent this barrier.

A few exceptions nevertheless apply in some countries. In Finland, a foundation may not routinely act as an intermediary, since an organization that only subsidizes other organizations will not qualify as a nonprofit organization. In theory, Germany allows a foundation to act as an intermediary, yet in practice the government might not grant approval of a foundation's original statutes if they provide for such foreign transfers, especially if transfers were intended to increase the capital of foreign organizations.[26] Similarly, new tax regulations that entered into effect on 1 January 2000 in Germany require activities carried out in the pursuit of 'international understanding', (a term typically used to refer to international activities allowed by the authorities to qualify as being in the public interest) to be specifically in the German public interest. Henceforth, the welcoming of foreign visitors to Germany, exchanges between Germans and foreigners in Germany, and exchanges of information qualify for tax privileges as long as they are 'intended and appropriate to promote international understanding'. German legislators were obviously concerned about preventing purely tourist programmes from qualifying as being in the public interest.[27]

---

[25] Frotiée, P. and de Monseignat, R , 'France Country Report' in George C. ed., p. 9; Alfandari, E. and Nardone, A., p. 181.

[26] Under German tax law, foundations may build up reserves only up to 33% of annual income from capital investments minus the costs of capital investments. As a result of the recent reform in Germany, foundations can also now add 10% more from other means for the purpose of building up its reserves. Foundations may not therefore accumulate too much capital. This reserve restriction would also apply when foundations make grants abroad so as not to allow foreign organizations to do what the German foundations themselves cannot do at home.

[27] *Verordnung zur Änderung der Einkommenssteurer-Durchführungsverordnung* (EstDV), 10 December 1999, *Bundesgesetzblatt* T1/99, No. 55, S. 2413.

One potentially significant private initiative that takes advantage of the general rule of using domestic qualifying intermediaries is the Transnational Giving Europe Agreement, which will be discussed below in 3.2.1.

2.4.2 Commercial companies

Commercial companies often escape these restrictions by deducting the 'donation' as a business expense rather than as a charitable donation. They can do this if the donation furthers their corporate objectives or can be considered as an advertising expense. Commercial companies having affiliates or subsidiaries in several countries might also be able to transfer the charitable deduction to a related company in the jurisdiction where the recipient charitable organization is located.

It is noteworthy that states impose higher burdens on deducting charitable donations (i.e. by restricting the deduction to donations made to organizations in the same country as the donor) than on deducting business expenses, which can be incurred in any country in the world. It does not seem logical that a French company can theoretically incur all its business expenses in a third country, for instance the Philippines, and still be able to deduct them from its total turnover, and without any of the ceiling limits that apply in the case of charitable donations, whereas a French corporate donor may only deduct a donation made to a domestic qualifying organization, up to a maximum ceiling of 0.3% of its annual turnover.

2.4.3 Deductibility of donations from a foreign donor's domestic income

More than half the countries surveyed allow foreign donors (i.e. non-resident donors) to deduct a donation from their income if the donors are also tax-payers in the host country. In this context, expatriates, who might generally be more inclined to give to foundations or other nonprofit organizations in their home country, are included in the group of non-resident donors.

A few countries, such as Luxembourg, the Netherlands, and Sweden, do not allow a foreign donor to make such a deduction.

In Finland and Sweden, no individuals (domestic or foreign) may deduct donations from their income. Only corporations may deduct donations to charitable organizations.

2.5 Restrictions on and taxes due by foundations receiving foreign donations

Most countries impose no restrictions on donations made by foreign donors. Only Bulgaria and Hungary require the approval of the currency authority if the donation is in foreign currency.

2.5.1 *Customs duties*

Foundations established in one of the EU member states and receiving in-kind contributions from outside the EU should be aware that they, the recipient organizations, might have to pay customs duties and/or VAT on the goods received.

Being a customs union, the EU applies common rules to all imports into the EU, irrespective of the member state serving as the port of entry. Therefore, common tariffs as well as common exemptions should apply throughout the EU. Countries aspiring to join the EU are in the process of adopting similar rules as a condition of their accession. Switzerland and Liechtenstein, which form their own common customs union and are members of the European Economic Area (EEA), also abide by similar rules as those in effect in the EU. The discussion below therefore deals indirectly with these non-EU countries as well.

European Council Regulation (No. 918/83) Setting Up a Community System of Reliefs from Customs Duty[28] provides a series of exemptions for certain products being imported, including some products that may be of particular interest to foundations and other nonprofit organizations. Some examples of items eligible for relief are:

- educational, scientific and cultural materials listed in an Annex to the Regulation (articles 50 *et seq.*)
- basic necessities imported by 'charitable or philanthropic organizations approved by the competent authorities for distribution free of charge to needy persons' (Article 65(1)(a))
- equipment and office materials sent free of charge to charitable or philanthropic organizations approved by the competent authorities, to be used solely for the purposes of meeting their operating needs or carrying out their charitable or philanthropic aims (Article 65(1)(c))
- articles specially designed for the educational, scientific or cultural advancement of blind persons (Articles 70 *et seq.*)
- articles specially designed for the education, employment or social advancement of physically or mentally handicapped persons other than blind persons (Articles 72 *et seq.*)

---

[28] OJ L 105/1 of 23 April 1983.

- goods imported by charitable or philanthropic organizations approved by the competent authorities where the goods are intended for distribution free of charge to victims of disasters affecting the territory of one or more member states (Articles 79 *et seq.*).

In principle, these exemptions should be applied uniformly to all eligible items being imported into one of the member states from outside the EU. In practice, however, they are interpreted and applied inconsistently from one member state to another.[29] For example, in interpreting the exemption for 'charitable or philanthropic organizations', the national authorities each use their own criteria, with no formal uniform guidelines and no reported administrative decisions to help determine qualification for the exemption.

Perhaps surprising is the fact that the customs authorities are the competent authorities to decide whether or not an organization qualifies for the exemption. Although this might make initial sense (since the customs authorities are the ones present at the port of entry where such determination is often made if the national rules do not require an advance ruling) customs authorities have little experience with the nonprofit sector and the criteria usually considered to determine whether or not an organization qualifies as a public benefit organization.[30] For this reason, the practice of the customs authorities is often very different from the practice of the other national authorities relating to charitable or philanthropic organizations. For instance, in the Netherlands, a jurisdiction renowned for its liberal interpretation of public benefit, the customs authorities interpret very strictly the exemption described under Article 65 of the Customs Regulation, basic necessities imported by 'charitable or philanthropic organizations'. In order for an organization to qualify for exemption under Article 65 in the Netherlands, it must be approved expressly by law. In light of this onerous requirement, only two organizations (Red Cross and Salvation Army) have been approved in the Netherlands for this exemption! In contrast, in the UK, all registered charities, as well as all other nonprofit organizations serving the welfare of the needy, qualify for the exemption.

The different interpretation given to the same situation by the national authorities in the various member states can cause unfair hardship to charitable foundations operating in a member state with a

---

[29] It is not possible to describe in this chapter all the differences in the implementation of this Regulation. A description of some of the reasons for disparate treatment is given merely to call the reader's attention to this issue.

[30] See generally Garcia-Andrade: Establishment, Amendment and Liquidation of Foundations (6) and Bater and Habighorst: Tax Treatment of Foundations and their Donors (2.2.1).

more restrictive interpretation. It also causes legal uncertainty in a domain where simple uniform rules should apply to the same situation. The European Commission does not seem concerned about resolving this problem by trying to ensure that the national authorities adopt similar criteria and guidelines for interpreting the exemptions provided under the Regulation.

2.5.2 VAT

As with customs duties, common rules apply to VAT throughout the EU.[31] The VAT rules, however, do allow the national authorities some freedom in determining how to achieve the common goals.

European Council Directive 83/181 of 28 March 1983,[32] as subsequently amended, provides several bases for exemption from VAT. Some of these exemptions, such as the exemption provided in Article 40 of the Directive, mirror exemptions granted in the Customs Regulation, in which case the customs authorities will usually be responsible for implementing both the customs and the VAT exemptions.

Where the VAT exemptions are different from the customs exemptions, the VAT authorities generally interpret them restrictively as they are very reluctant to grant exemptions for the import of items from outside the EU, as this would give a foreign supplier a competitive advantage over a local supplier who is subject to VAT. The Commission appears impervious to the argument that in the case of a donation, a foreign donor does not compete with a local supplier who is selling the same items. A charitable foundation that is to receive items that were donated from outside the EU would probably prefer paying VAT at the rate of 20%, for instance, to paying the full price to a local supplier of the same items. Therefore, whether the items are exempt or not, there would be no distortion of competition – the recipient would always prefer donated goods that are subject to VAT to goods for which it must pay the full purchase price.

The problem of inconsistent interpretations mentioned above in 2.5.1 for customs duty exemptions also applies to VAT exemptions.

2.6 Moving the foundation's seat abroad

Given that the laws applying to charitable foundations are deeply rooted in the historical and cultural traditions of the various countries

---

[31] Sixth Council Directive of 17 May 1977 on harmonization of legislation of member states concerning turnover taxes (77/388/EEC), OJ L145 of 13 June 1977; see generally Bater and Habighorst: Tax Treatment of Foundations and their Donors (2.1 as well as 2.5.1 above).

[32] OJ L 105/38 of 23 April 1983.

and that there are several built-in mechanisms for 'encouraging' foundations to remain active at home, not abroad, it is not surprising that foundations in most countries are not able to move their seat abroad without severe consequences, including dissolution and/or loss of tax privileges. Although the difficulty of moving their seat is not unique to charitable foundations, as companies and other legal entities in many member states also still face obstacles to their moving their seat, even within the EU, charitable foundations must confront the added barriers imposed by law and administrative practice to their conducting activities abroad. Charitable foundations, like other nonprofit organizations, are often dependent on their tax-exempt status for survival.

In countries where charitable foundations are incorporated on the basis of a specific law requiring that certain criteria be met, including perhaps that the foundation's seat be located in that jurisdiction,[33] moving the foundation's seat to another jurisdiction might deprive the foundation of its legal basis for its existence. It might therefore have to be dissolved and liquidated in the first country and then re-established in accordance with the laws of the new jurisdiction. This would be the case in Austria, Belgium, Finland, Greece, Portugal, Spain, and Sweden.

In other countries where the foundation's privileged status is linked to the benefits it provides to the community, as interpreted in a national context, a foundation's move of its seat to a foreign country might result in the loss of its tax privileges.[34] This would almost always be true for the tax privilege of having donations recognized by the charitable foundation as tax deductible for national donors. As seen above in 2.4, in general a donor may only deduct a donation made to a charitable organization established in the same jurisdiction in which the donor is a tax-payer. Thus the foundation's move to another jurisdiction would make it a foreign organization for tax-payers in its former jurisdiction.

In England, Ireland and Scotland, the type of consequences of such a move might depend on whether the charitable organization is established as a trust or as a company. Since a trust is established on behalf of defined beneficiaries, the state usually has a stronger interest in protecting the rights of the beneficiaries, which it would arguably not be able to ensure if the charitable trust were to move its seat abroad. In this

---

[33] For example, Article 30 of the Belgian Law of 27 June 1921 *accordant la personalité civile aux associations sans but lucratif et aux établissements d'utilité publique* specifically requires the seat to be located in Belgium.

[34] Ireland, Switzerland and United Kingdom.

context, a trust is deemed to move its seat abroad when either a majority of its trustees move outside of the jurisdiction, or the trustees move the trust property, (e.g. bank account) to another jurisdiction. In England and Wales, the Charity Commission usually requires a majority of the trustees to reside in England or Wales at the time of the trust's registration (*in personam* jurisdiction), presumably to be able to exercise control over the trustees and thus over the trust. Likewise, the Charity Commission might also require, although it is less clear in this case, the trust property to remain within the jurisdiction and their control (*in rem* jurisdiction). A trust wishing to move its seat abroad would also have to consider the very real possibility that its legal form would not be recognized in the European jurisdiction that would become its new home. Charitable organizations established in the form of a company, for example companies limited by guarantee, would not face the same obstacles to moving abroad and would probably be allowed to do so although, since the registered office would no longer be in the home jurisdiction, they would also have to be dissolved.

In all cases where a charitable foundation has to be dissolved before establishing a new entity in another jurisdiction, the foundation's governing body must consider whether the foundation's governing documents allow the transfer of capital to a foreign charitable organization. A foundation's governing documents generally contain a 'destination clause' that provides how the assets will be distributed upon dissolution. Often, the destination clause provides that the assets, after discharge of all debts and liabilities, must be given to some other charitable institution or applied for a charitable purpose similar to that of the dissolving body. Whether specifically stated or not, such a clause might presume an interpretation of 'charitable' within the meaning accorded under national law. Even where the stated purpose of the foundation allows activities abroad, the governing body might be duty-bound to apply the remaining assets in a way consistent with the national law, that is to say, for some organization or purpose that would qualify as 'charitable'.

In a few countries, a charitable foundation may move its seat if it obtains government approval or meets other legal requirements. Liechtenstein, the Netherlands[35] and Switzerland allow such a move as long as the home government approves it. Luxembourg, however,

---

[35] In the Netherlands, the Ministry of Justice must review the foundation's statutes, as amended to conform to the new state's requirements, and examine whether the new state provides for similar supervision to safeguard the proper use of the foundation's funds before taking its decision.

requires the host government's approval and recognition of the foundation's continued legal personality before allowing a charitable foundation to move its seat.

A foundation may not move its seat abroad in Estonia, Germany, and Slovenia. Although in Germany there is no legal provision that expressly prohibits a foundation from moving its seat abroad, in practice the supervisory authorities would view the moving of the German foundation's seat as being inconsistent with the founder's original intention of establishing a foundation for an everlasting period. If the authorities did allow a German foundation to move its seat, the foundation would have to be dissolved and liquidated in Germany before establishing a new foundation in the other jurisdiction.

2.6.1 *Dual registration*

Charitable foundations may have dual registration (i.e. registration in two states of a single entity) in Austria, Bulgaria, Cyprus and Italy. A foreign foundation may thus have a second seat in these jurisdictions.

A foundation wishing to take advantage of such a privilege must also verify that it is also allowed to do so under the law of its home jurisdiction. Some states, for example, might view a permanent establishment in a second jurisdiction as being contrary to the foundation's statutes or even the law of the home jurisdiction. The home jurisdiction's authorities might be concerned about its ability to exercise its supervisory authority over the foundation's activities in the second jurisdiction. Perhaps for these reasons, among others, dual registration is forbidden in Estonia, Finland, Germany, and Hungary.

2.7 General remarks

National barriers to cross-border giving continue to exist in many forms, some more apparent than others. In today's world, however, these barriers are no longer justifiable as a means of encouraging donors to give and foundations to act within national borders. In a Europe in which citizens are being asked to feel greater solidarity towards their fellow citizens in other states of the Union, and even in states aspiring to join the Union, these barriers violate the spirit of such a new European order calling for a People's Europe. They also prevent funding from going to regions that might need the resources most to help them raise their standard of living to a level enjoyed by others.

Instead, member states should be called to take appropriate action to eliminate these barriers and to promote cross-border giving. The European Commission, in its more recent calls for proposals, has begun to encourage organizations and enterprises in more than one member state to submit proposals together in an effort to increase the contacts between actors in the different member states. Member states should follow this lead and support similar cross-border contacts and activities. Foundations can also help by supporting cross-border activities and promoting greater interaction between people in various states throughout Europe. Recommendations for public and private action will be discussed in 3 below.

3 Instruments to overcome national barriers

The public instruments described below call for states or international intergovernmental bodies to take action to reduce or eliminate existing barriers to cross-border philanthropy. The private initiatives identified further below are examples of ways in which foundations can encourage cross-border activities and expand their own geographic scope of action.

3.1 Public instruments

The public instruments available to states for reducing national barriers include instruments that they can take up alone (unilateral measures), with another state (bilateral measures), or through regional intergovernmental organizations, such as the Council of Europe and the EU (multilateral measures).

3.1.1 Unilateral measures

States are first of all the master of their own laws. The legislators and politicians in each state have full influence over the legal and fiscal framework applying to charitable foundations and other nonprofit organizations residing, or engaging in activities, in their jurisdiction. If states wish to promote cross-border philanthropy, they can begin by amending their own laws in order to ensure that there is an enabling framework in place which does not prevent, discourage or discriminate against cross-border activities of foundations or their donors.

The Netherlands is a notable example of a country that has adopted a favourable legal and fiscal framework that does not discourage or discriminate against cross-border activities of foundations. Not only is it fairly simple for founders to establish a foundation in the Netherlands, which is an important consideration for foundations wishing to establish an affiliated foundation in a second jurisdiction, but the Dutch authorities also interpret public benefit to include benefit conferred outside their jurisdiction. A Dutch foundation may be active almost exclusively outside the Netherlands and still qualify as a charitable foundation with all its tax privileges.

All states are free to adopt unilateral measures that extend to foreign charitable organizations the tax privileges available to national organizations. They may also extend to their own tax-payers the same privileges when donating to foreign organizations as when donating to domestic organizations. By adopting unilateral measures, states can act as a model for other states to follow. Only a couple of states in Europe, however, have adopted unilateral measures, and even these require that the jurisdiction of the foreign organization extend similar privileges to their charitable organizations on the basis of reciprocity. For example, in Greece, Law 1160/1981 exempts Swiss charitable foundations from any tax or other form of duty on the basis of reciprocity. Similarly in Austria, the Federal Minister of Finance has discretion to extend tax privileges to foreign charitable organizations on the basis of reciprocity. In the Netherlands, the Ministry of Finance may also allow foreign charitable organizations to benefit from a reduced rate of gift and inheritance taxes (at a reduced rate of 11% instead of between 41% and 68%) on donations made by Dutch tax-payers. Disappointingly, however, the list stops here. The unilateral measures adopted to date have been isolated, not well publicized and limited in scope or effect.

In order for unilateral measures to be successful in encouraging other states to take similar action, larger states known for their developed philanthropy sector would have to adopt them. For instance, if Germany were to adopt a unilateral measure addressed to all states, not just to one state as in the case of Greece, other states wishing for their nonprofit organizations to be able to receive funds more easily from donors in Germany might be encouraged to adopt a similar measure.

3.1.2 Bilateral agreements (double taxation agreements)

Bilateral agreements between states dealing with tax issues usually focus on the avoidance of double taxation, not the extension of tax relief. The main concern of the states in entering into these agreements, as can be seen by the language in the OECD Model Tax Convention used as a reference for most such agreements in the areas of income tax as well as gift and inheritance tax, is to ensure that a tax-payer does not have to pay tax twice on the same income. Regrettably, the contracting states are not apparently concerned that a tax-exempt organization, such as a charitable foundation, that is resident in one country might be subject to tax in another country on income earned in that country, even though such income would be exempt from tax at home.

Very few bilateral double taxation agreements refer specifically to nonprofit organizations. In Europe, France, Germany and Sweden lead the pack with specific references to nonprofit organizations. Germany is also a notable leader with respect to gift and inheritance tax treaties granting benefits to foreign nonprofit organizations on the condition of reciprocity, as it has entered into five such treaties, almost all with European countries.

Of particular interest to foundations in the context of bilateral agreements is probably whether or not they will be subject to capital gains or income tax if they invest part of their endowment portfolio in securities or other investment instruments in another state. Foundations should be aware in this respect that bilateral commercial and investment treaties might also apply and include non-discrimination articles that prohibit treatment of foreign organizations that is less favourable than that applicable to national organizations or less favourable than that offered to organizations of any other state. The definition of 'organization' used in these treaties should encompass charitable foundations, especially to the extent that they can be considered investors with respect to their endowment assets.

On the whole, the effect of bilateral treaties on cross-border philanthropy has been disappointing. Not only are there few agreements that contain language specifically referring to nonprofit organizations, but also the language of the provisions does not fully reflect the particularities of the nonprofit sector. Instead of non-discrimination provisions which aim to prevent double taxation, the provisions should include express language that compels contracting states to extend tax privileges to nonprofit organizations and donors residing in their state and active in another contracting state, as well as to organizations and donors residing in the other contracting state and active in their state.

States negotiating future bilateral treaties or revising current treaties need to gather up the political will to include such positive language compelling contracting states to extend the tax relief granted to national nonprofit organizations and donors to nonprofit organizations and donors residing in the other contracting state. They must realize that it is in their mutual interests that both societies develop and advance. They must also understand that with such cross-border philanthropy, the roots of solidarity between the people of their respective countries will begin to grow, and hopefully later bear fruit.

3.1.3 Multilateral measures: Council of Europe

The Council of Europe is an important intergovernmental organization in several areas of interest to foundations and other nonprofit organizations, namely in human rights, culture, education, minorities, as well as the promotion of civil society in its newer member states in eastern Europe. The Council of Europe has also for years actively promoted a better tax treatment of NGOs, however, without many concrete results.

The most concrete example of the work of the Council of Europe in this area is the European Convention on the Recognition of the Legal Personality of International Non-governmental Organizations, discussed above in 2.1.1. As mentioned above, it is unfortunate that this Convention is limited to legal, not tax issues, applies only to international organizations, and currently has only nine signatory states.

Given that the Council of Europe currently has 41 members throughout Europe, it can offer a suitable forum for debating measures leading to an improved legal and fiscal framework for cross-border activities of nonprofit organizations and their donors. Moreover, it can be a useful partner to the EU in its plans to enlarge the Union towards the East. Together they can contribute enormously towards promoting a strong and vibrant civil society throughout Europe that brings a new stability and helps raise the standard of living for everyone.

3.1.4 Multilateral measures: European Union

The movement of several European states towards a common Union has drastically changed the course of Europe forever. The fact that several countries from diverse historical, cultural, religious and linguistic traditions could join forces in building their common future would have been unimaginable a little more than half a century ago. Ever since its inception, the driving force behind European integration was not the economic dimension alone, but the desire to safeguard peace, to contribute to civilization and to help raise the standard of living.[36]

---

[36] See preamble of ECSC Treaty.

European integration should not be viewed as a single phenomenon, but as a process responding to the changing reality of the member states. The member states began their cooperation by focusing on narrow economic issues. Yet over the years the member states have conferred more power on the European institutions to deal with many people-sensitive issues, such as environment, employment, food safety, asylum, international crime and social exclusion, to name a few. As charitable foundations and other nonprofit organizations have been traditionally active in all of these areas, it has become increasingly important for European institutions to decide how to work with these organizations when shaping new European policy.

With historically low public confidence in European institutions partially due to the democratic deficits reigning in their decision-making process, Mr Romano Prodi, the Secretary-General of the Commission, promised to restore public confidence by making the Commission more responsive to grassroots opinion and by strengthening the role of civil society through 'civil dialogue', that is by consulting representative civil society organizations during the legislative process.[37]

At a time when the EU is considering monumental institutional reform as well as enlargement of its borders to include countries in central and eastern Europe, it could benefit immensely by seeking greater cooperation with charitable foundations and other nonprofit organizations in the implementation of European policies as a means to complement their financial resources and to benefit from these organizations' valuable insight and knowledge.

Yet, in order for foundations and other nonprofit organizations to participate in the European decision-making process, through European organizations and networks that are created to represent the interests of citizens throughout Europe and are united around a common cause, European institutions and member states must reform the laws currently applying to these civil society organizations. At present, civil society remains largely outside the European Treaties.

In light of the continued contacts between member states at the EU level, the EU is the most logical forum for an initiative leading to

---

[37] One example of action taken to fulfil Mr Prodi's promise is the European Commission's draft Discussion Paper, 'The Commission and Non-Governmental Organizations: Building a Stronger Partnership' presented by President Prodi and Vice-President Kinnock and being circulated to non-governmental organizations, among others, for comments.

regional reform that improves the legal and fiscal rules governing cross-border giving. Whether the initiative should be taken by the member states themselves or by one or several of the European institutions (Parliament, Commission, Economic and Social Committee) will ultimately depend on the political balance of the moment. Yet, even if the European institutions are to play a role in launching an initiative, the influence of the member states on the ultimate success of such an initiative can not be underestimated. Ultimately, it will come down to whether or not the national politicians support such an effort.

Past European action and possible legal bases for action

In order for the European institutions to act, there must be a legal basis expressed in the Treaty of Rome, as amended by subsequent treaties. Since the original focus of the Treaty of Rome was economic integration, matters of primary concern to the 'social economy' fell to the wayside. The European institutions have as a result held only tepid discussions on action lacking a solid underlying legal basis.

To date, most of the action taken by the European institutions has focused on associations (e.g. Amended Proposal for a Council Regulation on the statute for a European association)[38] rather than on foundations, or has consisted of general studies of the voluntary sector (e.g. Communication from the Commission on Promoting the Role of Voluntary Organizations and Foundations).[39]

Although the current Amended Proposal concerning a European Association might appear to be a useful model for foundations to follow, the text of the Proposal is so severely flawed that they would do better to present their own proposals.[40] One serious flaw, for example, is the Amended Proposal's failure to resolve the fiscal issues arising for organizations conducting cross-borders activities. Moreover, the progress of the Amended Proposal has been held up for several years for political reasons related to the Proposal for a Council Regulation for a European Company.[41] Some member states have refused to allow the

---

[38] OJ C 236/01 of 31 August 1993.

[39] COM (97) 241 final; see Gallop, B., 'One Step Forward, Two Steps Back' in: *Alliance*, Vol. 3, 1.98, pp. 39–41 for a commentary.

[40] For a full discussion of this Amended Proposal, see Verbeke, L. and Gallop, B., 'Taxation, Legal and Self-Regulation Issues' in: L. Doyle, ed., *Funding Europe's Solidarity*, AICE publishers, 1996 pp. I–64 *et seq.*, and Gallop, B., *Alliance*, pp. 39–41.

[41] Com (89) 268 final. Guidelines for political agreement were agreed by the Council of Ministers on 20 December 2000 on the proposal for a Regulation for a European Company, sending the proposal to the European Parliament for a final consultation. These guidelines may pave the way for action on the Proposal for a European Association.

Amended Proposal for a European Association to be adopted before definitive action is taken on the Regulation for a European Company.

Another reason for foundations to initiate their own action is that by doing so they avoid inheriting the political problems related to the Amended Proposal for a European Association. With the European institutions (Commission, Parliament, and Economic and Social Committee) and the member states all currently giving particular attention to increasing the role of civil society, foundations might find this an opportune moment to launch an initiative and seek political support for action.

In order to determine the type of initiative that foundations should propose, they might usefully examine the more important legal bases in the Amsterdam Treaty that might support such an initiative. This would enable foundations to analyse the possible measures for proposal.

In its resolution on nonprofit-making associations in the European Communities in 1987,[42] the European Parliament identified several legal bases in the treaties that would enable the European institutions to take the appropriate action necessary to eliminate national barriers to cross-border activity on the part of foundations and other non-profit-making bodies. Among the more notable bases for this resolution were Article 2 ('the Community shall have as its task [...] to promote throughout the Community a harmonious development of economic activities, heightened stability, the raising of the standard of living and quality of life and solidarity among member states'); Article 12 (ex Article 6) (non-discrimination on the basis of nationality), and Article 18 (ex Article 8A) (elimination of barriers to Single Market). Reference to these articles as the legal bases for the Parliament's recommended action demonstrates the growing and important need, even in 1987, for the European institutions to attend to the non-economic aspects of the European Community, as it was then known.

Another legal basis that might be of interest to nonprofit organizations, including foundations, wishing to set up offices in other member states lies in Articles 43 to 48 (ex Articles 52 to 58) of the EC Treaty (freedom of establishment). Although nonprofit organizations are specifically excluded from the scope of these provisions by Article 48 (ex Article 58), case law shows some hope for organizations engaged in economic activities. Thus, an operating foundation wishing to establish an office in another member state to engage in an

---

[42] OJ C 99/205, 13 April 1987.

economic activity (e.g. publishing, purchasing art for sale/loan to museum, research) might be able to initiate a test case challenging a host country's refusal to extend its tax privileges to the foreign foundation, as such a refusal could be a barrier to its right to establish an office in another member state. However, if the foundation's only aim there was to engage in economic activities, the authorities might be justified to refuse it tax privileges on the basis that the pursuit of a nonprofit purpose was not its principal motivation for operating in their jurisdiction. The host jurisdiction could find added ammunition for its refusal on the basis of unfair competition principles if the foundation were competing against local for-profit entities. It would be a different case, however, if a host country's charitable organization were entitled to enjoy tax privileges when engaging in the same economic activities.

Bit by bit, however, as the process of integration has led to a Single Market, a Single Currency (11 member states in 2000, 12 member states in 2001), a Passport Union (Schengen, currently for 10 member states) and now a Common Foreign and Security Policy Area, it is no longer realistic or desirable to exclude nonprofit organizations from fully enjoying the benefits of this integration. It is unfortunate that the member states and the European institutions did not take advantage of the current round of institutional reforms being discussed at the present intergovernmental conference to take the appropriate steps to include at least one express provision in the revised Treaty that recognizes the key role to be played by civil society during the legislative and implementation processes. Increasing the intermediary role played by civil society organizations between citizens and the European institutions could have resulted in a reduction of the democratic deficits currently reigning in Brussels and a strengthening of the ties of solidarity among the citizens of Europe.

All it would take is for a core group of member states to push the European institutions and their fellow member states to begin considering reform. The European institutions are less likely to launch any initiatives of their own in these new areas without the express support of some member states. The support of member states is crucial for getting the reform on the agenda. It might perhaps be possible for a group of legislators who were involved in the recent reform processes in Germany, the UK and Italy to begin sharing their own experiences and identifying common areas still needing attention.

In fact, if the next European Treaty includes provisions expressly recognizing 'reinforced cooperation' or 'flexibility' as a policy (in other words allowing some European states to proceed in certain areas toward integration while others opt out of such plans) some member states could envisage adopting a common charity zone among themselves as an incentive for others to join later. The measures discussed below can be taken by either some or all of the member states, with the EU and its institutions providing a forum for the member states to discuss and adopt such measures.

Possible and realistic measures to be taken

In its Communication on Promoting the Role of Voluntary Organizations and Foundations in Europe, the Commission encourages member states to take appropriate action to make the legal and fiscal regimes applying to the sector more positive, clear and simple so that they are conducive to the sector fulfilling its potential.

Member states should review their laws applying to charitable organizations, including foundations, and amend where necessary and possible all definitions of public benefit so that they refer to the 'European' rather than the national community. Amending these definitions would be of prime importance, as it would encourage organizations and donors to think of themselves as European citizens interested in creating bonds of solidarity across their national borders. It would also help promote increased grassroots action, which is in line with the Community principle of subsidiarity – for action to take place at the level that is the most close to the citizen.

Mutual recognition

A next conceivable step would be for member states to extend their tax privileges to donors who contribute funds to qualifying organizations and foundations established in other European countries.

In order for member states to be willing to take such steps, the Commission might need to guide them by taking action that provides for mutual recognition of similar charitable organizations and foundations established in other member states. Whether or not the Commission or another European institution would however be useful in promoting action will depend on the balance of power between state and European institutions reigning at the time of action.

Member states would probably be more willing to agree to allow foreign organizations to qualify for the same tax privileges as national organizations if the other member states granted privileges to similar charitable organizations (i.e. used similar criteria for determining 'public benefit'). A certain degree of uniformity is therefore required if the member states are to extend their tax privileges.

In order to avoid disagreement that would sabotage the mutual recognition efforts, member states should identify either basic categories of purposes that they can all agree as qualifying as public benefit purposes, or a set of criteria, which if met, would ensure that an organization is acting for a nonprofit purpose. These categories or criteria could comprise a common core definition of 'public benefit' that would entitle qualifying organizations to be recognized in the other member states and to receive the tax privileges applying in those other states. Arguably, the task of agreeing to a common core definition would be easier if the member states first amended their laws to require that nonprofit organizations' activities conferred benefit on a European, rather than a national, community.

Agreeing to a common qualifying purpose clause would not preclude member states from allowing national organizations to qualify under national law for an additional purpose. For instance, a member state could decide to recognize a national organization pursuing a sports purpose and to grant such an organization the same privileges as other nonprofit organizations pursuing a purpose contained in the European core definition. If sports are not included in the core definition, however, other member states hosting this organisation's activities would not be obliged to extend tax privileges to it. Nor would they be compelled to extend tax privileges to donors residing in their jurisdiction who contribute funds to this organization.

Providing mutual recognition of all organizations that pursue one of the defined core purposes and that are duly established in one of the member states would eliminate any need for a new 'European' form of qualifying foundation

Supervision

An important consideration when contemplating mutual recognition of foundations is to ensure that foundations are subject to a similar level and degree of authority in the host jurisdiction. Since foundations are generally subject to greater state supervision than associations, member states would probably want to guarantee that foundations continue to be subject to similar supervision when acting in other member states. Likewise, if member states extend their tax privileges to allow donors who are national residents to deduct donations made to charitable foundations established in another member state, they will want to be sure that the donated funds are being used for a qualifying public purpose. For this, the supervisory authorities in the member state where the recipient foundation is located will need to ensure compliance with the common rules and take appropriate action against cases of abuse.

Ensuring similar supervision might be difficult given that the supervision varies so much from state to state.[43] In some states, it is the ministry of finance that exercises supervision, whereas in others it is another ministry or government body, or even the court. Likewise, in federal states such as Germany and Spain, there are various levels of supervision exercised by authorities at the different levels of government.

The member states would have to determine whether they prefer supervision by the host state authorities as a condition of the host state's extension of its tax privileges to foreign foundations active within its borders, or accepting that foreign foundations be subject to the supervision exercised in the home state, even when acting outside its borders. For the second choice to prevail, the member states would have to feel that supervision is adequate in all member states.

The most logical alternative would be a combination of supervision in the host and the home states. For example, certain issues relating to the establishment and governance of the foundation could be supervised by the home state, whereas certain activities conducted in the host state, such as fundraising and investments, could be subject to the rules and supervision in the host state. If a foundation engages in activities in another country, these activities should of course be governed by the local laws. The foundation would then be subject to the same rules as other foundations established in the host jurisdiction and engaging in similar activities.

Member states would also need exchange of information laws enabling them to obtain the information necessary to perform their own supervisory functions relating both to the foundations and to their donors.

Harmonization of tax privileges

Harmonization of tax privileges to foundations and donors is not absolutely required, although some approximation might be desirable to reduce the administrative burden and confusion of foundations

---

[43] See generally van Veen: Supervision of Foundations in Europe.

and donors who are active across borders. Moreover, to the extent that the privileges relate to direct taxes, as opposed to indirect taxes, harmonization will be much less likely at EU level because a decision requires unanimity.[44] Nevertheless, some approximation (or harmonization) would probably ultimately result from the foundations and other nonprofit organizations acting in a more open environment with reduced national barriers. Over time, increased forum shopping would probably encourage member states to take measures to attract foundations to their forum.

Enlargement process

Extending the reform described above to encourage donors in the European Union to make more dontaions to nonprofit organizations in countries applying for accession to the Union ('candidate countries') could contribute considerably to the enlargement process by providing much needed funds at a time when public funds seem to be diminishing. Individuals and corporations would hence be rewarded (or at least not penalized) for donating money to charitable organizations in candidate countries by receiving a tax deduction for their donations.

One way to promote giving to nonprofit organizations in candidate countries would be to ask the European institutions to assist member states in launching a special 'Enlargement Aid' programme. This programme could be established for an agreed period, for instance, until all the countries accede to the European Union, in an effort to raise public awareness of the need to contribute funds for the purpose of enlargement. Setting up a programme that would define common rules for fostering private donations to nonprofit organizations in the candidate countries could be a useful way of encouraging citizens to become involved in enlargement, even to become active supporters of a process that currently worries many. The Enlargement Aid programme could even involve special incentives in the form of additional tax privileges for participating private donors. Such a programme would thus provide nonprofit organizations with much needed additional resources to help the European institutions, member states and candidate countries bring these countries in line with European rules and policies before acceding to the Union.

---

[44] To date, harmonization efforts have focused on indirect taxes, such as VAT and more recently on withholding taxes on non-resident savings income. See generally Bater and Habighorst: Tax Treatment of Foundationsand their Donors.

The Enlargement Aid project could either be part of larger reform that would apply to donations thoughout Europe (for example, by extending the definition of public benefit and the applications of mutual recognition discussed above to include the candidate countries currently outside the European Union) or as a pilot project for further reform. As a pilot project, for instance, the member states and the European Union could use this historic opportunity of enlargement to agree a common definition of public benefit or of the organizational requirements that all charitable organizations would have to meet to qualify for these additional tax privileges. They could even begin establishing an accreditation system for eligible recipient organizations. Or, they might decide to designate certain national umbrella organizations through which private funds would pass, and who would decide, on the basis of agreed criteria, how to distribute the funds. The member states and the European institutions could afterwards learn from this Enlargement Aid programme and make recommendations for similar rules to apply within the European Union. In this way, by starting with a largely symbolic measure called 'Enlargement Aid' that does not require significant infrastructure to be established or money to be expended, enlargement can serve as the means of achieving deeper integration and stronger solidarity within the European Union.

3.2 Private instruments or initiatives

Foundations interested in being active across borders or in encouraging international philanthropy have several options available for doing so. These are described and discussed below.

3.2.1 Agreements

A foundation interested in becoming active in a host country might decide to seek partners there who can offer the requisite experience, contacts and insight. More importantly perhaps, the partner(s) sought will have knowledge of the applicable administrative and legal requirements and will be entitled to tax privileges, thanks to their status in the host country. A foundation might therefore find it well worthwhile to identify qualifying foundations or even associations in other countries to work with in order to facilitate its cross-border giving.

Once partners are found, the parties will want to enter into an agreement setting out the terms of their relationship, which can be tailored to suit their objectives. An agreement can be:

- formal or informal
- ongoing or project-specific
- targeted for certain fields of activities or more open (only limited to the stated objectives of the foundations in their respective statutes).

One example of an agreement is the Transnational Giving Europe Agreement, entered into between foundations in four European countries,[45] by which the party foundations each act as an intermediary in order to help donors in their country make a qualifying donation in a foreign jurisdiction.

One advantage of such an agreement is that it can provide for a procedure and rules to ensure that a party organization in the beneficiary country exercises the necessary responsibility over the transfer of the donation (i.e. to ensure that the donation is made to an appropriate beneficiary) and takes care of all reporting requirements. Thus an agreement can eliminate one of the principal difficulties a foundation faces when making grants abroad: the obligation to exercise responsibility over the grant in order to ensure that it is used in such a way as to fall within the foundation's charitable purpose. Moreover, it facilitates the task required of a foundation in many states of showing that the beneficiary organization is equivalent to a qualifying charitable organization in the home country.

Through an agreement, the parties can also decide in advance on the criteria to be used for identifying recipients of funds. Much work that is normally done each time a grant is made can hence be accomplished in advance in order to save time when making the grant.

3.2.2 Membership of associations

Foundations can join associations representing foundation interests and advocating improvements to the legal and fiscal environment applying to cross-border giving (e.g. EFC, Civicus, etc.). Through these associations, foundations can speak for cross-border giving reform with a stronger collective voice. They can also make useful contacts at other foundations that might prove to be suitable partners for joint action or cooperation.

Foundations can also join associations that are active in areas of interest to their programmes. In this respect, a foundation with a strong programme interest in alleviating poverty in Third World countries, for instance, might wish to join associations, or unincorporated networks or coalitions, engaged in alleviating poverty or related issues.

---

[45] Charities Aid Foundation (UK), *Fondation de France* (France), *Juliana Welzijn Fonds* (the Netherlands), and King Baudouin Foundation (Belgium).

3.2.3 International structure

As a legal person, a foundation may establish other legal entities as subsidiaries, sister organizations, affiliated organizations, and branch offices. These other entities may be located in other countries and be created to accomplish specified or like purposes of the foundation. A foundation may use these other legal entities to help it expand its international activities as well as to enjoy the tax privileges available in other countries; the Soros network of foundations, for instance, is currently present and active in more than 30 countries.

An international structure also allows the foundation to promote a more international perspective among its staff and contacts. The international exposure can only help to increase the exchange of ideas and values within the foundation's own internal organization and hence to enable the foundation to use these ideas and values for the benefit of its programmes.

If allowed by the host jurisdiction, a new organization may also be established in the form of a for-profit entity that is responsible for conducting an economic activity and channelling the profits back to the foundation, either as a dividend or as a donation. Many foundations in Germany are shareholders, even majority shareholders, of a GmbH or AG, thus assuring the foundation a steady flow of income as well as endowment capital.

European Economic Interest Grouping (EEIG)

A foundation engaging in an economic activity might moreover be interested in becoming a member of a European Economic Interest Grouping (EEIG), as allowed under European law.[46] The purpose of a grouping must be to 'facilitate or develop the economic activities of its members and to improve or increase the results of those activities; its purpose is not to make profits for itself'.[47] The EEIG's activities must be related to the economic activities of its members and must not be more than ancillary to those activities. Therefore, a foundation wishing to join at least two other legal entities or natural persons in other member states[48] to develop its economic activities can achieve its objectives by establishing an EEIG.

---

[46] EC Regulation 2137/85 of 25 July 1985, OJ L 199/1 of 31 July 1985 ('EEIG Regulation').

[47] Article 3 of EEIG Regulation.

[48] An EEIG must be comprised of at least two legal bodies (having their central administration) or two natural persons (carrying out their principal activities) in different member states.

An EEIG would only be a suitable option where all members already had similar economic activities that they wished to render somehow more efficient by joining forces. One example would be a foundation with a significant publishing activity that wished to cooperate with other legal entities, not necessarily other tax-exempt organizations, to conduct this activity.

The EEIG does not itself offer any special tax privileges. It merely provides a vehicle for several parties in different member states to work together and act under a common name. Members of an EEIG must enter into a contract setting out specified information, including how they will share the grouping's expenses and how they will apportion the profits earned from the grouping's activities.[49] Each member will be taxed on the profits apportioned to it in its home jurisdiction.

The members of an EEIG must register their contract in the state where the EEIG will have its official address. From the time of registration, an EEIG shall 'have the capacity, in its name, to have rights and obligations of all kinds, to make contracts or accomplish other legal acts, and to sue and be sued'.[50] Each member state shall decide whether or not an EEIG registered in its jurisdiction will enjoy legal personality. Even without personality, however, an EEIG enjoys many of the advantages of being a legal person. Yet, the members do not enjoy limited liability and may be held liable for the grouping's debts after a creditor first seeks recovery from the EEIG.

Becoming a subsidiary or affiliated organization

Alternatively, a foundation may be a subsidiary or an affiliated organization of another legal entity, such as an association that wishes to accumulate or raise funds in a given jurisdiction. Since foundations generally do not, and in some jurisdictions cannot, have members, allowing an association to create a foundation and then control the foundation's governing body can ultimately give the association's members an effective voice in decisions on the foundation's activities. In effect, an association will have created a foundation with indirect membership representation. Where the governing body is appointed by a 'parent' or other organization, it must of course act exclusively in the best interests of the charitable foundation being governed.

---

[49] Article 21 of EEIG Regulation.

[50] Article 1, paragraph 2 of EEIG Regulation.

The design that a foundation will choose for its activity will ultimately depend on several factors, including sources of additional funding, location of programme implementation, location of partners, and location of the requisite expertise. A foundation might wish to establish an organization in a jurisdiction where numerous potential individual or corporate donors are located in order to attract their funds with tax privileges. Similarly, if a foundation has a programme that requires a lot of activity in another jurisdiction or requires experts with certain skills or knowledge, it might make sense to establish an organization in that other jurisdiction in order to reduce the amount of travel and to ensure continuous contacts.

The legal and fiscal framework of the countries where the organizations will be established will also influence the ultimate design of the structure. In some jurisdictions, for instance, the type of activities contemplated will determine the legal forms possible. In Belgium, for example, an international association established pursuant to the Law of 25 October 1919 may only pursue one of five purposes: educational, philanthropic, cultural, religious or scientific. An organization wishing to pursue another purpose would therefore have to look at a different legal form to embody the new organization. In contrast, a foundation wishing to establish a presence in other jurisdictions, notably the Netherlands and Germany, would have a larger choice of legal forms as in these jurisdictions it is the purpose, not the legal form, that determines whether or not an organization qualifies as a nonprofit organization.

Parties interested in designing an international structure for their charitable activity should be aware that the related compliance costs are probably higher than for similar structures used by the for-profit sector. The for-profit sector has been more successful in gathering an international consensus in favour of reducing the costs of multinational and other international companies engaged in cross-border trade and investment. Reduced costs and barriers, they have argued, are necessary to increase the volume of cross-border trade and investment, which is essential for global sustainable growth.

Nonprofit organizations, and foundations in particular, are by contrast burdened by national compliance obligations imposed with the aim of keeping charitable funds and the related benefits at home. By conducting activities abroad, a foundation currently risks having its tax-privileged status reviewed or revoked.[51] Foundations engaging in

---

[51] See generally 2.3 and 2.4 above and Garcia-Andrade: Establishment, Amendment and Liquidation of Foundations; as well as Bater and Habighorst: Tax Treatment of Foundations and their Donors.

international activities must also comply with reporting requirements aimed at ensuring that the money is used abroad in furtherance of the foundation's stated purpose and is given to a qualified organization: often this organization must be equivalent to a charitable organization in the home country. Careful attention must therefore be given when designing an international structure so that the organizations involved are able to enjoy tax privileges in the jurisdictions where new entities are created, while avoiding any negative consequences arising from their increased international activity.

The nonprofit sector should moreover learn from the success of the for-profit sector's lobbying efforts and begin arguing more vociferously that reduced costs and barriers would lead to an increase in the cross-border giving essential for enhanced solidarity and regional stability.

3.2.4 *Hosting dependent foundations*

A 'dependent foundation' is a foundation or fund without legal personality that is usually administered or managed (hosted) by a qualifying foundation.[52] In this context, a qualifying foundation allows other donors to benefit from its expertise in administering and investing funds, selecting suitable grantees, and evaluating the results of the projects, while individuals or corporations provide the capital. Community foundations, given their inherent purpose of pooling funds from an indefinite number of 'smaller' donors, are particularly well suited to attracting individual and corporate donors interested in setting up a dependent foundation. Of course, however, other foundations can, and do, seek to host dependent foundations and can play a similar role.[53] By agreeing to host dependent foundations for individual or corporate donors interested in participating in cross-border activities, a foundation is thus able to carry out international activities without allocating its own resources.

Donors creating a dependent foundation benefit from the tax privileges enjoyed by the foundation. They will usually receive a tax deduction on money donated to establish or contribute to such a fund.

---

[52] In Germany, a dependent foundation may be administered or managed by any legal entity, whether or not such entity itself has charitable status, and may still qualify for tax benefits if the activities and purposes of the dependent foundation qualify for these benefits.

[53] Many foundations in Europe have expertise in hosting dependent foundations. In countries with relatively discouraging laws on foundations, such as France and Belgium, a single foundation in each of these jurisdictions virtually dominates the market for hosting dependent foundations. Faced with the restrictive legal environment for foundations, interested founders are discouraged from establishing their own foundation and thus compelled to establish a dependent foundation instead.

The same legal rules will apply to the dependent foundation as to the host foundation itself, yet a donor may define, within the confines of the law, separate conditions for the growth and distribution of the capital held in the dependent foundation. These conditions are often set out in an agreement between the donors and the host foundation.

3.3 General remarks

States have many options for improving the legal and fiscal framework applying both to charitable foundations that are active across borders and to their donors. They may begin by enacting favourable domestic laws that promote cross-border philanthropy and increase feelings of solidarity towards fellow citizens throughout Europe. They may continue by encouraging reform through bilateral and multilateral measures aimed at producing greater effect in the region. In this respect, action at EU level may prove the most logical and effective, given the continuous contacts and the solid institutional framework already in place.

Likewise, foundations and donors have several methods available to them for overcoming national barriers to cross-border activities and strengthening the links between organizations and donors in different European states. With professional advice, private initiatives may be designed to suit the parties' needs and objectives, while taking into account the legal requirements in the relevant jurisdictions.

4 Estate planning

Traditional grant-making foundations might be less tempted than associations to shop for the best forum for their activity because they are perhaps less restrained by the national barriers now in place; foundations may already invest freely in other member states, as investment is not legally tied to the home state, even though for political reasons they might feel obliged to invest in local stakeholders. Operating foundations, however, especially those relying on outside funding from donors, might find themselves in a similar position to that of associations and feel themselves hampered by the national constraints.

Individual donors motivated by the tax benefits that they will receive when creating a foundation might also be less inclined to forum shop for a favourable jurisdiction. If these donors wish to deduct the initial donation from their taxable income, they might be encouraged to establish a foundation in the jurisdiction where they are a tax-payer since a donation to a newly established foundation in a foreign jurisdiction is unlikely to give rise to an income tax deduction (see 2.4). A donor who is a tax-payer in more than one jurisdiction will be able to choose from a larger range of appropriate forums.

Individual donors, however, are not inspired soley by the tax effect of a donation in the current tax year. There are numerous other reasons why donors decide to establish a foundation, for example a personal desire to perpetuate the memory of someone, or a commitment to helping the local community or church. Both such reasons would obviously entail the selection of the home jurisdiction

Other donors, however, begin to think about creating a foundation as part of their estate planning – their planning for a future contingency (i.e. their death). In seeking advice from a professional, these donors will realize how estate planning can help them leave behind their own legacy, while perhaps also taking care of other considerations, such as reducing the tax burden on their heirs, avoiding the rules of forced heirship, or transferring the governance of a business to a separate legal entity in order to prevent the business being broken up and distributed to numerous heirs. All these considerations can be catered for by establishing a foundation, either in one's own country or abroad. These are the donors who will be particularly interested in shopping for the most favourable forum for their objectives.

Before designing a structure that fulfils a donor's estate-planning objectives, the donor must determine the laws that will apply to her or his estate upon death. The choice of law and the other main factors that a potential donor will need to consider when determining the most appropriate forum for her or his foundation are discussed below.

4.1 Choice of law

Potential donors need to be aware that their estate may be subject to the laws of several jurisdictions, depending on where their movable and immovable property is located, where their domicile (or habitual place of residence) is located, and their nationality. Each jurisdiction may apply a different rule in determining which law will govern the distribution of the property in the estate. Approximately half the jurisdictions surveyed apply the rules of a single jurisdiction to all property in the estate, be it movable or immovable property (unitarian states), while the remaining jurisdictions may apply the law of different jurisdictions to movable and to immovable property (schismatic states), the immovable property (real-estate) being governed by the law of the jurisdiction where it is located (*lex situs*).

Although it is not the objective of this section to describe all the rules applying in the various jurisdictions to the distribution of a person's estate upon death, the reader needs to be aware that a single estate may be subject to the law of more than one jurisdiction.[54] Therefore, persons with property in more than one jurisdiction, having more than one residence, having more than one nationality, or being married to someone with more than one nationality, should seek professional advice when designing an estate plan. These persons may draft and sign a testamentary will in more than one jurisdiction to cover the parts of the estate that will be governed by the laws of such jurisdictions. Since for succession purposes, it is the law of the connecting factor (whether domicile, habitual residence or nationality) at the time of death that is crucial, testators must be warned to review their estate plan again with professional assistance whenever one of these factors changes after the original estate plan is designed.

The discussion in this section is limited to the creation of a foundation, in particular a charitable foundation, as an estate-planning vehicle. To the extent that a foundation is a separate legal person,[55] it may own property in its own name. Thus, by transferring property to a foundation, a person is able to transfer property from her or his own estate to the foundation. As long as certain conditions are met, as will be described in 4.2 and 4.3 below, the property will no longer be subject to the succession laws, nor will the transfer be subject to succession taxes, thereby helping the donor to achieve her or his estate-planning objectives.

4.2 Claims in the estate: by heirs and the state

Establishing a foundation in another jurisdiction as an estate-planning vehicle may raise claims by certain heirs or the state, parties that would normally have an interest in a person's estate upon death. These parties might be concerned that the founder's primary objective for establishing a foundation abroad was to transfer property beyond their reach and hence to the detriment of their 'rights'.

---

[54] The determination of the law applicable to a person's estate may be made more simple with The Hague Convention on the Law Applicable to Succession to the Estates of Deceased Persons of 1 August 1989, which has not yet entered into force. So far, only Argentina, Luxembourg, the Netherlands and Switzerland have signed the Convention, yet only the Netherlands has ratified it.

[55] Only when a charitable trust is used does legal personality not exist. See generally 2.1 above.

A potential donor must therefore be aware of the rules applicable in the relevant jurisdictions that have been adopted to protect the interests of certain family members and the state. With careful advice and thought, however, a donor may design a structure that fulfils her or his estate-planning goals, which may include providing for a charitable legacy that continues after death, and does so in a legally scrupulous fashion, as described below.

4.2.1 Forced heirship

All member states of the EU, with the exception of England, Wales and Ireland, have 'forced heirship' rules aimed at protecting the rights of close heirs from being left too little upon the death of a family member. According to forced heirship rules, close family members are guaranteed a share of a given person's estate upon her or his death. The deceased (the 'testator' during her or his lifetime) may only dispose of a defined share of her or his property upon death (by testament) or during her or his lifetime (by an *inter vivos* transfer).

In Belgium, for example, a person with a spouse and two children must leave two-thirds (reserved share) of her or his estate to the children, to be divided equally between them, yet may leave the remaining one-third (unreserved share) to whomever she or he desires. If no testamentary provision for the unreserved share is made, it will be added to the reserved share. The spouse, however, may also have a *usufruct* (life estate) interest in some of the property in the estate. Consequently, someone wishing to leave a large part of her or his estate for charitable purposes may only bequest an amount that does not exceed the unreserved share of her or his estate to a charitable organization.

4.2.2 Calculation of rights

The forced heirship rules are compulsory and considered a matter of public policy. The state will therefore take all measures to have the forced heirship rules applied, even if the testator wishes to make other arrangements for her or his property. In fact, most jurisdictions have 'claw-back' rules allowing the heirs to recover property that the testator has given away during her or his lifetime to non-eligible persons or organizations. Of course, the heirs may only recover the property that exceeds the amount of the 'unreserved share' of the estate.

In some jurisdictions there is a time limit on how far back the heirs can travel to recover property. In other jurisdictions, such as Belgium, the claw-back period for civil law purposes is unlimited. Thus, for calculating the size of the entire estate in these jurisdictions and hence the size of the forced heirs' respective shares, the heirs can theoretically go back over the entire lifetime of the deceased.[56]

For tax purposes, however, the tax administration in Belgium uses a different time limit in determining what is considered a gift in contemplation of death, and thus subject to succession taxes.[57] The tax administration goes back three years before the person's death and includes all gifts made during this time in the calculation of succession taxes. In this respect, it should be noted that all gifts, those made to forced heirs and to others, are 'clawed back' and made subject to succession tax.

The tax authorities, for instance, would be highly motivated to enforce this three-year rule against a transfer made for charitable purposes so that the administration could collect the succession taxes due on such a transfer. In most jurisdictions, succession taxes are imposed at progressive rates calculated on the basis of the amount given and the closeness of the relationship between the deceased and the beneficiary. In Belgium, for instance, bequests to qualifying charitable foundations (*établissements d'utilité publique*) established in Belgium are taxed at only 6.6%, while bequests to strangers (someone not having a certain degree of kinship to the deceased), which include all charitable organizations established outside Belgium, are taxed at up to 80%![58] Similar rules apply in other jurisdictions, however, the tax rates of course vary from one to another.

Although the heirs may legally go back much further in time than the tax administration to 'reclaim' gifts, for reasons of evidence and legal certainty, the claw-back period is usually in practice limited to the same three years as used for tax purposes. Thus, any gift made more than three years before the death of the individual will for all practical purposes be free of claims by the forced heirs in Belgium.

---

[56] Article 922 of the Belgian Civil Code.

[57] Articles 7 and 8 of the Belgian Inheritance Tax Code. There is much debate among Belgian legal scholars on how these articles apply to the establishment of a trust or foundation in another jurisdiction. See e.g. Nudelhole, S., 'Trust et Fondation: Instruments Utiles de Planification Successorale', *Journée d'étude* , 28 January 1997.

[58] This is the rate applicable on amounts exceeding BEF7,000,000 (approximately €173,525).

4.2.3 Public policy rationale

It can be questioned whether forced heirship rules still serve a public policy today. The rationale underlying this public policy argument appears less justifiable when the forced heirship rules are used to prevent a testator from bequeathing a significant part of her or his estate to a charitable organization, established to serve a public benefit purpose. In such a case, the state should ask itself whether its policy should be to favour the transfer of property to certain family members, who may or may not have sufficient property of their own, or to favour the transfer of property for the benefit of society at large. Given that wealthy individuals are more likely to write a testamentary will than individuals with limited property to transfer upon death, the state should encourage such wealthy individuals to leave a significant amount of their property for charitable purposes rather than leaving it almost entirely to family members who would probably be able to live on a smaller portion. An exception from the forced heirship rules to allow charitable bequests upon death and during life would be a welcomed change in public policy that would surely benefit the public a great deal more.

4.2.4 Circumventing the forced heirship rules

A testator wishing to bequeath a significant share of her or his estate for a charitable purpose, perhaps to the detriment of her or his forced heirs, might still be able to do so by establishing a charitable foundation and transferring property to this foundation before death. The testator would have to take care to establish the foundation and transfer the property far enough in advance in order to avoid the claw-back provisions that could be used by the forced heirs or even the tax authorities. Where a testator establishes a charitable foundation in another jurisdiction, special attention should be paid to completing the transfer of property in sufficient time before death to avoid the prohibitive succession tax rates applied on bequests to foreign foundations.

By transferring property to a foundation established abroad, a donor can make it more difficult for the heirs and state to enforce their rights. Forced heirs wishing to recover property that they claim encroaches on their reserved share will first have to bring the claim before a court in their jurisdiction. If they succeed in proving their claim, they will obtain a favourable judgment that they must then try to enforce in the foreign jurisdiction where the foundation is located or has assets. Enforcing their judgment in non-EU jurisdictions will probably not be easy.

If the donor establishes the foundation in a jurisdiction that recognizes forced heirship rights, which includes almost all the EU member states, the forced heirs will have an easier time enforcing their judgment. Since the law of the foreign jurisdiction will also promote the same public policy aimed at protecting close family members from disinheritance, the authorities will be inclined to enforce the foreign judgment. The authorities in the enforcing jurisdiction would consequently execute whatever measures were appropriate to recover the property or its exchange value.

However if a donor establishes her or his foundation in an off-shore jurisdiction, or even a jurisdiction with an attractive banking environment, such as Liechtenstein or Switzerland, it will be more difficult for the heirs in a jurisdiction with forced-heirs rules to enforce their judgment. Many 'off-shore' jurisdictions have adopted measures that would impede any action by the forced heirs against property held by foundations or trusts[59] located there. In Liechtenstein, however, a special provision allows the forced heirs in other jurisdictions to bring an action to recover property donated to a foundation or trust established in this jurisdiction, yet allows the heirs to claw back only two years.[60] Therefore, irrespective of the claw-back period specified in the jurisdiction of origin where the judgment was obtained, the Liechtenstein authorities will only go back two years. Although under Liechtenstein law the heirs may recover property or its exchange value, their action cannot lead to the dissolution of the foundation itself.

---

[59] The discussion in this estate-planning section has focused on foundations, not trusts. As trusts do not have legal personality, the legal analysis of establishing a trust instead of an foundation as an estate-planning vehicle is different. Yet, the result is fairly close to that of foundations: the need to establish the trust in advance so that it is not the target of claims by forced heirs or the state (as a bequest) and to make sure that the delivery of property to the trust is genuine and irrevocable. The irrevocability requirement would argue against using a revocable trust, as this would cause the delivery to be deemed as being made upon death.

The reader's attention should be drawn to international efforts in recent years by the European Union and the OECD to eliminate harmful tax practices. These efforts have included measures that aim to improve cooperation with jurisdictions identified as 'tax havens' and to encourage these jurisdictions to demonstrate their commitment to increasing transparency and exchanges of information. If such 'tax havens' refuse to cooperate effectively with the international community, they will be deemed 'uncooperative' and 'defensive measures' might be taken against them to make it generally more difficult to conduct business there. The reader should be aware that these international efforts might in the near future cause such jurisdictions as Liechtenstein, Isle of Man, and Gibraltar, which are targeted by the international community, to change their laws in a way that would make them less attractive for estate-planning purposes as discussed in this chapter. Cyprus is one of a few countries that have already committed in advance to eliminating harmful tax competition by the end of 2005.

[60] Article 951 of the Liechtenstein Civil Code and Article 560(1) of the PGR.

In order for a foundation to prevent the enforcement of the forced heirs' claims, it must make sure that it does not hold assets in a country where the heirs would be able to enforce their judgment. It must therefore be careful how the funds are invested and where the property is located.

The need for a jurisdiction that does not recognize the rights of forced heirs is of significance only where there is a charitable legacy that exceeds the unreserved share of the estate. Otherwise, the heirs would have no claim against property transferred to the charitable organization. Nevertheless, a donor must still be careful about a claim by the tax authorities if the foundation is made within the time period before death that allows them to consider the transfer as being made in contemplation of death, and thus as a bequest subject to succession taxes. Time is hence the most important factor in designing and implementing a structure that fulfils all a donor's objectives for the foundation. It is essential for donors to seek estate planning advice far enough in advance.

Once the donor has a structure designed, she or he must then make sure that the initial capital is transferred in a genuine and irrevocable manner; or the donor's transfer will otherwise still be challenged.

4.3 Effective transfer of property

In order for the property to be transferred to the foundation and to be considered as leaving the individual's own estate, the transfer itself must generally be 'genuine' and 'irrevocable'. This means that the person must deliver the property to the foundation and surrender all claims of ownership over the property. It must allow the foundation to make all decisions governing the use or disposition of the property. The donor, however, may remain involved in the foundation's governance, provided that she or he does not have the right to recover the property.

On the other hand, if the person retains possession of the property, reserves the right to take back the property at any time, or fails to deliver the property to the foundation, the transfer will not be considered as made and the property will remain part of the person's estate. Since in these cases it will only be at the time of death that the transfer will become irrevocable – because the donor may no longer take back the property or otherwise exercise rights revoking the transfer – the property would then be considered as being transferred upon death instead of *inter vivos*. The transfer will hence be governed by the laws of succession, thus defeating the purpose of setting up a foundation as an estate-planning vehicle. The donor must therefore be extremely careful to transfer the property genuinely and irrevocably in advance.

In order to ensure that the donor succeeds in properly transferring the property, she or he must not retain too much discretion over the distribution of the income, especially in a way that she or he could personally benefit. Needless to say, to achieve the charitable purposes in jurisdictions using trusts,[61] instead of foundations, such as Jersey or Isle of Man, the donor is ill advised to set up a revocable trust.

In jurisdictions allowing family foundations or private foundations to be established for the purpose of paying the costs of education, health care, clothing, or support of members of one or more specified families (England and Wales,[62] Germany, Italy, Liechtenstein and Switzerland), donors might be able to establish a mixed foundation that has as its object both caring for the members of a family and providing support for a specified charitable or public benefit purpose. In Liechtenstein, for example, a mixed foundation may be set up to serve both family and public benefit purposes. Such a mixed foundation, however, will not enjoy the tax privileges available to charitable foundations. The capital and income will be subject to tax like other private benefit foundations. In Germany, a mixed foundation may use up to one-third of its income to support its donor, her or his immediate relatives, and the commemoration of the donor family without losing its charitable status.

A mixed foundation could be used as a vehicle for a donor concerned about donating too much of her or his wealth too early in life since the funds might be needed for care in later years. Well-drafted provisions in the foundation deed would allow the donor to transfer funds and property in a genuine and irrevocable manner and still be protected. As a member of the family defined as the beneficiary of such a mixed family foundation, the donor may also benefit from the foundation's provisions, as long as she or he needed financial support for health care or other specified purposes.

---

[61] See note 57 above.

[62] Family trusts are allowed under the first head of charity (the relief of poverty), for example, if a trust is established to relieve the *poor* descendants of a specified person.

4.4 Transferring the property to a foreign foundation

Since donors are not generally able to deduct a donation to a foreign charitable organization from their taxable income (see 2.4), donors interested in establishing a foundation in a foreign jurisdiction for estate-planning purposes will need to consider how to transfer their property to the foreign foundation in a tax-effective manner. Many of the ways available to individual donors wishing to donate money to a foreign charitable organization (e.g. having the property pass through a domestic qualifying organization) may also be used in this context. Once the foreign charitable foundation is established, the donor can use these mechanisms to increase the capital held by the foundation. The donor would nevertheless have to continue to give special attention to the time limits, mentioned above in 4.2, applying to claims by forced heirs and the state.

Individual donors with their own business may also create a company for their business and then transfer shares, even non-voting shares, to their foreign charitable foundation. Donors may thereby provide capital as well as income to the charitable foundation, without having to sell their business or relinquish control.

4.5 General remarks

With the help of professional advice, potential donors can design a structure that allows them to fulfil their estate-planning objectives, including providing for a charitable legacy after their death, while taking care of other considerations, such as reducing their tax burden, or the tax burden of their heirs, avoiding forced-heirship rules, and even transferring the governance of a business. On the European Continent, potential donors are well advised to begin their estate planning sufficiently early in order to avoid potential claims by the state or forced heirs. Time is of the essence to ensure that the donors' objectives are fulfilled.

5 Conclusion

At this historic milestone on the road towards the enlargement and democratisation of the EU, member states and European institutions alike would be wise to avail themselves of the considerable financial and intellectual resources of charitable foundations to ensure that these reforms are successful.

Yet, for foundations to be able to play their full role at a European level, member states, perhaps with the guidance of European institutions, should eliminate all national barriers erected against charitable foundations that are engaged in cross-border activities and their donors. Likewise, member states should promote enhanced feelings of European citizenship and solidarity by adopting a more enabling legal and fiscal framework that supports the expected role of civil society organizations in the development of an integrated Union. They can achieve this by providing for mutual recognition of similar charitable organizations and foundations established in other member states. Mutual recognition will be the key to bringing the laws of the various member states closer together on how they define public benefit organizations, and how such organizations and their donors are granted tax privileges.

Until the laws are reformed, however, foundations and donors can take their own initiatives to overcome the current barriers so that they can partake in their activities across borders. Professional advice should probably be sought in selecting the most appropriate jurisdiction and legal structure to meet their needs in light of current requirements.

By persevering in spite of the obstacles, foundations and donors can demonstrate the utility of their cross-border action and the need for reform. They can thus push the issue forward until there is the requisite political will to find a solution. Then, and only then, will foundations and other nonprofit organizations be able to fulfil their vital role by participating in the design and implementation of European policy on issues of importance to all European citizens.

Bibliography

Alfandari, E. and Nardone, A., *Associations et Fondations en Europe*, Lyon, Editions Juris Service, 1994.

Baron, E. and Delsol, X., *Les fondations reconnues d'utilité publique et d'entreprise*, Lyon, Editions Juris Service and AGEC, 1992.

Bater, P. ed., *The Tax Treatment of Cross-Border Donations*, IBFD Publications BV, Supp. 9/1997, p. 1.

Bierlaagh, H., Lyons, T. and Wheeler, J., eds, *The International Guide to the Taxation of Trusts*, Amsterdam, IBFD, 1999–2000.

Council of Europe, *The Legal Status of Non-Governmental Organisations and Their Role in a Pluralistic Democracy, Guidelines to Promote the Development and Strengthening of NGOs in Europe*, Multilateral Meeting, Strasbourg, France, 23–25 March 1998.

Council of Europe, *Seminar on the Application of the European Convention on the Recognition of the Legal Personality of International Non-Governmental Organisations* (ETS No. 124), Strasbourg, France, 9–10 February 1998.

Gallop, B., 'One Step Forward, Two Steps Back', in: *Alliance*, Vol. 3, 1.98, pp. 39–41 for a commentary.

George, C. ed., *International Charitable Giving: Laws and Taxation*, Kluwer International Law publishers.

Hondius, F., 'Das internationale rechtliche Umfeld' in: Bertelsmann Stiftung (ed.), *Handbuch Stiftungen,* Gabler Verlag, Wiesbaden, 1998, pp. 1156–76.

Nudelhole, S., 'Trust et Fondation: Instruments Utiles de Planification Successorale', in: *Journée d'étude,* 28 January 1997.

Salamon, L. M. ed., *The International Guide to Nonprofit Law*, New York etc., John Wiley & Sons, 1997.

Verbeke, L. and Gallop, B., 'Taxation, Legal and Self-Regulation Issues', in: Doyle, L. (ed.), *Funding Europe's Solidarity*, AICE publishers, 1996 pp. 1–64 *et seq.*

Zielinski, D., *Development of Civil Society for a Europe of Solidarity*, for the Council of Europe, May 1999.

Personal acknowledgments of country experts

Austria: Dr Friedrich Schwank, Lawyer, Law Offices of Dr Friedrich Schwank, Vienna, Austria.

Belgium: Nicole Van Crombrugghe, Partner, Lafili, Van Crombrugghe & Partners, Brussels, Belgium, with assistance of Bradley Gallop, Partner, BDG & Associates, Brussels, Belgium.

Bulgaria: Hristo Hristozov, Lawyer, Sofia, Bulgaria.

Cyprus: Yiannos G. Georgiades, Partner, The Law Office of Yiannos G. Georgiades & Co., Nicosia, Cyprus.

Czech Republic: Hana Marvanova, Lawyer, Prague, Czech Republic, with assistance of Bradley Gallop, Partner, BDG & Associates, Brussels, Belgium.

Denmark: Christian Harlang, Lawyer, Advokatfirma Christian Harlang, Copenhagen, Denmark.

England: Alison J. S. Paines, Partner, Withers Solicitors, London, UK.

Estonia: Daimar Liiv, Lawyer, Tallinn, Estonia.

Finland: Jouni Varpelaide, Partner, Varpelaide & Co Oy, Helsinki, Finland; Ralf Sunell, General Counsel, Finnish Cultural Foundation, Helsinki, Finland, with assistance of Bradley Gallop, Partner, BDG & Associates, Brussels, Belgium.

France: Bradley Gallop, President, The International Institute of Association and Foundation Lawyers, Inc., Brussels, Belgium.

Germany: Dr Klaus Neuhoff, Director of the Institute Foundation & Common Weal, University of Witten, Herdecke, Germany.

Greece: Helena Papaconstantinou, Lawyer, Law Offices of Papaconstantinou, Athens, Greece.

Hungary: Dr Zsolt Aradszky, Partner, Aradszky és Kepes Law Office, Legal Advisor of Non-profit Information and Training Centre (NIOK), Budapest, Hungary.

Ireland: John H. Hickson, Partner, A&L Goodbody Solicitors, Dublin, Ireland.

Italy: Claudia Cattrarin, Lawyer (Italian), Brussels, Belgium.

Liechtenstein: Dr Markus H. Wanger, Lawyer, Senior Partner of WANGER Advokaturbüro, Vaduz, Liechtenstein.

Luxembourg: Alex Schmitt, Partner, Bonn & Schmitt, Luxembourg, Luxembourg; Veronique Hoffeld, Associate, Bonn & Schmitt, Luxembourg, Luxembourg.

Netherlands: The International Institute of Association and Foundation Lawyers, Inc., with the assistance of Wino J. M. van Veen (dr. juris), Kennedy Van der Laan, Amsterdam, Netherlands.

Portugal: Domingo Marques, Partner, Escritoria de Advogados Domingo Marques, Braga, Portugal.

Scotland: Andrew M. C. Dalgleish, Partner, Brodies Solicitors, Edinburgh (Scotland), UK.

Slovenia: Dr Verica Trstenjak, State Secretary, Ministry of Science and Technology, Assistant Professor (part time) University of Mari Faculty of Law, Ljubljana, Slovenia; Vesna Petek, Accounting, Financial, and Tax Advisor, VGM Consulting, Ljubljana, Slovenia.

Spain: Mr Garcia-Andrade, Technical Director, Confederación Española de Fundaciones, Madrid, Spain.

Sweden: Helena Rempler, Lawyer, Mannheimer Swartling, Stockholm, Sweden.

Switzerland: Dr Stephan J. Schmid, Lawyer, Meroni & Schmid, Zollikon-Zurich, Switzerland.

▼　Appendices　▼

Appendix I

Comparative Survey: Legislation Governing Charitable Foundations in 24 European Jurisdictions

As described in greater detail in the Introduction to this book, a survey of the laws governing foundations in 24 European jurisdictions (all EU member states – with Scotland constituting a separate legal jurisdiction from England and Wales – Switzerland, Liechtenstein, Bulgaria, Cyprus, Czech Republic, Estonia, Hungary and Slovenia) was carried out by the International Institute of Association and Foundation Lawyers, Inc. through its members and other experts in these jurisdictions. The answers to the survey questions are summarized for easy reference on the following pages. Legal changes in Bulgaria, Germany and the UK through October 2000 have been included; the cut-off date for legal changes in the other jurisdictions was February 2000.

**Note: the materials contained in this
Appendix are © Bertelsmann
Foundation and the International
Institute of Association and Foundation
Lawyers, Inc. jointly.**

What is a foundation:
definition, purposes and legal capacity

1   Is the right of foundation guaranteed by law?

The right of foundation is guaranteed by legal provisions contained in either the Civil Code or in a specific foundation law in all jurisdictions except as follows:

Switzerland	Also implicitly guaranteed through the absence of restrictions.
Germany	The right of establishing a foundation is guaranteed through consistent case law interpreting a person's constitutional right to dispose of her or his property.
Finland Italy Portugal Slovenia	The right of foundation is guaranteed through the right of freedom of association.
England & Wales Ireland Scotland	The law does not recognize an entity specifically called a foundation but there is a statutory right to incorporate under company law. In addition, anyone may establish a charity provided it meets the necessary criteria as to its charitable purposes.

2   What is the basic definition of a foundation?

Austria	A legal person established upon an irrevocable transfer of assets, income from which to be applied for charitable or beneficial purposes.
Belgium	Law does not recognize foundations per se but *établissements d'utilité publique*, by which capital is dedicated by founders to a well-determined nonprofit project or goal.
Bulgaria	A legal person established *inter vivos* or upon death by unilateral articles of incorporation (i.e. deed) by which property is transferred gratuitously for the achievement of a nonprofit purpose.
Cyprus	Foundations can fall under the law of associations and institutes, or alternatively under the law of charities, and are defined as 'a whole property designed to serve a specific purpose'. It is not necessarily independent of government, as the government can participate in fundraising and administration, at the request of the founder.
Czech Republic	According to the Foundations and Endowment Trusts Act 'Foundations and endowment trusts are special property associations

	established pursuant to the law to accomplish generally beneficial objectives'.
Denmark	Criteria for foundations have been developed by administrative practice and precedent. It is not in an Act.
England & Wales	It is possible to establish an entity having the characteristics of a 'foundation', yet foundations as separate entities are not recognized and have no specific fiscal regimes. Whether an entity (being a trust or company limited by guarantee or having some legal basis, e.g. unincorporated association) qualifies as a charity will depend on its purposes and not its legal form.
Estonia	A foundation is a 'legal person in private law, which has no members, and which is established to administer and use its assets for objects mentioned in the articles of association'.
Finland	No statutory definition, but its commonly used definition is 'an amount of property functioning as an independent legal person and used for a specific purpose defined by the founder'.
France	Irrevocable dedication, by one or more individuals or legal entities, of property towards achievement of a public interest goal, memorialized in a private deed.
Germany	Foundation has no statutory definition, but its definition derives from history and court cases, and contains a number of criteria.
Greece	A foundation is 'an institution created by disposition of assets under a deed of establishment made either *inter vivos* or under testament, for the pursuit of a particular durable purpose'. A charitable foundation is a 'disposition of assets, made *inter vivos* or under testament, for the pursuit of a charitable purpose over a definite or indefinite period, fulfilment of which is entrusted by deed of establishment to natural persons or legal entities'.
Hungary	No legal definition as such, but the academic definition is 'an organization with legal personality in which assets are allocated for a well-defined purpose'.
Ireland	Law does not contain the concept of a foundation; a charitable company is the nearest thing to a foundation.
Italy	A foundation is a legal person, whose principal distinguishing characteristic is that its property is gathered to constitute an endowment, and which is dedicated for a specific public purpose.
Liechtenstein	Self-governing legal persons, established by a natural or legal (private, public or ecclesiastical) person with a permanent

	endowment for a specific purpose, in a deed, filed with the Public Registry.
Luxembourg	Establishments that pursue work, which may be philanthropic, social, religious, scientific, artistic, pedagogic, sportive or tourist, to the exclusion of any pursuit of material gain. This work shall be pursued using the funds dedicated to the foundation at its creation or during its life.
Netherlands	'A foundation is a legal person created by a legal act which has no members and whose purpose is to realize an object stated in its articles using property allocated to such purpose.'
Portugal	A legal person characterized by having assets dedicated to it permanently for the pursuit of a specified purpose of an altruistic nature.
Scotland	No foundations under Scottish law, but the definition of a foundation describes the concept of a body which can be created under the law, but which has no separate identity as a foundation. Such a body would be constituted as a trust or a company.
Slovenia	'Legal person formed to represent property tied to a specific beneficial and charitable purpose.'
Spain	Common definition is 'assets serving a general interest purpose'; the legal definition is 'non-profit organizations that under the will of the creators use permanently transferred assets for the fulfilment of general interest purposes'.
Sweden	A foundation is founded when money or property is separated to be administered by someone to permanently pursue a certain purpose (i.e. must have capital separated for a distinct purpose).
Switzerland	A 'corporate body, created by the dedication of assets for a specific purpose of a public, private or charitable character'. (NB not necessarily nonprofit.)

3 Qualifying purposes: how is public benefit defined?

Open definitions

Austria	'Advance the community at large.'
Cyprus	Activities must not pose a threat to the security of the country, public order, public health, public morals or the basic rights of individuals.
Czech Republic	All foundations must pursue generally beneficial purposes.

Denmark	If the purpose can be described as useful according to prevailing opinion in society, and is beneficial to a wide category of people in debt or difficult economic conditions, it has public benefit.
England & Wales	Advancement of religion, education, relief of poverty, and other purposes beneficial to the community.
Finland	Useful purpose; if 'solely and directly for public benefit or general good in a material, mental, intellectual, ethical or social sense'.
Germany	Not defined, but would have to have a charitable or nonprofit purpose, providing benefit to the public at large.
Greece	Any public, religious, or philanthropic purpose; any purpose beneficial to the public, either partially or fully.
Hungary	Involved in carrying out public benefit activities, broad categories of which are listed in Article 26/c of the Law 156 of 1997 on public benefit organizations.
Ireland	If a foundation wishes to attain the tax benefits for which charitable foundations are eligible, it must satisfy the definition of public benefit, by being for the relief of poverty, the advancement of religion, or education, or for other purposes beneficial to the community.
Italy	A socially useful activity.
Liechtenstein	A foundation's purpose must only qualify as 'charitable' in order for it to be eligible for tax privileges, but not to be able to register as a foundation. Charitable purposes, as broadly interpreted by the tax authorities, include social activities, religious activities and educational or academic activities.
Luxembourg	A public benefit serves a public interest.
Netherlands	Religious, life/contemplative (ideological), charitable, cultural, scientific, educational, or public utility (general interest; serving the well-being of the people within the relevant country).
Portugal	Must satisfy the requirement of social solidarity, by serving the public in some way (e.g. health; support of children, youth, families, social and community integration; resolution of the public housing problem; formation of educational and professional groups for citizens).
Scotland	Relief of poverty, advancement of education or religion, or other purposes beneficial to the community.

Slovenia	Generally useful or charitable aims (e.g. science, culture, sport, education, environmental protection, protection of natural features and cultural heritage, and religious aims).
Spain	General interest.
Switzerland	Must be set up for the benefit of an indefinite class of individuals, not specific persons.

Closed definitions

Belgium	Pursues a philanthropic, religious, scientific, artistic or pedagogical purpose, and is nonprofit.
Bulgaria	Development and affirmation of spiritual values, civil society, health protection, education, science, culture, engineering, technology or physical culture, support of the socially vulnerable, handicapped, support of social integration and personal advancement, protection of human rights and the natural environment, and other purposes determined by law.
Estonia	Objectives and activities that support science, culture, the cultural autonomy of minorities, education, sport, healthcare, social care, environmental protection, churches and confessions in the public interest.
France	Philanthropic; humanitarian; family-related; educational; scientific; social assistance; sports or cultural activities; purposes that contribute to the defence of the natural environment, enhance, promote and protect the national cultural heritage, or advance the French language and scientific knowledge.
Sweden	There is no general definition of public benefit. Under the National Income Tax Act, foundations that pursue the qualified purposes defined in the Act are exempt from income tax. Also, under the Inheritance and Gift Tax Act, foundations that pursue the qualified purposes as defined are exempt.

4   Permissible and prohibited/regulated activities

Commercial activities

Austria Cyprus Denmark Greece Italy Liechtenstein	Permitted provided they are charitable and within the objects of the foundation.

Portugal Slovenia Sweden	Permitted provided they are charitable and within the objects of the foundation.
Finland France Hungary Scotland Spain Switzerland	Permitted if not the main purpose.
Belgium Germany	Undertaking commercial activities risks loss of tax privileges.
Bulgaria	Permitted if they are not the main purpose (they should be 'additional'), they are related to their main activity, and the revenue generated is used for achieving the statutory purposes. Profits derived from commercial activities will be subject to tax.
Czech Republic	Permitted, provided that the activity does not occur on a regular basis, is only pursued as complementary to the principal activities described in the organization's governing documents and provides for a more effective use of property without jeopardizing the organization's public benefit services in any way.
England & Wales	Permitted if they are directly in pursuance of the charity's objects ('primary purpose trading'). Other commercial activities may not be undertaken directly.
Estonia	Permitted if not the main purpose, but there are restrictions in that a foundation shall not be a partner of a general or limited partnership, or manage a general or limited partnership.
Ireland	Permitted, provided that trade is conducted in pursuance of the charity's objects, or that trade is conducted by people who are the intended beneficiaries of the foundation.
Luxembourg	Permitted but taxed unless the activity achieves foundation's aims.
Netherlands	Permitted as above but taxed if the foundation is considered to be 'running an enterprise' (generally engaging in an economic activity in a durable manner).

Political and lobby activities

Austria Bulgaria Cyprus Estonia	Permitted, provided they are charitable and within the objects of the foundation.

Finland Greece Italy Netherlands Portugal Slovenia Spain Sweden Switzerland	Permitted, provided they are charitable and within the objects of the foundation.
Czech Republic Denmark France Germany Ireland Liechtenstein Luxembourg Scotland	Do not qualify as charitable.
Belgium	Not expressly prohibited, yet may prevent a foundation from being recognized as an organization entitled to receive tax-deductible donations.
England & Wales	Limited political and lobbying activities are permitted (see Charity Commission guidelines).
Hungary	Public benefit foundations may not engage in direct political activities (i.e. activities related to a political party or nominating a candidate in parliamentary or local elections at the county level or in the capital), must remain independent of political parties, and may not support (financially or in kind) political parties. Other foundations not having the special tax privileges attaching to public benefit organizations may engage in such activities. All foundations may engage in other political and lobbying activities.

Geographic restrictions

There are no geographic restrictions in any jurisdiction, except as follows:

Austria	A charitable foundation's activities must be carried out in Austria, unless the foundation is a development foundation transferring funds to Third World countries or the foundation has obtained a specific tax ruling on the basis of reciprocity in order to qualify for tax-exemption.
Belgium France	A foundation's activities must be carried out to a certain extent within national borders for the foundation to be eligible to receive tax-deductible donations.

806

Netherlands	None, as long as the foundation does not support or promote violent activities abroad.
Sweden	Activities must be partly in Sweden.

5 Does your jurisdiction have different legal types of foundation?

Yes, there are differences in:

Austria	Benevolent, charitable, ecclesiastical or religious, public benefit, public and private.
Bulgaria	Religious and non-religious, public and private, nonprofit with mutual benefit activities and nonprofit with public benefit activities.
Denmark	Any, as long as objects are constitutional, for example, religious, political, community, corporate, trusts, private and public.
England & Wales	Trusts, Companies limited by guarantee, Royal Charter bodies or those created by an Act of Parliament, Unincorporated Associations, Friendly Societies, Industrial and Provident Societies.
Estonia	Private.
Finland	Private, independent, pension, public, dependent.
France	Foundations and corporate foundations.
Germany	Foundations and trusts established under civil law, public law, and church law; and local, church, private and family foundations according to civil law.
Hungary	Private/public, special/public benefit.
Ireland	Companies, unincorporated associations, trusts.
Italy	Family, educational, religious, bank, military, cultural, development.
Liechtenstein	Private (charitable, ecclesiastical, family, enterprise and mixed purpose), employee benefits and public law foundations.
Portugal	Public utility, administrative public utility or private foundations.
Scotland	Trusts, companies.
Spain	National, regional, religious, labour, national inheritance, public.
Sweden	General, collections, collective agreements, profit-sharing.
Switzerland	Family, religious, employee's pension, for-profit, and charitable.

No, no differences in:

Belgium Cyprus Czech Republic Greece Luxembourg Slovenia	One legal type (for nonprofit or charitable purposes).
Netherlands	One legal type (can be for nonprofit or for-profit purposes).

Establishment, amendment and liquidation

6 Legal capacity

Foundations are recognized as legal persons in all jurisdictions except as follows:

England & Wales Ireland Scotland	In these countries a company limited by guarantee, which does have legal personality, can hold property, and a trust, which does not have legal personality, can hold property through its trustees.
Slovenia	Although there is no Civil Code to contain provisions on legal persons, a foundation is considered as having the status of a legal person because it holds property.

7 Is there a procedure for the acquisition of legal personality? If so, what?

Austria	The charter of a private law foundation must be approved by the appropriate authority. Legal personality is acquired upon such approval.
Belgium	A foundation acquires legal personality when its statutes are approved by the government in the form of a royal decree.
Bulgaria	A foundation must file with the Registry for legal persons with nonprofit purposes in the District Court where the foundation's seat is located. Religious foundations must have the approval of the Council of Ministers before applying for registration at the court. All foundations acquire legal personality upon filing with the Court Registry of the District.
Cyprus	A foundation must submit an application and the founding act to Registrar of Associations and Institutions at the Ministry of the Interior. The Registrar will accept to register a foundation by issuing a certificate. The foundation acquires legal personality upon issuance of this certificate.

Czech Republic	Legal personality is acquired upon registration at the Courts of Commerce.
Denmark	A foundation acquires legal personality upon the signature of a complying deed. The deed must also be sent to the local tax authorities. If the foundation, however, has commercial interests, it will only acquire legal personality upon registering the deed in the Danish Commerce and Companies Agency (*Erhvervs-og Selskabsstyrelsen*), a department of the Ministry of Industry. No government approval is required.
England & Wales	A charitable trust is validly constituted once the trust deed has been executed by the trustees although the trust itself does not acquire legal personality; it may act through its trustees who may acquire legal personality. A company limited by guarantee acquires legal personality when registered at Companies House.
Estonia	A foundation acquires legal personality upon registering the founding resolution and other pertinent information in the appropriate court.
Finland	Need approval of National Board of Patents and Registration to establish a foundation, then register within six months or permission expires.
France	Approval of application to Ministry of Interior for public interest status bestows legal personality.
Germany	A foundation's deed and statutes, delivered to Land authority. Legal personality is acquired upon approval by the appropriate Land authority.
Greece	A foundation may be created by notarial deed (*inter vivos*), by will or by bequest. In all cases, it must be approved by the Ministry overseeing the foundation's area of concern who recommends establishment by Presidential Decree. Legal personality is acquired when the Presidential Decree is published in the Official Gazette.
Hungary	A foundation acquires legal personality upon registration with the court.
Ireland	A charitable trust does not acquire legal personality. A company acquires legal personality under Irish Company legislation, which requires the filing of constituting documentation and an application for incorporation. The company comes into existence and therefore becomes a separate legal entity upon the issuance of a Certificate of Incorporation by the Registrar of companies.

Italy	Administrative act of recognition by state authority, done on a case by case basis.
Liechtenstein	A foundation must be inscribed in public register and must file the governing document.
Luxembourg	Deed must be sent to Ministry of Justice to get approval by grand-ducal decree. Legal personality is acquired upon promulgation of the grand-ducal decree.
Netherlands	Legal personality is acquired when established by formal notarial deed. No government approval is required.
Portugal	The foundation deed and statutes are embodied in a public deed, given to the administrative authority and the Department of Justice with a request for recognition. The recognition is then published in the Official Gazette. Legal personality is acquired upon recognition.
Scotland	A trust does not acquire legal personality. For a company, the memorandum of association and the articles of association must be registered at Companies House, for one to get a Certificate of Incorporation from the Registrar. Then, approval from the Financial Intermediaries and Claims Office (FICO) of the Inland Revenue is required, which will result in the charity being given a charity number.
Slovenia	Need state permission and property to establish foundation.
Spain	A notary must certify in a public document that the foundation has been created in accordance with the founder's will. Then, after certain formalities are fulfilled, the notary's document is filed at the registry of foundations. The registration authorities decide whether to approve the governing documents, while the supervisory authorities decide whether to approve the amount of the endowment and whether the foundation's purpose qualifies as serving a general interest. The foundation acquires legal personality after obtaining the approval of the registration and the supervisory authorities.
Sweden	Government approval is not required. Legal personality is acquired as soon as a foundation is established, i.e. the foundation's charter is executed and the money or property has been 'separated' for a specific purpose stated in the charter.
Switzerland	Must register at the Registry of Commerce (although family and religious foundations do not need to register), upon which legal personality is acquired.

8   Registration requirements

Austria Bulgaria Cyprus Czech Republic Denmark England Estonia Finland France Hungary Italy Liechtenstein Luxembourg Netherlands Scotland Slovenia Spain Sweden Switzerland	In all these countries, foundations must register with one or more public authorities.
Belgium	Does not require registration.
England & Wales	Most charities must register with a public authority, e.g. the Charity Commission, the Friendly Societies Commission, but some are exempt from such registration. In practice, all approach the Inland Revenue to obtain relief.
Germany	Some states do register foundations, but this is of no legal consequence with regard to a foundation's legal capacity or the accuracy of the contents of the entry.
Greece	None, but the Ministry of Finance keeps an unofficial list.
Ireland	There is no compulsory requirement for a company to register as charitable. A company will make a private application to the Revenue Commissioners for tax-privileged status.
Portugal	The deed must be notarized and transmitted to the Governo Civil and the Department of the Public Prosecutor, and is published in the Official Journal.

9 Nationality requirements

Austria Belgium Bulgaria Cyprus Czech Republic France Germany Greece Hungary Luxembourg Netherlands Portugal Slovenia Spain Sweden Switzerland	These countries have no nationality requirements with regard to members of a foundation's governing body.
Denmark	Requires that the managing director and at least half of the board members must live in Denmark; however foundation authorities can grant exemptions.
England & Wales	Have no nationality requirements with regard to members of a foundation's governing body although the residence of those members may be relevant for tax and other purposes where the entity is a trust.
Estonia	Requires that at least half of the members of the management board must reside in Estonia.
Finland	Requires that the members of the board of trustees and persons authorized to sign in the name of a foundation must reside in the European Economic Area (unless the Ministry of Trade and Industry grants an exception). The chairman of the board of trustees and at least one of the persons who, either alone or in conjunction with another person, has the right to sign in the name of the foundation must reside in Finland.
Ireland	In Ireland, as a condition for the grant of charitable tax-exemption, the Revenue Commissioners will require that a majority of the directors of a charitable company must be residents in Ireland for tax purposes. This is a private issue between the charitable body and the Revenue Commissioners in respect of the granting of tax-exemption. Under the Companies Act 1999, every Irish company must have one director who is resident in Ireland, or alternatively must put up a £20,000 bond against its tax and company law obligations.

Italy	Requires the director and members of the board to be residents in Italy, but not necessarily Italian citizens.
Liechtenstein	Requires one member of the foundation council to be a resident in Liechtenstein qualified as an advocate, professional trustee or accountant, or they must have corresponding qualifications and be serving as a foundation council member as an employee in a law, professional trustee or accountants firm or a bank. This requirement ceases if at least one member of the foundation council is a legal person that neither pursues commercial purposes nor has a managing director with a permit to run commercial enterprises.
Scotland	Requires a majority of the members of the governing body to reside in the country.

10 What are the legal and procedural requirements for amending the foundation's articles of incorporation (e.g. special quorum, special majority voting, governmental approval)?

Czech Republic France Ireland Portugal Scotland Spain	The articles of incorporation may be amended as provided in such articles or by-laws and must be amended if the purpose for which the foundation was created has been fulfilled, its assets have become insufficient for carrying out its stated purpose, or the goals of the foundation are deemed impossible to achieve and the articles explicitly permit amendments to be made.
Austria Belgium Denmark Finland Germany Greece Hungary Italy	Government approval is needed for any amendment.
Bulgaria	The articles of incorporation may be amended by the founder or according to a procedure established by the founder or by law. If the articles of incorporation may not be amended in one of these ways and need to be amended, the District Court at the seat of the foundation shall make the amendment, upon the request of an interested party, and shall do so in accordance with the intent of the articles of incorporation.
England & Wales	Foundations can amend their governing instrument if it permits such amendments, or by court approval (in certain circumstances) or with the approval of the Charity Commission (if a registered charity).

	Special majority voting requirements apply to certain changes if a company.
Estonia	The articles of incorporation may be amended by the members of the Supervisory Board when all the founders are no longer active in the foundation's management, the founders fail to agree on amendment, or this right is granted to the supervisory board by the articles of incorporation. The court's permission is required only when the amendment concerns the purpose of the foundation.
Liechtenstein	Government approval needed except where the articles of incorporation explicitly permit amendments to be made, whereupon no government approval is needed.
Luxembourg	If the founder has not determined the conditions of amendment of the articles of incorporation they may only be amended with the approval of the Minister of Justice and the majority of the acting members of the Board of Directors (*administrateurs*).
Slovenia	Prohibits any amendments to the articles of a foundation.
Sweden	If the articles do not permit amendments, a foundation may apply to the Judicial Board for Public Lands and Funds (*Kammarkillegiet*) for approval to amend its articles. Amendments concerning the purpose of the foundation always require the approval of the Judicial Board for Public Lands and Funds.
Switzerland	Articles generally cannot be altered as the above possibilities are rare.
Cyprus Netherlands	As above for Sweden, a foundation whose articles do not explicitly permit amendments of its articles may seek a court order authorizing such amendments.

11 Disposal of assets on liquidation

Austria Bulgaria Czech Republic Denmark England & Wales France Germany Italy Liechtenstein Luxembourg Portugal	Require that liquidated assets be spent in furtherance of the goals of the liquidated foundation, transferred to a similarly oriented foundation or for general charitable purposes in compliance with the will of the founder.

Scotland Spain Sweden	Require that liquidated assets be spent in furtherance of the goals of the liquidated foundation, transferred to a similarly oriented foundation or for general charitable purposes in compliance with the will of the founder.
Belgium Cyprus Finland Slovenia	As above, but the government serves as the intermediary between the liquidated foundation and any beneficiaries.
Estonia	Liquidated assets must be distributed among those entitled by the articles of association. If dissolved by founder's resolution, the assets are transferred to the founders unless the articles prescribe otherwise. If the articles of association do not prescribe this, then the assets go to the state, which shall use the assets in accordance with the foundation's objectives. If the foundation's objectives or activities are contrary to the constitutional order, criminal law or good morals, there is compulsory dissolution of the foundation, and the assets go to the state.
Greece	Assets of foundations dissolved under Presidential Decree are transferred to the state, provided law, deed of establishment or its articles of incorporation do not state otherwise.
Hungary	A foundation cannot be liquidated. A court can terminate the foundation and allocate its assets to another foundation with a similar purpose. Since the law on liquidation proceedings does not extend to foundations, the legal right of creditors remains unresolved under Hungarian law.
Ireland	A standard clause in the memorandum must state that the assets go to another charitable body, so that the money stays in the charitable domain. They cannot go back into private ownership.
Netherlands	Requires every foundation to include in its statutes a destination for assets or provide for procedures to determine a destination.
Switzerland	If provisions are not contained in the foundation's statutes, assets pass directly to the Federation, Canton or Community with which the foundation's aim was connected.

Tax treatment

12 What is the tax treatment in your jurisdiction of initial donations to a charitable foundation-in-formation for the constitution of its endowment?

Bulgaria Czech Republic Denmark England & Wales Finland France Germany Greece Hungary Portugal Scotland Spain Switzerland	Endowments are treated like donations.
Austria Belgium Luxembourg Netherlands	Charge flat tax rates of 2.5%, 6.6%, 6% and 11% respectively. Austria, Belgium and Luxembourg do not charge tax on donations of cash or other moveable property that can be transferred 'hand to hand' (*dons manuels*).
Cyprus	No specific provision exists in the income tax laws regarding initial donations. The matter has not yet been raised or examined.
Estonia	Initial donations are tax-exempt, under the new Income Tax Act, January 2000.
Ireland	Also treats endowments like donations; however a company limited by guarantee is subject to capital duty charged at 1% on amounts contributed to the company in exchange for membership rights. It is important therefore to ensure that any endowment is not made by reference to the acquisition of membership rights, but should be a gratuitous gift of funds to the company.
Italy	Although the law does not expressly address the tax treatment of initial donations, in practice they are treated like donations.
Liechtenstein	Imposes a gift tax on initial donations at a rate between 0.5% and 18%, depending on how close the relationship is between the least near beneficiary and the founder. The gift tax applies only to donations from Liechtenstein taxpayers. The donor and the foundation are jointly liable for the tax. If the foundation is deemed charitable, the foundation will nevertheless be exempt from paying this tax and the donor will also benefit from this exemption.

Slovenia	Such donations are tax deductible only after a foundation is created, constituted as a legal entity and governed by civil law.
Sweden	Only businesses benefiting from a donation (i.e. such as those given for scientific research) can deduct it from their taxable assets as a business expenditure. Employers can also deduct donations to Pension Foundations or Employee Foundations and, under certain conditions, contributions to profit-sharing foundations.

13 Who claims the tax relief deriving from donations?

Austria	
Belgium	
Bulgaria	
Cyprus	
Czech Republic	
Denmark	
Estonia	
Finland	
France	
Germany	The donor claims the tax relief.
Greece	
Hungary	
Italy	
Liechtenstein	
Luxembourg	
Netherlands	
Portugal	
Slovenia	
Spain	
Sweden	
Switzerland	

Bulgaria	
England & Wales	
Ireland	Both donor and donee claim the tax relief.
Scotland	

The mechanics of claiming tax relief

Austria	Only very limited tax benefits are available to donors making gifts to charitable foundations. Individual donors may only deduct from their taxes membership dues to churches or donations made to special institutions accredited by the relevant state revenue directorate. Donors claim the tax relief on their annual tax declaration.

Belgium	Charitable foundations that are entitled to receive tax-deductible gifts must give an 'acknowledgement of receipt' to all donors making a gift of BEF1000 (€24.79) or more in the same calendar year. Donors will then use this acknowledgement of receipt as justification for a deduction in the same amount from their taxable income, e.g. by attaching it to their tax declaration. Charitable foundations provide a copy of all acknowledgements of receipt to the Ministry of Finance.
Bulgaria	Donors may deduct the amount of their donations to a foundation engaging in charitable activities from their taxable income.
Cyprus	Donors must claim relief for donations made to approved charitable institutions by stating the sums given and names of the recipient institutions on their annual declaration form submitted to the Inland Revenue.
Czech Republic	Tax relief is claimed by the donor (tax-payer), who must submit a declaration of income shortly before the end of the half-calendar year.
Denmark	Donor must claim relief, not recipient (who pays no tax, unless supports family members, then must pay 20% tax).
England & Wales	In the case of income tax, this relief can be through Gift Aid or Payroll Deduction.
Estonia	Donors must report the amount of the deduction in their annual income declaration under the new Income Tax Act.
Finland	Donations are tax deductible, as long as the donee is named by the National Board of Taxation as a beneficiary of tax-deductible donations, a status received after being in existence as a nonprofit organization for at least one year. Initial donations are not tax deductible.
France	Foundations must give a 'contribution receipt' to all donors. Donors will then use this contribution receipt as justification for a deduction in the same amount from their taxable income, e.g. by attaching it to their tax declaration.
Germany	The foundation must give a certificate of deductibility which the donor gives to the fiscal authority.
Greece	Donors may only deduct contributions made in cash provided they do not exceed a certain percentage of their gross income. For gifts under GRD80,000, receipts are issued by the charity; gifts over GRD80,000 are annually deductible from income tax only if deposited directly into a special bank account of the donee institution.

Hungary	Foundations must issue a certificate of receipt of donation to donor, and keep their own copy. Donor attaches this certificate to tax form.
Ireland	The charitable body claims relief from taxation on its income and gains, and on the receipt of gifts and inheritances. The donor does not automatically get tax relief on donations. The donor will get a tax deduction only for certain contributions to certain charities, most notably corporate donations to designated charitable bodies which have enjoyed charitable tax-exemptions for at least three years.
Italy	Donors must give notice of gift to the Ministry of Finance and claim tax relief.
Liechtenstein	Tax deductions only for gifts of a minimum CHF100 per annum made to charities on the official list.
Luxembourg	Charitable foundations are exempt from paying gift tax. The donor can claim tax relief on annual income tax return for the donation to a foundation declared to be of public interest.
Netherlands	Foundations must give a receipt to all donors. Donors will then use this contribution receipt as justification for a deduction in the same amount from their taxable income, e.g. by attaching it to their tax declaration.
Portugal	One must claim tax relief at the local Finance Office of the city council within 30 days if one resides within the jurisdiction of that council, within 60 days if one resides outside the boundaries of that council, within 90 days if one resides in the islands, and within 180 days for residents abroad.
Scotland	Income tax may be recovered at the UK basic rate (not at the Scottish Variable Rate – SVR).
Slovenia	For claiming tax relief, a foundation must be constituted. The donor (individual or legal entity) claims the tax relief in its yearly tax declaration.
Spain	Tax relief recognized automatically, but more favourable tax treatment if certain criteria met. The beneficiary must then claim the relief.
Sweden	Donor must claim deduction on the annual tax return. Recipient of gift is subject to gift tax.
Switzerland	Donor can deduct the donation from taxable income if the foundation obtained exemption. The donor must claim the tax relief.

14 Must the foundation, once created, seek official exemption from taxation?

Austria Bulgaria Czech Republic England & Wales Finland France Germany Netherlands Scotland Slovenia Sweden	No
Belgium Cyprus Estonia Italy Liechtenstein Luxembourg Portugal Spain Switzerland	Yes
Denmark	Foundation does not pay tax, unless it is reluctant to use its revenue.
Greece	No, but there is a special procedure for exemption from VAT.
Hungary	Must apply for exemption from corporate tax of over 10% of its total income; the first 10% is exempt. Also exempt from local tax if activities below tax minimum in the last year (i.e. if did not pay corporate tax in the previous year).
Ireland	A charitable company obtains its charity number from the Revenue Commissioners, which results in exemption from most forms of taxation.

15 Is periodical renewal of exempt status required? If so, how often?

Austria Belgium Bulgaria Cyprus Czech Republic Denmark	Foundations in these countries do not have to renew their exempt status.

France Greece Hungary Italy Liechtenstein Luxembourg Netherlands Portugal Scotland Spain Switzerland	Foundations in these countries do not have to renew their exempt status.
England & Wales	There is no formal renewal procedure. Whether an organization can claim tax-exemptions will depend on its circumstances at the time. The Inland Revenue may challenge or restrict a charity's claims for tax-exemptions if the charity's activities do not comply with the exemption requirements (for instance, the application of property for charitable purposes).
Estonia	Annual renewal required, but imminent new government regulations may change this.
Finland	Ongoing.
Germany	Every three years.
Ireland	Ongoing.
Slovenia	Once a year, reviewed when annual report submitted to tax authorities.
Sweden	A foundation cannot seek official exemption from taxation. An advance ruling regarding income tax is only valid for a given time, but may be renewed.

16 How are foundations treated for tax purposes? (Specific exemptions or annual rates?)

Country	Exemptions	Special rates
EU Member States (current and future), Liechtenstein, Switzerland	**Customs**: The EU applies a single rate of customs tax to all imports of goods entering the EU from a non-EU country. EC Council Regulation No. 918/83 (O.J. L 105/1 of 23 April 1983), as amended, provides a series of exemptions for certain products being imported that might	

be of interest to foundations and other nonprofit organizations receiving these goods from outside the EU.

VAT: While different tax rates apply in different states, the tax base has been substantially harmonized by the EC 6th VAT Directive (O.J. No. L 145 of 13 June 1977), as amended, which provides for several bases for exemption that might be relevent to foundations and other nonprofit organizations receiving or supplying cerrtain goods or services.

Austria	corporate tax; income tax (except if from commercial activities); gift tax (on money or moveable assets)	donations of money and other personal property that can be transferred 'hand to hand' are exempt from registration tax, while gifts and inheritances consisting of property requiring a deed for delivery are subject to a registration tax at a reduced rate of 2.5% (6.5% where real property is involved) if made to a qualifying Austrian foundation
Belgium	corporate income tax; capital gains tax; real-estate and municipal tax generally exempt for property used for religion, teaching, medical care, holidays for the young and old, and associated activities	gifts and inheritances made to qualifying Belgian foundations are subject to a registration duty at the reduced rate of 6.6%. 'Hand-to-hand donations' (*dons manuels*) are not subject to tax as there is no need for an authentic deed for their delivery; income on non-charitable activities taxed at lower rate (28–41%)
Bulgaria	gift tax; inheritance tax; customs duties	
Cyprus	income tax; donors are exempt from capital gains tax, but charitable entities are not;	

	immovable property tax; import duties; municipal duties	
Czech Republic	gift tax; income tax; succession tax; real-estate tax	
Denmark	inheritance tax; generally not liable to tax on income, real property, or personal property	
England & Wales	income tax; capital gains tax; inheritance tax; stamp duty; VAT zero rates available for supplies of certain goods and services	charities are entitled to 80% relief from local rates with the remaining 20% being at the discretion of the local authority
Estonia	for listed foundations: income tax; VAT on goods imported as irrecoverable foreign aid	
Finland	income tax; inheritance tax; gift tax; national property tax (except municipal real-estate tax at the rate of 11.76%)	
France	income tax; gift and inheritance tax if made hand to hand (*dons manuels*) or in accordance with specific exemptions for certain types of beneficiaries or gifts; domestic dividend income; building and land tax for certain foundations	rents and farming income taxed at 24%; corporate income tax; income from interest on certain types of government bonds, certificates of deposit, treasury bills and certain dividends; income from dividends on certain real-estate companies taxed at 10%. Profit-related activities related to exempt purpose taxed at reduced rate; real estate transfer duties; certain transactions exempt from VAT
Germany	income tax; gift and inheritance tax; trade tax	sometimes VAT on related business income charged at 7% (though is usually not taxed at all); VAT on unrelated business income at 16% (or 7% for smaller charities or foundations, with turnovers below DEM60,000 or €30,612)

Greece	income tax; gift and inheritance tax; VAT; capital gains tax	
Hungary	income tax; local taxes (if income from activities stayed below the tax minimum); customs duties; duties on the acquisition of assets, and court and administrative procedures (if did not pay corporate tax in the preceding year)	
Ireland	income tax; capital gains; stamp duty on leases and transfers of land; gift and inheritance tax	
Italy	income tax (also on related commercial activities); tax on personal property; tax on real property; gift tax; inheritance tax	
Liechtenstein	profit taxes; gift and inheritance taxes if foundation qualifies as tax-exempt	capital tax of 1% of total assets
Luxembourg	income tax (except if from commercial activities); tax on real property for charitable foundations; tax on personal property for foundations whose purpose is religion, charity or public interest, except if they have an economic activity which is not only for the administration of the foundation's assets	gifts and inheritances made to qualifying Luxembourg foundations are subject to a registration duty at the reduced rate of 6%. 'Hand-to-hand donations' (dons manuels) are not subject to tax as there is no need for an authentic deed for their delivery
Netherlands	corporate income tax; private income tax; wealth tax; local property tax; inheritance tax (if gift does not exceed NLG16,167 or €7336)	gift and inheritance taxes reduced to 11% (from 41% to 68%) if the recipient foundation is mentioned on the list of charitable institutions; the donee must pay this tax
Portugal	corporate income tax; municipal tax; gift and inheritance tax; stamp duty	
Scotland	see England & Wales, above	

Slovenia	income tax; donations made to foundations are not subject to gift and inheritance taxes because legal entities that receive gifts are not subject to these taxes	25% tax on surplus profits on for-profit activities
Spain	income tax; tax on personal property; tax on economic activity, contracts and public documents (if obtained exemption); gift and inheritance taxes	
Sweden	income tax and gift inheritance tax for foundations with qualifying purposes.	
Switzerland	income tax; tax on personal property; cantonal gift and inheritance taxes; church taxes	

17 Can tax-exempt foundations automatically receive tax-privileged gifts?

Bulgaria Cyprus Czech Republic Denmark England & Wales Estonia France Germany Greece Hungary Ireland Netherlands Scotland Slovenia Spain	Tax-privileged gifts can be received automatically in these countries. The procedure is the same as that for tax-exemption.
Switzerland	As above with the exception of purely religious foundations.
Austria Belgium Finland Liechtenstein Luxembourg	Only limited categories of qualifying foundations can receive tax-privileged gifts.

Italy	Yes, provided they are recognized as ONLUS.
Portugal	Yes, if certified or approved by the government authorities.
Sweden	Foundations with qualifying purposes are exempt from gift tax.

18 What is the tax treatment of gifts to qualifying foundations?

Austria

Are monetary gifts tax deductible?	Yes, but only memberships dues for state-recognized churches or communities and donations for special institutions accredited by the relevant state revenue directorate.
Are in-kind gifts tax deductible?	In-kind gifts are not recommended because of the vagaries of the valuation practices.
Further details	Dues to state-recognized churches and communities may be deducted up to a maximum of ATS1000 (€72.67)per year. Donations for scientific research, publication or documentation to accredited donees are deductible as business expenses up to 10% of the prior year's taxable income.

Belgium

Are monetary gifts tax deductible?	Yes, but only to foundations with very specific purposes as listed in Article 104 Income Tax Act.
Are in-kind gifts tax deductible?	No, except for donations of works of art to museums, the value of which must be substantiated by an independent appraisal and approved by the Minister of Finance.
Further details	Individual donors may deduct the amount of their donations up to a maximum limit of 10% of the tax-payer's total net income, with an absolute maximum of BEF10,000,000 (€247,894). Corporate donors may deduct the amount of their donations up to a maximum limit of 5% of their gross revenue, not to exceed BEF 20,000,000 (€495,787).

Bulgaria

Are monetary gifts tax deductible?	Yes

Are in-kind gifts tax deductible?	No
Further details	Donors may deduct the amount of their donations up to a maximum limit of 5% before tax conversion, provided that the donations qualify under Article 23 subsection three of the Corporate Income Tax Act 1998. The donation should come out of the capital reserves account or from the owner. This deduction is permissible if the donations do not benefit the donor.

Cyprus

Are monetary gifts tax deductible?	Yes
Are in-kind gifts tax deductible?	No
Further details	Tax benefits for gifts to registered charities, whether individual, body corporate or non-corporate. Donations must be made in cash or by way of securities. Donations up to CY£20,000 in any year are allowed in full as a deduction from income. For amounts in excess of this, only 50% of the excess is allowed. The deduction allowed may not exceed the donor's income in the year in which the donation is made. There is no difference in restriction according to the various types of donor.

Czech Republic

Are monetary gifts tax deductible?	Yes
Are in-kind gifts tax deductible?	Yes
Further details	Individual donors may deduct the amount of their donations up to a maximum limit of 10% of the tax-payer's total taxable income, provided that they donate at least 2% of their taxable income, which is equal to not less than CZK1000. Corporate donors may deduct the amount of their donations up to a maximum limit of 2% (proposed legislation would increase this limit to 4%) of their taxable income, provided that they donate more than CZK2000.

Denmark

Are monetary gifts tax deductible?	Yes
Are in-kind gifts tax deductible?	No
Further details	Individual donors may deduct the amount of their donations up to a maximum limit of 15% of their taxable income, or DKK5000, whichever is less, provided that each donation exceeds DKK500. Corporate donors may deduct the amount of their donations up to a maximum limit of 15% of their taxable income.

England, Scotland & Wales

Are monetary gifts tax deductible?	Yes, if from net income, but not if the gift comprises capital cash.
Are in-kind gifts tax deductible?	No, not generally. Business (as opposed to individual) donors may, however, obtain tax reliefs on specific types of support given to charities. These specific types of relief are provided by law. Individual and business donors may also obtain tax relief on gifts of certain shares and securities to charities.
Further details	Individuals may make tax-deductible donations of any amount to registered charities by Gift Aid (individual donors deduct tax from their Gift Aid and give a Gift Aid declaration to the charity, which then reclaims the tax); or by payroll giving (employees can authorize their employer to deduct charitable donations from their pay before calculating pay as you earn tax, thereby allowing the employee to get tax relief at her or his top rate of tax). From 6 April 2000 to 5 April 2003, the government will pay a 10% supplement on all donations made under the payroll giving scheme in order to promote this method of giving.
	Companies may make tax-deductible donations of any amount to registered charities by Gift Aid (companies pay the full amount of the donation to the charity and then deduct this full amount from their total profits).

Individuals and companies, whether resident or non-resident in the UK, may get tax relief for gifts of certain shares and securities to a charity when calculating their income or profits for tax purposes. This tax relief is in addition to the tax relief available for gifts of shares, securities and other assets to charity when calculating capital gains. For income tax relief, the individual or company donor must dispose of the whole of the beneficial interest in any qualifying shares or securities to a charity either by way of gift or by way of a sale at undervalue.

Estonia

Are monetary gifts tax deductible?	Yes
Are in-kind gifts tax deductible?	Yes
Further details	Physical persons may deduct the amount of their gifts (donations) to listed foundations, not exceeding 5% of their total taxable income. Physical and legal persons may also deduct donations to listed foundations from their business income, not exceeding 10% of their total taxable sum. In-kind gifts are valued at local fair market value.

Finland

Are monetary gifts tax deductible?	Yes, for corporate donors; no for individual donors.
Are in-kind gifts tax deductible?	No
Further details	Only gifts by corporations are tax deductible, not gifts by private individuals. The minimum deductible donation is FIM5000 (€840) and for donations to purposes promoting science or art. The maximum deductible donation to any beneficiary in any taxable year is FIM150,000 (€25,200).

France

Are monetary gifts tax deductible?	Yes
Are in-kind gifts tax deductible?	Yes

Further details	Individual tax-payers may deduct an amount equal to 50% of the gift to a qualified entity. The total amount of the deduction from income tax for charitable gifts may not exceed 6% of taxable income for gifts to recognized public interest foundations or associations.
	Companies may deduct an amount equal to 0.225% of their annual turnover for gifts to qualifying entities. Gifts to entities designated to be of public utility may be deducted up to an amount equal to 0.325% of annual turnover. Excess corporate donations may be carried forward to the following five tax years.
	Donors may also claim a deduction for the value of the donation of property or services. Book value of property is deductible. Deduction for services is equal to the donors' cost of providing the services.

Germany

Are monetary gifts tax deductible?	Yes
Are in-kind gifts tax deductible?	Yes
Further details	Individuals, entrepreneurs, small companies, craftsmen, and members of liberal professions may deduct monetary and in-kind donations to qualifying nonprofit organizations from their taxable income up to 5%. Donations to organizations having scientific, higher education, benevolent and specifically recognized cultural purposes may be deducted up to 10% taxable income.
	Corporations use a formula (0.2% of total turnover plus salaries and wages) to determine the amount that can be deducted, even when the there is a loss in part generated by the donation.
	All tax-payers, whether subject to income tax or corporate tax, may deduct up to the sum of DEM40,000 (€20,452) per year for donations made to civil law foundations, not other nonprofit organizations. Percent limits mentioned above only apply to donations to foundations exceeding DEM40,000 (€20,452).

Greece

Are monetary gifts tax deductible?	Yes
Are in-kind gifts tax deductible?	No
Further details	Receipts are used by the charitable institution for gifts of less than GRD80,000. Cash gifts in excess of this amount annually are deductible from income tax only if they are deposited directly into a special bank account of the donee institution, opened for the purpose of receiving contributions. Cash gifts to charitable institutions are deductible to the extent that they do not exceed 10% of the tax-payer's gross income. Cash gifts to approved Greek nonprofit legal persons of the private sector with cultural purposes are nevertheless deductible up to 15% of the tax-payer's gross income.
	When tax deductible cash gifts made by the donor to a specific donee exceed in aggregate the amount of GRD100,000 annually, the donor may not deduct the excess of the amount unless she or he withholds tax at the rate of 20% of this amount.

Hungary

Are monetary gifts tax deductible?	Yes for corporate donors; no for individual donors.
Are in-kind gifts tax deductible?	Yes
Further details	A company donor's donation is defined as giving financial support or assets at book value, or intangible assets or objects at a calculated record value to a public benefit organization (by which the donor can reduce its pre-tax profits by the full sum of the donation, and for continuous donations, a further 20% of the donations in the years after the first donation – the total cannot exceed 20% of the pre-tax profits of the donor) or to a special public benefit organization (a company can reduce its pre-tax profits by 150% of the full sum of the donation, and for continuous donations, a further 20% of the donations in the years following the first donation – the total deduction cannot exceed 20% of the pre-tax

profits of the donor). For company donations to public benefit organizations and special public benefit organizations, the pre-tax profits cannot be reduced more than 25%.

Individual donor's donations are deductible from the consolidated tax base provided a copy of the certificate is kept. Here, a donation is defined as 'a sum of money'. For donations to special public benefit organizations, 35% of the amount paid is tax deductible, but the deduction cannot exceed 30% of the consolidated tax base. For donations to public benefit organizations, or other payments in the interest of the public, 30% of the amount paid is tax deductible, but the deduction cannot exceed 15% of the tax on gifts to special public organizations, or 35% of this tax if the gift is to both special public benefit organizations and public benefit organizations.

Continuous deductions are deductible at an additional rate of 5% of the sum donated. A continuous donation is financial support to public benefit organizations by a donor on the basis of a written contract for at least three years after the year of the contract, at least once per year with at least the same amount each year.

Ireland

Are monetary gifts tax deductible?	Yes
Are in-kind gifts tax deductible?	No
Further details	Gifts by corporations (as opposed to individuals) to approved charitable bodies (with minimum three years charitable tax status) of at least IRP250 and a maximum IRP10,000 per annum. A corporation may not get a deduction for more than IRP50,000 or 10% of its profits.

There is a personal income tax deduction and corporate income tax deduction for donations to fund approved projects in an approved educational institution for research, equipment, infrastructural development and increased skills training. The minimum deductible amount is IRP1000.

There is a personal income tax deduction and corporate income tax deduction for donations to disadvantaged primary and secondary schools. The minimum deductible contribution is IRP250; the maximum for an individual is IRP1000 and for a company it is IRP10,000 subject to an annual maximum of IRP50,000 or 10% of its profits (whichever is less).

For individual donations to approved Third World charities, the Irish standard rate of income tax can be claimed back from the Revenue Commissioners by the Third World charity.

Individual or corporate donors may achieve tax deduction against income in respect of covenanted payments for a period, which will or may exceed three years to a university or college in Ireland for teaching or researching natural sciences or to a recognized human rights body.

Italy

Are monetary gifts tax deductible?	Yes
Are in-kind gifts tax deductible?	Yes
Further details	All donations to a foundation will be tax deductible. Monetary gifts by individual donors will be tax deductible up to a limit of ITL4 million (€2,066) and up to 2% of the declared income for legal entities.

For in-kind gifts, some deductions will be allowed. If a donor seconds its workers to an ONLUS, it can deduct expenses relating to the workers' remuneration up to an amount of 0.5% of the donor's total expenses for staff. Food and pharmaceutical products, as well as goods produced by the donor company that are donated and related to the foundation's activity will be tax deductible for the donor. This applies to gifts made by all donors, whether or not resident in Italy.

Liechtenstein

Are monetary gifts tax deductible?	Yes

Are in-kind gifts tax deductible?	No
Further details	Tax deduction for individual or corporate donors will only arise from a gift of minimum CHF100 per annum and per tax subject to a limited number of charities in Liechtenstein and Switzerland on an official list.

Luxembourg

Are monetary gifts tax deductible?	Yes
Are in-kind gifts tax deductible?	Yes
Further details	Gifts to foundations are tax deductible up to a maximum limit of 10% of the net income of the donor or LUF20 million (€49,579), provided each gift exceeds LUF5000 (€123.95).

Netherlands

Are monetary gifts tax deductible?	Yes
Are in-kind gifts tax deductible?	Yes
Further details	For the calculation of gift and inheritance tax, each gift is valued at fair market value at the moment of acquisition. The same value must be used for the calculation of the deduction by the donor for private income tax and for corporate income tax purposes.

Portugal

Are monetary gifts tax deductible?	Yes
Are in-kind gifts tax deductible?	Yes
Further details	Individual donors may deduct the amount of their donations up to a maximum limit of 15% of their taxable income. Corporate donors may deduct the amount of their donations up to a maximum limit of 2% of their taxable income. The percentage at which each donation may be deducted will vary according to the purposes pursued by the foundation receiving the donation. For example, donations to foundations conducting activities of 'high social interest' are deductible at the rate of 130% of the value of the donation, or if the

donations are intended for a programme in certain specified areas, such as AIDS, prevention of social exclusion, or drug treatment, then they are deductible at the rate of 140% of the value of the donation.

Scotland

(See England and Wales)

Slovenia

Are monetary gifts tax deductible?	Yes
Are in-kind gifts tax deductible?	Yes
Further details	The donor may deduct the contribution from his or her tax base if it constitutes the endowment for humanitarian, cultural, educational, scientific, sports, ecological or religious purposes or given to people who, pursuant to special regulations, are organized to perform such activities or to serve the physically disabled. Total deductions for individual donors may not exceed 3%. For legal entities, this figure is 0.3% of the total yearly income. In-kind gifts are treated the same as monetary gifts (assessed at fair market value).

Spain

Are monetary gifts tax deductible?	Yes
Are in-kind gifts tax deductible?	Yes
Further details	If the foundation does not obtain favourable tax treatment, then gifts by individuals enjoy a benefit in the gross value of 10% of the amount given. There is a limit in the deduction of the amount given of 10% of the taxable income. Gifts given by legal entities to such foundations are not tax deductible.
	If the foundation obtains more favourable tax treatment, then gifts by individuals will be deductible at the rate of 20% of the amount given, up to a maximum limit of deductibility of 10% of the individual's taxable income. Gifts by a legal entity will be deductible (as an expense) from corporate income tax up to a maximum limit

of 10% of taxable income or one per thousandth of the entity's turnover.

In-kind gifts enjoy the same deductibility as monetary gifts, though the limit of deductibility is increased for artworks to 30% of taxable income or three per thousandth of an entity's turnover. In-kind gifts are assessed at fair market value by a special public agency.

Sweden

Are monetary gifts tax deductible?	No (see 'Further details' below)
Are in-kind gifts tax deductible?	No
Further details	Donations to foundations may not as a rule be deducted from the donor's taxable income, irrespective of the purpose of the foundation. However, if the donor carries on a trade or business that enjoys a direct benefit from the donation for its business activities, the donation may be tax deductible as a business expense.
	Employees may make tax-deductible donations within certain limits to pension foundations, employee foundations and profit-sharing foundations.

Switzerland

Are monetary gifts tax deductible?	Yes
Are in-kind gifts tax deductible?	No on federal level; yes on cantonal level.
Further details	Switzerland is a confederation consisting of 26 autonomous Cantons, each with its own jurisdiction in fiscal matters. In addition, the Swiss Federation (federal government) levies its own direct tax. Consequently, there are 27 different income tax laws existing in Switzerland. There is an upper limit for tax deduction of 5–20% of the donor's taxable income, depending on the Canton in which the donor's income is taxable. Tax laws frequently provide for a minimum amount to qualify for benefits (usually at least CHF100).

19 Are gifts (i.e. grants or social aid) by foundations to any third party (individual or organization) subject to taxation in your jurisdiction? If so, please explain

Austria Bulgaria Cyprus Czech Republic England & Wales Greece Hungary Ireland Italy Netherlands Scotland Sweden	These countries do not subject such gifts to taxation if the gift is given by a charitable foundation in pursuance of its purposes.
France Germany Spain	As above, but any taxes will fall on the recipient, not the donating foundation.
Belgium Denmark Luxembourg Portugal	Gifts are subject to tax payable by the donee. In Belgium and Luxembourg, registration tax is due only on gifts made in writing by deeds, whether immovable or movable property; it is not due on gifts of movable property that can be donated 'from hand to hand' (*dons manuels*). A reduced rate of 1.1% applies in Belgium when the gift is made to another nonprofit association or foundation established in Belgium. In Denmark, the gift would be added to the donee's income and taxed as such to the extent there would be liability. In Portugal, the tax liability of the donee will depend on the size of the gift.
Liechtenstein Switzerland	Taxes gifts, except in cases where the recipient is also tax-exempt.
Estonia	Generally taxes gifts. However, grants from foreign country governments, foreign governmental organizations and international organizations are exempt. Also, if paying grants is one of the organization's statutory purposes or if the selection of grants is made through public contest (competition) then the grants are tax-exempt, provided that they are not paid to the organization's own members or workers (new government regulations may change this).
Finland	Taxes stipends and grants by foundations for studies or scientific research or artistic work as well as prizes awarded for scientific, artistic or nonprofit activity if the aggregate amount of all the stipends and prizes received by an individual in any one year after

the deduction of costs necessary to acquire and maintain the income exceeds the annual amount of the state artist grant. If the beneficiary is not a nonprofit organization, it will have to pay tax at the rate of 30–40%, thus such gifts are not given.

| Slovenia | The grant is taxed if an individual is a donee and the grant is worth over DEM2500 (€1278) in kind or DEM1500 (€767) in money, but not if a legal entity is donee. |

Supervision of foundations

20 Which public/quasi-public authorities exercise supervision of the foundation's activities after incorporation/registration?

Austria	Authority which had given approval.
Belgium	Ministries of Finance and of Justice.
Bulgaria	Ministry of Justice, including the Special Central Registry at the Ministry of Justice.
Cyprus	The Attorney-General, the police, the Ministry of the Interior, the Ministry of Finance, the District of Land Officers, the Registrar of Companies and the courts.
Czech Republic	The Registry Court and the public.
Denmark	Local tax authorities.
England & Wales	Charity Commission, Companies House (if a charitable company), Inland Revenue, and Customs and Excise. Local authorities have a role in relation to local charities.
Estonia	Tax authorities and Registrar of nonprofit organizations.
Finland	National Board of Patents and Registration, the taxation authorities and auditors.
France	Ministry of Interior.
Germany	Differs between states; however, fiscal supervision is uniform throughout states.
Greece	Ministry of Finance; Council of National Bequests.
Hungary	Office of the Attorney-General.
Ireland	Irish Revenue Commissioners; the Commissioners for Charitable Donations and Bequests for Ireland.

Italy	Ministry of Finance.
Liechtenstein	Cabinet Secretary's Office (Government); Inland Revenue.
Luxembourg	Ministry of Justice; Public Prosecutor.
Netherlands	Public Prosecutor's Office and the District Court.
Portugal	Ministry of Finance.
Scotland	Financial Intermediaries and Claims Office; Capital Taxes Office; Scottish Charities Office.
Slovenia	State supervision by supervisory body of relevant Ministry.
Spain	Protectorados.
Sweden	County Administrative Board.
Switzerland	State supervision by the government of the municipality, Canton or Federation, and by the tax authorities.

21 Is there a special government unit responsible for relations with the charity/foundation sector? If so, which ones?

Austria Cyprus Estonia Liechtenstein Luxembourg Netherlands Portugal	These countries have no special government unit.
Slovenia Sweden Switzerland	These countries have no special government unit.
Belgium	Departments in Ministries of Justice and Finance.
Bulgaria	Ministry of Justice, including its Special Central Registry for legal persons with nonprofit purposes engaging in public benefit activities.
Czech Republic	Advisory body at government level headed by minister without portfolio.
Denmark	Danish Commerce and Companies Agency.
England & Wales	Home Office's 'Active Community Unit'; Charity Commission; Attorney-General.
Estonia	No special body, unless they fall under the Inspectorate of Religious Affairs.

Finland	National Board of Patents and Registration; Foundations Register.
France	'Association' correspondents in the departmental offices of the tax authorities (Ministry of Economy, Finance and Industry).
Germany	No national authority, but each state has its own supervisory system for legal matters.
Greece	Two departments in the Ministry of Finance; Council of National Bequests; depending on the purpose of the foundation, such supervision may be delegated to other ministries.
Hungary	Special department in the Ministry of Education.
Ireland	The Commissioners of Charitable Donations and Bequests for Ireland.
Italy	A new unit for this purpose is to be created in the Ministry of Social affairs.
Scotland	The Scottish Charities Office deals with compliance matters but there is no special government unit responsible for relations with the charity/foundation sector.
Spain	No special body, but it is intended that there will be one in the future.

22 Does supervision differ by level of government?

Austria	
Belgium	
Bulgaria	
Cyprus	
Czech Republic	
Denmark	
Estonia	
France	
Greece	No
Ireland	
Liechtenstein	
Luxembourg	
Netherlands	
Portugal	
Scotland	
Slovenia	
Sweden	

England & Wales
Finland
Germany
Hungary   Yes
Italy
Spain
Switzerland

23 What formalities are required of foundations to help the state's enforcement efforts to ensure compliance?

Austria	Compliance with the Civil Code investment requirements mandatory; full reporting required (including any major sale of assets).
Belgium	Annual accounts and budgets must be submitted and published. Receipt of large donations requires government approval.
Bulgaria	Annual reports containing specified information, including a certified financial report, must be filed with the Central Registry regarding their activities during the past year.
Cyprus	Accounts of money received and paid by the foundation must be kept by the trustees of the foundation, to be submitted to the Administrative Secretary at the end of the year.
Czech Republic	Annual reports, containing a summary of property and obligations of the foundation; an overview of persons who donated over CZK10,000, unless the donor remained anonymous, and how their money was used; an overview of the use of property; and an assessment of data from the annual statement of accounts and the auditor's report. The report must be given to the court that registered the foundation, and must be made available to the public.
Denmark	Annual accounts to local tax authorities (accessible to public); external audits.
England & Wales	Audited annual accounts and reports must be submitted to the Charity Commission (or other relevant regulatory authority). Tax returns and reclaims to the Inland Revenue and Customs and Excise. Accounts and reports to Companies House if a charitable company.
Estonia	Annually file accounts and activity reports (accessible to public); random audits (power of the tax authorities only).
Finland	Administration supervised to ensure compliance with the law and the by-laws of the foundation; Income statement must be submitted; itemization of balance sheet, annual report and audit report. Possible audit.

France	Must submit an annual information report accompanied by a financial statement to the appropriate prefecture and the Minister of the Interior. Receipt of large gifts requires government approval.
Germany	Possible audit and random reports required. Special reporting at the authority's demand; review of exempt status every three years; (basic regulations apply to all Lander; especially regarding oversight).
Greece	Annual budgets and statements of accounts of revenue and expenses; balance sheet of assets and liabilities; possible inquiry of foundation's bank accounts with banks or other institutions.
Hungary	Annual reports, simplified balance sheet (of calculation of profits and losses).
Ireland	The Revenue Commissioners will assess the charity for tax if the conditions for exemption have been breached.
Italy	Annual report presented to Parliament; specific audit mentioning commercial and related activities carried out.
Liechtenstein	Annually audited accounts complying with commercial accounting rules must be submitted to the Inland Revenue.
Luxembourg	Annual accounts.
Netherlands	Balance sheet and statement of income and expenditure; sometimes, financial and annual reports, particularly if foundation qualifies for reduced gift and inheritance taxes as a charitable institution; audit in some cases. No publication or filing is required.
Portugal	Annual activity reports including financial accounts and records to ensure that only charitable activities are conducted. All financial reports and records must be kept, and made available for tax department review.
Scotland	Prepare annual reports and accounts; external auditor must be appointed for larger charities; for smaller, must be independent examination.
Slovenia	Annual financial report.
Spain	Annual accounts and reports; external audit is required if at least two of the following are present within two years: the total value of all assets, or the net amount of income is greater than ESP400 million (€2,409,639), the average number of employees is over 50, or in 'special circumstances'.
Sweden	Review of annual reports from foundations required to maintain accounting records yearly, to examine whether the foundation's

capital is invested in an acceptable way and that the foundation complies with its purpose. There are also inspections if there is information from the public that the foundation does not comply with required formalities.

Switzerland	Accounts may be requested; professional audits are advisable.

24 (a) Is a foundation required to distribute a specific amount or percentage annually?

Unless otherwise required in a foundation's governing documents, the answer is no in the case of all countries except as follows:

England & Wales	No, but its tax relief may be restricted if its accumulations of income cannot be justified.
Finland	Approximately 50%.
Ireland	No, but the charitable body must be able to satisfy the Revenue Commissioners that the capital and gains which have enjoyed exemption from taxation will be applied to its charitable purposes only.
Scotland	No, except in certain specified circumstances which in practice would be extremely rare.
Spain	70% for stated purpose over three years.
Sweden	80% for purposes stipulated by law or in the governing documents of the foundation over previous five years.

(b) Is there a limit on the amount of reserves it can hold?

Unless otherwise required in a foundation's governing documents, the answer is no in the case of all countries except as follows:

England & Wales	No, subject to the charity demonstrating an appropriate and justifiable policy for their retention. The Charity Commission has recently issued guidelines on this subject.
Germany	Up to 33% annual income from capital investment, minus cost of capital investment.
Ireland	No, provided it can be justified.

(c) Are there any legal requirements regarding the investment of income?

The answer is no in the case of all countries except as follows:

Belgium Finland Luxembourg	Foundations may only possess such immovable property as is necessary for the pursuit of their purposes.
Czech Republic	The registered endowment of a foundation may not fall below CZK500,000. Assets comprising a foundation's registered endowment must remain in the form of monetary assets in a special bank account, real property, state-guaranteed bonds, patents or copyrights, or artwork yielding a permanent income. Assets comprising a foundation's registered endowment may not be used for investment purposes; other assets of the foundation, however, may be used for investment or other purposes. Foundations may invest only 20% of their property, excluding their registered endowment assets, in shares of a joint stock company, but may not hold more than 20% of the shares in any given joint stock company.
Finland	According to the Foundations Act, the board of directors must specifically ensure the proper management of the affairs of the foundation and a secure and profitable investment of the assets of the foundation.
Slovenia	Assets may not be transferred to another entity. Financial funds can be put into a special bank account, or can be used to purchase government securities. Funds may not be lent out. No more than 20% of assets (above endowment capital) can be invested in shares.
Austria Denmark England & Wales Hungary Ireland Scotland	It depends on the powers given in the governing document, but in the absence of specific provisions in the governing document, other regulations on investment will apply.

25 Do foundations have limited liability?

Austria Belgium Bulgaria Denmark Estonia Finland France	Yes

Germany		
Greece		
Hungary		
Italy		
Liechtenstein	Yes	
Netherlands		
Spain		
Sweden		
Switzerland		
Cyprus		
Czech Republic		
Luxembourg	No	
Portugal		
Slovenia		
England & Wales		
Ireland	Limited contractual liability for directors of companies limited	
Scotland	by guarantee but not for trustees of a charitable trust.	

26 Sanctions legally applicable to foundations, directors and board members

Austria

Civil sanctions:	Dissolution of foundation?	No
	Loss of legal personality?	No
	Same sanctions as for other legal persons?	No
	Dismissal/ disqualification of directors?	Yes
	Can board members be held civilly liable?	Yes
Criminal sanctions	Can board members be held criminally liable?	Yes
	Fine (F) or imprisonment (I) of directors?	Yes (F)
Fiscal sanctions:	Loss of tax-exempt status or other privileges?	Yes

Belgium

Civil sanctions:	Dissolution of foundation?	Yes
	Loss of legal personality?	Yes
	Same sanctions as for other legal persons?	No
	Dismissal/disqualification of directors?	Yes
	Can board members be held civilly liable?	Yes
Criminal sanctions	Can board members be held criminally liable?	No
	Fine (F) or imprisonment (I) of directors?	No
Fiscal sanctions:	Loss of tax-exempt status or other privileges?	No

Bulgaria

Civil sanctions:	Dissolution of foundation?	No
	Loss of legal personality?	No
	Same sanctions as for other legal persons?	Yes
	Dismissal/disqualification of directors?	No
	Can board members be held civilly liable?	Yes
Criminal sanctions	Can board members be held criminally liable?	Yes
	Fine (F) or imprisonment (I) of directors?	Yes (F & I)
Fiscal sanctions:	Loss of tax-exempt status or other privileges?	No

Cyprus

Civil sanctions:	Dissolution of foundation?	Yes
	Loss of legal personality?	No
	Same sanctions as for other legal persons?	Yes
	Dismissal/disqualification of directors?	No
	Can board members be held civilly liable?	Yes
Criminal sanctions	Can board members be held criminally liable?	Yes
	Fine (F) or imprisonment (I) of directors?	Yes (F & I)
Fiscal sanctions:	Loss of tax-exempt status or other privileges?	Yes

Czech Republic

Civil sanctions:	Dissolution of foundation?	Yes
	Loss of legal personality?	No
	Same sanctions as for other legal persons?	Yes
	Dismissal/disqualification of directors?	No
	Can board members be held civilly liable?	Yes
Criminal sanctions	Can board members be held criminally liable?	Yes
	Fine (F) or imprisonment (I) of directors?	Yes
Fiscal sanctions:	Loss of tax-exempt status or other privileges?	Yes

Denmark

Civil sanctions:	Dissolution of foundation?	No
	Loss of legal personality?	No
	Same sanctions as for other legal persons?	No
	Dismissal/disqualification of directors?	Yes
	Can board members be held civilly liable?	Yes
Criminal sanctions	Can board members be held criminally liable?	Yes
	Fine (F) or imprisonment (I) of directors?	Yes (F & I)
Fiscal sanctions:	Loss of tax-exempt status or other privileges?	Yes

England & Wales

Civil sanctions:	Dissolution of foundation?	No
	Loss of legal personality?	No
	Same sanctions as for other legal persons?	No
	Dismissal/disqualification of directors?	Yes
	Can board members be held civilly liable?	Yes
Criminal sanctions	Can board members be held criminally liable?	Yes
	Fine (F) or imprisonment (I) of directors?	Yes (F)
Fiscal sanctions:	Loss of tax-exempt status or other privileges?	No

Estonia

Civil sanctions:	Dissolution of foundation?	Yes
	Loss of legal personality?	No
	Same sanctions as for other legal persons?	Yes
	Dismissal/disqualification of directors?	Yes
	Can board members be held civilly liable?	Yes
Criminal sanctions	Can board members be held criminally liable?	Yes
	Fine (F) or imprisonment (I) of directors?	Yes
Fiscal sanctions:	Loss of tax-exempt status or other privileges?	Yes

Finland

Civil sanctions:	Dissolution of foundation?	Yes
	Loss of legal personality?	Yes
	Same sanctions as for other legal persons?	No
	Dismissal/disqualification of directors?	Yes
	Can board members be held civilly liable?	Yes
Criminal sanctions	Can board members be held criminally liable?	Yes
	Fine (F) or imprisonment (I) of directors?	Yes (F)
Fiscal sanctions:	Loss of tax-exempt status or other privileges?	No

France

Civil sanctions:	Dissolution of foundation?	Yes
	Loss of legal personality?	Yes
	Same sanctions as for other legal persons?	Yes
	Dismissal/disqualification of directors?	Yes
	Can board members be held civilly liable?	Yes
Criminal sanctions	Can board members be held criminally liable?	Yes
	Fine (F) or imprisonment (I) of directors?	Yes (F & I)
Fiscal sanctions:	Loss of tax-exempt status or other privileges?	Yes

Germany

Civil sanctions:	Dissolution of foundation?	Yes
	Loss of legal personality?	Yes
	Same sanctions as for other legal persons?	Yes
	Dismissal/ disqualification of directors?	Yes
	Can board members be held civilly liable?	Yes
Criminal sanctions	Can board members be held criminally liable?	Yes
	Fine (F) or imprisonment (I) of directors?	Yes (F)
Fiscal sanctions:	Loss of tax-exempt status or other privileges?	Yes

Greece

Civil sanctions:	Dissolution of foundation?	Yes
	Loss of legal personality?	No
	Same sanctions as for other legal persons?	Yes
	Dismissal/disqualification of directors?	Yes
	Can board members be held civilly liable?	Yes
Criminal sanctions	Can board members be held criminally liable?	Yes
	Fine (F) or imprisonment (I) of directors?	Yes (F & I)
Fiscal sanctions:	Loss of tax-exempt status or other privileges?	Yes

Hungary

Civil sanctions:	Dissolution of foundation?	Yes
	Loss of legal personality?	Yes
	Same sanctions as for other legal persons?	No
	Dismissal/disqualification of directors?	Yes
	Can board members be held civilly liable?	Yes
Criminal sanctions	Can board members be held criminally liable?	Yes
	Fine (F) or imprisonment (I) of directors?	Yes (F & I)
Fiscal sanctions:	Loss of tax-exempt status or other privileges?	Yes

Ireland

Civil sanctions:	Dissolution of foundation?	Yes
	Loss of legal personality?	No
	Same sanctions as for other legal persons?	No
	Dismissal/disqualification of directors?	Yes*
	*under company law, but not by the Commissioners of Charitable Donations and Bequests for Ireland	
	Can board members be held civilly liable?	Yes

Criminal sanctions	Can board members be held criminally liable?	Yes
	Fine (F) or imprisonment (I) of directors?	Yes (F)
Fiscal sanctions:	Loss of tax-exempt status or other privileges?	Yes

Italy

Civil sanctions:	Dissolution of foundation?	No
	Loss of legal personality?	No
	Same sanctions as for other legal persons?	No
	Dismissal/disqualification of directors?	No*
	*only possible as a criminal sanction	
	Can board members be held civilly liable?	Yes
Criminal sanctions	Can board members be held criminally liable?	No
	Fine (F) or imprisonment (I) of directors?	No
Fiscal sanctions:	Loss of tax-exempt status or other privileges?	Yes

Liechtenstein

Civil sanctions:	Dissolution of foundation?	Yes
	Loss of legal personality?	Yes
	Same sanctions as for other legal persons?	Yes
	Dismissal/disqualification of directors?	Yes
	Can board members be held civilly liable?	Yes
Criminal sanctions	Can board members be held criminally liable?	Yes
	Fine (F) or imprisonment (I) of directors?	No
Fiscal sanctions:	Loss of tax-exempt status or other privileges?	Yes

Luxembourg

Civil sanctions:	Dissolution of foundation?	Yes
	Loss of legal personality?	No
	Same sanctions as for other legal persons?	No
	Dismissal/disqualification of directors?	Yes
	Can board members be held civilly liable?	Yes
Criminal sanctions	Can board members be held criminally liable?	No
	Fine (F) or imprisonment (I) of directors?	No
Fiscal sanctions:	Loss of tax-exempt status or other privileges?	No

Netherlands

Civil sanctions:	Dissolution of foundation?	Yes
	Loss of legal personality?	No
	Same sanctions as for other legal persons?	Yes

	Dismissal/disqualification of directors?	Yes
	Can board members be held civilly liable?	Yes
Criminal sanctions	Can board members be held criminally liable?	Yes
	Fine (F) or imprisonment (I) of directors?	Yes (F & I)
Fiscal sanctions:	Loss of tax-exempt status or other privileges?	Yes

Portugal

Civil sanctions:	Dissolution of foundation?	No
	Loss of legal personality?	No
	Same sanctions as for other legal persons?	Yes
	Dismissal/disqualification of directors?	Yes
	Can board members be held civilly liable?	Yes
Criminal sanctions	Can board members be held criminally liable?	Yes
	Fine (F) or imprisonment (I) of directors?	Yes
Fiscal sanctions:	Loss of tax-exempt status or other privileges?	No

Scotland

Civil sanctions:	Dissolution of foundation?	No
	Loss of legal personality?	No
	Same sanctions as for other legal persons?	No
	Dismissal/disqualification of directors?	Yes
	Can board members be held civilly liable?	Yes
Criminal sanctions	Can board members be held criminally liable?	Yes
	Fine (F) or imprisonment (I) of directors?	No
Fiscal sanctions:	Loss of tax-exempt status or other privileges?	Yes

Slovenia

Civil sanctions:	Dissolution of foundation?	Yes
	Loss of legal personality?	Yes
	Same sanctions as for other legal persons?	No
	Dismissal/disqualification of directors?	Yes
	Can board members be held civilly liable?	Yes
Criminal sanctions	Can board members be held criminally liable?	Yes
	Fine (F) or imprisonment (I) of directors?	Yes
Fiscal sanctions:	Loss of tax-exempt status or other privileges?	Yes

Spain

Civil sanctions:	Dissolution of foundation?	No
	Loss of legal personality?	No

	Same sanctions as for other legal persons?	Yes
	Dismissal/disqualification of directors?	Yes
	Can board members be held civilly liable?	Yes
Criminal sanctions	Can board members be held criminally liable?	Yes
	Fine (F) or imprisonment (I) of directors?	No
Fiscal sanctions:	Loss of tax-exempt status or other privileges?	Yes

Sweden

Civil sanctions:	Dissolution of foundation?	No
	Loss of legal personality?	No
	Same sanctions as for other legal persons?	No
	Dismissal/disqualification of directors?	Yes
	Can board members be held civilly liable?	Yes
Criminal sanctions	Can board members be held criminally liable?	Yes
	Fine (F) or imprisonment (I) of directors?	Yes (F)
Fiscal sanctions:	Loss of tax-exempt status or other privileges?	Yes

Switzerland

Civil sanctions:	Dissolution of foundation?	Yes
	Loss of legal personality?	Yes
	Same sanctions as for other legal persons?	Yes
	Dismissal/disqualification of directors?	No
	Can board members be held civilly liable?	Yes
Criminal sanctions	Can board members be held criminally liable?	Yes
	Fine (F) or imprisonment (I) of directors?	Yes (F & I)
Fiscal sanctions:	Loss of tax-exempt status or other privileges?	Yes

27 Is a permit required before fundraising activities can be conducted?

Belgium	
Bulgaria	
Czech Republic	
Denmark	
Estonia	
France	
Hungary	These countries have no legal requirements.
Italy	
Spain	

Austria	Need written consent of the Premier of the Province for door-to-door solicitations.
Cyprus	Need a licence from the licensing authority (District Land Officer) in the district where the collection is to take place.
England & Wales	In certain circumstances the local authority's permission, or exemptions from the Charity Commission for door-to-door collections and public collections. Commercial participants and professional fundraisers must enter agreement with the charity in the stipulated form, and the public must be kept informed.
Finland	Need permission from the county government.
Germany	No, this is not needed unless fundraising is to become a permanent activity, and is not mentioned in the foundation's statutes.
Greece	Generally no, however a state permit is needed for the collection of money or valuable objects through coupons, lotteries, etc.
Ireland	Need a police permit, and a court licence to hold a lottery; to conduct door-to-door or public collections, a police permit is required.
Liechtenstein	No legal requirements must be met before a foundation can conduct fundraising activities. However, a foundation should make it clear whether it has exclusively charitable purposes, whether these have been acknowledged as such by the Liechtenstein Inland Revenue (which is different), and also whether they have been acknowledged as a Liechtenstein and Swiss charity, whose donors receive tax benefits (which is also different). These requirements are not regulatory or administrative, but originate from unfair competition, customer protection and principles of equity, which are not merely customary but also statutory.
Luxembourg	Yes, a grand-ducal decree is required.
Netherlands	Yes, a permit is obtainable from the local government (municipality) for solicitations in public places or from door-to-door.
Portugal	Need permission from the Governo Civil for the public collection of funds.
Scotland	Need the local authority's permission to conduct house-to-house and public collections; need a licence from the local authority to hold lotteries, and larger lotteries must be registered. Fundraisers must follow a code of practice, and must have an agreement with the charity.

Slovenia	No legal requirements for fundraising; restrictions relate only to games of chance, when it would be necessary to organize in line with the regulations.
Sweden	No, but a collection foundation may volunteer to be supervised by the Foundation for Collecting Supervision.
Switzerland	Public and door-to-door collections require permission.

28 What are the rights of third parties re receipt of information, initiation of enquiries, seeking government or judicial enforcement of legal or internal rules? Define who the third parties are. Is there a procedure to be followed to enforce these rights?

Austria	None.
Belgium	Creditors and reserved heirs may seek annulment of any decision that prejudices their rights, and they can demand dissolution of the foundation.
Bulgaria	According to the new law, all public benefit foundations must prepare an annual report containing certain mandatory information regarding its activities, expenditures and assets. Third parties have a right to review the annual report, which is available at the Central Registry.
Cyprus	A third party may file a complaint if his/her interests are affected, and may ask the police to conduct an enquiry. A third party may bring a civil action and claim damages.
Czech Republic	The general public can acquire information on the activities of the foundation from the foundation register kept at the Companies Courts. Anyone with a proven valuable interest can file a motion for a foundation to be dissolved.
Denmark	A third party's rights depend on the provisions made in the deed.
England & Wales	In relation to bodies registered with the Charity Commission third parties may make complaints or pass information to the Charity Commission (who may then conduct a 's.8 enquiry'). If they fall in certain categories they may, with the Charity Commission's consent, bring 'charity proceedings' in court. Third parties have the right to see charities' annual accounts (on payment of a copying fee). The Inland Revenue and Customs and Excise have their usual enquiry powers.

Estonia	A third party may demand information, examine accounts, activity reports, the auditor's conclusion, accounting documents. Third parties may seek judicial or governmental enforcement. Third parties are 'all interested persons whose rights are affected'.
Finland	Third parties may obtain information from the register of foundations.
France	Beneficiaries and interested individuals have limited rights to obtain information regarding a foundation's activities. They may also assert claims before the supervisory authority, which may result in administrative or judicial action.
Germany	Third parties have rights under some state laws to be informed via publication in the Gazette when the foundation comes into existence. Most registers are open to the public.
Greece	None, except that creditors and lawful heirs of the founder may attack the establishment of the foundation.
Hungary	Third parties may access documents regarding the operation of a foundation, and may appeal to the Public Prosecutor's office should they notice illegal activity.
Ireland	Third parties have no rights, unless the Commissioners for Charitable Donations and Bequests for Ireland or the Attorney General seeks to bring proceedings for misappropriation or wrongdoing.
Italy	Third parties may receive information; they may be protected, may initiate proceedings if the foundation's endowment is violated, or if someone has acted *ultra vires*.
Liechtenstein	Third party claimants and participants must prove their positions as such before being able to receive information, even internal information, and seek judicial assistance.
Luxembourg	Third parties with direct interest can seek judicial enforcement of legal and internal rules, by filing a request with the Civil Chamber of the District Court, resulting in the dismissal of administrators and/or dissolution of the foundation.
Netherlands	Interested parties can, in certain circumstances, ask for the foundation to be dissolved, the directors to be dismissed, or a decision to be nullified.
Portugal	Third parties do not have a statutory right to receive information. Foundations and other nonprofit organizations must provide information regarding their activities to the relevant supervisory authorities. Anyone with information regarding wrongful conduct by

	the foundation may present the information to the judicial bodies. Any wrongful conduct will be viewed in accordance with general principles of criminal law.
Scotland	Third parties are entitled to receive information. Any suspicions by a third party reported to the Scottish Charities Office or the FICO can be investigated.
Slovenia	Foundations must file a copy of their annual report each year by 28 February with a special public authority called Agency for Payment's Operation (APP). The public may review the information in the annual report by giving the name of the foundation to any of the several offices of APP throughout the country. A fee is charged to review the information.
Spain	Third parties are beneficiaries or interested individuals who have the right to obtain information regarding activities. A third party can assert a claim before the supervisory authority, which may result in judicial enforcement.
Sweden	All documents received by the County Administrative Board (CAB) are public documents; anyone can express their suspicions to the CAB if they think they should be inspected. Beneficiaries may plead their case against the founder.
Switzerland	Third parties have all the rights in question. Creditors and parties to a contract with the foundation can enforce legal rights.

29 What information is made public concerning laws, regulations, guidelines and administrative rulings governing foundations? Where can such information be obtained?

Austria	None of the above is available to the public in a user-friendly format.
Belgium	Legislative instruments are published in the *Official Gazette*. Law and general information available from the Ministries of Justice and Finance; Belgian Parliament has a website.
Bulgaria	Legislative instruments are published in the *Official Gazette*. A monthly newsletter will be published by the Central Registry and will contain information of interest to the general public, including the registration of nonprofit legal persons as well as denials and cancelled registrations.
Cyprus	Public may carry out a search at the Registrar of Associations for CY£10.00.
Czech Republic	Collection of Laws and Ordinances, and the Internet.

Denmark	All information on laws, regulations, guidelines and administrative rulings on the Internet.
England & Wales	Records of Register of Charities on the Internet; information from the Charity Commission by telephone; apply to charity for information.
Estonia	Published in the *State Gazette* and on the Internet; all Ministries have their own homepage.
Finland	Laws and decrees available in every public library, in many bookshops, and on the Internet too.
France	General information regarding relevant laws can be found on the website of the Ministry of Economy, Finance and Industry and be obtained from the 'association' correspondent in the departmental offices of the tax authorities.
Germany	Brochures published occasionally by the Ministry of Finance of a Land, the Ministry of Justice, or the Ministry of Interior, on the legal framework, obtaining status or establishing an association (rarely on foundations, though); mostly left to the private sector (such as charities, professional groups, publishers).
Greece	Such information is provided by the Department for Supervision of National Bequests.
Hungary	Regulations regarding foundations are published regularly; court decisions regarding foundations are published in a journal.
Ireland	Information regarding tax legislation is available on the Internet on the website of the Irish Revenue Commissioners at www.revenue.ie, while information regarding other legislation can be found at the website of the Irish Parliament (Oireachtas) at www.irlgov.ie/*Oireachtas*/frame.htm
Italy	Information is provided by the Ministry of Finance, and by the foundations; some foundations have their own websites.
Liechtenstein	Such information can be obtained at the Cabinet Secretary's Office and the Inland Revenue.
Luxembourg	Information is published in the *Memorial, Recueil des Sociétés et Associations* and the Luxembourg trade registry. This information is available on the Internet at http://etat.lu/memorial/
Netherlands	All legislation is published in the *State Gazette* and/or the *State Bulletin*.
Portugal	Information regarding tax legislation is available on the Internet on the website of the Ministry of Finance at www.dgci.min-financas.pt/SiteDGCI.nsf

Scotland	Company documents are public documents, and can be inspected for a fee. Trust deeds or the articles of association are available from the charity for a fee. General information is available from the Scottish Charities Office and the Inland Revenue, either in person, over the telephone, or a computer disc may be provided. Information and advice is also available from the Scottish Council for Voluntary Organizations.
Slovenia	The Foundations Act is well known, foundations are becoming increasingly popular, and the media also covers the setting up of foundations.
Spain	Information available in official legal publications, and on the Internet.
Sweden	The law is found in Swedish statute books; regulations, guidelines, and administrative rulings available from the appropriate authority.
Switzerland	Information in legal publications, published judgments. Some charities have their own websites on the Internet.

Cross-border issues

30 Are there restrictions on the extent to which charitable activities can be conducted and/or assets transferred for charitable purposes outside your country by a foundation?

Belgium Czech Republic Denmark England & Wales Finland France Greece Hungary Ireland Italy Liechtenstein Luxembourg Netherlands Portugal Scotland Slovenia Sweden	These countries do not impose any restrictions on the extent of activities conducted or assets transferred abroad, outside any restrictions found in the foundation's governing instruments.

Austria	Requires transfers abroad to be carried out in Third World countries or countries with specific tax rulings based on reciprocity. Any other transfers abroad do not receive tax benefits.
Bulgaria	Requires the approval of the Minister of Finance to transfer funds abroad and that donations of over DEM5000 (€2551) be declared for statistical purposes.
Cyprus	Requires a permit from the Central Bank of Cyprus to transfer funds abroad.
Estonia	No restrictions but the new Income Tax Act imposes several restrictions concerning transfers of assets to tax havens.
Germany	No restrictions, however investments must be made with a domestic bank.
Hungary	Requires authorization from the currency authority to transfer funds abroad.
Spain	No restrictions, however transfers of more than ESP250 million (€1,502,530) are subject to verification by the authorities and transfers of more than ESP500 million (€3,005,060) must be declared.
Switzerland	No restrictions, but donations must be channelled through a Swiss charity to be tax privileged.

31 Are there restrictions on a domestic foundation receiving a donation from a foreign source?

There are no restrictions in any country specifically imposed on foreign donations. See, however, the Bulgarian response to question 30 regarding declaration requirement for statistical purposes.

32 May a foundation move its seat to another jurisdiction? If so, what will be the formalities that the foundation will need to follow (e.g. government or judicial approval)? What will be the consequences of such a move (e.g. loss of tax privilege status, or dissolution)?

Austria Belgium Bulgaria Cyprus Hungary Italy Spain Sweden	Transferring the seat of a foundation abroad will result in its dissolution and liquidation in these countries (although there are no legal provisions concerning this). Note that the foundation's assets will have to be distributed according to the destination clause or the government's wishes, which probably means that they will have to be distributed to another entity in the same country.

Estonia Finland Scotland	A foundation may not move its seat abroad.
Czech Republic Luxembourg France	A foundation may move its seat to a foreign country without losing its legal personality, provided that the state to which the foundation moves recognizes the continuation of its legal personality. The foundation must satisfy any requirements imposed under the law applicable in the country of its seat.
Denmark	The consent of the Danish Minister of Justice is required and consent will only be granted if it is not practical to maintain the seat in Denmark.
England & Wales	Moving the seat (and ceasing to be tax resident) results in the withdrawal of tax privileges. For a company limited by guarantee, it is impossible to move the registered office out of the jurisdiction, as the company would cease to exist. It would have to incorporate in the new jurisdiction and transfer its assets to the new company.
Germany	A foundation wishing to move its seat to another state within the country will need the consent of the home state supervision authority first and then register with the relevant supervision authority of the new homeland. It is almost impossible to move a foundation to a foreign country.
Greece	Allows a foundation to move its seat to another jurisdiction provided that this is permitted in its governing document, and is consistent with the wishes of the founder as expressed in the purposes clause. In such a case, the formalities needed for amendment must be complied with.
Ireland	A company cannot change its place of incorporation but can in limited circumstances cease to be tax resident. If a charitable company ceases to be tax resident in Ireland it will almost certainly lead to a clawback of previously enjoyed tax-exemptions as well as an exit charge to capital gains tax on its assets.
Liechtenstein	A foundation may move its seat to another jurisdiction, if the laws and statutes do not otherwise provide and if the approval of the government has been obtained. Without such an approval the move of the seat would result in its dissolution by law. A move of the seat without the approval of the administration would be void. The general tax consequence of such a move would be that the foundation will no longer be subject to taxes in Liechtenstein but it will be in the new jurisdiction. Gifts to such a foundation would still qualify for a tax deduction if the foundation were to move to

	Switzerland and enter the official charities list there. In fact this might be easier than entering the official charities list in Liechtenstein. Therefore, Liechtenstein charities depending on gifts from Liechtenstein list might even consider moving to Switzerland for that purpose.
Netherlands	A foundation can move its seat to a foreign country only under very extraordinary circumstances (e.g. when the Netherlands is involved in a war). A transfer of the seat is possible only to countries that have an *inreisregeling* that allow legal persons from foreign jurisdictions to establish in their jurisdiction (*Wet vrijwillige zetelverplaatsing derde landen*). A resolution to move the seat to a foreign country other than in the above case will be null and void under Dutch law.
Portugal	A foundation may move its seat to another jurisdiction, by amending its governing document, but it will lose its fiscal benefits.
Slovenia	A foundation may not move its headquarters abroad, but may establish another legal person abroad.
Switzerland	A foundation will lose its Swiss tax privileges for itself and its donors.

33 May a foreign foundation conduct activities in your jurisdiction?

Will the foreign foundation have to obtain official approval or recognition from the authorities in your jurisdiction?

Does your state recognize the legal personality of a foreign foundation either under domestic law or under an international agreement?

Is it possible for a foundation to be established in both your state and another state (e.g. to be dually qualified in your jurisdiction and another jurisdiction?

The legal personality of a foreign foundation is generally recognized in all jurisdictions surveyed. Please see, however, the responses to Question 34 concerning the recognition of foundations set up as a charitable trust.

No jurisdiction grants tax relief to foreign foundations without first requiring such foreign foundations to obtain recognition from the authorities in the host jurisdiction. Official recognition is therefore recommended for tax purposes.

The following countries indicated that a foreign foundation is permitted to conduct activities in their jurisdiction. Additional notes on each country are given below where appropriate.

Belgium Czech Republic Denmark Greece Liechtenstein Netherlands Portugal Slovenia Spain Sweden Switzerland	No further details.
Austria Bulgaria Cyprus Italy	Official recognition is required; dual registration is allowed.
England, Scotland & Wales	A charity established outside the UK may not represent itself as a charity. The legal capacity of a foreign foundation would be recognized as an ordinary legal structure rather than as a charity. A foreign foundation must be managed or controlled from the UK, i.e. be subject to the control of the courts, in order to come within the definition of a recognized charity and be entitled to the usual tax privileges.
Estonia	Official recognition is required; dual registration is not allowed.
Finland Germany Hungary	Dual registration is not allowed.
France	Official recognition is required if a foreign foundation carries out activities in France on a permanent basis or wishes to acquire the same legal capacity as French foundations, for instance, to receive donations. Foreign foundations carrying out activities in France on an occasional basis need not obtain such recognition.
Ireland	There are no tax privileges for foundations not managed and controlled in Ireland; dual registration is not allowed.
Luxembourg	Recognition of a foreign foundation is automatic if it has valid establishment; certain restrictions applying to domestic foundations will also apply to a foreign foundation.

34 Is a charitable 'trust' recognized in law and in practice in your jurisdiction?

Has your jurisdiction signed and/or ratified the Hague Convention on the Law Applicable to Trusts and their Recognition?

Cyprus England & Wales Ireland Netherlands Scotland	Recognize a 'trust' in law; ratified the Hague Convention on the Law. Applicable to Trusts and their Recognition.
Liechtenstein Portugal	Recognize a 'trust' in law.
Austria Belgium France Luxembourg Switzerland	Do not recognize a 'trust' in law; recognize foreign trusts that are legally constituted in their home country.
Czech Republic Denmark Greece Hungary Slovenia Spain Sweden	Do not recognize a 'trust' in law.
Bulgaria	Does not recognize a 'trust' in law; has ratified the Statute of the Hague Conference on International Private Law in January 1999 and accession to the package of operative Hague Conventions is expected to follow.
Estonia	Does not recognize a 'trust' in law, but new legislation will change this.
Finland	The law does not recognize trusts, but according to the Finnish Income Tax Act trusts can be considered corporations or nonprofit organizations. This matter is unclear in practice, therefore advance ruling should be obtained to clear any matters relating to taxation.
Germany	Does not recognize a 'trust' in law, but recognizes foreign trusts that are legally constituted in their home country. Trust-like provisions in civil and public law do provide a degree of legal protection for German trust instruments.
Italy	Does not recognize a 'trust' in law; has ratified the Hague

Convention on the Law Applicable to Trusts and their Recognition; recognizes foreign trusts that are legally constituted in their home country.

35 Is a domestic donor able to receive any tax benefit from a donation that is made directly to a foreign charitable foundation?

Bulgaria Denmark	Yes, provided that the foreign charities fulfil certain local recognition or registration requirements.
Italy	Yes, with recognition as ONLUS.
Netherlands	Yes, with recognition as a public benefit organization by the Ministry of Finance.
Slovenia	Yes, if registered for a generally beneficial purpose.
Austria Belgium Cyprus Czech Republic England & Wales Finland Estonia Germany Greece Hungary Ireland Liechtenstein Luxembourg Portugal Scotland Spain	No
France	Donors may deduct donations made directly to a foreign charitable organization that conducts activities beneficial to the national community (i.e. France).
Ireland	Not generally, but Irish gift and inheritance tax contains an exemption for benefits received by a body to be applied for purposes that would be charitable under Irish law. This is slightly wider than the exemption in respect of income and capital gains tax. As a result, a foreign body receiving a gift or inheritance from an Irish person will enjoy this exemption provided the foreign body's objects are akin to charitable under Irish law.

Sweden	Only permits donations to be deducted as a business expense, not as a charitable donation; a donor that carries on a trade or business and enjoys a direct benefit from the donation for its business activities may deduct a donation made to a foreign charitable organization as a business expense.
Switzerland	No, except for donations to international organizations like UNICEF to which Switzerland belongs.

36 Can a foundation in your jurisdiction serve as a qualifying intermediary passing a donation from a donor in your jurisdiction to a charity in a foreign jurisdiction? If yes, can donations made to the qualifying intermediary foundation be donations qualifying for tax deductions or other privileges?

Austria Belgium Bulgaria Cyprus Denmark England & Wales Liechtenstein Luxembourg Netherlands Portugal Scotland Slovenia Spain Sweden Switzerland	Allow foundations to act as intermediaries, i.e. receiving gifts that are subsequently paid to foreign charities, as long as it is in accordance with the foundation's goals and the foundation makes the dispositive decision, i.e. the gift is subject to a request, not a binding instruction, and therefore also grant tax benefits.
Estonia	As above, but no cases yet exist.
Finland	An organization that only subsidizes nonprofit organizations is not considered to be acting in the public interest and does not therefore qualify as a nonprofit organization. The same applies to purely fundraising organizations. In principle, however, a foundation may act as a qualifying intermediary if passing donations from domestic donors to foreign charitable organizations is not its principal purpose.
Germany	A foundation may essentially serve as an intermediary for the transfer of funds (capital as well as donations) from a national donor to a foreign charity. However, this does not apply to funds received from donors explicitly as a contribution to the foundation's

endowment. To receive the approval of the supervisory authorities the statutes should ensure that funds may be used abroad. Funds can be used to pursue the stated aims both directly by making grants and indirectly by establishing foreign foundations with comparable aims. The key requirement under tax laws is that the funds must be disbursed immediately and timely (i.e. the same business year or the year after) for the purposes stated. According to tax laws the donor may get a certificate of deductibility for donations to foreign lands via a domestic intermediary, but not for the transfer of capital to endow or increase the capital of a foreign charity.

Ireland	Does not allow foundations to act as intermediaries. Yet, an Irish charity may act as an intermediary for raising donations in Ireland for application in a foreign country, provided that its objects are considered charitable under Irish law, which would normally be the case only with regard to donations raised for Third World countries. This would in principle require a charity established in a Third World country to establish a separate duly qualified charity in Ireland to act as the intermediary.
Czech Republic	A foundation must limit its activities to the Czech Republic. Only donations to charitable or nonprofit organizations that operate within the Czech Republic are deductible to their donors.
France Greece Hungary Italy	Serving as an intermediary is neither expressly allowed nor prohibited.

37 Does a foreign donor making a gift to a charity (i.e. foundation) in your country receive a tax benefit (deduction or credit) against tax payable to your government based on income earned in your country?

Austria	
Belgium	
Bulgaria	
Cyprus	
Czech Republic	
Denmark	Yes
England & Wales	
Estonia	
France	
Germany	
Greece	

Hungary Ireland Italy Portugal Scotland Slovenia Spain	Yes
Finland	The donor receives tax benefits only if it is a corporation that has taxable business income in Finland. Regardless of whether Finnish or foreign, individuals are not able to receive tax benefits.
Liechtenstein	Yes, if the charity is on the official list.
Luxembourg	No, unless foreign donors earn substantial amounts of their income from sources in Luxembourg, in which case they receive the same treatment as residents and their gifts to third parties (charitable foundations) are tax deductible.
Netherlands Sweden	No
Switzerland	Yes, depending on circumstances.

Appendix II

This Appendix provides a non-comprehensive list of legislation and administrative regulations governing charitable foundations in the 24 jurisdictions covered by the survey. The aim of the International Institute of Association Lawyers Inc. is to update and supplement this list so that it can be a valuable resource for all those conducting research in this area. For an up-to-date list please contact Bradley Gallop, International Institute of Association of Lawyers Inc., Rue Breesch 17 B-1020, Brussels, Belgium.
Email: bgallop@bdg-associates.com

Legislation

AUSTRIA

Civil legislation

Federal Foundation and Funds Act 1974
Privatstiftungsgesetz- PSG (Private Foundations Act) 1993

Tax legislation

Federal Fiscal Code, secs 34–47
Corporate Income Tax Act, sec. 5 (6)
Income Tax Law, sec. 4 (4)
Inheritance and Gift Tax Act, sec. 15 (1)

BELGIUM

Civil legislation

Associations Sans But Lucratif of 27 June 1921, Articles 27–56
Loteries et Paris (1851 and 1963)

Tax legislation

Income Tax Code, Articles 29 (1), 104 (3) to (5), 181, 200, 220–225
Inheritance Tax Code, Articles 59–60, 148–152

BULGARIA

Civil legislation

Regulation on the application of the Customs Act, Article 718
Law on Persons and the Family of 1949, as amended, Articles 131–133a, 149–154

Non-profit Legal Entities Act, S G No. 81/06.10.2000, of 2000

Tax legislation

Corporate Income Tax Act, Article 23
Local Taxes & Duties Act, Articles 38, 48
VAT Act 1999, Article 59
Decree on the Tax Registration of 15 January 1999, Article 2

CYPRUS

Civil legislation

Exchange Control, chapter 199 of the laws (1959 edition)
The Societies and Institutions Law 1972
Charities, chapter 41 of the laws (1959 edition)
Cyprus Broadcasting Corporation, chapter 300A of the laws (1959 edition)
Boy Scouts Association, chapter 34 of the laws (1959 edition)
Girl-Guide Association Law, 81/68
The Cyprus Red Cross Society Law 1967
Dianellos Orphanage, chapter 353 of the laws (1959 edition)
The Courts of Justice Amendment Law, 29/83
Cyprus Lotteries, chapter 74 of the laws (1959 edition)
The Capital Gains Law, 52/80
The Street and House to House Collections Law
Trustees, chapter 193 of the laws (1959 edition)
The Municipal Law, 111/85
The Hague Convention on the Law Applicable to Trusts and on their Recognition

Tax legislation

Income Tax Law, sec. 11
Capital Gains Tax Law 1980
VAT Law, 246/1990
Taxation of Immovable Property Law, 24/1980, sec. 18 (e)
Municipal Law, 111/1985, secs. 75 (f), 85 (2) & 105
The Value Added Tax Law, 246/90
The Customs and Excise Law, 109(I)/95
The Taxation of Immovable Property Law, 24/80

CZECH REPUBLIC

Tax legislation

Act 28/1996 on income tax, as amended
Act 588/1992 on VAT, as amended

Act 388/1992 on immovable property tax, as amended

Act 357/1992 on inheritance and gift tax and tax on the transfer of immovable property, as amended

Act 565/1990 on local taxes, as amended

DENMARK

Civil legislation

Bekendtgorelse as lov om erhvervsdrivende fonde (*3) Kapitels 1–12
Bekendtgorelse af lov om fonde og visse foreninger of 1984

Tax legislation

Law on Taxation of Foundations, secs 1 to 5
Corporate Income Tax Law, sec. 1 (1)
Tax Assessment Law, secs 8A & 12

ESTONIA

Civil legislation

Eesti Kultuutkapitali seadus 1997
Sihtasutuste seadus 1997
Mittetulundusuhingute saudus 1996
Riigi poolt eraoiguslike juriidiliste isikute asutamise ja nendes osalemise seadus 1996

Tax legislation

Income Tax Act, Articles 5, 12, 19
VAT Act, Article 5 (4)
Property Act, Article 29
Regulation no. 162 of 11 June 1996 'Order detailing how to maintain the list of nonprofit associations and tax-exempt foundations'
Regulation no. 484 of 27 December 1994 'Order and conditions for relief from income tax on non-governmental grants'

FINLAND

Civil legislation

Foundation Act 1930
Decree of 1989

Tax legislation

Income Tax Act, secs 1, 3, 20 to 23, 57
Act on Tax Relief for Certain Charitable Organisations 680/1976, secs 1 to 4

Income Tax Decree, sec. 2
Inheritance & Gift Tax Act, sec. 2
Real Estate Tax Act, sec. 13A
VAT Act, sec. 4

FRANCE

Civil legislation

Loi sur les fondations d'entreprise of 1990

Tax legislation

General Tax Code (*Code General des Impôts*), Articles 200, 206, 223, 238 *bis*, 795, 1655 *ter*
Law 87–571 of 23 July 1987 on the Promotion of Philanthropy
Instruction of 15 September 1998, BOI 4H-5-98

GERMANY

Civil legislation

Sections 80–89 of the Burgerliches Gesetzbuch
Foundation Laws of the German Länder: Baden-Württemberg of 1977, as amended
Bayern (Bavaria), as revised in 1996
Berlin, as revised in 1997
Brandenburg of 1995, as amended
Bremen of 1989
Hamburg, Law implementing the Civil Code sections 6–21
Hessen of 4 April 1966, as amended
Mecklenburg-Vorpommern of 1993
Niedersachsen of 1968 as amended
Nordrhein-Westfalen of 1977
Rheinland-Pfalz of 1966
Saarland of 1984, as amended
Schleswig-Holstein of 1972
Sachsen; Sachsen-Anhalt
Thüringen:The Foundation Law of the German Democratic Republic of 1990 – either unmodified (Sachsen); or with certain modifications (Sachsen-Anhalt and Thüringen)
(All texts reprinted in German in Seifart/von Campenhausen [ed. 2 1999] p. 819 ff. [MPI])

Tax legislation

General Tax Code (*Abgabenordnung*), secs 52 to 54
Corporate Income Tax Law, secs 1 (1), 5
Income Tax Law (*Einkommensteuergesetz*), sec. 10b

Income Tax Ordinance, sec. 48

Income Tax Regulations 1996 (*Einkommensteuerrichtlinien fur 1996*), para. 111

Inheritance & Gift Tax Law, sec. 13 (1)

GREECE

Civil legislation

Compulsory Law 2039/39, as amended

Law 2065/1992

Law 2238/1994

Law 2459/1997

Law 2579/1998

Law 3323/1955, Article 8 (6)

HUNGARY

Civil legislation

Parts 1–5 of the Public Benefit Organisations Act 1997 (CLVI)

Section 74A-74G of the Civil Code of 1959 (IV)

Tax legislation

Sections 3, 41 and 49B of the Personal Income Tax Act 1995 (CXVII)

Sections 18 of the Personal Income Tax Act 1996 (CXXVI)

Parts 1–5 of the Corporate Tax and Dividends Tax Act 1996 (LXXXI)

Act LXXXI of 1996 on Corporate Income Tax, secs 4, 7, 9

Act CXCVII of 1995 on Personal Income Tax, sec. 41 (1), Appendix 1

Act LXXIV of 1992 on VAT, sec. 7 (3), 71 (6)

Act C of 1990 on Local Taxes, sec. 3 (2)

Act C of 1995 on Customs Law, secs 114, 117 (3), 194

Act CLVI of 1997, secs 4, 14 (4), 16, 26 (n)

Government Decree no. 45/1996 of 25 March 1996

IRELAND

Civil legislation

Charities Act 1961

Charities Act 1973

Tax legislation

Taxes Consolidation Act 1997, secs 207–209, 235, 484 to 486A, 611, 792, Schedule 4

Capital Acquisitions Tax Act 1976, sec. 54

Finance Act 1984, sec. 108

ITALY

Civil legislation

Articles 11–35 and 2251–2271 of the Civil Code

Constitution Articles 11–33; *Leggi, Decreti e Ordinanze Presidentiale* (04/12/1997, no. 460)

Disposizioni di attuazione e transitorie del Codice Civil, Articles 1–30

Tax legislation

Law-Decree No. 460 of 4 December 1997

Income Tax Code, Articles 108 to 111

Law 1089/1939

LIECHTENSTEIN

Civil legislation

Personen- und Gesellschaftsrecht 1926, Articles 552–570 for Foundations and Articles 897–932 for Trusts

Tax legislation

Tax Law, Article 32

LUXEMBOURG

Civil legislation

Loi sur les of *Associations et Fondations Sans But Lucratif* of 1928, as amended in 1984 and 1994

Article 26 of the Luxembourg Constitution of October 17, 1868

Article 112 LIR (Luxembourg Tax Code)

Article 159 LIR

Paragraphs 17–19 of the '*Steueranpassungsgesetz*'

'*Gemeinnutzigkeits-Verordnung der 17–19 des Steueranpassungsgesetzes of December 16, 1941*'

Paragraph 4 of the '*Grundsteuergesetz*'

Article 931 of the Civil Code

Article 12 of the law of December 29, 1971

Article 157 LIR

Tax legislation

Income Tax Act, Articles 109 (3), 112, 159–161

Tax Law of 16 October 1934 (*Steueranpassungsgesetz*), paras. 17–19

Ordinance of 16 December 1941, paras. 1–10 (*Gemeinnützigkeitsverordnung*)

NETHERLANDS

Civil legislation

Title 6, Book 2, Articles 285–304 of the Dutch Civil Code

Tax legislation

Articles 1–36 of the Dutch Inheritance Tax Act
Articles 3, 17 and 18 of the Dutch Corporate and Income Tax Act
Corporate Income Tax Law, secs 2 (1), 4, 5, 6, 16
Individual Income Tax, sec. 47
Gifts & Inheritance tax Law, sec. 24(4), 32, 33

PORTUGAL

Civil legislation

Articles 185–193
Civil Code in Portuguese and relevant tax provisions

Tax legislation

Decree-Law 460/77 of 7 November 1977
Corporate Income Tax Code, Articles 9 to 11
Tax Incentive Statute, Articles 47 to 50
Inheritance & Gift Tax, Article 11 (16)
Property Tax Code, Article 50
Decree-Law 74/99 of 16 March 1999 (Patronage Statute), Articles 1 to 4

SLOVENIA

Civil legislation

Foundations Act 1995
Associations Act 1995

Tax legislation

Law on Income Tax (Official Gazette no. 71/93), Article 9
Law on Corporate Tax (Official Gazette nos. 73/93 & 20/95), Article 6
Law on VAT (Official Gazette no. 83/98)
Law on Citizens' Taxes (Official Gazette nos. 36/88, 48/90 & 7/93), Article 14

SPAIN

Civil legislation

Article 34 of the Spanish Constitution
Real Decreto 316/1996
Real Decreto 765/1995

Real Decreto 384/1996
Ley 24/12/1994, no. 30/1994
Ley 30/1994 [the most important general source]
Foundation Laws of the Spanish Autonomous Communities
Cataluña: Ley 1/1982
Galicia: Ley 7/1983
Canarias: Ley 1/1990
Navarra: Ley 1/1973
País Vasco: Ley 12/1994.
(Spanish texts reprinted in *Código de Fundaciones*, 1996 [MPI])

Tax legislation

Law on Foundations and Tax Incentives for the Private Sector in Areas of General Interest, 30/1994 of 24 November 1994, Articles 1 to 5, 42 to 43, 48 to 58, 59 to 63, 68

Corporate Tax Law 43/1995 of 27 December 1995, Articles 10, 14, 133 to 135

Individual Income Tax Law 40/1998 of 9 December 1998

Law on Value Added Tax 37/1992 of 28 December 1992, Article 20

SWEDEN

Civil legislation

Foundations Act 1994

Tax legislation

National Income Tax Act 1947
National Income Tax Act 1947:576, sec. 7
Inheritance & Gift Tax Act, sec. 3, 38
National Net Worth Tax, sec. 6 (3), 20

SWITZERLAND

Civil legislation

Articles 80–89 *bis*
Swiss Civil Code

Tax legislation

Federal Direct Tax Law of 14 December 1990, Articles 33 (1), 56, 59, 66
Federal Decree of 30 September 1955

Federal Law on Harmonisation of Cantonal and Communal Taxes of 14 December 1990, Articles 24, 26

UK

Civil legislation

England and Wales

Capital Allowances Act 1990, sec. 24(6)
Charities Act 1992
Charities Act 1993
Charitable Institutions (Fundraising) Regulations 1994
Charities (Accounts and Reports) Regulations 1995
Charities (Trustee Investment Act) Order 1961
Companies Act 1985, secs 4, 9 and 13
Companies Act 1989, secs 111, 112
Deregulation and Contracting Out Act 1994, secs 25–30
Finance Act 1982, sec. 129
Finance Act 1990, sec. 25
Finance Act 1991, sec. 68
Finance (No. 2) Act 1992, sec. 28
Finance Act 1998, sec. 47
Finance Act 1999, sec. 55
House to House Collections Act 1939
Inland Revenue Extra Statutory Concession C4
Local Government Finance Act 1988, secs 43, 53
Police, Factories etc. (Miscellaneous Provisions) Act 1916, sec. 5
Public Trustee Act 1906; SI 1998/1868 – The Gifts for Relief in Poor
    Countries (Designation) Order 1998
Trustee Act 1925, sec. 61
Trustee Investment Act 1961

Scotland

Law Reform (Miscellaneous Provisions) Scotland Act 1990

Tax legislation

Income and Corporation Taxes Act 1988, secs 9, 84, 86, 202, 345(2),
    338, 339, 505, 506, 832
Inheritance Tax Act 1984, (Capital and Transfer Tax Act 1984) secs
    58(1)(a), 70
Taxation of Chargeable Gains Act 1992, secs 256, 257
Income and Corporation Taxes Act 1988, secs 84, 86, 202, 339, 505 to
    510, Schedule 20
Finance Act 1998, secs 47–48
Taxation of Chargeable Gains Act 1992, sec. 256–257
Inheritance Tax Act 1984, sec. 23